The *Arabian Nights* in Contemporary World Cultures

The stories in the *Thousand and One Nights*, or the *Arabian Nights*, are familiar to many of us: from the tales of Aladdin, Sindbad the Sailor, Ali Baba and his forty thieves, to the framing story of Scheherazade telling these stories to her homicidal husband, Shahrayar. This book offers a rich and wide-ranging analysis of the power of this collection of tales that penetrates so many cultures and appeals to such a variety of predilections and tastes. It also explores areas that were left untouched, like the decolonization of the *Arabian Nights*, and its archaeologies. Moreover, it expands a narrative grammar, a grammatology which theories of fiction need. Unique in its excavation into inroads of perception and reception, Muhsin J. al-Musawi's book unearths means of connection with common publics and learned societies. Al-Musawi shows, as never before, how the *Arabian Nights* has been translated, appropriated, and authenticated or abused over time, and how its reach is so expansive as to draw the attention of poets, painters, illustrators, translators, editors, musicians, political scientists like Leo Strauss, and novelists like Michel Butor, James Joyce, and Marcel Proust, among others. Making use of documentaries, films, paintings, novels and novellas, poetry, digital forums, and political jargon, this book offers a nuanced understanding of the perennial charm and power of this collection.

Muhsin J. Al-Musawi is Professor of Classical and Modern Arabic Literature, Comparative and Cultural Studies, at Columbia University in New York. He is the editor of the *Journal of Arabic Literature* and the recipient of the Owais Award in Literary Criticism in 2002 and the Kuwait Prize in Arabic Language and Literature in 2018. He is the author and editor of numerous books, including *The Postcolonial Arabic Novel: Debating Ambivalence* (2003), *Arabic Poetry: Trajectories of Modernity and Tradition* (2006), *Reading Iraq: Culture and Power in Conflict* (2006), *Arabic Literary Thresholds: Sites of Rhetorical Turn in Contemporary Scholarship* (2009), *The Islamic Context of the Thousand and One Nights* (2009), *Islam on the Street: Religion in Modern Arabic Literature* (2009), and *The Medieval Islamic Republic of Letters: Arabic Knowledge Construction* (2015).

Figure 0 Edmund Dulac: Scheherazade frontispiece.

The *Arabian Nights* in Contemporary World Cultures

Global Commodification, Translation, and the Culture Industry

Muhsin J. Al-Musawi
Columbia University

CAMBRIDGE
UNIVERSITY PRESS

CAMBRIDGE
UNIVERSITY PRESS

Shaftesbury Road, Cambridge CB2 8EA, United Kingdom

One Liberty Plaza, 20th Floor, New York, NY 10006, USA

477 Williamstown Road, Port Melbourne, VIC 3207, Australia

314–321, 3rd Floor, Plot 3, Splendor Forum, Jasola District Centre, New Delhi – 110025, India

103 Penang Road, #05–06/07, Visioncrest Commercial, Singapore 238467

Cambridge University Press is part of Cambridge University Press & Assessment, a department of the University of Cambridge.

We share the University's mission to contribute to society through the pursuit of education, learning and research at the highest international levels of excellence.

www.cambridge.org
Information on this title: www.cambridge.org/9781108465557

DOI: 10.1017/9781108593847

First published 2021
First paperback edition 2023

A catalogue record for this publication is available from the British Library

Library of Congress Cataloging-in-Publication data
Names: Mūsawī , Muḥsin Jāsim, author.
Title: The Arabian Nights in contemporary world cultures : global commodification, translation, and the culture industry /Muhsin J. al-Musawi.
Description: Cambridge ; New York, NY : Cambridge University Press, 2021. | Includes bibliographical references and index.
Identifiers: LCCN 2021026864 (print) | LCCN 2021026865 (ebook) | ISBN 9781108474856 (hardback) | ISBN 9781108593847 (ebook)
Subjects: LCSH: Arabian nights – Influence. | Arabian nights – Adaptations. | BISAC: HISTORY / Middle East / General | HISTORY / Middle East / General | LCGFT: Literary criticism.
Classification: LCC PJ7737 .M745 2021 (print) | LCC PJ7737 (ebook) | DDC 398.2–dc23
LC record available at https://lccn.loc.gov/2021026864
LC ebook record available at https://lccn.loc.gov/2021026865

ISBN 978-1-108-47485-6 Hardback
ISBN 978-1-108-46555-7 Paperback

Was it an enchanting cap, or just Abdou's blue hat of wonders, somewhere in Saint Germaine, in Paris, with so many charming tales, that keep on unfolding as if vying with Marrakech storytellers, and those of Baghdad, Damascus, and Cairo, wonder upon wonder, an endless treasure?

Jabra

Contents

Figures

Acknowledgments

The story of my engagement with a *Thousand and One Nights* requires a book of its own. In 1975–76, I found myself involved in researching its place in French and English literatures and cultures. It took me away from my interest in Arabic narrative, poetry, and poetics. By then I had published books and articles, and the coming of the *Arabian Nights* was a surprise to those who were aware of my interests. By 1978, I had submitted and defended my doctoral dissertation on eighteenth- to nineteenth-century English criticism of the *Nights*. I continued my other interests, but the *Nights* has a compelling hold on one's mind, and I found myself entangled again in exploring its early genealogies, borrowings from other Arabic, Indo-Persian, and Greek sources. My focus turned, however, to its structure, semiotics, and extensively on its social dimensions as spaces that generate and define narrative, while getting impacted by the contours of performance and storytelling as a powerful discursive space with a storyteller whose survival depends, as always, on an excellent craft. I noticed soon after that there is a need for a third project on the Islamic context of the *Nights*; for no matter how narratively engaging, the *Nights* happened to grow in translation, appropriation, or borrowing, and creation in a specific milieu. By the 1990s, scholarship on the *Nights* began to multiply, and this rise in culture industry invoked another participation to encapsulate, synthesize, and theorize the nature and future of a collection that has been passing through ups and downs without losing some attraction. In one of the significant developments in this culture industry, the *Nights* found its place in academia. While this book is more focused on critical shifts and intellectual conversation since its appearance in Europe, it aims also to set the stage for further studies of the the presence of the *Nights* in the Global South.

In writing and preparing *The Arabian Nights in Contemporary World Cultures*, I was bound to incur many debts. I thank in particular my close friends Suzanne P. Stetkevych from Georgetown University and Roger Allen from the University of Pennsylvania for a careful reading of the manuscript. Their suggestions were invaluable. I am thankful to Nizar

Hermes from the University of Virginia and Tarek el-Ariss from Dartmouth College for their support. Hussein Kadhim from Dartmouth College, who teaches a core course on *Arabian Nights*, was helpful in tracing the early use of the phrase "*Arabian Nightism.*" Ulrich Marzolph was very helpful in providing articles and meticulous notes, and Aboubakr Chraïbi was no less so. I thank them both and also Richard van Leeuwen for being as helpful. My former student Omar M. Shafik Alhmashi, who was my voluntary assistant, helped not only in securing high-resolution images for illustrations by William Harvey and Arthur Boyd Houghton, alongside manuscript images, but also in putting final touches on the bibliography and preparing the index. My assistant Sarah Ariyan Sakha was no less helpful in preparing the bibliography. My gratitude goes as well to Ryan Damron, who was my work study assistant in 2008–9. Ryan proved to be an excellent support. He helped in a compilation of bibliographies for another *Nights* project that is yet unpublished. Under my guidance, he prepared a preliminary and select textual comparison between Haddawy's translation of Galland's incomplete manuscript and the Grub Street translation, as reproduced in Harrison's *Novelist's Magazine* (1785).

I express appreciation to the Schoff Fund at the University Seminars at Columbia University for their help in publication. The ideas presented have benefited from discussions in the University Seminar on Arabic Studies.

The cover for this book is by the late and renowned Iraqi artist Jawad Selim. I am grateful to the Mathaf: Arab Museum of Modern Art, Doha, for making this available, and to the Mathaf Curatorial and Collections team. I should thank my dear friend, the UAE intellectual Muḥammad al-Murr for making available the manuscripts which he possesses of King Jaliʿād and Wāq Wāq. Christine Dunn went over the manuscript with diligence and professional care, while the unique acquisition editor at Cambridge University Press, Maria Marsh, was extremely professional and helpful throughout. Her assistant, Atifa Jiwa, proved tactful and diligent in the preparation and production process. Many thanks go to both, as well as to the copyeditor, Muhammad Ridwaan, for his careful attention, and to Natasha Whelan, the senior content manager at CUP, and the production team, for their meticulous care. Because of the extensive use of footnotes and references to bibliographies, and encyclopedias, the bibliography is selectively organized. Even so, many items and entries could have been unwittingly missed. Hence, my apologies.

Introduction
The Stunning Growth of a Constellation

This study of the *Thousand and One Nights* addresses the place of what is commonly called *Arabian Nights* in contemporary world cultures.[1] It aims to study theoretical and philological undertakings, including poetics of prose and poetry, in conversation with social science. It explores and excavates the reasons for and effects of an enormous constellation of knowledge about and around the tales that has generated further projects to compile manuals, guides, companions, edited compilations, and encyclopedias.[2] These constellations and projects also build on, or converse with, cinematic production, theater, painting, music,[3] and other visual sites and spectacles. Since its early inception in translation, 1704–12/17 (*Les Mille et Une Nuit: Contes Arabes*), it has sustained an unequalled presence in cultural production. The enormous increase in scholarship on *A Thousand and One Nights* (the *Arabian Nights*) is further indicated by the multiplication of publications that take the tales as their focus and concern.[4] Whether this scholarship addresses issues of translation, the appropriation of the tales in visual culture, or in media, its growth evidences a massive production of published materials, one that

[1] *The Thousand and One Nights*, *Arabian Nights*, *Arabian Nights' Entertainments*, and *A Thousand and One Nights* are interchangeably used.

[2] Among the latest compilations of edited material, see Ibrahim Akel and William Granara, eds., *The Thousand and One Nights: Sources and Transformations in Literature, Art, and Science* (Leiden: Brill, 2020); and Orhan Elmaz, ed., *Endless Inspiration: One Thousand and One Nights in Comparative Perspective* (Piscataway, NJ: Gorgias Press, 2020).

[3] Although the most known were Farmer's writings, there was earlier G. W. Peck, "The Thousand and One Nights," *American Review* 5 (1847), 601–18; and, certainly, Henry George Farmer, *The Minstrelsy of "The Arabian Nights": A Study of Music and Musicians in the Arabic "Alif Laila wa Laila"* (Bearsden: Hinrichsen, 1945); and his "The Music of the Arabian Nights," *Journal of the Royal Asiatic Society*, 2 parts (October 1944 and 1945), 172–85, 39–60. Reflecting on Rimsky-Korsakov's and Ravel's inspired music, Tim Ashley wrote to *The Observer* about the scope of this inspiration; see Tim Ashley, "Eastern Promise," *The Observer*, August 20, 2005, www.theguardian.com/music/2005/aug/20/classicalmusicandopera.proms2005.

[4] See Ulrich Marzolph's bibliography: http://wwwuser.gwdg.de/~umarzol/arabiannights.html.

prompts us to speak of *A Thousand and One Nights* as a field of knowledge. Over time, this field has witnessed some radical transformations in relation to other fields and also within its own diversification of assets at certain moments in its historical processes. In other words, its appearance in France, and almost simultaneously in translation in English, was also conditioned by possibilities while opening up certain venues within each culture.

Conditions of possibility that may be applicable at a certain historical moment undergo change, mutation, or transformation in relation to other fields.[5] Studies of the reception of the *Nights* at different periods within each culture can tell us as much. The *Nights* has become a mirror of specific tastes and directions in cultures as a result of certain properties that are highlighted or appropriated in each translation or adaptation within an episteme, or "a total set of relations that unite, at a given period, the discursive practices that give rise to epistemological figures, sciences, and possibly formalized systems."[6] A cursory glance at the following can give us an idea of how the *Nights* reached even the grand minds of the Age of Reason and the pre-Romantic reaction: Denis Diderot's novel *Les bijoux indiscrets* (1748), Jean-Jacques Rousseau's *La reine Fantasque* (1755–56), and Francois-Marie Arouet's (Voltaire, 1694–1778) *Zadig* (1747), along with a prologue in which he finishes by acknowledging the widespread popularity of the *Nights*. The case is even more problematic when we study the notorious theorist for racist ideology, Joseph Arthur de Gobineau (1816–82), the author of *Essai sur l'inégalité des races humaines* (1853–55; *Essay on the Inequality of Human Races*). Pierre-Louis Rey argues how de Gobineau considers the *Nights* a Persian text, an

[5] See, as examples, Muhsin Jassim al-Musawi, "The Arabian Nights in Eighteenth-Century English Criticism," *Muslim World* 67 (1977), 12–32; and his *Scheherazade in England: A Study of Nineteenth-Century English Criticism of the Arabian Nights* (Boulder, CO: Three Continents, 1981); Rochelle Almeida, "A Thousand and One Nights in the Pedagogic Global Village: Cross-cultural Transnational Connections," in *La Réception mondiale et transdisciplinaire des Mille et une Nuits*, ed. Waël Rabadi and Isabelle Bernard (Amiens: Presses du Centre d'Études Médiévales, 2012), 17–30; Danielle Buschinger, "*Les Mille et une Nuits* et la littérature européenne: quelques rapprochements," in ibid., 117–39; and Sylvette Larzul, "Les Mille et Une Nuit d'Antoine Galland: Traduction, adaption, création," in *Les Mille et Une Nuit en partage*, ed. Aboubakr Chraïbi (Paris: Sindbad, 2004), 251–66. Digital surveys like Encounters with the Orient project, funded by HERA (Humanities European Research Area) can offer handy and accessible information (www.kent.ac.uk/ewto/projects/anthology/index.html). An effort to place the Enlightenment intellectuals in context of two categories, Arabic science and an irrational "Islam," is made by Rebecca Joubin, "Islam and Arabs through the Eyes of the Encyclopédie: The 'Other' as a Case of French Cultural Self-criticism," *International Journal of Middle East Studies* 32, no. 2 (May 2000), 197–217.

[6] Michel Foucault, *The Archaeology of Knowledge*, trans. A. M. Sheridan Smith (New York: Pantheon, 1972), 191.

understanding that led him to study Persian: "During his adolescence in Brittany, he had become enamored of the *Thousand and One Nights*. All he dreamed of were mosques and minarets, he said he was a Muslim, ready to make his pilgrimage to Mecca." Furthermore, as soon as he arrived in Paris in 1835, "he started taking Persian lessons with Quatremère at Le Collège de France, before giving into the Orientalist fashion of the time in a long poem entitled *Dilfiza* (1837)."[7] Almost every writer, philosopher, philologist, and theologian of note, in France, England, and Germany, was engaged with the tales in one way or another. In other words, and apart from the striking appeal that the tales engendered with the rest of society, the dialogue through which the learned engaged with the *Nights* for more than two centuries signifies this epistemic shift that was made possible by Galland's appropriated translation, and the multifarious and composite nature of *A Thousand and One Nights*. Its journey in one translation or adaptation or another to other cultures may not display the same set of conditions or responses that are applicable to Franco-Anglo orientations; and yet, this migration established the path for multiple transactions that have attracted attention. Hence, we read of its presence in Sicily, Slovakia, Argentina, Somalia, and almost everywhere else, not only in Europe and America, but especially in the Global South.[8] The current study is thus a theoretical continuation of explorations already initiated in

[7] https://heritage.bnf.fr/bibliothequesorient/en/joseph-gobineau-art.

[8] See, for example, Abdalla Uba Adamu, "'We Are Not in Baghdad Anymore': Textual Travels and Hausa Intertextual Adaptation of Selected Tales of One Thousand and One Nights in Northern Nigeria," in *Endless Inspiration: One Thousand and One Nights in Comparative Perspective*, ed. Orhan Elmaz (Piscataway, NJ: Gorgias Press, 2020), 35–59; Zubair Ahamed and Krishnaswamy Nachimuthu, "Reception of The Arabian Nights in Tamil: The Story of Medinatun Nuhas in Tamil Adaptation," in *Essays on The Arabian Nights*, ed. Risvanur Rahman and Syed Akhtar Husain (New Delhi: India International Centre, 2015), 25–39; Syed Hasnain Akhtar, "Reception of Alf Layla in India with Special Reference to Urdu," in ibid., 105–10; Sergio Gabriel Waisman, "The Thousand and One Nights in Argentina: Translation, Narrative, and Politics in Borges, Puig, and Piglia," *Comparative Literature Studies* 40, no. 4 (2003), 351–71; Kevin Windle, "The Slavonic Nights: Observations on Some Versions of *The Book of a Thousand and One Nights* in Slavonic Languages," *Modern Language Review* 88 (1993), 389–40; Francesca Maria Corrao, "The Arabian Nights in Sicily," *Fabula* 45, no. 3–4 (2004), 237–45; revised version in *The Arabian Nights in Transnational Perspective*, ed. Ulrich Marzolph (Detroit, MI: Wayne State University Press, 2007), 279–89; Magdalena Kubarek, "The Reception of One Thousand and One Nights in Polish Contemporary Literature," in *The Thousand and One Nights: Sources and Transformations in Literature, Art, and Science*, ed. Ibrahim Akel and William Granara (Leiden: Brill, 2020), 216–26; Manuela Cortés Garcia, "Les Mille et Une Nuit dans une zarzuela espagnole: El Asombro de Damasco," in *Les Mille et Une Nuit dans les imaginaires croisés*, ed. Lucette Heller-Goldenberg (Cologne: Romanisches Seminar der Universität Köln, 1994), 204–10; Justin St. Clair, "Mahfouz and the Arabian Nights Tradition," in *Approaches to Teaching the Works of Naguib Mahfouz*, ed. Waïl S. Hassan and Susan Muaddi Darraj (New York: The Modern Language Association of

Scheherazade in England (1981) and a couple of articles in 1977 and 1980:[9] a study of informed response, as demonstrated in the writings of poets, prose writers, critics, journalists, moralists, neoclassicists, and Romanticists.

A sequel to that research project, one that is also concerned with a broader field of narrative in diverse fields of production, is in order. Many colleagues have already participated in this endeavor in one way or another, and the present project derives power and acumen from their research and insights. It aims, however, to interrogate the place of the *Arabian Nights* in postindustrialist, postcapitalist world cultures; hence it adopts a theoretical line that focuses on the reasons behind every phenomenal rise in a field of knowledge called *A Thousand and One Nights* (*Arabian Nights*), as attested to by Marzolph's online bibliography.[10] That said, however, the current study departs from my earlier undertaking, not only in its historical perspective, the postcapitalist, postindustrialist world order, but also in its focus on new concerns, applications, theories of enunciation and narrative, and what Michel Foucault describes as "a modification in the principle of exclusion and the principle of the possibility of choices" in a "a new discursive constellation."[11]

On the scholarly and critical levels, my study intends to depart from current studies, edited volumes, and conference proceedings, with their strict application of either current literary theory and its emphasis on social science, or its rhetorical return to techniques that were popular once in concomitance with the vogue of structuralism. While not overlooking these approaches and making use of some of them at certain points, my study takes as its point of departure the critical and popular reception that I have already studied, examining in depth the postcolonial transactional activity that started more conspicuously in the 1970s in Europe, the United States, and all over the globe. Reception in its popular

America 2012), 105–17; Matthew Isaac Cohen, "Thousand and One Nights at the Komedie Stamboel: Popular Theatre and Travelling Stories in Colonial Southeast Asia," in *New Perspectives on [the] Arabian Nights: Ideological Variations and Narrative Horizons*, ed. Wen-Chin Ouyang and Geert Jan van Gelder (London and New York: Routledge, 2005), 103–14; and Thomas Lahusen, "Thousand and One Nights in Stalinist Culture: Far from Moscow," *Discourse: Theoretical Studies in Media and Culture* 17, no. 3 (1995), 58–74. See also Kamran Rastegar, *Literary Modernity between the Middle East and Europe: Textual Transactions in Nineteenth-Century Arabic, English and Persian Literatures* (London: Routledge, 2007).

9 al-Musawi, *Scheherazade in England*; and his "The Growth of Scholarly Interest in the *Arabian Nights*," *Muslim World* 70 (1980), 196–212.

10 As I have no intention to reproduce the bibliography that I sent to publishers in 2008, I find Ulrich Marzolph's updated online bibliography the best (https://wwwuser.gwdg.de/~umarzol/arabiannights.html). It shows the enormous amount of material written about the *Nights* in many languages.

11 Foucault, *Archaeology of Knowledge*, 67.

and critical form; the understanding or misunderstanding of Islam, the Arab, or the Orient; and the nature of navigation in texts, lands, and languages all provide a substantial threshold to the core of the book, its central argument, one that makes use of multiple documentaries, films, paintings, novels and novellas, poetry, digital forums,[12] and political jargon, to offer an updated and nuanced understanding of a text that at this point encapsulates world cultures. Whether we speak of globalization, worldism, literary theory, cultural dialogue, or "clash of civilizations," no other text can ever signify and encapsulate everything in its protean core, especially in relation to the first translated text that managed to play havoc with European cultures upon its first introduction in French and, probably, simultaneously in English.[13]

A dominating cultural climate constructs its temporal/spatial tropes and topoi in an age that, for better or worse, now takes pride in its media achievements that compress materiality into a cyberspace. Facts on the ground speak, however, of massive wars, migrations, displaced communities, and also reflect the growth of an astounding rhetoric as another venue for conflict, rapprochement, cold war, persuasion, and deception. This multidimensional universe, with its cultural scripts and the increasing domination of artificial intelligence, is another space that also makes use of Scheherazade's tales, her rich lexicon of intrigue, ruse, treachery, love, passion, and anxiety. It is not in vain to trace the *Arabian Nights* in this space, even in places that could have eluded the ingenuity of an artist or philosopher. Barry Blitt's cover for the *New Yorker*, January 25, 2021, is a case in point. It depicts the former US president Donald Trump lifted by a *rukh*, an enormous eagle. Blitt calls it "A Weight Lifted." But behind this, in the subconscious, the artist could have the *Arabian Nights* tale of the third mendicant, ʿAjīb Ibn Khaṣīb, the son of a king, in mind. He is lifted by the *rukh* to experience further trials that end up with the loss of an eye and consequent mendicancy.[14] ʿAjīb Ibn Khaṣīb has become a mask among modernist poets whose trials, troubles, and misfortunes confront them with difficult choices. The Egyptian poet Ṣalāḥ ʿAbd al-Ṣabūr's poem "Mudhakkirāt al-Malik ʿAjīb Ibn Khaṣīb" says as much, though the poet takes the early history of the king's son as a starting point to bemoan the absurdity of things

[12] See, on this point, Tarek el-Ariss, *Leaks, Hacks, and Scandals: Arab Culture in the Digital Age* (Princeton, NJ: Princeton University Press, 2019), 34–38.

[13] For some reason, what we have as extant copies of the English version relate to 1706. See, for example, James Holly Hanford, "Open Sesame: Notes on the 'Arabian Nights' in English," *The Princeton University Library Chronicle* 26, no. 1 (1964), 48–56.

[14] Husain Fareed Ali Haddawy, trans., *The Arabian Nights* [based on the text edited by Muhsin Mahdi] (New York and London: W. W. Norton & Company, 1990), 125.

around him.[15] In his usual propensity to empty the real of carnage and human loss, a propensity for simulacra, Jean Baudrillard references the *Thousand and One Nights* for the sake of contrast between recurrent time and real time in the war on Iraq. Procrastination, false advance, and retreat are levelled at the victim to exemplify "the recurrent time of *The Thousand and One Nights* – [as] exactly the inverse of real time."[16] The *Nights* is recalled only in relation to warmongers' Other.

Combined with the growth and mobility of global capital, its smooth or enforced flow through wars and the disintegration of the Soviet Union, followed by the fragmentation of nation-states, a new culture industry now forces its way alongside a newly emerging world of media fluidity. Whether in the tourist industry, film and TV production, or political rhetoric and economic transaction, Scheherazade's treasures are even more alluring and available than before. An enormous appropriation is taking place, one that suggests a number of classifications under which the present project, *The Arabian Nights in Contemporary World Cultures*, argues its point. There is first appropriation, including adaptation, as cultural production in response to the transactional dynamics of consumerist economies. Contemporary trends do not necessarily involve a complete departure from earlier appropriation, including intertextual allusions as pervasively seen, for example, in Victorian fiction.[17] New options and dialogue with another world order under a postcapitalist economy and powerful soft technologies impel moves in other directions.

A very recent example is the marketing of the new Disney production of Aladdin, in its adult and also earlier cartoon versions. Directed by Guy Ritchie, May 24, 2019, with a budget of 183 million USD, the version departs from its original like many other appropriations of the *Arabian Nights*, and it incites critics to speak of great art and cinematography at the expense of a familiar story (Figure 1).[18] Thus, while there is a newly

15 Ṣalāḥ ʿAbd al-Ṣabūr, "Mudhakkirat al-Malik ʿAjīb Ibn Khaṣīb" [Memoirs of King ʿAjīb Ibn Khaṣīb] (1961). It is included in *al-Aʿmāl al-Kāmilah* (1993), 419–42. See Muhsin Jassim al-Musawi, "Engaging Tradition in Modern Arab Poetics," *Journal of Arabic Literature* 33, no. 2 (2002), 195.

16 Jean Baudrillard, *The Gulf War Did Not Take Place*, trans. with an introduction by Paul Patton (Bloomington, IN: Indiana University Press, 1995), 65.

17 For a detailed and thorough reading, see Nancy Victoria Workman, "A Victorian 'Arabian Nights' Adventure: A Study in Intertextuality" (PhD diss., Loyola University of Chicago, 1989).

18 "The story that follows is surprising in that it is not the tale we have actually heard and known. It seems that the makers have taken a big risk. To be honest, their experiment has been well crafted. The plot gives a very impressive character arc for Jasmine. Though the story of Aladdin begins and ends in a familiar way, a different tale is told. We see the rise of a different Sultan, a feature that is neatly written and brought out. It has, for sure, befitted all the ongoing noble fights going on in our real world. Kudos to the team for tampering with the original story, introducing a motive to bring out a strong message."

Figure 1 Arthur Boyd Houghton: The African magician offers new lamps for old in the tale of Aladdin.

directed revival of scholarly and literary interest, along with productions for the cinema and theater, there is also "collateral" damage, as Jack Shaheen's comprehensive survey of cinematography shows. Raids on

Behindwoods.com, "Aladdin Movie Review," www.behindwoods.com/english-movies/aladdin/aladdin-review.html.

the *Arabian Nights* that are as violent as wars of intervention are in evidence.[19] Alongside objectified reproductions and highly informed presentations,[20] there are many others that have cursorily skirted the tales to intensify their stereotypes of the region. Orientalist paintings, broadcast productions, and satellite TV appropriations are in abundance, signifying a new turn in reception. This postcolonial, global capital turn rests on understanding the *Nights* as a manageable property, an appropriate commodity that can meet differentiated tastes while appealing to all as a shared cultural script.[21]

Appropriation is not only a method, but also a strategy, one that derives from a cultural script and conveys and disseminates a worldview of one sort or another. It appears in multifarious productions that take the *Arabian Nights* as a rejuvenating and perpetual property. Alongside this axial mapping is translation that presents the translator as a dynamic actor, an author who absorbs, clarifies, or obfuscates an appropriated and owned tale and forces her/his being as the ultimate authority on a text. As will be shown in Chapter 5, on archaeologies, processes of translation are bound to convey the contours of the mediating milieu and the character of the translator. Compilation, accretion, and translation are often in line with a cultural script that impacts cultural importation. However, economies of desire and communal and business-like transactions constitute the basis for reception, circulation, appropriation, translation, publication, publicity, and whatever that makes up a culture industry.

19 Steve Marble, "Jack Shaheen Dies," *Los Angeles Times*, July 13, 2017, www.latimes.com/local/obituaries/la-me-jack-shaheen-20170713-story.html. Shaheen convinced Disney to change a few things. Jack Shaheen, *Reel Bad Arabs: How Hollywood Vilifies a People*, 3rd ed. (Northampton, MA: Olive Branch Press, 2014). See also Christopher Wise, "Notes from the Aladdin Industry: Or, Middle Eastern Folklore in the Era of Multinational Capitalism," in *The Emperor's Old Groove: Decolonizing Disney's Magic Kingdom*, ed. Brenda Ayers (New York: Peter Lang, 2003), 105–14; Dianne Sachko Macleod, "The Politics of Vision: Disney, Aladdin, and the Gulf War," in ibid., 179–92; Timothy R. White and James Emmet Winn, "Islam, Animation and Money: The Reception of Disney's Aladdin in Southeast Asia," *Kinema* (1995), 58–59, https://doi.org/10.15353/kinema.vi.778; and Erin Addison, "Saving Other Women from Other Men: Disney's Aladdin," *Camera Obscura* 11, no. 131 (January–May 1993), 4–25.

20 Like Tim Supple's significant production for the theater of *One Thousand and One Nights*: Two Parts, Friday, June 17, 2011. This is part of the advertisement for the panel that followed: "Luminato 2011 examines modern takes on old stories, from its commission of One Thousand and One Nights, to Evie Christie's adaptation of Racine's Andromache, to Theatre Smith-Gilmour's production of LU XUN blossoms. Join One Thousand and One Nights' director Tim Supple, author Evie Christie, artistic director Dean Gilmour and renowned Columbia Muhsin al-Musawi, an expert on One Thousand and One Nights, for a rich discussion on the craft of adaptation and interpretation."

21 Susan Nance, *How the Arabian Nights Inspired the American Dream, 1790–1935* (Chapel Hill, NC: University of North Carolina Press, 2009).

We speak of Antoine Galland (1646–1715),[22] Edward William Lane (1801–76),[23] Sir Richard Francis Burton (1821–90),[24] and less of John Payne (1842–1916),[25] for example, because these translators present themselves and their texts as world treasuries emerging from metropolitan centers. The aesthete Payne was not a publicist, and his suave style keeps the copy in the dark, especially as it was soon to become Burton's ghost text.[26] Given the nature of *A Thousand and One Nights* as a common storytelling property, these translators are archaeologists, resuscitators, and founders of a tradition. Along the third axial pattern are narrative art, narratology, and a theory of fiction.[27] It includes metafiction, as shown in John Barth's novels,[28] and the Lebanese Elias Khoury's *The Children of the Ghetto: My Name*

[22] Antoine Galland, trans., *Arabian Nights' Entertainments: Consisting of One Thousand and One Stories, Told by the Sultaness of the Indies, to divert the Sultan from the Execution of a bloody Vow he had made to marry a Lady every day, and have her cut off next Morning, to avenge himself for the Disloyalty of his first Sultaness, &c. Containing a better Account of the Customs, Manners, and Religion of the Eastern Nations, viz. Tartars, Persians, and Indians, than is to be met with in any Author hitherto published. Translated into French from the Arabian Mss. by M. Galland of the Royal Academy, and now done into English from the last Paris Edition (London: Andrew Bell, 1706–17)*, 16th ed., 4 vols. (London and Edinburgh: C. Elliot, 1781). Other publishers, like Longman, issued many editions.

[23] Edward William Lane, trans., *The Thousand and One Nights, Commonly Called, in England, The Arabian Nights' Entertainments. A New Translation from the Arabic, with Copious Notes*, 3 vols. (London: Charles Knight, 1839–41). It came out first in 1838 in thirty-two parts.

[24] Richard F. Burton, trans. *A Plain and Literal Translation of The Arabian Nights' Entertainments, Now Entitled the Book of the Thousand Nights and a Night: With Introduction, Explanatory Notes on the Manners and Customs of Moslem Men and a Terminal Essay upon the History of the Nights*, 10 vols. (Benares [= Stoke-Newington]: Kamashastra Society, 1885).

[25] John Payne, trans., *The Book of the Thousand Nights and One Night; Now First Completely Done into English Prose and Verse, from the Original Arabic*, 9 vols. (London: Villon Society, 1882–84); John Payne, trans., *Tales from the Arabic of the Breslau and Calcutta (1814–18) Editions of the Book of the Thousand Nights and One Night, Not Occurring in the Other Printed Texts of the Work; Now First Done into English*, 3 vols. (London: Villon Society, 1884); John Payne, trans., *Alaeddin and the Enchanted Lamp; Zein ul Asnam and the King of the Jinn: Two Stories Done into English from the Recently Discovered Arabic Text* (London: Villon Society, 1889).

[26] There is more on this point in the following chapters, but among recent writings on Burton's use, see Anna Ziajka Stanton, "Vulgar Pleasures: The Scandalous Worldliness of Burton's 'Arabian Nights,'" *Journal of World Literature* (September 2020), 1–20.

[27] Gerald Prince, "Narratology, Narrative, and Meaning," *Poetics Today* 12, no. 3 (Autumn 1991), 543–52; where Prince sums up the term as "Narratology, as is well known, attempts to define the nature of narrative, its specificity, and to characterize the forms which it may take" (543).

[28] For more on Barth, see Lahsen Ben Aziza, "Romancing Scheherazade: John Barth's Self-perpetuating Narrative Machine from 'The Floating Opera' through 'Chimera'" (PhD diss., Dalhousie University, 1991).

Is Adam,[29] or in the Egyptian Ṭāriq Imām's *Ṭaʿm al-nawm* (*The Taste of Sleep*). Narrative and narratological experimentation present technical and thematic issues that often subvert and destabilize a cultural scene. Multiple theories of narrative emerge that take their cue from Scheherazade. French experimentation with Scheherazade was noticeable in the late eighteenth and early nineteenth centuries.[30] In English, the American Edgar Allan Poe was a pioneer, as was Meredith, along with a number of others before we reach Barth. Among early twentieth-century Arab writers, Ṭāha Ḥusayn and Tawfīq al-Ḥakīm collaborated in a joint novella, *al-Qaṣr al-mashūr* (1936; *The Enchanted Palace*). A vast thematic terrain opens up, and women writers find in Scheherazade a feminist pioneer, an adept in narration as to outwit a dominating masculine discourse.[31] Male writers may hold other views and present their women characters as unhappy with Scheherazade for accepting the role of a wife in the first place, as is the case with the mother Najwa in the Libyan novelist Hisham Matar's *In the Country of Men*. She thinks of Scheherazade as a "coward who accepted slavery over death," a "stupid harlot."[32] Throughout these and other worldwide engagements, the *Arabian Nights* appears liberal and open enough to offer imitators, adapters, translators, and architects of taste a wide scope for use and misuse that ranges between complicity in a dominating ethic and a postcolonial consciousness that interrogates the status quo.[33]

At a certain point, scholars and critics felt some unease with respect to a seemingly waning interest in the *Arabian Nights*. Pitted against their eighteenth- and nineteenth-century vogue, the tales are no longer a center of attention in periodical criticism. While there may be some justification

[29] Elias Khoury, *Awlād al-ghītū: Ismī Ādam* (Beirut: Dār al-Ādāb, 2016); trans. Humphrey Davies, *Children of the Ghetto: My Name Is Adam* (Brooklyn, NY: Archipelago Books, 2019).

[30] See Jennifer Lynn Gipson, "Writing the Storyteller: Folklore and Literature from Nineteenth-Century France to the Francophone World" (PhD diss., University of California, Berkeley, 2011), 29–34.

[31] See Fedwa Malti-Douglas, "Shahrazad Feminist," in *The Thousand and One Nights in Arabic Literature and Society*, ed. Richard G. Hovannisian and Georges Sabagh (Cambridge: Cambridge University Press, 1997), 40–55.

[32] Hisham Matar, *In the Country of Men* (New York: Dial Press, 2008), 15, 17, respectively.

[33] Ferial Jabouri Ghazoul finds in the absence of a definitive text enough license for marauding in redactions and editions. "If the text has been handled frequently in this promiscuous fashion, it is indicative that the text allows itself to be 'mishandled.' One cannot blame a Lane or a Galland for taking liberties with the text, for after all, texts get the treatment they deserve. . . . It is constructed so as to accommodate and incorporate different material, as in an anthology or a compendium." Ferial Jabouri Ghazoul, *The Arabian Nights: A Structural Analysis* (Cairo: National Commission for UNESCO, 1980), 17.

for such unease, we need to read the scene from a different perspective: Radical and at times drastic transformations enforce different cultural scripts that are heavily impregnated with utilitarian values and interests. Literary pursuits have suffered under postcapitalist culture, which has been developing other means of selling itself. Scheherazade's craftiness comes to writers' rescue, as shown in James Joyce's narratives. Playing on dreams for power and conversely presenting porters, mendicants, thieves, dreamers, beauty models, and rogues or respectable businessmen, it has been making its way into cultural production. Artists, poets, painters, and scholars can all find a thematic or narrative thread here and there that arouses curiosity and simultaneous appeal to some emerging taste.

The seeming surge in scholarly research and criticism is not generated by a specific book or undertaking, as some well-meaning scholars have argued. Whenever gaining momentum, a literary phenomenon speaks of and to a wider cultural script: a dynamic movement against the status quo, and a postcapitalist and neoliberal market that requires new approaches, tastes, fashions, and certainly adaptable and appropriate treasuries. German translations of the *Nights*, philological research, and narratology cannot be seen apart from a long genealogy of interest in folk literature.[34] Moreover and in tandem with this line of questioning presumptions regarding a specific case or edition as the one that generates interest, was it sheer coincidence that led three Iraqis to start working in the mid-1970s on the *Arabian Nights*? Ferial Ghazoul submitted her doctoral dissertation on a structural analysis of the *Arabian Nights* to Columbia University in 1978;[35] I published an article in 1976, "18th-Century English Criticism of the *Arabian Nights*,"[36] to be followed by my dissertation in 1978 that appeared in book form as *Scheherazade in England* in 1981; a year before another article appeared, "The Growth of Scholarly Interest in the *Arabian Nights*."[37] Almost around that same time (1972–84), the renowned philosopher and social scientist at Chicago and then Harvard, Muhsin Mahdi, took upon

[34] Mia I. Gerhardt, *The Art of Story-Telling: A Literary Study of the Thousand and One Nights* (Leiden: Brill, 1963); Sami Alahmedi, "Wieland und 1001 Nacht" (PhD diss., Leipzig University, 1969); and Katharina Mommsen, *Goethe und 1001 Nacht* (Berlin: Akademie-Verlag, 1960), were among many other efforts to establish that line of folk genealogical interdependency. See further notes on this topic in Chapter 7.

[35] Ghazoul, *Arabian Nights*. This was updated and expanded in Ferial Jabouri Ghazoul, *Nocturnal Poetics: The Arabian Nights in Comparative Context* (Cairo: American University in Cairo Press, 1996).

[36] See al-Musawi, "Arabian Nights." Two years earlier, Christopher Knipp published a survey of the reception of translations; see Christopher Knipp, "The *Arabian Nights* in England: Galland's Translation and Its Successors," *Journal of Arabic Literature* 5, no. 1 (1974), 44–54.

[37] al-Musawi, "Growth of Scholarly Interest."

himself the arduous task of writing firstly "Remarks on the 1001 Nights" (1973), and then editing the extant fourteenth-century Arabic manuscript of *Alf laylah wa-laylah* (*A Thousand and One Nights*) that appeared in 1984, to be followed by two volumes of manuscript classification and criticism.[38] He may have acquired this taste for a critical text from both his Chicago mentor, the Iraqi-born Nabia Abbott,[39] who unearthed a fragment of a manuscript of the *Thousand and One Nights*, and also in some way from his cherished advisor, the liberal political scientist and classical philosopher Leo Strauss (d. 1973), to whom Mahdi lent Enno Littman's translation of the *Thousand and One Nights* (1961–62).[40] Mahdi's tenure as James Richard Jewett Professor of Arabic at Harvard (beginning in 1969) could have been an incentive to balance his lifelong involvement in Islamic philosophy with some more literary research.

Another Iraqi, Husain Fareed Ali Haddawy, the translator of Galland's edited manuscript, wrote his dissertation on the Oriental tale in 1962.[41] Should we regard this as a turning point in scholarship, or should we instead look upon it as an initiation into a momentous cultural movement, one that began to take shape after the massive youth and workers' revolt of May 1968, the Vietnam War, the civil rights movement in America, the raging Cold War, and the serious revisionism undergone by European communist parties, especially in France and Italy?[42] The university campus could no longer be the same. These and similar events opened up troubling gaps in patriarchal structures and Eurocentric

[38] William A. Graham et al., "Muhsin Mahdi," *The Harvard Gazette*, April 21, 2011, https://news.harvard.edu/gazette/story/2011/04/muhsin-mahdi/; Muhsin Mahdi, "Remarks on the 1001 Nights," *Interpretation* 3 (1973), 157–68; Muhsin Mahdi, "Mazâhir al-riwâya wa-'l-mushâfaha fî usûl 'Alf layla wa-layla,'" *Revue de l'Institut des manuscrits arabes* 20 (1974), 125–44; Muhsin Mahdi, *The Thousand and One Nights (Alf Layla wa-Layla) from the Earliest Known Sources* (Leiden: Brill, 1984–94) [Part I: "Arabic Text" (1984[a]); Part II: "Critical Apparatus. Description of Manuscripts" (1984); Part III: "Introduction and Indexes" (1994). Contents of Part III: "Antoine Galland and the Nights," 11–49; "Galland's Successors," 51–86; "Four Editions: 1814–1843," 87–126; "Three Interpretations," 127–80].

[39] She was born in Mardin, Mosul in Iraq, and educated in Baghdad and later Bombay before moving to the United States. She died on October 15, 1981.

[40] There is more on this point later. See Rasoul Namazi, "Politics, Religion, and Love: How Leo Strauss Read the Arabian Nights," *The Journal of Religion* 100, no. 2 (April 2020), 193.

[41] Husain Fareed Ali Haddawy, "English Arabesque: The Oriental Mode in Eighteenth-Century English Literature" (PhD diss., Cornell University, 1962). See al-Musawi, *Scheherazade in England*, bibliography/unpublished material. For more, see https://libraries.indiana.edu/bibliography-doctoral-dissertations-middle-eastern-islamic-studies.

[42] See Julie Rivkin and Michael Ryan, "Introduction: 'The Class of 1968-Post-Structuralism par lui-meme,'" in *Literary Theory: An Anthology*, ed. Julie Rivkin and Michael Ryan (Malden, MA: Blackwell, 1998), 334–57.

university programs that had allowed no texts of color in their curricular offerings. It was then, and also in the mid-1970s, that Edward Said embarked on his project that appeared in book form as *Orientalism* in 1978, a devastating archaeological excavation of Western paradigms versus the colonized and people of color. Its wide scope and venture into philological inquiry to scathingly uncover representations of the "Orient" took the cultural scene by surprise and raised waves of both favorable and antagonistic response. Bernard Lewis's article is representative of the latter position;[43] it is propelled by fear of this challenge to an enduring academic status quo. The term "Orientalism" is no less problematic for Arab scholars whose training in the humanities had directed them toward literature as an apolitical pursuit. Thus, in the mid-1930s, the Egyptian scholar Aḥmad Ḍayf, for example, wrote "a critical historical study" on *Alf laylah wa-laylah* that credits European Orientalists with the *Arabian Nights* phenomenon: "For only European Orientalists were the ones to uncover its mysteries. They wrote books and long and short treatises about it."[44] Other Arab scholars, with the exception of Suhayr Qalamāwī,[45] continued to take a trivial approach to the tales and probably regarded them as unworthy of academic study.

In America in particular, the 1970s set the academic scene for a textual resurrection of *A Thousand and One Nights*. Scholarship takes a number of directions and interests to deal with translation, appropriation, reception, critical response, and specific analysis of certain structures in the heyday of structuralism and its poststructuralist aftermath.[46]

To recapitulate, and as a sequel to my *Scheherazade in England* (but now more geared toward a wider concern with the return of the *Arabian Nights*, especially in the academy, cinematography, and art), the present project is an archaeology of the work's genealogy, formation, dissemination, use, commoditization, and study in *contemporary* world cultures. The project can be neither smooth nor easy, not only because of massive production and academic interest, but also because we are witnessing

[43] Bernard Lewis, "The Question of Orientalism," *The New York Review of Books*, June 24, 1982, https://bit.ly/3cK4bvk.

[44] Aḥmad Ḍayf, "Baḥth tārīkhī naqdī fī alf laylah wa-laylah," *al-Muqtaṭaf* 86, no. 3 (1935), 265–70.

[45] Suhayr al-Qalamāwī, *Alf laylah wa-laylah* (Cairo: Dār al-Maʿārif, 1943).

[46] While human sciences made use of structuralism to situate human relational practices in a wider episteme, in poetics language sustains some independent entity as self-contained, with a relational structure whereby this elemental structure sustains value or meaning as a matrix of parallels, oppositions, and distributions. See more on poetics in Jonathan Culler, *Structuralist Poetics: Structuralism, Linguistics and the Study of Literature* (London: Routledge and Kegan Paul, 1975). Poststructuralism rejects the conceptualization of language as transparent medium connecting to an outside reality or truth, but rather a code or structure. It invests more in discontinuity and rupture.

other modes and methodologies of acquisition. The Internet offers enormous help nowadays, missed by earlier generations who had to cope with arduous perusal of archives and periodicals. Despite this internet luxury, scholarship still suffers from a number of omissions that relate to other cultures, especially Arabic. It is rare to find scholars writing on the *Thousand and One Nights* who have checked the relevant Arabic sources.[47]

As noted earlier, academic interest is on the increase because of a postcolonial consciousness that helped the accommodation of non-European writing in global and common core courses. Every year brings about new productions of the *Arabian Nights*, along with a multifarious use of its properties. At the extreme end of negative use, the tales are casually referenced or used to further early colonialist representations. Violent and abusive, these representations surge in times of war and aggression or sweeping reports on terrorism. In an ironic turn against Scheherazade's narratives gifts of wit, wisdom, love, and reason, the sumptuous palaces and valleys of diamonds of the *Arabian Nights*, not the dreams of cobblers and fishermen, incite greed, and generate motives for invasions that simultaneously present the invaded lands with their rich oil fields as harboring terrorists or accumulating weapons of mass destruction.[48]

There are other lines of inquiry, however, that can engage with a few individual cases traversing the world cultural spectrum while signifying textual filiation and affiliation. There is the female genealogy of women's writing since the days of Delarivier Manley and her *Almyna, or, The Arabian Vow* (1705–6), one that does not conclude with the Egyptian Suhayr Qalamāwī in her *Ḥikāyāt jaddatī* (1936; *My Grandmother's Tales*) and her doctoral dissertation of the same period on *Alf laylah wa-laylah*, completed under the supervision of the prominent man of letters Ṭāhā Ḥusayn. Nor would it conclude with Angela Carter or the Booker Prize winner A. S. Byatt. There is also Jorge Luis Borges's trajectory, because, in addition to his two significant essays, "The Translators of the Thousand and One Nights" and "The Thousand and One Nights," his writing is rarely free from some lineage to the *Arabian Nights*, its art, and translations or editions.[49] Alongside this long-cherished engagement, there is Barth's parodic and often sardonic tone that mocks his own textual affiliation with the *Nights*. A different but very defining line in visual culture is the one taken in 1974 by Pier Paolo Pasolini in his film

[47] See more in Ibrahim Akel, "Arabic Editions and Bibliography," in *Arabic Manuscripts of the "Thousand and One Nights": Presentation and Critical Editions of Four Noteworthy Texts; Observations on Some Osmanli Traditions*, ed. Aboubakr Chraïbi (Paris: Espaces et signes, 2016), 431–91.

[48] Shaheen, *Reel Bad Arabs*.

[49] More on this point in Chapters 4 and 6.

Il fiore delle mille e una note (*The Flower of the One Thousand and One Nights*), which terminates his Trilogy of Life (*Decameron* and *Canterbury Tales*). In the theatrical realm there is Tim Supple's contribution.

I examine specific instances of productions, writings, and critiques to present a comprehensive outlook, not a survey, of the underlying political, cultural, and economic dynamics that inform the return of the *Arabian Nights* to the scene since the mid-1970s. I adopt Tim Supple's 2011 production for the theater, Richie's Disney production of Aladdin, and certain rewritings of the *Arabian Nights* like Najīb Maḥfūẓ's *Layālī alf laylah* (1982; English translation: *Arabian Nights and Days*), or Andrei Codrescu's *Whatever Gets You through the Night* (2012), and Barth's *The Last Voyage of Somebody the Sailor* (1991), as three differentiated appropriations that, respectively, speak of and against closed systems of thought and practice; that rewrite the genealogical tree of translators as entrepreneurs, proprietors, and pundits; and that present globalization ironically as anchored in a three-pronged exercise in persuasion, coercion, and invasion. Never giving up on their presence as authors, their resort to this type of self-reflexive authorship, as is the case with Barth, is postmodernist in the first place. This postmodernist stance is sardonic, parodic, relativist, and fluid. It even ridicules modernist presumptions that reason and science lead to truth, or that Western democracy and the belief in progress are universal truths.[50] The postmodernist recourse to the *Nights* is often a reaction against modernist mimicry, and its Othering of cultures and nations, and the modernist faith in the transparency of language. Scheherazade offers uncertainties and vicissitudes of fortune, and the tales are open to readings and misreading. Postmodernists invest in Scheherazade and her translators, but it is often Galland's Scheherazade, the one that other translators cannot ignore, as she lays down the basic parameters for European texts ever since 1704–17. Since then, a culture industry has been engendered and generated that is uniquely its own. Borges sums up this verdict: "Galland established the canon, incorporating stories that time would render indispensable and that the translators to come – his enemies – would not dare omit."[51]

At this juncture, the *Arabian Nights*, and some tales in particular, serve as national, transnational, and global allegories. While at times they

[50] Basically, postmodernism opposes the modernist view of reason and science as conducive to truth. A postmodernist stance looks upon these as ideologies. Truth is relative and cannot be nailed down. The modernist understanding of a stable "self" is a myth for postmodernists because it is made up of a number of sociocultural elements that also mutate against modernist dichotomies in matters of gender, race, and ethnicity. Western production in these domains is held suspect.

[51] Jorge Luis Borges, "The Translators of the Thousand and One Nights," in *Selected Non-fictions*, ed. Eliot Weinberger (New York: Penguin, 1999), 106.

become sites of protest to be used in feminist readings, on many other occasions they assume larger meanings and lead us into the heart of urgent political, economic, and ideological issues. In Assia Djebar's (1987) *Sister to Scheherazade* and Fatema Mernissi's *Scheherazade Goes West* (2002), we as readers find feminism serving as an integral part of the dialogue on cultural dependency or emancipatory discourse. The late Egyptian scholar Suhayr Qalamāwī surveyed scholarship on origins and manuscripts. Her other chapters focus on content, especially borrowing from other books, and the presence of women. In the chapter on women, Qalamāwī sets the stage for nuanced readings of gender through storytellers' lenses. With her study, Qalamāwī brought to the attention of Arab scholars a book that had been relegated to the margins of popular literature, or folk narrative. In line with her supervisor's classification, *Alf laylah* is regarded as folk literature because the storyteller builds on the written to develop an embedded narrative for interested audiences, a viewpoint which is highly debatable.

In reading selected texts, it is the plan of this study to enable them to speak for themselves; produce their techniques and themes; and often engage or interrogate common practices and current theoretical applications. In a manner similar to my method in a recent book in Arabic on popular memory and the societies of the *Thousand and One Nights*,[52] this book hopes to initiate further discussion concerning the intricate or overt mechanisms of the *Nights* and their bearings on cultures, as well as their accessibility to one or other type of marauding. Although it is too early to attempt an adequate assessment of the main currents in twentieth-century criticism of the *Nights* and early twenty-first-century studies, it is hardly too much to suggest that what follows in the coming chapters indicates an increasing awareness of the aesthetic richness of the tales and the complexity of their sociocultural milieu. Compared to Victorian literary journalism, a considerable portion of twentieth-century treatment of the tales recognizes their composite nature, a recognition that is manifested at its best in the more or less specialized analyses of specific modes, thematic cycles, and artistic patterns.[53] Along with other factors, this specialized pursuit informs current academic research and thus indicates a drastic break from the reflective nineteenth-century reception of the *Arabian Nights*. Although its countless simplified versions still entertain children all over the globe, its so-called complete texts only attract the specialist. Thus, for the ethnologist, sociologist, and student of aesthetics, the *Nights* is a rich storehouse of

[52] Muḥsin al-Mūsawī, *al-Dhākirah al-sha'biyyah li-mujtama'āt alf laylah wa-laylah* (Beirut: al-Markaz al-Thaqāfī al-'Arabī, 2016).

[53] For a general overview, see Jan Pauliny, "Adaptation oder Ubersetzung? Tausend und eine Nacht im europäischen Literaturkontext," *Graecolatina et Orientalia* 15–16 (1983–84), 115–31.

information and modes that invites investigation and research, and even the growth or demise of genres.

Rather than a survey, this project is thus more focused on intersectional and interstitial spaces that specifically account for the presence of the *Nights* in narratology, politics, and arts and sciences. In a succinct note, Robert Irwin argues that it is easier to speak of what is not touched by *A Thousand and One Nights* (*Arabian Nights*).[54] Insofar as the tercentenary spectrum of the *Arabian Nights* is concerned, we are presented with further excavations in an expanding assemblage. Within this spectrum, Antoine Galland retains his place of honor, already celebrated by Leigh Hunt, a place that Jorge Luis Borges heralds early in 1936 in his "Los traductores de las 1001 noches." A year earlier, the Sorbonne-trained Egyptian academic Aḥmad Ḍayf had returned to Egypt to readdress the *Arabian Nights* in terms that resonate with French literary and philological emphases.[55] For publication purposes he chose no less than the staid and rigorous journal *al-Muqtaṭaf*, which had for some time been espousing scientism against what it had previously dubbed fictitious narratives of bygone dark ages.[56] Ḍayf had that in mind when he published a "historical critical research paper" that takes for granted what has been circulated and discussed in Europe: "This book is the most famous in storytelling, not only in Arabic but also in every other language." He adds: "Some European scholars argued that it is next to the Bible in fame because it is the most widely read, the most imaginative and strange, and the richest in fables and legends."[57] To cover also its massive presence in the Global South could make this project much larger.

If Borges is more concerned with translators and texts, the Egyptian scholar focuses on philological inquiries, classifications. His conclusion is important to the premise of modification in discursive contexts: "The book might have been written in standard Arabic, but, as people used it, they made changes and alterations, adding to it a great portion of their conversational tales and reports to meet the taste of the common folk."[58] This is only one suggestion among many that scholars have been proposing in their search for a definitive text. In the end, the *Arabian Nights* has gathered around it more than a 300-year period of culture industry that reflects epistemic shifts in world knowledge constructions.[59] To find Ḍayf

[54] Robert Irwin, *The Arabian Nights: A Companion* (London: The Penguin Press, 1994), 290–91.
[55] Ḍayf, "Baḥth tārīkhī naqdī."
[56] See Muḥsin al-Mūsawī, *al-Riwāyah al-ʿArabiyyah* (Beirut: Dār al-Ādāb, 1988), 49.
[57] Ḍayf, "Baḥth tārīkhī naqdī," 265. [58] Ibid., 270.
[59] Apart from reprints of Galland, Mardrus, and others, there are Jamel Eddine Bencheikh, André Miquel, and Touhami Bencheikh, ed. and trans., *Les Mille et Une Nuit: Contes*

and Borges writing on two sides of the *Arabian Nights*, its translators and its popularity, is coincidental, for sure, but how much do they tell us about the rise of new theories of translation, their relevance to a body politics, and their encapsulation of philological inquiry? Even Galland's incomplete Arabic manuscript raises questions about the viability of terms like equivalence, transference, appropriation, translation, recension, and redaction. What had previously been raised about translating Homer should also have been raised with respect to Scheherazade's travels to France, England, and Germany, before reaching almost everywhere else.[60] The search for an original has been always a preoccupation for philologists whose research has been inseparable from emerging ethnographic, ecological, and demographic theories in Europe ever since the late eighteenth century.[61]

Since the last decades of the twentieth century, authentication responds to a postcolonial consciousness to emancipate Scheherazade's narrative from the overwhelming imposition of early translators or appropriators. Editors and/or translators appear as facilitators rather than owners. They are in tune with writers' self-conscious engagements with Scheherazade's narratives. While engaging with postmodernism or more inclined to metafiction, the late twentieth-century rhetorical turn invests more in the presence rather than the death of the author, the new cultural entrepreneur or pundit who, as Codrescu shows, gives herself/himself a free hand in invading, fabricating, and rewriting translations and texts, patching together and collating shreds and pieces while authenticating them in marginal commentaries. An open market cultural economy is the rule of the textual land. Although the translator may be driven into the background, receiving slight or no recognition from the postmodernist author as the storyteller's double, the former's role is not negligible. After all, it is the translator who originates the phenomenal rise of this fictional

choisis, 2 vols., folio 2256–57 (Paris: Gallimard, 1996); and Jamel Eddine Bencheikh and André Miquel, ed. and trans., *Sindbâd de la mer et autres contes des Mille et Une Nuits: Contes choisis* IV, folio 3581 (Paris: Gallimard, 2001). See also Chraïbi's study of new tales, Aboubakr Chraïbi, *Contes nouveaux des 1001 nuits: Étude du manuscript Reinhardt* (Paris: J. Maisonneuve, 1996).

[60] Borges admired this dialogue between Matthew Arnold and F. W. Newman. See Jorge Luis Borges, "Some Versions of Homer," trans. Suzanne J. Levine, *PMLA* 107, no. 5 (October 1992), 1137. Arnold's "On Translating Homer: Last Words" was the last of a series of lectures, given as of Poetry at Oxford, collected and published in 1861; and F. W. Newman's response, *Homeric Translation in Theory and Practice: A Reply to Matthew Arnold, Esq.* (London: Williams and Norgate, 1861).

[61] See Edward Said, *Orientalism* (New York: Random House, 1979), 130; Anwar Abdel Malek, "Orientalism in Crisis," *Diogenes* 44 (Winter 1963), 107–8; and Muhsin Jassim al-Musawi, "Postcolonial Theory in the Arab World: Belated Engagements and Limits," *Interventions* 20, no. 2 (February 2018), 174–91.

genre that Martha Pike Conant in 1908 called the "Oriental Tale."[62] This is not a fortunate label, for Leigh Hunt among poets, Bagehot among essayists, and Robert Chambers among public intellectuals and cultural critics think of the *Arabian Nights* in particular as central to their culture.[63] The latter thinks of the *Nights* "amongst similar things of our own which constitute the national literary inheritance."[64] They recognize Galland more than any other translator as the one who deserves acclaim. Barth relies on his version, so have many others done to date.

Chapter 1, "The *Arabian Nights*: A European Legacy?" examines a referential framework that informed a cultural milieu and legitimized the use of the term "*Arabian Nightism*" in discussions that relate to presumed sumptuousness and lavish spending. However, that very phrase illustrates how the *Nights* permeates a consciousness and inhabits European and American culture in multifarious ways and contexts, ways that justify addressing it as a knowledge consortium, an epistemic inception that has continued to direct or challenge regimes of thought. Its trajectory in these cultures demonstrates constants and variables in reception and appropriation, and invites us to draw comparisons with its native culture in relation to issues of literacy and orality.

Chapter 2, "The Scheherazade Factor," takes its title from a conversation with Barth (1987) as a means of addressing the focus on the frame tale in contemporary writing. It reveals the central function of preliminary volatile sites, the preludinal site of nuptial failure that ushers the reader headlong into the main rupture, the garden scene, and its narrative function before the advent of Scheherazade. What is missing in scholarship, both old and contemporary, is redeemed here to draw attention to the role of the spectacle in exploding hierarchies, power structures, and racial and class distinctions. It draws attention to a number of narrative levels that need to be taken into account when we address the frame tale, not as a container, but a dynamic that offers storytellers the chance to embed other tales that are no less explosive. It shows also the implications of narrative functions in relation to issues of relativity, plight, desire, and joy.

Chapter 3, "Engagements in Narrative," discusses other aspects of narrative properties, taking as examples and models a number of writers from Bethlehem to Havana, to demonstrate two types of engagement with the *Nights*: firstly, its role in consolidating predispositions to the art of narrative, as in the case of the Palestinian-Iraqi novelist, critic, poet, and

[62] In a recent talk at George Mason University, I addressed this question. See www.facebook.com/avacgis and https://twitter.com/AVACGIS/status/1316437710219948039.

[63] For a study of these responses, see al-Musawi, *Scheherazade in England*. [64] Ibid., 38.

painter Jabra Ibrahim Jabra; secondly, its generous loans to writers across the globe. A narrative globe-trotter of a sort, Scheherazade is an ever-welcome guest and host in almost every culture. If she offers Michel Butor a number of tales, but especially that of the second mendicant of multiple adventures and transformations that converse with his experimentation in new fiction, it is Marcel Proust's self-reference for an unfinished narrative journey. Barth reads the frame tale as a dialectic between sex and narrative. The Egyptian Nobel Prize winner Najīb Maḥfūẓ presents the cosmopolitan female narrator as an adept who, even so, cannot dispense with her Sufi master's guidance so as to see behind the thick material barriers of arrogance, passion, vicissitudes, wide challenges, and the need to combat evil. Scheherazade is the trope for the *confabulator nocturne*, the nocturnal raconteur whose traces are still around.[65]

Chapter 4, "The 'Hostile Dynasty': Rewriting the *Arabian Nights*," parallels Borges's reading of a dynastic translational spectrum of anxieties. A forum for discussion initiated by Galland has involved a worldwide cultural community in anxieties that are expressed in reeditions, abridgments, and authentication processes; claims to fidelity to an original, though disputed, text; and unexpurgated or collated editions. The discussions that have erupted ever since the publication of Galland's *Thousand and One Nights* have set that same community on fire: Accusations and countercharges leveled over three centuries signify the existence of the *Nights* in world cultures as a knowledge consortium that invokes theories of translation, cultural interventions, conversations, and discussions among the most prominent intellectuals, artists, and fiction writers. Illustrators, film industry producers, and directors have also been participating in this dynasty, simply because they are part of one translation or another, though on certain occasions they stand on their own. If political dynasties of rulers are often biologically related, the *Nights* in Europe has its own textual dynasty: no translator or editor could ever be liberated from Galland's enterprise, not even Muhsin Mahdi, who reproduced Galland's Arabic manuscript after only portions of it had appeared in print early in the twentieth century. More important is the fact that the *Nights* was once also a platform in the ongoing racial/philological divide in language families Aryan and Semitic. *New* philology found in the *Nights* a viable means to discuss origins. The divide did not die, and is reborn in stock images, value judgments, and essentialisms.

[65] Nocturnal fabulator or storyteller. See Richard Hamilton, *The Last Storytellers: Tales from the Heart of Morocco* (London: I.B. Tauris, 2011). On a narrative level, see Rabih Alameddine's novel, *The Hakawati* (New York: Knopf, 2008).

Chapter 5, "The Archaeology of *A Thousand and One Nights*," complements the previous chapters in that it foregrounds archaeology in relation to two domains that will allow a history of the burgeoning of the *Nights* in its own lands to be laid out in terms of a body of enunciations and statements. A discursive genealogy suggests multiple productions that share only a basal root, that is, the frame tale of the two kings, but not the rest, such as "The Merchant and the Demon." The other domain includes early migrations of tales, and the major translational movement established by Galland. Both these domains have their own histories that effectively give place "to definite types of discourse . . . which are related to a whole set of various histories."[66] Within such discursive density, the issue of authorship is not visible. It wanes and disappears within large grids of narrative engagements. Furthermore, beginnings cannot be dissociated from a narrative corpus that possesses its own underlying theoretical bases before the advent of the novel as a bourgeois epic.

Chapter 6, "Signatures and Affiliates," starts with the understanding of the advent of the *Nights* as "a major event for all European literature," a point that Borges and other commentators argue passionately. To gauge the impact of this event, we need to differentiate the Romantic craze of William Beckford in his *Vathek*, *Episodes*, and "Long Story," his translators, and also his admirers from other cultures. Beckford was phenomenal in his ability to work across at least three cultures along with Arabic: French, English, and Jamaican. After all, his father and father-in-law made their fortune in Jamaica. Beckford was born there in 1709. His infatuation with and reproduction of the *Nights* is unique, but we have to place it in the context of a raging discussion involving many, but especially August Wilhelm von Schlegel (1767–1845), of the grotesque and Arabesque. Beckford's writing and personal penchant for challenging everything presents him as a filiate of a specific genealogy in the *Nights*. His approach is different, for instance, from that of the Brontës, Emile and Charlotte, whose writings bear the marks of a contained infatuation. They serve as the bridge for twentieth-century shifts in reading and response. A "murky sensualism," which Maxime Rodinson associates with "the Western bourgeoisie," prepares for the dialectic of rapprochement, engagement, and detachment that present the twentieth century and later as more experimental but also no less involved in substantiating the *Nights* in architecture, painting, reenactment of medieval travels, and the practice of parody and pastiche in a postmodernist anxiety and search for distinction.

[66] Foucault, *Archaeology of Knowledge*, 165.

Chapter 7, "Decolonizing the *Arabian Nights*?," throws us headlong into a controversial issue that reflects on the first chapter, but also complements every other chapter in that it takes the "Oriental mode" as a problematic that invites deconstruction. Does the connotation of the mode signify the anxieties of the pillars of the Enlightenment? It certainly does, and hence the need to devise an emancipatory discourse from a ruling Western rationality that presents everything, even the theory of the novel or narratology, as being necessarily Western. The role of philologists since the early nineteenth century regarding the production of knowledge is more relevant to the study and vogue of the *Nights* than has been hitherto noticed. Scheherazade's body, the matter and manner of the *Nights*, is no less the crux of discussion than the visible grouping of language in families Aryan and Semitic. That is why many twentieth-century narrative experiments are to be read as decolonizing in that they redirect attention to a literary text, not a document. In this sense, it is time to see the *Nights* as central to any study of grammatology where writing and script laws, conversation protocols, reiteration and repetition are sites of differentiation or confirmation. A grammar for narrative has to go beyond a few European texts that have occupied the scene.

Chapter 8, "Invitation to Discourse," concludes the discussion. It attempts to show how the *Nights* has been continually opening the gate for every kind of reading. Although this study, and this chapter in particular, is not a survey of scholarship, it selects instances that identify a genealogical line that brings all the players on board, showing how the often-marginalized Payne is pivotal to the twentieth-century scene, not only because he was Richard F. Burton's ghost translator, but also because he set the path for literary classification of the tales that nobody, not even Burton, can overlook. Twentieth-century scholars like Mia Gerhardt or Peter Heath cannot devise more typologies than Payne's, but they add what "conditions of possibility" allow. The chapter focuses on critical typologies, textual and genealogical criticism, the comparatists' pursuits, and literary criticism. The last of those categories covers genres and translational mediums, and the poetics of narrative. It also treats cultural criticism as being more nuanced than nineteenth-century readings of manners and customs. The chapter has to conclude with the question: Is there a possible conclusion to this ongoing enterprise?

1 The *Arabian Nights*

A European Legacy?

> During the bombardment of Sarajevo in 1994, a group of theater workers in Amsterdam commissioned tales, from different European writers, to be read aloud, simultaneously, in theaters in Sarajevo itself and all over Europe, every Friday until the fighting ended. This project pitted storytelling against destruction, imaginative life against real death. It may not have saved lives, but it was a form of living energy. It looked back to "The Thousand and One Nights" and forward to the millennium. It was called Scheherazade 2001.
>
> A. S. Byatt, "Why Scheherazade Keeps on Talking"

> [A]nd the first serial novel ever written, *The Thousand and One Nights*, are the greatest joys I have experienced.
>
> Jorge Luis Borges, "Literary Pleasure"

A Phenomenal *Arabian Nightism*!

As much as the *Arabian Nights* is fortunate in having inspired so many articles, books, films, paintings, and other forms of production in almost every language, it also suffers from manipulation or misuse. In both cases, a vast field exists, one that has been calling on scholars and research groups to tabulate and systematize its corpus and define its frontiers.[1] This book does not choose to *survey* influences, nor does it attempt to *chart* traces in fiction, poetry, film, and painting, a project that has already been undertaken by a number of researchers.[2] Instead it explores specific

[1] Alongside Marzolph's bibliography, and that of Akel, there is the Encounters with the Orient project, funded by HERA (Humanities European Research Area).

[2] For more on these, see Irwin, *Arabian Nights*; also his article, "The *Arabian Nights* in Film Adaptations," in *The Arabian Nights Encyclopedia*, ed. Ulrich Marzolph and Richard van Leeuwen (Santa Barbara, CA: ABC-CLIO, 2004), 21–25. For more, see Ulrich Marzolph, "The *Arabian Nights* International Bibliography," in *Arabic Manuscripts of the "Thousand and One Nights": Presentation and Critical Editions of Four Noteworthy Texts; Observations on Some Osmanli Traditions*, ed. Aboubakr Chraïbi (Paris: Espaces et signes, 2016), 493–564. On the film industry, see Alan Nadel, "A Whole New

instances that invite conceptualization and construction of an archaeological site. In particular, it focuses on narrative strategies and spectacles in a postcapitalist era. Hence, the effort is concerned with the enormous body of motifs, leitmotifs, images, narrative levels, and dynamics that sustain the presence of the most popular tales in cultural production. It also poses questions, not only concerning historical fluctuations in matters of reception and the absence of some tales or their devaluation in comparison with others, but also maps of reading and misreading.

The challenge posed by this recurrence/occurrence of absence and presence draws on a wide spectrum of differential but also cohesive elements. A world of labyrinths but also straightforward narratives continue to enthrall readers of texts and spectators of cinematic and theatrical production, albeit with variations. This world has also drawn the attention of structuralist critics who usually avoid unsystematic narratives or those that elude paradigmatic patterning. As a composite narrative corpus presided over by the narrator of narrators, Scheherazade, *A Thousand and One Nights* resists neat classification. Poised between its early burgeoning in written or orally narrated tales, and its transmutation in translations and redactions, this collective narrative body is differentiated by diversity, plurality, and vast geographical and cultural swathes. Narratives characterized by a seemingly smooth storytelling may produce a surprising detour somewhere in the middle or at the end. What distinguishes relevant sites of cultural production of the *Arabian Nights* since the enormous investment of late nineteenth-century scholars in philological and anthropological research is the specific focus on the characteristics of these tales. *A Thousand and One Nights* (*Les Mille et Une Nuit: Contes arabes*, baptized by the Grub Street translator in 1706 or before as *The Arabian Nights' Entertainments*) occupies a different space in this postcapitalist era. If it was then the preoccupation of monthlies, newspapers, circulating libraries, cafés, theaters, and drawing rooms, the academy and cinema have since taken over in this postindustrial, postcapitalist society. A large culture industry gathers momentum. Along with publication, distribution, promotion, and academic or cinematic investment and appropriation in visual arts, this industry tends to raise further questions not only about dissemination and reception, but also origination, genealogies, and

(Disney) World Order: Aladdin, Atomic Power, and the Muslim East," in *Visions of the East: Orientalism in Film*, ed. Matthew Bernstein and Gaylyn Studlar (New Brunswick, NJ: Rutgers University Press, 1997), 184–203.

history.[3] It invests even more in establishing a constellation of presence, a consortium of traces in contemporary world literatures.[4] A postcolonial or decolonial streak is noticeable in these engagements with a focus on Scheherazade as a pioneering feminist, a liberator; but, since the last decades of the previous century, she also looms large as a narrative fulcrum, a tendency that reminds us of a long French tradition that centers on her role as narrator, as Chapter 2 explains.[5] A multilayered hermeneutic, deeply interwoven with explorations into narrativity, narratology, and narratorial perspectives, is quite visible. Scheherazade's presence as narrator or protagonist reflects even on tales like Ali Baba or Aladdin that were once either seen as orphan or unidentified. Appropriated translations manage to give form to a composite whole.[6] Aladdin, Ali Baba, and even Sindbad,[7] prove more accessible to cinematic and visual production as they provide cinema industry and visual arts with color, variety, action, characters, and motifs. In all cases, the tales of *A Thousand and One Nights* are no longer confined to Victorian drawing rooms or middle-class theaters in Europe. They are the subject of academic study and multifarious

[3] See Dominique Jullien, "Hârûn al-Rashîd, du conte au feuilleton," in *Les Mille et Une Nuits. Catalogue of an Exhibition at the Institut du Monde Arabe*, ed. Élodie Bouffard and Anne-Alexandra Joyard (Paris: Institut du monde arabe, 2012), 147–50.

[4] See al-Musawi, *Scheherazade in England*; Ghazoul, *Nocturnal Poetics*; Irwin, *Arabian Nights*; Richard van Leeuwen, *The Thousand and One Nights and Twentieth-Century Fiction: Intertextual Readings* (Leiden: Brill, 2018); and Ulrich Marzolph, ed., *The Arabian Nights in Transnational Perspective* (Detroit, MI: Wayne State University Press, 2007). For a comprehensive survey of the field in Arabic, see Akel, "Arabic Editions and Bibliography."

[5] For a brief survey, see Gipson, "Writing the Storyteller." See also Dominique Jullien, *Les Amoureux de Schéhérazade. Variations modernes sur les Mille et une nuits* (Geneva: Droz, 2009); and Christine Chaulet-Achour, ed., *Les Mille et Une Nuit et leurs réécriture au XXe siècle* (Paris: L'Harmattan, 2005).

[6] See Paulo Lemos Horta, *Marvellous Thieves: Secret Authors of the Arabian Nights* (Cambridge, MA: Harvard University Press, 2017), 1–2, 30–31. Ruth Bottigheimer and Ulrich Marzolph provide more on this in the Zurich Conference Proceedings on 'Orphan Tales,' 2020. Forthcoming. On "Ali Baba," see Katia Zakharia, "Jean-Georges Varsy et l'Histoire d'Ali Baba: révélations et silences de deux manuscrits récemment découverts.' *Arabica* 62, 2016, 652–687. And Katia Zakharia, "La version arabe la plus ancienne de l'Histoire d'Ali Baba: si Varsy n'avait pas traduit Galland? Réhabiliter le doute raisonnable." *Arabica* 64, 2017, 50–77.

[7] As an example, see Aboubakr Chraïbi, "Galland's 'Ali Baba' and Other Arabic Versions," *Marvels & Tales* 18, no. 2 (2004), 159–169; revised version in *The Arabian Nights in Transnational Perspective*, ed. Ulrich Marzolph (Detroit, MI: Wayne State University Press, 2007), 3–15. See also Duncan B. MacDonald, "'Ali Baba and the Forty Thieves' in Arabic from a Bodleian Ms," *Journal of the Royal Asiatic Society* (1910), 327–86. For 'parenthood' of Galland's "Nuits" see Ibrahim Akel, "Quelques remarques sur la bibliothèque d'Antoine Galland et l'arrivé des Mille et une nuits en Occident." In *Antoine Galland et l'Orient des savants*. ed. by Pierre-Sylvain Filliozat and Michel Zink (Paris: Académie des Inscriptions et Belles-Lettres, 2017), 197–215. Hollywood's production of Aladdin, and Hallmark's production of the *Nights* with emphasis on Ali Baba, are two examples.

productions. Both efforts are intertwined. The interest of the academy in popular courses on aspects of the *Arabian Nights* and visual production of tales are both signs of contemporary culture: its visible consumerist sway. While the academy is increasingly bent on developing skills, the nod to the *Nights* and courses that are saleable among marginal humanities' requirements is not done as a favor to any. It is merely a complementary gesture to students' demands and needs. We need to agree with Lyotard's early discussion of *The Postmodern Condition*, namely, that the "transmission of knowledge is no longer designed to train an elite capable of guiding the nation towards its emancipation, but to supply the system with players capable of acceptably fulfilling their roles at the pragmatic posts required by its institutions."[8]

However, cinematic production, paintings, and other visual venues are more accommodating because they thrive on the demand for diversion and a bit of leisure outside the system's grip. The trend toward commercial, commoditized, and loose ends signifies an epistemic turn, a shift in knowledge acquisition, appropriation, and representation. But, no matter how overwhelming the tendency is in criticism, philological inquiry, and cinematic production, it cannot be dissociated from an enormous corpus that made the *Arabian Nights* the most phenomenal legacy in Europe and North America throughout the eighteenth and nineteenth centuries. Indeed, until 1904, tourist guides speak of *Arabian Nightism* as a dash of fantasy, lavish spending and wealth, allurement, and intrigue. In mid-nineteenth-century New York, when the discussion of budgetary issues with respect to the Erie Canal was at its height, John A. Dix, a former Regency Canal commissioner, lectured widely against high-spending projects, an "*Arabian Nightism*," "in the midst of the depression of 1837."[9] Thomas Cook's *Traveler's Handbook for Algeria and Tunisia* describes the population there in markets and tourist hangouts in this manner: "Take away the dash of *Arabian Nightism*, and they are the same Jewesses whom you may see on the high days and holidays taking their ease in European tight-fitting dresses on the Saint Eugène or Mustapha tramcars, with their red-lipped, moist-eyed children round them."[10] This was taken almost verbatim from George Augustus Sala, *A Trip to Barbary by a Roundabout Route*, 1866, Algeria. The *Arabian Nights* thus assumed

[8] Jean-Francois Lyotard, *The Postmodern Condition: A Report on Knowledge*, trans. Geoff Bennington and Brian Massumi (Minneapolis, MN: University of Minnesota Press, 1984), 48.

[9] See Ronald E. Shaw, *Erie Water West: A History of the Erie Canal, 1792–1854* (Lexington, KY: University Press of Kentucky, 2013), 347.

[10] Thomas Cook, *The Traveller's Handbook for Algeria and Tunisia* (London: Simpkin, Marshall, Hamilton, Kent and Co., 1913), 21.

the role of a fashionable and trendy referent to aspiration, intrigue, enchantment, mirth, abundance, lushness, but also strangeness and squalor. In *The Satire in Victorian Fiction*, Frances Theresa Russell speaks of *Arabian Nightism* in relation to George Meredith's *Shaving of Shagpat*, as a mode of mirth, satire, humor, a laughter that defuses enchantment.[11] On a more educational note, it was listed in 1920 among the American High School's thirty works of fiction.[12]

In other words, the *Arabian Nights* has drawn contours and initiated a tour de force pseudo-Oriental narrative, and also an accumulation of impressions, comparisons and analogies, speech habits, registers, and handy catchphrases that make up a common communication forum.[13] It stopped short of making itself widely known and celebrated in the academy, primarily because the academy was not yet open to a systematic discussion of this kind of literature. It seems that the case was different in North America, as Columbia University and a number of institutions and publishers found this mode of writing intriguingly popular.[14] Given the nature of other translations and their specific production intended to meet either the bourgeois drawing room needs or private subscription of limited and numbered copies, the Grub Street translation into English of Antoine Galland's version long remained uncontested. At the time the growing corpus around and about the *Arabian Nights* was more focused on Galland's version, although Susan Nance argues differently in her book on the *Arabian Nights* in America, for "Galland's rendition came across as burdened with French idioms and sounded to Americans more French than anything else."[15]

But the question concerning this version and its migration from Aleppo to France and, thence, England and the rest of Europe is rarely

[11] Frances Theresa Russell, *Satire in Victorian Fiction* (New York: Macmillan, 1920), 80.

[12] N. W. W., "Thirty Books of Great Fiction," *The High School Journal* 3, no. 4 (April 1920), 115. This brief note says: "Home Reading Course No. 6, prepared by the United States Bureau of Education, gives a list of thirty books of great fiction that should be in every high-school library. Teachers of English would do well to bring this list to the attention of their pupils and explain to them the Bureau's plan of issuing certificates to those who read the entire list."

[13] See, in particular, Harry Stone, "Dickens's Reading" (PhD diss., University of California, Los Angeles, 1955); and Margaret C. Annan, "The Arabian Nights in Victorian Literature" (PhD diss., Northwestern University, 1945).

[14] Martha Pike Conant got her doctorate from Columbia University, and had it published by Columbia University Press in 1908; see her *The Oriental Tale in England in the Eighteenth Century* (New York: Columbia University Press, 1908). For a survey, see Rasoul Aliakbari, "American Nights: The Introduction and Usage of the Arabian Nights within the US's Print Modernity," in *The Thousand and One Nights: Sources and Transformations in Literature, Art, and Science*, ed. Ibrahim Akel and William Granara (Leiden: Brill, 2020), 255–69.

[15] Nance, *How the Arabian Nights Inspired the American Dream*, 23.

contextualized.[16] In his multiple capacities – as translator, antiquarian, of Arabic, tutor in modern Greek, and first secretary to Charles-Marie-François Olier, marquis de Nointel's diplomatic mission to the Sublime Porte (1670–79), and again with the new ambassador, Gabriel-Joseph de Lavergne, Comte de Guilleragues (1628–84) – Galland received support and encouragement to conduct research, secure manuscripts, connect with the elite and scholars, and familiarize himself not only with the languages, science, and cultures of the Ottoman Empire, but also and primarily with trade and Levantine commerce.[17] But French interest in that region was inseparable from a large imperial project, as the mission of Louis XIV's astute minister Jean-Baptiste Colbert makes clear.[18] As shown by his biographers, and also summarized by Muhsin Mahdi, Galland made full use of his stay in Istanbul and the Levant, and improved his knowledge of the languages of the region.[19] England was no less bent on some kind of cultural acquisition that could pave the road for further incursions. The letter of King Charles I of England, dated February 15, 1634, shows how the British felt the need for knowledge, not only for its immediate appeal, but also because, "there is a great deal of learning that is very fit and necessary to be known, that is written in Arabike, and there is a great defect in both our Universities."[20] A draft of Archbishop Laud's letter in justification of this royal order speaks of manuscripts as being needful for British interests, "for the knowledge of those parts, is for some accommodation to trade."[21] Like manuscripts on "useful knowledge," the *Nights* has its supply of inventions, ruses, and claims to automation. The magic carpet, the flying horse, and open sesame or trapdoors are among just a few of the devices that Scheherazade's tales offer as gateways out of the mundane,[22] but its

[16] Gerald J. Toomer's book is an exception; see his *Eastern Wisdom and Learning: The Study of Arabic in Seventeenth-Century England* (Oxford: Oxford University Press, 1996); see also Raymond Schwab, *The Oriental Renaissance: Europe's Rediscovery of India and the East, 1680–1880,* trans. Gene Patterson-Black and Victor Reinking (New York: Columbia University Press, 1984).

[17] For a brief note, see www.britannica.com/biography/Antoine-Galland. For more, Mohamed Abdel-Halim, *Antoine Galland, sa vie et son œuvre* (Paris: A. G. Nizet 1964). See also Raymond Schwab, *L'Auteur des Mille et une Nuits. Vie d'Antoine Galland* (Paris: Mercure de France, 1964).

[18] See Mahdi, *The Thousand and One Nights* (1995), 13–19. [19] Ibid., 16–18.

[20] Cited in Toomer, *Eastern Wisdom and Learning,* 108–9. See also Dorothee Metlitzki, *The Matter of Araby in Medieval England* (New Haven, CT: Yale University Press, 1977).

[21] Toomer, *Eastern Wisdom and Learning.*

[22] In this sense, see Ibn al-Razzaz al-Jazari, *The Book of Knowledge of Ingenious Mechanical Devices (Kitab fi ma'rifat al-hiyal al-handasiyyah)*, trans. Donald R. Hill (Dordrecht, Holland: Dordrecht Publishing Company, 1974); and Bin Shakir Banu Musa, *The Book of Ingenious Devices (Kitab al-hiyal)*, trans. Donald R. Hill (Dordrecht, Holland: D. Reidel Publishing Company, 1979).

sumptuousness becomes also a yardstick to measure wealth. A *New York Times* reviewer wrote in 1851, that capitalist growth, the "Gold Rush boom overflowing from California," "almost surpass[es] in reality the gorgeous fictions of the Arabian Nights."[23]

The Travels of a "Coarse Book"

In a surprising turn in the history of ideas, a manuscript of a "coarse book, without warmth in the telling [It is in reality a worthless book of silly tales],"[24] as described by the renowned bibliophile of Baghdad Muḥammad ibn Isḥāq al-Nadīm (d. 990/91),[25] is to become the most famous book in world traditions. The translation, in Jorge Luis Borges's words, "is a major event for all of European literature."[26] The book was to undergo transformations in Baghdad before traveling to Aleppo, Damascus, and later Egypt, as I will show in Chapter 5. Once transported, it received its additional bonus. Instead of "a thousand fables" or tales, it was called *A Thousand and One Nights.* Borges's intervention on this point is worth citing: "The idea of infinity is consubstantial with *The Thousand and One Nights.*"[27] The word "one" in the title opens the gate for further accretion, not only because etymologically it connotes endlessness, and hence an invitation to a process of appropriation, acquisition, and replacement, but also because it invites Edgar Allan Poe and others to indulge in their own second night.[28] Its newness, appeal, and the frame story's tantalizing invitation, all work together to generate the "rental tale" and pseudo-Orientalism. Having once served as the encapsulating arch and dynamic for narrative, the frame tale provides further momentum to narrative, in that it accelerates the passion for imitation, abridgment, duplication, claimed continuations, and declarations of authenticity that D. B. MacDonald called "a weighty chapter in the history of the great publishing humbug."[29]

[23] Referenced by Nance, *How the Arabian Nights Inspired the American Dream*, 33.
[24] This is Nabia Abbott's more exact translation of al-Nadīm. See Nabia Abbott, "A Ninth-Century Fragment of the 'Thousand and One Nights': New Light on the Early History of the Arabian Nights," *Journal of Near Eastern Studies* 8, no. 3 (July 1949), 151.
[25] Abū al-Faraj Muḥammad ibn Isḥāq al-Nadīm, *The Fihrist: A 10th Century AD Survey of Islamic Culture*, ed. and trans. Bayard Dodge (New York: Columbia University Press, 1998), 714.
[26] Jorge Luis Borges, "The Thousand and One Nights," trans. Eliot Weinberger, *The Georgia Review* 38, no. 3 (Fall 1984), 567.
[27] Ibid.
[28] Edgar Allan Poe, "The Thousand-and-Second Tale of Scheherazade," *Godey's Lady's Book* (February 1845).
[29] See al-Musawi, *Scheherazade in England*, 11.

Since then, it has become an index and repertoire of reflections, impressions, insights, theorizations, and a catalyst in reminiscences, memoirs, confessions, narratives, reviews, poetries, and rigorous scholarship. Since the last decades of the twentieth century, an alien sibling, adopted and raised in eighth- to ninth-century Baghdad, has been enjoying a distinguished treatment in Western academies as a precious commodity. In eighth- to ninth-century Baghdad, as was also the case with Galland's fourteenth-century manuscript,[30] the collection was incomplete for a specific reason: the number of nights does not necessarily correspond to the number of tales. Al-Nadīm describes *Hazār afsānah* (also, *Hezār afsāne*: thousand stories), as follows: "although it was spread over a thousand nights, [it] contained less than two hundred tales, because one story might be told during a number of nights."[31] His other remark complements the first, in that it touches on the hosting milieu that was to participate in the production of the *Nights* and its companions in the narrative tradition: "The Arabs translated it [story collection, and *Hazār afsānah* as the first] into Arabic language and then, when masters of literary style and eloquence became interested, they refined and elaborated it, *composing what was similar to it in content*."[32] Although enjoying this privilege and probably popularity, the emerging composition as a postmaturation of *Hazār afsānah* that became available to storytellers could not have earned a strikingly visible place in the growing compendious tradition, had it kept the earlier title of *A Thousand Nights* that militates even against selective inclusion. Nabia Abbott, however, cites Abū Bakr Muḥammad ibn Yaḥyā al-Ṣūlī's (d. 946) *Akhbār*, to suggest that storytelling was so popular in Baghdad that the caliph al-Muqtadir's mother, Shagab, rigorously supervised the readings assigned to her grandson Muḥammad, the future caliph al-Rāḍī, in case he might be taught such popular tales. But al-Ṣūlī, as the future caliph's tutor and boon companion, was no ordinary figure insofar as these tales are concerned. He was a unique *shaṭranj* (ancestor of chess) player who created "al-Ṣūlī's Diamond," an unsolvable chess problem that nobody could tackle unless tutored by the chess master. Al-Ṣūlī also authored a chess book. He could well be regarded as one of the perpetuators of everyday material life in affluent Baghdad. There is much here to

[30] Already described by Chauvin, Zotenberg, Richard F. Burton, and Duncan Black MacDonald, as shown in the next chapters.
[31] al-Nadīm, *The Fihrist*, 714.
[32] Ibid., 713 (italics added). In Abbott's version: "The Arabs translated these into the Arabic tongue. Then the eloquent and the rhetoricians took them in hand and revised them and re-wrote them in elegant style and composed, along the same idea, books that resembled them" ("Ninth-Century Fragment," 151).

encourage us to draw comparisons between his book in relation to books on crafts, and also storytelling as a profession, something that ʿAmr ibn Baḥr al-Jāḥiẓ (d. 868 in Basra) adroitly and neatly describes in his character sketch of Khālid ibn Yazīd (Khālawiyah al-Mukaddī; i.e., the tramp).[33] This is the model that is recalled by the postmodern Basra short story writer Muḥammad Khuḍayyir: "I find myself walking along an alley in ancient Basra, mingling with its men clothed in their rough robes." He adds: "This is my feeling whenever in a crowded train, or settling in scattered cities, crossing wooden bridges, or small stone ones."[34] In other words, there was a time in Baghdad and Basra when storytellers made use of written material to devise their tale-telling in a thriving profession that requires improvisation, passion, and imagination. I connect crafts to storytelling because we often forget that it is in marketplaces, corners, squares, and somehow popular assemblies that storytellers and craftsmen find their customers. The postmodern Basra writer argues: "The memory of the storyteller is not larger than that of an apothecary or druggist where scents of herbs, seeds, and oils get mixed up ... but his hand reaches to the right flask and jar from among these as he distinguishes the familiar scent from every other."[35] This is Scheherazade's craft.

Let us assume, then, in line with the notes of the Baghdadi bibliophile Ibn Isḥāq al-Nadīm and before him Abū al-Ḥasan al-Masʿūdī (897–967), that there was a collection,[36] *Hazār afsānah*; and that it underwent accretion in time and led to similar collections by such refined minds like Muḥammad ibn ʿAbdūs al-Jahshiyārī. This last figure

> began the compiling of a book in which he was to select a thousand tales from the stories of the Arabs, Persians, Greeks, and others. Each section (story) was separate, not connected with any other. He summoned to his presence the storytellers, from whom he obtained the best things about which they knew and which they did well. He also selected whatever pleased him from the books composed of stories and fables.[37]

Al-Jahshiyārī is described as a prominent member of the caliphal court, "of a superior type."[38] This means that storytelling was so much in demand that the court felt its impact and power and thought of accommodating it so as to fit into its discursive repertoire. However, a system of adaptation, appropriation, and domestication was taking place to exclude coarse language, sanitize the whole, and include the entertainingly proper in matter and

33 Muhsin J. al-Musawi, "Abbasid Popular Narrative: The Formation of Readership and Cultural Production," *Journal of Arabic Literature* 38, no. 3 (2007), 261–92; expanded in "Abbasid Popular Narrative: The Formation of Readership and Cultural Production," in *Arabic Literary Thresholds* (Leiden: Brill, 2009), 17–51.

34 Muḥammad Khuḍayyir, *al-Ḥikāyah al-jadīdah* (Amman: Shūmān, 1995), 26.

35 Ibid. 36 More on this point in Chapter 7. 37 al-Nadīm, *The Fihrist*, 714. 38 Ibid.

manner. Moreover, the issue of orality, literacy, and refinement is scrambled: al-Jahshiyārī is focused on a multidimensional accretion of storytelling.

Knowledge Consortiums

The frame tale and its various accretions traveled across Arab lands to undergo further accumulation and appropriation in line with knowledge construction during the medieval period.[39] The presence in the text of vernaculars and dialects should not be taken as necessarily indicative of origins and origination.[40] In their travels, whether in written or oral form, the tales were bound to undergo changes. The fourteenth- or fifteenth-century Aleppo manuscript reached Galland in Paris at an opportune moment. The tales received recognition in France, and the rest of Europe soon after, due to a number of factors with which eighteenth-century contemporaries were to grapple.[41] But, once they had passed through other cultures and been translated by Galland (1704–12), *Contes arabes* proved to be a turning point in the book industry and economics of reception. Bodies of knowledge grew around it, with diversified interests in sociology, anthropology, philology, psychology,[42] economy, cuisine, literature, arts, architecture,[43] and history.[44] Galland opened the gate not only for narrative to diversify its preoccupations and assets, but also for a would-be thriving print industry that undertook a hastened serialized production with Galland's *Contes arabes*. A large investment in the so-called Oriental mode now occurred, not only because of the strong appeal of the mode as initiated by the *Nights*, but also because it interacted with an increasing dissatisfaction with a prescriptive knowledge that was dry and uninspiring. Around Galland's phenomenal success grew a body of

39 See Muhsin Jassim al-Musawi, *The Medieval Islamic Republic of Letters: Arabic Knowledge Construction* (Notre Dame, IN: University of Notre Dame Press, 2015), 133–34.

40 The poet and critic Jamāl al-Dīn ibn Nubātah al-Miṣrī (1287–1366) was stationed in Cairo and Damascus, and made a compilation of the Iraqi poet Ibn al-Ḥajjāj's (941–1001) notorious poetry, with its typical *zaṭ* dialect of a certain "low" quarter in Baghdad (ibid., 17, 134, 273).

41 See al-Musawi, "Arabian Nights," 15–24; Conant, *Oriental Tale*; and Knipp, "The *Arabian Nights* in England."

42 See, for example, Hans Dieckmann, *Individuation in Märchen aus 1001 Nacht: Märchendeutung u. Patiententräume in tiefenpsycholog. u. psychotherapeut Sicht* (Oeffingen: Bonz, 1974).

43 Jo Tonna, "The Thousand and One Nights and the Poetics of Arab-Islamic Architecture," in *Les Mille et Une Nuit dans les imaginaires croisés*, ed. Lucette Heller-Goldenberg (Cologne: Romanisches Seminar dans Universität Köln, 1994), 171–76.

44 For an overview of this scholarship, see al-Musawi, "Growth of Scholarly Interest."

knowledge that scholars to date have tried to explain. "Knowledge is and will be produced to be valorized in a new production: in both cases, the goal is exchange."[45] This knowledge involved members of the *encyclopédie* group, and thus is not merely a one-sided matter of narrative. At the time (1751–72), their work and its title claimed to be an *Encyclopedia, or A Systematic Dictionary of the Sciences, Arts, and Crafts*, a systematic initiation into knowledge construction. It was edited by Denis Diderot and Jean-Baptiste le Rond d'Alembert, and among its members were Montesquieu, Jean-Jacques Rousseau, Voltaire, André Le Breton, and many others who, in one way or another, responded to the *Nights* in ways that imply that they regarded it as being a constellation of social, political, historical, and economic matters, even if its supernatural element is downplayed in comparison with its freedom from religious ties. This diverse endeavor, with its multiple and divergent concerns, presents the *Nights* as "spaces of dissension,"[46] reflecting on the frame tale as being the threshold to territories of conflict, collision, intrigue, vicissitudes of fortune, and love and passion. The power of the *Nights* derives in the first instance from the invitation to narrate, as exemplified in the frame story, but redrawn or refracted in every cycle. Driven by conflicting motives and desires of a powerful and morose monarch and a vizier's daughter, Shahrayar and Shahrazad, the frame tale sets the stage for a number of dynamics: a good story for one's life, a ransom transaction, action, and ruse and reason.[47]

Although some characters are forcefully presented, such as the barber, the hunchback, and certainly Sindbad, Aladdin, and Ali Baba, the named characters and the anonymous appear through narrative as well-rounded people. To designate the superiority of one element at the expense of another is a matter of prioritization among strong narrative properties. The frame story generates disequilibrium on moral and narrative levels. Even though the story of the two royal brothers and their wives is free from marvels, the supernatural element that for many readers and scholars signifies a prominent feature, this natural supernaturalism presents more challenges than resolutions. Tzevtan Todorov and other structuralists find examples of this element to explain their theories of the fantastic in relation to narratology.[48] The disproportionate scale of

[45] Lyotard, *Postmodern Condition*, 5. [46] Foucault, *Archaeology of Knowledge*, 152.

[47] David Pinault, *Story-Telling Techniques in the Arabian Nights* (Leiden: Brill, 1992); Daniel Beaumont, "Literary Style and Narrative Techniques in the Arabian Nights," in *The Arabian Nights Encyclopedia*, 1–5.

[48] al-Musawi, "Growth of Scholarly Interest"; a focused discussion of Todorov's applications is on pages 206–8.

crime and punishment in the tale of "The Merchant and the Demon," or of reparation and rapprochement in the "Story of Qamar al-Zaman and the Princess of China," to cite two examples, has already attracted the attention of poets like Samuel Taylor Coleridge. Natural supernaturalism provides an encompassing narrative frame that can address the haunting fear of the unknown; that same unknown is another name for an endless narrative. The underlying natural supernatural system confronts the reader with the inadequacy of a human moral order in universal contexts. The "dreamer" in Coleridge was genuinely aware of that aspect in his response to Anna Laetitia Barbauld's complaint that his ballad *Rime of the Ancient Mariner* "was improbable, and had no moral." As I explained in an earlier study,[49] Coleridge noted this attitude along with her confession that she had never had a dream in her life. The association of this lack with her lamentation over so much improbability and absence of moral should place her at the opposite end of Coleridge's poetics, his "maze of metaphysic lore," something that she reiterates in her poem "To Mr. Coleridge."[50] For Coleridge, his poem needs to have no more moral than the *Nights*' tale of "The Merchant and the Demon." The demon's retribution sounds disproportionate as a response to a petty and unintentional gesture that put out the eye of the unseen demon's son.[51] As I argued in a previous study, alongside Todorov's reading of the marvelous, "the intrusion of the supernatural is a salient constant in the literature of the fantastic. Rather than merely symbolizing dreams of power, the existence of beings superior to us compensate for 'a deficient causality.'"[52] However, while this deficiency may apply to our human reason, it does not apply to the world of dreams. Etsuko

[49] al-Musawi, *Scheherazade in England*, 79–80.

[50] Lisa Vargo, "The Case of Anna Laetitia Barbauld's 'To Mr C[olerid]ge,'" www.usask.ca/english/barbauld/criticism/vargo98.html.

[51] The passage in Samuel Taylor Coleridge, *Table-Talk*, May 1830 (*Miscellaneous Criticism*), reads as follows:

> Mrs. Barbauld once told me that she admired the Ancient Mariner very much, but that there were two faults in it, – it was improbable, and had no moral. As for the probability, I owned that that might admit some question; but as to the want of a moral, I told her that in my own judgment the poem had too much; and that the only, or chief fault, if I might say so, was the obtrusion of the moral sentiment so openly on the reader as a principle or cause of action in a work of pure imagination. It ought to have had no more moral than the *Arabian Nights*' tale of the merchant's sitting down to eat dates by the side of a well and throwing the shells aside, and lo! a genie starts up and says he *must* kill the aforesaid merchant *because* one of the date shells had, it seems, put out the eye of the genie's son.

See al-Musawi, *Scheherazade in England*, 79–80, 89n20.

[52] al-Musawi, "Growth of Scholarly Interest," 196–212, 207. Years later, scholarship had not undertaken any reading other than this recapitulation of the fantastic. See, for example, Tim Fulford's surmise that the *Nights* and *Tales of the Genie* "placed humans in the hands of powerful figures who acted according to a logic of cause and effect inexplicable in conventional terms." Tim Fulford, "Coleridge and the Oriental Tale,"

Aoyagi, from the University of Tsukuba in Japan, suggests that our fascination with the *Nights* derives from its being "a work which has always been transfiguring itself."[53] While this applies to a formative period when incompleteness generates more storytelling, the European and American demand for supply involves other socioeconomic factors. If the European scene received much study, the American side remains in need of further exploration. Nance mentions the case of the New York publisher and journalist George Putnam who, in his 1853 use of Aladdin as metaphor, "sought to play Eastern storyteller in homage to the tremendous growth of New York City." Even the story of Aladdin "grows daily tamer and tamer." He adds: "We also are Aladdins, and for us the Genii of the lamp are working."[54] This immersion in the material life of a nineteenth-century expanding and prosperous but filthy and relatively unruly city contrasts with the Romantic orientation in a boundless universe of imagination. In all cases, the *Nights* has ever since become a referent and index of taste.

Like a Jar of Sicilian Honey? Or "Spaces of Dissension"?

This fascination must stem from the needs and expectations of various readerships. A. S. Byatt has much to say about the *Arabian Nights*, but, when selecting Qamar al-Zaman for reading (Figure 2), she has a reason:

> I like Kamar al-Zamen because it's a very long, rambling tale. It goes on and on into the separation of the lovers, the retrieval of the lovers, into the whole of the rest of their lives, fitting story within story, which is the essence of the Arabian Nights.[55]

This is only part of a prominent contemporary novelist's unequivocal preference for the *Arabian Nights* as the "best story." We need to search in Leigh Hunt's (1784–1859) writings for reasons behind this fascination. As he published more pieces on the *Arabian Nights* than any other figure in eighteenth- and nineteenth-century England, he deserves attention before we dig into a culture industry that has been on the increase ever

in *The Arabian Nights in Historical Context: Between East and West*, ed. Saree Makdisi and Felicity Nussbaum (Oxford: Oxford University Press, 2008), 218.

53 Etsuko Aoyagi, "Repetitiveness in the Arabian Nights: Openness as Self-Foundation," in *The Arabian Nights and Orientalism*, ed. Yuriko Yamanaka and Tetsuo Nishio (London: I.B. Tauris, 2006), 68.

54 Cited in Nance, *How the Arabian Nights Inspired the American Dream*, 33.

55 "A.S. Byatt reads from the 'Arabian Nights.'" From an interview with Colby Devitt of *The New York Times* on the Internet (April 9, 1999). https://archive.nytimes.com/www.nytimes .com/books/99/04/11/specials/byatt.html.

Figure 2 Arthur Boyd Houghton: The birth of Camaralzaman, 1896.

since the publication of Galland's translation. Hunt was once intrigued by a little blue jar in a shop window, especially because its label read: "Sicilian Honey." That jar, and the association with Sicily, led his memory to recall the brass bottles and jars in the *Arabian Nights*. An ordinary label and image thereby evoke recollections of a shared reading script that introduces his "unequaled" Christmas production,[56] *A Jar of Honey from Mount Hybla* (1847), which starts with the story of "The Fisherman and the Genie."[57] Thus his first introductory chapter reads: "A Blue Jar from Sicily, and a Brass Jar from the 'Arabian Nights'; and What Came Out of Each." Analogical sweetness lies at the base of his comparison. If a jar of honey from Sicily recalls the jar of unfolding marvelous tales, its other propensity for invoking the wonderful and strange prompts the poet and critic to argue that "The *Arabian Nights* appeal to the sympathy of mankind with the supernatural world, with the unknown and the hazardous, with the possible and the remote. It fetches out the marvelous included in our common-places."[58] Narrative fecundity and power derive from elemental components that collapse the marvelous and ordinary. Jars, leather bags, trapdoors, and caps are among many *Nights* properties that are associated with the marvelous, but their narrative property resides in the unfolding of storytelling. While enjoyable and enchanting, this storytelling is also taken seriously by some sedate minds that read the *Nights* as documents. Hence, the

[56] In 1847, the journal *Athenaeum* mentions that, in this book, as in his other writings, Hunt "is the prince of parlour-window writers." The book was published in London by Smith Elder and Co.

[57] He writes:

> To introduce it, however, even to them, in a manner befitting their judgment, it is proper that we call to their recollection the history of a previous jar of their acquaintance, to which the foregoing paragraph contains an allusion. They will be pleased to call to mind that eighteen hundred years after the death of Solomon, and during the reign of the King of the Black Isles, who was (literally) half petrified by the conduct of his wife, a certain fisherman, after throwing his nets to no purpose, and beginning to be in despair, succeeded in catching a jar of brass. The brass, to be sure, seemed the only valuable thing about the jar; but the fisherman thought he could, at least, sell it for old metal. Finding, however, that it was very heavy, and furthermore closed with a seal, he wisely resolved to open it first, and see what could be got out of it. He therefore took a knife – (we quote from Mr. Torrens's *Arabian Nights*, not out of disregard for that other interesting version by our excellent friend Mr. Lane, but we have lent his first volume, and Galland does not contain the whole passage; he seems to have thought it would frighten the ladies of his day) – the fisherman, therefore, "took a knife," says Mr. Torrens, and "worked at the tin cover till he had separated it from the jar; and he put it down by his side on the ground. Then he shook the jar, to tumble out whatever might be in it, and found in it not a thing. So he marvelled with extreme amazement. But presently there came out of the jar a vapour, and it rose up towards the heavens, and reached along the face of the earth; and after this, the vapour reached its height, and condensed, and became compact, and waved tremulously, and became an Ufreet (evil spirit), his head in the clouds, and his foot on the soil, *his head like a dome, his hand like a harrow,* his two legs like pillars, his mouth like a pit, *his teeth like large stones,* and his nostrils like *basins,* and his eyes were two lamps, *austere and louring.* Now, when the fisherman *saw that Ufreet,* his muscles shivered, and his teeth chattered, *and his palate was dried up,* and he knew not where he was."

Leigh Hunt, *A Jar of Honey* (London: Smith Elder and Co., 1847), 28.

[58] Cited from *Leigh Hunt's Literary Criticism*, in al-Musawi, *Scheherazade in England*, 83.

history of the *Nights* in France, England, and other countries and cultures, presents cases that offer no clear-cut demarcation between what Lyotard calls narrative and scientific or professional knowledge in a postmodern condition. However, this latter demarcation remains important for our reading, as contemporary fiction writers like Salman Rushdie in *Two Years Eight Months and Twenty-Eight Nights* (2015; a multiplication of 1001) draws on the Andalusian philosopher Ibn Rushd (Averroes) to engage with the dialogue between these two systems of knowledge.[59]

Reclaiming a Poetics of Storytelling

However, to fathom our contemporary and worldwide explorations of the hold of Scheherazade's tales, we need every now and then to go back and reclaim the views and sentiments of those earlier critics and poets whose massive engagement with Scheherazade retains a poetic touch which our postmodernity often skips, overlooks, or simply relegates to a margin in structural or deconstructionist poetics. Byatt situates this negligence in an ongoing theoretical understating of literary consciousness:

> Modernist literature tried to do away with storytelling, which it thought vulgar, replacing it with flashbacks, epiphanies, streams of consciousness. But storytelling is intrinsic to biological time, which we cannot escape. Life, Pascal said, is like living in a prison from which every day fellow prisoners are taken away to be executed. We are all, like Scheherazade, under sentence of death, and we all think of our lives as narratives, with beginnings, middles and ends.[60]

Hunt offers clues to this narrative treasury, even more than the distinguished high modern advocate of the art, Borges. In his celebration of "The Orient of Poets," in the *London Journal* of October 1834, Hunt draws a road map for critical pursuits of the *Nights*. He states:

> To us, the Arabian Nights are one of the most beautiful books in the world: not because there is nothing but pleasure in it, but because the pain has infinite chances of vicissitude, and because the pleasure is within the reach of all who have body and soul, and imagination. The poor man there sleeps in a door-way with his love, and is richer than a king. The Sultan is dethroned tomorrow, and has a finer throne the next day. The pauper touches a ring, and spirits wait upon him.

[59] Salman Rushdie, *Two Years Eight Months and Twenty-Eight Nights* (London: Jonathan Cape, 2015).

[60] A. S. Byatt, "Narrate or Die: Why Scheherazade Keeps on Talking," *The New York Times Magazine*, 1999, https://archive.nytimes.com/www.nytimes.com/library/magazine/millennium/m1/byatt.html.

You ride in the air; you are rich in solitude; you long for somebody to return your love, and an Eden encloses you in its arms. You have this world, and you have another. Fairies are in your moonlight. Hope and imagination have their fair play, as well as the rest of us. There is action heroical, and passion too: people can suffer, as well as enjoy, for love; you have bravery, luxury, fortitude, self-devotion, comedy as good as Moliere's, tragedy, Eastern manners, the wonderful that is in a common-place, and the verisimilitude that is in the wonderful calendars, cadis, robbers, enchanted palaces, paintings full of colour and drapery, a warmth for the senses, desert in arms and exercises to keep it manly, cautions to the rich, humanity for the more happy, and hope for the miserable.[61]

In Hunt's overview, themes, desires, dreams, and motivations are all collapsed, a fitting reflection of a poetic imagination that is enthralled by the collection. This tendency was to continue to appear in writings, but the turn to philological inquiry and anthropological research dominated for some time before the *Arabian Nights* could draw the attention of narratologists, and thereafter the academy. The turn is in line with formalist, structuralist, and other academic pursuits after the death of "new criticism." With the few exceptions of Todorov's interventions, a language of science takes over as it steadily applies social science, digital technology, and at times medical discourse, to account for narrative properties that relate to what Lyotard calls, "ideas of internal equilibrium and conviviality next to which contemporary scientific knowledge cuts a poor figure, especially if it is to undergo exteriorization with respect to the 'knower' and an alienation from its user even greater than has previously been the case."[62]

Early in 1908, Martha Pike Conant published her doctoral dissertation, *The Oriental Tale in England in the Eighteenth Century*, in which she set the scene for studies of reception and also narratological inquiry. She stipulates that the *Arabian Nights* "was the fairy godmother of the English novel."[63] She goes on to suggest, in "connection with the history of the novel" and against a lacuna in action and function in European narratives, that these newcomers lack characterization, but offer plot: "Stories of pure adventure, in fantastic and often brilliant setting, sometimes emotional or sentimental, never strong in characterization – they offered just that element of plot which was lacking in the periodical sketches."[64] She further explains that:

in the *Arabian Nights*, there are several tales that, in certain aspects, deserve to be called classical; *Ali Baba and the Forty Thieves*, or *Zeyn Alasnam and the King of the*

[61] Leigh Hunt's *London Journal* 30 (October 22, 1834), 233, cited in al-Musawi, *Scheherazade in England*, 47.
[62] Lyotard, *Postmodern Condition*, 7. [63] Conant, *Oriental Tale*, 243. [64] Ibid., 241–42.

Genii, for instance, despite their oriental decorations, are admirably simple, and well-proportioned.

Conant cannot escape the common process of collapsing the Oriental with the hyperbolic and profuse. She concludes, however: "[T]he *Arabian Nights*, as a whole, is a treasure-house of story perhaps unsurpassed in literature."[65] In a comparative framework that accommodates eighteenth-century French and English narrative traditions, she argues:

In France, the popularity of these fantastic and marvelous stories, restless in plot and exuberant in colour, had testified to a truant desire to escape from the strict artistic rules and classical ideals of masters like Boileau. Conditions were similar in England.[66]

Another reason for popularity and also the makeup of this art is its romantic character: No wonder that the growing demands of the reaction against pseudo-classism found a certain satisfaction in these extraordinary tales, which brought into the comparatively gray and colourless life of Augustan England the fascinating marvels of oriental legend, encompassed, even in the translations from the French, by something of the magical atmosphere and strange glamour of the East.[67]

Conant was certainly compromised by a prevalent equation that linked the land of the *Nights* with glamour, strangeness, and magic. In this study, the search for frames of reference to hold this comparative reading together in an otherwise massive and vast space requires that Hunt, Borges, and Barth be called on every now and then. Conant's critique of Augustan aesthetic strictures repeats what the engaging poet and critic Hunt mentions in his essay for the *London and Westminster Review* of October 1839, in which he discerns "the ultra-material skepticism of the prevalent metaphysics," and the total disgruntled distrust of imagination, fancy, and emotional propensity.[68] In Conant's search for more explanations, she adds that: "In varying degree, these stories show a love of adventure and of mystery; a desire to excite the feelings – of surprise, horror, or delight."[69] She recognizes, however, the impossibility of full accounting for popularity in relation to the characteristics of the collection: "It would be as difficult as superfluous to analyze the world-wide charm of these tales."[70] This is precisely the challenge that we confront when placing the *Nights* into contemporary world cultures.

[65] Ibid., 242. [66] Ibid., 247. [67] Ibid.
[68] Leigh Hunt, "New Translations of the Arabian Nights," *Westminster Review* 33 (October 1839), 103.
[69] Conant, *Oriental Tale*, 247. [70] Ibid.

In 1999, the novelist Byatt named the *Nights* "The Best Story Ever Told."[71] In the same vein as Barth, she also stresses the urge to narrate a good story: "We are all, like Scheherazade, under sentence of death."[72] In a bold suggestion that projects the Judeo-Christian tradition as a grand narrative, a historical construct, different from the free gifts of Scheherazade's *Nights*, she explains:

> The Judeo-Christian culture is founded on a linear narrative in time. It moves forward from creation through history, to redemption in the Christian case, and looks forward to the promised end, when time and death will cease to be. The great novels of Western culture, from "Don Quixote" to "War and Peace," from "Moby Dick" to "Dr. Faustus," were constructed in the shadow of this story. People are excited by millennial events as images of beginnings and endings. There is a difference between these great, portentous histories and small tales that are handed down like gifts for delight and contemplation.[73]

This is an important line of demarcation that cuts across cultural and sociopolitical and economic issues: narratives of apocalypse have to end "when time and death cease to be"; there is an end to be reckoned with, something that the *Nights* dispels as the tale leaves things open to conjecture, even when the destroyer of happiness is nearby. Conversely, master or grand narratives speak for a specific makeup of subjectivities, aspirations driven by greed, imperial wars, conflicts, formations of nations and empires, and centripetal/centrifugal exchange driven by interest and mercantilization. A master or grand narrative addresses exclusive totalities through detail.[74] The tales function as emancipatory narratives, but they are not allegories of emancipation. Scheherazade presents "gifts for delight and contemplation" to save her life, and by default, the lives of other women, and also eventually to please those who are outside the Abbasid (roughly 750–1258) or Mamluk (1250–1517) courts, the social fringes in squares and cafés. Borges provides a summary in an adroit generic comparison whereby allegory tends toward sadness and tedium, while the *Thousand and One Nights* offers "an unrestrained happiness."[75]

[71] See Byatt, "Narrate or Die," 105–7, cited in Robert L. Mack, "Cultivating the Garden: Antoine Galland's Arabian Nights in the Traditions of English Literature," in *The Arabian Nights in Historical Context*, 61.

[72] Ibid., 106. [73] Ibid. [74] Lyotard, *Postmodern Condition*, 48, 60.

[75] Jorge Luis Borges, "Arthur Waley, *Monkey*," in *Selected Non-fictions*, ed. Eliot Weinberger, trans. Esther Allen, Suzanne Jill Levine, and Eliot Weinberger (New York and London: Penguin Books, 1999), 254.

Shifts in Periodical Criticism of the *Nights*: Old and New

A noticeable marker in eighteenth- and nineteenth-century European periodical criticism is the relative *absence* of emphasis on the generative narrative power imparted by the frame tale. There are exceptions such as Poe's irreverent sardonic extra tale which Byatt also critiques: "Edgar Allan Poe's Scheherazade makes the mistake of telling her aging husband about modern marvels like steamships, radio and the telegraph. He finds these true tales so incredible that he concludes that she has lost her touch and has her strangled after all." Unlike the French engagement with Scheherazade's narratorial role,[76] writing in English throughout the eighteenth and nineteenth centuries is focused on actions, "narrative men," and customs and habits. Poe offers an early exception. Poe's counter use of the frame tale underlines its glaring absence in most periodical criticism. Preoccupied with genealogies, scholars were not drawn to narrative dynamics. However, periodical criticism of that period shows a concern with translation as mediating processes, and hence such terms as abridgment, cultivation, omission, fidelity, domestication, emasculation, and bowdlerization occur more often than issues of narrative profusion. Along with those issues, there were also phrases that suggest discursive limits: terms such as squeamish, prudish, priggish, and ultimately Mrs. Grundy.[77] These recurrent terms applied in a visible discursive space cannot be seen apart from what Michel Foucault speaks of as "discursive erethism," an expansive multiplication in this relation that operates in "the very space [of power] and as the means of its exercise."[78] The recurrent emphasis on an "Oriental moralist" versus Galland's translation evokes a tendency to emphasize and discuss sexuality. In his establishment of a cultural differential, *scientia sexualis* and *ars erotica*, or Europe minus Rome and the East,[79] Foucault highlights how "sex was driven out of hiding and constrained to lead a discursive existence."[80] Hence the significance of Richard Johnson's (Reverend Mr. Cooper), *The Oriental Moralist, or The Beauties of the Arabian Nights' Entertainments* (1797), which is no more than an abridged and "emasculated" selection to please "the sedate and the philosophical." Hunt has the following to say about this approach: "Forty years ago, a lover of the 'Arabian Nights' thought it necessary to pick his way into a public confession by the following polite style of concession to a 'severe taste.'"[81]

[76] For a good review, see Gipson, "Writing the Storyteller."
[77] Mrs. Grundy is a fictional character, unseen but watchful, in the comedy *Speed the Plough* (1798) by the English playwright Thomas Morton (1764–1838).
[78] Michel Foucault, *The History of Sexuality*, trans. Robert Hurley (New York: Random House, 1990), 1:32.
[79] Ibid., 32, 57. [80] Ibid., 33. [81] Hunt, "New Translations," 103.

A Decolonizing Critique

In line with the rise of novelistic criticism, early twentieth-century writers engage with the narratorial Scheherazade. The frame tale is seen as generator and preserver of a body of narrative that intrigues readers and narrators and provokes a desire for completion. E. M. Forester draws on Scheherazade to explain his theory of fiction in *Aspects of the Novel* (1927), but standard histories of literature often neglect to mention the linkage. If it ever appears, it is only in reference to a "road to Xanadu," or sources for imaginative recreations by poets.[82] In other words, Scheherazade has to remain an outsider for literary historians before the advent of new schools of thought that open the gate for theoretical and literary studies. We need outsiders to the hegemonic narratological discourse to decolonize theory and imbue it with other readings that take publication details as the starting point for an argument. Such outsiders may well agree with Borges that it is "the first serial novel ever written, *The Thousand and One Nights*."[83] Before him, the poet and translator John Payne argues that the *Arabian Nights* is "the most famous work of narrative fiction in existence."[84]

This study, *The Arabian Nights in Contemporary World Cultures*, is thus a response to this issue as being a complex of multiple trends in the makeup of cultural thought. In its effort to engage and disengage with ongoing theory in its specific English/French orientations in matters of prose poetics, it seeks also to develop a decolonizing critique that Byatt has addressed in terms of grand or master narratives versus small but captivating tales. Although cherished, used, and appropriated, the *Nights* remains marginal to literary theory despite the enormous amount of nineteenth-century criticism that argued for its inclusion. While often assessed in Romanticized or neoclassical terms, narratological explorations remain largely tied to a "Western canon of fiction." This can be viewed as a literary oversight, but it is not so when perceived in terms of other issues, especially in relation to religio-political stereotyping or dismissals of Otherness. Hence, while working across a two-way axial-proposition – the rise of a new turn in the novelistic tradition, and the

[82] John Livingston Lowes, *The Road to Xanadu: A Study in the Ways of the Imagination* (Boston, MA: Riverside Press, 1927).

[83] Jorge Luis Borges, "Literary Pleasure" (1927), trans. Suzanne Jill Levine, in *Selected Non-fictions*, ed. Eliot Weinberger (New York: Penguin Books, 1999), 28–31.

[84] John Payne, *The Book of the Thousand Nights and One Night*, "Prefatory Note," 1, ix–x. Also cited in Gerhardt, *Art of Story-Telling*, 80. Payne's statement runs as follows: "The present translation being intended as a *purely literary work* produced with the sole object of supplying the general body of cultivated readers with a fairly representative and characteristic version of the *most famous work of narrative fiction* in existence" (italics added).

commoditization of the *Nights* in a growing culture industry – this and the following chapters aspire to develop a grammar of narrative that can account for the connection between narrative, trade, global trafficking in cultural goods, and the stupendous growth of an *Arabian Nights* culture industry. Discounting the rhetoric of debasement as tied to imperialism, this growth is a very positive development, and it certainly helps generate a counternarrative discourse. While what was written, produced, and circulated about the tales before 1970–90 may have been meager, the late 1990s onward have witnessed a surge in a culture industry about the *Nights* that we need to explain.

A body of knowledge that takes Scheherazade as its focus or ploy is rarely free of cultural politics.[85] However, the poetics of narrative, its narratological dimension, gains momentum so as to present a constellation of motifs, styles, turns, narrative levels, actants, functions, and units that sediment other visible narrative congregations.[86] Although still struggling with the question as to where to place such a collection, literary theories have begun to give way to the forceful arguments propounded by some theorists of narratology as a comprehensive term to account for narrative properties, irrespective of common generic typologies involving folktales, popular storytelling, or novelistic experimentation. While bound to a hegemonic manipulation of a critical lexicon exemplified in an almost exclusive application to specific European narratives, narratology is still scant in its referential to other cultures, even to the *Arabian Nights* that was once, and still is, a European commodity.

However, new inroads have opened up in narrative, narrativity, and thence narratology involving the names and texts of such literary icons as Proust, Joyce, Angela Carter, Rushdie, Barth, William Butler Yeats, Umberto Eco, Byatt, Borges, Italo Calvino, Carlos Fuentes, Githa Hariharan,[87] and almost every other writer or poet. Moreover, the *Nights*, more than any other narrative, has been an inventory of multiple traces, as shown in its compelling invitation to painters, illustrators, musicians and musicologists, cinematic scripts writers and producers, tourist agencies, and almost every other venue and practice. The outcome is a body of knowledge that derives inspiration from, and also manipulation of, the *Nights*, offering new perspectives on narratology as a poetics/politics theory wider than what its pioneers and early theorists devised. Let us recall here that Yeats, Borges, and Byatt rate it first, or in the case of

85 Rana Kabbani, "The Arabian Nights as an Orientalist Text," in *The Arabian Nights Encyclopedia*, 25–29.
86 See Marzolph and van Leeuwen, eds., *The Arabian Nights Encyclopedia*, as an example.
87 For Githa Hariharan, see especially her *When Dreams Travel* (New Delhi and New York: Penguin Books, 2008).

Yeats second only to Shakespeare.[88] In matters of narrative theory, or narratology, Claude Bremond, and somehow Todorov, invested more in the *Nights* than any of their contemporaries. Gerald Prince and Roland Barthes made only occasional nods to the art of the *Arabian Nights*, but even those remain marginal to the overall drift of narrative theory. In this context, the question that confronts us is how to account for its rise in academic scholarship, with visible focus on *A Thousand and One Nights*, while there is simultaneously a meager attention to it in narratology. It is good to know, however, that narratology proper has been growing outside the immediate field of Arabic, Middle Eastern, and somehow comparative studies. However, the culture industry now displays a moderate interest in the *Nights* that is relatively better than was the case in the first six decades of the twentieth century.

Translations and abridgments of the *Arabian Nights* are deeply immersed in a collective unconscious. They can initiate, provoke, or recall familiar or totally strange inroads in architectural analogies,[89] fantasies, and urban planning. Similar inroads are noticeable in other fields of knowledge, as well as in cinematic and other visual productions, including painting. They often reveal the other side of the encounter with the Oriental tale, and the *Arabian Nights* in particular. There is bound to be some connection between this appropriation and imitation in the previously mentioned fields and a trendy authentication that was once advocated by late eighteenth-century owners of partial manuscripts, and later by Jonathan Scott,[90] Henry Torrens,[91] Payne, and Richard F. Burton, along with a number of Arabists and Orientalists. French and German cultural milieus were no less involved in this venture. Is this turn toward authentication, one that witnessed Mahdi's edition of Galland's incomplete Arabic manuscript, and Lyon's and van Leeuwen's editions, for example, a response to a supply and demand economy? Does it respond to the involvement of the academy in *Arabian*

[88] A. Norman Jeffares and K. G. W. Cross, eds., *In Excited Reverie: Centenary Tribute to W. B. Yeats* (London: Macmillan, 1965).

[89] Among many instances, the eminent American architect Bernhardt E. Muller designed in 1926 "an architectural fantasy" for the city of Opa-locka, using tales from *The Arabian Nights*. See https://chronicles.roadtrippers.com/theres-glittering-arabian-nights-themed-town-hidden-south/ and http://scholar.library.miami.edu/treasures/pages/manuscriptsarchives/hotdogstand.html.

[90] Jonathan Scott, trans., *Tales, Anecdotes and Letters* (London: Cadell and Davies, 1800); and Jonathan Scott, trans., *Tales Selected from the Manuscript Copy of the 1001 Nights Brought to Europe by Edward Wortley Montague, Esq.; The Arabian Nights Entertainments, Carefully Revised and Occasionally Corrected from the Arabic*, 6 vols. (London: Longman, Hurst, Rees et al., 1811).

[91] Henry Torrens, trans., *The Book of the Thousand Nights and One Night*, ed. William H. Macnaghten (Calcutta: W. Thacker, 1838).

Nights courses? Should we say that authentication is a postcolonial nod, intended to liberate the *Nights* from the early translators' grip? Is it only a whim on the part of translators and editors and their publishers? Or should we see it as being part of the rise of a new understanding of narrative as something larger than the properties of the nineteenth-century European novel? Whether authenticated or not, the *Nights* is no longer a source of information on the East as it was for eighteenth-century readers. The new turn toward authentication does not share with nineteenth-century major editions (by Lane, Payne, and Burton) and their scholarly apparatus the tendency to reproduce manners and customs, and cultural ethnographic and anthropological fields. In other words, we have a situation that requires further elucidation, something that the following chapters seek to address. Ultimately fresh fields of knowledge open up in geographies, traditions, histories, manners, and matters, and – when perceived closely – present challenging sites. Each of these dimensions reflects on the others, and can help us understand not only the perennial charm of a collection of multiple patterns of growth, but also its complex presence in an age of colonial expansion.

The appearance of the *Nights* as a mediated property in France, England, Germany, and the Netherlands could not have happened had the colonial expansive drive not been in effect. Interest in trade, natural resources, and markets required knowledge of other lands and people. As already mentioned, even Galland had to concede to this rising colonial drive and emphasize the informative power of the *Nights* with respect to manners and customs. This same drive entailed also the study of race, language, and land. Why was there a painstaking search for an original or authentic manuscript? Is this important for the narrative art? Is the translator not a second author? But questions such as these will have to wait until we reach Chapter 5, which aspires to situate the search for origins, not only in the massive philological drive to study the Other in terms of Semitic/Aryan dichotomy, but also in the context of the effort to place manuscripts in genealogical recensions. As scholars and philologists respond to a cultural script, they direct attention away from the narrative art toward its presumed authors and locations.[92] It is critics, literary researchers, narratologists, novelists, and poets who move in the opposite direction. In her attempt to study this differentiation between folklorists, historians, and literary critics, Mia Gerhardt suggests that the "student of folk narrative regards them all [tales] on the same level," whereas the "critic applies literary standards from the beginning, and singles out for study the one masterpiece, as the most rewarding. ... It is one of the

[92] See Malek, "Orientalism in Crisis."

striking qualities of the '1001 Nights' that the majority of its stories represent such masterpieces."[93] Concerning the literary critic and literary historian, Gerhardt suggests the following: "The literary historian will not rest content until he has found out all that is possible to find out about the man, and the milieu, behind the work," while the "literary critic ... accepts the anonymous encounter ... to give his undivided attention to the handiwork alone."[94] A more nuanced differentiation between literary historians and narrators is offered by Eco. The narrator as translator in his novel *The Name of the Rose* argues against "the misplaced sense of fidelity to my source."[95] He assures the reader that

> I now feel free to tell, for sheer narrative pleasure, the story of Adso of Melk, and I am comforted and consoled in finding it immeasurably remote in time ... gloriously lacking in any relevance for our day, atemporally alien to our hopes and our certainties.[96]

But Eco also retains the narrative suspense that derives from curiosity, castigating his tongue for so much loquacity: "But curb your impatience, garrulous tongue of mine. For on the day of which I am telling, and before its night, many more things happened that it would be best to narrate."[97]

However, do contemporary writers, critics, film producers and directors, and painters perceive scenes from the tales in the same manner as their nineteenth-century predecessors? Does a scene like the whipping and caressing of the dogs in "The Porter and Three Ladies of Baghdad" invoke explanations other than surprise or reflections on magic? What if we read it within the context of what a number of scholars like Lilie Chouliaraki articulate as a universal problematic that requires a response: "Does the ... text construe the misfortune of distant sufferers as a case of action – whose action or with what effects – or does it construe the scene of suffering as being of no concern to the spectators?"[98] The underlying ethos in the tale needs the incognito

[93] Gerhardt, *Art of Story-Telling*, 57. [94] Ibid., 59.
[95] Umberto Eco, *The Name of the Rose*, trans. William Weaver (San Diego, CA: Harcourt, Inc., 1983), 5.
[96] Ibid.
[97] Ibid., 39. See also Sabry Hafez, "The Name of the Rose: Time and the Dialectics of Parallel Structures," *Alif: Journal of Comparative Poetics* 9 (1989), 36–48. He argues:

> The power of the text lies in becoming the arena in which the powerless becomes the all-powerful. The other and more important structural parallel between this text and *The Arabian Nights* is the analogy between the violation of the taboo and the quest for truth. In many tales of *The Arabian Nights* the concealed treasure is guarded by many measures the most effective of which, the prohibition, is at the same time the most fallible. The secret is always hidden in a sealed box, which happens, in our text, to be a room or rather a labyrinth of rooms and book shelves: the Abbey's library.

[98] Lilie Chouliaraki, *Spectatorship of Suffering* (London: Sage Publications, 2006).

Commander of the Faithful to address a destabilizing challenge to a presumed governance of justice. Long ago, Payne raised questions about history as told in the *Nights*,[99] interrogating in particular the historicity and authenticity of this governance, an issue that shall receive more attention in due course.

Constants and Variables

With its perennial charm, the *Nights* has become a broad-scaled cultural presence, but in different garbs that attest not only to its unchanging properties, but also to its malleability. Constants and variables should have been present in its formative processes, accretion, and compilation. A corresponding system, probably with even more malleability, defines its travels outside its immediate habitat and milieu. Given its wide popularity and fame in Europe in particular, but also in almost every other culture, a knowledge spectrum gathers around it that is both centripetal and centrifugal. In one of the rare moments of exchange, this collection takes Baghdad, Cairo, and Damascus as its narrative points of departure. Hence, Borges's following surmise is not off the mark:

> The Thousand and One Nights appears in a mysterious way. It is the work of thousands of authors, and none of them knew that he was helping to construct this illustrious book, one of the most illustrious books in all literature (and one more appreciated in the West than in the East).[100]

Like the fisherman's net in the first cycle of stories in the *Arabian Nights' Entertainments*, narrative cities spread their web widely across the globe. The narrative constellation that gathers around the frame-tale nucleus functions as the epicenter, exactly like Abbasid Baghdad in relation to surrounding civilizations and nations.[101] A constellation of narrative grids builds around the frame story and its cycles. While in constant processes of appropriation and assimilation in an ongoing narrative cauldron, it also engages storytellers, philologists, compilers, critics, and scholars to explore this phenomenal rise. It invites journeying in genealogies, archives, means and methods of accommodation and response, and whatever is integral to human need, ambition, desire, and entertainment. This

[99] John Payne's translation of *the Book of the Thousand Nights and One Night*. Complete in nine volumes. Volume 9 has Payne's significant contribution, which appeared in book form in 1884. Payne published "The Thousand and One Nights" in *New Monthly Magazine*, 2 parts (January–April 1879), 2:150–74, 377–401.

[100] Borges, "The Thousand and One Nights."

[101] For a detailed reading of this analogy between the frame tale and Abbasid Baghdad as centripetal and centrifugal center, see Muhsin Jassim al-Musawi, *The Islamic Context of the Thousand and One Nights* (New York: Columbia University Press, 2009).

unabated but differential popularity over a period of three centuries provides the public with a culture industry that is diversified and rich, and therefore challenging. It is more so because the *Arabian Nights* is composite.

The archaeology of *A Thousand and One Nights* cannot be an easy task. Questions continue to arise, despite Pierre Daniel Huet's effort to provide a final word on origins of fiction in his *Treatise on the Origin of Romances* (which appeared as a preface to Marie de la Fayette's novel *Zayde* in 1670). It was made available in an English translation by Stephen Lewis (1715). John Dunlop's *History of Fiction* (1814) adopted the same line, a survey of a wide field that struggles to respond to a phenomenal growth in narrative that was driven by the rising readership throughout the eighteenth and nineteenth centuries. But the third millennium provides more explorations that build on a rich corpus of philological and literary inquiry.[102] The Austrian Orientalist Joseph Freiherr von Hammer-Purgstall's (1774–1856) explorations of the origins of the collection set the scene for further research.[103] No less so were the efforts of Silvestre de Sacy and, to a certain extent, Schlegel. More research is conducted to demonstrate what the American novelist and critic Barth calls the "Shahrazad factor."[104] Scholarship multiplies in such a fashion as to

[102] Wikipedia, s.v. "One Thousand and One Nights," https://en.wikipedia.org/wiki/One_Thousand_and_One_Nights.

[103] This is also touched on by Richard Burton in his "Biography of the Book and Its Reviewers Reviewed," *Supplemental Nights* 6 (1886–88), 311–66. See also Duncan B. MacDonald, "A Bibliographical and Literary Study of the First Appearance of the 'Arabian Nights' in Europe," *Library Quarterly* 2, no. 4 (October 1932), 387–420. For a summary, see M. J. de Goeje, who argues,

> Von Hammer concluded that the Thousand and One Nights were of Persian or Indian origin. Against this conclusion Silvestre De Sacy protested in a memoir (1833), demonstrating that the character of the book we know is genuinely Arabian, and that it must have been written in Egypt at a comparatively recent date. Von Hammer in reply adduced, in *Journ. As.* (1839), ii. 175 seq., a passage in the *Fihrist* (A.D. 987).

He also repeats what was already argued by the *Athenaeum* reviewer.

De Goeje says: "Maqrizi, describing the capital of Egypt, quotes from a work of Ibn Sa'id (c. A.D. 1250), who again cites an older author (Al-Qortobi), who, in speaking of a love affair at the court of the caliph Al-Amir (1097–1130), says 'what is told about it resembles the romance of Al-Battal, or the Thousand and One Nights.'"

See Michael J.de Goeje, "De Arabische nachtvertellingen," *De Gids* 50 (1886), 385–413. See also https://theodora.com/encyclopedia/t/thousand_and_one_nights.html. A full discussion was done by the *Athenaeum* reviewer when reviewing M. G. S. Trebutien's translation. See *The Athenaeum*: Weekly Review of English and Foreign Literature, Fine Arts, and Works of Embellishment 122 (February 27, 1830), 113–14.

[104] John Barth, "The Scheherazade Factor: Conversation with Alvin P. Sanoff," *U.S. News and World Report* (August 31, 1987), 55.

repeat antecedent quotes, critiques, and gleanings. On many occasions, the early third-millennium writer forgets that what he/she is arguing is already present in predecessors' writings. A recycled and reprocessed body of knowledge appears in this culture industry, a neatly drawn surplus that signifies an age of commodity, fetish, and spectacle. The 1990s interest is further augmented on the occasion of Galland's tercentenary. Investment in the *Nights* at conferences, symposia, collected and edited proceedings, film production, and critical inquiry attests nevertheless to a culture industry that exploits the *Nights* as a commodity. More than ever, the last five decades have demonstrated a surplus. This transactional activity across the audiovisual and print industries demands an archaeological exploration, not only to map out the genealogical and epistemic shifts in taste and interest, but also to open up further venues for discovery, already laid out in common and almost stock images such as Solomon's sealed jars and rings, and Ali Baba's cave.

Central to this archaeological excavation is storytelling, as being the most powerful technique intertwined with human beings' insatiable desire to talk and listen. As noted by Todorov, loquacity is held paramount, inciting others and eliciting action. However, verbal and nonverbal properties and images of copper vases, brass jars, magic rings, and flying carpets become household words all over the globe. Stories pour out of the fisherman's newfound brass jar, unfolding lands, lakes, people, wealth, and pleasure. These elements act in turn on readers as recipients, prompting and consolidating an American dream for gold,[105] or a voracious imperial desire to take over rich lands.[106] When we take into consideration the volume of interest in the *Nights* as generated and perpetuated by Galland and his successors, the question arises as to whose legacy stands foremost, not as a constant like the properties of the *Nights*, but as a variable, a cultural question that in turn generates still more issues about translation, mediation, transaction, and the waning value of origins. It was obviously an Arab legacy that made use of a Persian frame tale, as argued by Suhayr Qalamāwī,[107] and a few years later by Abbott, who points out a genealogy in view of the manuscript fragment that she analyzes and the writings of tenth-century Arab scholars. The collection easily made its way into a popular tradition as narrated and handed down by one generation to another. Eventually it has become part of a sociopolitical unconscious. However, as it has

[105] Nance, *How the Arabian Nights Inspired the American Dream*, 33, 39, 59.
[106] Edward Said, *Culture and Imperialism* (New York: Random House, 1993); Anne McClintock, *Imperial Leather: Race, Gender, and Sexuality in the Colonial Conquest* (London: Routledge, 1995).
[107] al-Qalamāwī, *Alf laylah wa-laylah*, 94–98, 163–77.

passed through appropriated translation, it has regained a compelling presence that no one, not even its detractors, can ignore. In this migration, it is transmuted into something else without losing its basic nucleus and properties. As a European legacy, it reminds readers, adaptors, manipulators, scholars, and everyone else that it is a transplant. In fact, Galland's title (*Les Mille et Une Nuit: Contes Arabes*) and its Grub Street translation into English as *The Arabian Nights' Entertainment* say as much.

2 The Scheherazade Factor

Scheherazade speaks to me mainly as an image of the storyteller's condition: Every one of us in this business is only as good as our next story. And there is a sense in which narrating equals living. We really are alive as human beings as long as we're still interested in telling anecdotes to one another.

John Barth, August 31, 1987

Through puns, Joyce destroys one word so several more are born from the ruins of the mangled term. So in its very definition, *Finnegans Wake* is a Scheheracharade, a vicoclometer, or kaleidoscope of collisions, a multiformograph, and a meanderthal, a story of meanders, a valley of labyrinths.

Carlos Fuentes

Allegory is a fable of abstractions, as the novel is a fable of individuals.

Jorge Luis Borges, "From Allegories to Novels"

The Empowering Dynamic

Taken as trope and metaphor, "an image for the storyteller's condition," Scheherazade has been pivotal to prose poetics as laid down in Todorov's *Poetics of Prose* and *The Fantastic*. She is not as yet necessarily central to narratology that remains tied to a few exemplary novels or stories. However, to vault over the preliminary staging of the Scheherazade/ Shahrayar encounter with betrayal without due recognition of the kitchen and garden scenes in the frame story may deprive the "Scheherazade factor" of its dynamic motivating acumen. The Scheherazade factor, so called by John Barth,[1] is closely related to the storyteller's vocation and circumstantial conditions of possibility. It also connects to the art as a nocturnal occurrence that opts to be surprising, captivating, and, hence, winning. Every tale is a deferral of an ending, and even wordplay works within this matrix of luring narrativity. It claims the past whenever

[1] See Barth, "The Scheherazade Factor."

there is a lacuna, a lack of a sustainable adventure, or when "literature of exhaustion" begs for refurbishment. The last category involves self-reflexivity, a metafictional discourse, as a self-testing experimentation that may act as deferral of failure and death. These three directions are noticeable in world cultures,[2] and they always build on *A Thousand and One Nights*, not only as a reservoir or treasury of narrative means, methods, tropes, and metaphors, but also as an attestation to the power of art as perpetuation and prolongation of life and, by implication, creative fecundity against impending aridity and death. Whenever this art opens up vistas of continuity and surprise, of challenge and further disequilibrium, we speak of a Scheherazade factor that is the staple of high modernist and postmodernist narrative. The story of the fisherman can exemplify this mushrooming or embedding process: the colored fish is surprising to the king, vizier, and escort (Figures 3 and 5). So is the story of the ensorcelled king (Figure 4) whose kingdom is turned into a lake with colored fish. Borges dwells on a side of Scheherazade's poetics in his reading of the fisherman's story and its explosion of tales and surprises:

> he goes down to a sea and cast his net. One morning he casts and hauls it in three times: he hauls in a dead donkey; he hauls in broken pots – in short, useless things. He casts his net a fourth time – each time he recites a poem – and the net is very heavy. He hopes it will be full with fish, but what he hauls in is a jar of yellow copper, sealed with a seal of Soleiman (Solomon). He opens the jar, and a thick smoke emerges. He thinks of selling the hardware jar to merchants, but the smoke rises to the sky, condenses, and forms the figure of a genie.[3]

This is how storytelling works: surprising events that open up a sequence of others, a pattern that we meet also in the story of the merchant and the demon, and in almost every secondary frame tale. But this is only one side of the Scheherazade factor, which signifies the power of storytelling. In Scheherazade's twenty-fifth night, we hear the ensorcelled king speak to his royal visitor – who is camping not far from the castle – of the spell cast on his domain as follows:

> after my wife turned me into this condition, she cast a spell on the city, with its gardens, fields, and markets, the very place where your troops are camping now. My wife turned the inhabitants of my city who belonged to four sects, Muslims, Magians, Christians, and Jews, into fish, the Muslims white, the Magians red, the Christians blue, and the Jews yellow.

[2] On the *Nights* as world literature, see also Sandra Naddaff, "The Thousand and One Nights as World Literature," in *The Routledge Companion to World Literature*, ed. Theo D'haen, David Damrosch, and Djelal Kadir (London: Routledge, 2011), 487–96. For a general check on traces, see: https://en.wikipedia.org/wiki/List_of_works_influenced_by_One_Thousand_and_One_Nights.

[3] Borges, "The Thousand and One Nights," 571.

SO STRANGE OF FORM AND SO BRILLIANT AND DIVERSE IN HUE
(Page 110)

Figure 3 Edmund Dulac: The fisherman showing his strange fish to the sultan.

This comes in response to the royal visitor's question concerning the colored fish brought to his palace by the fisherman.[4] Everything is taken for granted, and the spell cast by the queen takes place because she wants

[4] Haddawy, trans., *The Arabian Nights*, 61. References to this edition are in the text.

SUPPOSING ME ASLEEP, THEY BEGAN TO TALK
(Page 125)

Figure 4 Edmund Dulac: The ensorcelled king feigned sleep.

to have her way in running her personal life as long as she has the power to do so. The real bursts into marvels, and a magical realism becomes the narrative code as it is in the fisherman's tale. In applying some of Barthes's narrative codes, one can argue that the fisherman's habitual act of casting the net and his anticipation and response are daily occurrences that meet the proairetic code of actions. But a hermeneutic code of enigmas functions through every casting of the net where there is a paradoxical situation of expectation and disappointment. It applies also to the surprising brass jar, its sealed cap, and the demon's oath, swearing to kill the first person who rescues him after a series of waiting and disappointments. The same applies to the dying

GREAT WAS THE ASTONISHMENT OF THE VIZIER
(Page 135)

Figure 5 Edmund Dulac: The vizier's astonishment upon knowing the story of the fish in the Tale of the Ensorcelled King of Ebony Isles.

queen's lover in a rubbish shack on the outskirts of the city. The site connotes poverty, and hence is a semic code, while it also raises questions about the enigmas surrounding the queen's choice of a lover.[5] An underlying symbolic referent underlines the whole affair between the queen and her decrepit lover: Has he once been healthy and loving as her lamentations suggest? Does she suffer from a psychopathic condition, a pathological disorder? Does she take revenge against her husband, the king, for some inexplicable reasons? A referential code is summoned to explain a number of enigmas surrounding the fish, the queen, the ensorcelled king, and the debatable need for magical spells in the story of the queen.[6] The fishing net happens to spread worldwide, covering lands and people, who in this instance are turned into fish. The fisherman's net may be read as correlative to *A Thousand and One Nights* in its diversity, plurality, and resistance to strict systematization. It testifies also to its accessibility to multiple cultures and readerships, and its ongoing invitation to redactors and translators. Its primary narrator, Scheherazade, reproduces herself in multiple versions that pose further challenges to any attempt at strict structuration of narrative, or representation of female voices and bodies in this narrative corpus. The ensorcelled king's wife is not exemplary, nor are the three ladies of Baghdad, nor Aziza and Tawaddud for that matter. They exemplify motifs and assume a certain presence in readers' memories, but they defy compartmentalization.

The Scheherazade Factor and Serial Narrative

Regardless of Scheherazade's origination in other cultures, her transference and translation into French, English, German, and almost every other language complicates identification. As the named storyteller in folk tradition and also the narrator in print, Scheherazade appeared at an opportune time in French, English, German, and Dutch so as to raid a print culture that also made enormous use of her stories.[7] In

[5] For more on this tale, see Muhsin Jassim al-Musawi, "The 'Mansion' and the 'Rubbish Mounds': The Thousand and One Nights as Popular Literature," *Journal of Arabic Literature* 35, no. 2 (2004), 329–67.

[6] For a neat summary of Barthes's codes, see Marie-Laure Ryan, "Narrative Code," in *Encyclopedia of Contemporary Literary Theory*, ed. Irena R. Makaryk (Toronto: Toronto University Press, 1993), 599–600.

[7] See al-Musawi, *Scheherazade in England*, 33, where I mention the following sources: MacDonald, "A Bibliographical and Literary Study," 405–6; Richard F. Burton, "Terminal Essay," the Burton Club Edition (n.d., vol. 10); and W. F. Kirby, "Contributions to the Bibliography of the Thousand and One Nights," in Burton's *Book of the Thousand Nights*, 10:92–94 and 414–18, respectively. See also the British Museum Catalogue for editions; Victor Chauvin, *Bibliographie des ouvrages arabes* (Liege, 1900),

January 1723 the thrice weekly *London News* began a serialization of these tales "which occupied three years and four hundred and forty-five installments."[8] Soon after, serialization became a norm in dailies and periodicals. The division of the collection into *Nights*, something that was soon to trouble its first translator who was bothered by Parisians at night mimicking Dunyazade's call for more tales, turned into an incentive for installments. Even the sagacious Edward William Lane made use of that in his arrangement with the publisher in 1838 when his translation appeared in thirty-two installments.

The power of the Scheherazade factor, as incentive to and desire for narrative, finds itself repeatedly invoked. Whether spreading the fishing net or touching a lamp, a ring, or some other loaded object, these acts of incitement prompt narratives of adventure and, along with them, a number of tropes that happen to serve as leitmotifs in world narratives. Nineteenth-century European writers were not the only ones who made use of this treasury, for even Arab writers were belatedly drawn to it. Throughout, the frame tale functions as a dynamic for serial fiction, the *feuilleton roman*. The sister's presence can be linked to a readership that used to wait for Dickens's next chapter, demanding that he not let this or that character die.[9]

Before we draw on the properties of the Scheherazade factor, a recapitulation of the frame tale is in order. Significantly, all manuscripts and detractions have, albeit with seemingly slight variations, the same introductory or frame tale, that of King Shahrayar, Scheherazade and her sister, or maid or nurse,[10] Dunyazade. As pointed out by Muhsin Mahdi, the name Shahrazad means "of noble race," whereas Dinarzad, corrupted in translations and oral transmission as Dunyazade, means "of noble

4:25–26; and "Notes on Sales: 'The Arabian Nights,'" *TLS* (March 16, 1922), 176. *The Cambridge Bibliography of English Literature* assigns the period between September 1705 and March 1706 as the date of the first English translation. As early as December 16, 1706, Mrs. Manley's heroic drama *Almyna; or the Arabian Vow* was performed at the Theatre Royal. Mrs. Manley admitted in the preface that the theme was taken from Arabian sources, "with something of a Hint from the Arabian Nights Entertainments." After citing the preceding evidence, Adel M. Abdullah rightly concludes that this adaptation "corroborates the scanty evidence we have which points to the period between September, 1705, and March, 1706." See Adel M. Abdullah, "The Arabian Nights in English Literature to 1900" (PhD diss., University of Cambridge, 1963), 225.

[8] al-Musawi, *Scheherazade in England*, 11. There I mentioned, "After the renewal of the stamp tax on newspapers, William Parker's *London News* came to an end in April 1725, and his *Penny Post* began to appear instead in four pages. It continued to serialize the rest of the *Nights* as 'a front-page feature.'" See R. M. Wiles, *Serial Publication in England before 1750* (Cambridge: Cambridge University Press, 1957), 35, 38n2.

[9] The publisher Chapman and Hall made use of the illustrator Robert Seymour's idea to have his illustrations appear in installments to accompany a serialized novel. Seymour suggested the young Dickens who came up with *Pickwick Papers*, March 31, 1836. Seymour turned into a secondary figure, a status that bothered him and he committed suicide.

[10] More on this point in Abbott, "A Ninth-Century Fragment."

religion."[11] For a good reason, this frame is the most popular of the tales among readers of every age and culture. The German translator and scholar Enno Littmann came up with the classical categorization of the frame tale that was to undergo revisions later in the century. The frame story is of Indo-Persian origin, and consists of three different parts, originally independent stories, as shown earlier by Emmanuel Cosquin in *Revue Biblique* and *Etudes folkloriques*.[12] According to the latter, these parts are:

(1) The story of a king grieved by a disloyal wife, to be allayed and appeased when finding out that no less than his elder brother, the king, has suffered the same misfortune;
(2) the story of the giant demon whose captive bride deliberately betrayed him with a hundred males. This is the same as the tale told by the seventh vizier in the story of "Sindbad the Wise"; and
(3) the frame ransom story of a clever girl whose skillful storytelling averts the king's design to take revenge by keeping a bride for a night and have her murdered the next day to escape further betrayal.

Of these three parts, only the third seems to have belonged to the original framework story, as reported by al-Masʿūdī and by Ibn Isḥāq al-Nadīm in *al-Fihrist*. As already noted, the king, the clever daughter of the vizier, and Dunyazade were known. According to those sources, this story migrated at an early date from India to Persia, to undergo nationalization and appropriation, and to be subsequently combined with the other two parts of the frame story. Scholars have devoted some attention to the frame story as a complex of stories, developed deliberately to emphasize a multiple spectrum where many views and concerns speak for themselves beyond limitations and constraints.

Narrative Framing

To these views of the construction of the frame tale, I will add a number of notes.

Embedding involves the imposition of a frame that colors and appropriates the enframed. It acts on the material and operates on its stratagems. Every woman's tale thus has a stratagem of limits. The story of "The Porter and the Three Ladies of Baghdad," for example, has on its door the inscription not to ask and inquire. The inscription works with and against the curiosity of visitors who wish to explore the reasons behind this foreboding note. While the inscription is an invitation to

[11] *Thousand and One Nights*, 131. All further references are given in the text.

[12] Emmanuel Cosquin, "Le Prologue-cadre des Mille et une Nuits," *Revue Biblique* 6 (1909), 7–49; also in *Études folkloriques* (Paris, 1922), 265.

silence, it also generates curiosity and desire. In narrative terms, no intruder should ever be a narrator or interlocutor because narrative is an empowering domain, and action is entirely controlled by the three ladies who – before the coming of the Commander of the Faithful and his vizier – enjoy a sovereign status. This authority cannot be discredited unless there is a counter and contending one. Whence comes the girl's surprise at the audacity of the transgressor who insists on an explanation: "Haven't you read the inscription on the door, which is quite clearly written, 'Speak not of what concerns you not, lest you hear what pleases you not'" (77). The implications of power work within a dynamic of competitive politics. The ladies are only empowered within their domain, but a caliph can subsume this within his broader authority as the Commander of the Faithful. "Tell me who you are," says the girl, "for you have only one hour to live. Were you not men of rank or eminent among your people or powerful rulers, you would not have dared to offend us" (3). While the phrasing indicates power politics, it also negotiates a presence in the spheres of refinement or *ẓarf* etiquette. However, there is space for the Commander of the Faithful to resume authority and command, an explanation that normatively involves opening the gate for more narratives.

Women in the tales are actively involved in shaping events and are ready to pay for their transgression. The two queens set the prototype for the rest, including the giant demon's abducted bride, the women in the mendicants' stories, and others in the narratives of the barber and his brothers. Transgression as self-affirmation takes place even outside the domain of royalty and privilege.

The frame story offers itself easily to different interpretations and readings. Its "writerly" aspect, that is, openness to differentiated readings, has made it the subject of discussions, novels, novellas, short stories, and parody. It is read literally, metaphorically, and historically, and applied to attitudes, concepts, and images of the East. Among old Orientalized views, it is quintessentially the story of a despotic East, voluptuous, polygamous, and unscrupulous. Among early European defenders of women's rights, it serves as transposition of guilt to project internal European grievances onto an alien East.[13] Among contemporary feminists, it is the apt trope for women's ingenuity, wit, and resourcefulness to outwit and overrule patriarchal practices. For postmodernist fiction writers, like Barth, Scheherazade is the quintessential artist, as she/he is as good as her/his next story. To the aesthetes, Scheherazade is

[13] See Muhsin Jassim al-Musawi, *Anglo-Orient: Easterners in Textual Camps* (Tunis: University Publishing House, 2000), 15–16, 33–35, 108.

the artist par excellence, as art not only equals life, but also negates the idea of verisimilitude. Life becomes an effort to imitate art, in that, as long as she has a good story to tell, she secures survival against heavy odds and transforms the monarch and his like into better human beings.

The Frame Setting and Story

The frame story narrates adversity as a starting point to account for subsequent action and storytelling. It thus exemplifies disequilibrium, as narrative disorder generates further disorders or narratives. The Sassanid royal house suffers an unexpected misfortune due to the adultery of the two kings' wives, a misfortune that in the frame tale provokes not only revenge but also a need for a thorough understanding of human behavior. The kings cannot swallow betrayal as being possibly directed against them and have to view it in a universal context. As betrayal is not merely personal, but also involves royalty and universal applications of authority, it looms larger than the immediate retribution. In Kantorowicz's analysis in *The King's Two Bodies* (also used by Michel Foucault),[14] "The King's Body" is a double body: the transitory physical one and the unchanging symbolic one around which gathers

> an iconography, a political theory of monarchy, legal mechanisms that distinguish as well as link the person of the king and the demands of the Crown, and a whole ritual that reaches its height in the coronation, the funeral and the ceremonies of submission.[15]

This is how the sense of betrayal should be treated in discussions of the frame tale. The brothers' quest is thus meant to cope with betrayal as a calamity of enormous proportion. It reflects on the ensorcelled king of the black islands and his betrayal, which only another royal person can set right and repair.[16] The complexity of the frame tale does not end here, as the following subsections explain. There is first its "writerly" aspect. The frame tale acts like a mirror for the readers' agenda and priorities, but it operates as well on their intimate and perennial desires. Moreover, it includes catalytic narrative ingredients interspersed in the collection, including introductory geographical and historical settings, such as the Sassanid royal palaces, meadows, and gardens; the emphasis on human

[14] Ernst Kantorowicz, *The King's Two Bodies: A Study in Medieval Political Theology* (Princeton, NJ: Princeton Classics, 1957).

[15] Michel Foucault, *Discipline and Punish: The Birth of the Prison*, trans Alan Sheridan (New York: Random House, 1977), 28–29.

[16] See Haddawy, trans., "The Tale of the Enchanted King," in *The Arabian Nights*, nights 22–27, 56–66. Further references to this edition are in the text. For a study, see al-Musawi, "The 'Mansion' and the 'Rubbish Mounds.'"

and supernatural agents in collaboration or confrontation; residuals and leitmotifs that prepare for action and accelerate controversy, like gardens, windows, and sealed boxes and caskets; human desires like sex, food, and curiosity that act as overridingly uncontrollable impulses, leading to disequilibria; and faith in human reason as being in line with God's vision of the universe. Thus begins the anonymous narrator:

> It is related – but God knows and sees best what lies hidden in the old accounts of bygone peoples and times – that long ago, during the time of the Sassanid dynasty [Persian dynasty, ca. AD 226–641] in the peninsulas of India and Indochina, there lived two kings who were brothers. (3)

The story preempts criticism on grounds of authenticity and reliability, and leaves things in the hands of God, the all-knowing and omniscient. We are informed that the oldest brother, King Shahrayar, is "a towering knight and a daring champion, invincible, energetic, and implacable" (3). The emphasis on power and magnanimity is deliberate, as it sets the stage for a tragic flaw in his character. Both nostalgia for the younger brother[17] and later disappointment and resignation to fate contribute to his frailty and weakness. These factors are also behind his quest for further recovery of power by taking revenge on women. While he was ruling India and Indochina, "to his brother [Shahzaman] he gave the land of Samarkand to rule as king" (3). Overwhelmed with a longing for his brother, the older king sent an invitation to his younger brother, Shahzaman, to visit, which the latter happily accepts. Shahzaman thus displays a flaw of sentimentality that will be augmented by his excessive love for his wife. Thus, camping outside the city with his brother's vizier, the younger king returns one night to his palace to bid his wife goodbye, only to find her "lying in the arms of one of the kitchen boys." Although killing both, the young king is no less troubled and morose, a demeanor that bothers the older king, Shahryar. The implications of the double body of the king also apply to the younger brother.

A cursory reading of the plight of the young king could run as follows: The young brother could not join his brother on his hunting and camping errands. One day, while he was left behind, the young king was surprised to see through his window his brother's wife with twenty slave girls, ten white and ten black, in the garden of the palace. The ten black slaves were men dressed as women. "Then the ten black slaves mounted the ten girls, while the lady called 'Masʿud, Masʿud!' And a black slave jumped from

[17] Fedwa Malti-Douglas has drawn attention to this point: "This longing, seemingly at the outset quite natural is, however, problem-generating, since it sets in motion the events that will follow." Fedwa Malti-Douglas, *Woman's Body, Woman's Word: Gender and Discourse in Arabo-Islamic Writing* (Princeton, NJ: Princeton University Press, 1991), 15.

the tree to the ground, rushed to her, and raising her legs, went between her thighs and made love to her. Mas'ud topped the lady, while the ten slaves topped the ten girls, and they carried on till noon" (5). The scene concludes as follows: "When they were done with their business, they got up and washed themselves" (5). The scene sets the stage for the unfolding dramatic events, as the young king looked upon his misfortune in relative terms, for "'my misfortune is lighter than that of my brother,' he said to himself" (5). His depression left him, and he "continued to enjoy his food and drink" to the surprise of his brother, who demanded an explanation. As every calamity is only so in relative terms, the brothers decided to desert the world and its privileges until they can find who might be unluckier:

> Let us leave our royal state and roam the world for the love of the Supreme Lord. If we should find someone whose misfortune is greater than ours, we shall return. Otherwise, we shall continue to journey through the land, without need for the trappings of royalty. (8)

The choice here is either a full resumption of royalty in its "double body of the king," or mendicancy. As I intend to offer further readings of sites of betrayal later on, it suffices now to perceive things from the brothers' angle.

Relativity of Individual Blight

Insofar as the narrative proceeds, this seeming resignation operates within a stoic frame of reference, one obviously tinged with the copyists' or storytellers' Islamic faith in predestination. However, it is couched in relativism so as to perpetuate dramatization. When the kings come to a meadow by the seashore, they decide, "to sleep on their sorrows." They wake up to resume journeying in the morning, but they "heard a shout and great cry coming from the middle of the sea." The preparation for the event is of great narratological value. Set against their sorrows and saddened mood, the cry unsettles placidity and quietude, and accelerates action. In terms of popular faith verging on superstition, the waterspout at sea indicates the presence of evil jinn, as Lane explains in his notes to his translation of *The Thousand and One Nights* (1838), collected later in book form by his nephew, Stanley Lane-Poole, under the title *Arabian Society in the Middle Ages: Studies from the Thousand and One Nights* (37). When the "sea parted . . . there emerged a black pillar that, as it swayed forward, got taller and taller, until it touched the cloud" (37). As if duplicating Mas'ud in the garden scene, they climbed "a very tall tree, sat hiding in the foliage," watching the black demon carrying a large glass chest with "four steel locks" (37).

Further dramatization now takes place, as the demon "pulled out a full-grown woman" whom he addressed as the most charming bride "carried away on ... [her] wedding night," telling her he "would like to sleep a little" (9). It was then that she looked up at the tree and saw them, pointing to them to come down and make love to her, or she would awaken the demon. Collecting their wedding rings, she added these to the ninety-eight which she has collected from others "under the very horns of this filthy, monstrous cuckold," who tried to keep her "pure and chaste, not realizing that nothing can prevent or alter what is predestined and that when a woman desires something, no one can stop her" (9–10). This statement of hers invokes two motivations: the accelerated coincidence that justifies any occurrence under the auspices of fate, and the wiles of women, as a motivation that Scheherazade's tales have to counteract within the underlying relativism. The immediate response of both kings is to believe in both fate and the treachery of women, whence follows their decision to go back to their kingdoms and "never to marry a woman for good" (10). Whether they are forced into it or otherwise, their submission to seduction and the threat to awaken the demon means that they are no less implicated in betrayal than their wives. They also succumb to a divide between human beings and demons, something that even royalty is unable to defuse without the help of other powers. Shahrayar's vizier now has to get him a woman from among the daughters of princes, officers, merchants, and even the common people. As death awaits them every dawn, "all the girls perished." At a later stage, Scheherazade forced the vizier, her father, to agree to her proposal to marry the king, her design being to put an end to a reign of vengeance and terror.

But her willful decision is countered by her father's warning, duly accompanied by maxims and wise sayings. Here he sets the tone for storytelling within a male tradition that assigns knowledge to men, including knowledge of the esoteric, the language of animals, and the masculine code that prevails among humans, birds, and animals. At this point, narrative is functioning on the levels of symbolic code, as a patterning of male/female pervades his discourse. It also functions on a referential code level, as cultural norms are invoked as part of the vizier's discourse. He relates the story of "The Bull and the Ox," embedded within another between the merchant and his wife, and the dog and the rooster. These are designed to deter Scheherazade from a seemingly hasty decision, offering examples that counsel her not to "misbehave," to give up curiosity, and not "imperil" herself (11). The rooster advises beating as a way of controlling curiosity. Beating and containment are narrative equilibriums intended to counter such curiosity, which is itself a dynamic narrative impulse. They also stand for the authoritarian patriarchal code that is unitary, as opposed to multiplicity and diversity. But Scheherazade reads through these maxims. "These tales don't deter me from request," she says (15). She even makes an early claim for a counter narrative, telling her father, "If you wish, I can tell you many such tales" (15).

An Underlying Complexity

The frame tale is multiembedded, for the first part of betrayal and disenchantment involves the story of the demon and the glass-box bride; the second, between the vizier and his daughter, contains the story of the bull and the ox, the merchant and his wife, and the rooster and the dog. The third part includes the rest, while involving narrative in complexity that shatters dichotomies, platitudes, and generalizations. However, the underlying pattern that questions them is civilizational, not impulsive, cultural not natural. Basically, it emanates from a cultural consciousness that works by design and intent versus an authority that applies power, maxims, and selective experiential application. We are told that Scheherazade

> had read the books of literature, philosophy, and medicine. She knew poetry by heart, had studied historical reports, and was acquainted with sayings of men and the maxims of sages and kings. She was intelligent, knowledgeable, wise, and refined. (11)

The emphasis on the "sayings of men" is worth noticing as it is referentially inclusive of both patriarchal discourse and her nonpatriarchal plan to expose presumptions against women's wiles. It also encapsulates her plan to reform, albeit through multiple correctives and critiques, not to overthrow or weaken a system. Her stories to the king, as perpetuated by her sister's or maid's desire to hear more tales, keep the king awake, curious to hear more and more for unlimited time, as the phrase "one thousand and one nights" indicates. By the end of that time, Shahrayar's character has undergone change, and his mistrust of women is replaced by some recognition of gender equality and marital advantage. Such is the impact of storytelling on a person's temper and nature. As explained earlier with reference to Chesterton and the high modernists like Proust and Joyce, storytelling, or narrative proper, is a counterstratagem to silence, another name for death. Thus, an underlying complexity supplies narrative with a perpetuity, which is another name for life.

Based on the combination of challenge and acceptance of risk, narration as an act is here also rich with a woman's presence. Both function in unison, for the king derives satisfaction from this meeting, where he can fully enjoy a sense of supremacy to compensate for his loss and discard his fear of further loss of virility. The early disturbing and disheartening scene in the garden implies to him his failure to satisfy his wife, while his bloodthirsty pledge is a self-styled mechanism aimed at publicizing his virility. While Scheherazade accepts the risk, her beauty, education, and resourcefulness work together, not only to engage his attention, but also to direct this attention to the main preoccupations of human concern: historical records and archives, supernatural and uncanny events, and contemporary or relevant situations culled from all walks of life. In this sense, narration is an act of containment and resistance, not only to the emerging king's misogyny, but also to any acquiescence to hegemony. Beauty and narration are cunningly interwoven, whereas poetic insertions are liberated from male voicing so as to fit into multiple acts of storytelling that are so multivoiced as to break down absolutist maxims. Story and discourse work in unison. The frame becomes a trope for liberty because both narrative multiplicity and Scheherazade's eventual pragmatic achievement and successes (as a liberator of womankind) transcend both frames and borderlines. In the end, this is what Elias Khoury wants his narrator, the displaced and forlorn Palestinian Adam, to announce: "The writer who added the frame to the stories of Scheherazade was a footling as every other writer who fears the story that comes to us for nothing, that explodes inside us as water explodes inside the belly of the earth."[18] It is not meaning, however, that makes the frame story so central; rather it is its encasement and incarceration that incites release and lets stories pour out endlessly. It offers readers the chance to go beyond pettiness and lose themselves in a sea of stories.

The Dynamics of the Frame Tale

The frame tale uses pairing to disturb racial and social demarcations, for black men and white women mix and make love, royalty and slaves do the same in the garden scene and the royal bedroom. The storyteller plays on the perennial, too, as the slave, Masʿud, acts like an ape, an action that the two kings are themselves to perform in crisis. Nature overrules culture, and all resort to raw nature under duress, limits, and/or sexual deprivation. The frame tale functions through dichotomies, too, for the palace and the glass box indicate confinement, and meadows and gardens signify

[18] Khoury, *Awlād al-ghītū*; Khoury, *Children of the Ghetto*, 426.

freedom and laxity. Moreover, the night signifies privacy, including private sexual intrigues, but the day is the time for orgy and public sex. In both cases, symbolic and referential narrative codes are available to ground a seemingly smooth story of betrayal and revenge. The kings' quest, or the mention of journeying, paves the way for unexpected happenings and shocking scenes that invoke narrative and human transformation. Like traps and incarcerations, glass boxes and their like are storytelling frames and limits: They incite a human desire for freedom. Not all writers read the frame story as argued here. Khoury, for one, has a different interpretation with respect to the narrative frame that has always received more attention than single stories and cycles. He allows his narrator Adam to reflect on the major narrative encasement as follows: "I think the character of the king with his insane desires is merely an excuse that became transformed into a fact with the construction of the frame story." He adds that this frame tale: "[M]ust have [been] added in recent times in the belief that by doing so he would give the stories meaning."[19] This conjecture that takes the form of justification concludes against any superimposition of meaning, for narrative art in *A Thousand and One Nights* is available for its own sake, and not for some pragmatic value. Adam surmises that the "meaning is a mistake," for "Scheherazade fell in love with her stories, and when she was victorious and, after giving birth to three sons, won the king's goodwill, she entered the lethargy that leads to death."[20] The distracted Palestinian turns in the end and before his death into a mouthpiece for art for art's sake.

The Missing Preliminary Volatile Sites

As the frame tale is given so many twists and interpretations by novelists like Khoury and others,[21] the rest of this study of the frame tale engages with a specific lacuna in scholarship created by the way in which scholars vault over sites of betrayal and orgy.[22] It argues against a limitation of the frame tale to the Shahrayar/Scheherazade binary. Although it occasionally applies a grammar of motives, and a poetics of prose validated over decades among narratologists, this study proposes to offer another reading that questions and deconstructs common representations of women

[19] Khoury, *Children of the Ghetto*, 426. [20] Ibid.

[21] For a review of writings in Arabic, see Maher Jarrar, "The *Arabian Nights* and the Contemporary Arabic Novel," in *The Arabian Nights in Historical Context: Between East and West*, ed. Saree Makdisi and Felicity Nussbaum (Oxford: Oxford University Press, 2008), 297–315.

[22] This part of my reading of the frame tale was planned as a lecture at Duke University upon an invitation from miriam cooke to whom it is dedicated.

as passive ideological constructs. The frame tale of the collection disputes such readings. As the most appealing narrative for formalists, literary historians, and philologists, the frame tale of the two brothers and their nameless wives, finishing with the presence of a defiant but clever Scheherazade, has over time received only a partial reading that either focuses on the morose king and the defiant heroine or on the frame tale as artifice for narrative embedding. In the following reading, the neglected parts of the frame tale are given their due as being the most dynamic on semantic and syntagmatic levels. Their narrative presence in terms of utterance, motifs, speech acts, societal and normative attributes, and categories is explored.

The frame tale involving the two brothers and their wives is often explored and studied in terms of cause and effect, a sequence of events that the presence of Scheherazade and her narrative alternately suspend and generate. Scheherazade stops bloodshed through her nocturnal narration, involving its own variety of narrative strategies and outcomes. That understanding is ironically in line with Arab classicists' reading and summation of that enveloping frame. In an age of equipoise suspended between high Romanticism and striding utilitarianism, Edgar Allan Poe was the first in Europe and America and, probably, the only storyteller and poet who destabilizes and debunks this common reading, one that has survived over the ages. Throughout a period of 300 years, and since the publication of Antoine Galland's translation of *Contes Arabes* (1704–12), the binary structuration of named kings versus anonymous women has prevailed, imposing a binding narrative law that is rarely questioned. As far as I know, no critic has ventured to question the binary of anonymity and naming in the first part of the frame tale. Readers and reviewers are alike in being so intrigued by the power of narrative that their critical faculty gets numbed and thence accepting the narrator's prioritization of kings at the expense of their wives. A patriarchal structure is imposed that only the advent of Scheherazade and her sister or maid can destabilize.

Even when early twentieth-century Arab writers like Ṭāhā Ḥusayn and Tawfīq al-Ḥakīm ingeniously ventured to break up the frame tale binary of the authoritarian king or emperor Shahrayar, they are still focused on empowering Scheherazade as the heroine who takes revenge on both the king and compromised authors. In their joint *al-Qaṣr al-masḥūr* (*The Enchanted Palace*, 1937) and al-Ḥakīm's play *Shahrazād* (1934; French 1936; English 1945), the beheaded queens whose story establishes the cause-effect sequence have no place. In line with al-Ḥakīm's philosophical turn, Shahrazad duplicates the beheaded heroine so as to lead the emperor Shahryar away from the flesh toward a yearning for knowledge, a yearning for secrets that downplays issues of adultery, jealousy, and rancor. Shahrazad now strives to draw him back to her body while enjoying her success in recreating a new man who may question her narratives but is bedeviled by a mania that wanderlust cannot dispel.

Narratologists who use the tales as case studies jump over the first bedroom and garden scenes and find themselves more at ease with such popular narratives as Sindbad the Sailor, for example, to argue against other novelistic theories. In one of his arguments against Henry James's reading of narrative as "an illustration of character" (66),[23] Todorov, for instance, argues a different case with ample examples from the available European (i.e., French) version of the *Arabian Nights*: "Every new character signifies a new plot. We are in the realm of narrative-men" (70). With focus on immediate or unmediated action, the latter is wrested away from the psychologism proposed by James, a psychologism that takes action as a manifestation of character.[24] To James, plot is transitive in relation to character. This is not where Todorov stands. Nor is it where scholars like Ferial J. Ghazoul detect repetitive patterns as in a geological, not a biological, order.[25] A new story is born through embedding. Todorov traces the narrative structure in the *Arabian Nights* that derives "from a predicative literature: the emphasis will always fall on the predicate and not on the subject of the proposition" (67). "A best known example of this effacement of the grammatical subject is the story of Sindbad the Sailor," an impersonal tale where narrative works as a series of actions (67). To modify James's articulation, he argues: "Hence it would be more accurate to say that psychological causality duplicates the causality of events (of actions) rather than it takes its place" (69). Ironically, Poe also uses the same voyages in "The Thousand-and-Second Tale of Scheherazade," first published in 1845, but for the purpose of something else: to humorously let Shahrayar dispute and scorn the whole idea of a credulous king who passively listens to tales. Poe's story engages headlong with the advent of Scheherazade and her narrative mechanism to flaunt and dispute the presumed credulity of the king. Poe's Shahrayar falls asleep every now and then and ridicules the narrator. The enchantment is dispelled, and the narrative is under the scrutiny of a cynic. There is more reason to bring Poe in this argument, not only because of his

[23] Tzvetan Todorov, "Narrative Men," in *The Poetics of Prose*, trans. Richard Howard (Oxford: Basil Blackwell, 1977), 66–79. References are in the text.

[24] Henry James, *The Art of the Novel* (New York: Oxford, 1948).

[25] Ghazoul, *Nocturnal Poetics*. Srinivas Aravamudan's comment on Todorov is worth noting; see Srinivas Aravamudan, "The Adventure Chronotope and the Oriental Xenotrope: Galland, Sheridan, and Joyce Domesticate *The Arabian Nights*," in *The Arabian Nights in Historical Context*, 243–44. The same view is to be found in his *Enlightenment Orientalism: Resisting the Rise of the Novel* (Chicago, IL: University of Chicago Press, 2012), 56–57.

drawing on Sindbad that he shares with Todorov and other narratologists, but also because his redrawn narrative of the frame tale should have opened it up to further exploration. His recounting reads as follows:

It will be remembered, that, in the *usual version of the tales*, a certain monarch, having *good cause to be jealous* of his queen, not only puts her to death, but makes a vow, *by his beard and the prophet*, to espouse each night the most beautiful maiden in his dominions, and the next morning to deliver her up to the executioner.

Having fulfilled this vow for many years to the letter, and with a religious punctuality and method that conferred great credit upon him as a man of devout feelings and excellent sense, he was interrupted one afternoon (*no doubt at his prayers*) by a visit from his grand vizier, to whose daughter, it appears, there had occurred an idea.

Her name was Scheherazade, and her idea was, that she would either redeem the land from the depopulating tax upon its beauty, or perish, after the approved fashion of all heroines, in the attempt.

Accordingly, and although *we do not find it to be leap-year, (which makes the sacrifice more meritorious,)* she deputes her father, the grand vizier, to make an offer to the king of her hand. This hand the king eagerly accepts – (*he had intended to take it at all events, and had put off the matter from day to day, only through fear of the vizier,*) – but, in accepting it now, he gives all parties very distinctly to understand, that, grand vizier or no grand vizier, he has not the slightest design of giving up one iota of his vow or of his privileges. When, therefore, the fair Scheherazade insisted upon marrying the king, and did actually marry him despite her father's excellent advice not to do anything of the kind – when she would and did marry him, I say, *will I nill I*, it was with her beautiful black eyes as thoroughly open as the nature of the case would allow.

It seems, however, that this *politic damsel (who had been reading Machiavelli, beyond doubt,)* had a very ingenious little plot in her mind. On the night of the wedding, she contrived, *upon I forget what specious pretence*, to have her sister occupy a couch sufficiently near that of the royal pair to admit of easy conversation from bed to bed; and, a little before cock-crowing, she took care to awaken the good monarch, her husband, (who bore her none the worse will because he intended to wring her neck on the morrow,) – she managed to awaken him, I say, (*although, on account of a capital conscience and an easy digestion, he slept well,) by the profound interest of a story (about a rat and a black cat, I think,)* which she was narrating (all in an under-tone, of course,) to her sister. When the day broke, it so happened that this *history* was not altogether finished, and that Scheherazade, in the nature of things, could not finish it just then, since it was high time for her to get up and be bowstrung – a thing a very little more pleasant than hanging, *only a trifle more genteel!* (italics added)

Behind the veneer of comicality and humor, there is a repartee that undermines public acceptance and prepares for another criterion for what Poe terms the grotesque and Arabesque. This deliberate rewriting with parenthetical and often humorous interjections deprives the frame tale of its seductive hold, frees readers from its captivating spell, as related by Leigh Hunt from among the Romantics and Walter Bagehot from among the High Victorians. Poe turns the prelude into a farce of one sort or another and undermines the very properties that have secured its popularity that James Mew, E. M. Forster, and many others highlight, such as suspense, narrative mechanisms, strangeness, wonder, and the enduring hold of specific names that crept into Victorian poetry and novels. In Poe's version, it emerges as prosaic and plain enough to invite sarcasm. The elaborate frame tale's bedroom and garden scenes are effaced and replaced with "having good cause to be jealous of his queen"; while the two brothers are Islamized as if they were not Sassanid. Poe's version is also unconcerned with the beheaded queens.

Pre-Scheherazade Women Actors

Storywriters like Poe and twentieth-century grammatologists are drawn to sequential narratives that are also the most appealing and popular over the ages. Hence their focus is on narrative men as narrative representations, or events of no psychological depth. Both men and women are mere artifacts. But what if we claim the beheaded queens of the prelude as actual players whose deliberate action, that is, betrayal, explodes power structures? What if we suggest that proper names have a hold on memory whenever there is some link between action and name, like Anīs al-Jalīs, for example? However, how is it possible for the anonymous queens to survive properly in narrative along a pendulum of equilibrium and disequilibrium without a claim to some rebelliousness, an explosive desire to thwart codified rule and ethics and confront danger? I do not intend to argue against Todorov's selections from the *Arabian Nights*, especially the popular tales like Sindbad, but would like to question the phrase "narrative men," and replace it for the time being with "narrative women," not because I am more attuned to women's voices, but rather because, in the phrasing and application to these tales, I detect another instance of empowering masculinity in a narrative that can exemplify narrative women. Whenever action is undertaken by a doer like the queens, narrative women are only envisaged as agents whose very action generates response. Without their action there are no tales, no morose and bloody kings, and, certainly, no every-night damsel including Scheherazade. By contrast, Todorov certainly uses a common phrase for human beings to present a human situation, but I am afraid that it ends up by citing only males as grammatical subjects. Admittedly, a substantial part of the *Arabian Nights* involves the narrative of male *actants* or agents, but the other portion involving women incites action and response: It often explodes a situation, sets it in motion and hence disequilibrium, and traps men in response. After all, Todorov also suggests the following: "The meaning (or function) of one element in the text is its ability to enter into correlations with other elements in this work and with the work as a whole."[26]

As we will note in the following text, the opening part, the prelude, does not function as a narrative supplementation, but as a very integrative beginning to the paradigmatic and syntagmatic units that make up the structure of the frame tale. A close reading of this part of the frame tale is bound to change our usual reading of this frame as a point of confrontation of authority, power, and pomp with art. This modification in a poetics of prose beyond gendered classification and in cognizance of doers or agents can better explain the opening part of the frame tale.

As already mentioned, *A Thousand and One Nights* rarely appears as narrative proper in critics' or grammatologists' readings despite the efforts of Claude Bremond and Todorov to redirect their reading into a central space between fiction proper and the fantastic. A counter reading applies the other extreme by presenting the tales as representations of social life. While these nights play on verisimilitude, the uncanny, the wonderful, and the supernatural, their power derives from illusion working craftily in a rich treasury of discursive space that offers much to grammatologists. More often, especially in the frame tale, women play dynamic roles that undermine the narrator's voice as it alternates with that of the grammatical subject, that is, Shahrayar and royal power. These dynamic roles deconstruct any illusionism that surreptitiously imposes and encodes a circumscribing ideology. They happen to play and navigate within a liminal space between presence and absence, deference and defiance. This dynamic does not depend solely on the role of Scheherazade in the frame tale. Nor does it rest totally on the artifice of embedding.

Before the appearance of Scheherazade in the tale, women have exercised a degree of personal freedom and power, as their actions provide a set of motifs that, in Boris Tomashevsky's grammar, determines a dynamic situation. These motifs, Propp's/Joseph Bedier's constants or functions, generate action without necessarily succumbing to narrative ethos as probably endorsed by the narrator, the second-rate historian whose version of the frame tale lacks firsthand accountability. In

[26] Cited from *Communications* in Roland Barthes, "An Introduction to the Structural Analysis of Narrative," *New Literary History* 6, no. 2 (Winter 1975), 244n20. See also Roland Barthes, "Introduction to the Structural Analysis of Narratives," in *Image, Music, Text*, trans. Stephen Heath (New York: Hill and Wang, 1977), 79–124; and *A Barthes Reader*, ed. Susan Sontag (New York: Barnes and Noble, 2009), 212–49.

challenging normative ethos, female subjects explode the hierarchal myth along with its patriarchal structures. When freed from customary associations rooted in habits of thought and reading, the reader's mind may question narrative transmission, interrogate its makeup, and reject it as a basic mode of legitimation. Both the secondary historian who begins the narrative and the two monarchs present the case for violent response and beheading of the two queens and damsels as being legitimate, a right of royalty sustained by a tradition of similar practices. The hurried pace of the prelude and its production as a transmission can act disarmingly on the reader's mind, leading to a passive attitude that accepts whatever is communicated as transmitted history that has established itself in a revered tradition. Jean-François Lyotard, for one, cites transmission as an opportunity to "formulate prescriptions that have the status of norms," prescribing thereby "utterances with pretension to justice."[27]

Although more applicable to a "postmodern condition," Lyotard's conceptualization can fit into a narratological framework that has much to say about a surprising wave of appropriation involving the frame tale in dozens of feminist and other writings. Scholarship on the tale also partakes of this "postmodern condition," and multifaceted readings treat the tales as a fulcrum for critical inquiry.[28] Passive readings under the spell of these tales often forego questioning a tale and its underlying substratum: ignoring Fredric Jameson's point that genres "are essential literary institutions or social contracts between a writer [here a storyteller] and a specific public, whose function is to specify the proper use of a particular artifact."[29]

These are not Todorov's concerns, nor are they the dominating preoccupations of critics of the art. It is to Todorov's credit, however, that he brings forcefully to the discussion the role of structure. Even when he applies the established hypothesis that the "act of narrating is never, in the *Arabian Nights*, a transparent act, on the contrary, it is the main spring of the action" (73) – for as already argued in early twentieth-century writings, "narrating equals living" (73) – he lets this hypothesis grow into a grammatology. In both *The Poetics of Prose* and *The Fantastic*,[30] he takes his examples from Sindbad and the mendicants in "The Porter and the Three Ladies of Baghdad" to establish a structured cosmology where life

[27] Lyotard, *Postmodern Condition*, 31.
[28] A different and highly intelligent argument is offered by Malti-Douglas, "Shahrazad Feminist."
[29] Fredric Jameson, *The Political Unconscious: Narrative as a Socially Symbolic Act* (Ithaca, NY: Cornell University Press, 1981), 106.
[30] Tzvetan Todorov, *The Fantastic: A Structural Approach to a Literary Genre*, trans. Richard Howard (Ithaca, NY: Cornell University Press, 1975); Tzvetan Todorov, *The Poetics of Prose*, trans. Richard Howard (Oxford: Basil Blackwell, 1977).

and death, presence and absence, wound and healing, evolve as paradigms. These give life to what preceding and contemporary grammatologists and narratologists present in terms of motifs, functions, and the narrative act, something that, in Genette's terms, is explicative, predictive, thematic, persuasive, distractive, or obstructive.[31] The narrative act assumes significance in these tales because, as Todorov argues in line with what is already accepted and as the frame tale suggests, the "absence of narrative signifies death," a stance that acquires further evidence from similar absences and narrative death, as in the tale of the physician Duban, the dervish in princess Parizades, and many others. Around this conclusion gather a number of warnings, forebodings, clashes of will, and violations of specific sets of oaths, or simply a failure to perceive the complexity of human behavior as in the kings' sense of unfathomable betrayal.

The Preludinal Site of Nuptial Failure

To be sure, the death/life or silence/loquacity binary holds narrative together. The case is even more so in the frame tale. Scheherazade's storytelling provides the necessary proof. But the first part of the frame tale, the prelude that sets up the scene, does not adhere to this binary. The raconteur as secondary historian admits us to a royal life of conviviality, sociability, longing, hunt, and subsequent calamity. In this prelude, there is little talk but more voyeurism. In the bedroom and the garden scenes, there are spectacles. Both reader and kings are spectators, and the spectacle unfolds as in cinematic close-ups. Hence, this early turn to the spectacle manages to contravene common approaches to the frame tale, the enveloping framework that gives rise to the ongoing marvelous story-machine that translators, adaptors, appropriators, and narrative entrepreneurs over the ages have never tired of mining, acting throughout as storytellers' doubles. While Poe overlooks the scenes and replaces them with "a reason for jealousy," translators often tamper with them, laying emphasis instead on the issue of surprise, shock, and *punishable* adultery: One instance occurs between the queen and the kitchen boy and the other with the slave Mas'ud. Translators address themselves to an audience, which, especially in the case of Galland and his English translator, and Lane, is presented as squeamishly opposed to such explicit scenes that are central to the frame tale. Lane exaggerates this sense even more and empties the first part of the frame tale of whatever serves to challenge

[31] Gérard Genette, *Narrative Discourse: An Essay in Method* (Ithaca, NY: Cornell University Press, 1983), 92–94.

a bourgeois drawing room sensibility. Galland's taste takes his addressee and her like into consideration as he trims the tale and rewrites those sections that lack the kind of modesty that he is upholding. The relevance of these omissions or modifications to narrative grammatology cannot be regarded as minor, especially in the case of Galland's translation in its status as the primary source for all, including Lane and his late eighteenth-century Egyptian manuscript. Poe provides us with an early dismissal of this part in his critical rewriting. Hence the need to view Poe's dismissal of the two scenes in the context of Galland's account and his proclaimed sense of "modesty." Galland's version of the second scene, the one in the garden, reads as follows:

Whilst he was thus swallowed up with grief, an *object presented itself to his view*, which quickly turned all his thoughts another way. A *secret gate* of the Sultan's palace opened all of a sudden, and there came out of it twenty women, in the midst of whom marched the Sultaness, who was easily distinguished from the rest by her *majestic* air. This princess, thinking that the King of Tartary was gone a hunting with his brother the Sultan, came up with her retinue near the windows of his apartment; for the prince had placed himself so that he could see all that passed in the garden without being perceived himself. He observed, that the persons who accompanied the Sultaness threw off their veils and long robes, that they might be at more freedom; but was wonderfully surprised when he saw that ten of them were blacks, and that each of them took his mistress. The Sultaness, on her part, was not long without her gallant; she clapped her hands, and called – "Masoud! Masoud!" and immediately a black came down from a tree, and ran to her in all haste.

Modesty will not allow, nor is it necessary to relate, what passed between the blacks and the ladies; it is sufficient to say, that Schahzenan saw enough to convince him that his brother had as much cause to complain as himself. This amorous company continued together till midnight; and, having bathed all together in a great pond, which was one of the chief ornaments of the garden, they dressed themselves, and re-entered the palace by the secret door, all except Masoud, who climbed up his tree, and got over the garden-wall the same way as he came. (Grub Street translation, reproduced in *Novelist's Magazine*; italics added)

The notion that the king "saw enough" does not minimize the overwhelming impact of the spectacle. Although the scene is curtailed, limited, castrated, and sanitized, Galland's omission and underlying *modesty* and superfluity only make the spectacle that much more suggestive. The detail that the translator's modesty shuns opens the door for conjecture. The consequential sense of wrath and distrust of women sets the stage for further action. It is this scene, with all its omissions and modifications, that triggers narrative. Galland follows the secondary historian complacently whenever hierarchy and class distinctions apply. The bare thread of narrative serves the purpose of entertainment but not instruction. The garden scene, as will be shown shortly, derives a great narrative power not only in terms of functions, but also as a spectacle that replaces words with images and scenes. A different grammatology applies. Instead of limiting analysis to verbal structuralist poetics, we need to account for the garden orgy not only as a spectacle, but also as staging, a frequent performance to which the actors are used. A scene unfolds with twenty actors, and the young king as audience. The garden scene has therefore a mixed grammar of motives whereby the visual and verbal coalesce. The case is less so in the bedroom scene that in Galland's version replaces the kitchen boy with "one of the meanest officers of the household" as befitting his sense of decorum. Verbal narrative leaves little space for the spectacle as it reads in the following excerpt:

> But willing once more to embrace the queen, whom he loved entirely, he returned alone to his palace, and went straight to her majesty's apartment; who, not expecting his return, had taken one of *the meanest officers of the household to her bed, where they lay both flat asleep, having been there a considerable time.*
>
> The king entered without any noise, and pleased himself to think how he should surprise his wife, who he thought loved him entirely as he did her: but how strange was his surprise, when, by the light of the flambeaux which burn all night in the apartments of those eastern princes, he saw a man in her arms! (*Novelist's Magazine*; italics added)

The secondary historian who relates what is already in circulation passes over these scenes with neither condemnation nor approval. The recurrence of queens' choices in the preceding text, and in the tale of the ensorcelled king of the black islands, alerts us to what is of greater interest to James: the psychological depth. Do the queens have their revenge on royalty through this choice? Is the raconteur making a point in this selection? Why do translators either bypass the scene as reported or make modifications as Galland does in deference to propriety? James's psychologism, which Todorov underestimates, is important to the spectacle. How do the kings take betrayal as a double body-blow: as rulers and, on a strictly personal level, as males? Do they feel as if they have been missing a convivial life with their wives, free of sumptuousness and grandeur? In a reading of the spectacle, Jacques Rancière makes the following remark in his *Emancipated Spectator*: "What human beings contemplate in the spectacle is the activity they have been robbed of; it is their own essence become alien, turned against them, organizing a collective world whose reality is that dispossession."[32] This is particularly important in view of the garden scene, the gathering of so many in a broad daylight orgy. The kings' personal angst has to assume larger

[32] Jacques Rancière, *The Emancipated Spectator*, trans. Gregory Elliott (London and New York: Verso, 2011), 7.

proportions in the context of a world that has run wild against their royal pomp. Narratologists are unconcerned with these questions, even though, as noted earlier, they are central to the structure of the tales that have taken Europe and later the world by surprise.

Throughout the collection, translators leave an indelible mark of their presence that is most often social, economic, political, and cultural. Their variations on the frame tale also signify its gravitational pull. Even when such a genius as Poe (1809–49) is the first to radically deviate from facile imitation or appropriation in the long tradition of the Oriental tale in his *Tales of the Grotesque and Arabesque*, the frame tale still traps and urges him to adopt different alternatives, as in "The Thousand-and-Second Tale of Scheherazade," first published in 1845, during the heyday of realism. In the opening paragraph, Poe sets the tone for the ironic twist to the structure of the frame tale and the denouement of the collection; an ironic and probably humorous gesture unwelcome to the Romantic sensibility. He writes:

> I was not a little astonished to discover that the literary world has hitherto been strangely in error respecting the fate of the vizier's daughter, Scheherazade, as that fate is depicted in the "Arabian Nights"; and that the denouément there given, if not altogether inaccurate, as far as it goes, is at least to blame in not having gone very much farther.

Poe reads, retranslates, and rewrites at one and the same time. Thus, he continues: "It seems, however, that this politic damsel (who had been reading Machiavelli, beyond doubt,) had a very ingenious little plot in her mind." He intervenes, comments, parodies, and invents in a unique metafictional style that has to endure a long wait before it is adopted by some late twentieth-century writers to engage, not with Poe, but with another genius, Jorge Luis Borges. Both Poe and Borges might have led criticism and scholarship on *A Thousand and One Nights* in another direction that could have enriched both narrative and translation theories.

In line with Borges, Todorov writes of retranslations as processes of addition and suppression; each is "a secondary speech act," a "new tale which no longer awaits its narrator" (78). Translations and their editors rarely take a careful look at narrative variables, visual and verbal, as are encountered in the frame tale. All recognize the enveloping structure that courts and incites embedding, which, in Todorov's phrasing, is "the narrative of a narrative" (72). But it is also rare to find among critics, including Bremond, Greimas, and Todorov, someone who takes into consideration the components that unlock a sequence of mystery and suspense. They also rarely take into account James's "psychologism" that

Todorov critiques. James's mind was focused on a nineteenth-century European tradition that is bourgeois in its direction and concern, while structuralists other than Todorov veer away, perhaps too sharply, from interpretive criticism and its obsession with character as the locus for subjectivity and modernity. The *Arabian Nights* has made some gains in Romantic criticism but received no serious attention from James and his fellow critics. However, structuralists brought something new to the study of the tales that invites further analysis, interpretation, and critique. The case is even more inviting in the case of the frame tale, and its explosive preludinal part.

What Does the Muslim Chronicler Tell?

The frame tale is not only a dynamic of cause and effect, a proliferation of active and static motifs in Tomashevsky's terms;[33] nor is it only an opening, a rupture in a monarchic structure of power, or a devastating shock to the sustained binding ethos of a familial or societal mechanism. It is all these at once; it also opens a binary of life and death that narratively plays out loquacity and curiosity as the irrevocable dialectic in human life. The frame tale situates time in narrative, as Todorov notes, and not narrative in time: Thus, narrative unaccountability in the opening sentence of the frame tale in the early fifteenth-century manuscript ("it is related") appears as a moment of unease that the narrator, in the garb of a Muslim chronicler or historian, soon qualifies as being as unescapably disputable as ancient myths, legends, and accounts, for "God knows and sees best what lies hidden in the old accounts of bygone peoples and times" (3). As a disclaimer, the qualification may sound sublative, or even a mere formula intended to appease listeners or readers. But it is not so. It sets the tone for these narrative women to raise doubts about everything told or narrated. The question here was posed in an earlier article of mine on cultural production and narrative in particular, during the Abbasid period when prominent writers were involved in the discussion of reliability and invention.[34] Based on Nabia Abbott's manuscript fragment, we can be sure that the frame tale was available in written form by the end of the ninth century, meaning that the discussion of fictionality and reliability was part of the ongoing controversy with respect to invention and historicity, fabrication, and reliability. The secondary historian who relates what is already in circulation resorts to Muslim historians'

[33] Boris Tomashevsky, "Thematics," in *Russian Formalist Criticism: Four Essays*, comp. Lee T. Lemon and Marion J. Reis (Lincoln, NE: University of Nebraska, 1965), 62–95.
[34] al-Musawi, "Abbasid Popular Narrative."

unaccountability regarding "*asāṭīr al-awwalīn*" (fables of the ancients) to shrug off responsibility, especially on issues pertaining to faith and courtly life. This equivocal position is bound to inform the narrative of narratives, the embedding technique.

The prologue's first two lines set the frame tale in motion: To claim the garb of a second-degree historian, a narrator of narratives has to establish a substantial process of gathering and dispersing where spatial, temporal, and descriptive attributes have to work together to offset the equivocation of the first two lines: "during the time of the Sassanid dynasty, in the peninsulas of India and Indochina, there lived two kings who were brothers. The older brother was named Shahrayar, the younger Shahzaman" (3). With these pieces of information, the reader is led into a history with its proper geography. By contrast, and in the framework of Genette's narrative levels or diegetic relations, the narrator steps outside the narrated world as an extradiegetic-heterodiegetic figure; but only seemingly so, as will become clear in due course. At this point in the prologue, the chronicler narrates "what he is absent from."[35]

Now that we have a common or substantive noun as in the names of the two royal figures, we can resort to Todorov's association of names with attributes. In the opening scene that introduces the two kings, we are placed in the realm where agency combines attributes and characteristics that are not only denominative but also explicable and descriptive: "such an expression," argues Todorov, "is equivalent to an entire proposition, where its denominative aspects constitute the subject" (110). But more than descriptive, the predicate reflects on the denominative very closely so as to produce in our minds the magnitude of power, authority, and mastery:

> His power reached the remotest corners of the land and its people so that the country was loyal to him, and his subjects obeyed him. Shahrayar himself lived and ruled in India and Indochina, while to his brother *he gave* the land of Samarkand to rule as king. (3, italics added)

In the end, we have an emperor and a king; and power sustains loyalty in what we can describe as a hegemonic order. Loyalty is inclusive, and their households are the first to abide by it. The moment that desire intrudes, order (equilibrium) witnesses a passage to probable disorder. To comply with his brother's desire to see him, Shahzaman has to prepare for his journey and join the vizier's (wazir's) caravan for a night before starting the journey. So far desire has played a minimal preparatory function; but, as soon as it doubles in force, it leads him back to the palace: Shahzaman

[35] Genette, *Narrative Discourse*, 248.

returns to his city "to bid his wife goodbye." We are in the realm of surprise. Narrative women here function at this often-neglected nub. Desire operates now within a commonly upheld social practice, but it soon opens the gate for action. Desire creates a narrative positionality, a rupture, a wound that is to trigger action. What is already produced as yearning for a family reunion between brothers initiates another desire, to "bid his wife goodbye" and only to find her lying "in the arms of one of the kitchen boys" (3).

Before tracking effect and affect,[36] we need to define the moment as semantically the most loaded, while syntagmatically it is a heightened series of narrative units that build up and lead to an acute function, an explosion that the narrator has to sketch cursorily before looking at the effect: "when he saw them, the world turned dark before his eyes" (4). The betrayal assumes a magnitude in correspondence with pomp and power: "I am king and sovereign in Samarkand, and yet my wife has betrayed me and has inflicted this on me" (3). As seen and perceived by the sovereign, the bedroom spectacle is relatively private; but we assume that there are guards who are to be called on to clean up the site. A hierarchy and power are asserted through the infliction of death. The upsurge of anger, as the "world turned dark," cannot be quelled by death, and hence another functional dynamic has to operate. Moreover, while betrayal sets the stage for bloodshed, and hence a probable end to narrative, its magnitude will sound less so in comparison to the next betrayal scene. A gradation of response is in full play.

Questions remain, which are raised by this scene and which readers sidestep under the spell of a captivating narrative. The betrayal scene is more often regarded from the perspective of the agent, the king: Why

[36] Gregory J. Seigworth and Melissa Gregg argue in "An Inventory of Shimmers," in *The Affect Theory Reader*, ed. Melissa Gregg and Gregory J. Seigworth (Durham, NC, and London: Duke University Press, 2012), 2:

Affect can be understood then as a gradient of bodily capacity – a supple incrementalism of ever-modulating force-relations – that rises and falls not only along various rhythms and modalities of encounter but also through the troughs and sieves of sensation and sensibility, an incrementalism that coincides with belonging to comportments of matter of virtually any and every sort. . . .

Hence, affect's always immanent capacity for extending further still: both into and out of the interstices of the inorganic and non-living, the intracellular divulgences of sinew, tissue, and gut economies, and the vaporous evanescences of the incorporeal (events, atmospheres, feeling-tones). . . .

At once intimate and impersonal, affect accumulates across both relatedness and interruptions in relatedness, becoming a palimpsest of force-encounters traversing the ebbs and swells of intensities that pass between "bodies" (bodies defined not by an outer skin-envelope or other surface boundary but by their potential to reciprocate or co-participate in the passages of affect).

should the narrator, the storyteller, refrain from further explanation of the other agent's (queen's) motivation for betrayal? Why is she in an extramarital relationship with "one of meanest kitchen boys"? If an explanation were to be offered at this stage of narration, narrative would lose its underlying structure, embedding as narrative of narrative. Mystery lies at the basis of this mechanism. The human being remains a bundle of desires in the absence of a guiding cause, a counter system that certainly involves the narrative in complication. The queen's desire for a kitchen boy or his like is to be repeated in the tale of the petrified "King of the Black Islands."[37] Even so, this desire begs for analysis. It shows that the queen is already involved in a licentious relationship with the kitchen boy. Deception, if that is the name for betrayal, has already been going on, but now it is discovered because of the king's unexpected visit. Power and pomp fall to the ground as mere superficial accessories when compared with the human desire for transgression, deviation, and realization of selfhood in terms of lust. The narrator leaves no space for the queen to deliver a speech like William Morris's Guinevere in "The Defense of Guinevere." However, we are confronted with a dynamic and explosive action that should raise questions as to the nature and reasons behind it. An action of this magnitude is depicted summarily in half a sentence. Power has its discourse, but not the queen. But has the queen considered the consequences? Why the risk? We are not placed into a plain realm of psychologism. It is up to the reader to determine the reasons for this extramarital relationship. But we are definitely placed in a different realm of action whereby women's silence, repressed or self-chosen, forced or driven to absence, offers us another nonverbal narrative. Agency and action coalesce, inviting us as readers to take account of the indivisible speculations of both James and Todorov.

The scene as related does not appease or assuage the curiosity of the king, nor that of his entourage. Its effect and affect do not end with a termination of the queen's life. What is repressed and remains as mystery opens up the narrative. As is always the case with curiosity, there is risk and possibly death. The betrayal scene and its aftermath signify action at its highest degree. One can argue this action in the context of James's psychologism that studies "action" as a viable access to a personality, a perspective that justifies the search for reasons behind a massive transgression. As already shown, Todorov looks at such narratives as the *Arabian Nights*, the *Decameron*, the *Saragossa Manuscript*, and the *Odyssey* as "a limit-case of literary a-psychologism" because they are "characterized by intransitive action," as action unfolds as important in

[37] al-Musawi, "The 'Mansion' and the 'Rubbish Mounds.'"

itself.[38] For him, the *Arabian Nights* has laid emphasis on the "predicative,"[39] in that the "predicate ... not the subject of the proposition" draws so much attention and focus to the extent of the "effacement of the grammatical subject."[40] The proposition differentiates widely between the two. Todorov leaves no space for the unsayable and repressed that should have substantiated and complemented the present perspective with respect to narrative women.

If we accept Todorov's hypothesis that "a character is a potential story," and that every "new character signifies a new plot" and hence "the realm of narrative men,"[41] then the queen or "his wife" is no less substantive for being a common not a proper noun. Adopting his phraseology for a different discussion, her "denominative aspects" as queen and wife constitute a positionality, while her descriptive attributes of a privileged status provide the predicate.[42] However, the secondary historian as narrator undertakes two functions to sabotage this positionality; the queen appears only as a common noun, a queen, which nevertheless, and according to Todorov, has the dual denominative and descriptive function that allows the character to appear "equivalent to an entire proposition: its descriptive aspects for the predicate of the proposition whereas its denominative aspects constitute the subject."[43] Although repressed and with no proper name, the queen is deliberately involved, and has been for some time, in this extramarital relationship with a kitchen boy. The episode falls within the category of narrative "verbs" that, again in Todorov's narratology, apply to a passage from one state of equilibrium to disequilibrium.[44]

But Todorov's "grammar," which he applies to the poetics of prose in general, and the short story or tale in particular, should not misdirect our reading. A common noun, queen or wife, used and pursued in this narrative instead of a proper name, which is Shahzaman, has to raise questions, for example, as to its implications in terms of gender. Barbara Godard suggests, in line with Belsey, that "gender differences structure social relationships at all levels and are essential to narrative, whose grammar is grounded in defense and opposition of marked and unmarked pairs."[45] This premise offers us other opportunities to pursue the realm of narrative women where a queen, a wife, generates an astounding series of actions and reactions. These are of no ordinary consequence to the frame tale narrative because they present a complex or dialectic of cause/effect/affect. The act of killing is

[38] Todorov, "Narrative Men," 66–67. [39] Ibid., 68. [40] Ibid., 67. [41] Ibid., 70.
[42] Todorov, "The Grammar of Narrative," in *Poetics of Prose*, 110. [43] Ibid.
[44] Ibid., 111.
[45] Barbara Godard, "F(r)ictions: Feminists Re/Writing Narrative," in *Gender and Narrativity*, ed. Barry Rutland (Ottawa, ON: Carleton University Press, 1997), 87–114.

not a terminus; action stems from affects that also lead to questions and further action. A destabilizing act such as the queen's transgression not only undermines the status quo, but also operates on the king's body and feelings. He is no longer the same. Hence, although deprived of a proper name, Shahzaman's wife cannot be dismissed from narrative as a passing presence.

Thus, the first part of this inquiry focuses on the transformative aspect of narrative as a series of effects and affects on the younger brother, King Shahzaman. "[W]henever he found himself alone and thought of his ordeal with his wife, he would sigh deeply, then stifle his grief" (4). The secondary historian as narrator makes a point by providing an elaborate description of the deterioration of the king's body, with special emphasis on emotions and feelings as these operate on his physique. After all, he is very attached to his wife: "willing once more to embrace the queen, whom he loved entirely." No wonder, then, that Shahzaman, "would fret with anxiety. His spirit would sag," and he "ate less and less, grew pale, and his health deteriorated. He neglected everything, wasted away, and looked ill" (4). In "psychologism," this state depicts a person who is not only shocked by betrayal, but also by a sense of unrequited love, frustration, and intense bereavement. This representation invites the reader to weigh consequences in favor of the king: His love for her is more than his love for the kingdom, as he "*neglected everything*, wasted away, and looked ill" (italics added). In terms of wording, the narrator assigns only a few words to royalty and prestige or power. With a sustained emphasis on loss of health, the reader's empathy turns toward the king and works on the unconscious so as to deprive the queen of a voice. In that silence, we are not in a position to know; silence leaves the reader with the image of the queen as the culprit. In a neat reading of genres and using Jameson, Godard applies his suggestion that genres are "essentially literary institutions or social constructs between a writer and a specific public."[46] In this case, the reader gets "interpellated" into "the encoded ideologies of every day."[47]

On narrative levels, let us consider the matter by applying the narratology of Todorov and Bremond, before turning to Genette. How far does this early turn in the frame tale shift positions that are of consequence to narrative levels and specifically the relation of the frame tale to the embedded tales? If "embedding designates one of the three ways in which sequences can be combined syntactically into more complex forms: linking; embedding; alternation," then we are confronted early on with transformative actions that generate further shifts in structural and psychological levels and place the frame narrative into

[46] Jameson, *Political Unconscious*, 105–6. [47] Godard, "F(r)ictions," 117.

the complexity of "linking; embedding; alteration."[48] Genette suggests as much when, in redefining these relations, he adopts a functional perspective,[49] stating, however, that the province of narratology is not that of "interpretation."[50] Is it possible, then, to understand the physical and psychological changes undergone by the young king Shahzaman separately? Are they disconnected from functions? Does Shahzaman's love not act as a propelling and compelling motivation that forces him to return to the bedroom? Isn't the act of killing the queen and the "meanest kitchen boy" quickly passed over by the secondary historian? Does he not relate what is already in circulation as being a natural or justifiable response to transgression? Does this response calm the king down? As manifestations of bereavement and loss, affects evolve as a dynamic action that triggers and generates a narrative sequence. The province of narratology necessarily includes interpretation.

For the sake of convenience, let us go over the consequences of Shahzaman's health condition. The younger king's state is presented as so noticeable that his brother Shahrayar's curiosity increases. Curiosity is problematic at this juncture because it opens the door for further explosive action:

> When King Shahrayar looked at his brother and saw how day after day he lost weight and grew thin, pale, ashen, and sickly, he thought that this was because of his expatriation and homesickness for his country and family. (4)

The narrator gives in to "psychologism" at this point. The presumed homesickness for family faces us with the early conjecture that Shahzaman's disappointment does not stem necessarily from betrayal as much as it derives from the reasons behind that betrayal, reasons that his feelings for the queen could not justify. The "dejection . . . because of his homesickness for his country," which the narrator voices as Shahrayar's conjecture, is inclusive of yearning for country and family. As such, Shahrayar's surmise allows for his brother to stay behind and not participate in the planned hunting trip.[51] A seemingly intransitive action, this

[48] Cited from Claude Brémond, *Logique du récit* (Paris: Éditions du Seuil, 1973); Todorov, *The Fantastic*; and Introduction to *Poetics* (University of Minnesota Press, 1981) in Didier Coste and John Pier, "Living Handbook Book of Narratology," www.lhn.uni-hamburg.de.

[49] Genette, *Narrative Discourse*; *Palimpsests: Literature in the Second Degree* (1981); *Narrative Discourse Revisited* (1983; 1988). See also Coste and Pier, "Living Handbook Book of Narratology."

[50] Genette, *Narrative Discourse*, 87.

[51] Although not accounting for this part of the frame tale, Aravamudan's comment on Todorov is worth noticing; see his "Adventure Chronotope and Oriental Xenotrope," 243–44.

nonparticipation opens the gate for the most explosive action that is to establish the process of embedding in syntactic and distributive or integrational forms in connection with the rest of tales. The well-known garden scene has to be broken into a number of semantic and syntagmatic units to allow for a better structural reading that may account for narrative diversity (5).

In his reading of James in "The Secret of Narrative," Todorov suggests that the absence of knowledge provokes the presence of a "narrative" in James's "Sir Dominick Ferrand."[52] Lack of knowledge regarding Shahrayar and Shahzaman's dejection anticipates and leads to the garden scene where Shahrayar's wife repeats the other queen's bedroom scene, but on a more carnivalesque scale that involves twenty males and females. Disguised and masked along with the queen's partner in the top of a tree, we are led to a stage where everyone has roles to play, concluding with a sexual orgy. Royal pomp is turned upside down, and the primitive connotations of someone in the tree being called on to make love to the queen situate us in the realm of carnival. For the participants and the queen in particular, it is jovial to frequently enact the scene, but not necessarily for the spectator and the kings, who are bound to pass through "the Double Body" of the king's implications and personal pain. It is even more so because the same scene occurs on a daily basis and is watched twice by the young king and once by his brother. In this position as voyeurs or spectators, they compromise themselves because "[e]very spectator is already an actor in her story; every actor, every man of action, is the spectator of the same story."[53]

The Garden Site: The Spectacle

However, the scene unfolds with Shahzaman gazing as a voyeur: "from the window overlooking the garden, [he] watched the birds and trees" (5). "While agonized over his misfortune, gazing at the heavens and turning a distracted eye on the garden," his gaze is drawn to what follows. The voyeur's gaze will soon be implicated in a self-reflexive brooding that takes into account not only the even number of twenty-two males and females, but also the nature of the event's staging, something that smacks of regular performance in a closed garden that has all the conflictual and paradoxical implications of biblical and sacrilegious dimensions. Shahrayar's queen and her maids and slaves are performers and actors, but she is the one in charge of the stage. In

[52] Todorov, *Poetics of Prose*, 147. [53]Ranciére, *Emancipated Spectator*, 17.

other words, action as character and character as action create a realm of narrative women.

The queen's narrative is quelled and repressed, as the death scene makes clear, but it still finds voice in the reflections of the dejected young brother who is to undergo psychological transformation from dejection to mirth at a scene of such magnitude. To see the workings of this scene as spectacle, let us break it up, as it appears in the original of Galland's translation, into the narrative units that make up such a spectacle:

Stage:
"[T]he private gate of his brother's palace opened, and there emerged, strutting like a dark-eyed deer, the lady, his brother's wife, with twenty slave girls, *ten* white and *ten* black."

Performers/Actors:
"Then they sat down, took off their clothes, and suddenly there were ten slave-girls and ten black slaves *dressed* in the *same* clothes as the girls" (5).

Action:
A. "Then the ten black slaves *mounted* the ten girls, while the lady called, 'Masʿūd, Masʿūd!' and a black slave jumped from the tree to the ground" (5).
B. "(He) rushed to her, and raising her legs, went between her thighs and made love to her" (5).
C. "Masʿūd topped the lady, while the ten slaves topped the ten girls, and they carried on *till* noon" (5).

Denouement:
A. "when they were done with their business, they got up and washed themselves."
B. "Then the ten slaves put on the same clothes again, mingled with the girls, and once more there appeared to be twenty slave-girls."
C. "Masʿūd himself jumped over the garden wall and disappeared, while the slave-girls and the lady sauntered to the *private* gate, went in and, *locking* the gate behind them, went their way" (5, italics added).

The scene, with its staging, performance, action, speech acts, and performers, cannot be hurriedly dismissed as a preparatory narrative to justify the kings' mania. Everything in the scene invites analysis. A number of syndromes are in action: retribution and betrayal; the appearance of black slaves in relation to human desire or to an exchange of roles between slaves and masters; the binary of culture and nature; and the raw and the cooked. Each invites a follow-up as each embedded narrative connects to those elements; only rarely does it deviate as a separate dynamic working on its own. The kings are to duplicate the role of Masʿūd in their first encounter with the outside world beyond their lands; Harun al-Rashid and Jaʿfar will duplicate the same scene in "Nur al-Din and Anis al-Jalis"; the queen in the tale of the ensorcelled king of the black islands will wreak vengeance and destruction on the king and his people when her love for the black slave is disrupted. Quantitative and qualitative gradations assume significance; and calamity is measured accordingly. Affects emerge as relational. The garden recalls other narratives and connects with other scenes throughout the *Arabian Nights*.[54] The same scene has its own narrative and philological particulars.

The act of "locking the gate behind them" suggests a number of things: This is a customary orgy that requires a secure place, private and unattended by others. Like any act of secrecy, the emphasis on "locking behind" provokes questions as to the frequency of such an orgy, a frequency that the brother, and hence the narrator, is soon to prove. The queen, the lady or the brother's wife, is behind the action and hence the narrative. Her husband, Shahrayar, appears passive in comparison, at least until disequilibrium sets in again. The spectacle is to be reenacted again to dispel Shahrayar's doubts and to demonstrate the magnitude of this transgression.

Before analyzing the hunting trip as a narrative foil to the orgy, it is worthwhile to reflect on narrative distributional functions that enable us not only to trace affects, but also and primarily to see them in relation to the transformations undergone by each brother. The outcome of such transformations gathers momentum in such a way as to present curiosity as a constant motif that grows in stature, while provocation is one culmination of a series of remarks, tracings, and attributions that can be interpreted as variable motifs in Propp's typology – in line with Bédier. Along with his reading of the morphology of the fairy tale, Propp's interventions in "Fairy Tale Transformations" (1924) are important, especially in relation to (1) prioritization of religious form; (2) application of the fantastic in relation to the rational; (3) the belatedness of humor in relation to the heroic treatment; (4) the antecedence of logical form; and (5) the priority of the universal over the national.

[54] See T. G. J. Maynard, "The Literary Relevance of the Enclosed Garden as an Image in the Oriental Tale, 1704–1820" (PhD diss., University of London, 1970).

These interventions may sound irrelevant here, especially in the context of a prelude that is more realistic and plausible, exempting the demon in the abducted bride's tale. They nevertheless highlight the chronicler's tone, as being an Islamic one, the logicality of the queens' revolt, the kings' anger, and the universal dimension of vicissitudes of fortune. In one case, the hunt that takes ten days provides structural and sociopolitical outlets that should not be overlooked. On the narrative level, it offers a paradoxical pause and action. The emperor Shahrayar enjoys the time off as an excursion in manliness that is also highly appreciated and admired by poets and writers in both Indo-Persian and Arabic traditions. The royal household also enjoys this time off and has its alternative plans to make maximum use of it. This private space, the household, is open to its own players, namely, the queen's entourage, as the rest accompanies the master Shahrayar on his hunting trip. Now we have two contending spaces: the wilderness, the right space for the hunt, and the palace and its vicinity. Each has its own protocols and rules that the narrator does not detail. It is left to the reader or the listener to figure them out. The hunt and the hunted, "the pursuer – the hunter, companions, his steed, hounds, or falcon – and the pursued, whether the prey be oryx, onager, gazelle, hare, quail, or fox," stand for this race and parade of chivalry and knighthood.[55] It provides the ironic twist for what takes place in the narrative: The hunter is the one to be betrayed. The queen rejects being the prey. There is neither equivalence nor reenactment of the hunt. She is her own master, the one in charge of the staged garden scene as a jovial one that involves no hunt and no prey.

On the structural level, the hunt provides the excuse for absence and presence: Shahrayar has to be out hunting; and hence enables the brother to gaze unseen. Also, as a show of masculinity and prowess, the hunt suffers deflation in the garden scene where a contending masculinity – black, naked, and free of pomp – prevails. A counteraction takes place that opens up bloodshed and, along with it, narrative.

As the drift of my reading shows, the frame tale is not an ordinary enclosing or enveloping narrative. The narrator switches roles with the dejected brother. His focalized perspective provides the reader with the garden scene at the very moment when he is absorbed in an interior monologue that allows us to gauge and assess his dejection, something that only a greater misfortune can defuse. As readers we are given

[55] Jaroslav Stetkevych, *The Hunt in Arabic Poetry: From Heroic to Lyric to Metapoetic* (Notre Dame, IN: University of Notre Dame Press, 2015), cover.

a wider scope of narrative motifs, dynamic and static, and an insight into distributional and integrative functions, to use Roland Barthes's terms.[56] But, narratologists stop short of reading into the nonverbal, the unsayable, the inexpressible, and the repressed. The narrator's concession to authority and power and deference to a patriarchal norm leave the main actors silent. There is action on part of the queens, but no speech. And, if there is an utterance, it is the call to Masʿūd to exercise a monkey-like jump, followed by the sexual scene. It is this silence that should be interrogated every now and then. The frame tale only picks up on this when a nontemporal nonhuman authority is involved, like the monster, the abductor of the young bride. The scene that can be exchanged with that of the garden and places the two brothers, emperor and king, in the top of a tree following the appearance of the enormous monster from the sea replicates Masʿūd's role. They are free from pomp now and retain their naturalness as human beings as long as they are in open space. They end up making love to the young, abducted bride, but she is given a voice to explain a woman's idea of revenge. No matter how controversial this speech may be, it admits us to a woman's voice, a narrative gesture that the two queens have never been allowed, with the sole exception of the summons to Masʿūd to come down.

Between the garden scene and that of the abducted bride, we confront one of the most loaded pieces of narrative instigated and generated as such by the two queens who have no share in the narrator's privileged ability to gaze, interpret, and narrate. They act.

The universalization of Shahzaman's predicament is worth noticing because it fits into a normative ethic that is long sustained by patriarchal tradition. As he "pondered over his calamity and great misfortune, his care and sorrow left him" because "[t]his is our common lot," and "from what I have seen, everyone suffers". Ultimately, he "kept marveling and blaming life" (5), a stance that is to be confirmed for him by the abducted bride's act of seduction and speech.

The narrator is in no hurry to address Shahzaman's psychological transformation, in his role as extradiegetic narrator alternating with the character Shahrayar. He gives the young king "ten days" to "enjoy food and drink" with "zest," to regain "color" and weight and to emerge now as "lighthearted and free" (6). These depictions can be placed within Barthes's schema of predicative functions. They are there, however, to

[56] Based on Benveniste, Barthes discusses this in his "Introduction to Structural Analysis," 242. See also *A Barthes Reader*, 218, where he sums up the discussion of levels by saying: "Levels are operations."

draw the attention of Shahrayar, who has to understand the reason behind this change. Again, the narrator is in no hurry to satisfy such curiosity, which, ironically, is already known and conveyed to the reader and listener. An ironic situation arises as Shahrayar almost compels his brother to explain the reasons behind this transformation, a proposition with which the narrator duly plays. Shahrayar has to fulfill his curiosity piecemeal. As such, he asks Shahzaman at least to "explain the first cause" for his dejection, a cause of which we are already aware (6). The narrator's interjection that enables Shahrayar to comment with amazement "at the deceit of women" and the prayer to God "to protect him from their wickedness" only deepens the ironic situation while also speaking to a patriarchal norm. One can suggest that the manuscript tradition sustains that norm with some reference to the Divine. However, an integrative, and also distributional, function is prepared for in his retort: "By God, had I been in your place, I would have killed at least a hundred or even a thousand women. I would have been furious; I would have gone mad" (7). This ironic foreshadowing betrays the hand of professionals and redactors. When he persists in asking for the reason behind the change during the ten days of the hunting trip, he is made aware of his wife's garden orgy. A new addition to that narrative is Masʿūd's mastery of the situation. He addressed the queen as follows: "What do you want, you slut? Here is Saʿd al-Dīn Masʿūd" (8). In line with the carnival atmosphere, this coarse language sounds normal. It evokes joy and laughter: The queen "laughed and fell on her back" (8). Again, this scene foreshadows a scene in "The Tale of the Enchanted King," where similarly foul language invades sanitized royal discourse.

This culmination of action explodes the seeming equilibrium of the ten-day hunting trip. The narrative is in danger of dying, along with the repressed voice and death of the queen and her entourage. The temporary turn to piety, renunciation of royalty in search of "the love of the Supreme Lord" (8), can easily terminate a narrative. But this is not the narrator's plan. The entry into the world of a huge and enormous monster, "a black demon, carrying on his head a large chest with four steel locks" (8) that he will soon unlock to "pull out" a "full grown woman" of a "beautiful figure," a "face like the full moon, and a lovely smile" (9), this entry brings into the frame tale another woman who can voice her discontent and revenge on the demon. What is important for this sphere of women's action and narrative is the abducted bride's role as the contending power, one that is capable of forcing them to come down from a Masʿūd-like position in a tree to make love to her: "[M]ake love to me and satisfy my need, or else I shall wake the demon, and he will kill you" (9). The term "satisfy my need" places her, her need, and her language at the intricate nexus of a contaminated discursive space where a charged and challenging statement can invoke an appeal to the natural while seemingly also supporting a commonly held belief, one that receives Richard F. Burton's endorsement,[57] namely, that women surpass men in sexual desire. The bride compels them to give her their rings to be added to "the ninety-eight rings of different fashions and colors" (9). As there have been as many encounters and departures as reflected by the number of collected rings, the acquisition of rings testifies to multiple marriages. These rings also testify to the temporal dimension of storytelling, something that is suspended by the monster's abduction as a supernatural act. The act of ring acquisition might carry more weight if contextualized in terms of the challenges confronting the marital institution that suffers a series of inconceivable ruptures. Her explanation responds to acquisition as an act of revenge implemented by an abducted bride, a human agent, against no less than the monster or the demon:

> A hundred men have known me under the very horns of this filthy, monstrous cuckold, who has imprisoned me in this *chest*, *locked* it with four *locks*, and kept me in the middle of this raging, roaring sea. (9, italics added)

Although her demand is meant as an act of defiance and challenge, the following statement can also be used by the two brothers to support a normative maxim: "great is women's cunning" (10), which conversely implies their naivety as males:

> He has guarded me and tried to keep me pure and chaste, not realizing that nothing can prevent or alter what is predestined, and that, when a woman desires something, no one can stop her. (9–10)

A relative universal order is established as the two brothers muse and ponder over happenings that are larger than their own predicament. However, the narrator leaves us with important verbal clues such as chest, lock, garden, bedroom, locked door, all of which suggest containment and generate transgressive action on the part of the prisoners: women.

It is at this juncture that we need to examine encasement as semantic narrative incarceration in the frame tale. Rather than just a stepping-stone, a dynamic for embedding processes, the preludinal part of the frame tale is no less functional than the *qaṣīdah* prelude. It

[57] https://sourcebooks.fordham.edu/pwh/burton-te.asp.

sets the stage for serious issues that relate to narrativity and gender, patriarchy, authority, and rebellion, the slave and master binary, and a dozen other issues that sustain narrative accumulation over ages, through rewriting, redaction, abridgment, appropriation, translation, both East and West, and narrative engagements with its mechanisms.

3 Engagements in Narrative

From Bethlehem to Havana: Imaginative Flights of the *Nights*

The "Scheherazade factor" functions as a dynamic and trope. As a trope, it cuts across the tales, and draws attention to other women who have no less important roles to play than the narrator of narrators, Scheherazade. In Jabra Ibrahim Jabra's (1919–94) autobiographical atlas of a Bethlehem childhood, *al-Biʾr al-Ūlā* (English translation: *The First Well: A Bethlehem Boyhood*), the small town is given a dense and substantial representation in retrospect by Jabra's consummate and nuanced narrative skill that receives impetus from a child's reading of a serialized *Arabian Nights*. The discovery of the *Nights* was not an ordinary one, but its significance to this chapter cannot be overestimated. The child came across the *Nights*, as Jabra notes in *The First Well*,[1] in Louis Cheikho's *Majānī al-adab fī ḥadāʾiq al-ʿArab*.[2] But his brother Yusuf was able to smuggle "two collections of yellow leaves under another heap of magazines and newspapers," returning home with "his booty, or what remained of it, and he began to read with such deep joy that he added it to his books." He "realized that they were serialized in nights, and guessed that they must be *A Thousand and One Nights*."[3] The child read "The Tale of Masroor the Merchant and His Beloved Zayn al-Mawasif." Like his European counterparts, Jabra found himself in a web of enchantment, but, as he notes, "[I] was irritated because I did not know what happened to Masroor and Zayn al-Mawasif after they began to play chess, for the next leaf was about eighty pages later and exactly one hundred nights afterward."[4] This is only

[1] Jabra Ibrahim Jabra, *al-Biʾr al-Ūlā: The First Well: A Bethlehem Boyhood*, trans. Issa J. Boullata (Fayetteville, AR: University of Arkansas Press, 1995).

[2] Louis Cheikho, *Majānī al-adab fī ḥadāʾiq al-ʿArab* (Beirut: Maṭbaʿat al-Ābāʾ al-Yasūʿiyyīn, 1882); see Jabra, *The First Well*, 131.

[3] Jabra, *The First Well*, 131. [4] Ibid., 128.

a preparatory but nevertheless foundational threshold, for an identification process occurs, one that situates Jabra, the prominent translator, writer, novelist, and critic, on the same level as the most renowned writers of Europe who were no less attached to such tales.[5] This is foundational because it is associated with writing. Jabra first explains the identification process that takes place through reading: "Zayn al-Mawasif offered me the most delicious food, and I played chess with her on a board of ebony and ivory and exchanged poetic verses with her, the like of which I never read in my school books."[6] The association between chess, projection, and Scheherazade's storytelling is important because when these three operations get collapsed we perceive the ingenuity behind the art that flourished in the tenth century, as noted by Abū Bakr Muḥammad ibn Yaḥyā al-Ṣūlī in his (d. 946) *Akhbār*. The renowned *shaṭranjī* (chess player) is also known for his tutorials, narratives, letters, and poetry.[7] Isn't storytelling a maximization of ingenuity and craft?

This differentiation between "school books" and the *Arabian Nights* might remind us of Sissy Jupe in Charles Dickens's *Hard Times* (1854). Behind this differentiation between "useful knowledge" and imaginative narrative is Dickens's philosophy of the mission of art in a utilitarian environment. Although less attuned to a similar reading, Jabra's adult reflections endow the child's readings with connotations that relate to his growth as a renowned artist. Moreover, there is no reason to doubt his record of brother Yusuf's box of assorted journals and books. An identification process that aligns him with Masroor is footnoted as the reason behind his own first short story:

> It was about a man who dreams of a beautiful girl. In the morning, when he wakes up, he feels that passion had taken hold of him, so he paints her with oils on a large canvas so that her image may remain before his eyes and he may express to her his love in confidence. One day, he meets the sweetheart of his dreams, and lo and behold, she looks exactly like the picture he had painted.[8]

Jabra is obviously in conversation with the high modernists and their aesthetic values, but the process is significantly tied to the Scheherazade factor with which John Barth among many writers in world cultures engages. Emphasis is laid on the aesthetic process: an Oscar Wilde's rich narcissistic production that takes Zayn al-Mawāṣif as a prolongation of desire. The Scheherazade factor is a dynamic germinator for writing. Though it initiates yearning and then identification, its ultimate reach is an aesthetic experience that, for now, contains a high dose of postmodernity. A self-reflexive turn problematizes the issue of

[5] More in al Musawi, *Scheherazade in England*. [6] Jabra, *The First Well*, 128.
[7] See Chapter 1, n33. [8] Jabra, *The First Well*, 128n.

inventiveness in an age of mechanical production. While seemingly linear, however, this genesis has vertical movements that correspond to artistic aspirations, flashbacks, authorial intrusions, reflections, and recapitulations. Jabra differs from Michel Butor and other experimentalists, however, in espousing Scheherazade head-on, without going into Butor's appropriation of Scheherazade's second mendicant, in "The Porter and Three Ladies of Baghdad," as a rite of passage in Butor's *Portrait de l'artiste comme jeune singe* (*Portrait of the Artist as a Young Monkey*), his maturation from an ordinary but intuitive disciple into a writer whose struggle with narrative art remains unresolved. In a parallel structured nightly subtext, the second mendicant, the son of a king transformed into a monkey, has masterly qualifications in calligraphy and broad knowledge, but has to attain redemption on the road to narrative proper.

Butor's Second Mendicant and the Narrative Globe-Trotter

This nightly subtext complements the daily one, the imaginary and the real, and signifies the postmodernist engagement with the *Nights* as a protean narrative, fecund and inviting, coherent but also surging with possibilities. Jennifer Waelti-Walters takes this rite of passage, its realization in Butor's *Portrait*, as necessarily comparable to James Joyce's *Portrait of the Artist as a Young Man*. It paved the way for his subsequent narratives that retain modernist appropriations of an art of narrative, established in Scheherazade's tales, and given self-reflexive directions early on in the twentieth century. Based on Butor's negotiation with Scheherazade's core tales, she calls these "*Mille et une nuits*."[9] While Jabra the child grew through this connection with Scheherazade into Jabra the novelist, the Cuban Abilio Estevez let his characters in *Thine Is the Kingdom* morph into Scheherazade-like narrators who survive death through narrative.[10] As in *A Thousand and One Nights*, possibilities abound, and time does not count, nor does space: The old retain youth, and they in turn change gender under the purview of storytelling that is atemporal, if not eternal. The wounded boy can be a guide to an adult, and an old man can change into that boy, and then in turn to Scheherazade: A realm of fantasy is opened up that is also in conversation with the real. One element in this narrative engagement with the Scheherazade factor plays out as follows:

9 Jennifer Waelti-Walters, *Michel Butor* (Amsterdam and Atlanta, GA: Rodopi, 1992), esp. 10, 80. See also her article, "Michel Butor and The Thousand and One Nights," *Neophilologus* 59 (1975), 213–22.

10 Abilio Estevez, *Thine Is the Kingdom: A Novel*, trans. David Frye (New York: Arcade Publishing, 1999).

You are authorized to call me Scheherazade. It seemed the light was becoming intimate. Surprisingly, the man became young again, turned, to my astonishment, into the Wounded Boy with his handsome Honthorst face, and from there he went on to become a woman, a beautiful woman. As the cruel sultan is eternal, she exclaimed in a powerful and even more mysterious voice, Scheherazade has found herself obliged to use countless pseudonyms throughout countless centuries.[11]

Thus, Scheherazade of *A Thousand and One Nights* is reborn in narrators and novelists whom Estevez selects from all over the globe.[12] This narrative metamorphosis adheres to a source that the alter ego substantiates with images of an Oriental woman. "She turned toward me, eyebrows raised, the lovely hand on her breast covered with shining rings." In keeping with a source as made available in translation, Scheherazade is credited with brilliance:

Scheherazade was (she is, I am, I will be) a brilliant woman, who decided (I decided, I decide, I will decide) to tell story after story to save her life, she realized (I realize, I will realize) the life-saving possibilities that words have (and will have), she had the insight that storytelling was (is, will keep on being) the only way (the only way!) to gain eternity.

As a trope for fictional narrative, Scheherazade reclaims eternal presence, beyond time and space. She roams as a narrative globe-trotter, atemporal and free. Although bearing the stamp of authorial intrusion, this intervention, to argue the case for narrative as lifesaving and hence eternal, is a landmark in a fictional trend that is self-celebratory. It is also a defensive strategy as novelists undergo anxiety and fear of imaginative aridity. Metafictional discourse betrays a hard-fought battle to endow fiction with a new life after realism has exhausted its urban possibilities. It also invades a territory occupied by critics who are enthralled by specific exemplary novels.[13]

Hence, the author's alter ego, Sebastian this time, has to place the narrative in its frame story, that is, *A Thousand and One Nights*: "And it was like in those tales of the *Thousand and one nights* where the magic words open doors that seemed closed for ever, or allow the djinn to appear and resolve any problem and load us down with treasures."[14] Variations on the power of words, in amulets, pronouncements, speech acts, and

[11] Ibid., 307. Also cited and studied in van Leeuwen, *The Thousand and One Nights in Twentieth-Century Fiction*, 108.
[12] See, for example, the list of names under a subsection: "Dostoyevsky."
[13] Muhsin Jassim al-Musawi, section "On Arabic Metafiction: Convergence with Postcoloniality," see chapter 9, "Cultural Contestation and Self-definition," in *The Postcolonial Arabic Novel: Debating Ambivalence* (Leiden: Brill, 2003), 337–73.
[14] Estevez, *Thine Is the Kingdom*, 302.

narrative have been a staple in postmodernist theorizations. Although there is a large body of allusions in the writings of high modernists like Joyce's *Ulysses* and Marcel Proust's *Remembrance of Things Past*, the credit should go to Jorge Luis Borges who, ahead of many, reinvents the Scheherazade factor, as an ongoing repetitive art that dallies with deferrals without giving up on the presence of death as the other name for narrative equilibrium.

Confabulación Nocturna: *Reinventing Scheherazade*

The fear of losing one's inventiveness is almost a distinctive feature in postmodernist writing. With the encroachment of postcapitalist economies, mechanical production, and the competing venues of cyberspace and visual prominence, anxieties abound and drive writers to align themselves with the narrator of narrators in her stratagem to beat challenge and death. Storytelling turns into a mechanism for survival. Todorov highlights this dichotomous tension between silence and speech in his reading of the Baghdad barber's loquacity: To narrate is to survive and defer death.[15] Todorov also thinks of speech acts, storytelling for that matter, as stemming from a situation: Had Scheherazade not been in that situational problematic, she could have told her stories to another audience, or found another vocational direction. In *The Poetics of Prose*, Todorov advocates for the equation between narrative and life as follows:

> The speech act receives, in the Arabian Nights, an interpretation which leaves no further doubt as to its importance. If all the characters incessantly tell stories, it is because this action has received a supreme consecration: narrating equals living.[16]

Years later, and in line with an earlier comment by G. K. Chesterton,[17] Wendy Faris also writes to this effect. In this context, Chesterton's conclusion is pertinent, especially if we realize that it was written in 1901: "Never in any other book, perhaps, has such a splendid tribute been offered to the pride and omnipotence of art."[18] As if recapitulating, Faris explains:

> When Scheherazade staves off her death for 1001 nights by telling a continuously enthralling chain of stories to her captor, the king, she dramatizes an intriguing

[15] Todorov, *Poetics of Prose*, 75. [16] Ibid., 74–75.

[17] G. K. Chesterton, "The Everlasting Nights," in *The Spice of Life and Other Essays*, ed. Dorothy Collins (Beaconsfield, UK: Darwin Finlayson, 1964), 58–60.

[18] Ibid.

aspect of all literary discourse, its capacity to simulate the postponement of human death through prolongation of fictional life.[19]

But because situations decide speech acts, not all story writers are so sanguine as to accept this equation between narration and life. Cynics like Edgar Allan Poe, whom Estevez lists first in the subsection devoted to novelists and storywriters, provides a Shahrayar who thinks of new achievements in science as unbelievable nonsense. While also satirizing the scene in America, Poe looks upon these achievements as alien to a storytelling that has its make-believe play on the limits between the real and the imaginary. In the end, the king is dissatisfied with this drastic departure from the art:

"Stop!" said the king – "I can't stand that, and I won't. You have already given me a dreadful headache with your lies. The day, too, I perceive, is beginning to break. How long have we been married? – my conscience is getting to be troublesome again. And then that dromedary touch – do you take me for a fool? Upon the whole, you might as well get up and be throttled."[20]

The sardonic touch here does not stop Poe from deploying the Scheherazadian urge to speak to an auditor: His king grumbles and his Scheherazade is annoyed by his snoring, but the narrative goes on. There is no end in Scheherazade's original, as long as the One stands for ad infinitum; a point on which modernists and postmodernists often reflect. Like every imaginative and powerful writer, Borges also lives with the fear of one day losing one's imaginative fecundity. Meanwhile he has to speak and write. Borges's parable, "Someone," reflects on this One from a different angle: as a trope for an ongoing *confabulatio nocturni*. We know that Leo Strauss of Chicago reads in numerology, and in 1001 in particular, some esoteric deep layer meant for the elect to decode.[21] Faris draws attention to this piece as a parable for "the imaginary composition of *A Thousand and One Nights* in a nostalgically elegiac tone."[22] In Faris's translation of the piece, there is a dusty plaza, probably like the ones we meet in Badīʿ al-Zamān al-Hamadhānī's (968–1008) *Maqāmāt*, where there is a surrounding circle of people.

The man talks and gesticulates. He doesn't know (others will) that he belongs to the lineage of *confabulatores nocturni*, to the nighttime rhapsodizers, which Doublehorned Alexander assembled as consolation to his sleeplessness. He thinks

[19] Wendy B. Faris, "1001 Words: Fiction against Death," *The Georgia Review* 36, no. 4 (Winter 1982), 811.
[20] Poe, "The Thousand-and-Second Tale of Scheherazade."
[21] Namazi, "Politics, Religion, and Love," 193.
[22] Faris, "1001 Words," 821. Reference to Borges, *Historia de la noche*, 27.

he's speaking to a few people for a few coins and in a lost yesterday he weaves the Book of the Thousand and One Nights.[23]

As shown in his series of reinventions, Borges duplicates and reinvents a tradition where the storyteller of old times, the *confabulator nocturni*, is reborn in others who roam the world in search for good audiences. Borges plays on oral storytelling that earlier Arabic accounts relegate to a second place even after the translation of the Indo-Persian frame tale into Arabic.[24] His faith in the *Nights* as also symbolic of inventiveness and improvisation led him to claim that his own short story "The Two Kings and the Two Labyrinths," included in *Ficciones* and published first in the magazine *El Hogar*, is part of the *Arabian Nights*.

More akin to "Narrative Engagements" is the mise en abyme, a narrative within itself, in that almost all the inside core frame tales like "The Fisherman and the Genie," or "The Porter and the Three Ladies," are miniature tableaus of the Scheherazade–Shahrayar container-motivator tale. Although diversifying the application and giving it further narrational dimensions, Borges's specific focus on the obscure 602nd night brings to light the self-reflexive embedding whereby the king listens to his own story. He draws attention to this in a number of places, but here is one in his famous "Translators of the Thousand and One Nights," written in 1934–36: "Is it not portentous that on night 602 King Schahriah [*sic*] hears his own story from the queen's lips?"[25] He explains: "Like the general framework, a given tale often contains within itself other tales of equal length: stages within the stage as in the tragedy of *Hamlet*, raised to the power of a dream." He quotes Tennyson's "clear and difficult line" to support the conclusion: "Laborious orient ivory, sphere in sphere," or mise en abyme.[26] This is not a repetitive speech act, nor is it a representational narrative unit, but rather a deliberate deployment of a narrative reflexivity that is soon to become a staple in postmodernist fiction. Borges gets entangled in this disputed case of night 602. He often references it whenever the question of ad infinitum arises. In "The Garden of Forking Paths," the narrator says:

I remembered too that night which is at the middle of the *Thousand and One Nights* when Scheherazade (through a magical oversight of the copyist) begins to relate

[23] Borges, *Historia de la noche*, 27.
[24] See Abbott, "A Ninth-Century Fragment." Also, more on this point in Chapter 5.
[25] Borges, "The Translators," 109.
[26] For more on this use of Andre Gide's formula, see Gabriel Garcia Ochoa, "The Mystery of Borges' Night 602," *Comparative Literature Studies* 55, no. 3 (2018), 620, where Rodriguez Monegal is cited on mise en abyme as a "typically Borgesian" trope. Emir Rodriguez Monegal and Roberto González Echevarría, "Borges and la Nouvelle Critique," *Diacritics* 2, no. 2 (Summer 1972), 34.

word for word the story of the Thousand and One Nights, establishing the risk of coming once again to the night when she must repeat it, and thus on to infinity.[27]

Notwithstanding the confusion surrounding night 602, as a reflection on the frame story, Borges repeats this whenever there is an occasion. Again, he is another *confabulator nocturni.* In "Metaphors of the Thousand and One Nights," he reiterates:

the dream divides into another dream and then another, and so on, entwining in a static labyrinth. In this book is *the* Book. The careless Queen tells the King their own half-forgotten story. Distracted by the din of past enchantments they forget who they are . . . and dream.[28]

Borges's theory of writing, and of fiction in particular, has a number of elemental patterns, and one of them is circularity,[29] while among other pieces are labyrinthine forms, and the immortality of the text, or more so of a writer, not a person as he makes it clear in "The Double." It is the writer who survives the mortal. Borges's poetics is larger than these elemental patterns, but, for the sake of argument, let's work with these three as stepping-stones to his prose poetics. The circular form enchants him, and hence he never tires of referencing night 602. In "When Fiction Lives in Fiction" (1939),[30] he speaks of the *Nights* as follows:

None of them is as disturbing as that of night 602, a bit of magic among the nights. On that strange night, the king hears his own story from the queen's lips. He hears the beginning of the story, which includes all the others, and also –monstrously – itself. Does the reader have a clear sense of the vast possibility held out by this interpolation, its peculiar danger? Were the queen to persist, the immobile king would forever listen to the truncated story of the thousand and one nights, now

[27] Jorge Luis Borges, "The Garden of Forking Paths," trans. Donald A. Yates, in *Labyrinths: Selected Stories and Other Writings* (New York: New Directions, 1964), 25.

[28] Jorge Luis Borges, "Metáforas de Las Mil y Una Noches," *Historia de la noche* (1977). Translation by Jack Ross first published in *Magazine* 1 (2003), 36–38, https://dinarzade.blogspot.com/2006/09/metaphors-of-1001-nights.html.

[29] Ibid. Evelyn Fishburn argues these as "key concepts": "If we think of the key concepts associated with Borges's fiction we will surely come up with the following: infinity, the labyrinth, entertainment (diversion), mirrors, duplication, embedding, and centrality." See Evelyn Fishburn, "Traces of the *Thousand and One Nights* in Borges," *Middle Eastern Literatures* 7, no. 2 (2004), 213–22. Also in *Variaciones Borges* 17 (2004), 47.

Philip Kennedy suggests that there are ideas about "narrative generation and ontology in the Nights" that were "carried over" in Borges's fiction, like "the idea of infinity, the idea of the labyrinth, and the idea of embedding and mise en abyme." See Philip Kennedy, "Borges and the Missing Pages of the Nights," in *Scheherazade's Children: Global Encounters with the Arabian Nights*, ed. Philip Kennedy and Marina Warner (New York: New York University Press, 2013), 200.

[30] Jorge Luis Borges, "When Fiction Lives in Fiction," trans. Esther Allen, in *Selected Non-fictions*, ed. Eliot Weinberger (New York: Penguin Putnam, 1999), 161.

infinite and circular . . . In *The Thousand and One Nights*, Scheherazade tells many stories; one of them is, almost, the story of *The Thousand and One Nights*.

The association between these two, infinity and circularity, runs through Borges's writings where Scheherazade's *Nights* is his constant frame of reference. Even when blaming great books for bad titles, the *Thousand and One Nights* is exempted:

Except for the always astonishing *Book of the Thousand Nights and One Night* (which the English, equally beautifully, called *The Arabian Nights*) I believe that it is safe to say that the most celebrated works of world literature have the worst titles.[31]

Scheherazade's titles in French, English, and in original Arabic, or in *Hazār afsānah*, attest to infinity; the tales of the *Nights* are more so than many other titles because of this suspended time between life and death or storytelling and sleep, the latter being the other name for death. Ad infinitum is found not only in *The Book of Sand*, but, as Borges argues, also or more so in that odd-numbered *One* in the *Book of Thousand Nights and One Night*. He writes in "Metaphors":

The Book of the Nights.
The Nights are Time, which never sleeps.
Keep reading as the day declines and
Scheherazade will tell you your own story.

It holds more charm, as it opens up space for accretion. Technically, it is the trapdoor that lures and opens up subterranean spaces for more action, and thence more tales. Even the physical lack of parts of the *Nights* in different translations begs for completion. Hence, in Borges's bookshelf, *The Book of Sand* is to end behind volumes with missing parts: "I thought of putting the Book of Sand in the space left by the Wyclif but I chose at last to hide it behind some imperfect volumes of the Thousand and One Nights."[32] As noted by scholars, Borges's tales like "Dr. Brodie's Report" and "The South" call for narrative accretion, or more properly invention and addition.[33] To have "Dr. Brodie's Report" manuscript in the first volume of Lane's translation means its availability to be part of the growing corpus of the *Nights*. In one sense, Borges is like the copyists

[31] Borges, "H. G. Wells' Latest Novel," in *Selected Non-fictions*, 193.
[32] See Fishburn, "Traces," 216. "The Book of Sand," translated from the Spanish by Jorge Luis Borges, http://archives.evergreen.edu/webpages/curricular/2010-2011/naturalorder/Readings/Week_09/The_Book_of_Sands.pdf. Borges concludes: "I thought of fire, but I feared that the burning of an infinite book would be just as infinite and suffocate the planet with smoke."
[33] See Kennedy's engagement with Fishburn, "Traces," 201.

whom he equivocally associates with an accrual enterprise: "The need to complete a thousand and one segments drove the work's copyists to all sorts of digressions."[34] Night 602 is the most "disturbing" because it includes and nests others. This is the "infinite involution," a "stage on the stage," which Borges assigns to *Hamlet*.[35] As noted by Kristal and Fishburn, he rewrote "The Chamber of Statues" and "The Story of the Two Dreamers," crediting Gustav Weil, the translator, with its authorship, while crediting Burton with his own invention, or his rewriting of a story like "The Two Kings and the Two Labyrinths."[36] *A Thousand and One Nights* allows this process, and Borges is no different from copyists and storytellers,[37] or even from translators like Galland whom he celebrates as a probable inventor of "Aladdin,"[38] a surmise that is partially not far off the mark.[39] In an article on *A Thousand and One Nights*, Borges writes in defense of invention: "Some have suspected that Galland forged the tale. I think the word *forged* is unjust and malign."[40] He explains his rejection of the accusation: "Galland has as much right to invent a story as the *confabulatores nocturni*." Borges has not covered as much translational territory as Galland, but he is no less a *confabulator nocturni*. "Why shouldn't we suppose that after having translated so many tales, he wanted to invent one himself, and did?"[41] Isn't Borges claiming the same for himself, as someone who was so immersed in the tales that they became his property?[42] Part of his inventiveness shows well in "The South," where the *Nights* in Weil's translation offers the protagonist Dahlmann some balance to an otherwise menacing external world. Conceptualization or recall of the *Nights* functions as a barometer to a character's response, but it also acts as the other half of experience that cannot be absent from thinking and everyday life. Thus, there is a reciprocal transaction between the tales and Borges, who is always equipped enough to accrue and revise.

[34] Borges, "When Fiction Lives in Fiction,"161. [35] Ibid.

[36] See Efraín Kristal, *Invisible Work: Borges and Translation* (Nashville, TN: Vanderbilt University Press, 2002), 71–74; and Fishburn, "Traces," 148.

[37] Reflecting on Italo Calvino's accusation of Borges as the one who invents "The Tale of the Two Kings and the Wazir's Daughters," Robert Irwin corrects Calvino, mentions that it exists in the Breslau edition, and appears in Burton's supplementary nights, vol. 2. See Irwin, *Arabian Nights*, 283–84.

[38] Borges, "The Thousand and One Nights," 573.

[39] There'll be more on this point later, but see Horta, on Galland's interventions and Lucas's travelogues, *Marvellous Thieves*, 46–48, 62.

[40] Borges, "The Thousand and One Nights," 573. [41] Ibid.

[42] For other scholarly notes on inventiveness, see Ochoa, "The Mystery," 626.

Borges's Poetics of Prose

Along with circularity, or because of it, a body of elemental functions mushrooms and presents Borges's connections with the *Nights* as a narratological complex that has to be central to current discussions of the art. Inventive supplementation is at the basis of Borges's poetics, and it certainly lays the ground for a number of elemental patterns which make up his poetics of prose.

Its immediate venue is the labyrinth. It finds a succinct architectural depiction in Borges's "The Immortal." The narrator/protagonist says: "A labyrinth is a structure compounded to confuse men; its architecture, rich in symmetries, is subordinated to that end."[43] Addressing the ancient place he finds himself in, he explains, "It abounded in dead-end corridors, high unattainable windows, portentous doors which led to a cell or pit, incredible inverted stairways whose steps and balustrades hung downwards."[44] In that dreamlike exposition where time and space are collapsed, the labyrinth is inseparable from a circular space. "I went down; through a chaos of sordid galleries I reached a vast circular chamber; the ninth (through another labyrinth) led to a second circular chamber equal to the first." Bewildered by these sites and their numbers, his "misfortune and anxiety multiplied them," where the "silence was hostile and almost perfect."[45]

In applying this to Arabesque, there are similarities and differences. There are symmetries and interruptions, but there is also repetition, replication, encasement, and circularity. Borges is drawn to this involute structure that makes up a significant part of his dreamlike or silhouette-like writing. This is his contribution to the art, and to the reading of *A Thousand* and *One Nights* in world cultures. Through direct or indirect rewriting (appropriation or distanced allusion and deployment), he endows the art with a peculiar twist where the narrator is rarely a vital visible actor. Its significance for our reading of "Narrative Engagements" stems from its intricate association with an aesthetic form that deliberately evades an immediate conclusion. While offering diversion, it traps the reader or listener, implicating the latter in a web of enchantment or challenge. Scheherazade's tales, at least the ones that sustain a core over time and survive processes of replacement and deflection, provide an enchanting web that makes Borges claim in unison with other voices, "The centuries go by, and we are still hearing the voice of Scheherazade." Storytellers replicate some tales, or resort to reflexive mirrors of one-night caliphs to teach the real a lesson. The same is true with night 602.

[43] Jorge Luis Borges, "The Immortal," trans. James E. Irby, in *Labyrinths*, 111.
[44] Ibid., 110–11. [45] Ibid., 109.

Borges's familiarity with Scheherazade's art has invited expansive research, but what begs more attention is his method of appropriating it to other sites, people, and action that makes up his own contribution to the art, as the modernist Scheherazade. His art often implies recognition, autobiographical traces, or highly layered revenge motifs as in "Emma Zunz."[46] The *Nights* compels the reader to forget, not because it is just entertaining, but also and primarily because its encasements, embedding, and reflexive mirrors operate like a maze. In "Metaphors" he brings a number of motifs in a tapestry that dizzies by its very ordained intricacy:

> **The second metaphor** is the web of a tapestry, which up close looks like a chaos of colors and arbitrary lines, a dizzying expanse of chance – but secret laws delimit it. Just like that other dream, the Universe, the Book of the Nights is made up of master-numbers and motifs: seven brothers and seven voyages, three Kazis and three wishes for whoever sees the Night of Nights, the dark-haired beauty in whose arms the lover watches three whole nights, three Wazirs and three punishments, and, behind all the others, that first and final number of the Lord: The One.[47]

Readers and scholars are aware of the discussion of the title, the presence of One, not only as a probable deviational track from the Indo-Persian frame, but also and more importantly as infinity. Borges relates this to an ongoing discussion of Arabesque, its mazelike designs, that is often assumed to reference the unrepresentable: the "final number of the Lord: The One." Later scholars like Strauss associate numbers in the *Nights* with esoteric knowledge. Borges brings this to the discussion of narrative art: does the infinite exemplified in "The One" readdress the narrative art as negotiation between the finite and the infinite? The limited and the vast? Or does it separate the two as incommensurable? The case is not so clear-cut for Borges, who reads secrets and riddles in everything that departs from the formidable norms set by nineteenth-century fiction. Hence, there are no clear-cut demarcations in his narrative. Borges is not alone in collapsing elemental patterns of labyrinthine narrative inroads, for as he concludes in "The Translators of the Thousand and One Nights": "The threshold is confused with the mirror, the mask lies beneath the face, no one knows any longer which is the true man and which are his idols."[48] More to his taste is this easy faring, "And none of it matters; the disorder is as acceptable and trivial as the inventions of a daydream."[49] In his essay "Partial Magic in the Quixote," Borges reflects on a self-reflexive narrative that allows protagonists to judge the author in a novel or story of which they are part. In this interplay

[46] See Fishburn, "Traces," 154. [47] Borges, "Metáforas"; trans. Ross, *Magazine*.
[48] Borges, "The Translators," 109. [49] Ibid.

between protagonists as actors and readers, narrative releases itself from narcissism. In this same article, Borges repeats his focused reading of night 602 as it stands for a corpus of *A Thousand and One Nights*. And notwithstanding deliberate interpolations by copyists, the tale generates further cycles, "now infinite and circular,"[50] while the "effect (which should have been profound) is superficial, like a Persian carpet."[51]

Borges's "Partial Magic in the Quixote" serves the purpose of "Narrative Engagements" and the Scheherazade factor, not only because of its reiteration of night 602 as another large frame tale that compels the king to listen to his own story, and thence pass through a therapeutic process. Its series of reflections on mise en abymes and other forms of reflection replicate Borges's poetics of prose, in that it allows little or no space for subjectification. Borges's "Immortal" presents a poet or a writer as larger and ever more present than a person. Freed from the power of time and space, the writer/poet or rhapsodist offers an ontological experience that is revelatory in a conceptualization of the infinitum. Scheherazade is a figure for the archetypal narrator, not a specific person. The archetypal narrator can be a scribe, a copyist, a translator in this exchange of roles, but all the credit goes to *confabulator nocturni*. He is the one who "transcribed in Bulaq the travels of Sindbad the Sailor." Invoking disquieting and destabilizing anachronisms and anomalies, the narrator is focused on a case, even at the expense of reliability: "it is strange that the latter [Homer] should copy in the thirteenth century the adventures of Sindbad, another Ulysses, and should discover after many centuries, in another kingdom and a barbarous tongue, the forms of his Iliad."[52] Homer is reborn in Pope's translation, and *confabulatores nocturni* are collapsed with scribes, historians, and rhapsodists: "In the seventh century of Hegira, in the suburb of Bulaq, I transcribed with measured calligraphy, in a language I have forgotten, in an alphabet I do not know, the seven adventures of Sindbad and the history of the City of Bronze."[53]

But is it only the basic faith in narrative as a transcending art that stands behind such a large script of collapsed narratives? Or does this tie in well with even larger distrust of rampant individualism? Borges's significant interventions at this juncture lead us to issues of cultural periodization and literary trends, issues that relate to modernity and modernism, the focus on the subject, and the faith in progression as perpetuated by positivist philosophy and its conditions of possibility in an industrial

[50] Jorge Luis Borges, "Partial Magic in the Quixote," trans. Anthony Kerrigan, in *Labyrinths*, 195.
[51] Ibid. [52] Borges, "The Immortal," 117. [53] Ibid., 116.

age. These interventions also confront us with postmodernist suspicions of these certainties and absolutes, the remnants of positivism. In "The Nothingness of Personality" (1922), Borges critiques the nineteenth century as follows: "The last century was rootedly subjective in its aesthetic manifestations. Its writers were more inclined to show off their personalities than to establish a body of work."[54] He explains, "There is no whole self,"[55] and "The self does not exist."[56] He does not confuse this with one's sensations:

> I don't deny this consciousness of being, nor the immediate security of *here I am* that it breathes into us. What I do deny is that all our other convictions must be adjusted to the customary antithesis between the self and the non-self, and that this antithesis is constant.[57]

Moreover,

> the sensation of cold, of spacious and pleasurable suppleness, that is in me as I open the front door and go out along the half-darkness of the street is neither a supplement to a pre-existing self nor an event that comes coupled to the other event of a continuing and rigorous self.[58]

Does this articulation cope with the archetypal narrator, Scheherazade, or with Borges the writer, not the individual? It does. In "The Double," he offers this split between the two, the writer beyond the reach of time, the immemorial, and the individual who is only a mortal. His affiliation with Scheherazade, and indeed with a long list of texts and authors like Cervantes, backgrounds this split that is coterminous with someone who describes himself as a good reader.[59] By the banks of the River Charles, Cambridge, Massachusetts, the old man notices a young one sitting there: "I turned to the man and spoke. 'Are you Uruguayan or Argentine?'" The young man is Argentine, and lives in the same place, and hence: "'In that case,' I resolutely said to him, 'your name is Jorge Luis Borges. I too am Jorge Luis Borges. We are in 1969, in the city of Cambridge.'"[60]

As argued by scholars, to verify identities, the young man tells the other person that he "is here in Geneva, on a bench, a few steps from the

[54] Jorge Luis Borges, "The Nothingness of Personality," trans. Esther Allen, in *Selected Non-fictions*, 6.

[55] Ibid., 4, 6. [56] Ibid., 8. [57] Ibid., 4. [58] Ibid.

[59] "I once said, 'Others brag of the books they've managed to write; I brag of the books I've managed to read.'" "Prologue to the Collection," trans. Eliot Weinberger, in *Selected Non-fictions*, 513–14.

[60] Jorge Luis Borges, "The Double," in *Collected Fiction*, trans. Andrew Hurley (New York: Penguin, 1998), 412. Also cited in Kennedy, "Borges and the Missing Pages of the Nights," 196–97.

Rhone," and the old man has to mention things unknown to a stranger to the lived space, such as the following:

> In the wardrobe closet in your room, there are two rows of books; the three volumes of Lane's translation of the *Thousand and One Nights* – which Lane called *The Arabian Nights Entertainment* with steel engravings and notes in fine print between the chapters.[61]

Listed and emphasized as the iconic identification marker, the *Nights* should be seen as central to Borges's narrative and narratology. In his prose poetics, he has to separate the two, the writer who transcends time and space, and the mortal who is bound by the corporeal. In "Borges and I," Borges writes: "The other one, the one called Borges, is the one things happen to." Then he adds:

> I live, let myself go on living, so that Borges may contrive his literature, and this literature justifies me. It is no effort for me to confess that he has achieved some valid pages, but those pages cannot save me, perhaps because what is good belongs to no one, not even to him, but rather to the language and to tradition. Besides, I am destined to perish, definitely, and only some instant of myself can survive in him.[62]

This self-effacement is a marker in Borges's writings. One may conclude with Dominique Jullien that the "repetition of this process of self-effacement to the point of weariness is an inherent part of Borges's myth of literature, which endlessly reenacts the birth of the author as Nobody."[63] However, the specific mention of language and tradition brings us back to significant issues raised by T. S. Eliot, even more so in Joyce's *Finnegans Wake* (1939), and later by Barthes and Foucault. Is it the text that is to survive? But is the text not a mosaic, a tapestry of quotes that assemble in a writer's subconscious and verbal or nonverbal lexicon that presents writing as a complex operation in dialogue with writings and readings that happen to make the present writer's register? Insofar as "Narrative Engagements" is concerned; this elemental pattern allows an idealization of texts and even authorship to survive in a vast matrix of script whereby great minds feed each other.

The Ever-Unfinished Work: Scheherazade's Proust

The inventory of allusions to Scheherazade which Proust made in his seven volumes (*À la recherché du temps perdu* (English translation: *In Search of Lost Time* – also *Remembrance of Things Past*)) remains unfinished as *A Thousand and One Nights*: Overtaken by illness and ultimately by death, Proust broke

61 Ibid.
62 Jorge Luis Borges, "Borges and I," trans. James E. Irby, in *Labyrinths*, 246–47.
63 Dominique Jullien, "Biography of an Immortal," *Comparative Literature* 47, no. 2 (Spring 1995), 159.

off in 1922 what he had started in 1909. Self-situated in an enclosed private space, the narrator sustains a freedom from time imposition as it impacts the outside world.[64] Memory operates on a past that probably recalls Scheherazade's *kān wa-kān*, "once upon a time" songs and narratives that defer death. Art rules supreme, and high modernists like Proust find this narrative engagement with the Scheherazade factor much to their taste in their confrontation with historical time. The narrator's maturation or metamorphosis is as central to this narrative as it is in *A Thousand and One Nights*: Shahrayar is not a model, but stands for a futile search for gratification, the perpetuation of erotic desire as exemplified in the submission to the power of time in those onetime nightly marriages. The narrator has to submit to other choices, to reconstruct all in art as the most exemplary triumph on the eroding power of time. He morphs into Scheherazade in these seven volumes with their reminiscence of things past. To ensure art triumphant, he has a model in Scheherazade, not only to restructure spatial-temporal life, but also to intertexualize this remembrance with Scheherazade's "once upon a time." His canvas of reproduction extends to many names, but these are "his pastiches of Flaubert, Balzac, Renan, and the Goncourts." Edward Said adds: "In making over the authors he imitated, Proust set himself the aim of producing them from the opening to the conclusion of a passage."[65] The matter is more personal in the case of Scheherazade as it relates to the life and career of Proust as an artist. In *Time Regained*, and almost reaching toward an end, and probably to stave off death, Proust recapitulates in another remembrance of Scheherazade, which often appears in studies of his groundbreaking work. He writes:

> And I should live in the anxiety of not knowing whether the master of my destiny might not prove less indulgent than the Sultan Shahrayar, whether in the morning, when I broke off my story, he would consent to a further reprieve and would permit me to resume my narrative the following evening. Not that I have the slightest pretension to be writing, in any way, a new version of the *Thousand and One Nights* . . . you can make a new version of what you love only by first renouncing it. So my book, though it might be as long as the *Thousand and One Nights*, would be entirely different.[66]

[64] See Daniel Beaumont, "Bedtime Story: The *1001 Nights* in Proust's À la recherche du temps perdu," in *Tradition and Reception in Arabic Literature: Essays Dedicated to Andras Hamori*, ed. Margaret Larkin and Jocelyn Sharlet (Wiesbaden: Harrassowitz, 2019), 221–32; van Leeuwen, *The Thousand and One Nights and Twentieth-Century Fiction*, 117–28; and Dominique Jullien, "Ailleurs ici: Les Mille et Une Nuit dans À la Recherche du Temps Perdu," *Romanic Review* 79 (1988), 466–75.

[65] Edward W. Said, *The World, the Text, and the Critic* (London: Vintage, 1991), 157.

[66] Marcel Proust, *Time Regained*, trans. Andreas Mayor, in *On Remembrance of Things Past*, trans. C. K. Scott Moncrieff and Terence Kilmartin (New York: Random House, 1981), 3:1101–2. Also in Faris, "1001 Words," 817.

It is the art of reinventing Scheherazade for a new audience that keeps Proust narrating a series of stories, recollections, and reminiscence, things past that create an external reality that settles nevertheless in a subconscious and demands to be narrated, or so it sounds, to defer the sword raised by "the master of my destiny." Proust's struggle with "things past" is a struggle for a continuum which he knows sustains the life of art, but not the person. The sword of time, the ever-concluding reminder in each story in the *Nights*, in terms of dawn interruptions or ultimate death, inhibits Proust's influential work, and generates the endlessness of "things past."

What worried Proust is also in the mind of Barth. In his short contribution to *Book Week* (1965), he declares the kind of rapport between him and the frame tale in *A Thousand and One Nights*: "The whole frame of these thousand nights and a night speaks to my heart, directly and intimately – and in many ways at once, personal and technical."[67]

Barth's Linking: Sex and Narrative

Barth fits well in a genealogy of novelists and storywriters, like Proust, Joyce, Nabokov, Gide, and Borges. Like them, he finds himself intrigued and challenged by the frame tale and its multiple equations between narrative and erotica, storytelling and life, loquacity and survival. Moreover, like them, he is brought to experimentation as an exhaustion of possibilities, metaphysics of a sort that forces writers to come to terms with a fictitious nature of being. Scheherazade, and for him Dunyazade in particular, are key players in this fictitious universe which he tries to explain in his theorization of the literature of exhaustion, its exhausted sources, and need for replenishment. More self-reflexive than many of his postmodernist contemporaries, Barth invests in a series of parallel structures that hang on a major one that is succinctly argued by Fedwa Malti-Douglas in her reading of Scheherazade's feminism in relation to two major structural interpretations: the temporal life-saving and the psychological healing power of narrative. She argues: "Shahrazad shifts the problem of desire from the area of sex, the realm of Shahrayar's trauma, to the superficially more distant and more malleable world of the text."[68]

[67] John Barth, "Muse, Spare Me," *Book Week* (September 26, 1965), 28; reprinted in *The Sense of the Sixties*, ed. Edward Quinn and Paul J. Dolan (New York: Free Press, 1968), 440–44; cited in Faris, "1001 Words," 822.

[68] Fedwa Malti-Douglas, "Narration and Desire: Shahrazâd," in *Woman's Body, Woman's Word* (Princeton, NJ: Princeton University Press, 1991), 22. Malti-Douglas referenced a number of scholars on this point:

Abdelkebir Khatibi, *La Blessure du nom propre* (Paris: Denoel, 1986), 168–69: "If Chahrazad escapes death by telling a story every night, it is because her discourse undoes

Such a self-conscious, self-reflexive endeavor finds its prototype in *A Thousand and One Nights*, in night 602 which Borges highlights and repeatedly alludes to as a staged mirror spectacle, as argued in the preceding text. Barth suspects that Borges "dreamed this whole thing [night 602] up,"[69] which nevertheless is traced in volume six in *Supplemental Nights* of Burton's Club edition.[70] Whether invented, revised, or quoted and referenced, this night becomes pivotal to a self-reflexive experimentation. Let us recall that Barth, who claims that his interest in *A Thousand and One Nights* is focused on the frame tale, and Sindbad, Ali Baba, and Aladdin, is the same person who can write in "The Literature of Exhaustion" (1967): "I myself have always aspired to write Burton's version of the 1001 nights, complete with appendixes and the like, in ten volumes."[71] His justifications for Borges's interest in, or invention of, night 602 provides more dimensions to his Scheherazade factor, as a narrative dynamic that is more inclusive and generative than structuralist poetics as exemplified in Todorov's significant contributions. Barth's reading of Borges's focus on the controversial night 602 is argued along three axial narrative directions, which are based on the consideration of this specific night as "an instance of the story-within-the-story turned

the patriarchal frenzy, transcends it in a novelistic consciousness." Cf., also, Kattan, "Du recit," 174–75; Susan Gubar, "'The Blank Page' and the Issues of Female Creativity," in *Writing and Sexual Difference*, ed. by Elizabeth Abel (Chicago: University of Chicago Press, 1982), 73–93. On desire and writing, see, for example, Raymond Jean, *Lectures du desir* (Paris: Editions du Seuil, 1977), 7–28.

69 See John Barth, "Literature of Exhaustion," *Atlantic Monthly* (August 1967), 28–35. Also available online, as part of *The Friday Book: Essays and Other Non-fiction* (London: Johns Hopkins University Press, 1984), 73, http://people.duke.edu/~dainotto/Texts/barth.pdf.

70 Evelyn Fishburn cites a number of studies that have some reflections on this night; see her "Readings and Re-readings of Night 602," *Variaciones Borges* 18 (2004), 35–42. The reference is to Sir Richard Francis Burton, *Arabian Nights*, 16 vols. (vols. 10 and 6 of *Supplemental Nights*). Printed by the Kamashastra society for private subscribers only: Benares, 188–88, in Fishburn, "Readings and Re-readings," 38. Fishburn further documents this by another note: See the Introduction in 1:10–12 of the *Nights*, and its repetition in 6:257–72 of the *Supplemental Nights*, 40, whereby she quotes from a 1919 print, in 17 volumes, 16:259:

> SHAHRAZAD AND SHAHRYAR. King Shahryar marveled at this history and said, "By Allah, verily, injustice slayeth its folk! And he was edified by that wherewith Shahrazad besoke him and sought help of Allah the Most High." Then said he to her, "Tell me another of thy tales, O Shahrazad; supply me with a pleasant story and this shall be the completion of the story-telling," Shahrazad replied, "With love and gladness! It hath reached me, O auspicious King, that a man once declared to his mates, I will set forth to you a means of security against annoy. A friend of mine once related to me and said: – We attained to security against annoy, and the origin of it was other than this; that is, it was the following: (The Tale of the Two Kings and the Wazir's Daughters)."

Fishburn, "Readings and Re-readings," 40.

71 Ibid., 69.

back upon itself."[72] Barth finds himself in Borges's narrative preoccupations; first a self-conscious turn destabilizes our sense of reality, for the metaphysics of being is no longer self-assured when fictional characters change into readers or authors, reminding us of "the fictitious aspect of our own existence." Even more to Borges's liking, and to Barth as ephebe, is the mechanics of *regressus in infinitum*, whereby there is an endless breeding and distribution of motifs.

No less relevant to Scheherazade's "accidental gambit" is this *regressus in infinitum* as "an image of exhaustion, or attempted exhaustion of possibilities." What we have here is Barth's reflections on his writing strategies as an outlet to revive fiction beyond the exhausted genre of the bourgeois epic. Part of this resuscitation is through the Scheherazade factor. While very much involved in a *regressus* narrativity, Barth thrives on building frames within frames, as he does in "Dunyazadiad," in *Chimera*.[73] His short story "Dunyazadiad" is a deliberate parodic practice in deconstruction. It responds to current views and prospects to explode a seemingly placid crest, problematize and open up black holes, and enable him as author to place the narrative within the rising concerns of the 1960s. Thus, the sister is the author's alter ego who addresses everything, including the reasons behind lack of revolutionary movements:

> Political science, which she [Sherry] looked at first, got her nowhere. Shahryar's power was absolute, and by sparing the daughters of his army officers and chief ministers (like our father) and picking his victims mainly from the families of liberal intellectuals and other minorities, he kept the military and the cabinet loyal enough to rule out a coup d'état. Revolution seemed out of the question.[74]

Scheherazade's (Sherry's) story is told by the young sister, who hands the reins to an omniscient narrator to reflect on the young sister's story. We are told that Scheherazade often runs out of tales, but a genie is available to help out, recalling readings in the treasury of *A Thousand and One Nights*. As if this is not enough, there are other linguistic and speech act tricks that enable the narrative to grow and to turn upon itself. "As if" is a speech motif that allows the reliable and incredible to coalesce. Dunyazade is no less successful in her tales told to Shahzaman, who is so enthralled and drawn to her as to offer her a razor blade to castrate him, meanwhile requesting her to tell a story that proves to be no less staving off of death than Scheherazade's. Barth plays on frame structures and is even more self-reflexive than his counterparts in the novelistic tradition.

[72] All citations from the "Literature of Exhaustion" are to the preceding reference; ibid., 73.
[73] John Barth, "Dunyazadiad," in *Chimera* (New York: Fawcett, 1973). [74] Ibid., 13.

Why Invest More in Dunyazade?

More than others, he invests more in the sister, and centers her in narrative to build a parallel narrative structure with an innovative parallelism between a "dramatic" narrative structuration, on the one hand, and "sexual intercourse," on the other.[75] Or, as Barth would like his Missy to tell us ("Missy: A Postscript to *The 1001 Nights*," 2015/16), that these nightly or dawn interruptions in her mom's narrative are like "the narrative equivalent of *coitus interruptus*."[76] More involution, rewriting, postscripting is done in such late pieces as "Missy,"[77] which may not be Barth's most impressive piece, but functions as a postscript, because it has all the stylistic mechanics and Americanized humor exemplified in his affiliated narratives with the *Nights*. As the daughter, Missy is to fill out narrative gaps, as Barth would like that to be: The king, her father, pardons her mother and requests Sherry as follows: "Oh, one more thing, dear: please retell all those thousand-and-one-night stories to my scribes, so they can write them down for our kids and grandkids and the world in general. Okay?" She adds: "Can you imagine? But Mom, being Mom, said, 'Sure, hon, just give me a year or three.' (Do the math: 1001 divided by 365 equals 2.7424657 or thereabouts.) And by Allah, she did it, one way or another: came up with 267 stories (including the tales-within-tales and tales-within-tales-within-tales), plus about ten thousand lines of verse for good measure."[78] Barth works within the grandmother's frame, but he builds a genealogical generational tree that also demonstrates changes in speech acts and parlance, as the granddaughter Missy is the third-generation breed who speaks, acts, and communes like urban American teens. This makes up part of his literature of replenishment. There is nevertheless an art that staves off death: yarn spinning. The granddaughter is to deliver Americanized tales, for, as her mother tells her when she was a kid, there is always "Once upon a time."

> I remember asking her for my usual bedtime story one night when I was a little girl – imagine Mom having to spin out bedtime stories for us kids before going in for sex-and-storytelling, copulation-and-fabulation, with Dad! But she did it, one way or another. That particular night, e.g., when she couldn't come up with a story for me, she said, "Once upon a time, Missy, there was a story that began, quote Once upon a time there was a story that began double-quote Once upon a time there was a story that began triple-quote Once upon a time there was a story that began – et cetera, ad infinitum."[79]

[75] The reference is to ibid., 32–33, also cited by Faris, "1001 Words," 814.
[76] John Barth, "Missy: A Postscript to *The 1001 Nights*," *The Iowa Review* 45, no. 3 (Winter 2015–16), 161–64.
[77] Ibid. [78] Ibid., 163. [79] Ibid.

While the mother, Scheherazade, "was too busy cooking up her entertain-me-or-die concoctions," Missy enjoys the companionship and help of Aunt Doony, Dunyazade. The shift toward the sister in Barth's narrative is more conspicuous than what we find in other postmodernists. His Dunyazade plays further on her dual role in the frame tale, that of the voyeur and auditor. In the words of Malti-Douglas, "it is Dunyazad who links sex and narration by first witnessing the act, then requesting the story."[80] Missy is also Barth's alter ego who reflects on his reading of *A Thousand and One Nights*. Throughout his writing in relation to the collection and its frame tale, Barth highlights two elements: the Ground Situation, which Missy speaks of as her status, which is unstable, but requires, as a second element, some action to move forward: "Dramatic Vehicle (enter Scheherazade), which then Complicates some Conflict through the story's Rising Action to its Climax and Denouement – much like the course of intercourse from titillation through copulation to orgasm and Ah!"[81]

The association between art and sex that takes its cue from the frame tale's nuptial chamber is pivotal to Barth's narratology. Without the king's insatiable desire, there is no reason for a narrative strategy to stave off death. Even when switching emphasis from Scheherazade to another character, Yasmin as Sindbad's daughter in his *Last Voyage of Somebody the Sailor*,[82] Barth redraws narrative roles and functions while emphasizing the sexual drive. The flap cover describes the novel as "rambunctious, sexy, and full of narrative jinks." As a postmodernist rewriting of Sindbad, it makes two significant departures, along with the often discussed interludes and frame story: mimetic depiction of reality as an adolescent practice exercised by the other contending character in the narrative, the stranded Simon Behler, who admits that in that early age, he was given to a "rendition of reality."[83] The present narrative where Behler and Sindbad tell their stories is more in line with a recreation of the real, a reinvention, not duplication. Behler cautions Sindbad and audience that "in my stories there are no genies or one-eyed giants to be swallowed whole. Nature's laws are not transgressed."[84] Behler, Sindbad the Stranger, the Stranded, is after all a site for multiple names and heteronyms, meaning that characters from the collection are reborn in new times and locations that still need Scheherazade's "narrative men" as archetypes.

[80] Malti-Douglas, "Narration and Desire," 21. [81] Barth, "Missy," 164.
[82] John Barth, *The Last Voyage of Somebody the Sailor* (Boston, MA: Little, Brown and Company, 1991).
[83] Ibid., 27. [84] Ibid., 71.

The other departure from Sindbad's *Voyages* is the assembly that brings together Sindbad, Behler as the Stranger, as a postmodernist travesty, a pastiche, of the Arab seafarer, a raucous charade, a flaunting excursus in what is perceived as an alien Islamic culture. The assembly, as a public space for conversations, a heteroglossia, where there are a number of narratives and comments, allows for a dialogic interaction and gives Barth's narrative some space to surpass the beginning of the original tale in which Sindbad addresses his double, the porter or Sindbad of the Land. If we address these issues on narrative levels, we can say that Barth overstretches the original, peels off its luster, and subsequently attempts to derive his own rewriting of the original and its specificities. The assembly where a discussion of difference between the original and the American version takes place is, to use one of Harold Bloom's titles, Barth's "map of misreading." He overdoes Borges's suggestion that the "thousand and one nights," as a "collection of fantastic tales duplicates and reduplicates to the point of vertigo the ramifications of a central story in later and subordinate stories, but does not attempt to gradate its realities, and the effect ... is superficial, like a Persian carpet."[85] The assembly allows some relevant voices, including the seafarer, Ibn al-Hamra, the daughter Yasmin, and Behler the Stranded, opportunities to narrate or recapitulate. Authorial commentaries through Behler the Stranded collapse the new Iraq and the East with a medieval past that Barth obviously observes from a privileged postindustrialist, postcapitalist perspective.

Barth's Sindbad in *The Last Voyage* is not merely Borges's "deliberate anachronism" as in "Pierre Menard, Author of the Quixote," but a measured misreading of both the Arab and Muslim past and present.[86] Unconcerned with cultural spectrums, and possibly unaware of storytelling genealogies that apply to the *Nights*, the narrator invades the avowed narrative property of the company, representing them as a credulous group whose very credulity prevents them from perceiving the real. Ibn al-Hamra is given leave by the host to differentiate between two narrative levels, one represented by "the host's [Sindbad's] compelling and exemplary tale of his second expedition," as this "quite fits the bill"; while "our visitor's [Behler the Stranded's] ... falls short." The representation of Ibn al-Hamra is taken out of context and is made to appear as Barth's contender whose knowledge derives from a modernized literary stance that accepts natural supernaturalism in fiction and welcomes action

[85] Borges, "Partial Magic," 195.

[86] See Wang Jianping, "Imagining Iraq and the Cultural Politics of Misreading: John Barth's *The Last Voyage of Somebody the Sailor*," *Journal of American Studies of Turkey* 21 (2005), 29.

and plot. Against these platitudes are inserted Behler's open dismantling of spatiotemporal verities, and his counternarrative of "urination, masturbation, and ... regurgitation" (136). Before going over these juxtapositions, the narrator, Barth's alter ego, allows Ibn al-Hamra and the host enough space to advocate for a narratology that Barth holds suspect. His deliberate anachronism and lack of good acquaintance with the Arabic literary tradition turns these differentiations into personal projections. Ibn al-Hamra is empowered by the host's approval to argue natural supernaturalism as the "real stuff," a "homely Islamic realism":

> The high ground of traditional realism, brothers, is where I stand! Give me familiar, substantial stuff: rocs and rhinoceros, ifrits and genies and flying carpets, such as we all drank in with our mothers' milk and shall drink – Inshallah – till our final swallow. Let no outlander imagine that such crazed fabrications as machines that mark the hour or roll themselves down the road [referring to Baylor's Omega Timex and locomotive] will ever take the place of our homely Islamic realism, the very capital of narrative – from which, if I may say so, all interest is generated. (136)

The narrator's sense of unease at the ongoing modern theory of fiction, the reason for his projections onto another landmark in an alien culture, leads him to question even early structuralists' reading of the *Nights* as action-driven narrative. Ibn al-Hamra is made to speak of action as follows: "Speak to us from our everyday experience: shipwreck and sole survivorhood, the retrieval of diamonds by means of mutton-sides and giant eagles, the artful deployment of turbans for aerial transport, buzzard dispersal" (136).

These "ground-verities" are contrasted with Behler's "profitless sideshows as human copulation" (136). One can read these as Barth's ironic interventions against his critics and the advocates of conventional fiction writing. Deriving his understanding of the Orient from Lane's heavily annotated translation and Burton's expansive excursus into anthropological detail, Barth defines this fiction as grounded in realism, that is, natural supernaturalism; but it also edifies. Thus Ibn al-Hamra turns edification into a fiasco of some sort, for a "story without a moral is like a meal without mint tea" (137). Ibn al-Hamra criticizes the "still-stranded somebody" for his failure to construct a well-plotted narrative, the staple of fictional conventions: "he will not deign to knit the ravels of his plot" (137).

But rather than beaten, Barth's alter ego doubles down, and asks for an audience to prove that he has something worth listening to, like good storytelling. The emphasis is laid on fiction and time, or rather the collapse of time as in a dream:

> Of six voyages . . . the third jumps not another seven years but four times seven, to the voyager's forty-second birthday: a leap in time that should gratify my impatient critic. And it fetched me not to an island virgin but to a virgin island, where I am not only reapproached the Boundary you've heard me speak of-between that world of my stories and this of their telling. (138)

With this he catches the attention of Sindbad who resumes the *Nights*' role of adventurers and narrators, admonishing all, "By Allah . . . we will not let our brother go till we've heard that story" (138). Now Barth and his alter ego are on firm ground: They can raise curiosity, the dynamic for action. At this juncture, Ibn al-Hamra loses, and even Yasmin and the dancer turn their attention to Behler. In other words, Barth has his take against novelistic conventions, but, in leveling blame against a ninth-century narrative in "deliberate anachronism," he intentionally violates narrative protocols and repeats what late eighteenth-century and early nineteenth-century European Romantics projected on to the Orient in their oblique devaluation of contemporary regimes of thought. William Beckford's *Vathek* and Byron's pseudo-Eastern poems, along with Poe's rewriting of the frame tale, should have been in the back of Barth's mind.

While not lacking in humor and irony, but overloaded with stereotyped stock images of an Orient presented as stagnant, Barth's novel revels in outdated Eurocentric explications. Thus, we listen to such authorial parenthetical projections like denying Arab culture any "autobiography," for the latter belongs to Europe and, now, Barth's culture![87] Apart from a deconstruction of Sindbad's voyages as driven by greed and brutality against fellow merchants, in the presentation of Yasmin as the voyager's daughter who has to concede to male authority in line with her culture (73), he multiplies a pile of stock images. Even if we accept the suggestion that it is an imaginary narrative of a Behler in a state of delirium or lunacy, stock images and misrepresentations abound. The ultimate structure of narrative, with six unnumbered voyages for Sindbad and six numbered and relatively orderly for Behler as Sindbad's double, is more than a mere concession to a cultural script or spectrum: There is a deliberate structure that speaks for an author as the arbiter on matters other than the ones he is known for – his infatuation with the art that he associates with Scheherazade. His "mechanical birds and bracelets that measure time" turn Behler into Poe's Scheherazade, whereas Sindbad exchanges roles with King Shahrayar: Though Sindbad is better equipped than Poe to compare these to his "sleeping wale overgrown with trees and beaches" (60), a "bit of realism in a sea of fantasy" (60). This is problematic, not

[87] Thus we read about Sindbad's daughter, Yasmin: "Raised as she had been in a culture in which autobiography was all but unknown." Barth, *Last Voyage*, 519.

because he misconstrues Poe's satirical but misanthropic perspective in "One Thousand-and-Second Tale of Scheherazade," which A. S. Byatt has addressed, but also because he invades Borges's referential frame to build up a mythopoeia of almost everything that is equally fascinating and repelling. He takes from Borges's "Immortal" his "Zahir," and probably the idea of the double in the original Sindbad of the Sea and Sindbad of the Land, as well as other themes found in a number of Borges's tales to construct his own alternating narratives of the Baghdadi/Basri seafarer and his host, Somebody the Still-Stranded (190). But there is a difference: Borges the Writer lives the experience of the impartial scribe across time and space, "I transcribed in Bulaq the travels of Sindbad the Sailor,"[88] whereas Barth rewrites to demonize the original and its cultural script. However, *The Last Voyage* is fascinating because Barth flaunts and exposes systems and regimes of conventions, be they literary or philosophical. This sardonic and at times debasing tone runs throughout his articles, as collected in *The Friday Book*. Literary modes, including those of narrative, are held suspect, not because he is more inclined to atemporality, but mainly because he associates them with existential contemporaneity. He argues,

> the difference between the fantasy we call reality and the fantasies we call fantasy has to do with cultural consensus and with one's manner of relating to the concept-structure involved. It goes without saying that one generation's culture's realism is another's patent artifice.[89]

Barth could have applied this to other cultures, including that of the tales, instead of a series of picturesque and also racial appellations.

Barth's Scheherazade factor is centered on inventiveness, as is shown in Sindbad's response to his guest's request to be heard. To theorize this, he resorts to means of deflection and sarcasm. To prove the efficacy of his narratological mechanism, he turns against the novelistic tradition, using throughout the common and shared background of narrative repertoire, *A Thousand and One Nights*. The *Nights* suffers in this transaction, but it gains in keeping Barth in its orbit, exactly like King Shahrayar, waiting for the next best story.

What Goes Wrong with John Barth's Postmodernism?

As postmodernity operates in postcolonial or liberal space, it takes different directions in writings, as we notice in Barth's novels and criticism. As a touchstone for a flowing storytelling and also as a symbolic signpost,

[88] Borges, "The Immortal," 117. [89] Barth, *The Friday Book*, 222.

a trope, for rejuvenation, the *Nights* for Barth is also an intertext, with an enormous repository of details, names, motifs, and adventures. It offers itself to him, or so he believes, as a terrain for intercultural dialectics where no single identity detracts from another and no one vies for ascendancy. The whole drive in his writings is toward parody, the demystifying of originality as a Romantic staple. While this can work well in short narratives, it proves more difficult in longer ones, especially because Barth has an agenda at the back of his mind, a deliberate interrogation of certain literary traditions and techniques. In other words, Barth negotiates his strategies in intercultural space where each position is set against another. In a sustainable struggle, however, juxtaposition is highlighted in his parodic *Last Voyage of Somebody the Sailor*.[90] Bringing Sindbad and the American Behler face to face, Barth the parodist exercises postmodernist poetics to the extreme, as if to take literature to task for its well-established traditions of tight narrativity and serious tone. Even Sindbad is made to pay for his narratives despite their open-endedness in a new voyage, an endless yearning to move into the mysterious and boundless. Scheherazade is in danger of exhaustion. To "The Destroyer of Delights," the personified death that concludes every tale in the *Arabian Nights*, Scheherazade admits the impossibility of virginity in narrative: "[A] virgin story there can't be anything you haven't heard." Shahrayar and death exchange positions, for both equate virginity with life, and exhaustion with death. Like other parodists, Barth finds himself entangled in issues that obviously touch some sensitive chords in his person, like virginity, family, and age. His Yasmin dissolves into images to cope with the parodist preoccupations, and Scheherazade exchanges place with him every now and then.

Faithful to the vocation of the parodist, Barth needs this intertext to debate, challenge, ransack, distort, and love. His postmodernism is self-conscious and parodic as practiced by his contemporaries. He is no less bent on critiquing the modernists' concerns with the subject or their shy espousal of representation as reflective of reality. He shares with them an underlying ironic tone that is also self-referential and ambiguous. He is less concerned with destabilizing subjectivity that Linda Hutcheon associates with capitalism.[91] His use of Sindbad's *Voyages* as subtext to parody and engage with is a challenge to modernist aspiration to an autonomous and refined creation as distinctively separate from popular culture. But the question that arises whenever we read his *Last Voyage* is: How does he parody Sindbad's seven voyages? Why? And how does this parody and

[90] Barth, *Last Voyage*.
[91] Linda Hutcheon, *Politics of Postmodernism* (London: Routledge, 1991), 15.

pairing sound in the year that witnessed the publication of *The Last Voyage*, and also the massive war on Iraq? His strayed voyager or Behler ends up stranded in Basra and the Gulf that witnessed the most vicious attack on an embattled and retreating Iraqi army. Behler is there, sea-stranded, and challenged. However, he is not at loss. In fact, he insists on a separate identity, as if subscribing to traditional stereotyping of the East. Stretching his postmodernity to the utmost, Barth evidently populates his textual terrain with this opposition and engagement to revitalize a literature already exhausted and drained. However, as parodist he makes his intertext pay for the effort. Stereotypes reappear in abundance, and his Arabs have no intelligent talk to offer other than innate preoccupations with virginity, sex, the body, and domestic affairs. What Mark Edmundson says rings true, for Barth the parodist is entangled in "the tradition of cultural perception and misperception that has been called Orientalism."[92] Postmodernism can never identify with postcolonial theory and poetics despite many arguments that argue for the common ground that both share. Within their deconstructionist methodologies, both share challenge to authority, essentialism, and closure. Nevertheless, while deconstruction is both the means and end for postmodernist poetics, it is never so for postcolonial theory. Barth's *Last Voyage* shows the problems involved in parody that allows free space for experimentation but cannot halt the stream of stereotypes that overcrowd the mind. Ghazoul is right in suggesting that he "anchors the work in his own harbor and invests it with his predilections and anxieties."[93] While the parodist in Barth cannot be tasked for his discursive strategies, those same strategies work in line with a bent for racial stratification. His women, for instance, come from both Baghdad and America, but Yasmin, Kusia, and Jayda are singled out for manipulation. They rarely appear as actors. Subjected and exposed to a penetrating gaze, their portraiture converses with Orientalists' paintings. However, Barth's women are resourceful, burlesquing tradition and turning patriarchy upside down. Indeed, Yasmin's unknown loss of virginity is meant to subvert social and literary patriarchy. Misleading the sociopolitical authority and deluding it into self-satisfaction and complacency, Yasmin thwarts and challenges systems of closure, in life as in narrative. Her paradoxical role between early complicity and subsequent subversion sounds as another trope for a racial acculturation whereby her encounter with Behler and company turns her into a rebel. The colonialist civilizing mission takes over the otherwise parodic narrative. Nevertheless, and in line with the poetics and politics of parody as a postmodernist strategy,

[92] Cited in Ghazoul, *Nocturnal Poetics*. [93] Ibid., 129.

The Last Voyage becomes a voyage in an enormous ocean of narrative, where contradictions abound, and where no closure is possible.

Barth's association with Scheherazade's tales is never short-lived. Hence, he never aggrandizes his American Behler, though he sustains him as a separate identity. The implications of this kind of parody emanate from its mixture of text and context, popular narratives and autobiographical detail, past and present, and self and Others. As an ideal storyteller, Scheherazade is Barth's real love, and Barth as parodist is at pains to argue this infatuation narratively in juxtaposition with his own personal life. He never belongs to the East, but he identifies with Scheherazade. Indeed, his Behler leads a drab life, and so does his family. Disconnected and forlorn, he needs to make the most of his present situation to delve, like the Romantics, into a land of narrative fecundity and richness. In other words, the parodist suffers liminality in relation to Romanticism and postmodernist poetics, debating premises, while negotiating literary affiliations with Scheherazade. As if undergoing the anxiety of authorship, he takes leave of her to come upon Sindbad, wrestle with him, and engage his narrative voyages with a mixture of attachment and revulsion before embarking on a further narrative excursion. In an attempt to bring the old narratives and Behler's figurative ones into a storytelling marathon over six evenings at Sindbad's dinner table, Barth the parodist never loses sight of his anti-Romantic drive. Rather than a return to a dream world, Behler's involvement in Sindbad's narrative and life is a revisionist reading of the past to cope with the present. It is an American dilemma first, as many intellectuals try to make sense of tradition through a recourse, albeit parodist, to the ancient heritage, as the only filiatory, or textually genetic, bond that occupies memory.

Tim Severin's Enactment of a Medieval Sindbad and Visual Experimentation

With this reading, the *Arabian Nights* is simultaneously a site of independence and rupture. As a mixture of parody, travesty, burlesque, and raids on current responses to Sindbad's voyages, Barth's *Last Voyage* is an attempt to terminate an enchantment that the *Nights* continues to hold. In the process it creates its own traps, as its reflections on the Irish Tim Severin's voyage, book, and film indicate. Thus Barth's Julia Moore and Baylor the Sailor (Behler) in *The Last Voyage* change direction in approaching the *Nights*: Instead of perceiving it as fictitious with possible historical material, it is presently perceived as factual by the Irish adventurer whom Barth reproduces to allow some space for his own fictitious characters:

Mr. Tim Severin is persuaded on good evidence that the seven voyages of Sindbad the Sailor, as retold by Scheherazade in *The Thousand and One Nights*, are amplified echoes of actual expeditions on the limits of the known world by Arab maritime traders between the eighth and eleventh centuries. (322)

Disheartened but jealous nevertheless of this supremacy of the factual, Barth's character Moore traces archival material to understand the venture that will turn art upside down:

From illuminated manuscripts of the period, Julia Moore has learned, Severin and his associates are working up designs for a careful replica of a medieval Arab trading vessel. If he can find the required funding, he intends to have the vessel built by isolated Arab craftsmen who still employ such ancient methods as sewing ship's timbers together with ropes of coconut fiber – and then, with a mixed crew of Arabs and Europeans, navigate her by medieval techniques from Sindbad's famous starting place (or somewhere farther down the Persian Gulf if international politics rule out Basra), across the Arabian Sea to India and "Serendib" (now Siri Lanka), across the Bay of Bengal to Sumatra and Malaysia, and up the South China Sea all the way to mainland China, the fabled "Al-Sin" of Sindbad's time. (322–23)

Using initials for Behler or Baylor, Barth is on his own meditating with Moore on ways to be part of this adventure. In other words, his "replenishment" schema requires some invigorating input from a simulacrum that duplicates an origin that exists vaguely in a book, now Edward Powys Mathers's translation of Mardrus's *The Thousand and One Nights* (324). But Severin is adamant in reproducing an authentic, geographical venture:

He wishes the whole ship's company except himself could be indigenous – cameramen, sound technicians, divers, and scientists as well as deckhands – because experience has taught him that the essential moments of such replicated adventures are those when with nothing in sight suggests the Here and Now. (325)

To have Moore on board is out of the question: "The Sindbad project organizer is polite but both busy and wary: it is *his*, for *his* book, his film, his *National Geographic* piece, etc." (324).

Whether rephrasing Severin's reluctance to have a female on board or speculating in line with his stereotyping of the medieval and contemporary Arab, the narrator recapitulates:

A woman crew member, moreover, absolutely will not do, given the large "native" crew he anticipates, with their unWestern notions of gender difference and the primitive conditions of life aboard a crowded Arab boom. Besides, did Sindbad ever sail with a woman aboard? (324)

In a succinct reading of Sindbad's children in multiple translation mediums, the intralingual, interlingual, and intersemiotic – as theorized by Roman Jakobson[94] – Ghazoul adds that this journey falls within the intersemiotic medium.[95] She quotes from Severin's account his belief that there were real journeys like Sindbad's, and that fiction only tried to capture geographical voyaging:

> The more I delved into the legend of Sindbad, the more I suspected that he was no mere fictional hero of children's tales. Rather, he was a composite figure, an amalgam of the Arab sea captains and merchants who ventured to the limits of the known world in the golden age of Arab sail between the 8th and 11th centuries.[96]

This successful project, sponsored by Sultan Qābūs ibn Saʿīd of Oman, brings to the affiliates of the *Nights*, its ardent devotees and initiates in its art, another legacy that connects with a past and sets in motion a number of other productions and writings. To have it reproduced in Barth's *Last Voyage* is not coincidental. It either inspired Barth to parody it, to retain the voyages to a metafictional space, or incited further recapitulations on his part to expand his canvas and include an experience that went into film and book.[97]

Compared with the Egyptian Najīb Maḥfūẓ, Barth has had a long relationship with the *Nights*. Maḥfūẓ could have claimed what Ibn al-Hamra articulates in Barth's narrative: "Give me familiar, substantial stuff ... such as we all drank in with our mother's milk" (136). The Egyptian novelist was not given to a postmodernist pastiche, but he synthesizes narrative properties and reproduces the *Nights* in a short readable form that also provides an oblique criticism of authoritarianism.

[94] Roman Jakobson, "On Linguistic Aspects of Translation," https://complit.utoronto.ca/wp-content/uploads/COL1000H_Roman_Jakobson_LinguisticAspects.pdf.

[95] Ferial Jabouri Ghazoul, "Sindbad the Sailor: Textual, Visual, and Performative Interpretations," in *Scheherazade's Children*, 243–62.

[96] Tim Severin, "In the Wake of Sindbad," *National Geographic* 162, no. 1 (July 1982), 2–41.

[97] Ghazoul describes these as follows:

> Cameramen and filmmakers David Bridges and Richard Greenhill were on the ship to keep visual records. Severin recorded the voyage textually in 1982 through an article and a book. Severin's Sindbad Voyage and a film with the same title (directed by David Bridges, scripted by Tim Severin, and narrated by Brian Hayes) reproduce the same wonder and amazement we experience when reading the Sindbad voyages in the *Nights*.

Ibid., 256.

Najīb Maḥfūẓ's Cosmopolitan Female Narrator

Novelists like Barth and Maḥfūẓ differ in carving their narratorial inroads through a number of navigations between rewriting and creative and invigorating parody, self-reflexive and metafictional stratagems, and a concatenation of elemental devices of much alethic density in a world of event and landscape. Significantly, they also make use of a textual terrain to expound on a diversified landscape of "communitarian" exchange, whereby characters turn into readers/listeners and stories open up on to an exterior space.

Maḥfūẓ's *Layālī alf laylah* (1982; English translation: *Arabian Nights and Days*, 1995) signals the possibility of rewriting an *Arabian Nights* without the need for Barth's inhibiting preoccupation with replenishment as an alternative to exhaustion in the narrative field. He is no less involved than many postmodernists in collapsing a number of narrative strategies to present a very readable *Arabian Nights*, a *Nights* that speaks to Roland Barthes's surmise, "narrative is international, transhistorical, transcultural: it is simply there, like life itself."[98] This *Arabian Nights and Days* has as prologue the conclusion of the usual thousand and one nights: "Three years he [the vizier Dandan as Scheherazade's father] had spent between fear and hope, between death and expectation" (1). The father's fears are soon dissipated as stories transform the sultan into a just, serene, and compassionate ruler. Faced with so many challenging events in which evil supernatural beings play on the greed and ambition of individuals, the ruler allows space to Sufi masters, the vizier, and Scheherazade to come up with solutions. However, people regain power, and participate in the establishment of a less chaotic society. Sindbad comes back after seven voyages with lessons that reflect obliquely on the situation in Egypt (211–15). In other words, Maḥfūẓ relies on the original *Alf laylah wa-laylah*, uses it as intertext and subtext, collapses and rewrites some of its tales, lets the supernatural intervene, but he also enables the common public to function in protest, discussion, and action. Maḥfūẓ navigates smoothly between the original and the new production, and his parody is tamed to fit into the narrative fabric of his writing in the 1970s, which leaves behind the bourgeois epic structure of his novels of the 1950s and 1960s. The noticeable turn of the 1970s is entrenched in popular culture and lore. As I argued in *The Postcolonial Arabic Novel* (2003), Maḥfūẓ's use of *enchâssement* is postmodernist in that it is "a combination of embedding, inclusion and interwoven narration." Furthermore, "through juxtaposition, duplication, parallelism, coordination,

[98] Roland Barthes, "Introduction to the Structural Analysis of Narratives," in *A Barthes Reader*, ed. Susan Sontag (New York: Barnes and Noble, 2009), 212.

subordination, intertextuality, gradation, embeddings and distortion," the Egyptian Nobel Prize winner "has recreated the tales to regroup the socio-political morals of the original, providing them with a contemporaneous drive."[99]

But, no matter how different modernist and postmodernist fictional narrative techniques may be, there is an awareness of the narrative art that impels experimentation with form. Proust is different from Carlos Fuentes, and Barth is different from Maḥfūẓ. They all share the *Arabian Nights* as a common property that speaks to their achievement and ordeal. Thus, Fuentes admits: "When I was a young man, I wrote to live. Now, at 54, I write not to die. Like Scheherazade in the 'Arabian Nights,' I'll live as long as I have another story to tell."[100] The author of *The Death of Artemio Cruz* and *Terra Nostra* has more affinities with Maḥfūẓ than with Barth.

Navigational ironies in these fictions between texts and locales speak more to what Gerald Prince means by "conditions for intelligibility."[101] As my reading takes Maḥfūẓ's *Arabian Nights and Days* (or as the original title has it: *Nights of the Thousand Nights, Layalī alf laylah*) as a case study, I will limit this reading to narratological modes with specific bearing on modal structures that situate Maḥfūẓ's *Arabian Nights and Days* in a cosmopolitan postmodernist novelistic tradition with some postcolonial underpinnings.

A Narrative Grammar for Maḥfūẓ's Scheherazade

Maḥfūẓ locates Scheherazade at a crossroads, spatially, epistemologically, and ontologically: spatially, in an undefined silhouette of a palace where she is held between life and death; epistemologically between boundless affluence and Sufi austerity and disinterestedness; and ontologically in constant negotiation with being and nothingness. Paradoxically, she starts where her prototype ends, meaning that exteriority takes over at the point when her narrative comes to an end. Yet, she

[99] Muhsin Jassim al-Musawi, "Scheherazade's Gifts: Maḥfūẓ's Narrative Strategies in *Layalī alf laylah*," in *The Postcolonial Arabic Novel*, 376.

[100] Arthur Holmberg, "Carlos Fuentes Turns to Theater," *New York Times*, June 6, 1982.

[101] See Prince, "Narratology, Narrative, and Meaning," 547, where he makes reference to the post-1960s generation of critics who try to make sense of these conditions. He argues as follows:

> to Diesel (1976, 1980, 1988), Pavel (1980, 1988), and Ryan (1980, 1985), narrative semantics has been proving to be a particularly fertile and promising subject. As these works emphasize, narrative intelligibility is based upon the relationships, in the narrative universe, between a world designated as real – what is, what was, what will be, what could be – and more or less adequate representations, perceptions, and notions of that world.

is alive, and the structural equivalence between wound and narrative, speech and life, has to be substituted with another sequence of events or another mode of tension whereby desire functions as the repressed unconscious, and it is perhaps therein that its "double nature" resides.[102] The narrator is privileged only as a narratological subject who is the recipient of reports from the outside world and whose presence gradually leads the sultan to fuse the narrative of the real, the encroaching world, with the narrator's early narrative. In terms of typology of octants, as expounded by Barthes,[103] she is a catalyzer, dispatcher, and index rather than a nucleus, an expansion than a cardinal, or a focus well positioned to presumably devise and impact the unfolding of events. But, if taken beyond functional typologies and confounded with the author as excavator, decipher, decoder, appropriator, exploiter, and hijacker of a medieval text, Maḥfūẓ's Scheherazade undermines a dynastic frame of succession, dismantles its teleological resolution of happiness ever after, and instead establishes a constant dynamic of shifting power relations. The sultan's withdrawal and bathing in the elusive waters of eternity (that have their prototype in Gilgamesh's wondrous sea) is shattered not, as in the Akkadian prototype, by an overwhelming slumber that allows the snake to steal the eternal life secret but by irresistible curiosity, which is primarily libidinal and the source for the ever-virgin quest, and hence for further narrative. While leading into the latter, curiosity is as risky as life itself because, as Todorov argues, "If loquacity saves from death, curiosity leads to it."[104] Taking as a point of departure the end of a prototypical narrative of suspense, Maḥfūẓ's novel rewinds old stories to fit into an external world that forces itself on the sultan, stripping him of his grandeur, immersing him into the mundane real, and emancipating him from the egoism of a sovereign subject. In narratological terms, narrative opens up under the impact of Sufism and marvelous happenings on to an exterior that sets the stage for the sultan's wayfaring. Maḥfūẓ's novel opens with Scheherazade's father's concerns after she spent the three years of storytelling "between fear and hope, between death and expectation; three years spent in the telling of stories; and thanks to those stories, Shahrazad's life span had been extended."[105]

[102] See Todorov on this matter in *Poetics of Prose*, 105. "The paradox and tragedy of desire proceed from its double nature. We desire at the same time desire and its object." Equating desire with speech, he argues, "words imply the absence of things, just as desire implies the absence of its object." He concludes, "Words to things what desire is to its object" (105–6).

[103] Barthes, "Introduction to the Structural Analysis," 93–95.

[104] Todorov, *Poetics of Prose*, 75.

[105] Naguib Mahfouz, *Arabian Nights and Days*, trans. Denys Johnson-Davies (Arabic, 1982; New York: Anchor Books, 1995), 1.

While worrying about his daughter's fate, the vizier Dandan is curious to know what is in the sultan's mind now. He is relieved to hear the latter say: "Her stories are white magic. ... They open up worlds that invite reflection" (2). It is now the exterior world that overwhelms the sultan with ongoing troubles, including the intervention of the supernatural, and leads in the end to his wayfaring.

This wayfaring has water as subtext, not only to complement land and air and hence compose a universal order, but also to endow moral and physical transformation with existential and symbolic analogues. Growing as a semantic field of fluidity and consequent transformation, waters are not a neutral player. While seemingly offsetting the wound through purgation in the sultan's case, water fails to clean a conscience; and hence the permanence of the quest. By contrast, the metamorphosis of the all-knowing omniscient character like the police chief Gamsa is an unprecedented (not in the original text) verbal construct that undergoes double transformation through invitations to escape human limits. Gamsa is an amalgam of supernatural beings and humans driven by desire for unlimited power. His dive into the waters to equate his other half of the sea is a way to make use of what Todorov calls "chance time," an "extra temporary hiatus" that appears "between two moments of real time sequence."[106] But this given escape endangers the narrative, as it empties the character of that invariant desire, the libidinal craving and its unconscious recesses that account for the narrative flow.[107] However, it dovetails with the Sufi subtext, the one from which Maḥfūẓ's Scheherazade presumably inhales, and whose source is no other than her mentor, Sheikh al-Balkhi. Scheherazade is made to reiterate her doubts that the sultan can ever be free from a quintessential evil. Thus, even when giving up the kingdom and seeking comfort in the wilderness, he cannot overcome his libidinal craving. Duplicating the second mendicant of the original, he only echoes the tavern owner Seduri in the *Epic of Gilgamesh* who tells Gilgamesh that, as a human, he cannot attain eternity. Maḥfūẓ is obviously torn between giving credit to Scheherazade as basically Sufi and disinterested, and his knowledge that this ends the story and its motivational libidinal craving. Shahrayar is trapped by the latter. The under waters that have brought him youth are a "visible displacement" that, for Riffaterre, means the "loss of narrativity,"[108] hence he has to open the forbidden door, the symbolic gateway to narrative.

[106] Todorov, *Poetics of Prose*, 91, 94.
[107] Michael Riffaterre, *Fictional Truth* (Baltimore, MD: Johns Hopkins University Press, 1990), 87.
[108] Ibid., 91.

The dialectic in these shifts is no ordinary matter, for Todorov's basic equilibrium/disequilibrium pendulum builds on the fantastic modal of human desire for power.[109] But this universal principle should not blind us to the particular: There must be a powerful urge behind the narrator's/author's choice of prototypical text to question this site of power and to turn equilibrium upside down, to interrogate its seemingly rational contracts that have been holding up the very outcome of modernity, its structure of a nation-state. Written ahead of the popular revolutions by more than three decades (1982), but soon after the massive popular protests against President Anwar Sadat's open-door market economy (1979), as a blatant revocation of a "benefits for compliance contract" with the state, the street sets an intelligible narrative condition for Maḥfūẓ's cobbler, Maʿrūf, who is picked up from among many other characters of the original. Tempted by the mysterious person, the Devil or any site of power, to enjoy fantastic excursions that he declines to exploit for evil ends, the shoemaker unsettles the privileged and the powerful, but tantalizes the souls of the downtrodden. Upon rejecting villainous designs, he is forsaken and almost driven to the gallows. There lies the seed for revolt, as the people take to the streets to defend him as one of them, untainted and intact. The narrator has already prepared conditions of intelligibility for this shifting politic in an astrological prediction of future rule by the riffraff.

Astrology serves a similar purpose to dreams or the intrusion of the fantastic, a kind of coincidental occurrence, a "chance time."[110] The overall diegesis makes use of interlaced textual unities that structurally tear down any epical possibility or its political equivalent of dynastic rule. The narrative voice recedes in this interlacing where there are other contending voices: of genies who exercise the role of human power politics, Sindbad who comes back laden with stories and lessons, or Ugr, the loquacious barber whose realist or representational poetic is offset especially by voices from which the arch narrator Scheherazade presumably inhales: the Sufi Sheikh al-Balkhi and the madman, as the ultimate metamorphosis of the executed police chief Gamsa. Metamorphosis amounts to more or less another cycle in shifting politics. Even a Sufi politic of disinterestedness, despite its equilibrium, has a function in this shifting power politics. As long as it poses a challenge to corruption,

[109] See Todorov, *Poetics of Prose*. In his reading of motivation, Todorov speaks of two types of episodes: those describing a state and those describing a passage from one state to the other. The first is from equilibrium to its opposite, and he thinks of this as static and reiterative (111). In terms of the grammar of narrative, the re/iterative is the adjectival predicated on a change of state.

[110] Ibid., 94.

malevolent practices, and unlimited human desire, it initiates disequilibrium. In other words, the narrator straddles the fence already erected between a violent system that permeates a whole power network and a Sufi critique of that power. In terms of a reconfigured subjectivity, Scheherazade perhaps derives much-needed substance more through Shahrayar's withdrawal from the scene than from scattered reference to the Sufi sheikh's teaching. One can say that Sufism fits neatly in Bourdieu's concept of predisposition as an early inculcation that retains power ever after. But its function as a nonradical politics of rejection based in disinterestedness provides for the conditions of intelligibility where events and actions make up a diegetic space. The propositions, conflicts, desires, and contradictions decide the veracity of this narrative.

Apart from the conflation between postmodernism and postcolonialism, pastiche and ironic or self-reflective strategies, and the critique of power in its local and regional dimensions, Maḥfūẓ's Scheherazade is the narrative catalyst only insofar as it offsets and unsettles the contending patriarch as quintessential power politics. Only in this sense, survival opens up rather than concludes narrative. Hence, Maḥfūẓ's seeming departure is the gateway to textual doubling whereby scenes are played out anew and narrative descriptive strategies converge in what Riffaterre may call "diegetic implementation of narrative models."[111] By reversing the order of the original through a seeming engagement with an unfolding textual present of events and speech, there is what Riffaterre calls the "actualization of structures, the ways in which models are fleshed out with the description of characters and settings, and the representation of the thoughts and speeches of these characters."[112]

Loquacity and the Language of the Mad

Maḥfūẓ's text as a condensed embedding extends an exterior referent that is no more than a combined convention and politic. Scheherazade rarely appears in these concatenations such as the imaginary kingdom of Ibrahim, the water carrier. The latter squanders a newfound treasure on an imaginary exercise as an alternative sultan presiding justly over an orderly kingdom beyond time, an intertext for the "psychological unconscious."[113] It is meant, as in the original, to challenge the so-called real with a fictitious ideal. In this sense, it functions as mise en abyme, a subtext, a mini-narrative, in Riffaterre's terms,[114] whereby the narrative "is to the subject as an object is to its sign."[115] Maḥfūẓ is more

[111] Riffaterre, *Fictional Truth*, xiii. [112] Ibid. [113] Ibid., 86. [114] Ibid., 27.
[115] Ibid., 28.

focused on debunking, if not exposing, the limits of realistic representation. Whereas barbers stand foremost for curiosity and loquacity,[116] Maḥfūẓ stretches the barber Ugr's fecundity. The tale spinner whose curiosity leads to unpredictable and calamitous outcomes remains out of touch with differentiated social segments. Unexplored territory remains a challenge to his curiosity and dream of "virgin girls." The latter is Maḥfūẓ's trope for the desire to explore and penetrate, a desire that is maximized in Shahrayar's unabating will to conquer. Both open up and paradoxically close narrative. The spinner cannot function like a sultan with unlimited power, nor can he uncover the secrets of the wealthy who "answered without any encouragement, wary of his intrusion" (115). The limitations of the spinner are deliberately spelled out:

> In ordinary circumstances nothing distracted him from what was happening, for he was a deeply-rooted minder of other people's business, making mountains out of molehills and regarded in his shop as a spinner of tales before being a barber, deriving interest and pleasure from news and exaggerated rumors. (103)

As if critiquing his early career as a realist, Maḥfūẓ casts doubts on the unlimited trust in representation. There is no character that can unsettle the realistic paradigm other than a madman who can untie knots and sever causal consequences. In unison with Sufi unworldliness and poets' imaginative flights, madness speaks the language of gods. In Michel Foucault's reading, the poet and madman occupy "a marginal position" as their "words unceasingly renew the power of the strangeness and the strength of their contestation." They load "all signs with a resemblance that ultimately erases them."[117] In other words, it is only with such transpositions from verisimilitude and temporality that fiction accedes to truth.[118]

At this juncture, the language of the mad is worth pondering, not only because of its association with poetry, its eradication of rationalized barriers, but also because it leads us back to issues of narratology, narrative, and meaning, to borrow Prince's title.[119] The narrator has to establish verisimilitude to sustain links with readers. In Riffaterre's explanations it is "a system or representations that seems to reflect a reality external to the text, but only because it conforms to grammar"

[116] Todorov writes: "If all characters incessantly tell stories, it is because this action has received a supreme consecration [in the *Arabian Nights*]: narrating equals living." *Poetics of Prose*, 73.

[117] Michel Foucault, *The Order of Things: An Archaeology of the Human Sciences* (New York: Random House, 1994), 50.

[118] In Riffaterre's unusual surmise, "fiction obtains when the mode of the diegesis shifts from the narrative to the poetic." *Fictional Truth*, 111.

[119] Prince, "Narratology, Narrative, and Meaning."

as rules.[120] In Maḥfūẓ's case, this grammar extends even beyond "substitutability," the sequential generation of "synonyms and functions" denoting "unchanging semantic structure of the given."[121] It responds to readers' consensus with respect to the language of the mad. Only the mad can transgress without the restraints of rules and reason. Hence, Shahrayar has to know what the madman says, for the latter, adds Shahrayar, "winked at me with a boldness possessed only by madmen" (131). Madness is another face for wonders that belie reason and question the human's staunch attachment to rigid applications. Narrative offers one gateway that may well enact another reality; as long as it carves a grammar of correspondence with readership/listeners. Maḥfūẓ lets his sultan recognize these wonders: "The days and nights have taught us to pay attention to such wonders and to knock at the door of the inscrutable so that it may open wide and reveal light" (104).

The "inscrutable" may include detective fiction, but its presence here in Maḥfūẓ's world as the other half of reality answers to narratologists' explication of plausibility or its lack. While repetition has a dialectic of its own as both a consolidation and initiation of "fictional truth," wonders and their external counterparts outside the text substantiate a truth that narrative tends to stress even when courting self-reflexivity. Maḥfūẓ lets his Scheherazade respond to Shahrayar's recollection of a story from the street upon an incognito encounter with a forlorn young person by saying, "The fact that stories repeat themselves is an indication of their truth" (98). In order not to give up on ironies, Maḥfūẓ also looks upon people's actions and outcomes as the structural substratum for a fictionality that has been the paradoxical solace and reality of human life. Thus, a character facing death is made to respond to shows of sympathy: "It is an old story with which the elderly warm themselves: the story of love, madness, and blood" (137).

This surmise only draws attention to the tale as a sign system that reflects on readership's reception of narrative. The surmise sounds apodeictic because, to cite Riffattere, "a specific fact is inserted into a generalizing syntagm."[122] As readers we nod in approval because narrative has always involved such vindication. As such, there is no effort to mask fictionality, but rather to market it as repetition.

Retaining the proper names of the frame story that have served as emblems over time and across cultures, Maḥfūẓ's text functions in a number of capacities: primarily as subtext, stagehand, a mnemonic, to a large text of stretches and scenes, and as a trope whose foil is the original book.[123]

[120] Riffaterre, *Fictional Truth*, xiv. [121] Ibid. [122] Ibid., 9.
[123] Ibid., 60, 52, respectively.

Sufism as Critique of Power

Maḥfūẓ's fictional reconstruct generates verisimilitude not only in relation to an original, but also through allusions to any state machinery. The unique departure from the original resides in Scheherazade's Sufi education that places her within a benevolent order that espouses feminism as a drive for equality and justice. As a narrator, she influences unfolding events and occurrences only in her capacity as a leading trope in a Sufi matrix that unsettles contenders by default. Hence, exchange of roles between the sultan and Scheherazade occurs only as a convention that requires a scene of recognition: "I am not wise, but also I am not stupid," concludes Shahrayar, "How often have I been aware of your contempt and aversion!" (217). These are words that are placed in the mouth of a defeated sultan who in the process changes into a self-blaming Malamati Sufi:[124] "Do you know why I kept you close by me?" he asks. "Because I found in your aversion a continued torment that I deserved" (217). A Malamati Sufi inhabits a borderline between symbols, emblems, and human agonies that are bound to infect a biographer, in her capacity as Maḥfūẓ's female narrator of the pursuit for meaning in a seemingly somber and humorless intertext. The cosmopolitan arch-narrator functions as a foil that evokes a gloss, a discourse that invokes decoding. Although Maḥfūẓ spreads across the narrative a number of Scheherazade's rejoinders, somber comments on the news, and her own reading of the sultan's reported transformation, these are often residual. Todorov's too sweeping reading of the *Arabian Nights* as a "predicative literature," focusing on the predicate "and not on the subject of the proposition," may specifically apply to Maḥfūẓ's narrator, where, through embedding and predication, there is an "effacement of the grammatical subject,"[125] its impersonality in an otherwise highly condensed narrative. As a trope, Scheherazade is not the story, but its sign – to evoke Riffaterre one last time,[126] of "an ideological telos," a female jailbreak from a closed system.

Maḥfūẓ's rewriting of the *Nights* provides a coherent text that gains in impetus and "fictional truth" because it is not inhibited by Barth's preoccupations, or by the postmodernist self-reflexivity that engages with the *Nights* in translation.[127] Each translation or redaction leaves its marks on writing, as Chapter 4 argues.

[124] Malamati Sufism is the "way of blame." Its practitioners incur blame through a deviation from strict application of Islamic rituals.

[125] Todorov, *Poetics of Prose*, 67. [126] Riffaterre, *Fictional Truth*, 69.

[127] For a good reading of Maḥfūẓ's rediscovery of the *Nights* as nation, narration, and worldview, see Wen-Chin Ouyang, *Poetics of Love in the Arabic Novel* (Edinburgh: Edinburgh University Press, 2012), 127–158, 128.

4 The "Hostile Dynasty"

Rewriting the *Arabian Nights*

> Translations are a partial and precious documentation of the changes the text suffers.
>
> Jorge Luis Borges, "The Homeric Versions"

> Lane translated against Galland, Burton against Lane; to understand Burton we must understand this hostile dynasty.
>
> Jorge Luis Borges, "The Translators of the *Thousand and One Nights*"

These two epigraphs from Jorge Luis Borges (1899–1986), which serve as paratextual mottos, are meant to define the drive and intention of this chapter: its reading of "translation" as a multiple refashioning of a disputable text. Because of the lack of a definitive manuscript earlier than Antoine Galland's incomplete one, and the concomitant popularity of the latter in France, and almost everywhere else but especially in England, the stage has been set since 1704 for conjecture, fabulation, fabrication, and hunt for manuscripts. Galland's incomplete and appropriated translation has ever since become the most vital dynamic in a tireless hunt for manuscripts, and has incited in turn authenticated translations, collated versions, and recourse to Galland as the most readable as Robert Mack's reproduction indicates.[1] But translation is not only a navigation or negotiation between two lexical spaces, it is a transformation of one kind of speech, the verbal, into other mediums, which nineteenth-century British pantomime made use of for the theater, while French and British journalism fed on it in serialization. You need to keep your readers expectant and in waiting, like the Shahrayar of *A Thousand and One Nights*, or like the less known minister, Ibn Saʿdān, in relation to Abū Ḥayyān al-Tawḥīdī's *Nights*. I will return to this point in due course. Insofar as the subject matter of this chapter is concerned, the second epigraph from Borges also sets the stage for a number of dynasties: textual, visual, and audiovisual. The tales have

[1] Robert L. Mack, ed., *Arabian Nights' Entertainments* (Oxford: Oxford University Press, 1995).

morphed into illustrations, paintings, engravings, TV and cinematic production, songs, music, architecture, and almost everything that the cyberspace accommodates. In 1934, Borges was focused on texts, but his definition of the hostile dynasty of male translators fighting to prove their superiority to a predecessor can also apply to other fields. In this third millennium, the most challenging domain is audiovisual. Nevertheless, there is a genealogy here as it is in every part of this book: It burgeons in the contested space of contending registers and relevant claims to authenticity.

A Translation Dynasty?

Borges's pertinent and informative phrase for Scheherazade's chain of translators sums up the history of *A Thousand and One Nights* in Europe, but it also and discreetly raises the question with respect to the legitimacy of archival and manuscript material in another language. Historically speaking, dynasties and clans have male blood genealogies as the base for dynastic rule, even when mothers hail from other regions, races, and religions. Within these dynasties, the quest for power happened to be a dynamic and conclusive factor in the makeup of political history. What supports Borges's "dynastic" term for the chain of translators is the fact that these translations or renditions borrowed from, relied on, and engaged with an "original": Galland's translation and his archive (including manuscripts, oral narratives, and notes).[2] Yet, this legacy, an archive on its own, does not collect "the dust of statements that have become inert once more";[3] it is an ongoing engagement with a domain that is taking different dynamic directions. Thus, even if there is a single translator, like van Leeuwen into Dutch,[4] or Rafael Casinos Assens's first complete translation from Arabic into Spanish (1954), and Malcolm Lyons's into English,[5] their translations are conversant with a worldwide phenomenal transterritorial, transtextual enterprise. Their

[2] Ruth B. Bottigheimer, "East Meets West: Hannā Diyāb and The Thousand and One Nights," *Marvels & Tales* 28, no. 2 (2014), 302–24; Ulrich Marzolph, "The Man Who Made the Nights Immortal: The Tales of the Syrian Maronite Storyteller Ḥannā Diyāb," *Marvels & Tales* 32, no. 1 (Spring 2018), 114–29. For more, see Jack Ross's neat summary of editions in English, https://mairangibay.blogspot.com/2008/12/new-translation-of-arabian-nights.html; and also Horta, *Marvellous Thieves*, 19–21, 31–33, 35–52, 68–77.

[3] Foucault, *Archaeology of Knowledge*, 129.

[4] Richard van Leeuwen, *De vertellingen van duizend-en-één nacht* (1999) used the Bulaq edition (Cairo 1835), the Calcutta edition (1842), and the edition by Muhsin Mahdi (Leiden 1984).

[5] Malcolm C. Lyons and Ursula Lyons, *The Arabian Nights: Tales of 1001 Nights*, 3 vols. (Harmondsworth, UK: Penguin, 2008). Malcolm Lyons used the Macnaghten edition, that is, Calcutta II; but Ursula Lyons added Aladdin and Ali Baba, and an ending to *The Seventh Voyage of Sindbad* from the Antoine Galland eighteenth-century French edition; the volume is introduced and annotated by Robert Irwin.

sources are no longer a single authenticated text. In other words, and to qualify Oliver Goldsmith eighteenth-century *Citizen of the World*, the translator is a citizen of texts. World cultures had become aware of *A Thousand and One Nights* as an overwhelming narrative power in 1704–17. In view of a history initiated by Galland's venture, his "translation" and its genealogical tree should be seen as a European phenomenon.[6]

Galland's Afterlife

Long before Borges, Leigh Hunt (1784–1859) saw Galland as the gate-opener:

> It was he that first opened to Europe this precious source of delight; he it was whose taste and enthusiasm led the way to the taste and enthusiasm of others, and without whom perhaps Lane himself would not have been ultimately led to favor us with his more accurate version.[7]

As Borges argues concerning Galland's inclusion of orphan and other tales: "Galland established the canon, incorporating stories that time would render indispensable and that the translators to come – his enemies – would not dare omit."[8] Furthermore, Galland's edition has been sustaining a tradition because there is around it and over a 300-year span a large corpus of literary criticism, poetics, memoirs, and reminiscences whose authors happened to be the architects of a literary and artistic tradition. In 1934–36, Borges wrote: "Two hundred years and ten better translations have passed, but the man in Europe or the Americas who thinks of the *Thousand and One Nights* thinks, invariably, of this first translation."[9]

Borges and, before him, the English poet and critic Hunt, enumerated many aspects of the empowering narrative and its thematic features; but to place this in a theoretical frame, we need probably to accept Walter Benjamin's premise that "a translation issues from the original – not so much from its life as from its afterlife."[10] This articulation offers a venue for the argument of this chapter: No hostile textual dynasty can ever exist without this empowering afterlife as enjoyed by Galland's version. Hence the issue of an original loses ground as long as this afterlife entails

[6] See, in particular, MacDonald, "A Bibliographical and Literary Study"; also his "On Translating the Arabian Nights," *The Nation* 71, no. 6 (August 1900), 167–68, 185–86; Knipp, "The *Arabian Nights* in England"; al-Musawi, *Scheherazade in England*; and Irwin, *Arabian Nights*.

[7] Hunt, "New Translations," 110–11. Also cited in al-Musawi, *Scheherazade in England*, 45.

[8] Borges, "The Translators," 92. [9] Ibid., 93.

[10] Walter Benjamin, "The Task of the Translator," in *Illuminations: Essays and Reflections*, trans. Harry Zohn (New York: Schocken Books, 1968), 71.

a process of transformation and metamorphosis as argued by Benjamin. Every translational effort has something of this afterlife, and all translations are also further transformations of an original. Is there anyone in this chain of translators who has not sustained this afterlife, its diversified routes in reaching the reading public? In Freudian terms, applied by Harold Bloom in *The Anxiety of Influence* (1973) and *A Map of Misreading* (1975), there is an enormous anxiety that distinguishes this dynasty. In this case, however, there is more than the repression that Bloom traces among poets. The massive reception of *A Thousand and One Nights*, or *Arabian Nights' Entertainments*, has been generating, and still does, literary and cultural distinction in national and world literatures. This distinction is not only symbolic, but also financial, as the art of production, binding, and illustration shows, a point that I will discuss in due course.

In other words, there are many reasons behind this anxiety, unease, and hostility, but, no matter how the hostile dynasty argues against Galland's, this translation "is the one charged with the special mission of watching over the maturing process of the original language and the birth pangs of its own."[11] The dearth of information on an "original" text for *Alf laylah wa-laylah* (*A Thousand and One Nights*),[12] before the late fourteenth or early fifteenth-century manuscript that Galland received from Damascus and supplemented with a number of tales (that include Ali Baba and Aladdin), constricts authentication possibilities. Hence, our original is no other than Galland's manuscript. Its *afterlife* began in 1704, due to a number of factors that my earlier study, *Scheherazade in England* (1981), attempted to identify. Both the reception given to this version and the enormous number of imitations, pseudo-translations, and subsequent recognized translations attest to this *afterlife*. Nobody made any discovery of an earlier manuscript than Galland's, not only because some supplementary tales were either narrated or written down by the Syrian Maronite, Ḥannā Diyāb, or simply improved on by Galland, but also because of the nature of the compilation, its evolutionary growth that probably helped in its translatability. Galland's *Contes Arabes* had already won him a readership, even before including Diyāb's tales (1709).[13] Benjamin conceives of translation as a "mode," meaning that "a specific significance inherent in the original manifests itself

[11] Ibid., 73. [12] Abbott, "A Ninth-Century Fragment."

[13] For a well-edited edition in Arabic of Galland's diaries, see Muḥammad Muṣṭafā al-Jārūsh and Ṣafā᾽ Abū Shahlā Jibrān, eds., *Min Ḥalab ilā Bārīs* (Beirut/Baghdad: al-Kamel Verlag, 2017), 408–74. As noticed by Christiane Damien, Galland's manuscript ended abruptly in night 282; which Galland translated in 1704–6. By 1709, he became acquainted with Ḥannā Diyāb, starting probably with Aladdin as a written text by Diyāb. See ibid., 477–78. For more, see Horta, *Marvellous Thieves*, 33–35, 83–85.

in its translatability."[14] As he further contends, the question of fidelity is still contentious: Does Galland's version "reflect the great longing for linguistic complementation"? Is it "transparent"? That is, "it does not cover the original, does not block its light, but allows the pure language, as though reinforced by its own medium, to shine upon the original all the more fully."[15] Does Galland's translation "lovingly and in detail incorporate the original's mode of signification, thus making both the original and the translation recognizable as fragments of a greater language, just as fragments are part of a vessel"?[16]

The Authentication Mania

Especially in the English-speaking world, where the tales have been drawing wide readership, the struggle for "authentication" has turned into mania. While some suspected that the Grub Street (1705–6) translation might lack definitive fidelity to Galland's version, others were hard pressed to find an alternative to his version, even if that meant a collected one from late eighteenth-century Egypt or other places.[17] A few translations done at the turn of the eighteenth century are worth mentioning. The Rev. Edward Forster did his translation in five volumes in 1802 (London: Miller), with an extensive preface, which G. Moir Bussey expanded in "an explanatory and historical introduction" in 1839. He also "revised and corrected" Forster's.[18]Richard Gough translated and edited Galland's French edition in four volumes in 1798 (London: Longman). William Beloe had three volumes *of Arabian Tales; or, A Continuation of the Arabian Nights* (London: Faulder, 1794). D. B. MacDonald paid special attention to Edward Finter's translation of the *Arabian Nights' Entertainments*, translated into English from the Arabic with a new collection of tales, in five volumes (1810).[19] The claim to surpass the Grub Street translation into English or to improve on Galland's French edition were rampant, but they indicate a philological turn among a new class of scholars who claim intimate knowledge of Arab culture. More visible are other efforts like Jonathan Scott's (1811) retranslation of Galland's, alongside his unique translation of the Wortley Montague manuscript;[20] Henry Torrens's translation of the first fifty nights from Calcutta II (1838); Edward William Lane's translation

[14] Benjamin, "The Task of the Translator," 71. [15] Ibid., 79. [16] Ibid., 78.
[17] To understand references to "originals" or Arabic manuscripts the following information might be useful: Calcutta I is the Shirwanee edition of two volumes, 1814–18; Bulaq edition named after its press in Cairo has two volumes, 1835; Breslau edition has eight volumes, 1825–38; Calcutta II is W. H. Macnaghten edition of four volumes, 1839–42.
[18] For more, see al-Musawi, *Scheherazade in England*, 151.
[19] See my note in ibid., 152. [20] This manuscript is at the Bodleian Library, Oxford.

(1838, in thirty-two parts, and in 1839–41, in three volumes; from the Bulaq edition as cross-checked against Calcutta I and Breslau); and John Payne's *The Book of the Thousand Nights and One Night* (1882–84), which became the base for Richard F. Burton's translation, *The Book of the Thousand Nights and a Night* (1885–88). Burton used Payne's version extensively throughout volumes 2–10, and 1–3 *Supplemental Nights*.[21] Payne's translation was and still is a literary piece that sets another afterlife for the *Arabian Nights*, that of literary textuality. Payne's and Burton's friendship and Payne's focus on his own aesthetic concerns helped in the realization of Burton's unique transaction that simultaneously confirms and deviates from the hostile dynasty.

To understand this recognition outside the context of Burton's combativeness, we have to reflect on the more complicated relationship with Lane. When addressing what he calls "restorative citation of antecedent authority," Edward Said argues how this "citationary way" operates in Burton's dealing with Lane's *Arabian Nights*. Indirection means "citing his predecessor, challenging him even though he was granting him very great authority."[22] Payne's study that accompanied the *Nights* is no less important, not only because it gave Burton a lead to counterbalance Lane's copious notes on manners and customs in Egypt and thence to produce an important "Terminal Essay," but also because Payne helped in setting the stage for the double role of the translator as scholar and critic. With Lane, Payne, and Burton, a solid tradition is established to conceptualize an Orient as a field of study, a space for a Romanticized projection or ethnographic and anthropological reproduction. In all cases, the empire looms large as the purveyor, custodian, and the power in charge: as it claims resurrection of dead regions and languages, and resuscitation of cultures. Throughout, the translator and philologist have a part to play, even if it were a personal whim, as the case was in Payne's refined translation, a characteristic of which Burton made full use.

Incitement to Undo Expurgation?

The significance of Burton's *The Book of the Thousand Nights and a Night* (1885–88), for this reading, stems from its comprehensive coverage of

[21] For more on this point, see Thomas Wright, *The Life of Sir Richard F. Burton* (London: Everett, 1906); and Thomas Wright, *The Life of John Payne* (London: T. F. Unwin, 1919). See also Wiebke Walther, *Tausend und eine Nacht* (Munich and Zurich: Verlag, 1989).

[22] Said, *Orientalism*, 176.

tales that were in Macnaghten or Calcutta II and others that happened to circulate in the first half of the nineteenth century, along with Galland's additions. But, this significance also derives from the enormous anthropological apparatus, and the archaic style and the revelry in erotica. No less important is his thorough subjective reading of his predecessors and contemporaries in the "Terminal Essay" (vol. 10) and "The Biography of the Book and Its Reviewers Reviewed" (vol. 6, *Supplemental Nights*). If we ever think of the evolution of the term "expurgated" or "unexpurgated" since Lane's Victorian edition, it has definitely gained currency because of Burton's project and Lady Burton's later attempt to calm down the storm caused by that private edition by reproducing a trimmed version of her husband's translation. Her project was also commercially driven because she offered the new edition to the market and to the drawing room readership that might have been repelled by rumors about her husband's privately circulated version. In the second half of the nineteenth century, and especially in Burton's "Biography of the Book and Its Reviewers Reviewed," a battle over the body of the *Nights* was unleashed between bourgeois ethics of propriety and decorum as preserved in Lane's edition of the most popular book and opponents who revolted against conformity as shown in Burton's edition and soon in the French version of J. C. Mardrus. Lane's edition was claimed by pro-Burton reviewers as the reason for this incitement to speak out, overloading the *Nights* with everything that can present an uninhibited Orient, and Arab culture, that serves the projections of a generation of translators and editors against a restrictive metropolitan one. The *Nights* has become a bedrock for transgression. Every other translation venture, even Mardrus's version of 1899 (*Le livre des mille nuits et une nuit*) with its unsubstantiated claims to a Tunisian manuscript lineage,[23] translated into English in 1923 by Edward Powys Mathers,[24] has to take into account every other translation, and also such compilations as Bulaq, Calcutta II, and Breslau. Most probably Mardrus found Burton's copious notes necessary to expand on scenes of pleasure that won him the favor of such prominent figures like Andre Gide and Proust.[25] Mia Gerhardt

[23] J. C. Mardrus, *Le livre des mille nuits et une nuit* (Paris: Fasquelle, 1899).

[24] Edward Powys Mathers, trans., *The Book of the Thousand Nights and One Night: Rendered from the Literal and Complete Version of Dr. J. C. Mardrus; and Collated with Other Sources*, 8 vols. (London: The Casanova Society, 1923).

[25] David Steele, "Galland and Mardrus: André Gide's reading of The Arabian Nights," in *La Réception mondiale et transdisciplinaire des Mille et une Nuits* (Medievales 51), ed. Waël Rabadi and Isabelle Bernar (Amiens: Presses du Centre d'Études Médiévales, 2012), 336–56; Évanghélia Stead, "Joseph-Charles Mardrus: Les Riches Heures D'un Livre-Monument," *Francofonia* 69 (2015), 105–25; on Burton and Mardrus, 109. The first-rate bibliographer Aboubakr Chraïbi (email, April 24, 2020), provided me with the

makes this comment with respect to the edition: "it has no affinity whatever with the '1001 Nights,' but all the more with the boulevard literature of Paris 1900s." She adds: "[H]e diffused among the public a distorted and oversexed image of the book he pretended to translate."[26] But, apart from his "lack of regard for the original text," Gerhardt credits Mardrus with a better handling of poetry, though in a way that "happens to suit him." She agrees that he has some "spirited, swift moving pages," even when he "indulges in the affected and cloying prose-style of his day."[27] Enno Littmann published a six-volume translation into German in 1921–28. Primarily based on Calcutta II, this celebrated translation offered the *Nights* in full with its poetry and lewd passages, though those parts are Latinized. The act of distancing lewdness using an archaic medium presents a unique case between fidelity and evasion.

The earliest translations from Galland are worth discussion for a number of reasons. They show an expanding reading public that, in due time, would become the source for state management and imperial undertaking. In England, France, and somehow the Netherlands, the interest in the Arab East was never smooth or transparent. Translation was part of a political/commercial penchant, an interest in lands that the *Nights* presents as bountiful. The translator appears as the self-styled epic hero, destined to resurrect a dead manuscript, and hence self-authorized to edit as befitting a cultural script of which he is a part. Benjamin does not elaborate on the multiple roles of translation, but he does make a suggestion with respect to bringing the local flavor of an original/target

following notes to suggest Mardrus's use of Burton's edition. He wrote: "About Mardrus and Burton, there are at least three connections:

- The title of Burton was *The Book of the Thousand Nights and One Night* . . . And Mardrus did the same: first 3 vol. (1899–1900) *Les Mille nuits et une nuit,* and vol. 4 to 16 (1900–1904), he used the title : *Le livre des Mille nuits et une nuit*, exactly as Burton
- The eroticization of the text
- Most important perhaps : Mardrus used 4 stories from the Wortley Montague manuscript which were translated into English only by Scott and ... Burton (see Sylvette Larzul, *Les traductions françaises des Mille et une nuits* . . ., L'Harmattan, Paris, 1996, p. 148). Chauvin said that Mardrus used Scott, as we can read in Larzul, but no one compared . . . Mardrus to Burton . . .

These stories are: L'histoire compliquée de l'adultérin sympathique, Chauvin n° 439.
And, inside the 'Diwan des faciles facéties et de la gaie sagesse':
Les aiguillettes nouées, Chauvin n° 146
Les deux preneurs de haschisch, Chauvin n° 279
Le kadi père-au-pet, Chauvin n° 107"
Victor Chauvin, *Bibliographie des ouvrages arabes,* Vols. 5 to 7 for the *Nights* are on archive .org and Chauvin gives the references for Scott and Burton and Wortley Montague manuscript.

[26] Gerhardt, *Art of Story-Telling*, 103. [27] Ibid., 104.

to the translator's own language. In "The Task of the Translator," he borrows from Rudolf Pannwitz the latter's articulation of "the laws of fidelity in the freedom of linguistic flux."[28] Pannwitz argues that "[t]he basic error of the translator is that he preserves the state in which his own language happens to be instead of allowing his language to be powerfully affected by the foreign tongue." He further explains, "Particularly when translating from a language very remote from his own, he must go back to the primal elements of language itself and penetrate to the point where work, image, and tone converge."[29] Moreover: "He must expand and deepen his language by means of the foreign language."[30] If we are to use Pannwitz's criterion, then Galland, Lane, Burton, and a number of other translators have something of the original in their translation. Along with some formulaic openings, conversations often bear the stamp of the original. Galland might fail the test because of a heavy French dose in matters of "decorum." Thus, Sir Walter Scott (d. 1832) stressed Galland's French climate. In the "Dedicatory Epistle" to *Ivanhoe*, he agreed that *Contes Arabes* were less "purely Oriental in their first concoction," but were "eminently better fitted for the European market, and obtained an unrivalled degree of public favor which they certainly would never have gained had not the manners and style been in some degree familiarized to the feelings and habits of the Western reader."[31] More importantly, it is this very debate about Galland's version that generated, even before Lane's, a series of partial translations or reeditions. As alluded to earlier, Beloe translated some additional tales in *Miscellanies* (1795), while Gough issued a "valuable" edition of 1798, and Forster decided to translate from the French (1802). However, G. S. Beaumont retranslated Galland (1811, 1814, 1817). Scott's *Tales, Anecdotes and Letters* (1800) and *Arabian Nights' Entertainments* (1811) followed soon after.[32] These works did not mark the end for this

[28] Benjamin, "The Task of the Translator," 80. [29] Cited in ibid., 81. [30] Ibid.

[31] Cited from Scott's "Dedicatory Epistle," in al-Musawi, *Scheherazade in England*, 13.

[32] In Burton's "Terminal Essay," Part 8, there is the following note on Jonathan Scott's project:

> In 1811, Scott published an edition of the Arabian Nights' Entertainments, in six vols., Vol. 1 containing a long introduction, and Vol. 6, including a series of new tales from the Oxford MS. (There is a small paper edition, and also a large paper edition, the latter with frontispieces, and an appendix including a table of the tales contained in the manuscript.) It had originally been Scott's intention to retranslate the manuscript, but he appears to have found it beyond his powers. He therefore contented himself with reediting Galland, altering little except the spelling of the names, and saying that Galland's version is in the main so correct that it would be useless repetition to go over the work afresh. Although he says that he found many of the tales both immoral and puerile, he translated most of those near the beginning, and omitted much more (including several harmless and interesting tales, such as No. 152) toward the end of his manuscript than near the

genealogy that Galland had set in motion: Henry Weber published *Tales of the East* (1812), the Rev. George Lamb translated Joseph von Hammer's version (1826), and in 1838 Torrens published the first volume of the unexpurgated *Nights* in Calcutta.[33] All these versions and editions demonstrate some anxiety, but they also testify to the popularity of the *Nights* and the wish to be part of a thriving culture industry. By contrast, the hostile dynasty is not necessarily restricted to the known versions or translations that happened to capture attention. The ones just mentioned, as well as the innumerable others that claimed authenticity, had their audiences. Their fault was their untimeliness and incompleteness. Notwithstanding Torrens's termination of his important project to continue translating an unexpurgated version in 1838 after learning about Lane's, the issue of timely translations remains pivotal, both before and as it is now.

The Explosive Transactional Enterprise

Uncertainties and anxieties between Galland's sweeping success and his textual descendants before Lane happened to take place at a time when France, England, and somehow Germany were undergoing transformations politically, socially, and industrially. Even so, a word on Galland's version is still overdue. Apart from availing himself of some nights, giving names to the ladies in the story of "The Porter and Three Ladies of Baghdad," giving up on formulaic openings, and "abandoning the lean structure of the original,"[34] along with tampering with the bath scene in "The Porter and Three Ladies of Baghdad," and the omission of poetry that he thought irrelevant to a flowing narrative, he was as faithful as possible to his manuscript (Appendix A). Scott found it so in justifying his reluctance to produce a new translation.[35] An example of Galland's letting the original "deepen his language" is the anecdote that drove him to do away with the sister's call on Scheherazade to start the narrative. The anecdote, mentioned by von Hammer, and cited in *Scheherazade in England*,[36] works both ways, and it certainly offers something worth

beginning. The greater part of Scott's additional tales, published in Vol. 6, are included in the composite French and German editions of Gauttier and Habicht; but, except Nos. 208, 209, and 215, republished in my "New Arabian Nights," they have not been reprinted in England, being omitted in all the many popular versions that are professedly based upon Scott, even in the edition in four vols., published in 1882, which reprints Scott's preface.

[33] For more, see ibid., 42. [34] See Mahdi, *The Thousand and One Nights*, 39, 44–49.

[35] Burton, "Terminal Essay," vol. 10.

[36] "Galland was so responsive to his audience that he dispensed with the original introductory note to each tale, after some Parisians had made fun of it. 'The Parisians, returning

considering regarding the vagaries of translation and the "task of translator." Held between a desire to "deepen" the French and a counter one to stay bound to it, Galland sets the scene for a number of trends in the translational zone, including the *querelle du roman feuilleton*. The thrice-weekly *London News* began serializing the *Arabian Nights' Entertainments* on January 6, 1723, in 445 instalments over a period of three years. Before that, the Churchman's *Last Shift* serialized "The Voyages of Sindbad the Sailor" in weekly parts in 1720, followed by another extract from the *Nights*. Many other weeklies did the same to win over more readers. Galland's version never lost its hold. Payne, the poet and eminent translator of the *Arabian Nights*, wrote to the *New Quarterly Magazine* of January 1879:

> Indeed, it seems to me that this first effort, imperfect as it was, to *transplant* into European gardens the magic flowers of oriental imagination, can never entirely be supplanted, and that other workers in the *field* can only hope to *supplement* and not to *efface* it.[37]

The careful wording highlights a number of things: It builds on the "garden" analogy that was popular in eighteenth-century criticism and acquired more impetus in Richard Johnson's (Rev. Mr. Cooper's) *The Oriental Moralist*.[38] The *Nights* is a transplant; and all translations and editions struggle to habituate this version, to "supplement and not efface it." Payne overviews the whole endeavor as a *field* of knowledge, and not as single efforts by individual translators.

You need to be a Lane to hit the Victorian taste for a drawing room version, an annotated one that could also meet the needs for "useful knowledge," which was celebrated in a metropolitan culture. To place him within Benjamin's "tasking" properties, Lane would fail because of his authorial imposition on a script, his enormous omissions, and heavy scriptural lexicon.[39] Burton was to take into account the translations by Galland and Lane. He was at peace with Payne, not only because he was to make a very substantial use of Payne's translation (1882–84), but also because Payne wrote in the style of his age, a highly aesthetic turn with a heavy dose of Pre-Raphaelite poetics. This did not escape the attention

from their nocturnal revels,' said Jos. Von Hammer, relating an anecdote originally reported by Michaud, 'would often stop before his door, and awake him from his soundest sleep, by calling loudly for him. Galland would open his window, to see what was the matter, and they would cry out: "0 vous, qui savez de si jolis contes, et qui les racontez si bien [, racontez nous en un!"'" See al-Musawi, *Scheherazade in England*, 13.

37 Cited in ibid., 77 (italics added).

38 See al-Musawi, "The Arabian Nights"; and Mack, "Cultivating the Garden," 51–81.

39 For a detailed study of Lane's translation and consequent critical response, see chapters 4–5 in al-Musawi, *Scheherazade in England.*

of the devoted scholar of *A Thousand and One Nights* MacDonald, who saw how it partook of the "richness and strangeness of Wardour Street furniture and of medieval tapestries."[40] Other cultures have similar hostile dynasties; otherwise, how can we explain retranslations? Are they not driven by a number of factors, including a grievance against a predecessor, a desire to prove some literary merit when empires invested in translation from other cultures? Moreover, the new ventures had the market in mind. Publishers and authors worked together in meeting the increasing demand for "unexpurgated" editions. The search for authentication and complete editions corresponds to what Foucault defines for other histories as "a regulated and polymorphous incitement to discourse."[41]

To Familiarize or Exoticize?

In more than one sense, the history of the *Arabian Nights* in European cultures sums up both the history of empires and the East/West dichotomy. Beginning in 1704 with Galland's two volumes of *Les Mille et Une nuit, Contes Arabes*, and concluding the twelfth in 1717 as translation and appropriation of the available twenty-one cycles of tales with their Arabic core of nine,[42] Scheherazade's *Arabian Nights' Entertainments*[43] as it was inscribed in its English Grub Street translation (1705–6) underwent adaptation to meet the receiving milieu, its expectations, needs, and habits of reading.[44] As I argued in *Scheherazade in England* (1981),

[40] MacDonald, "On Translating the Arabian Nights," 168.

[41] Michel Foucault, "The Repressive Hypothesis," in *The History of Sexuality*, trans. Robert Hurley (New York: Random House, 1990), 1:34.

[42] For details, see H. Zotenberg, *Histoire de 'Alā' al-Dīn, avec Notice sur quelques manuscrits des Mille et une nuits et la traduction de Galland* (Paris 1888), which contains the Arabic text along with a study of certain MSS. See also Chauvin, *Bibliographie des ouvrages arabe*, vol. 4; and MacDonald, "A Bibliographical and Literary Study." Confusion of dates insofar as Galland's version is concerned continued, and Jorge Luis Borges wrote in 1934–36: "Twelve exquisite volumes appeared from 1707 to 1717, twelve volumes that were innumerably read and that passed into various languages, including Hindi and Arabic." See Borges, "The Translators."

[43] See al-Musawi, *Scheherazade in England*, 3, 33n3.

[44] Let me mention in passing that my argument for translations as appropriations and for the *Nights* as a mirror of taste was and has been widely accepted since 1981. Taking over editorial responsibility after the late Allan Grant, the brilliant scholar and intellectual Peter L. Caracciolo apologized in writing for not being fully aware of my contribution. See Peter L. Caracciolo, ed., *The Arabian Nights in English Literature: Studies in the Reception of the Thousand and One Nights into British Culture* (New York: St. Martin's Press, 1993). See also Nancy Victoria Workman, "Reviewed Work: *The 'Arabian Nights' in English Literature: Studies in the Reception of 'The Thousand and One Nights' into British Culture* by Peter L. Caracciolo," *Victorian Studies* 33 (Spring 1990), 521; and Mohammad Shaheen's book review, "The *Arabian Nights* in English Literature," *The Yearbook of English Studies* 22 (1992), 312.

Galland's version proved popular for taking into account those very habits and predilections. While preserving the outlandish, Galland made the East an available property to be both possessed and criticized, accommodated and plundered. However, it is to the credit of Galland that his translation elicited and still elicits contradictory responses with respect to issues of exactitude or faithfulness. Robert Irwin collapses previous views, suggesting that it was done in the vein and temper of other French humanists who "argued that good taste took precedence over strict accuracy in translation," for Galland's "aim in translating the *Nights* was not so much to transcribe accurately the real texture of medieval Arab prose, as to rescue from it items which he judged would please the salons of eighteenth-century France."[45] However, ahead of him and much in tune with Burton's "Terminal Essay," but with Borges's gusto, the latter wrote in 1934–36: "Word for word, Galland's version is the most poorly written of them all, the least faithful, and the weakest, but it was the most widely read."[46] He adds, "Galland's discretions are urbane, inspired by decorum, not morality."[47] Although there remains a great deal of the mysterious and veiled, Galland's East was made available to be analyzed, investigated, enjoyed, loved, and, simultaneously, repelled. In a reflection on Littmann's observation that *A Thousand and One Nights* is "above all, a repertory of marvels," Borges comments that the "Universal imposition of this assumption on every western mind is Galland's work; let there be no doubt on that score."[48] While foreshadowing the Enlightenment's taste for classification and comparison, Galland's version evidently met the Romantic aspiration for freedom and change. Unchallenged for a long time, his French compatriots were later to work with Galland's text, adding to or updating it, but never superseding it. An acclaimed Arabist like Caussin de Perceval edited and supplemented Galland's with more volumes in 1806. The same situation would distinguish Edouard Gauttier's venture, whose supplementation and use of other available redactions brought to the French literary scene in 1822–25 an input that was concomitant with trendy redactions.

In both cases, then, Galland's *Nights* was not alien to a dual tendency to study the Other, reach for its strangeness, exoticize it, and view it in relation to a so-called European tradition. It also fits well with a rising desire to appropriate its habitat and exercise a sense of self-fulfillment against imaginary failures. Both impulses were not at variance with that growing colonialist discourse that had never been absent since early missionary efforts to convert Muslims or to combat Islam. More importantly, both were bound to provoke philological, anthropological, and

[45] Irwin, *Arabian Nights*, 19. [46] Borges, "The Translators," 93. [47] Ibid.
[48] Ibid., 96.

cultural studies, which took the *Nights*, along with literary and travel accounts in translation, as their starting point in preparation for the expanding imperial enterprise. The effort was so enormous that Romantics of a sensitive temper, like Hunt, were seriously bothered by this disenchanting endeavor. They insisted, but to no avail, on keeping the *Nights* away from dissection and exacting scholarship, a collection of tales to offer an "Orient of Poets."[49]

The East of poets was no less tantalizing for being so "airy," beyond time and place. However, this Romanticized view of the East gave way to another, which framed it in an East of the past, but whose life presently is a repetition within dormancy, asking for a Napoleon, or, in the case of the British, a Cromer to revitalize the land and to draw the domains of Scheherazade back to civilization! Indeed, Scheherazade's attraction became synonymous with her habitats – rich, tantalizing, and waiting for the imperial savior. Lane's text provoked further response, interest, translations, and studies of Muslims and Arab communities. Upon its first appearance, it gave impetus to interests of different paths and agenda. Borges recounts the following upsurge in *Nightism* in a pre-Bloom anxiety of influence, for "Lane translated against Galland, Burton against Lane; and to understand Burton we must understand his hostile dynasty."[50] He, as early as 1934–36, looks upon the translation mania as no more than an attempt to beat the precursor: "To be different: this is the rule the precursor imposes: Lane will follow the rule: he needs only to abstain from abridging the original."[51]

Conditions of Possibility/Conditions of Intelligibility

The appearance of a translation and its passage through appropriations cannot be viewed as an aberrant happening; it responds to conditions of possibility within a certain climate of ideas that enable or direct that appearance. Its intrinsic quality, which is also that of a translator, is better off when possessing the marketable and transactional features. But there is yet more, something that Borges's reading of anxiety may not admit: a condition of possibility. While there may be idiosyncrasies and personal whims, there must have been reasons, before as they are now, that compel the translator to take a different path. Each translator answers to a milieu. This is why Borges qualifies an early statement:

[49] Leigh Hunt, The editorial to his *London Journal*, October 1834, and also my survey of his writing in *Scheherazade in England*, 46–48.

[50] Borges, "The Translators," 92. [51] Ibid., 95.

The original is not professionally obscene; Galland corrects occasional indelicacies because he believes them to be in bad taste. Lane seeks them out and persecutes them like an inquisitor: His probity makes no pact with silence: he prefers an alarmed chorus of notes in a cramped supplementary volume.[52]

When reflecting upon reasons, Borges endorses the milieu proposition: "One reason for this was that he destined his work for the 'parlor table,' a center for placid reading and chaste conversation."[53] While Burton's "Terminal Essay" attempts to vindicate his translation against all precursors, but also against his immediate ghost, Payne's translation (1882), Borges's reading draws a map of translation and mistranslation. Both are important to read against the "task of the translator." Every review of critical response or philological inquiry into origins has to take account of the "Terminal Essay." Surrounded by a group of scholars like W. F. Kirby (himself a translator of an 1882 select tales not included in Galland and Lane; and a compiler of a bibliography of the *Nights*), Burton formed a conversational workshop, a team, which is a significant sign in the genealogy of a book that its European originator, Galland, initiated with Paul Lucas, Diyāb, and others.[54] More than any translation, Burton's received so much vituperative or celebratory criticism that he was incited to write another long survey on the "biography of the book and its reviewers reviewed."[55] Predominantly focused on anthropological detail and somehow on stylistic peculiarities that attempt to bring into English the sense of an original text as probably vouchsafed in Benjamin's essay on translation, this criticism for or against Burton often falls short of accounting for such sublime passages in Burton's understanding of the *Nights*:

Viewed as a tout ensemble in full and complete form, they [the tales] are a drama of Eastern life, and a Dance of Death made sublime by faith and the highest emotions, by the certainty of expiation and the fullness of atoning equity, where virtue is victorious, vice is vanquished and the ways of Allah are justified to man. They are a panorama which remains kenspeckle upon the mental retina.[56]

Such a powerful statement, which I once placed as the paratext for a chapter, is to prove a challenge to scholarship ever since.[57] It encompasses in a nutshell themes, techne, and stylistic shades of meaning. Burton's contemporaneous translations, such as Mardrus's, have to add a dose to this understanding. The latter deliberately chose the full title *The*

[52] Ibid., 94. [53] Ibid.
[54] See Chapter 2, n8. For more on Paul Lucas, see Horta, *Marvellous Thieves*, 57–58, 77–79.
[55] Burton, "Biography of the Book." [56] Burton, "Terminal Essay," 139.
[57] See chapter 5, "A Panorama of Eastern Life," in al-Musawi, *Scheherazade in England*, 115.

Book of Thousand Nights and One Night (*Livre des mille nuits et une nuit*, 1899) to compete with Galland who eliminated the "original's repetition." However, Mardrus was only following MacNaghten with his *Book of the Thousand and One Nights* (1839), Payne with his *Book of the Thousand Nights and One Night*, and, finally Burton, with his *Book of the Thousand Nights and a Night.*[58] Nevertheless, no matter how hard Mardrus tried to use "rhymed prose and moral predictions," "it is his infidelity, his happy and creative infidelity," says Borges, "that must matter to us."[59] Otherwise, his version could have proved flat and placid. The difference between Gerhardt's dismissal and Borges's celebration of this infidelity is a difference between an exacting scholarship and a creative imagination.

While Galland's remained unchallenged in France for long, this was not the case in Germany. Four translations appeared in Germany, by Gustav Weil (1839–42), Max Henning in his "expurgated" edition (1895–97),[60] Felix Paul Greve (1912–13), and Littmann (1923–28).[61] Weil's edition signifies the rising tension in culture industry between translators and publishers. His German publisher authorized the editor and writer, August Lewald, to delete what was deemed offensive. Henning used "Bulaq and Breslau," along with "Zotenberg's manuscripts and Burton's *Supplemental Nights*."[62] Greve's is also one of Burton's descendants. Borges's assessment of Littmann is often fair, but, if he critiques him for something, it is the inexcusable commensurability with German. But, it is to Littmann's credit that he translates in the wake of unexpurgated renditions, and hence the "most ineffable obscenities do not give him pause; he renders them into his placid German, only rarely into Latin."[63] Littmann's translation has the advantage of common sense, and the style "is always lucid, readable, and mediocre."[64] The original is not an elegant classical Arabic, not in Galland's Arabic manuscript. Between the origination of this phenomenal rise in *Arabian Nightism*, and the claims to unexpurgated editions, there runs the in-between translation zone where a triangulation takes place. Von

[58] Ibid., 103. Mardrus's translation was celebrated among the same circles that subscribed to Burton's. See B. Bjersby, *Interpretation of the Cuchulain Legend in the Works of W.B. Yeats* (Upsala: Lundquist, 1950), 127n3.

[59] Borges, "The Translators," 106.

[60] Max Henning, trans., *Tausend und eine Nacht. Aus dem Arabischen übertragen*, 24 vols. (Leipzig: Reclam, 1895–99).

[61] Enno Littmann, trans., *Die Erzählungen aus den Tausendundein Nächten: Vollständige deutsche Ausgabe in zwölf Teilbänden zum ersten mal nach dem arabischen Urtext der Calcuttaer Ausgabe aus dem Jahre 1839 übertragen von Enno Littmann*, 6 vols. in 12 (Frankfurt: Insel Verlag, 1976).

[62] Borges, "The Translators," 107. [63] Ibid., 109. [64] Ibid.

Hammer was behind a real recension of tales not found in Galland's in his *Die noch nicht uebersetzten Erzaehlungen der Tausend und einen Nacht* (Stuttgart, 1823), which became Zotenberg's Egyptian Recension. Although von Hammer's French translation was lost, Zinserling (1823) translated them into German, and they made their way into English at the hands of Lamb (1826) and into French by Trebutien (1828).[65] The search for manuscripts turned into a mania, and affected scholars of high caliber like Sir William Jones, who obtained manuscript, portions of which were brought to light by John Richardson (1740/41–95) in his *Arabic Grammar* (1776; 2nd ed. London, 1801); whereas Joseph White's projected complete edition never materialized except for a specimen. The herpetologist, physician, and longtime resident of Aleppo Patrick Russell (1727–1805) bought a manuscript that he described in his *Natural History of Aleppo* (1794) and in his February 1799 long letter to *Gentleman's Magazine*.[66]

[65] G. S. Trébutien, trans., *Contes inédits des Mille et une Nuits*, extraits de l'original arabe par M. J. de Hammer, 3 vols. (Paris: Dondey-Dupré, 1828). Richard Burton emphasizes the importance of von Hammer's recension. In his "Terminal Essay," part 8, he explains:

> Several complete copies of The Nights were obtained by Europeans about the close of the last or the beginning of the present century; and one of these (in 4 vols.) fell into the bands of the great German Orientalist, Joseph von Hammer. This MS. agrees closely with the printed Bul. and Mac. texts, as well as with Dr. Clarke's MS., though the names of the tales sometimes vary a little. One story, "The two Wazirs," given in Von Hammer's list as inedited, no doubt by an oversight, is evidently No. 7, which bears a similar title in Torrens. One title, "Al Kavi," a story which Von Hammer says was published in "Mag. Encycl.," and in English (probably by Scott in Ouseley's *Oriental Collections*, vide antea p. 491) puzzled me for some time; but from its position, and the title I think I have identified it as No. 145, and have entered it as such. No. 9a in this as well as in several other MSS., bears the title of the Two Lovers, or of the Lover and the Beloved. Von Hammer made a French translation of the unpublished tales, which he lent to Caussin de Perceval, who extracted from it four tales only (Nos. 21a, 22, 32 and 37), and only acknowledged his obligations in a general way to a distinguished Orientalist, whose name he pointedly suppressed. Von Hammer, naturally indignant, reclaimed his MS., and had it translated into German by Zinserling. He then sent the French MS. to De Sacy, in whose hands it remained for some time, although he does not appear to have made any use of it, when it was dispatched to England for publication; but the courier lost it on the journey, and it was never recovered. Zinserling's translation was published under the title, "Der Tausend und einen Nacht noch nicht uebersetzte Maehrchen, Erzaehlungen und Anekdoten, zum erstenmale aus dem Arabischen in's Franzoesische uebersetzt von Joseph von Hammer, und aus dem Franzoesischen in's Deutsche von Aug. E. Zinserling." (3 vols., Stuttgart and Tuebingen, 1823.) The introductory matter is of considerable importance, and includes notices of 12 different MSS., and a list of contents of Von Hammer's MS.

[66] D. B. MacDonald, "Alf laila wa-laila," *The Encyclopedia of Islam*, supplement (Leiden: Brill, 1938), 12. See also al-Musawi, *Scheherazade in England*, 28.

Arabists, Orientalists, and Philologists

These specimens and projected translations, along with those of Scott and Forster, are important for at least two reasons. In the first place, they indicate a rising tide for British-oriented translation to satisfy the demands of a consumer society in an expanding empire. In that respect, British Arabists and Orientalists were competing with French philologists, and the battle adopted the *Arabian Nights* as the testing ground and fulfilling achievement. Whether for or against Galland, in this hostile dynasty the conversation was not an ordinary one. Richardson for one argues that, "the deviation from the original [in Galland's version] is greater than even a free translation seemed to require."[67] The second reason relates to what MacDonald suggests, namely, that Russell's manuscript led "naturally to the first attempt at an edition of the Nights in Arabic," as shown in the derivative Calcutta I edition of "the first 200 Nights" in 1814, which derived in part from L. Langles's *Les Voyages* (1813).[68] Maximilian Habicht's Breslau edition (1825–38), which was "continued by Fleischer," was behind a new genealogy, that of "a new recension" that bewildered specialists.[69] Does this relate to the hostile dynasty? Does Habicht's version matter in the same manner as Mardrus's, for example? It does because it was also behind other amalgamated editions, hybrid texts, and intertextualities.

Habicht's version (1825; Galland's, supplemented from Caussin, Gauttier,[70] Scott, and from a disputed Tunisian MS) is a challenge to this hostile dynasty. In MacDonald's "A Preliminary Classification of Some MSS of the *Arabian Nights*,"[71] it was a "literary myth and enormously confused the history of the *Nights*." Being a fabricated collection of a number of renditions, it falls outside the center of this hostile dynasty; but its claim to be so is obviously driven by the mania for authentication accelerated by the culture industry. Another reason could be Habicht's ambition to be at the center of a literary movement where there was no lack of eccentrics. However, its very defects as "vulgar" and not

67 Cited in al-Musawi, *Scheherazade in England*, 28.

68 MacDonald, "Alf laila wa-laila," 12.

69 Ibid. Max Habicht, Fr. H. von der Hagen, and Carl Schall, *Tausend und Eine Nacht*, Arabische Erzählungen, 1824–25, 12 vols., ed. Karl Martin Schiller (Leipzig: F. W. Hendel, 1926). See also Max Henning, trans., *Tausend und eine Nacht. 1895–99*, ed. Hans W. Fischer (Berlin and Darmstadt: Deutsche Buch-Gemeinschaft, 1957).

70 Edouard Gauttier, trans., *Les Mille et Une Nuit, contes arabes, traduits en français par Galland. Nouvelle édition revue ... avec les continuations et plusieurs contes, traduits pour la première fois du persan, du turc et de l'arabe*, 7 vols. (Paris: Société de traduction, 1822–23).

71 *Journal of the Royal Asiatic Society* (1909), 685–704.

"grammatically and lexicographically 'improved' by learned shaiks" make it closer to storytelling.

While lagging behind the main core of French–English–German production, other cultures either abridged or translated the previously mentioned major editions, and occasionally were able to come up with local manuscripts. Such was Mikhail Salye's translation into Russian from Calcutta II in eight volumes (1929–39), supplemented with tales from a manuscript in the National Library of Russia. Much earlier was Alexey Filatyev's translation from Galland's in 1763–74, followed by Yulia Doppelmayr's (1889–90) version that also uses Galland's. Lyudmila Shelgunova's (1894) translation reverts to Lane, while another anonymous translation (1902–3) relied on Mardrus. It was only in the second half of the nineteenth century that other cultures made use of the available major editions, as shown in Appendix B. Does the "hostile dynasty" apply in this case? It does so only within their immediate cultural milieu. The Russian example shows how each translator has something different either in supplementation or in alignment with one of the major editions. Taken together as a movement that surged in activity in the late eighteenth and early nineteenth centuries, it cannot be seen outside conditions of possibility and intelligibility. The surge in authentication, translation, rewriting, and supplementation signifies an epistemic stage in the history of cultural production, especially when seen in relation to the division of labor in culture, the rise of social science, and the focus on literariness as an empowering domain in the colonialist enterprise.

Whose Translation?

In matters of translation, and the search for a definitive text, we have to concede the impossibility of such a goal. In MacDonald's words, the "whole subject, for lack of a definite basis and a Vulgate text, was involved in uncertainty and semi-fraud."[72] When it comes to prioritizing translations, the matter of a reliable manuscript is ridden with confusion. We end up with Galland's manuscript as the oldest extant version, and with our understanding of him as the most capable of bringing forth the art of storytelling in the culture of Paris and Versailles. Echoing Galland's admirers throughout two centuries, MacDonald adds: "He was a born story-teller; he had a flair for a good story and a knack to re-tell it well."[73] His descendants have to cope with the art of retelling in print, visual industry, and virtual space. The matter is not related to an extant manuscript, and the merits or deficiencies of a first translation, which this

[72] MacDonald, "Alf laila wa-laila," 10–11. [73] Ibid., 10.

chapter and the next discuss, but to the properties of a produced text. How does it relate to a canon? Does it initiate a canon? Or is it superseded by another and hence displaced? When read in context of its massive appeal and popularity, and its reaching into the depths of souls and minds, the *Nights* assumes larger impact than any other single book, exempting probably the Bible. Hence, we can argue that each new translation is an act of displacing a predecessor. This dynastic usurpation of power is as applicable to texts as to kingdoms. Each translation speaks to an audience because of its specific properties. Even when applauding Galland for being the first in this hostile dynasty, later editors, redactors, and translators situate him within a specific context, and often in association with a dawn of enchantment. As Burton argues in Part II of his "Terminal Essay":

> we must not forget that it is wholly and solely to the genius of the Gaul that Europe owes "The Arabian Nights' Entertainments" over which Western childhood and youth have spent so many spelling hours. Antoine Galland was the first to discover the marvelous fund of material for the story-teller buried in the Oriental mine; and he had in a high degree that art of telling a tale which is far more captivating than culture or scholarship.

Burton was not the first to recognize this pioneering role, nor was he the first to address Galland's knack for storytelling: Hunt and other nineteenth-century writers were no less drawn to this art.[74]

However, the properties of each translation or redaction differ. For translations, we need not only account for semiotics, styles, and narrative patterns in translations or editorial appropriations as indices of a taste that is impacted in turn by this culture industry, but also consider them in terms of methods and means of manipulation in science fiction, the film industry, and educational programs. Moreover, they often come accompanied with illustrations for a purpose, as shown in the following text. Visual culture, print, and illustration set the road away from storytelling. Hence, to follow up on dynastic genealogies, it is tenable, perhaps, to reinstate that as the *Arabian Nights* tales herald and hence anticipate current artificial intelligence experimentations, and electronic achievements, so do "open sesame" and its like in the tales seem to materialize and open further venues for the human imagination. Translators intervene in these as much as in ethnographic and anthropological spaces to appropriate the text and reproduce it as a fashionable entity. No matter how scholarly and committed to the field the ongoing translation, redaction, or reprint industry is, it signifies a stage in postindustrial global cultures that reflect on and make use of this legacy in their own ways.

[74] See al-Musawi, *Scheherazade in England*, 81–83.

A survey of translations worldwide will tell us that cultures come upon specific translations in certain times. This also applies to individual writers. Borges read the available translations and discussed them, but he specified Lane's in his veiled autobiographical sketch.[75]

The renowned traveler, anthropologist, translator, and critic Burton (1821–90) was not primarily concerned with establishing a genealogy of the *Arabian Nights* and its linguistic transformations in translation, nor was MacDonald, whose massive philological inquiry into the first appearance of the *Thousand and One Nights* was unmatched in its time.[76] Like Payne (1842–1916) in his informative reading of the "history and character" of *A Thousand and One Nights*,[77] Burton's "Terminal Essay" and "Biography of the Book"[78] deal not only with reviewers of his translation, but also with translators and translations, along with extensive remarks on a cultural "anthropology."[79] But his towering figure overwhelms the scene, and we are confronted with a spirit rebelling against Victorian prudery and squeamishness, probably exemplified by Lane's Victorian translation of 1838–40. Burton's role as translator, editor, anthropologist, ethnographer, erudite scholar, and a disenchanted pillar of a cultural empire cannot be overestimated. His voluminous work in its unexpurgated edition, and also Lady Burton's version, went through abridgments and one-volume editions. He also collects tales that escaped the attention of many preceding redactors and accretes. In other words, he draws attention once more, and quite vigorously, to *A Thousand and One Nights* as no less of a British property than any other mandated or colonized region. Likewise, was not Mardrus's endeavor a marker in a rising colonial French venture?[80] It is "the most readable of them all," writes

[75] See "The Double," in Borges, *Collected Fictions*, 412.

[76] See D. B. MacDonald, "Lost Manuscripts of the 'Arabian Nights' and a Projected Edition of That of Galland," *Journal of the Royal Asiatic Society* (1911), 219–21; D. B. MacDonald, "A Missing MS of the Arabian Nights," *Journal of the Royal Asiatic Society* (1913), 432; and D. B. MacDonald, "A Preliminary Classification of Some MSS of the Arabian Nights," in *A Volume of Oriental Studies, Presented to E. G. Brown on His 60th Birthday*, ed. T. W. Arnold and R. A. Nicholson (Cambridge: Cambridge University Press, 1922), 304–21; and MacDonald, "A Bibliographical and Literary Study."

[77] On Payne, see Chapter 1, n99. He also published a translation of *Alaeddin and the Enchanted Lamp and Other Stories* (London 1901) where he prefaces this with a historical sketch of Galland's encounter with the Syrian Maronite "Hanna" in 1709. Payne also mentioned the existence at the Bibliothèque Nationale of two manuscripts containing Aladdin and two tales that were included in Galland's version.

[78] Richard F. Burton, *Supplemental Nights to the Book of the Thousand Nights and a Night*, 6 vols. (London: Burton Club Edition, 1886–88). These complement his *Plain and Literal Translation*.

[79] Burton, "Biography of the Book."

[80] For some bibliographic listing and comparative quotes from different translations, see http://journalofthenights.blogspot.com/search/label/mathers%2Fmardrus.

Borges, but Mardrus "does not translate the book's words but its senses," and probably "these smiling diversions are what infuse the work with such a happy air, the air of a far-fetched personal yarn rather than of a laborious hefting of dictionaries."[81] More to the point is the issue of "infidelity" that sits comfortably in the French fin de siècle and responds discreetly to the colonial monopoly of culture: "It is his infidelity, his happy and creative infidelity, that must matter to us."[82]

Unconcerned with translational politics proper, Borges came up with some uncontested conclusions with respect to the genealogical order and merits of recognizable translations.[83] The blind Argentine with a fecund memory and enormous acquaintance with world literature and English in particular does not know Arabic, a point which Elias Khoury references in his metafictional work, *The Children of the Ghetto: My Name Is Adam* (2016). Borges was so discerning as to come up with a reading that takes the *Nights* as a global commodity. The translated text, Galland's in particular, becomes so available and so well known as to intrigue everyone, regardless of the source language and its authenticated or forged manuscripts. Other faces of this global commodity are addressed in due order. Thus, Borges writes that, by including tales other than the ones in his fifteenth-century manuscript, "Galland established the canon, incorporating stories that time would render indispensable and that the translators to come – his enemies – would not dare omit."[84] Galland decided to include the three most famous tales of Aladdin, Ali Baba, and Sindbad (which he had translated earlier in 1701)[85] in response to a demanding reading public and a publishing industry that was growing fast in Europe. Burton drew comparisons with predecessors' versions, but his attack is focused on the eminent Victorian Orientalist Lane (1801–78), whose translation spoke to a Victorian middle class and its learned society. Its power lies in the extensive notes and semirealistic detail that addressed an age that valued representation, a shadowy image of the East. In Borges's neat conclusion each translator "annihilated" a predecessor. But, if translations are indices of taste, readership, and politics of a masochistic bourgeoisie in the heyday of empire, it is time to engage more with a whole culture industry, and not only with the print side that MacDonald aptly describes as the great "publishing humbug." In this cultural transaction, translations are able to impact cultural artifacts,

[81] Borges, "The Translators," 106. [82] Ibid.

[83] Faten I. Morsy, "Frame-Narrative and Short Fiction: A Continuum from 'One Thousand and One Nights' to Borges" (PhD diss., University of Essex, 1989).

[84] Borges, "The Translators," 92.

[85] See Wen-Chin Ouyang and Geert Jan van Gelder, *New Perspectives on Arabian Nights: Ideological Variations and Narrative Horizons* (London: Routledge, 2005), xi.

writings, and audiovisual and media productions. They are able to provide contexts, matrices, symbols, catchphrases, and stereotypes. In other words, they are at the center of material conditions that constitute a cultural script. Each newly claimed translation has a readership, and indeed a very significant one, as publishers' registries, writers' response, readership, and publication data convey. We need to keep in mind that in England in particular, the *Arabian Nights' Entertainments* (1704–6), as its anonymous Grub Street translator baptized it, was next only to the Bible in popularity and vogue. Forster says as much in his 1802 translation, which Bussey revised in 1839. Forster concludes, "[T]heir magic name has served as escort or convoy to a prodigious importation of contraband merchandise, without the 'Thousand Nights' having lost any of their popularity or favour."[86] Forster also covers the ongoing philological discussion of the *Nights*, arguing throughout his preface with or against current views and reviews.

The Issue of Aryan/Semitic Language Families

The unabated translation movement with respect to the *Nights* cannot be taken lightly, not only because of its immediate relation to the culture industry throughout these three centuries, but also because, ever since its early advent, the *Nights* has become a subject of philological exploration, especially in matters of origin and its presumed Indo-Persian evolution. Indeed, Muhsin Mahdi finds it surprising how the views of Friedrich Schlegel and von Hammer-Purgstall continued in the writings of Oestrop.[87] He argues against these views that were also met with opposition by other scholars of Arabic like Silvestre de Sacy and Lane:

> How did they come to think that a collection of stories presumably originating in ancient India could survive transmission from one culture to another, from one language to another, and from one storyteller to another and yet remain identifiable in eighteenth-century Paris or Cairo as belonging to a particular ancient nation?[88]

In more than one sense, the keen interest in the origins of *A Thousand and One Nights*, and hence in manuscripts, during the last decades of the eighteenth century and early nineteenth century, was at the center of a vigorous philological inquiry. Drawn to this rising field, many scholars

[86] *Arabian Nights' Entertainments*, trans. the Reverend Edward Forster: Carefully revised and corrected by G. Moir Bussey, with an explanatory and historical introduction. Illustrated by twenty-four engravings from designs by R. Smirke (London: J. Thomas, 1839) (the 1842 edition is used), 62. Also 1864 edition, vi.

[87] Mahdi, *The Thousand and One Nights*, 4. [88] Ibid., 1–2.

of "Oriental" languages participated in the structuring of philology as a discipline which Ernest Renan would think of as "the exact science of mental objects . . . It is to the sciences of humanity what physics and chemistry are to the philosophic sciences of bodies."[89] Associating philology with modernity, and philologists as "the founders of modern mind," or Europe,[90] Renan of 1848 was only building on the ground work done by de Sacy, Schlegel, and many others. What brought this philological drive together was the absolute faith in "the reclassification of languages into families, and the final rejection of the divine origins of language."[91] To Schlegel, "the Indo-European family was artistically simple and satisfactory in a way the Semitic, for one, was not."[92] Promoted by a group of influential philologists, the absurd Aryan versus Semitic grouping has since become the segregationally cultural yardstick that has led the conversation astray away from manuscripts as "literary" texts, and not documents. To understand the mania for editions, translations, and origins in relation to this racial divide, we can cite the aristocrat, novelist, and racist theorist Joseph Arthur de Gobineau (1816–82), author of the infamous *Essai sur l'inégalité des races humaines* (1853–55; *Essay on the Inequality of Human Races*), who, as was noted in the Introduction, rewrote the Oriental mode to fit his own Aryan race theory.[93]

In a reverse movement, and since the late nineteenth century, authentication is no longer a pressing issue. More important is the amalgamation of texts, which necessarily means a departure from a racially devised textual lineage. With the rise of a pluralist approach or the amalgamation of multiple editions, the issue of translation as an afterlife takes the discussion further, and relatively away from single texts as documentary records. In his reading of how new history, as different from traditional history, "transforms documents into *monuments*," Foucault suggests that "in our time history aspires to the condition of archaeology, to the intrinsic description of the monument."[94] The *Nights* passed through different transformations, depending on its redactors/translators, illustrators, and editors. The recent drift is toward reading it as fiction, not history or document for that matter, against a long memory steeped in enormous white mythologies that have proved resilient in late capitalist consumer culture, as reprints of illustrated nineteenth-century versions demonstrate.[95]

89 Cited in Said, *Orientalism*, 133. 90 Ibid. 91 Said, *Orientalism*, 135. 92 Ibid., 98.
93 https://heritage.bnf.fr/bibliothequesorient/en/joseph-gobineau-art.
94 Foucault, *Archaeology of Knowledge*, 7.
95 For a listing of illustrated editions until 1936, see Kazue Kobayashi, "The Evolution of the *Arabian Nights* Illustrations: An Art Historical Review," in *The Arabian Nights and Orientalism: Perspectives from East and West*, ed. Yuriko Yamanaka and Tetsuo Nishio (London: I.B. Tauris, 2006), 190–93. More on this point in Chapter 7.

While annotation or substantial introductory and terminal essays tend to historicize a text and situate it within an understanding imposed and guided by the translator/editor and publisher and their consumer economy, twentieth-century criticism often – but not always – engages with the "intrinsic" characteristics of a specific version or more than one. Does this literary pursuit of a text as narrative negate annotation that was once the pride of nineteenth-century scholarship? Only partly. Annotations reappear in many reprints of earlier editions, and they often make their way into recent literary criticism, undergoing thereby a process of approval or denial. In other words, they are treated as documents of a certain milieu, as will be shown in Chapter 7. Like illustrations, with a difference in matters of script and visual surface, annotation and explanatory essays address specific readerships in the age of consumer economies and colonization.

In Celebration of the Visual: Illustrations

Even reprints of Galland, like the 1840 edition that had Clément-Pierre Marillier's (1740–1808) illustrations along with many other foreign artists, carried the dissertation of the renowned de Sacy to defend his thesis against other Orientalists or Arabists. The German edition of Weil (1838–41) with Friedrich Gross's illustrations was almost a German response to Lane's remarkable version (1838–41), with its William Harvey illustrations. On other occasions, reprints of translations like the Pickering and Chatto edition of Scott's (1890) found it reasonable and profitable to have the prolific Welsh artist Stanley L. Wood's (1866–1928) illustrations instead of those of Robert Smirke (1811). Ever since Galland's sweeping success, the battle for authentication and representation of the *Arabian Nights* has never been an ordinary one. Galland's successors were often driven to justify their endeavor and explain their alignment with or departure from his version. Thus, nineteenth-century annotation remains central to the study of illustrated translations/editions. Hence the question: Can we address translations without their illustrations? The same question partially applies to other visual appropriations: A cinematic production stands by itself in relation to an amalgamated version. Illustrations that have begun to accompany print editions substantiate the text while making use of the heavy annotations of translators/editors, like Lane and Burton. They feed each other to the presumed benefit of the reader whose visualization of the scene or character might be blurred by her/his immediate milieu. Until very recently, French, British, German, and other painters and illustrators fought hard to endow each translation with claimed uniqueness, or some distinction that has been feeding the hostile dynasty. Each new production vies for a better place than its contemporary or predecessor.[96] Each translation in its own language or in its multiple travels to other languages wears that apparel to win over readers after being tested and proved successful, especially in early French and English translations. The Danish reprint of Galland's (Hague, 1714–30) has the advantage of David Coster's engravings, which demonstrate not only the disposition to account for one's immediate milieu,[97] like Galland's deliberate appropriation, but also the hazy imaging of the Oriental Other. Coster's Westernized versions were part of an eighteenth-century outlook that tended to impose its own style on the Other.[98] The same can be said about the renowned French artist Marillier's engravings. Although attempting representations, his illustrations are tied to Galland's version, his imposition of the French style on imported material. In other words, it is not a lack of curiosity on the part of engravers that incapacitated the art movement with respect to the *Arabian Nights*, but rather a hegemonic outlook that strove to absorb and assimilate the alien. Hence, the need to examine some versions not only as indices of hostile dynasties, but also and more importantly as registers of colonial and postcolonial involvement. The accelerated print industry and compelling demand made selections of appropriate versions a priority, as attested to by the number of sales, reprints, pirate copies, forgeries, adaptations, and serializations that were the staple of the Victorian period in particular. The reprints, adaptations, serializations, and illustrations and engravings, along with the stupendous amount of literary criticism, demonstrate how a popular book can function as an index of taste. The *Athenaeum*, a mirror of Victorian culture, was so involved in their assessment and the interest in illustrations that it had then a number of specialists to care for the reading and analysis of reception and taste. Although Galland's version – and similar manuscripts like Russell's – continued to be the original for every

[96] Terry Reece Hackford, "Fantastic Visions: Illustration of the Arabian Nights, " in *The Aesthetics of Fantasy Literature and Art*, ed. Roger C. Schlobin (Notre Dame, IN: University of Notre Dame Press, 1982), 143–75; Felix Tauer, "Einige Randglossen zu Tausendundeiner Nacht," *Acta Universitatis Carolinae, Philologica 1, Orientalia Pragensia* 1 (1960), 13–22. See also Felix Tauer, "Tausendundeine Nacht im Weltschrifttum als Gegenstand der Lektüre und der Forschung," *Irrgarten der Lust: 1001 Nacht, Aufsätze, Stimmen, Illustrationen* (Frankfurt: Insel Verlag, 1968), 122–47.

[97] See Robert Irwin, "The Arabian Nights: A Thousand and One Illustrations," *The Guardian*, March 12, 2011, www.theguardian.com/books/2011/mar/12/arabian-nights-illustration.

[98] For samples, see Margaret Sironval, *Album Mille et Une Nuits: Iconographie Choisie et Commentée* (Paris: Gallimard, 2005), 50–51, 82, 134–35.

following translator,[99] it was not the Victorians' most popular text. Even the illustrations of Edward Francis Burney for the 1785 edition, with the collaboration of Henry Coulbert and Thomas Stothard, could not sustain popularity with the Victorians. They were more attracted to Harvey's illustrations for Lane's translation, which went into a number of prints in 1838, 1840, 1847, 1850, 1853, 1854, 1857, 1859, 1863, 1865, 1883, and 1889. Across the Atlantic, it was reprinted in 1847, 1848, 1853, 1856, 1882, and 1883. Publishers like John Murray, Routledge, Chatto and Windus, and Harper and Scribner were all involved in the venture. A mention should be made of Smirke (1753–1845), whose nomination in 1804 as keeper to the Royal Academy of Arts was not sanctioned by George III because of his revolutionary politics. His illustrations of Forster's edition of Galland (1802, 1810, and 1811)[100] signify an important turn in the art: They have that haziness that keeps to the story while opening the gate for imaginative flights. This edition could not sustain competition, however, with Lane's translation as illustrated by the celebrated engraver Harvey (1796–1866; Figures 6, 7, and 8).[101] Lane's was the edition where illustrations complement the text.[102] With Lane's keen interest in the art, Harvey was not given the chance for flights of imagination. A sharp realistic outline depicting specific scenes helped in presenting Lane's edition to a drawing room readership that could visualize a scene as Eastern.

Illustrations in Victorian texts vary in value and perspective. But one may define these in terms of literary and popular attitudes. Harvey's illustrations, for instance, cater to the mainstream, in the sense that they emphasize detail in a manner that reminds the reader of the realism of Victorian fiction. Although leaving a touch of strangeness and exoticism here and there, Harvey follows the text, and one can tell that Lane supervised the art very closely. The Orientalist who spent years in Egypt and who appropriated the tales to meet the needs of a Victorian audience was keen on sustaining a smooth narrative good for family

[99] Maurits H. van den Boogert, "Patrick Russell and the Arabian Nights Manuscripts," in *Scholarship between Europe and the Levant: Essays in Honour of Alastair Hamilton*, ed. Jan Loop and Jill Kraye (Leiden: Brill, 2020), 276–98.

[100] Edward Forster, *The Arabian Nights*, 5 vols. (London: William Miller, W. Bulmer and Co., 1802).

[101] Tales from the *Arabian Nights' Entertainments*, trans. E. Forster, Willoughby's Illustrated Standard Edition.

[102] Sironval, *Album Mille et Une Nuits*, 62, 84, 87.

Figure 6 William Harvey: Kamar ez-Zeman disguised as an astrologer from E. W. Lane, 1839–41 edition.

reading. In keeping with his bent for extensive annotation and ethnography, Lane's eye was on detail. Harvey was no less infected by the prevailing taste; his illustrations fit well into a mainstream Victorian art. Soon after, the painter, draughtsman, and illustrator Arthur Boyd

Figure 7 William Harvey: Barber standing at his door.

Houghton (1836–75; Figure 9) proved even more meticulous in realistic detail.[103] Both share the emphasis on figures rather than background. As usual with mainstream art, women figures receive less attention in the paintings of both, and the detailed focus on Oriental dress is there, as if to provide the reader with a deeroticizing perspective at a time when the empire was making every effort to master the knowledge of the East.

[103] Allan Life, "Scheherazade's 'Special Artist': Illustrations by Arthur Boyd Houghton for The Thousand and One Nights," in *Haunted Texts: Studies in Pre-Raphaelitism*, ed. D. Latham (Toronto: University of Toronto Press, 2003), 211–36.

Figure 8 William Harvey: Abu-al-Hasan on the couch of the Khaleefeh.

Harvey occupies a middle ground between Smirke and Houghton. The latter brought the art of portraiture to its zenith. The density of lining, sharp focus on specific scenes of action, and a mixed Eastern touch make Houghton's drawings significant to the art of illustrating the *Arabian Nights*. A very popular edition that enlisted the contributions of Victorians of every spectrum and taste, including the Pre-Raphaelites like John Everett Millais (1829–96), was the *Dalziel's Illustrated Arabian Nights* (London, 1863, 1865, 1869, and 1888 by Ward Lock and Tyler). The illustrators were George J. Pinwell (1842–75), John Tenniel (1820–1914), Houghton, J. D. Watson (1832–92), and Thomas B. Dalziel (1823–1906). Both George (1815–1902) and Edward Dalziel (1817–1905) carried out the engravings for the edition. Millais, Tenniel, and

Figure 9 Arthur Boyd Houghton: The travelers resting on reaching Damascus.

Watson illustrated the *People's Edition of the Arabian Nights' Entertainments*. There was a *Pictorial Penny Arabian Nights' Entertainments* in 1845, in four pence-halfpenny parts. Soon after, there was Willoughby's *Illustrated Standard Edition* in one-shilling parts (1852–54) with its 600 engravings by French artists.

The Power of Illustrated Nights

Lane's edition became a standard Victorian text, and the Dalziels made use of it. They "entered into a contract with the house of Ward and Lock to produce a series of popular standard works, fully illustrated to be under the able editorship of Dr. H. W. Dulcken," of which the *Arabian Nights* was the first. With its many illustrators, the Dalziel edition veers away from the mainstream as it accommodates the eclectic mode at large. Their Pre-Raphaelite tastes, aesthetic aspirations, along with a realistic bent promoted by H. W. Dulcken,[104] speak for the mid-Victorian period at large. The middle-class readership, and also the most cultivated reader found it appealing, as indicated in the number of reviews it received. Its reprints in the twenty-first century say as much.[105] Women appear in these illustrations, but mostly in a Pre-Raphaelite pose, carefully dressed, with a languid look, which also keep them in a distance, as heavenly as Rossetti's "Blessed Damozel." Millais's paintings, with their Pre-Raphaelite interest in color and detail, were the prototype for both Burton's close friend and illustrator of his translation Albert Letchford (1866–1905) and the French-born British color illustrator Edmund Dulac (1882–1953).[106] Payne's translation was even more interested in the dreamlike side of life, its exoticism offering a subjective outlook whose concern is personal and more aesthetic than representational.[107] Letchford was more interested in scenes of intrigue and adventure, like the scene of the charming lady with her urge to control a man and

[104] Upon the suggestion of the editor for Barnes and Noble Classics, I was asked to edit and introduce Dulcken's edition, 2006.

[105] *Dalziels' Illustrated Arabian Nights' Entertainments, the Text Revised and Emendated by H. W. Dulcken* (USA: Palala Press, 2018).

[106] For a sample from each, see Sironval, *Album Mille et Une Nuits*, 143–44.

[107] See John Payne's *The Book of the Thousand Nights and One Night: Now Completely done into English prose and verse from the Original Arabic, by John Payne. Bassorah Edition. Numbered 98 of 500, Printed for Subscribers Only, 1901. 8vo. Red Cloth, Illustrations by Albert Letchford and Adolphe Lalauze.* https://en.wikisource.org/wiki/The_Book_of_the_Thousand_Nights_and_One_Night/Illustrations. The Villon Society describes the corpus as follows: "The first 9 represent the traditional 'conservative' canon of the tales. Volumes 10–12 consist of tales from the important Breslau and Calcutta (1814–18) editions which had not been included in the more conservative editions. And the final three volumes offer supplementary 'Oriental Tales': the first features tales that were collected by the earliest French translators and added to their compilation – ironically these apocryphal tales include some of the most famous of the Arabian Nights stories – those of Aladdin, Ali Baba and some of the Sindbad tales. Volumes 14 and 15 are not really part of the Payne Translation – the former is Persian Letters written in French in 1721 by Montesquieu, while the latter contains The Thousand and One Quarters of an Hour/Tartarian Tales by Thomas-Simon Gueullette written in 1715 in imitation of the newly popular *1001 Nights*. These last two are included in this series because they were issued uniform with volumes 1–13 to complete the 15 volume Oriental Tales."

Figure 10 Albert Letchford: Aziz and Azizah.

imprison him after testing his manliness and fidelity (Figure 10).[108] His black-and-white illustrations impart a hazy vision, a silhouette, that incites imagination. Such illustrations of dynamic scenes fit well into

[108] *Alf Laylah wa-laylah* (Būlāq; al-Muthannā repr.), 1:250, night 16. The tale is reproduced in full in Payne's and Burton's. See Burton, *The Thousand and One Nights*, 3:125–28.

both Payne's and Burton's translations. Engaging women in action and sexual intrigues provides some release from prudery, but it also fights back a dominating discourse of discrimination against women in private and public life. This was not the case with Tenniel's drawings. His 1861 designs, like "The Sleeping Genie and the Lady,"[109] exploits to the full the stereotypical Eastern elements of fantasy, exoticism, opulence, strangeness, grotesqueness, terror, and desire. It certainly makes use of the realism of Harvey, but is also designed to cater to Victorian fantasy, repression, and Manichean displacements. Every desire is predicated on the Other, and both humor and terror are there to account for the human scene in its veiled pronouncements and arts.

While manifesting the response of the illustrator to the tales and the equal release of personal inhibitions and desires, these illustrations also cater to the tempers of the reading public. Scott's edition with Smirke's illustrations did not entirely disappear from the scene, nor did Forster's edition as adorned with Smirke's illustrations. The latter's "The Sleeping Genie" proved to be of abiding appeal to the Victorians, for instance. Dickens wrote about it, and recollected it in his "A Christmas Tree":

> Down upon the grass, at the tree's foot, lies the full length of a coal-black Giant, stretched asleep, with his head in a lady's lap; and near them is a glass box, fastened with four locks of shining steel, in which he keeps the lady prisoner when he is awake. I see the four keys at his girdle now. The lady makes signs to the two kings in the tree, who softly descend. It is the setting of the bright Arabian Nights.[110]

Seen in context of the collection's frame story, the illustration could have invoked different readings and insinuations that touch on Victorian squeamishness. But the descent of the kings speaks also for repressed desires as much as it suggests the hypocrisy of power and authority. In its many versions, the tale brings together more than a Victorian issue, and may well deserve analysis in view of the predilections of Victorian illustrators and writers. Early illustrated editions, like Forster's, Scott's, or Galland's, for that matter, were reissued a number of times and, as mentioned before, invited the participation of new illustrators. Some were adapted for children, like Albert Ludwig Grimm's 1889 reprint that made use of chromolithography to include "eight original water colors."[111]

[109] Haddawy's translation of Galland's manuscript (Norton, 1990), prologue, 8–10. On illustrations, see Maria Popova, "A Visual History of Arabian Nights," *The Atlantic*, January 20, 2012.

[110] Charles Dickens, "A Christmas Tree," in *Household Words, Conducted by Charles Dickens*, no. 39, Saturday, December 21, 1850.

[111] See Donald Haase, "The Arabian Nights, Visual Culture, and Early German Cinema," *Fabula* 45, no. 3–4 (2007), 1; revised version in Marzolph, ed., *The Arabian Nights in Transnational Perspective*, 245–60.

From 1850, there were further illustrations by Tenniel, Levilly, and Gustave Doré.[112] A different illustration of great popularity is the one based on al-Nashshar's dream in the tale of "The Barber's Fifth Brother." Smirke had already offered a version, which was followed by Tenniel and Houghton,[113] among many others. The illustration and the tale were very much in vogue. Appealing to the Victorian fear of mobility, but, in line with the tendency to social climbing, the story also warns against over-active imagination. We need to go back to Dickens's *Hard Times* and his critique of Utilitarianism and John Stuart Mill to understand the ramifications of the discussion of the issue in the face of the growing pragmatism of the period. In an extended daydream, the peddler marries the Grand Vizier's daughter, but, in the middle of the dream, he kicks over his precious glassware. There is always another figure in the picture, the next-door tailor, who looks through a side window and laughs. As has been noted, Tenniel's Alnaschar (al-Nashshar) also becomes the stereotype for the different Other. With a long-hooked nose, it is the typical Victorian image of Otherness, whereby desires and inhibitions are predicated on the Other. However, the illustrated children's book industry was soon to make use of the *Arabian Nights*; and artists like the prolific and resourceful Walter Crane (1845–1915) had *Aladdin's Picture Book* (1876). Along with these efforts, the Anglophone Dulac's illustrations for the retold stories by Lawrence Housman (1907) deserve attention, not only because of retelling as another track in "translation," a departure from appropriation, but a reorientation in the target culture, that is, the British, and the assimilation of the alien, but also because Dulac brought the Franco-British traditions together, merging the mainstreams of European visual artistry (Figure 11). Dulac also set the path for twentieth-century celebrations of *Arabian Nights*' artistry as being an influential tide that is bound to impact every other audiovisual production. The Housman edition was translated into French and German, and Dulac's paintings marked a turn toward book illustration being regarded as a discipline by itself.

By the end of the century, Dulac's illustrations were a celebration of a balanced and striking use of color. Designed with relish and love for life and exquisite adventure, and also informed by his interest in Persian miniatures, his illustrations have become among the most valued. Dulac's involvement in this industry cannot be overestimated: His collaboration with the *American Weekly* in 1925 and his dynamic role in designing cover paintings derived from the *Arabian Nights* placed his work at the center of a thriving publishing industry.[114] Although different from

[112] For samples, see Sironval, *Album Mille et Une Nuits*, 130, 162; 63, 72, 73, respectively.
[113] Ibid., 64. [114] C. White, *Edmund Dulac* (London: 1976), 120, 190, 200–205.

SHE GAVE ORDERS FOR THE BANQUET TO BE SERVED

Figure 11 Edmund Dulac: The banquet in the Fairouz Shah story.

Dulac, Henri Mattise drew his *Arabian Nights* scenes from texts and notes, only to undergo a strong avant-garde twist whereby the illustrations are rich with pure undiluted color and a sense of ruling serenity. The females of the *Nights* appear still and colorful.[115] Other painters like Eric Fraser, Kay Nielsen, and Edward Julius Detmold continued innovation in book production. In 1958, Fraser was commissioned by the Folio Society to illustrate the first two volumes of the English translation of Mardrus's French edition. Mardrus's edition in French was serialized in *La revue blanche*, itself a forum for new trends in art.[116] Mardrus's

115 Sironval, *Album mille et nuits*, 229–231.
116 Georges Bernier, *La revue blanche; ses amis, ses artistes* (Paris: Hazan, 1991). On this point see, Richard van Leeuwen, "The Iconography of the Thousand and One Nights

1926–32 edition also included Léon Carré's illustrations. In the words of Irwin, these illustrations "conjured up a strange fantasy world, redolent with Elizabethan woodcuts and science fiction."[117] Active participation in illustrating the *Arabian Nights* operates within this hostile dynasty of grand translators. But publishers have found this culture industry quite profitable regardless of whose version they are using. In 1948, the Pantheon Press, for example, published "in a special edition of ten, a book in portfolio containing lithographs in color by the Russian-French Marc Chagall (1887–1985) that illustrates episodes from the *Arabian Nights*."[118] Chagall's distinctive rural outlook, subtle color, deregulated patterns, inventiveness, and fantasy bring to the art a new streak that complements and also supersedes the urban limits of the hostile dynasty.[119]

The emerging conversation between images and texts is not uniform. There were instances of deviation from the mainstream realism of Houghton and Harvey, for example, as there were also anticipatory ones by Marillier (Paris, 1785) and Smirke.[120] Engravings, illustrations, and theatrical and cinematic productions launch another line of translation that should redirect our textual discussion toward audiovisual arts as befitting an age of the spectacle. Hence, Mardrus's version is important for other reasons. It continues the tradition of supplementing the text with paintings and embellishments. This visual supplementation of the *Arabian Nights* has substantiated an Orient that is an upgraded representation of the nineteenth-century version. It is not eerie, but it is certainly different and Other. While also appealing to fin de siècle literati and the aesthetic movement, as, for example, in Dulac's paintings, the history of engravings, paintings, and illustrations for the tales is associated not only with an ever-growing readership and changes in the social fabric, but also with "translation" from one medium to another: from script to image.

and Modernism: From Text to Image," *Relief* 4, no. 2 (2010), 213–36, www.revue-relief.org.

117 Robert Irwin, "The Arabian Nights: A Thousand and One Illustrations," *The Guardian*, March 12, 2011, www.theguardian.com/books/2011/mar/12/arabian-nights-illustration.

118 Henry S. Francis, "Chagall's Illustrations for the One Thousand and One Nights," *The Bulletin of the Cleveland Museum of Art* 37, no. 3 (March 1950), 57–59.

119 Marc Chagall, *Arabische Nächte; 26 Lithographien zu 1001 Nacht, München* (Zürich: R. Piper & Co Verlag, 1975). See also Marc Chagall, *Arabian Nights* (Munich: Prestel, 1999). The UAE short story writer Muḥammad al-Murr has gathered many of these illustrated editions; see his catalogue of books, *Shaghaf al-layālī al-ʿArabiyyah* (Sharjah, UAE: Sharjah Institute for Heritage Publications, 2019). See also *Four Tales from Arabian Nights* (New York: Pantheon Books, 1948) for the complete set of twelve signed and numbered lithographs in colors, on laid paper.

120 Sironval, *Album Mille et Une Nuits*, 126.

The French Orientalist Léon Georges Jean-Baptiste Carré's (1878–1942) illustrations for the *Book of One Thousand and One Nights* correspond with Dulac's, and both bring forth color, virtuosity, and specific emphasis on languor as shown in facial features.[121] Under the glaring sun of the presumed East, visibility is captured as a trap, as Foucault argues in a different context.[122] Artists before Chagall and the French Henry Matisse (1869–1954) play the role of voyeurs. A dreamlike Orient with languid women and carefully delineated background appears, one that speaks more to French and English audiences.

Whenever trying to come up with a historiography for a pictorial tradition of the *Arabian Nights*, it is difficult to draw clear-cut borderlines. While there are transformations and genealogical transmissions, there are also ruptures and discontinuities. There is, however, a gradual departure from textual subordination toward experimentation. In other words, there is a parting with the hostile dynasty. Art is elevated to the utmost, and the very frame story of a lady buying her life through narrative becomes, especially in Dulac's illustrations, the very symbol of art as improvement on life. It is no longer representational or imitative, and the interest of Harvey in documentation, for instance, is no longer binding. Each illustration stands by itself as a piece of art with a story to tell and a scene that addresses and targets the reader. Art redeems itself and signifies nothing but itself. Scenes of magic and intrigue are there, but they stand on their own, self-sufficient and sovereign. In the works of the Matisse and Chagall, for instance, the art of illustration comes full circle, and the tales are no less evocative of response than literature. Matisse's participation in illustrating the *Nights* was not a minor event. His "fauvism" imbibed the scene with vigor and vivid expressionistic use of color, and helped in establishing a movement with as many followers as opponents. His understanding of art is summed up in his saying: "What I dream of is an art of balance, of purity and serenity, devoid of troubling or depressing subject matter." Often produced as independent albums, illustrations, especially by Chagall, speak of themselves as independent entities, sovereign in a "palace of art,"[123] but not necessarily in line with Tennyson's late Romantic subjectification. Irwin suggests, "Over the course of three centuries a new iconography of wonder had been created."[124] Contemporary scholars have found in this phenomenal

[121] See ibid., 66, 72, 81, 92, 123, 125, 130, 150, 220; 57, 66, 78, 89, 138, 142, 151, 154, 158.

[122] Foucault, *Discipline and Punish*, 200.

[123] Alfred Lord Tennyson's poem, "The Palace of Art," www.poemhunter.com/poem/the-palace-of-art-2.

[124] Irwin, *Guardian Books*.

upsurge in illustration a clear-cut disconnect with the primary texts of *A Thousand and One Nights*. Leeuwen goes so far as to suggest that the "iconography of the *Thousand and one Nights* has absorbed the texts and has perhaps even *become* the *Thousand and one Nights*."[125] To be sure, there is a departure from mid-nineteenth-century illustrations, but a sustainable illustration genealogy is still there, impacting visual culture. Reprints of the primary texts and illustrations are as popular as ever, and the culture industry still makes use of these. Moreover, rare editions are auctioned for prohibitive prices. However, alongside the rapidly developing print industry, the rise of experimentation in art and literature, and also the demand for illustration and book covers, artists have found themselves free to experiment widely in the world of the *Arabian Nights*. Unshackled by the hostile dynasty, they are free to give rein to their imagination in a large hybrid textual-visual space, which, in selections and titles for visual production, still converses in multiple ways with an archaeology of the *Nights*.

[125] van Leeuwen, "Iconography."

5 The Archaeology of *A Thousand and One Nights*

> The concept of the "definitive text" corresponds only to religion or exhaustion.
>
> Jorge Luis Borges, "The Homeric Versions"

> The Arabs "have highly polemical natures; they are the annihilators among the nations. Their fondness for destroying or throwing away the originals when the translations are finished characterize the spirit of their philosophy."
>
> Friedrich von Schlegel, *Philosophical Fragments*

> [I]t may turn out that archaeology is the name given to a part of our contemporary theoretical conjecture.
>
> Michel Foucault, *Archaeology of Knowledge*

Invoking these paratextual snippets from three intellectuals separated from each other by a century or more, and also by grounding and affiliation,[1] I plan to draw the prospects and limits of this archaeology of *A Thousand and One Nights*. The search for a definitive text is not peculiar to Orientalists or Arabists, as Borges's nod to the ongoing controversy surrounding Homer shows. There is no definitive text for a multifarious growth like the *Arabian Nights*, not only because of the migration of texts, their transformation, transference, transmission, and storytellers' articulation and manipulation, but also because there is a dearth of a sustained chain of original manuscripts that Schlegel assigns to the "spirit of... [the Arabs'] philosophy" that obliterates originals. Erroneous as it sounds, this surmise implies that the Arabs were preceding Walter Benjamin in a literal understanding of translation as an afterlife that supersedes the original. He argues: "a translation issues from the original – not so much from its life as from its afterlife."[2] In the case of *A Thousand and One*

[1] Friedrich von Schlegel (d. 1829), *Philosophical Fragments*, trans. Peter Firchow (Minneapolis, MN: University of Minnesota Press, 1998), 49.
[2] Benjamin, "The Task of the Translator," 71.

Nights, the issue is even more complicated. Whereas Nabia Abbott's significant finding in 1949 of a fragment of the book of *Alf laylah* that belongs to the early ninth century sets the stage for reorienting origins and migration of texts,[3] it also raises further questions and thence generates more research, often in line with D. B. MacDonald's early classification of sources. She was not focused on the absence of *one* in the title before it became visible in the tenth century. Although Abbott's groundbreaking contribution does not raise this as a problematic, it is so for an archaeological study of the *Arabian Nights*.

Contexts of Evolution of *1001 Nights*

The translators of *A Thousand and One Nights* are even more perplexed than Abū al-Ḥasan ʿAlī ibn al-Ḥusayn al-Masʿūdī and Abū al-Faraj Muḥammad ibn Isḥāq al-Nadīm with respect to the evolution of the Thousand Tales as they get transformed to the *Thousand Nights*. They both wrote of *Hazār afsānah* (before Thousand Fanciful Tales; or *Khurāfāt*) as being a translation of a book from a Persian source in eighth-century Baghdad during al-Manṣūr's caliphate (754–75 CE). The early ninth-century fragment relates selections from a book called the *Thousand Nights*, containing urban and Bedouin tales, probably alongside others from Persian, Indian, and Greek sources. Al-Nadīm specifically addresses the effort of "the eloquent and the rhetoricians" to "re-write" the tales in an elegant style. Ibn ʿAbdūs al-Jahshiyārī (d. 942) is mentioned as one of them. An obvious demand for storytelling prompted a compilation movement generated by a specific literary elite.[4] Whether in translation, redaction, revision, or rewriting and accretion, the tales as we know them have passed through varying processes that relate to reading publics and tastes.

In other words, we have a translated eighth-century Persian text, followed by an Arabic one that made use of the frame tale, to morph even further into an elegant one, which still bears the title *Thousand Nights*. Even if one Masʿūdī manuscript bears the title of *Thousand Nights and*

[3] Abbott, "A Ninth-Century Fragment."

[4] Apart from what is listed in *Fihrist*, it is good to know the following: Abū ʿUthman ʿAmr ibn Baḥr al-Jāḥiẓ, *The Epistle on Singing-girls of Jahiz*, ed. with trans. and comm. A. F. L. Beeston (Oxford: Aris & Phillips, 1980); Abū al-Muṭahhar Muḥammad ibn Aḥmad al-Azdī (fl. late fourth/tenth century), *Ḥikāyat Abī al-Qāsim al-Baghdadī*, ed. A. Mez (Baghdad: Maktabat al-Muthannā, 1902). Part of the book on singing-girls is reproduced, probably by copyists, in Abū Ḥayyān al-Tawḥīdī, *Kitāb al-imtāʿ wa-l-muʾānasah*, ed. Aḥmad Amīn and Aḥmad al-Zayn (Beirut: al-ʿAṣriyyah, n.d.). See also Jaakko Hämeen-Anttila, "al-Azdī, Abū l-Muṭahhar," in *Encyclopedia of Islam*, vol. 3, ed. Kate Fleet, Gudrun Krämer, Denis Matringe, John Nawas, and Everett Rowson, http://dx.doi.org/10.1163/1573-3912_ei3_COM_23693.

One (which, as an exact title, opens up a morphological growth),[5] Abbott's fragment and the Persian source suggest otherwise. However, Chraïbi claims the second half of the tenth century as the time when a *Thousand and One* was in use. This is an important intervention, especially when we become aware of such use in al-Yamānī's book *Muḍāhāt* (around 358/969) where he uses *Alf mathal wa-mathal* (*A Thousand Exemplary Accounts and One*).[6] Until the end of the tenth century, there was no "One" after the *Thousand Nights*, other than in one Masʿūdī manuscript, but there were many coeval titles that had a "thousand and one."[7] It is this "One," however, that should have been the effect and ultimate outcome of the preceding revisionist and editorial or creative movement in the narrative domain. It is also a gate opener for further processes of expansion and replacement. And, no matter how we perceive subsequent compilations, they all attest to a *One Thousand and One Nights*, a title that resists containment, and leaves the door open for storytellers to work on an available written corpus. In its transformation, marvels, and growth as a constellation, since the tenth century it had become an exemplary book, as testified to by no less an authority than Ibn Aybak al-Ṣafadī (1296–1363) in *Aʿyān al-ʿaṣr*, who used the term *Kitāb laylah wa-alf laylah* (*The Book of One Night and a Thousand Nights*) as a yardstick for excellence and perfection.[8] This is a unique case of a literary production that was available as a series of written or rewritten texts, which storytellers made use of over a long period. However, it was not a one-track narrative navigation because Ibn ʿAbdūs summoned storytellers, not only to expand the available treasury of Arabic, Persian, Indian, and Greek selections, but also to localize the narrative and tailor it to be appropriate to his taste as a member of elite society. The written texts were in turn to become the material for oral tradition, and not the other way round. A regression in narrative style was only part of the pact between storytellers and the common public.

To the credit of the French translator Galland, the post-tenth-century title of a manuscript was preserved: His *Les mille et Une Nuit, contes arabes traduits en français* ("*The Thousand and One Nights*, Arab stories translated into French") sets the stage for a dynastic rivalry among translators, duly noticed by Borges. Payne and Burton tried to prove their meticulousness in playing around the "One": Is it *Thousand and One Nights*, or *Thousand Nights and One Night*? Or even *Thousand Nights and One*? Payne settles for

[5] Aboubakr Chraïbi, "Introduction," in *Arabic Manuscripts of the "Thousand and One Nights": Presentation and Critical Editions of Four Noteworthy Texts; Observations on Some Osmanli Traditions*, ed. Aboubakr Chraïbi (Paris: Espaces et signes, 2016), 21.

[6] Ibid., 21. The referenced book is al-Yamānī, *Muḍāhāt amthāl kitāb Kalīla wa-Dimna*.

[7] See Chraïbi, "Introduction." [8] Ibid., 22.

The Book of the Thousand Nights and One Night; but bent on distinction, Burton comes up with *The Book of the Thousand Nights and a Night*. The "One" incited, and it still incites, reflections, parodies, pastiches, and more tales. The manuscript, about which both Arab classicists al-Masʿūdī and al-Nadīm wrote, has "Thousand Tales," the additional "One" was most probably not in the material under their purview. Yet, that same milieu invited the "One" as a narrative locus, instigator, germinator, and dynamic host. It certainly signifies processes of reading and reception. In spatial correspondence between texts and contexts, or the *One* and Baghdad, both generated growths and functioned as centripetal/centrifugal fulcrums: both host narrative, and, for that matter, both accommodate people, life, and action.[9] Narrative as loquacity signifies life, as noticed by Todorov in his "Narrative Men." It also signifies the barbers of Baghdad as necessarily inquisitive and talkative in a thriving urban center. That is Scheherazade's lesson.

Archaeology requires an understanding of the available discursive space that relates to the specific and general in the formation of knowledge systems whereby *A Thousand and One Nights* functions. It certainly

> indicates a possible line of attack for the analysis of verbal performances; the specification of a level – that of the statement and the archive; the determination and illumination of a domain – the enunciative regularities; the positivities; the application of such concepts as rules of formation, archaeological derivation, and historical *a priori*.[10]

To become a name for perfect performance, a constellation over three centuries of a series of archival transformations and processes, and to gain an exemplary status in the fourteenth century, the *Nights* is no longer a book, but a tradition that strongly relates to the theoretical conceptualization of fiction. The case is even more so when we take into account the kind of accretion that took place early on in the eighth century when *Hazār afsānah* made its welcome presence in Arabic. Sooner than later, it accommodated in translation the tale of "The Merchant and the Demon," which, according to MacDonald in view of René Basset's significant reading, antedates the Persian import,[11] and hence easily

[9] For a discussion of how Baghdad soon after its establishment in 762 turned into a centripetal/centrifugal epicenter, see al-Musawi, *The Islamic Context of the Thousand and One Nights*.

[10] Foucault, *Archaeology of Knowledge*, 206.

[11] René Basset, "Notes sur Les Mille et Une Nuit," *Revue des Traditions Populaires* 9 (1894), 377–80; 11 (1896), 146–87; 12 (1897), 146–52; 13 (1898), 37–87, 303–8; 14 (1899), 20–37, 687–89; 16 (1901), 28–35, 74–88; 18 (1903), 311–14; Duncan B. MacDonald, "The Earlier History of the Arabian Nights," *Journal of Royal Asiatic Society* 3 (1924), 353–97; MacDonald, "Alf laila wa-laila (A.)"; MacDonald, "A Preliminary Classification."

found its place there as modeled on the story of the Bedouin Khurāfah, presumably communicated by the Prophet. As Abbott argues, in line with Enno Littmann's (d. 1958) belief in the existence of a substantial portion of Arabic narrative in these formations: "Whether the Khurāfah-Mohammed link is an invention or not, the tale itself was definitely known in the last quarter of the eighth century, hence affording, along with similar tales, ready basis for comparison with the Persian Afsāna."[12]

Basset's 1901 article is based on al-Sharīshī's (d. 1222) commentary on the *Maqāmāt* of al-Ḥarīrī (d. 1122).[13] The reported story by the Prophet details a ransom motif, exactly in the manner followed in the tale of "The Merchant and the Demon," whereby the life of the Bedouin Khurāfah was paid for by fantastic and wonderful narratives, as will be explained in the following text.[14] MacDonald traces Basset's reference to an earlier source, namely, al-Mufaḍḍal ibn Salamah's (early tenth-century) book, *al-Fākhir fī al-amthāl* (*The Superb in Exemplary Sayings*). This kind of activity within what MacDonald calls "the work-shop from which the materials of the *Nights* came" should have included not only H. Ritter's Constantinople manuscript of *Kitāb al-ḥikāyāt al-ʿajībah*,[15] but also other narratives like *A Hundred and One Nights*.[16] The activity in this workshop was not lost on the early nineteenth-century translators, editors, and detractors of the *Arabian Nights*. Nor was it lost on Payne and Burton, and the following generation of translators. But little was done to interrogate the remnants of *Hazār afsānah* in the final constellation of *Alf laylah*, the one that ends up in an incomplete Galland manuscript of three volumes that was partially used by MacDonald,[17] and produced in Arabic in full by Brill, with Muhsin Mahdi as editor.[18] Such activity required an engagement with a body of knowledge that has the nature of an archive. Furthermore, it urges us as readers and explorers to understand its prospects and methods. As Michel Foucault shows in his reading of epistemic formations, the "archive is first the law of what can be said,

[12] Abbott, "A Ninth-Century Fragment," 157.
[13] For an excellent review of this literature, see Chraïbi, "Introduction," 26–27.
[14] For extensive quotes, see ibid., 35–37.
[15] H. Ritter, *Kitāb al-ḥikāyāt al-ʿajībah wa'l-akhbār al-gharībah: Tales of the Marvelous and News of the Strange*, ed. Hans Wehr; trans. Malcolm C. Lyons (London: Penguin, 2014).
[16] Bruce Fudge, trans. and ed., *A Hundred and One Nights*, with a foreword by Robert Irwin (New York: New York University Press, 2016).
[17] Duncan B. MacDonald, "The Story of the Fisherman and the Jinnî: Transcribed from Galland's MS of 'The Thousand and One Nights,'" in *Orientalische Studien: Th. Nöldeke zum 70. Geburtstag gewidmet*, ed. Carl Bezold (Giessen: Toepelmann, 1906), 1:357–83. See also MacDonald, "Lost Manuscripts"; MacDonald, "A Missing MS"; Duncan B. MacDonald, "From the Arabian Nights to Spirit," *Muslim World* 9 (1919), 336–48; MacDonald, "A Preliminary Classification"; and MacDonald, "The Earlier History."
[18] See also his earliest article, Mahdi, "Remarks on the *1001 Nights*."

the system that governs the appearance of statements as unique events."[19] But Foucault's view of the archive is pivotal to this reading of narrative morphology because it dispels the notion of a container, as it is not "that which collects the dust of statements that have become inert once more, and which may make possible the miracle of their resurrection; it is that which defines the mode of occurrence of the statement-thing; it is *the system of its functioning*."[20] *Hazār afsānah* was received with enthusiasm and underwent transformation and accretion in *Alf Laylah*, and that in turn acted, in the words of Chraïbi, "as a creative stimulus."[21] There is a dialectic relationship between statements (here narratives), their enunciation, and grouping "together in distinct figures, composed together in accordance with specific regularities."[22] The archive in this interpretation is that "which determines that they [i.e., the statements] do not withdraw at the same pace in time, but shine, as it were, like stars, some that seem close to us shining brightly from far off, while others that are in fact close to us are already growing pale."[23]

This reading may well apply to the mounting scholarly interest in *A Thousand and One Nights*, especially efforts that update and modify nineteenth-century research in the history of the book. In this connection, we have to appreciate Abbott's resurrection of an early ninth-century fragment of tales, a fragment that recalls earlier philological inquiry, especially MacDonald's classifications. It generates further research toward a better understanding of the collection in relation to the frame tale of Scheherazade/Shahrayar, and also in dialogue with a narrative corpus that calls for etymological, philological, historical, and religion-cultural exploration. Abbott's fragment is thus pivotal to this exploration, not only because it corroborates the narratives of the tenth-century Baghdadi scholars, but also because it establishes a plausible inventory of three narrative processes: translation from Persian sources, emulation and further narrative accretion, and resurrection of fabulation within its conditions of presumed occurrence, as accounts by humans who endured astounding experiences. These partake of ransom-like motifs that are central to the art of storytelling in the *Thousand and One Nights*.[24] These processes are of significance for an archaeology of the *Arabian Nights* as a narrative body that is well-established in tradition, and more in dialogue with classical Arabic script than hitherto recognized.[25] To cope with these

[19] Foucault, *Archaeology of Knowledge*, 129. [20] Ibid. [21] Chraïbi, "Introduction," 27.
[22] Foucault, *Archeology of Knowledge*, 129. [23] Ibid.
[24] Pinault, *Story-Telling Techniques*, 16–30.
[25] Chraïbi, "Introduction," is probably the most exhaustive documentation of origins, history, and classification of manuscripts; the present reading is indebted in many places to Chraïbi's scholarship (see 15–64).

processes, Abbott's findings are important. They become significant against a background that she describes as follows: "Extant manuscripts representative of this class of literary productivity [light and entertaining literature] consist of trade or private copies, usually dating from periods considerably later than that of the original work."[26]

Furthermore, her expertise in paleography enables her to deduce that "the 'Nights' manuscript is most probably the oldest Arabic book extant to come out of the Asiatic provinces, if not indeed the oldest book extant of all Islam, the Qur'ān alone excepted."[27] This fragment does not claim to be a full text of the *Nights*. It is "A Book of Tales from a Thousand Nights," as communicated by Abbott, and it starts midway as merely a selection of a larger volume of an Arabic *Thousand Nights* that was familiar with *Hazār afsānah*. Its Arabic says as much:

كتاب فيه حديث الف ليلة

So, we have a book of selected tales that belongs to the early ninth century; it references another book from which it derives tales that has as the title *Thousand Nights*. In all probability the full text belongs to the eighth century, as Abbott argues; and that a translation of *Hazār afsānah* (Thousand Fanciful Tales) already existed.[28] Insofar as style is concerned, it is in standard Arabic. If we accept Abbott's conclusion, it is the oldest extant paper book. Abbott's argument tends toward Iraq as the place for a complete translation of *Hazār afsānah*; a translation that gave way to appropriation, or "imitation" in Abbott's terms. The questions about this hypothesis never end. She raised some of them herself, as, for example, the reason for the silence of such polyglots like al-Jāḥiẓ (d. 868) and Ibn Qutaybah (d. 889) with respect to the book. Valid as the question is, both polyglots showed more interest in other fields, and had probably taken the growth of such a narrative corpus for granted. Chraïbi comes up with a conclusion to the effect that an extant and coeval narrative corpus was the direct milieu for appropriated material.[29] But the question raised in Abbott's significant undertaking still begs an answer. A century-long silence may well sound disturbing in the context of an archival exploration. In the first half of the tenth century, we have al-Mas'ūdī's significant mention (which I will discuss in due course). In the second half, there is the bibliophile al-Nadīm's elaborate discussion of storytelling

[26] Abbott, "A Ninth-Century Fragment," 131. [27] Ibid.

[28] Persian was still in use for matters of administration and state protocols in al-Shām under the Umayyads. See al-Musawi, *The Medieval Islamic Republic of Letters*; see also George Saliba, *Islamic Science and the Making of European Renaissance* (Cambridge, MA: MIT Press, 2007).

[29] Chraïbi, "Introduction."

activity in relation to translation, transference, or independently as a two-sided activity by the learned and storytellers. Devoted scholars wrote about a mid-fifteenth-century (perhaps late fourteenth-century) manuscript,[30] of which MacDonald published "The Tale of the Fisherman and the Genie."[31] The gap between an early ninth-century manuscript of a work that made use of a collection called *Alf laylah* and the mid-fourteenth century is not an ordinary one, but there are references to it throughout that period.[32]

Domains of Statements: Divided Readerships

More urgent is the early lacuna: What happened in almost eighty years of the ninth century? Could it be that there was a mention of the *Nights* in others works that are lost to us? Again, Abbott was not carried away by a specific hypothesis; and, as is becoming a scholar of her caliber, she allows enough space for a double argument that accounts for a differential reading or diversified audiences. The elite and common people could have shared some readings, but they surely differed widely in matters of taste. Abbott's translation of al-Ṣūlī's report on the future caliph al-Rāḍī's retort – when rebuffing the servants who invaded the tutoring session to show his books to his grandmother, but came back with the books – is worth mentioning:

> Tell them who sent you, "You have seen these books and found them to be books of tradition, jurisprudence, poetry, language, history, and the books of the learned-books through the study of which God causes one to benefit and to be complete. They are not like the books which you read excessively such as *The Wonders of the Sea*, *The Tale of Sindbad*, and the *Cat and the Mouse.*"[33]

There were, then, varied readerships. Even among the elite, there were different tastes and books. The future caliph castigated the grandmother and her servants for excessive interest in narratives that he deems of less or no value. Knowledge is classified as beneficial or worthless as it is played out in the court and outside it. This is why such situations beg for some archaeological explication to "reveal, with archive, the discursive formations, the positivities, the statements, and their conditions of formation,

[30] M. H. Zotenberg, "Communication relative au texte arabe de quelques contes des Mille et une Nuits," *Journal Asiatique* 8, no. 9 (1887), 300–303; M. H. Zotenberg, "Notice sur quelques manuscrits des Mille et une Nuits et la traduction de Galland," *Notices et extraits des manuscrits de la Bibliothèque National* 27 (1887), 167–235; MacDonald, "A Preliminary Classification," esp. 307.
[31] MacDonald, "The Story of the Fisherman and the Jinnî."
[32] Chraïbi, "Introduction."
[33] Cited and translated from Abbott, "A Ninth-Century Fragment," 155.

a specific domain,"[34] which is, in the case of this chapter, the domain of storytelling as a discursive battleground. What matters to us is the existence of these narratives that al-Nadīm listed in his *Fihrist*. However, the storytelling profession, and the existence of some well-known storytellers,[35] was visible throughout the eighth through tenth centuries. In the second half of the tenth century, Ibn ʿAbdūs gathered them to help in the compilation of his *Alf samar*, or *Thousand Entertaining Night Stories*. That, however, can wait until we have considered al-Masʿūdī's note, using Abbott's translation from the Arabic text of *Murūj al-dhahab* (*Meadows of Gold*):

> Many of those well acquainted with their *akhbār* (pseudo-historical tales of ʿAbid [ʿUbayd] ibn Sharyah and others of the court of Muʿāwiyah) state that these *akhbar* are *apocryphal, embellished, and fabricated*, strung together by those *who drew nigh to* the kings by relating them and *who duped* their contemporaries with memorizing and reciting them (as authentic. They state, furthermore), that they are of the same type as the books which have been transmitted to us and translated for us from the Persian [Pahlavi], Indian and Greek – books composed in like manner as the above mentioned – such as the book of *Hazar Afsana*, or translated from the Persian to the Arabic of a Thousand Khurafat, (fantastic tales) for *khurafa* in Persian is called *afsana*. The people call this book *A Thousand Nights* [*and a Night*]. It is the story of the king and the wazir and his daughter and her nurse [or maid, or sister, or the vizier and his two daughters] named Shirazad . . . and Dinazad [Dinarazad] and such as the Book of Farza [Jaliʿad] and Shīmās and what is in it of the stories of the kings of India and their wazirs [see Figures 12, 13, 14, and 15]. And such as the Book of Sindbad and other books of this nature.[36]

As already noted, raconteurs were not well thought of because they used to fabricate what they claimed as translations and dupe their contemporaries into thinking likewise. This means that there was an already active tradition of fictitious narratives during the Umayyad period (661–750 CE). The question of reliability would be raised at some point, but fabrication and invention were the rule of the day because of the rising demand for fiction. Al-Masʿūdī's intervention should not be taken lightly because there is an underlying assumption that what we read as translations, possibly including *Hazār afsānah*, are fabrications or inventions of the late Umayyad period. In the absence of a manuscript, we have no proof that there was such a Pahlavi book. Authorities like al-Masʿūdī, al-Nadīm, and Abū Ḥayyān al-Tawḥīdī took it for granted as a translation. In an age

[34] Foucault, *Archaeology of Knowledge*, 207.

[35] Abbott, "A Ninth-Century Fragment," 150.

[36] al-Masʿūdī, *Murūj al-dhahab*, 4:90–91, Abbott's translation (emphasis added); cf. Silvestre de Sacy, "Les Mille et Une Nuit," *Memoires de l'Academie royale des inscriptions et belles-lettres* 10 (1833), 30–64, esp. 38–41, 62–64; MacDonald, "The Earlier History," esp. 362–63.

بسم الله الرحمن الرحيم
وبه استعين هذه حكاية بعض
الملوك مع من اضمر وله العداوة حكي انه
كان احد الملوك له اعداء اخفياء وذلك
ملك حديث السن لم ينتبه لبغض حساده
وكانت زوجته متيقظة لهم قالت له يوما
من الايام اعلم ايها الملك اما من احد
ولي الامارة الا وصار له اعداء يحسدونه
وانت قد وليت سلطنة عظيمة فاولى ان
يكون لك اعداء [illegible] ولكن ابدي لك
مما تتخلص به من ورطة مكرهم وما ذلك
الا بالاعتماد على من ولاك هذه السلطنة
ثم بالحذر ممن يتظاهر لك بالصداقة فانهم
لو امكنهم ان يخلعوك من هذه الامارة لم
يبقوك فيها لحظة ولكن وجدوك

وجدوك عاجزا فاعطوك هذا الملك ورفعوك هذه
الرفعة ولو كان كذلك لما قدروا ان يصنعوا بك هذا
الصنيع ولا وجب عليك ان تخضع لهم هذا الخضوع

الست تعلم انهم كانوا لابيك عبيدا ووزرك اباهم وولاة
امورهم ليحكم كما تحب وانت مرعوب القلب كانك
لم تلد الملوك حتى تجزع ممن جعله الله لك خفا
تحت موطئ قدميك وقد قيل ان لم يكن قلبك حديدا
فلا تستطيع ان تكون ملكا فان البهيمة لها قلب ضخم
وانما يفزعوك هؤلاء بالنكث بك وترك الطاعة لك

Figure 12 Opening manuscript page: The Story of King Jaliʿad and the Wazir Shimas.
Source: Courtesy of Muḥammad al-Murr.

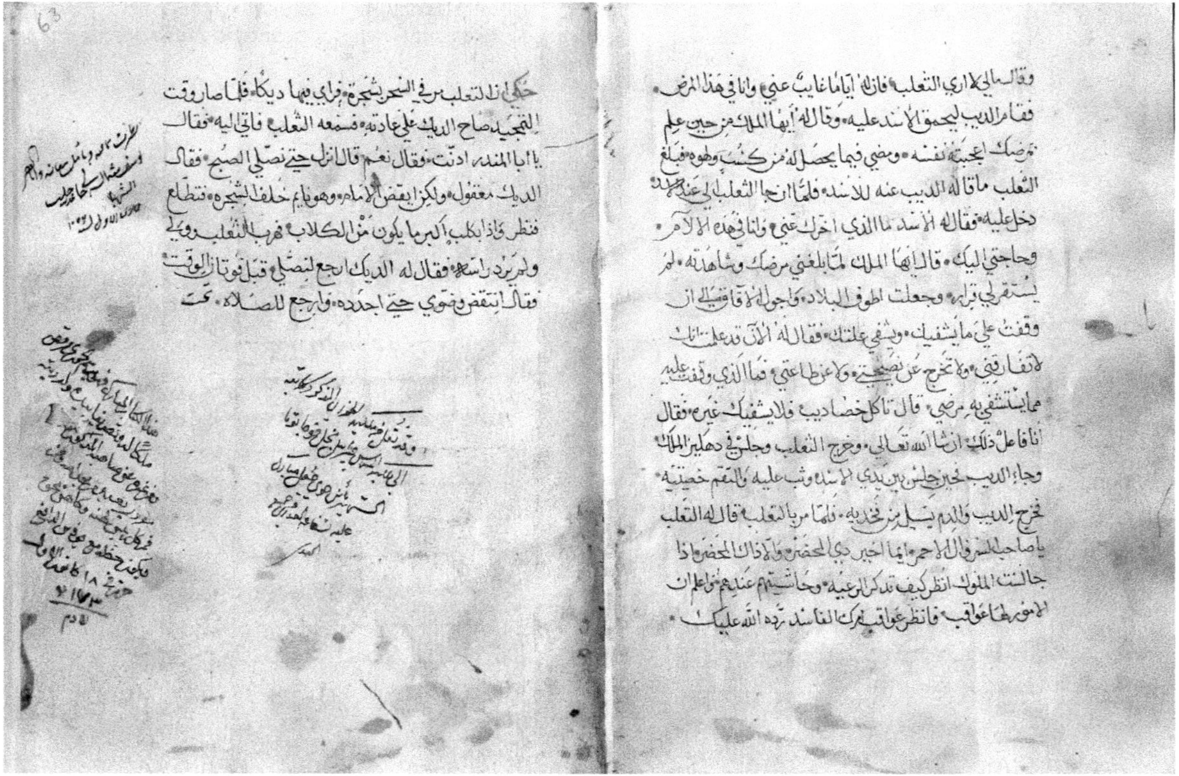

Figure 13 Last page: The Story of King Jaliʿad and the Wazir Shimas.
Source: Courtesy of Muḥammad al-Murr.

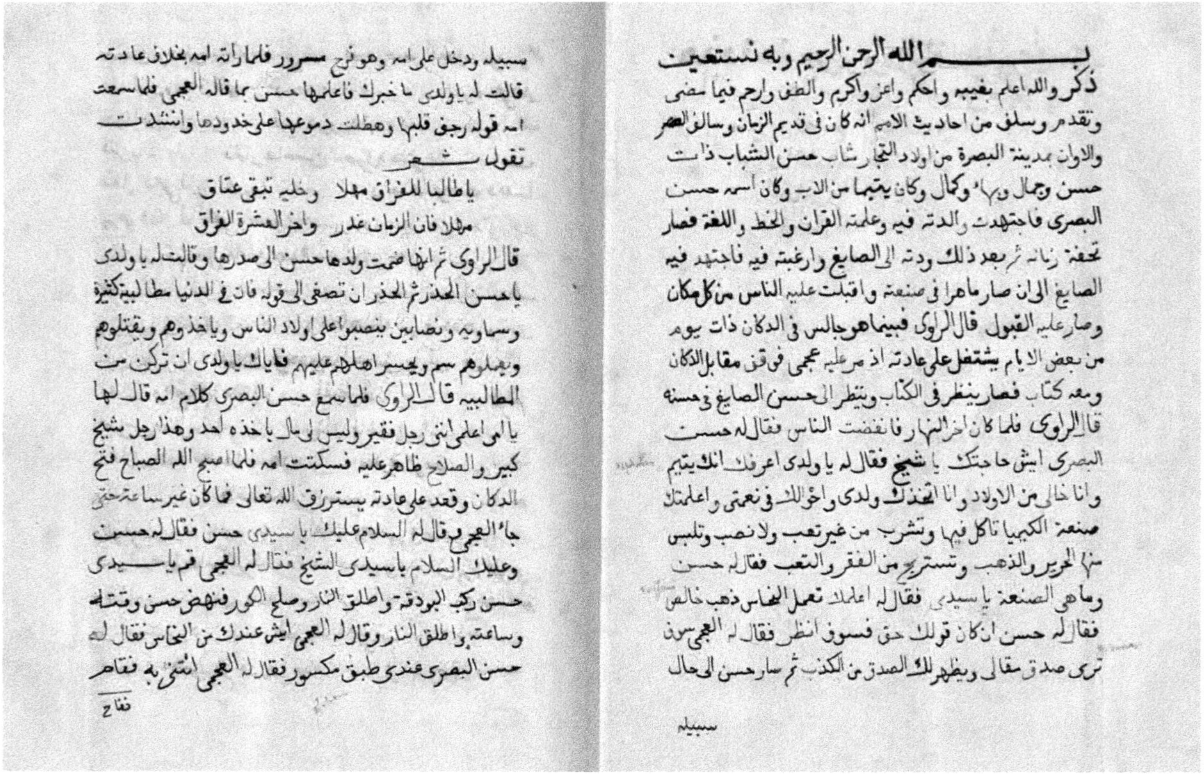

Figure 14 Opening manuscript page: The Story of Wāq Wāq.
Source: Courtesy of Muḥammad al-Murr.

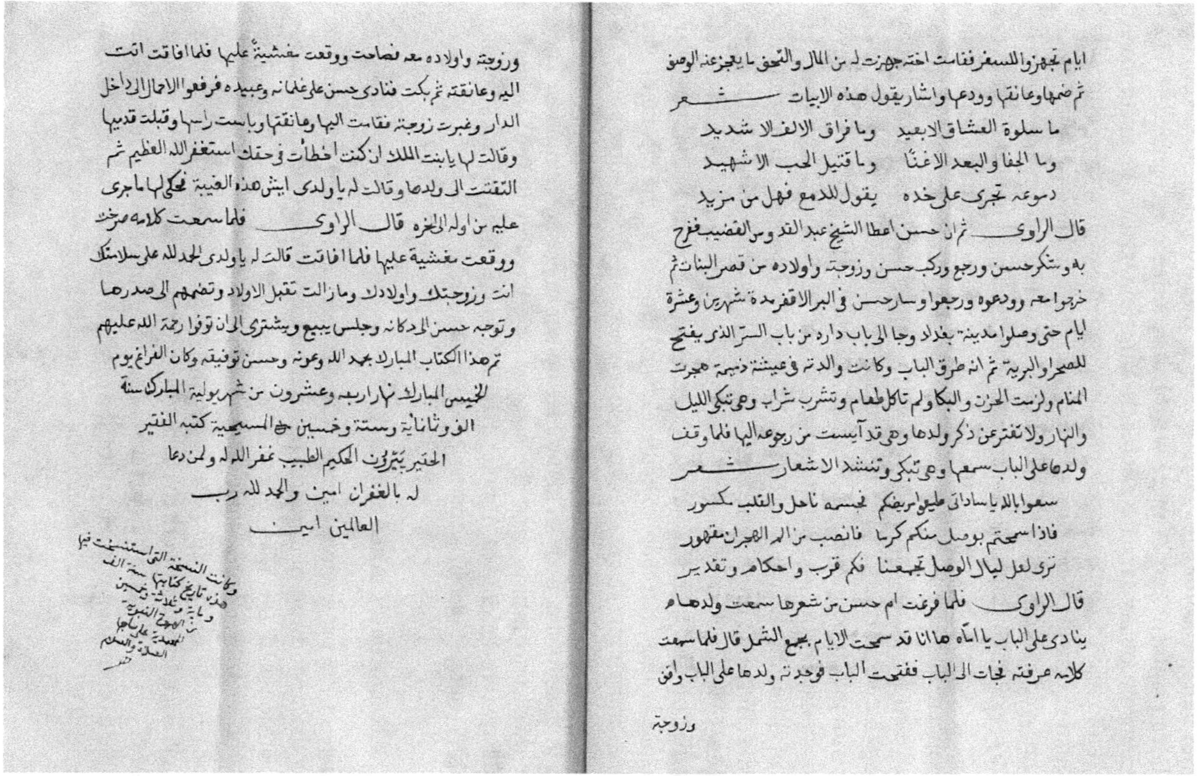

Figure 15 Last page: The Story of Wāq Wāq.
Source: Courtesy of Muḥammad al-Murr.

that was known for fabricating the Prophet's *ḥadīth* and using every means to revile his family according to the first caliph Muʿāwiyah's instructions, al-Masʿūdī's comment carries more weight than hitherto recognized.[37] The raconteurs' purpose was to have access to kings and be their boon companions. With regard to other details on this group in Muʿāwiyah's court, and the equation between *khurāfāt* and *Hazār afsānah* and their availability since the Umayyad period, al-Masʿūdī's statement is less informative than al-Nadīm's extensive reference to an art of storytelling. However, it does provide us with a continuous understanding of the varieties of narrative that happen to share a number of what postmodern discursive analysis terms "a well-determined set of discursive formations" with "describable relations between them."[38] The last examples that al-Nadīm mentions, and along with the emphasis laid on *khurāfah*, situate the discussion of narrative in a sociopolitical, but also entertaining, context. People in authority were in need of diversion, but they were also looking for edifying and instructing narrative. Although uninterested as yet in a rigorous comparative framework between *khurāfah* and *afsānah*, al-Nadīm at least reminds his readers of a number of narratives that were in demand. The narrator or storyteller was to please kings and caliphs. In this elevated profession, the raconteur was no less important than the epistolographer or the court poet. As a "systematic description of a discourse-object,"[39] archaeological explorations in this growing body of knowledge do not suggest continuities. They rather dwell on ruptures, and the absence of references to the *Thousand Nights* between the date of Abbott's fragment and al-Masʿūdī's statement, 920–45, is not necessarily a matter of lost books and manuals.

Raconteurs and Scribes

The rise of the professional scribe, the chancery epistolary art, and the raging discussions on poetry and translation blur other cultural productivities. Alongside this rise, there was also the proliferation of raconteurs since the eighth century, like ʿUbayd ibn Sharyah and Ibn al-Kalbī (737–819), before the explosion in the storyteller's profession where Ibn al-Maghāzlī and others were to make a visible social presence in the tenth century.[40] By the second half of the tenth century in Baghdad, Ibn ʿAbdūs was able to compile a written collection of what was circulating as tales at the time. This dialogue between the written, the translated, transferred,

[37] See Wilfred Madelung, *The Succession to Muhammad* (Cambridge: Cambridge University Press, 1996); and Ibn Abī al-Ḥadīd, *Sharḥ Nahj al-balāghah*, 20 vols., ed. Muḥammad Abū al-Faḍl Ibrāhīm (Beirut: Dār al-Kutub al-ʿIlmiyyah, n.d.); also in 2 and 4 vols.

[38] Foucault, *Archaeology of Knowledge*, 158. [39] Ibid., 140.

[40] For more on this, see al-Musawi, *The Islamic Context of the Thousand and One Nights*, 223.

and/or imitated and the oral tradition was the source for an enormous body of knowledge, one that has led Europeans to speak of an Oriental origin for fiction ever since the sixteenth century. Furthermore, the fragment that Abbott came cross among the possessions of the Oriental Institute (Chicago) specifies a migration indicated by the specific call by Dinazad (Dinarazad) for Syrian and Bedouin tales:

> The third significant fact is provided by the fragmentary text itself, namely, tales of Syrian and Bedouin Arab origin are singled out for special mention. The Bedouin Arab was, as he is still today, a "familiar figure of fact and fiction in all the Arab provinces of the empire."[41]

As argued by Abbott, this should mark a departure from an original text that had Baghdad as its habitat, one that offered a welcome to translations of narrative. The issue of writing appears as another problematic: How was *Alf laylah* transmitted if the derivative fragment was the oldest paper script extant at the time? Leather, parchments, and other scrolls could have been viable means even for an extensive narrative corpus. We have a large number of authored texts that were available before the appearance of fine paper. As Abbott shows, Samarqand paper took over soon after, and "gained rapidly and steadily over the leather and parchments imported from Persia and the papyrus that came from Egypt."[42]

This explains why we need to look at the scene in terms of an archaeological study, as "it operates in a great number of registers; it crosses interstices and gaps; it has its domain where unities are juxtaposed, separated, fix their crests, confront one another, and accentuate the white spaces between one another."[43] We need a bibliophile to step in and argue the case in view of these spaces. Al-Nadīm writes:

> The first who made separate compilations of *khurāfāt* into books and placed these latter into libraries and in some gave speaking parts to beasts were the early Persians. Thereafter the Ashghanian kings, who were the third dynasty of kings of Persia, became deeply absorbed in these. Thereafter that (kind of books) increased and spread in the days of the Sassanian kings. The Arabs translated these into the Arabic tongue. Then the eloquent and the rhetoricians took them in hand and revised them and re-wrote them in elegant style and composed, along the same idea, books that resembled them.[44]

As already noticed, this is an important intervention on the bibliophile's part. Narrative processes involve translation, transference, emulation, and genuine narrative cycles that resembled the Persian *khurāfāt*. Such narrative processes took place in an active cultural context. As

[41] Abbott, "A Ninth-Century Fragment," 145. [42] Ibid., 147.
[43] Foucault, *Archaeology of Knowledge*, 157.
[44] Abbott, "A Ninth-Century Fragment," 150–51.

Abbott suggests,[45] the issue of *khurāfāt* is central to these processes. Apart from the new turn toward regionalization/localization of narrative (Shāmī or Bedouin) in the fragment, the translation of the Persian *Afsānah* as *khurāfāt*, as designated in al-Nadīm's and also al-Masʿūdī's statements, does not show in the fragment, nor does it show in the tenth century's multiple uses of "Thousand and One," as carefully documented by Chraïbi.[46] However, and following MacDonald's lead, Abbott hints at the use of the term *khurāfah* as a proper name, authenticated in a narrative allegedly mentioned by the Prophet to one of his wives who had dismissed some report as "*khurāfah.*" Chraïbi's well-documented interventions present this use as significantly intertwined with the etymological root that descends from a proper name of a person who was – according to the narrative assigned to the Prophet – kidnapped by the jinn, and who came back with marvelous and fantastic narratives. Even if we presume the report was fabricated, and argue against the authority of Ibn Ḥanbal (780–855), the mere circulation of the narrative as being the Prophet's response to his wife's dismissal of a fantastic story as *khurāfah* indicates a visible presence in a cultural script that was in search for Islamic authentication and legitimacy. Before going further, we need to return to al-Nadīm's statement:

> The first book that was made along this (*khurāfāt*) idea was the book of *Hazār Afsānah* which means a Thousand *khurāfāt*. The reason for its composition was that one of their kings whenever he had married a woman and passed a night with her, killed her on the morrow. Presently he married a maiden of royal descent, possessed of understanding and knowledge, who was called Shahrazad. And when she was first with him, she began telling him *khurāfāt* carrying the story along at the end of the night in such a way as to lead the king to preserve her alive and to ask her on the following night for the completion of the story until she had passed a thousand nights. And the king had a stewardess (*qahramanah*) who was called Dinarzad and she assisted her in that. The truth is – Allah willing – that the first to whom stories were told at night was Alexander the Great. He had people who used to make him laugh and tell him *khurāfāt*, not that he was seeking pleasure thereby but only as a means of keeping vigilant and on his guard. After him the kings used for that purpose the book of *Hazār Afsānah*. It contains a thousand nights and less than two hundred night stories, for the narration of a story often lasted through several nights. I have seen it in its entirety several times. It is in reality a worthless book of silly tales.[47]

Al-Nadīm saw the book *Hazār afsānah* many times, but, if it originates during the Umayyad period, are we sure it is a full-text translation? Apart from al-Nadīm's explanation that *afsānah* means *khurāfāt*, and that the

[45] Ibid., 151. [46] Chraïbi, "Introduction."
[47] Abbott, "A Ninth-Century Fragment," 151.

collection was extant in his time, the bibliophile al-Nadīm expands on what al-Mas'ūdī reports on the issue of the frame tale. The translation of a "worthless book of silly tales" speaks rather of the tenth-century cultural milieu that was extremely rich in literary and cultural productivity. It looked down on the Persian collection, but welcomed the appropriation of selected tales from Indian, Persian, and Greek sources that were to appear alongside its local/regional tales. Ibn 'Abdūs used such principles to compile "superior" narratives in the manner followed in anthologies and compendiums, but with more focus on the division into nights as *nocturnal* (*samar*) narratives. Al-Nadīm speaks highly of the endeavor:

Ibn 'Abdūs al-Jahshiyārī, the author of *Kitāb al-wuzarā'*, began to compile a book in which he made choice of a thousand night stories, *alf samar*, out of the night stories of the Arabs, Persians, Greeks, and others, each part independent in itself and unconnected with another. He summoned the tellers of night stories and took from them the best of what they knew and in which they excelled. Then he selected from books of night stories and *khurāfāt* what was to his taste and what was superior. So, out of all these, he brought together 480 nights, for each night a complete story consisting of fifty pages, more or less. But death overtook him before he had accomplished his intention of completing (the collection of) a thousand night stories. I have seen several parts of the collection in the handwriting of Abī al-Ṭayyib the brother of al-Shāf'ī.[48]

Now, previous to this compilation of Ibn 'Abdūs, there were several figures who composed night stories and *khurāfāt*, giving speaking parts to people, birds, and beasts. Among them were 'Abd Allāh ibn al-Muqaffa', Sahl ibn Harūn, and 'Alī ibn Dāwūd, the secretary of princess Zubaydah bint Ja'far (d. July 10, AD 831), wife and double cousin of the fifth Abbasid caliph Hārūn al-Rashīd.

Should we think of Ibn 'Abdūs as heir to the last three names and others like them? Or should we rely more on what was related by 'Amr ibn Baḥr al-Jāḥiẓ in his delineation of the storytelling craft and practice as superbly described by Khālawiyah the mendicant to his son? Or soon after by Abū al-Muṭahhar al-Azdī in *Ḥikāyat Abī al-Qāsim al-Baghdādī*, where the latter is described in terms that supersede Abū al-Fatḥ al-Iskandarī, the primary character in al-Hamadhānī's (d. 1007) *Maqāmāt*, in detail, ruse, physiological description, and focus on narrative, not plot?[49] In other words, we have professional writers, translators, and/or editors, like the

[48] Ibid.

[49] al-Azdī, *Ḥikāyat Abī al-Qāsim al-Baghdādī*, 46, 76–86, 88. See more on this in Muḥsin Jāsim al-Mūsawī, *Sardiyyāt al-'aṣr al-'Arabī al-Islāmī al-wasīṭ* (Beirut: al-Markaz al-Thaqāfī al-'Arabī, 1997), 157–74. In English, see Devin Stewart, "The Maqāma," in *Arabic Literature in the Post-classical Period*, ed. Roger Allen and D. S. Richards (Cambridge: Cambridge University Press, 2006), 145–58; and Jaakko Hämeen-Anttila, *Maqama: A History of a Genre* (Wiesbaden: Otto Harrassowitz Verlag, 2002).

three mentioned by al-Nadīm, who were more in the domain of writing, and the other group of raconteurs and fabulators who were so visible in the streets and marketplaces that market inspectors and conservative jurists regarded them as being dangerous.[50] However, Ibn ʿAbdūs's effort was not alien to an active and thriving culture in the Baghdad of his times. "To meet the demands of the newly emerging reading publics, the literati had to develop other means and terms of literary production."[51] Writing down and inscribing narrative was prioritized for a number of reasons. Alongside a growing reading public, there was also a fear among the literati that their store of memorized stories was dwindling and fading; or their circulated tales were being defiled. Upon returning to Baghdad in 971, Abū ʿAlī al-Maḥāsin al-Tanūkhī (d. 994) wrote:

> As for the tales, whatever I stored in memory began to dwindle and fade, and the meaning and theme of material orally narrated by people suffered distortion, to the extent that that those who reported what we had already heard began to put into it things that defiled and distorted it.[52]

In view of these fears and the demand for "superior" storytelling, Ibn ʿAbdūs's effort was timely. The emphasis on "his taste" and "superior" endeavor speaks of a specific tendency among the learned to further earlier ninth-century efforts to mainstream nocturnal narratives. Whether some of his 480 nights found their way to the collection that reached Europe is a question that nobody can answer, not only because of lost manuscripts, but also because of the nature of such compilations as necessarily in conversation with migration, tastes, and the intrinsic dynamics of narrative sustainability. However, al-Nadīm's reference to Ibn ʿAbdūs is important for the carefully drawn line between "silly" tales and others that were arranged and elevated to the standard of acceptable narrative. So, where are we to place Khurāfah's tales of ransom motifs and ensorcelled humans? While we have to agree with Chraïbi and his team in "The *Thousand and One Nights*: Sources and Functions in Medieval Arabic Islam," namely, the need to consider "any manuscript with the frame story of Shahrayar and His Brother," as legitimate in the genesis of the constellation and its surrounding corpus,[53] we still also need to explore the cultural context of this genealogy.

While taking into account the rise of transmission as methodological authentication, and its application to *ḥadīth* as an obligatory practice, Khurāfah's tales from the world of jinn resonate with many a verse in

[50] For more on this point, see al-Musawi, *The Islamic Context of the Thousand and One Nights*, 213–18, 221–24, 234–36.
[51] Ibid., 215. [52] Ibid. [53] Chraïbi, "Introduction," 15.

the Qurʾān. In other words, there is a world where the divides between the natural and the supernatural are blurred.[54] However, there was also a parallel tendency in tandem with the rising urban centers that rewrote the ethics of survival beyond Islamic regulatory standards and provisions. Alongside many treatises, poems, and epistles on the increasing demands of urban life, al-Jāḥiẓ offers characters that rewrite the Islamic script on avarice, for example. As argued elsewhere,[55] the standing reliance on both the acceptable and questionable, the canonized and deviational, shows narrative "as an egalitarian art." In his portrayal of Khālid ibn Yazīd (otherwise Khālawayh the *mukaddī*, also written as *mukdī*, "tramp"), and theft, or between the *qaṣṣ* (storytelling) as profession and vagabondage, al-Jāḥiẓ gives voice to Khālawayh whose letter to his son provides a unique instance of a profession at a certain time in the history of material culture. While stressing that professions are equal in a changing society, both vagabondage and *qaṣṣ* can bring one some wealth: "If my wealth goes, I will be a *qāṣṣ* or a vagabond, as I was a tramp. My beard is abundant and white; my throat is voluble and robust; my demeanor is good, and people find me appealing."[56] Apart from the emphasis on physiology, there is the art of storytelling, or its equal, that is, the art of mendicancy and beggary.[57] Had these instances been outside the domain of *A Thousand Nights* and its specific frame story? Why did Ibn ʿAbdūs gather storytellers? And what was al-Tanūkhī afraid of when writing of/on tales? Scheherazade's fecund memory is very much like that of al-Tanūkhī, Abū al-Faraj al-Iṣfahānī, and al-Masʿūdī or al-Nadīm. Even without a frame, there was once in Baghdad, Damascus, and Cairo a massive body of narrative that was available to other writers like Ibn ʿAbdūs and al-Tawḥīdī. How should we deal with the problem of manuscripts of tales with or without the *Hazār afsānah* frame that Chraïbi rightly raises as one way of inventorizing manuscripts that he counts as reaching one hundred? Whatever connects to *Hazār afsānah* falls within the corpus of *A Thousand and One Nights*; but this corpus was to undergo detraction and accretion as necessarily tied to the roles of storytellers, publics, and locations. Thus, another inventory of tales that makes its way from famous narrators, storytellers, translators, and historians is absolutely necessary to construct

[54] For more, see Amira El-Zein, *Islam, Arabs, and the Intelligent World of the Jinn* (New York: Syracuse University Press, 2009).

[55] al-Musawi, "Abbasid Popular Narrative," 283–84.

[56] Abū ʿUthmān ʿAmr ibn Baḥr al-Jāḥiẓ, *al-Bukhalāʾ*, ed. Ṭāhā al-Ḥājirī (Cairo: Dār al-Maʿārif, n.d.), 12–13, 53.

[57] Clifford Edmund Bosworth, *The Medieval Islamic Underworld: The Banu Sasan in Arabic Society and Literature* (Leiden: Brill, 1976).

a history for *A Thousand and One Nights*, which the *Athenaeum* reviewer starts with his reference to Ibn Saʿīd al-Qurṭubī's *al-Muḥallā bi-l-ashʿār* (*Adorned with Verses*),[58] to be followed by MacDonald's quote from al-Maqrīzī's *Khiṭaṭ*, then by S. D. Goitein.[59] There, as reported by many and familiar to Europeans through an article in the *Athenaeum* in 1839, the comparison is drawn between the stories spun around the Bedouin woman and Ibn Mayyāḥ and the tales of *al-baṭṭāl* (the loafer) and *A Thousand and One Nights*.[60] Earlier, and in mid-ninth-century Baghdad, ʿAbd Allāh ibn ʿAbd al-ʿAzīz al-Kātib had claimed ʿAbd Allāh ibn al-Muqaffaʿ (d. 756) was the translator of *Hazār afsānah* into Arabic.[61] Scholars like Chraïbi doubt this claim because of the known elevated style of Ibn al-Muqaffaʿ. Chraïbi offers a different hypothesis, namely, that Ibn al-Muqaffaʿ "did translate *something* connected with our *Nights*, [and] that *something* is now lost."[62] The matter of style is disputable on the basis of Abbott's fragment; and content varies according to the original, especially if we think of the frame story in particular as no less instructive with respect to the human condition than his other works. The

58 The reviewer for the *Asiatic Journal* 30, 117 (September–December 1839), 84, was impressed by the growing academic interest in the *Nights*, noticing that it "is becoming more than ever an object of grave attention and research." The reviewer might be C. Forbes Falconer as Burton guessed (see the "Terminal Essay" in the Burton Club Edition [n.d., 10:87]) for he, in Burton's conjecture, could hardly be distinguished in style and substance from the *Athenaeum* reviewer of the *Nights* in the late 1830s. Victor Chauvin, *Bibliographie des ouvrages arabes ou relatifs aux arabes*, 12 vols. (Liège: Vaillant-Carmanne, 1892–1922), 4:116, identified the latter as Falconer. Although Chauvin's reference was to the authorship of the September 28, 1839, item, the reviewer, as I notice, made cross-references to his other writings: nos. 572–74 (October 13, 20, 27, 1838), 737–39, 759–60, 773–75, and nos. 622, 624 (September 28, 1839; October 12, 1839), 741–42 and 773–75, respectively. Let me venture to say that both Chauvin and Burton were mistaken in this identification, for in the late 1830s the outstanding Spanish Orientalist Don Pascual de Gayangos (later Minister of Public Education and Senator in Spain), and later translator of al-Maqqarī (where the reference to the *Nights* is made), worked as a reviewer of Oriental works for the *Athenaeum*. His citations from manuscript material accessible at the British Museum testify to his authorship of the aforesaid contribution, for during his residence in England the British Museum put him in charge of cataloging its Andalusian manuscripts. The book, which was translated by the same reviewer, is al-Maqqarī's *Nafḥ al-ṭīb min ghusn al-Andalus al-raṭīb*, trans. P. de Gayangos, *History of the Mohammaden Dynasties in Spain*, 2 vols. (London, 1840–41). For more on the involved history of storytelling, see Jabrī, *Majallat majmaʿ al-lughah al-ʿArabiyyah fī Dimashq* 47, no. 1 (January 1972), 3–9. See also al-Mūsawī, *al-Dhākirah al-shaʿbiyyah*, 38–40.

59 S. D. Goitein, "The Oldest Documentary Evidence for the Title Alf Laila wa-Laila," *Journal of the American Oriental Society* 78 (1958), 301–2. See further notes on this point later.

60 Drawn upon by al-Maqrīzī, and also Shihāb al-Dīn ibn Faḍl Allāh al-ʿUmarī, *Masālik al-abṣār fī mamālik al-amṣār*, ed. Mahdī al-Najm and Kāmil Salmān al-Jubūrī (Beirut: Dār al-Kutub al-ʿIlmiyyah, 2010), 14:91n3.

61 See Chraïbi, "Introduction," 17, referencing Hilāl Nājī, *al-Mawrid* 2, no. 2 (1973), 59.

62 Ibid.

availability of sixteenth- and seventeenth-century Ottoman manuscripts can be helpful. The more demanding and urgent question concerning a genealogy of narrative and its accrual processes is: How and what tales could have been hosted by the frame story? One way is to check on early storytellers, and then the tales that made their way to the grand hostess. *Dhayl zahr al-ādāb, aw Jam' al-jawāhir fī al-mulaḥ wa-l-nawādir* by Ibrāhīm ibn 'Alī al-Ḥuṣrī al-Qayrawānī (d. 1022)[63] can provide us with a viable start because it relates a series of rarities, night narratives, anecdotes, and sayings. He duplicates what polyglots like al-Tanūkhī enumerate as a practice in collecting material, for he also makes sure to collect "from among the rare tales of the ancients and the moderns, the jewels of the sane and the deranged, and the singularities of the fraudulent and the virtuous, the wonders of the magnanimous and the stingy, the novelties of the ignorant and the learned." He includes "the ploys of the heedless and insightful, snippets from philosophers and wise men, and the ingenuities of supplicants and the storytellers." Moreover, he selects from among "the wonders of plebes and elite, the delights of dignitaries and rabble, the banquets of parasites and guests, the accounts of dissolute and eunuchs, and snippets from women and children."[64] By conversing with such human varieties and selecting what is "embroidered" in his *Flowers of the Arts*, al-Ḥuṣrī was part of a tradition that, by the end of the tenth century, had reached its zenith in Shams al-Dīn al-Muqaddasī (b. Jerusalem, 945–91) and his impressive geographical work, *Aḥsan al-taqāsīm fī ma'rifat al-aqālīm* (*The Best Divisions for the Knowledge of the Provinces*),[65] where he makes a specific mention of a long list of roles he had to perform to gather this massive constellation with many narrative snippets that resonate with tales in *A Thousand and One Nights*.[66] More so is Abū Yaḥyā Zakariyyā ibn Muḥammad al-Qazwīnī's (d. 1283) *'Ajā'ib al-makhlūqāt* (*Wonders of Creation*).[67] The reader has to ask which came first: the *Nights*, Sindbad tales, or al-Qazwīnī's book, especially

[63] See al-Ḥuṣrī al-Qayrawānī, *Zahr al-ādāb wa-thimār al-albāb*, ed. 'A. M. al-Bajāwī (Cairo: al-Bābī al-Ḥalabī, 1970); also A. M. al-Bajāwī's Dār al-Jīl edition, under the title *Jam' al-jawāhir* (Beirut: Dār al-Jīl, 1987), 3. For more on al-Ḥuṣrī, see Georges-Francois Montillet, "The Flowering of Adab: The Life and Works of Abū Ishāq al-Husrī" (PhD diss., Yale University, 2013).

[64] *Jam' al-jawāhir*, 3. Montillet's translation is used with substantial alterations, 131–32.

[65] Shams al-Dīn al-Muqaddasī, *Aḥsan al-taqāsīm fī ma'rifat al-aqālīm*, ed. M. J. de Goeje, Bibliotheca Geographorum Arabicorum, vol. 3 (Leiden: Brill, 1906).

[66] Kratignati Iulianovich Krachkovski, *Istoria Arabskoi Geograficheskoi Literatury* (Beirut: Dār al-Gharb al-Islāmī, 1963–65); in Arabic: *Tārīkh al-adab al-jughrāfī al-'Arabī*, trans. Ṣalāḥ al-Dīn 'Uthmān Hāshim (1987), 232–33.

[67] Abū Yaḥyā Zakariyyā ibn Muḥammad al-Qazwīnī, *'Ajā'ib al-makhlūqāt wa-gharā'ib al-mawjūdāt* (Beirut: Dār al-Sharq al-'Arabī, n.d.), 118. See Travis Zadeh, "The Wiles of Creation: Philosophy, Fiction, and the 'Aja'ib Tradition," *Middle Eastern Literatures* 13, no. 1 (2010), 21–48. For Sindbad prototypes, see al-Mūsawī, *al-Dhākirah al-sha'biyyah*, 558–60.

Figure 16 Edmund Dulac: The old man of the sea.

in matters associated with wonders, like rocs and the old man of the sea (Figure 16) whom the author references as reported by Yaʿqūb ibn Isḥāq al-Sarrāj. The latter narrative has its echoes in night 557 (2:26, Būlāq).[68]

Whose Authorship among So Many Names?

The navigation between narratives and narrators or performers was a deliberate strategy to meet the increasing demand for entertaining and

[68] al-Mūsawī, *al-Dhākirah al-shaʿbiyyah*, 559.

useful knowledge. Although al-Jāḥiẓ was almost a common property to the extent that al-Qāḍī al-Fāḍil once said that no writer escaped the impact of al-Jāḥiẓ,[69] the latter was in turn indebted to Ibn al-Muqaffaʿ, Ibn Najīʿ, Ibrāḥīm ibn al-Sindī ibn Shāhik, al-Aṣmaʿī, Abī ʿUbaydah, Muḥammad ibn al-Jahm, and Ṣabāḥ ibn Khāqān. Ibn ʿAbdūs tried to organize narrative, have it tabulated, and make it available to a privileged class. In his case, as with al-Ḥuṣrī, sources were either individuals (transmitters, reporters, and storytellers) or written material. Al-Ḥuṣrī's sources were no less than al-Jāḥiẓ, Isḥāq al-Mawṣilī, al-Aṣmaʿī, Ibn al-Muʿtazz, Abū al-ʿAynāʾ, Ibn Jāmiʿ, Abū al-ʿĀliyah, and al-Haytham ibn ʿAdī.[70] He also enlists those figures known for their entertainments, like Abū Dulāmah, Abū al-ʿIbar, ʿAbd Allāh Abū al-Sāʾib, Ibn Jāmiʿ, and many others. In his *Fihrist*, al-Nadīm mentions Abū ʿAlī ibn Hammām's book on *riwāyāt wa-nawādir* (stories and anecdotes), Jarīr ibn ʿAbd Allāh's *Kitāb al-nawādir*, and Ibn Qutaybah Muḥammad ibn Muslim al-Kūfī's *al-Ḥikāyah wa-l-Maḥkī* (Tales and What Is Being Told). Under the same title there are two more books by Jaʿfar ibn Muyassar and Abū Sahl al-Tuwayjī; whereas al-Masʿūdī mentions Ibn al-Maghāzalī.[71] Al-Nadīm makes mention of a notorious fabricator/fabulator by the name of Ibn Dallān. Mamluk Cairo could have added more names and titles to this repertoire. A legitimate question is: How much of these narratives made their way to the frame tale? Even if we assume that the tale of Khurāfah's abduction and fantastic ransom adventures passed through a narrative filter to emerge in the tale of "The Merchant and the Demon," this should enable us to understand narrative activity as an ongoing process of improvement. Early comparatists like H. F. Amedroz wrote in 1904 how a story related by al-Tanūkhī and his son ʿAlī found its way to Ibn al-Jawzī's *al-Muntaẓam*, then to the thirteenth-century *al-Ḥikāyāt al-ʿajībah*, and *A Thousand and One Nights*. He concludes:

It is interesting to contrast the two narratives, and to note how the story in the "Nights" differs from the original as told by Ibn al-Jauzi. The inevitable loss to truth caused by the exercise of the imagination should find its compensation in the heightened interest of a picturesque narrative, but in this instance the original seems to be in every way the better story. Indeed, in the reversion from fiction to fact the tale will be found to have lost all its evil, whilst retaining all its grossness – the latter, however, being quite inconsiderable. It depicts the course of true love, not a wholly smooth one, but marred by no such traits of excessive temper and

[69] See *Kitāb al-tāj*, ed. Aḥmad Zekī Bāshā (Cairo: al-Amīriyyah, 1914), 29n2. See also al-Mūsawī, *Sardiyyāt al-ʿaṣr*, 34.
[70] See on this al-Mūsawī, *Sardiyyāt al-ʿaṣr*, 38–54.
[71] For more, see al-Musawi, *The Islamic Context of the Thousand and One Nights*, 223.

wanton cruelty as disfigure the Steward's Story. Nor do any of the minor deviations from the original amount to improvements.[72]

Before moving to Muhsin Mahdi's reading and Julia Bray's sequel to it, it is worthwhile to read the conclusion to this early comparative study of structure in view of what structuralists speak of as distributional or integrational factors. Amedroz thinks that the *Arabian Nights*' conclusion is less dramatic than the original, a point which Mahdi does not deny. He explains:

The remainder of the story told in the "Nights" differs in spirit as in letter from our version. In place of the bride's exaggerated resentment and wanton cruelty to her husband, followed by his tame submission to conjugal happiness with her, we find her behavior to be as probable as it is pleasing.[73]

Mahdi finds it better to start with a genesis of *ḥadīth*s (reports or narratives). "The storyteller used the version reported by al-Muḥassin al-Tanūkhī in his book *al-Faraj ba'd al-shiddah* [*Deliverance after Stress*]."[74] "The other version is transmitted on the authority of his son ʿAlī, who reported it on the authority of his father."[75] In a later essay included in his second volume of *A Thousand and One Nights* (1995), Mahdi became aware of Amedroz's 1904 essay, but the direction of his study remains concerned with two things: the historicization of a source insofar as it differs from the burgeoning tale in the *Nights*; and an extensive reordering of a structure. The first point is the drift of the argument in both authored versions. He suggests historicization as necessarily bound to a milieu in a certain time:

What would have seemed impossible to the audience of the historical report in tenth-century Baghdad could very well seem possible to the audience of *1001 Nights* version in fourteenth-century Damascus or Cairo, which consisted of semi-literate men and women who remembered nothing to gainsay what they had heard about what might have happened in eighth- or ninth-century Baghdad: for all they knew, this was history, or else they were only too willing to transform the fictional version back into history.[76]

In the updated version, which appears as appendix 3 in Mahdi's, the latter justifies the need for such comparative studies of the migration of

[72] H. F. Amedroz, "A Tale of the Arabian Nights: Told as History in the 'Muntazam' of Ibn al-Jauzi," *Journal of the Royal Asiatic Society* (April 1904), 276.
[73] Ibid., 279.
[74] ʿAbbūd al-Shāljī, *al-Faraj ba'd al-shiddah*, 5 vols., ed. al-Muḥassin al-Tanūkhī (Beirut: Dār Ṣādir, 1978).
[75] Muhsin Mahdi, "From History to Fiction: The Tale Told by the King's Steward in the *1001 Nights*," *Oral Tradition* 4, no. 1–2 (1989), 65.
[76] Ibid., 79.

narratives between "history" and its varieties and storytelling: Scholars turn away from the study of origins and historical backgrounds and find studies of textualities more "profitable." His conclusions with respect to the divergence between the tale and the origin makes an important contribution to any analysis of the nature of both. Every instance of divergence has one reason or another behind it. However, Bray corroborates what both Amedroz and Mahdi have already reached. She emphasizes the "deliberately structured thematic patterns in the *Faraj* stories, which need to be taken into account in any evaluation of their historical content."[77] I must add, however, that a first step in this direction should start with a study of al-Tanūkhī's conceptualization of narrative, not only in *Faraj*, but also in *Nishwār*, a point that I have tried to address in other places.[78] Furthermore, the dramatic conclusion of the original or the trimming of details, and the collapsing of acts in the tale highlight the genesis of storytelling as necessarily tied to specific readerships at certain moments that demand narratorial management on the distributional or integrational levels. In his synthesis of what Benveniste and then Todorov address as narrative levels, or metonymic units of meaning, Roland Barthes speaks of the distributional level as that of same-level narrative, whereas the integrational one operates vertically from one level to another.[79] In commenting on Todorov's distinction in the manner of Russian Formalists between *story* as a logic of actions and a "syntax" of characters, and *discourse* as "comprising the tenses, aspects and modes of the narrative," Barthes reaches an important conclusion with respect to practical criticism. He argues, "To understand a narrative is not merely to follow the unfolding of the story, it is also to recognize its construction in 'storeys,' to project the horizontal concatenations of the narrative 'thread' on to an implicitly vertical axis."[80]

The tale of the cloth merchant received attention as a historical account that made its way into *A Thousand and One Nights*,[81] but it is not the only one. The close resemblance between the two is more visible, to be sure, and it is one of the tales that also circulated widely in *al-Muntaẓam*, and then in Dāwūd al-Anṭākī's (d. 1599) *Tazyīn al-aswāq*.[82] There are a number of reasons behind this easy migration: its compactness as a story, its accessible discourse, and the neat concatenation in its

[77] Julia Bray, "A Caliph and His Public Relations," in *New Perspectives on the Arabian Nights*, ed. Wen-Chin Ouyang and Geert Jan van Gelder (London: Routledge, 2014), 27–38.
[78] See al-Mūsawī, *Sardiyyāt al-ʿaṣr*, 18–28; and al-Musawi, "Abbasid Popular Narrative."
[79] Barthes, "Introduction," 86. [80] Ibid., 87.
[81] "The Steward's Tale: The Young Man from Baghdad and Lady Zubaida's Maid," in *The Arabian Nights*, trans. Husain Haddawy, 228–37.
[82] Dāwūd al-Anṭākīʾ, *Tazyīn al-aswāq bi-taʿṣīl ashwāq al-ʿushshāq* (Beirut: ʿĀlam al-Kutub, 1993).

distributional and integrational narrative levels. While it is true that the original narrative is historically couched in the time of the Abbasid caliph al-Muqtadar, a time when narratives were encouraged and some social mobility was visible, the version in the *Nights* (nos. 121–29, Brill) is obviously tampered with in its Cairene milieu, as shown by the interest in Hārūn al-Rashīd's time, the use of mixed idiolects, and the typical Cairene verse (no. 121, Brill, p. 304). The departure from the origin happens in cases in which actual dramatic action is not involved. In other words, it happens on the distributional level of symbols, rules, and social practices. Both origin and tale agree on the following: the son's inheritance and meeting the slave girl from the caliphal entourage who is prepared to be the stewardess (*qahramānah*). As there is often some reciprocity and/or complementarity, the palace and the marketplace have to make concessions for love. What is missing in the son's case is the motivation to rise up socially, while she is missing love. The best place for meeting is the market where his cloth shop is the most appropriate site for such overt/covert meetings. Hierarchy is upheld in the original as in the tale because no marriage can take place without the palace's agreement firstly to free the *mamlūkah* (slave girl) and then to facilitate the marriage. The tale tightens space to allow a rapid sequence of action. Hence even the masjid has not to be far from the marketplace and the river (which was the case in Baghdad topography until very recently).[83]

A number of tales that were reported as historical accounts found their way into the *Nights* whenever the possibility of switching names, locales, and residuals is available. Narratives that sound different from the outset find their way into the frame tale: for instance, such is the one reported by al-Jāḥiẓ in his *al-Maḥāsin wa-l-aḍdād* on the authority of the prominent Basran school philologist Abū al-Ḥātim al-Sijistānī (d. 869).[84] This narrative speaks of the caliph's suffering from insomnia, and thus sending for al-Aṣmaʿī and the poet al-Ḥusayn ibn al-Ḍaḥḥāk (al-Khalīʿ – i.e., the profligate or dissolute) for diversion.[85] The latter's narrative finds its way into nights 328–31 (Būlāq), but, instead of the boon companion and poet, we have as narrator ʿAlī ibn Manṣūr al-Khalīʿī (the dissolute) al-Dimashqī. Both address the caliph Hārūn al-Rashīd of the *Arabian Nights*. They are both poets and boon companions, and both come upon the house of the charming damsel in Basra. But, instead of the anonymous lady in the

83 See for more al-Mūsawī, *al-Dhākirah al-shaʿbiyyah*, 77–82.

84 Abū ʿUthmān ʿAmr ibn Baḥr al-Jāḥiẓ, *al-Maḥāsin wa-l-aḍdād*, ed. Fawzī ʿAṭwī (Beirut: al-Sharikah al-Lubnāniyyah, 1969), 183–89, 282.

85 Full name: ʿAbd al-Malik ibn Qurayb al-Aṣmaʿī (ca. 740–828); and Abūʿ Alī al-Ḥusayn ibn al-Ḍaḥḥāk (778–870).

historical narrative, we have in the tale Budūr bint Muḥammad ʿAlī al-Jawharī. Both narrators are aging, and hence are addressed as sheikh. Al-Ḥusayn ibn al-Ḍaḥḥāk comes upon a house where a Basran damsel looks around, expectant and hopeful; whereas the tale makes the narrator's thirst a reason to stop by a spacious house with a large door that is ajar, allowing him to hear from afar moaning and whimpering. Both narratives focus on estrangement and reunion or integration. Separation takes place because the male lovers come upon their beloved in a love scene with another damsel. Only the intervention of the sheikhs and a series of poetic exchanges bring them together.[86] A similar migration takes place in night 279. The origin goes back to Ibn Ṭayfūr's (d. 893) *Kitāb Baghdad*. It relates the story of the singing slave girl ʿArīb, whose master has taken every measure to get her the best education, until she is famed for her singing, knowledge, poetry, and refinement. Her love for Ḥātim ibn ʿAdī has driven her once to prepare a rope to escape from her master's palace to meet her lover. She is then the slave girl to the caliph al-Maʾmūn, and repeats the same escape to join the poet Jaʿfar ibn Ḥāmid. Stories around her multiplied, and narratives switched her name to Būrān bint al-Ḥasan ibn Sahl, who was to become the caliph's wife. Ibn ʿAbd Rabbihi relates the story on the authority of Ḥammād ibn Isḥāq al-Mawṣilī as he heard it from his father, who was in the company of the caliph al-Maʾmūn during an incognito nocturnal adventure when they came across a large basket of thick palm leaves dangling from the wall of a palace, waiting for whoever took the risk of using it to be pulled up inside. The "historical" narrative, the one presented in books as factual, was reported as the story behind the caliph's marriage, but one can tell that both the "historical" narrative and the tale are fabricated because they used common stories reported in *Kitāb al-aghānī* (*The Book of Songs*), and its like. The same occurs in nights 279–82 (Būlāq) where the storyteller makes use of what is available as a historical account in *Kitāb al-mukāfaʾah* by Ibn al-Dāyah, and a century later in al-Khaṭīb al-Baghdādī's *Tarīkh Baghdad*, and Ibn al-Jawzī's *al-Muntaẓam*.[87] Ibn Khallikān later reports the same account, without the emplotment found in *Alf laylah*, that is, the mamluk's refusal to divorce the slave girl whom the caliph would like to have on that night. The historical source mentions a prominent figure, ʿĪsā ibn Jaʿfar, as sitting on the right side of the caliph. In reporting the caliph's address to the prominent judge and jurist Yaʿqūb Abū Yūsuf al-Qāḍī, who is the speaker in the following text, the historical account reads thus:

[86] See al-Mūsawī, *al-Dhākirah al-shaʿbiyyah*, 101–4.
[87] Ibn al-Jawzī, *al-Muntaẓam* (Beirut: Dār al-Kutub al-ʿIlmiyyah, 1992), 9, 77–79.

"Do you know why I brought you here, Yaʿqūb?" asked the caliph.

"No."

"I call on you to witness that this [man ʿĪsā ibn Jaʿfar] has a slave girl whom I asked him to have as gift, but he refused. I asked him to sell her, he also refused. And by God, if he will not relent, I'll have him killed."

I [Yaʿqūb Abū Yūsuf] looked at ʿĪsā: "What is the merit in this slave girl that you deny her to the Commander of the Faithful, and allow yourself to challenge authority as if you were in the same status?"

He [ʿĪsā] rejoined: "You could have waited for my response before castigating me."

"So what is there as an answer?" asked Yaʿqūb Abū Yūsuf.

"I [ʿĪsā] took a binding oath that I divorce and manumit all I have, and relinquish what I own as alms if I ever sell or offer this slave girl as gift."[88]

Suhayr Qalamāwī argues that the *Nights* was the source of one motif,[89] the mamluk's refusal to divorce, that migrated in the opposite direction to the historical narrative. According to Ibn al-Jawzī (9:78), the caliph was infatuated with a slave girl, and he sent for the Qāḍī Abū Yūsuf, urging him to make arrangements to have the girl in a legitimate manner. Three difficulties arise: she was married, she was a slave (not a free woman), and the mamluk as husband swore not to divorce her. However, the caliph also swore to make love to her that night. This kind of a three-knotted morphological development relies more on speech – the oath as speech act – than physical action. In the historical narrative as well as in the tale, a legal language takes over. The narrative evolves as navigation in this verbal territory where indices of motifs cannot obtain. The Būlāq edition and its early nineteenth-century versions make use of that as part of a corpus, especially as Hārūn al-Rashīd is the protagonist in both. In the tale, the narrative rewrites the motif: instead of coming at the end of the first narrative plot, it appears first as incitement to action. Other verbal pronouncements as active incitements come later, like the effacement of divorce, and the legal clearance of a slave girl. Residuals abound, and they occupy the discursive space as long as these relate to codes, customs, and regulations associated with a caliphal entourage and life as in historical accounts. In the tale, emphasis is laid on motivation, the caliph's desire to have the slave girl in a formal Islamic marriage. This is why the mamluk's refusal appears as a high point in the dramatization of a verbal encounter between authority and Islamic jurisprudence. The divergence between

[88] Ibid. [89] See al-Qalamāwī, *Alf laylah wa-laylah*, 105.

the historical narrative and the tale, especially in names and roles, is important: as the historical origin speaks of a slave girl (*mamlukah*), her husband was a prominent individual. In the tale, the husband has to be a slave (*mamluk*). Everything that follows works in line with jurisprudence: only an adept like the judge Abū Yūsuf can work things out and surmount litigated obstacles.

Divergence might take a drastic direction insofar as discourse is concerned, or what Barthes describes in line with Todorov: whatever that comprises "the tenses, aspects and modes of narrative" and also the narrative grammar with a focus on "logic of actions and a syntax of characters."[90] Night 39 (Būlāq 1:128), for example, has the structure of a narrative that is available in al-Khaṭīb's *Tārīkh* (3:177), Ibn al-Jawzī's *Akhbār al-ẓurrāf wa-l-mutamājinīn* (132), and Yāqūt's *Muʿjam al-ʾudabāʾ* (7:69). All use Abū al-ʿAynāʾ Muḥammad ibn al-Qāsim's (d. AH 283) report on his reasons for leaving Basra after buying a certain slave: as in night 38, the slave has one defect – one lie a year. No one imagined that it could be so devastating. Also, the merchant of the *Nights* and Abū al-ʿAynāʾ never thought that the slave whom they had bought was an adept in litigation, medicine, and rhetoric. In this and other tales of a historical origin, it is noticeable that the storyteller and redactor invade these domains whenever they have at their disposal dramatic events, and urban tricks and ruses. Humor is also sought for because it is appealing to all audiences in an urban setting.

Other Instances of the Migration of Tales

On other occasions, the historical narrative migrates smoothly to the hosting *Nights*, as in night 682 (Būlāq), which Shihāb al-Dīn ibn Aḥmad al-Abshīhī (d. 1450) also collected from earlier sources.[91] This is the story of Hind bint al-Nuʿmān with al-Ḥajjāj ibn Yūsuf al-Thaqafī.[92] The same happens in night 407 (Būlāq, 1:587–88). The narrator is the poet Diʿbil al-Khuzāʿī (murdered in 861). The dramatic situation is the same, but variations occur on the distributional level that include poetic pronouncements. The *Nights* narrative maximizes affect through a narrative turn that hastens action. Instead of just leading the lady to the house of the poet Muslim ibn al-Walīd (d. 823), as in *al-Aghānī* (19:48–47), the narrator says: "I stood up in haste, and began to kiss her hands, saying I never thought that time could ever afford me such an

[90] Barthes, *Image, Music, Text*, 87.
[91] Shihāb al-Dīn ibn Aḥmad al-Abshīhī, *Tahdhīb al-Mustaṭraf fī kull fann mustaẓraf* (Beirut: Dār Ṣādir, 1999), 80.
[92] See al-Mūsawī, *al-Dhākirah al-shaʿbiyyah*, 127–30.

opportunity: follow me."[93] Another historical anecdote that easily found its way into the *Nights* (night 152, Brill, pp. 347–49) is one which is mentioned by both al-Masʿūdī (*Murūj al-dhahab* [*Meadow of Gold*], 4:9–10, 231–32) and Ibn ʿAbd Rabbihi's *al-ʿIqd al-farīd* (third ed. 1983, 87). The typical officious and inquisitive barber gets in a boat containing a group of people whom he thinks are crashing a party. When he is captured by the police and about to lose his head, he admits to his inquisitiveness. While the tale builds on a common motif in the *Nights*, conveying a lesson that unrestrained curiosity can bring about misfortune, the historical source and also the *Nights* offer an understanding of Manichaeism, its prophet Mani, rituals, and obligations. A heretic denomination that was tried and punished during the caliph al-Maʾmūn's reign, its practitioners were adept at making their case, something that baffles the barber who is punished for his unrestrained curiosity. Other stories that undergo some drastic turns in *A Thousand and One Nights* relate to psychiatry and psychology, like the tales that al-Tanūkhī included in *Nishwār*, such as "The Tale of the Woman of Hell" who belongs to a prosperous family but suffers from a passion for collecting coffins.[94] Less harrowing but startling nevertheless is the story of the old woman who tricks strangers into entering the house where a series of gruesome adventures follow. The tale morphed into the story of ʿAzīz and ʿAzīzah.[95] Such narrative treasures proved to be a textual mine worth raiding.[96]

Genesis and Episteme

Storytellers and redactors need tales with a surprising turn of events, an irony, humor, and a rich repertoire of urban life like that of Abbasid Baghdad. Compendiums and historical narratives had become an available source worth raiding and accommodating to live up to the number of *1001 Nights*. If we take into consideration manuscripts predating Galland's translation, not his manuscript, as inventorized by Ibrahim Akel,[97] issues of early genesis remain problematic. Apart from the evolution of a title, from "thousand" to "thousand and one," there should be an understanding of the theoretical base for the growth

[93] See Abū al-Faraj al-Iṣfahānī, *Kitāb al-aghānī* (Cairo: GEBO, 1993), 19:47–48; Būlāq, 2:587–88, night 407.

[94] Abū ʿAlī Muḥassin al-Tanūkhī, *Nishwār al-muḥāḍarah wa-akhbār al-mudhākarah*, ed. ʿAbbūd al-Shālchī (Beirut: Dār Ṣādir, 1971–73), 5:274–83.

[95] Ibid., 7:123–25.

[96] al-Mūsawī, *Sardiyyāt al-ʿaṣr*, 22–23.

[97] Ibrahim Akel, "Liste des Manuscrits Arabes des Nuits," in *Arabic Manuscripts of the "Thousand and One Nights": Presentation and Critical Editions of Four Noteworthy Texts*, ed. Aboubakr Chraïbi (Paris: Espaces et signes, 2016), 64–114.

of a taste, and the consequent vogue for some tales at the expense of others. Both the arrival of the "One" and the field of narrative grammar are interrelated. But the case is not as simple as it sounds, not only because the additional "One" in *A Thousand and One Nights* incites parodies and ironic narrative twists by Edgar Allan Poe and others, but also because the road to this "One" was already opened up in an ongoing narrative accretion in which Ibn ʿAbdūs and other litterateurs were involved. Notwithstanding the mention of the full title of *A Thousand and One Nights* in one of al-Masʿūdī's *Murūj al-dhahab* (*Meadows of Gold*) manuscripts, textual approximation for a century or so to an already disputable textual territory like *Hazār afsānah* in terms of frame and title cannot be dismissed. The three basic references to *Hazār afsānah* in al-Masʿūdī's *Murūj al-dhahab*, al-Nadīm's *Fihrist*, and al-Tawḥīdī's *al-Imtāʿ wa-l-Muʾānasa* are already problematic whenever read in the context of the writers' full statement. The first alludes to fabricated narratives whose authors claim them as translations, the second addresses its existence in relation to wider endeavors in narrative, and the last switches performers in the frame tale so as to have the male speaker al-Tawḥīdī acting as Scheherazade addressing Ibn Saʿdān as Shahrayar. The latter asks him on the next night, "Come over so we can make our night saucy and brazen, and have some substantial share of drollery as solemnity proved tiring."[98] On another night, al-Tawḥīdī resumes Scheherazade's role: "I came back another night and read for him from this art on omens, portents, augury, and coincidence."[99]

By contrast, the taste for narratives of this sort is not homogeneous. Although we have a relatively substantial corpus of theoretical speculations on narrative by such prominent figures like Ibn Qutaybah, al-Jāḥiẓ, al-Tanūkhī, al-Masʿūdī, Ibn ʿAbdūs, al-Tawḥīdī, al-Azdī, and al-Ḥuṣrī, this has to be read in the context of class and authority distinctions. As long as narratives work within a privileged domain of discussion, like entertaining historicized accounts, the court is very much in support. The common people should have their own selections and appropriations, but what usually reaches us in manuscripts speaks of a dominant taste. Hence, although not against narrative per se, the court tries hard to halt the invasion of an art that challenges its standards of noble education, an attitude documented by al-Ṣūlī among others. Thus, there is a need for a comparative outline of two different receptions, Arab and European. Although we cannot speak of an outright dismissal like the conservative neoclassical one in

[98] al-Tawḥīdī, *Kitāb al-imtāʿ*, 2:50. [99] Ibid., 163.

Europe,[100] al-Nadīm's assessment of *Hazār afsānah* as insipid and silly can be read as a specific tendency in literary criticism that held refinement in taste and writing in high regard, a point toward which the young Abbasid prince Muḥammad (the future caliph al-Rāḍī) was disposed as opposed to other members of the caliphal house. When read in the framework of their massive genealogies over time and the specific turns and thresholds that they take, narrative and storytelling cannot be viewed outside available discursive practices. Furthermore, by collapsing history, education, entertainment, social practice, and familial and societal economies, narrative appears as an epistemological field. If we modify Foucault's conceptualization of the episteme, we can argue with him that it is "a total set of relations that unite, at a given period, the discursive practices that give rise to epistemological figures, sciences, and possibly formalized systems." Also, the episteme "is the totality of relations that can be discovered, for a given period, between the sciences when one analyzes them at the level of discursive regularities."[101] The nature of narratives, histories, anecdotes, practices, tutorials, storytellers and their roles, and the genealogies of migration from one field to another, along with the effort of the "learned" to tabulate this corpus, all allow us to place this movement in totalities that operated alongside philosophical and scientific knowledge. By the same token, we can better understand the final migration of the *Nights* to Europe where it struck root. In this powerful transaction, a transplant took Europe by surprise so as to make the repetition and mention of *Nights* equivalent to a process of alluring storytelling.

Early Arab Narratological Findings

There is something more that is missing in nineteenth-century European explorations of Arabic narrative. Preoccupied with origins and/or authentication, Arabists, like the *Athenaeum*'s highly informed reviewer, put aside the issue of Arabic narratological explorations. As is the case with his contemporaries, his focus on the *Nights* excludes relevant research in issues of narrative growth, amalgamation, migration, and interfusion. In Arabic, the popularity of the term *Nights* to connote nocturnal storytelling is no less corroborated by the continuous fusion of tales, anecdotes, histories, and their like. Although narrative traveling and transfusion is customary, it is more conspicuous in the linkage of *A Thousand and One Nights* to other sources. The tenth century witnessed a deliberate attempt

[100] See my review of these attitudes in *Scheherazade in England.*
[101] Foucault, *Archaeology of Knowledge*, 191.

to write down tales for fear of getting them distorted, forgotten, or lost, as noted earlier in relation to al-Tanūkhī's (939–94) dismay at finding a dearth in assemblies in Baghdad in AH 360, "instead of the old richness and brilliant disputations." Then there was the other problem of distortion and dilution. A distrust of oral communication should alert us to other issues that nineteenth-century scholarship did not address. Was the tenth century active in storytelling? Or did the art suffer? Does al-Tanūkhī's statement express his own disillusionment rather than the status of the literary scene?[102] Did later attempts at writing down the products of storytelling represent a counter movement to oblivion, as argued by al-Tanūkhī in justification of his new projects? In his *Fihrist* al-Nadīm provides a long list of collections and their authors. There was a thriving art, as al-Ṣūlī tells us, that al-Tanūkhī deliberately overlooks to make a case for his own significant contributions. While these and similar references speak of a large reservoir of tales that was in the process of accumulation and that incited and invoked the attention of the literati throughout the tenth century and after, the so-called *dilution* and *distortion* of this reservoir is what matters in tracing the growth of *A Thousand and One Nights*. The question pertaining to the movement between the textual and oral is on the mind of some scholars of orality and literacy, such as Eric A. Havelock in his *The Muse Learns to Write*. Addressing habits of circulating copies "to form the basis for further reading," he raises the question: "Did these habits affect the style of the texts that were being used in this way, preserving the vestiges of orality in a form of composition ostensibly literate?"[103]

A comparison between what al-Tanūkhī relates and the tales as they appear in the *Nights* collection indicates a surviving skeleton, a plot. Even so, the residual part of these tales is of some significance.[104] As I have pointed out elsewhere, the tale in the collection makes use of punishment and retribution, for instance, as significations of class consciousness and enforcement of class borders.[105] The attempt to theorize storytelling since al-Tanūkhī's time should direct us to changes in taste, a consequence of urbanity, and social mobility. Al-Ḥuṣrī would try his hand at recording a preliminary theorem for narrative in his *Dhayl*

[102] al-Tanūkhī, *Nishwār*, 1:1, 3:10; al-Tanūkhī, *Table-Talk*. See also al-Mūsawī, *Sardiyyāt al-ʿaṣr*, 16–22.

[103] Eric A. Havelock, *The Muse Learns to Write: Reflections on Orality and Literacy from Antiquity to the Present* (New Haven, CT, and London: Yale University Press, 1986), 47.

[104] For information on tales that are related in other accounts as history, see Amedroz, "A Tale of the Arabian Nights"; and Mahdi, "From History to Fiction."

[105] See al-Mūsawī, *Sardiyyāt al-ʿaṣr*, 21–25; and Muḥsin Jāsim al-Mūsawī, *Mujtamaʿ alf laylah wa-laylah* (Tunis: University Publications Center, 2000), 43–140.

zahr al-ādāb.[106] When seen in the context of surviving manuscripts, like *Mi'at laylah wa-laylah* (transcribed in 1776, but belonging to the thirteenth century),[107] and *al-Ḥikāyāt al-'ajībah wa-l-akhbār al-gharībah* (probably transcribed in the fourteenth century), alongside a rich narrative repertoire, we can put together a burgeoning Arab theory of narrative between the ninth through twelfth centuries.[108]

Early ninth- to tenth-century pronouncements as reported in a number of books, but especially in al-Jāḥiẓ's *al-Maḥāsin wa-l-aḍdād*, al-Iṣfahānī's *Aghānī*, al-Mas'ūdī's *Murūj*, al-Tanūkhī's *Nishwār* and *al-Faraj*, and then Ibn 'Abd Rabbihi's *al-'Iqd al-farīd* (*Unique Necklace*), offer materials that can facilitate our reading of narrative transmission, migration among texts, and the ultimate settlement in *A Thousand and One Nights* repertoire over a long period of accretion. In one of the many tales that speak of Abbasid times, especially as reported by Isḥāq ibn Ibrāhīm al-Mawṣlī,[109] the latter addresses what al-Iṣfahānī thinks of as Būrān bint al-Ḥasan ibn Sahl. Upon being asked by her how he was able to collect so many tales and anecdotes, al-Mawṣlī's response was as follows: "I have a neighbor who was a boon companion to some kings, and he was knowledgeable and had a solid memory . . . until I became one of his close companions. What you heard was what I received from him."[110]

While refraining from exposing his own identity, al-Mawṣlī was able to act as raconteur. The act tells us of a thriving climate, one in which caliphs, princes, and prosperous people were in a position to court narrators. While laying the ground for further reflections, these narratives were to undergo selection, analysis, and description. Late tenth-century and early eleventh-century litterateurs were to perform the role that we usually associate with nineteenth-century periodical criticism in Europe. Along with philological excavation, they provided insights on the art of narrative. Thus, al-Tawḥīdī's seeming dismissal of *Hazār afsānah* should not be read at face value: He defines narratives according to their content and corresponding audience. *Hazār afsānah* kept its name during his lifetime, while other narratives based on the *Nights* happened to take over. His

[106] See al-Mūsawī, *Sardiyyāt al-'aṣr*, 33–54. For *al-Ḥikāyāt al-'ajībah*, see Hans Wehr's edition (Wiesbaden, 1956).

[107] It was most likely of a Maghribī origin. A French translation by Maurice Gaudefroy-Demombynes appeared in 1911. Claudia Ott discovered the oldest extant manuscript, 1234–35 (85 nights). Ott's German translation appeared in 2012; and the English one appeared in 2016. I am grateful to Nizar Hermes for this detail. See also Ulrich Marzolph, and Aboubakr Chraïbi. "The Hundred and One Nights: a Recently Discovered Old Manuscript." *Zeitschrift der Deutschen Morgenländischen Gesellschaft* 162, 2, 2012, 299–316.

[108] See Irwin, *The Arabian Nights*, 91–95.

[109] See Ibn 'Abd Rabbihi, *al-'Iqd al-farīd* (Beirut: Dār al-Kutub al-'Ilmiyyah, 1983), 8:156–67.

[110] More on this in al-Mūsawī, *al-Dhākirah al-sha'biyyah*, 112.

audiences are not homogeneous: Those who read *Hazār afsānah* happened to fall passively under the impact of its collapse of the real and improbable, the fictitious and impossible, that happened to "appeal and humor without any advantage." He recognizes this as an issue of human temperament, its attachment to whatever falls under the category of pleasing narratives. This is especially so when read in relation to his reliance on antecedent authority: "Address these souls with narratives because they can easily suffer effacement."[111] He concludes that not to get rusty, these souls need new appealing narratives. This understanding of a heterogeneous readership and tastes or predispositions has already been stressed in Ibn Qutaybah's *ʿUyūn al-akhbār*, which he compares to a banquet that has "various and different dishes to meet the desires of diverse tastes."[112] This recognition of plurality defines his understanding of writing as necessarily heterogeneous.[113] Al-Tanūkhī adds more in this direction, not only because he would rather cover these instead of "leaving pages blank," but also because his collection of anecdotes and narratives in *Nishwār* admits diversity, appropriation, inclusion of various professions and interests, and assimilation of related matter that he felt "would suffer injustice if not written down."[114] Later in the tenth century, scholars as critics speak of the narrative art in relation to reception. Thus, al-Ḥuṣrī passes this judgment: "[I]t is said the narrator [transmitter] is one of the scoffers, and the listener one of the tellers."[115] The art of narrative has its own demands on the narrator, who "should be light in allusion, fine in speech, refined and dexterous, brisk and graceful, not sluggish or clumsy, nor violent and ignorant, ready for every occasion."[116] The last notion is important at a time when boon companions were still sought after. He argues for an inclusive narrative that, to make its case, moves easily between vraisemblance and exemplary mention, strangeness and disputation, asking readers not to turn away whenever they come across swearing, a curse, or something silly.[117]

Arabic Classification of Narrators

Had nineteenth- and early twentieth-century European Arabists and Orientalists given more attention to a wide narrative spectrum, the

[111] al-Tawḥīdī, *Kitāb al-imtāʿ*, cited in al-Mūsawī, *al-Dhākirah al-shaʿbiyyah*, 73.
[112] Ibn Qutaybah, *ʿUyūn al-akhbār* (Beirut: Dār al-Kutub al-ʿIlmiyyah, 1986), 1:45–49.
[113] Ibid. [114] al-Tanūkhī, *Nishwār*, 1:1, 3:7. See also al-Mūsawī, *Sardiyyāt al-ʿaṣr*, 18.
[115] *Dhayl* or *Jamʿ al-jawāhir*, ed. ʿAlī Muḥammad al-Bijāwī (Beirut: Dār al-Jīl, 1987), 4. See also al-Mūsawī, *Sardiyyāt al-ʿaṣr*, 34, in which I used Maḥmūd Aḥmad Shākir (Cairo: al-Maṭbaʿah al-Raḥmāniyyah, 1934).
[116] *Dhayl* or *Jamʿ al-jawāhir*, 9. See also al-Mūsawī, *Sardiyyāt al-ʿaṣr*, 34.
[117] al-Qayrawānī, *Zahr al-ādāb*, 5, where the author cites Ibn Qutaybah.

conditions of possibility and intelligibility that make production conceivable, we could have a better understanding of the archaeology of the *Nights*. Al-Ḥuṣrī's efforts to theorize enchâssement can easily apply to the *Nights* as a phenomenal presence that elicited the responses of prominent tenth-century scholars and bibliophiles. Taking advantage of the accumulating narrative corpus, al-Ḥuṣrī argues for the following:

(1) narrative coherence that connects parts and portions, including poetry and reports; (2) elision when necessary; (3) a middle ground narrativity whenever necessary; and (4) a combination of resemblance, reported speech, alongside the strange and wonderful.

The narrators whom al-Ḥuṣrī applies and relies on are as follows: (1) The narrator in charge, the encasing narrator, like al-Ḥuṣrī; or, in the case of the *Nights*, like the anonymous second-rate historian who communicates what is related in chronicles. In Genette's terminology, this can be referenced as a "extradiegetic-heterodiegetic-paradigm."[118] (2) The witness-narrator like al-Aṣmaʿī or al-Ṣūlī; in Genette's system, this is intradiegetic-homodiegetic, when narrators tell their own story or in which they participate. (3) The narrator as protagonist like al-Ḥasan ibn Sahl or Abū al-ʿAynāʾ; this can be the extradiegetic-homodiegetic-paradigm, in which the narrator relates his own story. (4) Procreated narrators who appear in a transmitted narrative, like al-ʿAtābī and al-Ḥamdūnī; and hence the term "intradiegetic-heterodiegetic," as applied to Scheherazade's storytelling. And (5) the narrator/addressor like al-Tawḥīdī.[119]

With these narrators dealing with an enormous body of narrative, alongside prominent compilers like al-Tanūkhī, al-Masʿūdī, and al-Iṣfahānī, the *Nights*, as both descendant and independent, was to grow beyond the limits set by early nineteenth-century recensions, a fact that is proved by successive translations, editions, and selections. In the wake of philology as the "science of humanities" in Renan's stipulation, the popularity of the *Arabian Nights* with the rising reading public brought it to the attention of philologists as "the founders of modernity."

European Archaeological Explorations

Centuries later, in a different culture, the *Nights* – with its accommodation of the *Hazār afsānah* frame tale – made its way through eighteenth-century European culture before forcing itself on mainstream trends in literary criticism. Landmarks for the textual, literary, and historical study

[118] Genette, *Narrative Discourse*, 248.
[119] For more, see al-Mūsawī, *Sardiyyāt al-ʿaṣr*, 42–54.

of the *Nights* had already been laid down in Europe in the first decades of the nineteenth century. Aside from Edward William Lane's (1801–76) enduring contribution to the sociological interest in the tales in its colonial dimension, his endeavor to establish a "sound" text, albeit with scriptural tone and style, still elicits scholarly interest.[120] No less pertinent is the British periodical criticism of the years 1838–41, which, while highly informed by the British imperial quest, was mainly provoked by Lane's significant achievement. As a sign of this encompassing imperial spirit, this criticism took into account German and French contributions to assimilate or debate within a broad colonial spectrum. While the evangelical spirit was bent on replacing Eastern cultures with that of the empire, the Orientalist was keen on preserving local traditions to ensure a better and solid acculturation beyond the vagaries of change. Lane was no minor figure in this encounter, as his lexicon, studies of the "manners and customs" of the Egyptians, and translation of *A Thousand and One Nights* elicited further communications and interests. A case in point is the *Athenaeum*'s effort to elucidate the involved history of the *Nights*, a point that was noted earlier. Although taking into account contemporaneous views of Silvestre de Sacy, Joseph von Hammer, Schlegel, and Lane, the unnamed *Athenaeum* critic of the 1830s was fully aware of the pitfalls of basing final judgments regarding the date of composition on scattered references to historical events.[121] No great value must be set on these allusions in a book that went through many redactions and underwent a number of omissions, changes, and interpolations. A "careful and critical examination of the tales," he contends, "would convince the reader that they were chiefly composed by illiterate persons, unacquainted with the history of their country; and it is unfair, therefore,

[120] See, for example, Gerhardt's comments, *Art of Story-Telling*, 62, 252–53.

[121] The views of these philologists and literary historians were widely known at that time. Apart from their original appearance in French and German, the writings of de Sacy and von Hammer were available in English. De Sacy's discussion of the Syrian origin of the *Nights* appeared in the *Asiatic Journal* 28 (July 1829), whereas the Austrian Orientalist Joseph von Hammer-Purgstall's (1774–1856) documentary evidence respecting the genesis of the framing tale appeared in his article "On Arabian Poetry," *New Monthly Magazine* 13 (January 1820), 15–16n, and in the introduction to his version of the *Nights*, which was done between 1804 and 1806, but was made available in a German translation of his French version in 1825. Edward William Lane's survey of the question of origin and date of composition formed a large portion of the introduction and concluding "Review" to his translation. All these views were discussed by Hunt, "New Translations of the Arabian Nights"; B. E. Pote, "Arabian Nights," *Foreign Quarterly Review* 24 (October 1839), esp. 143–45; and John Payne, "The Thousand and One Nights," Part I, *The New Quarterly Magazine* 11 (Jan. 1879), 154–61. For Schlegel's observations and Henry Torrens's rejoinder, see the latter's "Remarks on M. Schlegel's Objections to the Restored Editions of the Alif Leilah, or Arabian Nights Entertainments," *Journal of the Asiatic Society*, n.s. 25 (1838), 72–77.

to assume the accuracy of some particular date referred to, considering the numberless anachronisms contained in the work, and urge it as an argument either in favor or against opinions respecting the authorship, or age when written."[122] Disapproving of Lane's conclusion that the social and cultural setting points to an Egyptian origin, the reviewer observed that Islam regulates and models manners and customs in the whole Muslim East, establishing social conformity to which the *Nights* plainly attests. The conformity issue would soon influence other views as well, as I noted in my study of Walter Bagehot's "The People of the Arabian Nights."[123] As for the very distinctive Egyptian traits, the *Athenaeum* reviewer urged that they be seen in light of the tendency of copyists and compilers to impose their own regional predilections on the text.[124] The critic, as philologist and literary historian, sets evaluative standards that were in tune with later scholars' readings, including Littmann, MacDonald, and Mahdi. A differentiation is to be made, however, between the early textual morphology of the corpus, and its later use by storytellers in its multiple migrations, a point that drew the attention of Abbott. But early on, when the debate on origins was at its height, the *Athenaeum* critic had his say on the archaeology of the *Nights*.

Well acquainted with the narrative tradition, the *Athenaeum* reviewer acknowledged the existence of some historical romances anterior to the Abbasid era. These he distinguished from the *Nights*, not only because they depict a chivalrous and warlike atmosphere, but also because they hardly refer to domestic practices.[125] He regarded these romances as true to the spirit of pre-Islamic Arabian society. However, following the urban expansion in Iraq, Syria, and Egypt, such tales gave way to a new narrative art that drew quite heavily on mercantile manners and aspirations. Rather than developing a sociological interpretation of the evolution of the *Nights*, the *Athenaeum* reviewer was bent on proving that the increasing urban demand for entertainment drove storytellers not only to invent or record accounts of adventure and roguery, but also to ransack the light literature of neighboring nations. Like contemporary scientists and philologists, Arab storytellers, he argued, must have appropriated a portion of this literature during a period of commercial and cultural expansion. Thus, although largely Arabian and Muslim in spirit and temper, the *Nights* contains some sporadic foreign elements. To round off his genetic criticism of the tales, the reviewer partly sided with von Hammer,

[122] *Athenaeum* 572 (October 13, 1838), 73–77.
[123] See Walter Bagehot, "The People of the Arabian Nights," *National Review* 9 (July 1859), 44–71. For a study of this art, see al-Musawi, *Scheherazade in England*, 101–11.
[124] *Athenaeum* 622 (September 28, 1839), 742.
[125] Ibid. 572 (October 13, 1838), 738–39.

concluding that the Indo-Persian *Hazār afsanāh* (which the Arab historian al-Mas'ūdī [896–956] had mentioned in his *Meadows of Gold*) was "either in whole or in part translated into Arabic, and served as a ground work to the various collections of tales circulated in the East."[126]

Beyond these insights into the early history of the *Nights* (which were also addressed later by 'Alī Aṣghar Ḥikmat in 1960),[127] the *Athenaeum* critic came across another piece of external evidence to corroborate the existence in the twelfth century of a work called *A Thousand and One Nights*. He referred to Shihāb al-Dīn Aḥmad ibn Muḥammad al-Tilimsānī al-Maqqarī's (1577–1632) "History of Spain under the Moslems."[128] The book is among the pertinent documentary evidence of von Hammer, Torrens, Ritter, and Abbott.[129] Taken together, this significant documentation, as well as the reviewer's effort to reconstruct the historical growth of the *Nights*, must be considered basic to the foundations upon which subsequent scholarship has established its readings of origins. Goitein's finding of the twelfth-century loan record corroborates al-Maqqarī's reference.[130] Aside from minor disagreements regarding the history and volume of some cycles, twentieth-century scholars such as Littmann, MacDonald, and Abbott have reached conclusions that are not different from those of the *Athenaeum* reviewer who translated al-Maqqarī's work at a later stage. They conclude that the framing tale was borrowed from the Islamized *Hazār afsānah*, around which clustered a few Arabized and numerous genuine Arabian tales that continued to accumulate until the early sixteenth century. The *Athenaeum* reviewer's method is no less rewarding than the substance of his argument. Rather than confusing the general with the particular and treating the collection as homogeneous, he demonstrates some awareness of the component parts and genres that comprise the whole. By pointing

126 Ibid., 738. The writer for the *Asiatic Journal*, n.s. 30, 117 (September–December 1839), 83, fully developed this point. The *Nights*, he noticed, "is rather a vehicle for stories, partly fixed and partly arbitrary, than a collection fairly deserving, from its constant identity with itself, the name of a distinct work, and the reputation of having wholly emanated from the same inventive mind." As for the foreign elements, he qualified von Hammer's early sweeping conclusion, postulating that a "work there may have been similar to the *Arabian Nights*, whether in Persian, Pahlavi or Arabic, we will not dispute; but we cannot imagine that this has furnished anything but the ground-work of what we now call the *Arabian Nights*."

127 See 'Alī Aṣghar Ḥikmat, "Min Hazār Afsan ilā Hazār distān: Dirāsah tarīkhiyyah li-kitāb alf laylah wa-laylah," *al-Dirāsāt al-Adabiyyah* 4 (1960), 5–35.

128 British Museum MS. no. 7, 334, fol. 136. The book, which was translated by the same reviewer, is *Nafḥ al-ṭīb min ghuṣn al-Andalus al-raṭīb*, trans. P. de Gayangos, *History of the Mohammaden Dynasties in Spain*, 2 vols. (London, 1840–41).

129 The citation was transcribed from Ibn Sa'īd al-Qurṭubī. See *Athenaeum* 622 (September 28, 1839), 742; and Enno Littmann, "Alf layla wa-layla," *EI*, 1:361.

130 Goitein, "The Oldest Documentary"; and MacDonald, "The Earlier History."

to the need for separating possible interpolations from core tales, he touches on a topic that has engaged the attention of a number of scholars, ranging from August Müller and Oestrup to Horovitz and Elisseeff. While specific reference culminates in Abbott's finding of an early ninth-century fragment bearing the title *Kitāb ḥadīth alf laylah*, along with a number of lines that provide the justification for storytelling,[131] there are scattered references to the mention of *A Thousand and One Nights*. A Cairene Jewish bookseller has such a reference in his loan record in the twelfth century.[132] However, the Egyptian historian al-Maqrīzī (d. 1442) indicates that the collection was in circulation in the late eleventh century.[133]

While the search for folk literature in association with the "spirit" of a nation was paramount in the sweeping German Romanticism, the *Nights* turned into a monument for the identification of a number of separate realities: its archetypal frame tale and substantial weight in Schlegel's thought was taken to indicate the power of the Aryan race. Its supernaturalism is no less so, especially as it negates monotheism. This corresponds to a similar negation of religion and the divine origins of language in a striding modernity exemplified in Renan's thought, and led by empires in relation to their Other. Whatever follows in the search for manuscripts was in one way or another connected with this philological drive, as the theorizations for Sanskrit origins indicate. Moreover, a noticeable line in the study of origins relates to Max Müller's school, which, in Robert Irwin's reading, "influenced Benfey and Cosquin in their attempts to find Indian (and therefore Aryan) sources for the *Nights*' tales."[134]

This was not an ordinary matter. Despite its seeming quantitative marginality in comparison to the massive popular celebration of the Oriental mode, this racist streak had its formidable presence in the colonialist discourse. Its proponents infiltrated the mode to redirect it away from "Orientals" toward a counter vigorous race that was meant to feed the empire. Again Pierre-Louis Rey's summation of Gobineau's short story collection is worth attention. He writes: "his *Nouvelles asiatiques* (1876) illustrated this nostalgia. Three of the six tales ('L'Illustre Magicien,' 'Histoire de Gambèr-Aly,' 'La Guerre des Turcomans') depict with both humour and tenderness the failings of modern Persians (dissimulators, versatile, taken in by anything shiny)." By contrast, "two others ('La Danseuse de Shamakha' and 'Les Amants de Kandahar') exalt individuals who, amid the mountains of the Caucasus or

[131] Abbott, "A Ninth-Century Fragment."
[132] See Goitein, "The Oldest Documentary," 301.
[133] al-Maqrīzī, *al-Khiṭaṭ* (Cairo: Būlāq, 1854), 1:448.
[134] Irwin, *The Arabian Nights*, 215.

Afghanistan, have managed to keep the strength of character and nobility of their original culture."[135] By situating the last two tales in the mountains of the Caucasus, the presumed birthplace of the Aryan race, Gobineau draws upon his racist theory that became central to colonialist ideology.

While Arabic scholarship was not enthusiastically drawn to popular culture, the Schlegel school in European scholarship was more interested in reading the tales as manifestations of culture and life, and indices of the spirit and language varieties of the region. The *Athenaeum* reviewer was not alone in interrogating many platitudes adopted by Schlegel and others; but his recapitulations were in response to an ongoing discussion that received further impetus after the publication of Lane's annotated edition.[136] Lane was keen on establishing that the work was by one single author who composed it between 1475 and 1525.[137] De Sacy had already dwelt on this issue (as documented by Chauvin and Littmann).[138] In these interventions de Sacy debated both single authorship and connectedness with Persian and Indian collections, dismissing the early reference by al-Masʿūdī (336/947, reedited in 346/957) as spurious. Opposing such views were von Hammer's contributions,[139] where he builds his argument on al-Masʿūdī, stressing therefore the genuineness of this as evidence of a collection of non-Arab origin. Late in the century, de Goeje resumed the discussion of origins.[140] His effort falls more into the framework of an increasing interest in the biblical and mythical, as he tries to demonstrate that the framework story is connected with the Book of Esther. August Müller was no less involved in the mythical, but his scholarship enabled him to go beyond philology to study the layers of the whole, as in his interventions on the subject.[141] He accorded these tales Baghdadi and Egyptian origins. Theodore Nöldeke and Oestrup were more articulate in Littmann's view because they built on careful

[135] https://heritage.bnf.fr/bibliothequesorient/en/joseph-gobineau-art.

[136] This and the following paragraphs build on al-Musawi, "The Growth of Scholarly Interest."

[137] Edward William Lane, preface to *The Arabian Nights' Entertainments* (London: 1838–41).

[138] Silvestre de Sacy, *Journal des savants* (1817), 678; *Recherches sur l'origine du recueil des contes intitules les Mille et une nuit* (Paris: 1829); and in the *Memoires de l'Academie des Inscriptions & Belles-Lettres* 10 (1833), 30.

[139] Wiener Jahrbücher, 1819, 236; *JA*, 1e serie, x; 3e serie, viii; preface to his *Die noch nicht uebersetzten Erzaehlungen*.

[140] *De Arabische Nachtvertellingen*, De Gids, 1886, iii, 385; and "The Thousand and One Nights," *Encyclopedia Britannica*, xxiii, 316.

[141] *Bezzenbergers Beitraege*, xiii, 222; and his article in *Die deutsche Rundschau*, xiii (July 10, 1887), 77–96.

analysis of texts.[142] As noticed in the preceding text, Oestrup's views, severely criticized by Mahdi for their racist predilections, were popular in the early twentieth century, as they were translated into Russian by Krymski,[143]and into German by Rescher;[144] and into French by Galtier (Cairo, 1912).[145] Further discussions of origins were by Horovitz[146] and by Littmann.[147] As already discussed, the search for origins received further impetus with Abbott's findings in 1949 of a papyrus dating from the ninth century that mentions Shahrazad and Dunyazade, whereas the interest in Galland's originals goes back to Zotenberg and, later, MacDonald, culminating in Mahdi's meticulous reading of genealogy. Zotenberg drew attention to the core stories that are less than 300, but that accumulated because of redactors' desire to match the number as mentioned in the title. The Bibliothéque National manuscript of Galland, which took France and Europe by surprise in 1704 as *Les Mille et Une Nuit*, was the core for Zotenberg, which could have belonged to the fourteenth century, and that was different from another seventeenth-century Bibliotheque National manuscript 1491A comprising 870 nights. The later manuscript, which was brought by the French consul general Benoît de Maillet, contains all Galland's core stories. Along with other manuscripts, this core nucleus led Zotenberg to conclude that the original core as made available in Galland's manuscript was the culmination of the early Arabic modification and elaboration on the *Hazār afsanah* frame, a point that MacDonald took to heart. He used the argument to develop a genealogy for Galland's version with a root in that framing story, and with a number of descendants since the fourteenth century. However, these culminate in a late eighteenth-century text that was produced under an Egyptian sheikh's supervision with a total of 1001 nights usually referenced as "Zotenberg Egyptian Recension," or ZER. An earlier mention of a collection in Jean-Louis Asselin's (1772–1822) diary of July 10, 1807, did not materialize in an edition, and the sheikh who was working on this collection could be any among the Cairene sheikhs in late

[142] "Zu den aegyptischen Maerchen," *ZDMG* (1888), 68; and Oestrup's *Studier over 1001 Nat* (Copenhagen: 1891).

[143] *Izsliedowanie o 1001 no'i* (Moscow: 1905).

[144] Oskar Rescher, *"Oestrups Studien über 1001 Nacht" aus dem Daenischen nebst einigen Zusaetzen* (Stuttgart: 1925); and "Studien über den Inhalt von 1001 Nacht," *Der Islam* 9 (1919), 1–94.

[145] Emile Galtier, "Fragments d'une étude sur Les Mille et Une Nuit," *Mémoires de l'Institut français du Caire* 27 (1912), 135–94.

[146] Josef Horovitz, "Die Entstehung von Tausendundeine Nacht," *The Review of Nations* 4 (April 1927).

[147] Enno Littmann, *Tausendundeine Nacht in der arabischen Literatur* (Tübingen: J. C. B. Mohr, 1923); Littmann, "Alf layla wa-layla"; and his "*Tausendundeine Nacht*," in *Irrgarten der Lust: 1001 Nacht. Aufsätze, Stimmen, Illustrationen* (Frankfurt am Main: Insel, 1968), 15–42.

eighteenth-century Cairo. However, a later recension could have been by ʿAbd al-Raḥmān al-Jabartī (1754–1822), whom Lane described as:

> so delighted in their perusal that he took the trouble of refining the language of a copy of them which he possessed, expurgating or altering whatever grossly offensive to morality without the somewhat redeeming quality of wit, and adding many facetiae of his own, and of other literati.[148]

This led to the Būlāq and also to the MacNaghten or Calcutta II editions. According to Mahdi, Galland's core *Nights* belongs to a Syrian manuscript family, whose presence is central to all subsequent descendants, including the late eighteenth-century ZER and its Būlāq, and MacNaghten or Calcutta II descendants. MacDonald was keen on producing *A Thousand and One Nights* in a reliable version with the core stories as its text. Mahdi used Galland's for his 1984 Leiden edition of 282 nights and provides a survey and exhaustive analysis of the family of the text and its descendants. All manuscripts of incomplete nights or single stories seem to belong to the second half of the eighteenth century, and early nineteenth century.

In sum, the philological inquiry, on the one hand, and the demanding market, on the other, led to the following editions as the base for translational enterprises: Shirwanee or Calcutta I (1814–18, 2 vols.), Breslau (1825–38, 8 vols.), Cairene, Būlāq (1835, 2 vols.), and Calcutta II or MacNaghten (1839–42, 4 vols.). For the Arabs, and probably for Near Easterners, the tales are always there as part of a popular culture before gaining some "writerly" legitimacy in the early twentieth century. As discussed earlier, in Barth's *The Last Voyage of Sindbad the Sailor*, one character, Ibn al-Hamra, is made to associate supernatural mechanisms with "traditional realism," and Sindbad's voyages with a totality of an Arab culture: "such as we all drank in with our mothers' milk and shall drink – Inshallah – till our final swallow." Barth insists on Easterners' credulity and hence his reluctance to read Arabic culture as a complex formation of multiple shades, strips, styles, ways, and functions: popular, colloquial, slang, classical, formal, elitist, poetic, prosaic, metonymic, metaphorical, imitable, and inimitable. Notwithstanding Barth's postmodernist travesties, what is traceable in this postmodernist drive is the lingering impact of the Schlegel–Renan school of thought, its notorious racism and reluctance to see what lies beyond the theoretical paradigmatic frame within which it imprisons itself.

[148] Edward William Lane, trans., *Thousand and One Nights*, ed. Edward Stanley Poole (London: Bickers, 1877), chapter 1, 1:66n18. See also al-Musawi, *Scheherazade in England*, 111–12n3.

6 Signatures and Affiliates

> Such is the primary meaning it has for us, and this is of *The Thousand and One Nights*. There is something we feel as the Orient, something I have not felt in Israel but have felt in Granada and Cordoba. I have felt the presence of the East, and I don't know if I can define it; perhaps it's not worth it to define something instinctively. The connotations of that word we owe to *The Thousand and One Nights*.
>
> Jorge Luis Borges, "The Thousand and One Nights"

To write on the *Nights*' affiliates and filiates is a challenge, not only because this undertaking is beyond the reach of one individual, but also because the *Arabian Nights' Entertainments* happens to permeate cultures, individuals, and lives in intractable ways. Affiliates are by thousands, as they include all readers and writers who express affinity with the *Arabian Nights*; but filiates are those who derive inspiration and sustenance from the tales, and whose texts and production convey a textual genesis that is more powerful and intimate than even a biological connection. Efforts expended on traces, echoes, imitations, departures from the frame tale, origins of fiction, rewritings of one tale or another, and also metafictional excursions on the art of writing are too overwhelming to be surveyed.[1] Single studies and some scholarly surveys (like Robert Irwin's chapter 10 in his *Companion*) have laid the groundwork for further research.[2] Other issues relate first to the genesis of this composition. Edward William Lane was quite plain about the difficult task of accounting for a work of this nature: "To discover the origins of the tales of the 1001Nights is in most cases impossible."[3] Engaging with the *Athenaeum* reviewer (no. 622, 741), and the inference

[1] See Marzolph's exhaustive bibliography: wwwuser.gwdg.de/~umarzol/arabiannights.html.

[2] For Robert Irwin, see his *Arabian Nights*. See also van Leeuwen, *The Thousand and One Nights and Twentieth-Century Fiction*; and Aida Azouqa, *Magical Realism between East and West: The Arabian Nights, Gabriel Garcia Márquez and Novelists of the Arab World* (Lewiston, NY, and Lampeter, UK: The Edwin Mellen Press, 2019).

[3] Lane, *The Thousand and One Nights*, 3:683.

that the *1001 Nights* "may have been imitated by various persons in different ages and countries," Lane recapitulates that he finds nothing improbable in the supposition, nor does he disagree that

> an altered and augmented edition of the *1001 Nights* may have served as the immediate model, and in some degree as the ground-work of the 1001; but I cannot think that the latter work is merely the last of several editions of the former, augmented in successive ages.[4]

Borges sums up the issue of genesis in this manner: "It is the work of thousand authors, and none of them knew that he was helping to construct this illustrious book, one of the most illustrious books in all literature."[5] This leads us to what Chapter 5 suggests: that there is a body of composite nature that took the frame tale of the two brothers as a container and generator of further tales with formulas that endow the whole with connections and narrative filiations required by the division into nights. The latter practice is in keeping with the role of "*confabulatores nocturni*, men of the night who tell stories," as mentioned by Baron von Hammer-Purgstall and "cited with admiration by both Lane and Burton, the two most famous translators of *The Thousand and One Nights*."[6] As for the title, Lane's review shows no rigorous engagement other than saying: "The title of the '1001 Nights' I suppose to have been adopted partly for the purpose of distinguishing this work from the '1000 Nights'; but not solely with this view; for even numbers are deemed by the Arabs unlucky."[7] If we assume that a composition of this volume was augmented and continued to take shape over time, always driven by the storytellers' skill and the desire to meet the demands of audiences and readers, then its departure from an origin relocates it in ever-growing grids of affiliations. To draw a biological schema, the departure from origins, that is, *Hazār afsānah* and its early ninth-century Arabic outgrowth, sets it free to acquire narrative affiliations, a process that concludes with the Orientalist restorative effort of emendation, supplementation, and ultimate assimilation. Although applying this triad process to culture, Edward Said offers an exemplary model that we can apply to the *Nights* in its movement from origin, to augmentation and restoration. As a working frame, an analogy to encompass a genesis from filiation to affiliation to a "restored authority" of cultural constructs, Said argues: "What I am describing is the transition from a failed idea or possibility of filiation to a kind of compensatory order that, whether it is a party, an institution, a culture, a set of beliefs, or even a world-vision,

[4] Ibid., 678–79. [5] Borges, "The Thousand and One Nights," 568. [6] Ibid., 569.
[7] Ibid., 677.

provides men and women with a new form of relationship." He calls this "affiliation but which is also a new system."[8] However, this new system will be used "to reinstate vestiges of the kind of authority associated in the past with filiative order" to provide "a restored authority."[9]

This genesis may sound inapplicable to the *Nights*, simply because it is only a composition, a book, and not a historical order with some hierarchical structures. But, unless we adopt this schema in terms of origins, growth, and restoration through translation or adaptation, we are bound to miss the genealogy of the *Arabian Nights* as an epoch-changing event.

Why a "Major Event for All of European Literature"?

While it was not epoch-changing in its native burgeoning and traveling before its translational transaction, its phenomenal advent in Europe and rise to popularity placed it in a sustainable cultural system. Again, Borges offers a way out:

> It might be said that the Romantic movement begins at the moment when someone, in Normandy or in Paris, reads The Thousand and One Nights. He leaves the world legislated by Boileau (d. 1711) and enters the world of Romantic freedom.[10]

Moreover, with its captivating hold on the Romantics in particular, it brought along with it a body of representations called "the Orient": "With the Romantic movement, the Orient richly entered the consciousness of Europe."[11] What Borges calls a "major event for all of European literature," also initiates a triad of filiation, affiliation, and restoration. It gives birth to narratives and poetics that bluntly claim legitimacy through textual assimilation, titles, metafictional reflections, and icons. The affiliatory stance shows more in departures from the two brothers' frame tale or specifically from the Scheherazade/Shahrayar framework. Before exploring aspects of these trajectories, the third part of the process, the restorative authority, requires some further analysis.

The restorative effort shows a scholarly deployment of exhaustive research that signifies a restoration of authority to claim the *Nights*, not only as a document worthy of some Orientalists' attention and research, but also as a cherished legacy in an Orientalist/Arabist grid. Lane offers us significant insights with respect to this restoration because his intervention is in dialogue with the interventions of others like de Sacy, von Hammer, the *Athenaeum* reviewer, and many others. He sets the stage,

[8] Said, *The World, the Text, and the Critic*, 19. [9] Ibid.
[10] Borges, "The Thousand and One Nights," 572. [11] Ibid., 567.

and, before him, Patrick Russell and the Rev. George Lamb, for further discussions of the involved history of the *Arabian Nights*. He starts his review with the following:

> The literary history of the *1001 Nights* was involved in the utmost obscurity until the celebrated Von Hammer pointed out an important passage, to which I have often alluded in Golden Meadows of El-Mesʿoodee, written about the middle of the tenth century of our era, or the year of the Flight 333 (A.D. 944–5).[12]

Von Hammer also "brought to light, last year (1839) a far more important and decisive testimony respecting the Hezār Afsāneh, shewing it, beyond all doubt, to have been the archetype of the *1001 Nights*."[13] While all this historical corroboration of a genealogy of *A Thousand and One Nights* is already explored by later scholars,[14] it derives further significance for the present argument because it navigates delicately between two prominent Orientalists who differ on issues of authenticity, title, and other details of origin. Lane has to depart from both de Sacy and von Hammer on a number of points.[15] In other words, a philological inquiry into origins, growth, and the role of public reciters over time presents us with a systematic endeavor to have the history of the book tabulated, classified, and presented in relation to three milieus: its point of origin, whether it is Baghdad, Aleppo, Damascus, or Cairo; early eighteenth-century Europe (1704), where it was forever transplanted in a land where "literature is legislated by Boileau" who "never suspected that his rhetoric is threatened by that splendid Oriental invasion";[16] and late eighteenth- to nineteenth-century Europe, where it underwent authentication, annotation, and documentation. The endearing, readable Galland's version that opened the gate for Romanticism has to pass through the restorative authority of the *new* philology. The undying *Arabian Nights*, as Borges claims it,[17] has to undergo a restorative process to fit into the rising field of social science and to be claimed as a European rectification of an incomplete and disputable case. Insofar as the Europeanized *Nights* is concerned, the viability of this schema can be tested in a number of ways. There is no need to undo the research on the Oriental mode, pseudo-Oriental tales, and so forth. These are important contributions that lay the ground for archaeological excavation that is inclusive with respect to the field of inquiry, but still very selective to draw:

[12] Lane, "Review," *The Thousand and One Nights*, 3:674. [13] Ibid., 675.
[14] See, for example, MacDonald, "The Earlier History." [15] Lane, "Review," 3:677.
[16] Borges, "The Thousand and One Nights," 567. [17] Ibid., 574.

(1) Filial engenderment, or what Wendy Faris calls Scheherazade's "children";[18]
(2) Affiliative concomitance and departure or difference; and
(3) Ultimate restorative undertaking that betrays such variables as John Barth's parodic mode of simultaneously covering up and exposing a Eurocentric dismissal of Otherness.

Restoration generates further efforts not only to edit Galland's manuscript (Mahdi's Brill edition, 1984), and get it translated, but also to recreate a new text out of a number of editions. Recensions are collapsed into new editions, as in Malcolm C. Lyons's "new translation," Leeuwen's Dutch edition, the French edition of Jamel Eddine Bencheikh, and André Miquel's *Les Mille et Une Nuit: Contes choisis.*

Filiates: The Romantic Craze – The Matter with William Beckford's Vathek

In a neat observation on narrative fiction in eighteenth- to nineteenth-century Europe, Said suggests that it "is based on the filial device of handing on a story through narrative telling," adding that "the generic plot situation of the novel is to repeat through variation the family scene by which human beings engender human duration in their action."[19] Apart from generic formulas and the division in nocturnal storytelling, the frame tale and almost every major (i.e., frame) tale in the *Nights* is one of rupture and search for a more assuring genetic link. Whether read literally or metaphorically, the conclusion in some manuscripts that Scheherazade has by then offered tales worthy to be written down and children to ensure dynastic continuity has been a subject of controversy with respect to the role of the savior of women and "creator" of tales and offspring. Direct textual genesis in this drama of survival implies that her direct descendants are not only fiction writers and poets who are brought up on her tales and continue to be caught in her magic web, but also those whose writings are saturated with leitmotifs, icons, images, and issues of narrative and survival. There are many who still appear under this category, but for the sake of convenience we can probably think of William Beckford of Fonthill in his *Vathek* (in French, 1782; in English, 1786) and

[18] Wendy B. Faris, "Scheherazade's Children: Magic Realism and Postmodern Fiction," in *Magic Realism: Theory, History, Community*, ed. Lois Parkinson Zamora and Wendy B. Faris (Durham, NC: Duke University Press, 1995), 163–90; see also Faris, "1001 Words," 815. Years later Irwin used the "Children of the Night" as a title for chapter 10 of his *Companion*; whereas Philip Kennedy and Marina Warner used *Scheherazade's Children* as a title for an edited volume.

[19] Said, *The World, the Text, and the Critic*, 117.

its continuation, Leigh Hunt in his poetry and criticism, the Polish traveler, polyglot, linguist, and Knight of Malta, Jan Potocki, in his *Manuscript Found in Saragossa* (1815), Samuel Taylor Coleridge, John Keats, the Brontës, James Joyce, William Butler Yeats, Marcel Proust, John Barth, and many others.

An impressionable and avid reader of the *Arabian Nights* like Beckford fits well the description as filiate. The *Arabian Nights* brought forth his latent leanings for ancient Persian satraps. Identifying with unbridled power and sites of sumptuous wealth, he dreamt of soaring on the "Arabian bird roc."[20] The wealth that he inherited from his father helped generate in him a sense of identification with some Eastern satraps in an "Aladdin-like retreat," or any embodiment of sultanic magnificence.[21] As Paul Elmer More suggests, Beckford's Fonthill palace is a symbol of some Romantic craze: "It was as if someone in that staid century had gained control over a group of Genii out of the *Arabian Nights* and had set them to raising a magic structure for his delectation."[22] His *Vathek*,[23] and *The Episodes of Vathek*, in particular are sites of filiation where Beckford is more at home.[24] With Samuel Henley's extensive endnotes, *Vathek* was not a minor event in the history of the *Nights*, but "a classic of English literature," as Irwin suggests.[25] Henley's 122 pages of endnotes prepare for the emerging new philological exploration, manifested in Lane's copious edition of the *Nights*, and show also the disparity between text and scholarship, or between the art of storytelling and eventual ethnographic scholarship, a point that was not lost on the *Monthly Review* of May 1786, which discerned how these endnotes are "of a character entirely different from that of the work."[26]

Source material, including his attempt to translate Edward Wortley Montagu's manuscript of the *Nights*, might have led him to envision the caliph *Vathek*, but Beckford put into the character some of his own yearning for a never-ending pleasure. As his "Long Story" of 1777 indicates, there was in him that insatiable craze for wealth, power, and

[20] Lewis Melville, *Life and Letters of William Beckford of Fonthill* (London: Heinemann, 1910), 21.

[21] Paul Elmer More considers Beckford's *Vathek* "one of the main documents to anyone who wishes to study the sources of the romantic movement," and the image of the damned with flaming hearts that concludes the book as the "essential type and image of the romantic life and literature." Paul Elmer More, *The Drift of Romanticism* (New York: Houghton Mifflin, 1913), 33.

[22] Ibid., 36.

[23] William Beckford, *The History of the Caliph Vathek* (London: Cassell and Co., 1887).

[24] For Beckford's readings, see al-Musawi, *Scheherazade in England*, 39, 49–51; and for a detailed study of his art, see Muhsin Jassim al-Musawi, *Anglo-Orient: Easterners in Textual Camps* (Tunis: Markaz al-Nashr al-Jāmiʿī, 2000), 173–97.

[25] Irwin, *The Arabian Nights*, 248.

[26] *The Monthly Review* (May 1786), 450.

freedom. His many *dramatis personae* seemed more real to him than the shadows of the outside. "I will seclude myself if possible from the world," he explained, "and converse many hours with you, Maisour and Nouronihar. I am determined to enjoy my dreams and phantasies and all my singularity, however irksome and discordant to the worldlings around."[27]

Beckford's *Vathek* has stimulated some critical and scholarly attention for a number of reasons: In Borges's words, "*Vathek* is a mere curiosity, 'the perfume and suppliance of a minute'" but it "foretells, in however rudimentary way, the satanic splendors of Thomas De Quincey and Poe, of Charles Baudelaire and Huysmans."[28] Borges enumerates Beckford's readings, to conclude that the French original, published by Perrin and "revised and prologued" by Mallarmé, is not as good as Henley's translation in English; it "is unfaithful to the translation."[29] *Vathek* remains powerful, however, for its "interior infinite of the individual."[30] Making use of his source material, as noticed by Lonsdale, and investigating other accounts of immediate relevance, Beckford set the stage for the romantic rebel.[31] In deriving the prototype for his romantic rebel from the annals of the Muslims, Beckford was in tune with the growing vogue of the Oriental tale, but his narrative took a direction that was Romantic in the main. It was, as he said, "the creation of . . . [his] own fancy."[32] Taking leave of the source, *Vathek* grows into a work with the very inhibitions and troubles of Romanticism. "It cost one three days and two nights of labor. I never took off my clothes the whole time. It made me ill."[33] Beckford's attachment to his text, his immersion into it, and his reluctance to leave it unfinished testify to a Romantic infatuation that exists to justify itself for itself, regardless of historical accuracy or exactitude.

Muslim historiography becomes a cultural terrain, one to which Beckford could displace whims and idiosyncrasies without jeopardizing his immediate status as a "trivial type of millionaire: distinguished gentleman, traveler, bibliophile, builder of palaces, and libertine."[34] The defects and faults of his immediate "wretched world without" are predicated on an Orient that his selective reading and imaginative faculty

[27] J. W. Oliver, *Life of William Beckford* (London: Oxford, 1932), 31–32.

[28] Borges, "On William Beckford's *Vathek*" (1943), trans. Eliot Weinberger, in *Selected Non-fictions*, 238.

[29] Ibid., 238–39.

[30] Mikhail Bakhtin, *Rabelais and His World*, trans. Helene Iswolsky (Bloomington, IN: Indiana University Press, 1984), 44.

[31] Roger Lonsdale, "Introduction," *Vathek* (London: Oxford, 1970), 167–70.

[32] Andre Parreaux, *William Beckford, auteur de Vathek, 1760–1844* (Paris: A. G. Nizet, 1960), 201–14.

[33] Ibid. [34] Borges, "On William Beckford's *Vathek*," 236.

helped create. According to a systematic transposition of codes and signs, Beckford comes up with a Romantic creation of this Orient that is boundless enough to accommodate aspirations and nurture repressed desires. It is there to entertain projections and to be accepting, supine as a soft yielding woman, the penetrative presence and gaze of all. It is also a site for nameless people, who move, revolt, rejoice, or die. It is peopled by groups of cripples, eunuchs, concubines, jesters, mutes, and naked boys.

While the Romantic "interior infinite" generates pre-Napoleonic models, whose prototypes are already available in Islamic historiography, the Romantic grotesque in the description of the Giaour – who appears as the satanic embodiment of temptations and the craving for unlimited power – provides subversive strategies counteracting state mechanism without necessarily coming into direct conflict with the empire. Interdependence and dialogue among texts and contexts keep the narrative in tension, for *Vathek* works not only among a grid of texts, but also in an Orientalized context that was informed by the powerful discourse of its times. "Beckford's *Vathek* of 1787," writes Kiernan, "may be seen as an Orientalized version of the old Faust legend that Goethe rediscovered in the same age of violent change, as the Elizabethans had done in theirs."[35]

Schlegel on the Grotesque and Arabesque: The Counterdiscourse

Although overlooked by Bakhtin in his reading of the grotesque, Beckford's *Vathek*, especially in its veiled autobiographical thrust, fits well into the generic characteristics of the subjective grotesque.[36] Apart from its satraps and interior infinite, Beckford's Romantic grotesque works its way against "dogmatism, completeness, and limitation."[37] Its multifarious growth, and appropriation of the carnivalesque, the ironic and the Menippean, present it as an intersection of the miscellaneous, ironic, scandalous, and abusive with the polite, pitting it thereby against a dominating essentialist discourse. Bakhtin considers *Tristram Shandy* the norm for this subjective grotesque, as a departure from the "carnival spirit" of the medieval and Renaissance periods. Theorizations for this mode, however, are to be traced in the writings of Friedrich Schlegel and Jean Paul (d. 1825; Johann Paul Friedrich Richter).[38]

In collapsing the grotesque with the Arabesque, Schlegel offers a reading that may apply to Beckford's *Vathek*. Rather than suggesting fantasy as central to the concept, Schlegel, according to Bakhtin's

[35] Victor Kiernan, *The Lords of Human Mind* (London: Serif, 1969), 136.
[36] Bakhtin, *Rabelais*, 36–37. [37] Ibid., 44. [38] Ibid., 37.

surmise, "sees its essence in the fantastic combination of heterogeneous elements of reality."[39] Reality in both assumes a variety that resists uniformity toward "the breaking up of the established world order."[40] Schlegel's applications to Shakespeare, Cervantes, Sterne, and Jean Paul do not touch upon the reasons for the use of Arabesque as a viable alternative to the grotesque. But, when seen in relation to a wider intertext, Schlegel looks upon alternating images and modes of expression in a fantastic succession as typically Arabian, an understanding that runs through his major discourse on the Arabic language and writing, and stamps his philological inquiry with absolutist formulas. However, the grotesque was bound to receive great attention in an age of radical challenge to official culture. Discrediting official claims for respectability, propriety, rationality, and composure, the Romantic consciousness was more responsive to the disruptive forces of the inner self. This consciousness is drawn to the infinitude suggested, for Schlegel, by the Arabesque.

Bakhtin accepts many of these theorizations, for the subjective grotesque carries within it symptoms of contamination and revolt. If the Renaissance grotesque is one of gaiety and mirth, turning the "frightening in ordinary life . . . into amusing or ludicrous monstrosities,"[41] then the Romantic scene presents a "terrifying world" which is "alien to man,"[42] driving the "gay and joyful tone" out of laughter. In this world, sarcasm, satire, fear, recurrence of masks, individual isolation, darkness, and heterogeneity become the hallmarks of a universe where the devil dwells as "the greatest humorist of all."[43] Even when set within a larger context of sociopolitical dynamics, including those of the empire, such motifs and tropes should highlight shifting positionalities and draw attention to patterns of historic reversibility in intersections where "insertion of history into a text, and of the text into history" call for a better reading of such works as *Vathek*. In Norman Fairclough's reading of Kristeva's view of "this inherent historicity of texts,"[44] no significant writing is born in a void, nor could it be an alien growth with no actual contribution to change. Rather than a matter of sources, the origination of *Vathek*, for instance, is more answerable to its immediate European, especially English and French, culture.

In its multiplicity of styles as well as in its humor and mirthless laughter, *Vathek* resists closure. Even its characters reach such a recognition, for there is an ongoing struggle that is not necessarily rewarding, a point that would not be favored by classical canons. Arguing in general for the grotesque and camivalesque, Bakhtin says, the "image of the

[39] Ibid., 41. [40] Ibid. [41] Ibid., 47. [42] Ibid., 38. [43] Ibid., 42.
[44] Norman Fairclough, *Discourse and Social Change* (Cambridge: Polity Press, 1992), 526.

contradictory perpetually becoming and unfinished being could not be reduced to the dimensions of the Enlighteners' reason."[45] Distinguished by ambivalence and hybridity, this genre and its variants could never have met the approval of that age: "This abstract rationalism and antihistoricism, this tendency to generalization and nondialectic thought ... prevented the Encyclopedists from grasping theoretically the nature of ambivalent festive laughter."[46]

Festive laughter, irony, and heterogeneous discursivity are aspects of both the carnivalesque and grotesque. The conflation is nowhere more visible than in the description of the rolling Giaour. To Bakhtin, every language act or communicational activity has a purpose; in that context there is a purposeful drive to unmask or disclose whatever lies hidden under the veil of ranks and claims of distinction. In both the seventeenth and eighteenth centuries, rationalism and classicism, says Bakhtin, "clearly reflect the fundamental traits of the new official culture," which was, like "the ecclesiastic feudal culture," also "authoritarian and serious, though less dogmatic."[47] In other words, works that fit into the genre of the grotesque destabilize and subvert the hierarchy of genres, as well as ranks and positions, a case that finds many a manifestation in Beckford's Giaour in *Vathek*.

Beckford's Giaour stands for the Romantic grotesque in more than one sense. His comic gestures, eccentric postures, grimaces, and abusive language endow him with the very "essence of the grotesque,"[48] to use Bakhtin's words regarding the mask. However, more important is that the mask is "related to transition, metamorphoses, the violation of natural boundaries, to mockery and familiar nicknames."[49] The appearance of the Giaour at court carries within it a great deal of mockery, something that is alien to the primitive roots of the mask with their colorful life and richness. In there, the Giaour's presence "hides something" and, like the Romantic mask, "keeps a secret, deceives."[50] Hence, regenerative humor almost disappears, and instead there remains irony, "somber hue," setting the stage for the Devil and its representations with their sarcastic infernal laughter. It is here that Beckford's *Vathek* seems to apply the Romantic grotesque, as shown by Jean Paul, whereby destructive laughter becomes the sign and message of the infernal power, as "the greatest humorist of all would be the devil."[51] Elaborating on transformation and change, Bakhtin traces the loss of regenerating laughter to a historical outlook that imposes its stamp on generic evolution or regression. Regardless of sociopolitical dynamics, Bakhtin looks upon the emerging

[45] Bakhtin, *Rabelais*, 118. [46] Ibid. [47] Ibid., 101. [48] Ibid., 40. [49] Ibid. [50] Ibid.
[51] Ibid., 42.

Romantic mask as an ultimate break with rationalism, but its significant structural difference from the medieval and Renaissance grotesque is reset in terms of outlook or world view, not in conditions of possibility. Nevertheless, Bakhtin's argument applies not only to feasts, inversions, and scenes of bodily indulgence, but also to the representation of the Giaour, his presence at court, dealings with the caliph, and his surprising unveiling of a demonic character. With respect to the laughter of this mask, Bakhtin notes: "Laughter was sent to earth by the devil, but it appeared to men under the mask of joy, and so they readily accepted it. Then laughter cast away its mask and looked at man and at the world with the eyes of angry satire."[52]

Vathek, Satraps, and Interior Infinite

Does *Vathek* depart from the *Arabian Nights*? It collapses many elements in the collection: metamorphosis, mask, grotesquery, mirth, colorful characters, and the tension between power and beauty. These pass through a mind given to rebellion and transgression that selects and condenses to rework the *Nights' Entertainments* in such a manner as to spite his own society.

What the two kings of the frame tale understand is the impossibility of controlling human desire through pomp and power. They are derided by circumstance and forced by the bride with many rings to recognize disorder as coexistent with uniformity and compliance. This is a thread that runs throughout the *Nights*. *Vathek*'s sultan of Fonthill is no less incited to find a way out of restrictive society and culture. The jinn of the *Nights* metamorphose into the Giaour to play out the interior infinite of the caliph of Fonthill. Beckford takes his readers back in history to a region that is evoked by the *Arabian Nights* and similar tales. The narrative builds on dialectics of need and motivation, whereby interdependency is underscored but distinctions are paradoxically focused. As if in a carnival, limits are transgressed and interdependency between high and low is underlined as being in the nature of things. It is the caliph, with all his grandeur, who needs the "hideous" stranger. The latter is the monstrous Other, the invading alien who embodies the fear that inhibits rising empires. Instead of responding to the caliph's question, the Giaour is reluctant to answer, looking the caliph in the eye before bursting into laughter. Partaking of carnivalesque transgression, the Giaour's silence and subsequent laughter go against expectations, for the Giaour's silence is thought to be occasioned by "the awe which his [the caliph's] presence

[52] Ibid., 38.

inspired."[53] Yet, this "taciturnity" of the so-called merchant or stranger turns out to be a show of disrespect. In narrative, silence is death, as it signals the end of communication; but conversely it provokes action, for either the caliph will order the Giaour's death or the latter will take the initiative to save his neck. Instead, "the man, or rather the monster ... thrice rubbed his forehead, which, as well as his body, was blacker than ebony ... opened wide his huge eyes, which glowed like fire-bands; began to laugh with a hideous noise."[54]

This transgression of hierarchy is bound to lead to some radical transformation whereby the world, in Stallybrass and White's reading of Bakhtin, is turned "topsy-turvy, of heteroglot exuberance, of ceaseless overrunning and excess where all is mixed, hybrid, ritually degraded and defiled."[55] As Bakhtin argues for the carnival, the Giaour's act signifies "suspension of all hierarchical rank, privileges, norms, and prohibitions."[56] Although Beckford's narrative makes use of the carnivalesque, it is rather an accommodation of travesty, parody, and grotesquery.

The Giaour's appearance is not merely a technique of destabilization and disequilibrium, usually looked upon in Todorov's poetics as vital to narrative progression. The Giaour is certainly a destabilizing force, an alternating presence whose dealings with the caliph are central to the dramatic structure of *Vathek*. But he is also the rogue who gains the caliph's tacit agreement to transform the whole city into a site of comic, but grim, processions. Indeed, when turning himself into a rolling ball, the Giaour becomes an embodiment of a narrative that rolls on, gathering everything in its path, words of piety and abuse, creating as such a universe of unbridled urgency where ranks, emotions, and languages blend and fuse into each other regardless of caste, class, or official barriers. In other words, as a work that filiates with the *Nights*, *Vathek* should not be regarded in terms of correspondence in structures and themes. Its uniqueness stems from an ingrained indoctrination in the *Nights* at a time when its author was working on a translation of the Montague manuscript. For an imagination like Beckford's, the act of translation is one of absorption, distillation, and displacement.

Affiliates: The Brontës and After

The *Nights* serves as a defining matrix for an "interior infinite," the sense of freedom through one form of transgression or another. The artist,

[53] Lonsdale, *Vathek*, 6. [54] Ibid.
[55] Peter Stallybrass and Allon White, *The Politics and Poetics of Transgression* (London: Methuen, 1986), 8.
[56] Bakhtin, *Rabelais*, 10.

author, and suspected serial killer Thomas G. Wainewright (1794–1847) felt that he was the concentration of all the sultans, as he interiorized them through the *Nights* and imitations or translations. The craving for the vastness and freedom predicated on an imaginary Orient is the source for a filiation that differs from an affiliatory stance undergone, for example, by Walter Bagehot. Bagehot recollects how reading the *Nights*, and Aladdin in particular, led into a "cavern stored with the precious rarities of an Eastern fancy." A "dim mingling of identities" takes place "which we sometimes have in sleep, it is not Aladdin but our self and yet not our self but Aladdin, who gazes on the Jewel-bearing fruit-trees, marries the Vizier's daughter and controls the resources of the lamp." When looking back, Bagehot is no longer in the same position. There is a time before and a time after: Once upon a time, "we suffer and triumph with Sindbad, taste vicissitude with Camaralzaman, enjoy the shrinking fondness of Zutulbe, travel upon the enchanted carpet or mount the flying horse."[57] Now, he is more of a voyeur whose gaze penetrates the scene and whose mind looks upon recollections as passing moments, remembered but not sustained. Tennyson recalls them as cherished recollections of a palace of art, and not as material images or representations of an Orient. Thus, the brilliant poet and critic Arthur Henry Hallam, whose premature death Tennyson mourned in a long poem, "In Memoriam," remonstrates against any expectations of mere Eastern trappings in Tennyson's "Recollections of the Arabian Nights": "let nobody expect a multifarious enumeration of viziers, Barmecides … trees that sing, horses that fly and Gouls that eat rice pudding," for Tennyson "places us at once in the position of feeling" where there is "one of those luxurious garden scenes" in the caliph's pavilion. As Hallam, and later John Sterling, noticed, Tennyson was unconcerned with "topics, images, variations, and originalities."[58] His recreation caters to no pseudo-Oriental or other mode. His recollection of the fair Persian, with her impressive singing to the lute-luring Sheikh Ibrahim into some forbidden pleasure, grows into this imaginative recreation of a realm of art where life aspires to attain that enervating and enchanting state of things. Thus, a reader may well agree with J. H. Buckley that "Haroun's Baghdad to the young Tennyson is essentially the city of eternal artifice, in a realm of self-subsistent reality beyond all movement and desire."[59]

As a floating trope intended to predicate desires, an Anglo/Franco-Orient or, in Hunt's wording, "The Orient of Poets," takes a number of

[57] Bagehot, "The People of the Arabian Nights," 46–47.
[58] For these, see al-Musawi, *Scheherazade in England*, 53–55.
[59] Jerome Hamilton Buckley, *Tennyson: The Growth of a Poet* (Cambridge, MA: Harvard University Press, 1960), 39.

forms. These accommodate the latter's desire for justice, love, beauty, and repose; but it also includes Beckford's satrapism, Byron's brooding melancholy, Goethe's and Nerval's search for redemptive spontaneity and purity, and Tennyson's recreation of a city of arts. Once there, however, the Romantic is prone to her/his craving for the exotic, putting the complexity of life aside for fear of shaking her/him out of the ongoing reverie. Byron's "authenticity" is half-true, or, as Borges suggests, he is "more important for his image than for his work,"[60] for his poetry shows how he restructures experience according to an underlying paradigm of Otherness, which, in Homi Bhabha's Lacanian reading, remains "at once an object of desire and derision."[61] Byron fits within a genealogy that includes Bagehot, and probably many others who predicate their misgivings on an alien Other.

One can cite the Brontës, Charlotte and Emily,[62] for example, as a bridge between the positivists, with their claim to outgrow early attachments to the *Nights*, and Proust or Joyce and, in poetry, Yeats. The writings of the Brontës show an absorption of the tales that also differs from that of Hunt, for example, and Gérard de Nerval (d. 1855), in that they thoroughly embed Scheherazade's tales in their textual fabric. The difference emanates from a revisionist disposition intended to outgrow the basal tale and redirect its properties not only to their own desires and inhibitions, but also to an informing cultural and political milieu.[63] Their biographer and devoted scholar, Winifred Gerin (d. 1981), argues:

> of their (the Brontës) own earliest children books *Aesop's Fables* and the *Arabian Nights' Entertainments* appear to thousands to have been their favorites. Thousands of children before and since the Brontës – Thackeray and Beckford among them – read these books, but in few can they have generated so lively a creative impulse.

She adds:

> So intense was their immersion in a book that they had only to read to identify themselves with the characters; from this to acting the parts in dramatized

[60] Borges, "The Thousand and One Nights," 567.

[61] Homi Bhabha, *The Location of Culture* (London and New York: Routledge, 1994), 67.

[62] The Brontës read Galland's translation of the *Arabian Nights' Entertainments* (London, the 1787 ed.) and Sir Charles Morell's *Tales of the Genii* (London, 1764). See Winifred Gerin, *Emily Brontë: A Biography* (Oxford: Clarendon, 1971), 15. See also, for the same, Winifred Gerin, *Charlotte Brontë: The Evolution of Genius* (Oxford: Clarendon, 1967), 25–27, 43, 45–46. For more information, see Fannie Elizabeth Ratchford, *The Brontës' Web of Childhood* (New York: Russel & Russell, 1964), 4:12, 14; Laura L. Hinkley, *The Brontës: Charlotte and Emily* (New York: Hastings House, 1945), 25.

[63] For a detailed reading of the Brontës, see al-Musawi, *Anglo-Orient*, 133–62. Some portions are rewritten from that early critical account.

reconstructions of the stories was but a step (this they called, establishing a play) and then to add to the original plots was a natural consequence of their tireless invention.[64]

The implications of this early infatuation with the tales can be far reaching as Proust's *Remembrance of Things Past* testifies. The Brontës' adult effort to rewind that early absorption and locate it within the poetics and politics of the age is crucial to our understanding of textual and contextual sites. Alongside this absorption was the infatuation with Byron's Eastern poems, *Vathek*, and Robert Southey's "Thalaba the Destroyer."[65] Between subservience and revolt are gray areas that require some archaeological exploration. As Gerin explains:

On Charlotte, the influence of this early belief in magical powers was deep and lasting; the effort to combat it became more than the adolescent's usual painful squaring with reality; the creative artist in her suffered a life-long struggle to overcome the lure of the fabulous, in which she had not only believed but participated in childhood.[66]

Thus, Rochester is modeled on her early heroes like Zamorona, who, in Gerin's words, is "lifted from the Arabian Nights."[67]

The presence of the *Nights* permeates *Jane Eyre* (1847), especially the story of the two monarchs, the king of the Black Isles, and the Hārūn al-Rashīd cycle of tales which shows an embittered, restless caliph. Although asking his sword-bearer Masrour for diversions, he is also prone to tease out a number of options on his own, as Rochester is doing. *Jane Eyre*'s Rochester resembles Hārūn not only in his humor or his possession of a horse – though not a servant – named Masrour, but also in his sultanic attitude to Jane Eyre and women in general. In his feeling of remorse and his craving for amusement, Rochester is no different from Hārūn. Rochester even attempts to emulate Hārūn, who roams the city incognito to redress wrongs or to unite lovers.[68] Rochester's masks tend not only to test Blanche

[64] Gerin, *Charlotte Brontë*, 25.

[65] Byron's influence on the Brontës was deep. See Winifred Gerin, "Byron's Influence on the Brontës," *Keats-Shelley Memorial Bulletin* 17 (1966), 1–19. Perhaps Charlotte was influenced by Southey's *Thalaba* that owed its theme and imagery to Arabian mythology. See William Haller, *The Early Life of Robert Southey* (New York: Octagon, 1966), 256. Charlotte wrote to Southey asking for advice. See Gerin, *Charlotte Brontë*, 109. John Martin's paintings, which influenced Charlotte, are about such Near Eastern themes as the fall of Babylon and Nineveh. Also, Charlotte was interested in his "Sadak in Search of the Water of Oblivion," which is based on a scene from *Tales of the Genii*. Charlotte wrote a description of this engraving. See Gerin, *Charlotte Brontë*, 43.

[66] Gerin, *Charlotte Brontë*, 27. [67] Charlottë's "My Angria & Angrians," in ibid., 45–46.

[68] Charlotte Brontë, *Jane Eyre*, introduced by D. Leavis (London: Penguin, 1966); Charlotte Brontë, *Jane Eyre*, with appendix and notes by Reynold Clark (London: Longman, 1964), 14:131; 15:144. Hereafter citations are in the text.

Ingram's fidelity and her feelings toward him, but also to ascertain Jane's. With the monarchs of the *Nights* in mind, Charlotte Brontë presents Rochester as another monarch who expects obedience and compliance. Jane only disputes this role when it applies to her as a second wife. The narrative rarely raises questions against his amorous exploits with Celine, Giacinta, and Clara. Rochester disguises himself as a fortune-teller, a gypsy, exploring the double lives of others. Throughout, his teasing and taunting of women is licensed with little narrative opposition. Even his representation of Bertha Mason, the wife in the attic,[69] is justified in the narrative through a climactic fire scene that presents her as dangerous and wild. Bertha is the dark figure, who is associated with darkness and thence with promiscuity and secrecy. What the *Nights* offers in tales, especially in the Hārūn cycle and the frame tale, is redrawn so as to have Rochester tamed and domesticated by a plain Jane whose role is to please and entertain him by her narratives. More important than these parallels, however, are the heroines' courage, eloquence, deep insight, and capacity for understanding and defeating their masters' designs. When Scheherazade resolves to marry Shahrayar, her father cries,

> have you lost your sense, daughter, that you make such a dangerous request to me? You know that the Sultan has sworn by his soul that he will never lie above one night with the same woman, and to order her to be kill'd the next morning... Pray consider well to what your indiscreet zeal will expose you. (1:14)[70]

Similarly, when Mrs. Fairfax becomes acquainted with Rochester's intention to marry Jane, she warns Jane of the dangers of such a marriage:

> "I am sorry to grieve you," pursued the widow; "but you are so young, and so little acquainted with men. I wished to put you on your guard. It is an old saying that 'all is no gold that glitters'; and in this case I do fear there will be something found to be different to what either you or I expect." (24:293)

They embark on such an adventurous course to satisfy their inner craving for excitement, challenge, and active participation in life, but also because they are presented narratively as different from their "sex." In other words, it is this difference that, as both tales argue, grants them equal standing. Jane's method of counteracting Rochester's imperiousness and playful humor is basically the same as Scheherazade's. Both use their gifts to win their "masters'" favor and to compel them not to pursue their former designs. Scheherazade, the most entertaining and intelligent figure ever depicted in literature, summons all her mastery of the art of

[69] Susan Gubar, "'The Blank Page' and the Female Creativity," in *The New Feminist Criticism*, ed. Elaine Showalter (London: Virago, 1989), 243–63.
[70] Galland, trans., *Arabian Nights' Entertainments*.

storytelling to capture Shahrayar's attention and to pamper his susceptibility to suspense, until, after the passage of a thousand and one nights, Shahrayar changes his attitude to women and becomes devoted to Scheherazade. Thus, Scheherazade's tales contribute much toward liberating the sultan from prejudice against women, and also sweetening his temper (4:311).

Similarly, Jane submits herself voluntarily to become Rochester's wife, though she knows of his sexual exploits on the continent and, later on, of his marriage to Bertha. Charlotte Brontë's heroine clearly attempts to emulate Scheherazade. Thus whenever Rochester summons her to his presence, for example, she "prepares an occupation for him" (24:299), telling him a story, showing him a picture, or asking him to sing, always "pampering that susceptible vanity of his; but for once, and from motives of expediency, would e'en soothe and stimulate it" (24:299). Instead of letting him exercise his taunting and teasing traits – as his habit with others – she is able to employ his own method in dealing with him, thus disarming him by her playful humor and her sarcastic submission until he is divested of his sultanic imperiousness and of his virile exploits. Like Scheherazade, she has Rochester to admit her success. Shahrayar sets the prototype for a concluding scene of resignation, concluding the tales by telling Scheherazade: "I receive you entirely into my good graces, and I will have to be looked upon as the deliverer of the many damsels, I have resolved to have sacrificed" (4:312). Similarly, Rochester tells Jane: "I never met your likeness. Jane, you please me, and you master me – you seem to submit, and I like the sense of pliancy you impart; and while I am twining the soft, silken skein round my finger, it sends a thrill up my arm to my heart." He adds, "I am influenced, conquered; and the influence is sweeter than I can express; and the conquest I undergo has a witchery beyond any triumph I can win" (24:289).

Within this Scheherazade–Jane frame, the *Nights* images of witchcraft and the recurrence of smitten humans into apes or dogs undergo a Victorian trimming. The Jamaican Bertha, whom Rochester loved and married while accumulating wealth there, is pitted against Jane: the wild creole against a pleasant, intelligent English Jane. The dark Bertha suffers containment for being the human representation of the colony.[71] To counteract identification with natives or creoles, Jane emphasizes her Englishness in a manner that echoes that of settlers in the far reaches of the empire. It is only when read in this context that Jane's imaging of her Englishness against all Others makes sense. However, her political

[71] A general reading is by Patrick Brantlinger, *Rule of Darkness* (Ithaca, NY: Cornell University Press, 1990), 177.

positionality against patriarchy at large maximizes her role against early Victorian politics. Her job as a nurse also involves her in a subversive activity of a sort. In Gilbert and Gubar's analysis, Jane is "more dangerous to the order of society" for yearning "to escape entirely from drawing rooms and patriarchal mansions."[72] In this, she may sound like Scheherazade in the sense that she appeases Rochester and stoops to conquer.

But, by working simultaneously as both Rochester's narrative agent against the silenced Bertha and the latter's scribe, especially in her suicide scene, Jane also emerges as a typically Victorian neurotic creation. In Gilbert and Gubar's words, Bertha is "Jane's truest and darkest double" (360).[73] But this division betrays a common personality split, brought about by a number of factors, including readings and contacts with other nations and cultures. It is also the outcome of the colonial enterprises as an amalgam of contradictions. Caught up in the pursuit of interest among creoles whom he exploits, derides, and paradoxically desires, Rochester is also the epitome of colonial hybridity. This is where Charlotte Brontë swerves from, and also desires, her *Arabian Nights* as a site of riches to be gained and expectations to be achieved.

Jane Eyre and *Wuthering Heights* (1847) share some preoccupations that relate to a strain of transitionality in Victorian thought regarding issues of change, the rights of women, and the politics of enfranchisement, advancement, and expansion. The *Nights* provokes questions of relevance, and also nourishes desires and dreams of fulfillment. While immediacy and relevance have set the two novels within typically middle-class issues of achievement and domestic settlement, the dialogue with other texts and contexts, English and "Oriental," has involved them in resistance and challenge, endowing them, as it were, with an acumen for subversion. Both are ridden with contradiction, and the use and misuse of figurative strategies, along with other narrational traps and tropes that continue to draw the attention of many writers from every position and platform.

While both *Jane Eyre* and somehow *Wuthering Heights* draw on readings in the *Arabian Nights*, Byron's poetry, and Beckford's *Vathek*,[74] especially in the latter's Giaour, they diverge from there to fit more into the context of Victorian writing. Ridden with conflict and uncertainties, they

[72] Sandra M. Gilbert and Susan Gubar, *The Madwoman in the Attic: The Woman Writer and the Nineteenth-Century Literary Imagination* (New Haven, CT: Yale University Press, 1979), 338.
[73] Ibid., 360.
[74] Emily Brontë, *Wuthering Heights*, with a preface by Charlotte Brontë, ed. Frederick T. Flahiff (Toronto: MacMillan, 1968).

demonstrate the enormous shift in rewriting the *Arabian Nights* for a Victorian audience. Even when seemingly submerged in "white feminism,"[75] there is a counterdiscourse of parody, humor, and satire that defies closure and implicates narratives in contradictions. In the sultan/slave dichotomy of *Jane Eyre*, as much as in the love/marriage binary of *Wuthering Heights*, history is questioned, redrawn, and discredited. In both novels, history is disrupted and challenged by its claims of progress and justice. Creoles and dark figures are summoned back to the center, in the shape of Bertha, or in the form of a no less peripheral Other than Heathcliff, the unwanted hybrid of colonialist enterprise abroad. Deprived of name and language, to be stationed at the heart of the colonizer's domestic bliss, Heathcliff is a test not only for presumptions of equality, charity, and humility, but also for avowed racial superiority, as well as relevant issues of passion and love.

Murky Sensualism of the Western Bourgeoisie

In the case of Charlotte Brontë's Jane, Scheherazade is divided into two, each part being played off against the other. The defiant voice of the queen is accommodated by the plain nurse to promote a white feminist discourse in the line of Wollstonecraft, whereby "Western feminist writers rhetorically define their project as the removal of Eastern elements from Western life," as Zonana aptly argues.[76] As for Scheherazade the narrator, with her strategy of appeasement and domestication, she is only retained by Jane to be divested of her identity and site, in a manner that relates her to another strain in thought since the Renaissance. According to this Eurocentric drive, it is good to borrow from Islam and the Arabs, but acknowledgment is instead to be given to some Greco-Roman origin and lineage. Thus, what is retained of Oriental residue in narrative serves another purpose: to shift the blame for the backward status of English women from the immediate English context to the distanced Other. The East is deliberately recalled only to suggest uncongeniality and difference.[77]

[75] Joyce Zonana, "The Sultan and the Slave: Feminist Orientalism and the Structure of *Jane Eyre*," *Signs* (Spring 1993), 615.
[76] Ibid., 615.
[77] Winifred Woodbull, *Transfigurations of the Maghreb* (Minneapolis, MN: University Minnesota Press, 1993), 4: "despite the relative marginality of feminist discourse in the West, they [Western women] contribute to the production and perpetuation of Western power and privilege." She further argues: "Western subjects – specifically, Western women – are identified with modernity, rationality, individual autonomy and freedom, all of which depend symbolically and materially on the backwardness, mystification, subordination, and unfreedom of their third-world other-opposites."

Yet, such an interpretation covers only part of Jane's strategy of appropriation. While overtly opting for difference, there is inside Jane a great deal of attachment to that strain of *Arabian Nightism* that connects her to Byron and the Romantics. There is much Byronic Orientalism in her grounding and background that involves enormous fusion of figures and residue in her narrative. But, to escape this entanglement, Jane develops her parodic politics of "continuum" and "ironic difference," to bring about a text fraught with "contradictions" that, in another context, Hutcheon deems typical of parodic feminism.[78] Indeed, contradictions only manifest and correspond to the neurotic in *Jane Eyre*, for "wandering between two worlds," to use Matthew Arnold's apt analogy for intellectuals in a changing world, Jane is no less divided than many of Tennyson's personae. As grounding entails and explains a bent of mind, her subsequent striving for release and also for proper "Englishness" only testifies to another side of an identity crisis in an age of change inside and expansion and exploitation outside. Thus, within this context, it is not surprising to find Jane resorting to some parody of *Arabian Nightism* whenever impersonating Scheherazade to pamper her sultan, or to playfully remind him of this different English site. It is in line with her neurosis that Rochester is presented as a medley of the Byronic dark figure with a mysterious past and brooding mind (15:144), an "emir" (18:181) or sultan, a collaborator with colonialist authority who has "battled through a varied experience with many men of many nations" (131), and a person of some "English" proportions who is ready to settle for plain Jane and enjoy the "sweet wind" of Europe! Yet, it is Rochester's "new face" that hangs in the "gallery of memory," "masculine . . . dark, strong, and stern" (113), and whose person she swears solemnly to give her life "to serve" (18:202). Throughout, Jane exploits the tactical behavior of "a lamb-like submission and a turtle-dove sensibility," not only to appease him, but also to "fostering his despotism more" (24:274). Tracing in him Shahrayar's "susceptible vanity" (24:271), Jane frames him among figures from her *Arabian Nights* in its Byronic twist.

In other words, a divided neurotic mind is bound to salvage a similar textual hybrid, a creation from texts and contexts, ridden with tensions and oppositions that entail the reader's corresponding indecision as to its very formation, generation, and aftermath. Patched and retailored, Rochester is no more English than Jamaican or Oriental, a configuration of sites that only represents aspects of coloniality in its enterprising stage. But, when maimed in the fire scene, presumably caused by the caged wife Bertha, and domesticated in Jane's latest version

[78] Hutcheon, *Politics of Postmodernism*, 94.

of him, Rochester is no more than her own excessive perverse cry for rape, to use Fanon's phrase, which has been accentuated through representations of the virile but dangerous Other. Reminiscent of an entire middle-class culture, she only partakes of what Maxim Rodinson describes as that "murky sensualism, the unconscious masochism and sadism of the peaceful Western bourgeoisie."[79]

To follow Jane's own narrational representation, we may compare Rochester to Heathcliff. The latter is brought into the Eamshaws's household, a "gipsy brat" or "as dark almost as if it came from the devil" (41). Rochester, however, is met on the road, heading for Thornfield, with a dark face and stern complexion, a heavy brow, whose looks are "superb, impetuous" with a horse named after the caliph's sword-bearer Masrour. With the specific reference to the Prophet "Mahomet," Rochester is meant to be associated with the caliphs of Scheherazade, rather than with her cobblers, fishermen, and calendars. Roaming incognito hereafter, Rochester is presented to assume the definite airs of Hārūn, the caliph who has attracted the attention and love of Tennyson and Yeats. Yet, he is also the morose character whom John Payne has studied as the archetype of the neurotic and schizophrenic.[80] Attracted specifically to this latter lineage and association, Jane imparts, and inscribes on to him as site, her own longing for some irredeemable past of virility, passion, and difference of some Romantic abundance. In Fanon's words: "the Other will become the mainstay of … [her] preoccupations and … desires."[81] Distanced as such, Rochester fuses into a paradigm of Romantic historiography, especially attuned to the Romantics' own love for the outlandish, the boundless, and the mysterious. In Bhabha's postcolonial reading of Lacan, Rochester is the stereotype fetish object whose appearance occasions this very projection of desire. But, distanced imaginatively in place and time, Rochester as Shahrayar or Hārūn resists containment or identification. Thus, Jane will develop a Scheherazade disposition for wit and storytelling that tends to disarm Rochester, while gradually dissociating herself from any Eastern linkage. Henceforth, Scheherazade as

[79] Maxime Rodinson, *Europe and the Mystique of Islam*, trans. Roger Veinus (Seattle, WA: University of Washington Press, 1991), 58. Cited in al-Musawi, *Scheherazade in England*, 46n44, 66, and as follows: Maxime Rodinson, "The Western Image and Western Studies of Islam," in *Legacy of Islam*, ed. Joseph Schach and C. E. Bosworth, 2nd ed. (Oxford: Clarendon, 1974), 48. Cited also in Samar Attar, *Borrowed Imagination: The British Romantic Poets and Their Arabic-Islamic Sources* (Lenham and New York: Lexington, 2014), 21.

[80] John Payne, "The Thousand and One Nights," in two parts, *New Quarterly Magazine* (January–April 1879), 1:161.

[81] Frantz Fanon, *Black Skin, White Masks*, trans. Charles Lam Markmann (New York: Grove Press, 1968), 170.

woman is to be relegated to the background, along with women of dark skin like Blanche and Bertha, who are either to be alienated figuratively (17:157, 159, 18:181), or to be swept away to ensure total possession of the object of desire.

While Charlotte Brontë's intertextuality draws on some available images and tropes common to the pseudo-Oriental genre, she also shares with her generation certain visions and codes with respect to lands outside Europe. The central passage in the sultan/slave dialogue conveys a level of humor, irony, and playfulness that cuts across racist and colonialist figurative discourse. Rochester impersonates Shahrayar when he says: "I receive you entirely into my good graces, and I will have you to be looked up on as the deliverer of many damsels I have resolved to have sacrificed." While rephrasing the conclusion to the *Nights* frame story, this conclusion functions also as parody of the frame tale and its epilogue and partakes therefore of subversion, as it manipulates popular repertoire to deflate gender and class strictures. Incongruity emerges, however, whenever discourse and dramatic action are in disharmony. While Jane claims subordination, her playful resistance debunks and ejects male chauvinism and class distinction. Hence, echoes of feminist achievement in the Scheherazade motif tend to tame masculinity through both coincidence and contrivance. Losing grace and resolution, Rochester is to admit subordination rather than equality: "I have never met your likeness, Jane, you please me, and you master me . . . I am influenced-conquered" (23:250). This resignation splits Rochester in two. The conquered part is the dark stern self, the site upon which is predicated the "murky sensualism, the unconscious masochism and sadism," as noted by Rodinson. It is the other half that is the site of Jane's wish fulfillment, as it vaults over colonial arrogance and duplicity and the negation of Creoles, to present the triumph of plain Jane against antagonistic arrogance and pomp. The burden of the empire and its violence against natives is shifted and projected as Otherness. Duplicity, cruelty, and pomp are disposed of as Oriental in what Fanon calls the "unreflected imposition of culture."[82] But, according to the Jane–English and Rochester–Easterner divide, there remains a greater contradiction whenever drama is enacted within Rochester as an amalgam of so many characters. Rochester's playful description of Jane as "deliverer of many damsels," whom he "would not exchange for the Grand Turk's whole seraglio" (24:269), recalls and parodies texts of mutiny and rebellion, an offshoot of Scheherazade's achievement. There is so much duplicity and exploitation in

[82] Ibid., 191.

Rochester's enacted history in Jamaica, Europe, and Thornfield that unsettles Jane's allusions.

We may remember that Rochester's enterprise abroad, a period of "prurience" and "degeneration" (27:306), covers the largest part of (his)story. In that discursive space allotted to his exploitation of women "such as the ladies of Carthage" (20:218), Rochester impersonates many European travelers who practice and claim a sense of identity through difference, and accentuate superiority through shows of virility.[83] It is during that period of "prurience," which is also one of great enterprise and exploitation, that Rochester develops a male Eros that is significantly invested with a sense of superiority, patriarchy, and absolute power. Burton is only a latecomer to that imperial lexicon.

Rochester is "flattered" by women, sought for by no less than "tall, dark and majestic" Bertha, "the boast of Spanish Town for her beauty" (27:305–6). Although self-critical now of that "prurience" and "rashness, the blindness of youth" (27:307), the whole passage levels the blame on that "fecundity" and "sexual promise" that, according to Said's analysis, elicits "complex responses, sometimes even a frightening self-discovery."[84] Yet, while playfully challenging this part of his character, Jane forgives the "worldly, dissipated, restless man" (20:217) because she is more taken with his "sternness," which "has a power beyond beauty" (22:245). Needed to meet the narrator's innate desire for this side of Rochester, to have "the powerful Negro [black] bruise her frail shoulders,"[85] as in the garden scene in Scheherazade's frame tale, the Eastern element is so well articulated that it stands for every sign of the hidden, mysterious, and virile in Rochester.

When Jane situates her "model of Eastern emir" (18:181) among native Jamaicans and Creoles (126–27), Charlotte Brontë destabilizes her figurative strategy of race and color.[86] In both *Wuthering Heights* and, especially, *Jane Eyre*, color functions in issues that relate to virility and licentiousness. The frame tale garden scene in the *Arabian Nights*, the figure of Beckford's Giaour, and Byron's Eastern poems all inform this visibility of color. A plateau of signs and icons where color polarity reigns appears in both conversations with other texts and paintings that make up the dominant discourse in nineteenth-century Europe, especially in England and France. In collapsing texts and intertexts, along with a latent desire to blame Others for problems and vices already existing in England, Charlotte Brontë's text partakes of what Fanon describes as

[83] Said, *Orientalism*, 187–88. [84] Ibid., 188. [85] Fanon, *Black Skin*, 167.
[86] Susan L. Meyer, "Colonialism and the Figurative Strategy of *Jane Eyre*," *Victorian Studies* 33, no. 2 (Winter 1990), 247.

the "Manichean," whereby the colonial world looks upon the native as the "quintessence of evil." The blacks, eunuchs, cobblers, strangers, and exiles of the *Nights* flood the unconscious and present a number of narratives and poems as sites of the colonial encounter and its aftermath in modern and postmodernity's textual and virtual space. Rochester's discourse on that side of the world is not that of an emir or chief because it resonates with images of bestiality, madness, and drunkenness, which culminate in one total image of repugnance and aversion. To him, people in Jamaica are of "alien" nature, "obnoxious" tastes, and "common" cast of mind (27:206). Their females are there to "flatter" him. They, like Bertha, "lavishly displayed for [his] pleasure ... [their] charms and accomplishments" (27:206). Men are no better, for they suffer inferiority, tending therefore to "envy" him for his exploits. Others, like Dick Mason, are his subordinates, showing no more than "dog-attachment" to him (27:206). While betraying a colonialist and racist sense of superiority, these words also convey hatred for natives, but not for the exploited land. In Mannoni's analysis, "this is the world from which the colonial has fled because he cannot accept men as they are," according to an innate "desire for a world without men [i.e., people]."[87]

Positioned in England like the returning Nabobs of India, however, Rochester adopts that Manichean demarcation to the extreme: The colonized is a beast in comparison with the English. Taking plain Jane as the exemplary English woman, he argues, "compare these clear eyes with the red balls yonder, this face with that mask, this form with that bulk" (26:294). Enforcing an antifeminist discourse that resonates with that of the two brothers in the *Nights* frame tale, Rochester's Anglicized preference is no less disciplinary than other forms of containment and control already detected and analyzed by feminists. As every physical feature entails moral associations, it is Jane who has "discretion," "foresight, prudence, and humility" (23:250) against Bertha's savagery. In other words, people of different complexions and color serve, according to some "unreflected imposition of culture,"[88] as paradigmatic evil (*Jane Eyre*, 307), conversely enhancing thereby a European essence of beauty, sweetness, and reasonableness (20:217) that, in Jane's view, is bound to blossom "like a rose" (25:280). This is where the narrative joins colonial discourse in total spite of natives. Analogy and rhetorical accumulation of epithets cater to some innate desire to escape reasoning. As Fanon explains, the "European has tried to repudiate this uncivilized self" or bypass that "inordinately black hollow" in memory.[89] But for that to happen, there is a "mechanism of projection" at hand, an act of

[87] Quoted in Fanon, *Black Skin*, 107–8. [88] Ibid., 191. [89] Ibid., 190.

"transference" that ascribes evil to "someone else." Positioned as English in England, Rochester looks upon Bertha as "wholly alien." Deprived of voice and caged in the attic, Bertha becomes a site for disparagement by Rochester and Jane, for both belong to a discourse that has already made its paradigms for good and evil. "To identify an active, aggressive woman with Truth," writes Alicia Ostriker, "is to defy a very long tradition that identifies strong females with deception."[90] She is the "mysterious lunatic" (26:292), a "beast or human" who "groveled ... snatched and growled like some strange wild animal" with "a quantity of dark, grizzled hair," hiding "its head and face" (26:293). This restoration of the colonial encounter on the soil of England recalls the accounts of many travelers who, after their return, are positioned to write on their exploits against the little that they perceived and desired. Scheherazade's mirth, even in grim sites like the ensorcelled king of the Black Isles and the smitten sisters in "The Three Ladies of Baghdad," is turned upside down. Englishness becomes a privilege, and Rochester has to suffer a purgatorial fire and to emerge maimed and disfigured to regain an uncontaminated self.

Jane Eyre and *Wuthering Heights* are not duplicates of the *Nights* and Byron's Eastern poems. Nor are they pseudo-Oriental tales. They rewrite specific features and properties of the *Nights* for a Victorian audience, and this explains their popularity in postcolonial discourse and feminist writings.

Shifts in Reading the *Nights*

From now on, the *Nights* rarely functions as an overall subtext: Single stories evoke reminiscences, impressions, dialogues, images, icons, and an array of semiotic tableaus. This is how Joyce's *Finnegan's Wake* operates. Other affiliates take similar roads: They cherish their memory of the tales. Instead of apologizing for once being so enamored, they retain that memory to perceive reality anew, as Salman Rushdie does in *Haroun and the Sea of Stories*,[91] or in *Midnight's Children*,[92] and especially in his *Two Years Eight Months and Twenty-Eight Nights* (2015). The last of those works, with its added-on numbers that make up a thousand and one, engages sites of rationalist thought in Islamic culture to cope with contemporary realities and challenges. The eminent Andalusian philosopher Ibn Rushd (Averroes) is recalled as the main character, who, with the help and support of good jinn – the wizards of human knowledge – combats

[90] Alicia Ostriker, "The Thieves of Language: Women Poets and Revisionist Mythmaking," in *The New Feminist Criticism*, 320.
[91] Salman Rushdie, *Haroun and the Sea of Stories* (London: Granta, 1990).
[92] Salman Rushdie, *Midnight's Children* (London: Jonathan Cape, 1981).

evil powers and warmongers. Apart from the title that recalls the *Nights*, and manipulation of supernatural beings, the allegorical pattern relies on story-within-a-story structure to present narratives that resonate with pressing inhibitions and concerns. Erica Wagner wrote an eloquent critique for the *Observer*, stating that Rushdie's one thousand and one days is the novelist's way of envisioning another reality beyond our world, a reality that also negotiates the present. Always enraptured and thrilled by the *Nights*, Rushdie summons Dunia, the jinnia, to Ibn Rushd to wage a war against evil and dark jinn:

> One day, a beautiful orphaned girl who calls herself Dunia arrives at his door; being a rational man Ibn Rushd doesn't guess that she is a jinnia, a great princess of those supernatural creatures who are made, we learn, of smokeless fire. The jinn are fascinated by humankind, and Dunia more than most. And so, a little less than 1,000 years later, the descendants of the philosopher and the jinn will find themselves called on to rise up in battle against those dark jinn who would destroy the earthly world.[93]

This is how Wagner sums up the plot, which is also a love letter to New York, its fight against death, like Scheherazade's fight for survival through storytelling.[94]

Rushdie feels he is one of Scheherazade's children, and, as his narrator Saleem Sinai says in *Midnight's Children*:

> Now, however, time (having no further use for me) is running out. I will soon be thirty-one years old. Perhaps. If my crumbling, over-used body permits. But I have no hope of saving my life, nor can I count on having even a thousand nights and a night. I must work fast, faster than Scheherazade, if I am to end up meaning-yes, meaning-something. I admit it: above all things, I fear absurdity.[95]

Indeed, *Midnight's Children* is semantically placed in a textual field whereby the narrator, born at midnight, on the eve of India's independence from the British, is to be in limbo, exactly like his own birthday when a nurse switched the baby from destitute parents to his present well-to-do parents. This limbo, a liminality that defies certainties and absolutes, echoes the uncertainties bedeviling storytelling as Scheherazade fights for her life and survival through narrative. It is the narrative of Indian politics since independence.

[93] Erica Wagner, "Two Years, Eight Months and Twenty-Eight Nights by Salman Rushdie Review – Stories Told against Disaster," *The Guardian*, September 13, 2015, www.theguardian.com/books/2015/sep/13/two-years-eight-months-twenty-eight-nights-review-salman-rushdie.

[94] Ibid. [95] Rushdie, "The Perforated Sheet," *Midnight's Children*, 1.

I, Saleem Sinai, later variously called Snotnose, Stainface, Baldy, Sniffer, Buddha and even Piece-of-the-Moon, had become heavily embroiled in Fate – at the best of times a dangerous sort of involvement. And I couldn't even wipe my own nose at the time.[96]

Liminality and hybridity afflict the narrator as they agonize a nation where politicians are in search of absolutes that are impossible to attain. What eases the narrative and offers it some mirth is Rushdie's intertextualizing strategy that lets the novel navigate smoothly between the real and surreal, the natural and the fantastic, as if things happened this way. Sindbad's valleys of diamonds, and the mendicants' adventures in lands of plenty where faith is tested, are recalled to reflect on emerging conflictual sites of promise and disenchantment.

One Kashmiri morning in the early spring of 1915, my grandfather Adam Aziz hit his nose against a frost-hardened tussock of earth while attempting to pray. Three drops of blood plopped out of his left nostril, hardened instantly in the brittle air and lay before his eyes on the prayer-mat, transformed into rubies. Lurching back until he knelt with his head once more upright, he found that the tears which had sprung to his eyes had solidified, too; and at that moment, as he brushed diamonds contemptuously from his lashes, he resolved never again to kiss earth for any god or man.[97]

It is easy to read a "secular" message in this quote, but the disdain for diamonds places the grandfather more in a Sufi line of practice than in rationalist discourse. Adam Aziz is typical of many who combine faith with rationalism, but who also suffer the pangs of remorse upon leaving traditional practices that are once the source of repose and certitude. Upon taking the decision not to "kiss earth for god or man," Adam also navigates with Sindbad and the mendicants among promises of a paradisiac hereafter and a hard reality that impels him to perceive reality as it is, with "diamond-free eyes." The narrator recapitulates:

This decision, however, made a hole in him, a vacancy in a vital inner chamber, leaving him vulnerable to women and history. Unaware of this at first, despite his recently completed medical training, he stood up, rolled the prayer-mat into a thick cheroot, and holding it under his right arm surveyed the valley through clear, diamond-free eyes.[98]

At these moments of hard choice, the *Nights* creeps in to oust other icons and sites of power. Commodities make up one's surroundings. They have their numbers, connotations, and allusions, but none can be like the magic number of the *Nights*: "1001, the number of night, of magic, of alternative realities – a number beloved of poets and detested by

[96] Ibid. [97] Ibid. [98] Ibid.

politicians, for whom all alternative versions of the world are threats." This is the crux of the novel. The unfolding postindependence history, partisan conflictual politics, and social and religious lives of people in Kashmir and elsewhere are set in conversation and conflict with "alternative realities" that poets and writers as Scheherazade's children envision.

The celebration of storytelling is what matters among affiliates, and they are as many as Scheherazade's tales. It is so not only because they see it as more telling than historical accounts, but also because it elevates their profession as writers. Storytelling delays the end, but it also gives life. This is how Elias Khoury thinks of it in an otherwise metafictional journey among texts to dispel the silence surrounding the destruction and erasure of Palestinian villages and life. In his *Awlād al-ghītū: Ismī Ādam* (2016; English translation: *Children of the Ghetto: My Name Is Adam*, 2019), Khoury questions a number of things that are subjects for discussion. To account for the narrator's resurrection of accounts that have been kept locked and silenced for years, he compares his profession, resuscitating the hidden and numbed, to Scheherazade's: "Scheherazade was the first narrator. She gave birth to children and told a thousand stories, every one of which became a person who narrates."[99] Like Adam's memoirs and notebooks that find voice in this narrative, storytelling has no other function than itself: to "delay death," which is also another invitation to fight the horror that comes with memory. Khoury might have in mind a number of writers, but especially Ṭāhā Ḥusayn and Tawfīq al-Ḥakīm in their writings of the 1930s. Their joint novella, *al-Qaṣr al-masḥūr* (1936; *The Enchanted Palace*) reflects on al-Ḥakīm's play *Scheherazade* (1934), which presents her as an Egyptian goddess, or even Bidpai,[100] who tells King Dabschelim instructive parables and stories in *Kalīlah wa-dimnah*, presumably translated from a Persian source by ʿAbd Allāh ibn al-Muqaffaʿ (d. 139 [756/57]).[101] The tale revolves around Scheherazade as the abductor of al-Ḥakīm to teach him a lesson on how to present her (17). Thus upon meeting her, al-Ḥakīm expresses surprise at being kidnapped by the person who inspired him to write his play. She retorts: "Didn't you abduct me and imprison me in a large size book?" (39–40).

Not all affiliates care for the frame story of the *Nights*. The case is so in Garcia Marquez's novels.[102] His use of the "City of Brass," Sindbad's voyages, and tales of exploitation endows his writing with some *Nightism* that is not as visible as is the case with other writers who claim

[99] Khoury, *Awlād al-ghītū*, 200.
[100] Ṭāhā Ḥusayn and Tawfīq al-Ḥakīm, *al-Qaṣr al-masḥūr* (Cairo: Dār al-Nashr al-Ḥadīth, 1936), 92. Further references are in the text.
[101] For a discussion of *al-Qaṣr al-masḥūr*, see al-Mūsawī, *al-Riwāyah al-ʿArabiyyah*, 31–37.
[102] For more, see Azouqa, *Magical Realism*.

Scheherazade by name. "Garcia Marquez uses the *Arabian Nights*' hyperbolic marvelous to accentuate their [Native Americans'] plight." Reflecting on the functional use of the hyperbolic, Aida Azouqa detects in *One Hundred Years of Solitude* a resemblance to "The Fourth Voyage of Sindbad the Sailor."

A Postcolonial or a Postmodernist Scheherazade

Variations on the *Arabian Nights* in Arabic fiction are many, and writers and critics like Jabrā Ibrāhīm Jabrā never tired of mentioning the *Nights* as a reference while they also stressed its difference from the modern novel in its search for climactic points and development of characters. He critiques the *Nights* as series of adventures that rarely "grow organically."[103] He adds in another article that the *Nights* is a mixture of the real and the fantastic, but its power lies in its invigoration of the imaginative faculty that changes someone like Shahrayar into a better person.[104] One can tell that Jabrā reads the *Nights* in the 1950s in terms of the modern European novel, but not its subsequent postmodernities that resort to patching, metafiction, parody, travesty, and irony to cope with multiple realities, simulacra, and transgeneric experimentation. The Egyptian Yaḥyā al-Ṭāhir ʿAbd Allāh (d. 1981) wrote *Ḥikāyat li-l-amīr ḥattā yanām* (1979; *Tales to Put the Prince to Sleep*), Maḥmūd al-Wardānī wrote *Awān al-qiṭāf* (2002; English translation: *Heads Ripe for Plucking*, 2008), and Jamāl al-Ghīṭānī came up in 1976 with *Waqāʾiʿ ḥārat al-Zaʿfarānī* (English translation: *The Zafarani Files*, 2009). While using the *Nights*, these novels invoke postmodernist techniques to account for sites of political and social upheaval. Before the burst of postmodernist practices, experimentation was already gathering momentum in "peripheral" regions where indigenous narrative, linguistic innovations, and openness to the world, and Europe and America in particular, have led to new writing.[105] What Jabrā dismissed as lacking organic unity, other writers eagerly embrace to make use of such techniques as interruptions, repetition, accumulation of events, and stylistic diversity as more appropriate to meet their limbo situation. In a neat conclusion, Richard van Leeuwen argues: "Authors such as Macedonio Fernández, and later Roberto Arlt and Jorge Luis Borges, developed their work in the context of Argentine modernism,

[103] Jabrā Ibrāhīm Jabrā, "al-Dhirwah fī al-adab wa-l-fann," *al-Adīb* (February 1950), 3–7. See al-Mūsawī, *al-Riwāyah al-ʿArabiyyah*, 26–28.

[104] Jabrā Ibrāhīm Jabrā, "al-Riwāyah wa-l-insāniyyah," *al-Adīb* (January 1954), 31–36.

[105] Eleni Kefala, *Peripheral (Post)Modernity: The Syncretist Aesthetics of Borges, Piglia, Kalokyris and Kyriakidis* (New York: Peter Lang, 2007); and van Leeuwen, *The Thousand and One Nights*, 300–15.

budding capitalism, and debates about the cultural identity of their country."[106] He adds that the following generation, especially Ricardo Piglia (d. 2017), felt bound to these predecessors. "Like them, he is also concerned with the effort to construct a certain cultural coherence out of disparate elements and a variety of centripetal forces."[107] Like many who belong to the post-1960 generation, Piglia inherits from predecessors and the *Nights* a number of properties that resist closure and "organic" narrative. Just as life is a series of interruptions, deferrals, formulas, repetitions, and surprise, so have postmodern narratives to accommodate them, as Italo Calvino does in *If on a Winter's Night a Traveller.*[108] This multiple narrative of disequilibrium and disorder works within a sea of narrative where the legendary American Indian regains imaginative and experiential fecundity and presence to be the "Father of Stories," a "reincarnation of Homer, of the storyteller of the *Arabian nights*, Popol Vuh, Dumas, Joyce."[109] A "man of immemorial age, blind and illiterate," opens the gate for a fertile land that signifies the replenishment for which Barth is searching. It is this immemorial man who is Borges's "Immortal." The dream of automatic storytelling that attracts the postmodernists works smoothly throughout this narrative, as the narrator thinks of this flow of narrative as a labyrinth, a web, where parts and units reflect on each other, or simply initiate disorder or chaos to begin anew. Scheherazade is a model there because the search for unity is impossible in her labyrinthine narrative. Calvino's narrator explains:

> I'm producing too many stories at once because what I want is for you to feel, around the story, a saturation of other stories that I could tell and may be will tell or who knows may already have told on some other occasion, a space full of stories that perhaps is simply my lifetime, where you can move in all directions, as in space, always finding stories that cannot be told until other stories are told first, and so, setting out from any moment or place, you encounter always the same density of material to be told.[110]

Issues raised by structuralists like Todorov with respect to disorder reverberate in Calvino's narrative. His views and also whims of automatic inventiveness place him at the center of experimentation where Scheherazade becomes a model for particular departure from the highly compact novel as theorized by Henry James, Conrad, D. H. Lawrence,

106 van Leeuwen, *The Thousand and One Nights*, 300. 107 Ibid.
108 Italo Calvino, *If on a Winter's Night a Traveller*, trans. William Weaver (Orlando, FL: Harcourt, Inc./Helen and Kurt Wolff, 1981).
109 Ibid., 117. Also in Michael Wood, "A Romance of the Reader," *New York Times*, June 21, 1981, www.nytimes.com/1981/06/21/books/a-romance-of-the-reader.html.
110 Calvino, *If on a Winter's Night a Traveller*, 109. Also van Leeuwen, *The Thousand and One Nights*, 325.

Flaubert, and many others. Calvino reflects on this literature machine in an article that also echoes experimentations in mechanical verse and automatic poetry. He writes, "[T]he true literature machine will be one that itself feels the need to produce disorder, as a reaction against its preceding production of order."[111] His conjectures are not necessarily deep, but they are in line with a postmodernist metafictionalist streak that cinematic production tries hard to resist to come up with a cohesive film.

How Does the Cinema Cope with Postmodernism?

While Scheherazade's affiliates in the cinema industry are many, indeed as many as the ones who marauded the tales to glean and appropriate stereotypes, there are very few who approached the *Nights* as systematically and thoughtfully as Pier Paolo Pasolini in *Il fiore delle mille e una notte* (1974; *The Flower of the Thousand and One Nights*). Unconcerned with the frame tale, and starting where he finds sites of love, intrigue, and adventure, Pasolini partially retains for the *Nights* its storytelling practice.[112] This experience also coincides with a postmodernist tendency to self-conscious production while working with present realities that converse with a past. The film is often thought of as being the most autobiographical among his films. This last production in his trilogy, *Decameron* (1971) and *Canterbury Tales* (1972), is unique in its difference from the common resort to the frame story as a way of constructing a selection of scenes. Although criticized for its bent for the erotic, Pasolini opens the film with the story of "Nur al-Din and Zumurrud," before covering other unique tales of sexual encounter and learning as in "Aziz and Azizah." Colin MacCabe draws attention to specific properties in the film that distinguish it as a production. While Pasolini checked different versions of *A Thousand and One Nights* (and shot scenes in a number of places including Yemen, Esfahan [Iran], Eritrea, and Nepal), he also let his recent frustrated experience in love show in his selections of sites and stories.

> He would now search for his vision of a precommodified culture not in the beginnings of modern Europe and the present-day lumpen proletariat but in more distant times and places and in the contemporary third world, creating his most exultant vision of simple sex outside of commodity exchange.[113]

[111] Italo Calvino, "Cybernetics and Ghosts," in *The Uses of Literature*, trans. Patrick Creagh (San Diego, CA: Harcourt Brace & Company, 1986), 13.

[112] Michael James Lundell, "Pasolini's Splendid Infidelities: Un/Faithful Film Versions of The Thousand and One Nights," *Adaptation: The Journal of Literature on Screen Studies* 6, no. 1 (2013), 120–27.

[113] Colin MacCabe, "*Arabian Nights*: Brave Old World," The Criterion Collection, November 13, 2012, www.criterion.com/current/posts/2552-arabian-nights-brave-old-world.

While highlighting the erotic, Pasolini rarely deviates from the selected tales, giving them the power of local life where the fringes of the society profusely appear.

This turn in cinematic production is rarely followed up, but there are still some entertaining productions, like Hallmark Entertainment, broadcast over two nights (April 30 and May 1, 2000) that sustain some storytelling properties of the *Nights* while focusing on some tales of adventure, surprise, and humor. Ali Baba opens the scene after the frame tale, followed by that of the hunchback, then Aladdin (Figure 17), the sultan and the beggar that takes the story of the sleeper awakened and retailors it as in Najīb Maḥfūẓ's *Layālī alf laylah* (1982; English translation: *Arabian Nights and Days*, 1995), and the three princes whose one-year quest brings about harmony among them. Well produced, this Hallmark Entertainment also "worked within a set of clichés, stereotypes and audience expectations."[114] A different approach was taken by Tim Supple in his significant production for the theater in 2011. As his text, Supple used a version prepared by the Lebanese novelist Ḥanān al-Shaykh that lays more emphasis on "Moorish" expositions of virility. It is nevertheless an important step in theatrical appropriation of the *Nights* as a composite work with a frame tale. Like in Maḥfūẓ's *Layālī alf laylah*, it also collapses scenes and tales to produce a total impression of a colorful life of fortunes and vicissitudes. Alongside this effort to regain a corresponding meaning to the *Arabian Nights* is the recognition of its presence in a digital age. Tarek el-Ariss offers a significant reading, not only of some traces and echoes in social media, but also the digital conversation that brings the *Nights* to the virtual space as no less informing leaks and scandals than other forms of production.[115] Thus, we are in the presence of visual and virtual spaces that take the *Nights* as a malleable property worth accommodating in a new digital but challenging age.

From Opa-locka to Baghdad: Emancipated Architecture

As scholarship finds some material worthy of study in this virtual and cinematic industry,[116] it is logical to explore other production sites that show the power of the *Nights* in world cultures. Like the history of illustrations, the history of the film industry made definite progress in

[114] Robert Irwin, "A Thousand and One Nights at the Movies," in *New Perspectives on Arabian Nights: Ideological Variations and Narrative Horizons*, ed. Wen-Chin Ouyang and Geert Jan van Gelder (London and New York: Routledge, 2005), 100.
[115] el-Ariss, *Leaks, Hacks, and Scandals*.
[116] See, for instance, Warner's *Stranger Magic*; and Irwin, "A Thousand and One Nights at the Movies."

ALADDIN IN THE CAVE
(Page 262)

Figure 17 Edmund Dulac: Aladdin in the cave.

the first decades of the twentieth century. In her neat historicizing of the vogue of *Nights* industry, Catherine Lynn shows how it grew rapidly alongside other variations in performance art: "When Terry Ramsaye wrote one of the earliest histories of the movies in 1926, the title, *A Million and One Nights: A History of the Motion Picture*, further suggested the new industry's fix on the theme."[117] This was the topic for the Opa-locka project of 1926.[118] What started as a dreamlike fantasy was soon to materialize in a Florida town. The story of that dream connects well with Pasolini's motto of multiple dreams, for the Opa-locka developer and aviator Glenn Curtiss's (d. 1930) real estate project found in the New York architect Bernhardt Emil Muller (d. 1964) the right person to have his dream of an *Arabian Nights* town come true. Muller explains:

> I described to him how we would lay the city out on the basis of the stories [*Arabian Nights*], using a story for each of the most important buildings, naming the streets accordingly. In each building we would tell the story by means of mural decorations and wrought iron work carrying out the various features of the story. The style of the architecture would be governed by the country in which the story was supposed to have taken place. Mr. Curtiss was fascinated with my ideas, and I made plans to actually create the phantom city of my mind.[119]

Opa-locka turned fantasy into a real town, with its bank, gas station, city hall, hotel, marketplace, houses, and streets that connect to the *Arabian Nights*. Emphasis was laid on an exterior show, a façade, that can capture the eye. Muller and his team were no ordinary architects and city planners; they brought along with them experience, knowledge, and art. Muller was thoroughly imbued with the *Arabian Nights* to make this dream materialize. This took place when the tales were very popular in late nineteenth- and early twentieth-century America.[120] In her attempt to cover the enormous consumption of the *Nights* in the context of a growing consumer culture, Susan Nance suggests:

> all century Oriental tales had been making their way through multiple venues of fashion, theater, advertising, stage and costume design, circuses, and more, all of it culminating in elaborate high-budget theater productions like Robert Hichens's desert romance *Garden of Allah* (1904), which moved quickly into the cinema.[121]

Lynn situates the Opa-locka venture within a worldwide vogue:

[117] Catherine Lynn's important study, "Dream and Substance: Araby and the Planning of Opa-Locka," *The Journal of Decorative and Propaganda Arts* 23 (1998), 169.

[118] Bernhardt E. Muller, "Arabian Nights in America: Fascinating Architectural Fantasy," *Country Life* 55 (November 1928), 67–69. For the history of the town, see Frank S. FitzGerald-Bush, *A Dream of Araby: Glenn H. Curtiss and the Founding of Opa-locka* (Opa-locka, FL: South Florida Archaeological Museum, 1976).

[119] Bernhardt E. Muller, "Bernhardt Muller's Dream of Arabian City in Florida Is Reality," *Opa-locka Times*, February 23, 1927, 1. Also cited by Lynn, "Dream and Substance," 164.

[120] See Nance, *How the Arabian Nights Inspired the American Dream.* [121] Ibid., 201.

Like Irving's volumes, tales derived from *The Arabian Nights* enjoyed great popularity during the early twentieth century. That popularity was enhanced by musical works and ballets based on the tales, and it was extraordinarily broadened by the early movies they inspired.[122]

She explains:

During these years, while school children and their parents everywhere were reading the tales, *The Arabian Nights* was also inspiring major works of performance art elaborately produced in the cultural capitals of Europe and the United States. Nikolai Rimsky-Korsakov based his symphonic suite, Scheherazade, on the theme and in 1910 his music inspired Sergei Diaghilev, the great Russian shaper of the modern ballet, to mount his production of the same name.[123]

Relatively free from imperial politics that impacted and permeated British and French culture, the American scene has its open conversation with the tales down to the 1930s. More than an affiliate, however, was the renowned American architect Frank Lloyd Wright (d. 1959), who was so enraptured with the *Nights*, and "The Fisherman and the Demon," that he had a mural named "The Fisherman and the Genii from the Arabian Nights" over the fireplace in his children's playroom in his house in Oak Park, Illinois, in the 1890s.[124] In Lynn's words and rephrasing of Wright's,

In the surviving Oak Park mural the fisherman is realistically rendered sitting to one side of the great half-round scene dominated by the central figure of the enormous, abstractly rendered figure of "the Genii … done in straight line pattern."[125]

This detail may sound insignificant, were it not for the fact the Wright was invited to Baghdad to design an opera house in May 1957. At the age of ninety and under the spell of the *Nights* and the visit, Wright drew up "organic" designs to retain for Baghdad its glory in a present context, elaborately designing therefore an opera house, archaeological museum, post office, bazaar, university campus, and gallery for contemporary art. Although other famed architects, including Walter Gropius, Le Corbusier, Josip Lluís Sert, and Alvar and Aino Aalto, were also invited and commissioned by the Iraqi government development board, Wright thought of Baghdad as being different from any other city: It is the city of the *Arabian Nights*. Thus, he pleaded with Iraqi engineers and architects

[122] Lynn, "Dream and Substance," 167. [123] Ibid., 169.
[124] See Neil Levine, *The Architecture of Frank Lloyd Wright* (Princeton, NJ: Princeton University Press, 1996), 25.
[125] Lynn, "Dream and Substance," 25.

to derive motifs from their own culture, and not to be lured by Westernized replicas. On May 22, 1957, he implored Iraqi architects:

> Now in the push of modernism, modernization, that ancient strength should not be weakened and lost and that background of your own culture should now be developed so genuinely, so broadly and so individually that it still has so many phases of beauty that no architect should come here and put a cliché to work.[126]

His elaborate designs for Baghdad never materialized, but they certainly were in the minds of a generation of Iraqi architects who tried to make use of his notions to retain a touch of the past in new architectural designs and urban planning. His Baghdad opera house design on the Pigs' Island in the middle of the Tigris around its bend is a gorgeous work of art that is also carefully drawn to connect the two sides of city. He renamed the island "the Isle of Edena,"[127] with all the properties of an *Arabian Nights* tale, with something of Aladdin's lamp as symbolic of exuberance and imagination. When transferred to Tempe, Arizona, the project had to undergo material and symbolic changes that speak of the vicissitudes of the *Nights* under changing circumstances. Joseph Siry summarizes this change as follows:

> Adaptation of the Baghdad scheme to Tempe entailed changes in overtly symbolic forms. While the portal arches flanking the Baghdad Opera House were to have roundels containing scenes from *The Arabian Nights*, the arch roundels of precast concrete flanking the Gammage Auditorium were to have sculpted cast-metal bas-reliefs of Arizona history.

He adds:

> In the Tempe auditorium's domed crown, Wright replaced the figure of Aladdin and his lamp atop Baghdad's dome with a statue of "the individual, his majesty the American citizen, with his lamp, the imagination," housed in a domical metal and glass lantern, evoking the water domes on the site.[128]

Wright is not a frame tale fan; and his contributions partly retain for the *Nights* its composite nature.

[126] Joseph M. Siry, "Wright's Baghdad Opera House and Gammage Auditorium: In Search of Regional Modernity," *The Art Bulletin* 87, no. 2 (June 2005), 272.
[127] As cited by Siry, Wright explains the location as follows: "The Garden of Eden was located at an old city named Edena, which was on the great canal taken from the Tigris and Euphrates. And that's about 120 miles, I guess, south of Baghdad. So we are calling this little island the king put his hand on and gave me specifically, the Isle of Edena." Ibid., 273.
[128] Ibid., 287.

Authenticating a Pastiche? Codrescu's Transgeneric Frame

While Wright was not alone in working with the *Nights* as more than a frame tale; other artists, architects, painters, and writers show how it resonates with contemporary concerns, as women's writings demonstrate.[129] Other writings show different interests and concerns without abandoning the representation of Scheherazade as a female narrator. The Romanian-born American poet, novelist, essayist, screenwriter, and commentator Andrei Codrescu chose Wilhelm Vita's painting of Scheherazade (1891) as cover for his *Whatever Gets You through the Night.*[130] A very Orientalized presentation of an uncovered upper part of a lush but languid storyteller strikes the reader as counter to the mounting depiction of Scheherazade as symbolic of the triumph of art. His text, with its *ḥawāshī* (explicatory margins) on its right, left, and bottom, negotiates a place between translators/editors, annotators like Lane and Burton, and fiction writers. He claims awareness of the power of the *Nights*, and he has to prove his mastery of the art:

> The *Nights* are themselves a sea of stories that drowns the poor writer who, driven by hubris or fascination, lowers herm's innocent pirogue on its waves; suddenly there is no land in sight. J. L. Borges has compared the *Nights* to a vast "cathedral"; B. Odăgescu compared their attraction to that of "a moth to the flame." Both of them ground their metaphors in important motifs: Borges in the Alhambra, Odăgescu in the magic lamp of Aladdin. (23n20)

To place himself among the recognized devotees of the art of storytelling, he claims humility and lineage to Sheherezade: "But to us, just out for a foolish cruise, the *Nights* became an angry sea we trust to navigate safely by following closely the sound of Sheherezade's voice weaving salty vastness from the lighthouse of Sharyar's bed" (23n20). The reader may conclude that Codrescu is as good as his claim: He rewrites the frame tale, explores narrative possibilities, and engages with translators as if they were necessarily new to his readers (74nn39–41). He denies contextual readings of the *Nights* as "exclusive Arabic imaginary" because the *Nights* "are a world, a world, moreover, that deconstructs the imperial and theological worlds set up by Islam in various phases of self-consciousness" (75n41). He is right there, but he has also to admit that the tales converse with manners, customs, and what Raymond Williams

[129] For a review of these, see Muhsin Jassim al-Musawi, "Prefatory Thresholds: Scheherazade Avenged," in *The Postcolonial Arabic Novel: Debating Ambivalence* (Leiden: Brill, 2003), 1–19.

[130] Andrei Codrescu, *Whatever Gets You through the Night* (Princeton, NJ: Princeton University Press, 2011). Quotes are in the text.

includes under "structures of feeling." His immediate ghost is not Rushdie, Eco, Balzac, or "The blind Argentine writer, Jorge Luis Borges" (75n42). He wrestles with Barth, who "wrote a robustly heterosexual history of Sheherezade (whom he called 'Sherry')" (75n42), all to prove that he can work along Scheherazade's narrative style without necessarily giving in to pastiche and parody, Barth's preferable gateways. Both of them struggle to claim lineage to the archetypal storyteller. To elevate her role is to aggrandize theirs. Codrescu argues his case as follows: "Sheherezade changed the human paradigm from accounting to storytelling. She did so at the peril of her life and of her afterlife. Insofar as she risked her life for others, she was a hero, like Prometheus" (97n61). He recapitulates: "She is a historical hero, a proto-feminist, and a mortal with a biography encompassed by the single word *Storyteller*" (97n61). He even goes out of his way to suggest like Maḥfūẓ that her "Master-Teacher was a Sufi who taught her to spin-dance" (98n64). In this recapitulation, he sets a trap for himself: He imposes another cage or context on an imaginary! Codrescu may have been aware of Maḥfūẓ's *Layālī alf laylah*. Like Maḥfūẓ, he also collapses a few tales and augments the role of the Sufi master, but his main focus is on rewriting the frame story and buttressing its summary-like narrative with details. With mirthful psychologizing of "Sharyar," Codrescu explains: "Thinking further, Sharyar realized that his present misfortune had begun with an uncharacteristic impulse, nostalgia" (30). He repeats what Fedwa Malti-Douglas argued in 1991. Nostalgia is the motivation for his brother's visit, the latter's discovery of the garden scene, and the eruption of a series of misfortunes before Scheherazade's precarious advent. Taking the role of the storyteller, and directing action away from the written frame tale, Codrescu has this to say on the end of the kings' quest: "they had no way of knowing that looming over the parting was the Storyteller's fast-spinning spindle that would shortly fold time and generate more creatures than were now living" (32). Although deliberately confusing the frame tale with an Islamic text to digress on circumcision, Codrescu cannot forget that he is a male storyteller even in moments that ask for narrative intervention to draw a comparison between a discursive space under the king's rule, and a popular one during his absence:

> in the king's absence, solemnity, praise, and elevated sentiments had fallen in disuse. Rough and prurient humor, rude chants, lewd dances, and ironic or downright parodic recitations were the preferred entertainments in the Vizier's easygoing empire. (34)

Within this discursive navigation, the storyteller in Codrescu digresses further on circumcision as a Shahrayar's new fixation; a disposition that drives the young Scheherazade to safeguard herself along with Dinarzad, sleeping "lightly with a curved knife under her pillow" (46). She even reports how her master-teacher went to the king to "argue against the circumcision of females," citing "the Koran as proof." Moreover, he told the king that he had no right to slaughter his wife because "women guilty of lewdness should be committed to the house until four witnesses testified against them"; hence his action was "a breach of the Law" (47). Codrescu enjoys these digressions even though the frame tale was set in pre-Islamic times and regions. Spinning tales born out of the written sources become Codrescu's art as a storyteller who is vying for a place in the tradition of Barth, Borges, and, especially, Burton. He is aware of Burton, the "spinner," who "began to spin the story of what happened before Sheherezade assumed her storytelling destiny" (76). Codrescu demands his share in spinning tales, and "Sheherezade" has to explain the second mendicant's tale differently: "the story is not about a monkey who can write. It is about a girl who can fool a king" (93). In other words, he has to be a spinner, like Burton, or Eco, "who was Burton's Lachesis, confined himself to stretching a paragraph from the *Nights* into the book-length tale *The Name of the Rose*" (76n42). Though he spares no one, Codrescu uses his margins to place Burton as the center of a phenomenal culture industry that incorporates Orientalism, postmodernism, and high or low modernities. In one sweeping gesture, he includes Balzac, Rushdie, Eco, Barth, and many others, and concludes as follows:

> For the full flavor of the rhymed prose and fanciful poetry of the arrogant and erudite Burton, go to the source. You will be rewarded by a kind of languorous paralysis, brought about by Burton's vigorous libertinage and his intimate acquaintance with Arabic and Arabs, an intimacy that made it possible for him to keep his colonial Englishman's prejudice intact, and to mythologize his subjects simultaneously. Orientalism is in full bloom here, and its grotesque flowers are still headily appealing to the senses. (77n44)

Codrescu is not without whims, stock images, and stereotypes. His anxiety with respect to predecessors testifies to Borges's "hostile dynasty." His own dynasty differs, however, because it includes a vast canvas of names and modalities, illustrating his wide readings, affiliation with Scheherazade and her children, and difficult negotiation for independence. Navigating through and among a sea of storytelling, Codrescu draws a fine conclusion to this chapter while preparing in his marginal notes for an overview of the state of the field, which is the *Arabian Nights*, where multiple directions occur to disengage with a legacy of appropriation and framing. In its digressions and margins, his work also raises questions as whether pastiche, irony, and digression are decolonizing strategies toward the emancipation of a book.

7 Decolonizing the *Arabian Nights*?

> We are in Egypt not merely for the sake of the Egyptians, though we are there for their sake; we are there also for the sake of Europe at large.
>
> Arthur James Balfour

There are a number of ways to "decolonize" a book that cannot be spoken of as one definitive text. One way is to read and approach *A Thousand and One Nights* as a book free from a body of paraphernalia, stereotypes, and representations that Edward Said associates with a movement that began to take shape by the early nineteenth century as "Orientalism." By that term, Said meant "a Western style for dominating, restructuring, and having authority over the Orient."[1] This is differentiated from "great Orientalist works of genuine scholarship," like de Sacy's and Edward William Lane's as compared with that of Renan and Gobineau.[2] A popular book like the *Nights* is bound to suffer in this transaction. As much as it has benefitted from this popularity, attention, and interest, it has also become a commodity for cheap use, handy platitudes, and study. As part of the increasing colonial interest in the lands of the *Nights*, the book with a complex history between literacy and orality settled in Europe with the translation of Galland, whom Said admired as a great Arabist. What happened thereafter in the field of philological scholarship takes a number of directions, one of which is what Said defines in a different instance as "flexible *positional* superiority."[3] Within the larger context of new philology as cherished by prominent Orientalists, the *Nights* as a storytelling book was to benefit and also lose in ethnographic pursuits that relegate its "literary" side to the background. New philology set the stage for the study of language, grammar, and origins, and helped establish a very conspicuous tradition of annotation and discussion beyond the literary merits of the tales or their folklorist mix. The discussion has also to

[1] Said, *Orientalism*, 3. [2] Ibid., 8. [3] Ibid., 7.

include a circle of Arab storytellers (among them, Ḥanna Diyāb, the Syrian priest Dom Denis Chavis,[4] and Michel Sabbagh[5]) and sheikhs (i.e., learned scholars), who, if they appear at all, are consigned to an auxiliary presence, as suppliers of tales, or, in the case of Lane, as philologists, copyeditors, and teachers.[6] However, and much in line with Galland's praise for "the surprising quantity and diversity of narratives, admirably linked to each other," whereby he concludes that "the Arabs surpass other nations in this sort of composition,"[7] Robert L. Mack reproduced Galland's Grub Street version.[8] He also takes the lead from Richard Johnson (1733/34–1793; i.e., Rev. Cooper's *Oriental Moralist*) to conclude that "the *Nights* is just as likely in its influence to disfigure as to enhance."[9]

Emancipatory Poetics from a Western Rationality

These issues relate also to releasing the *Nights* from its heavy paraphernalia and resurrecting it from piles of scholarship that obfuscate and muddle the literary properties of available texts. Notwithstanding the problematic nature of these texts, the need for a poetics of the *Nights* remains paramount to the art of narrative. A postcolonial narratology is still too slow to gather momentum. As Gerald Prince puts it in his "On a Postcolonial Narratology": "(Postcolonial) narratology can not only permit the (re) assessment of indefinitely many texts; it can, also, perhaps function as a rhetoric and indicate unexploited narrative forms."[10] To situate this properly within an ongoing argument on decolonization, one can reference Catherine E. Walsh who argues, "decoloniality seeks to make visible, open up, and advance radically distinct perspectives and positionalities that displace Western rationality as the only framework and possibility of existence, analysis, and thought."[11]

Walsh is not concerned with specific entities like the *Nights*, but her interrogation of "Western rationality" is relevant to this chapter. It is this rationality that builds its argument on a comparison between Occident and Orient, between reason and imagination and intuition, the general

[4] Dom Chavis and M. Cazotte, trans., *La Suite des Mille et une Nuits, Contes Arabes*, Cabinet des Fées 38–41, 4 vols. (Geneva: Barde & Manget, 1788–89).

[5] Mahdi, *The Thousand and One Nights*, 51–72.

[6] Lane, "Review," vol. 3.

[7] Mahdi, *The Thousand and One Nights*, 20.

[8] Mack, ed., *Arabian Nights' Entertainments*.

[9] Mack, "Cultivating the Garden," 69.

[10] Gerald Prince, "On a Postcolonial Narratology," in *A Companion to Narrative Theory*, ed. James Phelan and Peter J. Rabinowitz (Maiden, MA: Blackwell, 2005), 379.

[11] Catherine E. Walsh, "Decoloniality in/as Praxis," in *On Decoloniality: Concepts, Analytics, Praxis*, ed. Walter D. Mignolo and Catherine E. Walsh (Durham, NC, and London: Duke University Press, 2018), 17.

and the particularized detail (as specially noticed by Samuel Johnson in *Rasselas*), and, in the end, between modernity and the divine.[12] Disturbed and shaken up by the phenomenal rise of the Oriental tale, and the Arabian tales in particular, this rationality resorts to the Oriental mode to counteract a style associated with the *Arabian Nights* and its imitations. Not ready to concede the ground to the Oriental mode, both Voltaire in *Zadiq* (1747) and Johnson in *Rasselas*, for example, inhabit the subgenre to flaunt, redirect, and control its political and philosophical direction. In opposition to the "Oriental style" that was in vogue in eighteenth-century France and England,[13] Jacques Cazotte was to ridicule the phenomena as a parade of "fadaises" (follies) in his *1001 fadaises, contes é dormir debout* (1742, *Thousand and One Follies: Tales That Send You to Sleep Standing Up*). Of paramount significance was the birth of this paradox in the fabric of rationality, its use of the so-called Oriental style for its own purposes, as a habitat intended to reach the emerging audience, and also to sabotage that style as it was understood at that time. Voltaire was ready to pass the following dismissive judgment on a large body of knowledge, most of which was inaccessible to him: "Orientals have always made prodigious use of metaphor, without measure and without art." He adds: "Their excessively lively imagination has never allowed them to write with method and wisdom."[14] Even those commentators, like Walter Bagehot (1856), who were brought up on these tales as formative influences would write in a similar vein so as to end up prioritizing the pedestal of Greco-Roman poetics. If we read this in context of a hegemonic rationality discourse, then a rising new philology emerges with an essentialist fulcrum that considers the Orient "endowed with a 'historical' subjectivity" that is "non-active, non-autonomous, non-sovereign with regard to itself."[15] Seen as such, with the *Nights* as exemplary of waywardness and lack of "method and wisdom," the eighteenth century prepares the fieldwork for the upcoming discourse of Renan who speaks of and for modernity as the Occident versus the Orient, and the Semites in particular:

Therefore we refuse to allow that the Semitic languages have the capacity to regenerate themselves, even while recognizing that they do not escape – anymore

[12] See Muhsin Jassim al-Musawi, "Rasselas as a Colonial Discourse," *CIEFL Bulletin*, n.s. 8, no. 1 (June 1996), 47–60. See also Samuel Johnson, *The History of Rasselas, Prince of Abissinia* (Harmondsworth, UK: Penguin Books, 1976), 61.

[13] On the philosopher, to become France Comptroller, Anne Robert Jacques Turgot's use of the term in 1760, see Madeleine Dobie, "Translation in the Contact Zone," in *The Arabian Nights in Historical Context: Between East and West*, ed. Saree Makdisi and Felicity Nussbaum (Oxford: Oxford University Press, 2008), 39.

[14] Cited in ibid., 40.

[15] Malek, "Orientalism in Crisis," cited in Said, *Orientalism*, 97.

than other products of human consciousness – the necessity of change or of successive modification.[16]

Presented as passive and lacking in the will and power for growth or "regeneration," Orientals and especially Semites are shown as waiting for the civilizing Occident, a point that Johnson's Imlac advocates in a grave authoritarian tone. Thus, when asked for the reasons behind the European conquest of the Asiatics and the Africans, Imlac's answer is unequivocal: "They are more powerful, Sir, than we," answered Imlac, "because they are wiser, knowledge will always predominate over ignorance, as man governs the other animals" (11:30).[17] Other statements that speak of the Orient as the source and cradle of Romanticism, as in Friedrich Schlegel's *Über die Sprache und Weisheit der Indier* (1800), or even Galland's celebration of the *Nights* as a sign of distinction in imaginative fiction, can be held suspect.

Anxieties over the "Oriental" Mode

But because this chapter opened with an investigation of the emergence of the *new* philological inquiry, in tandem with an intensive reading of Arabic poetry and poetics, narratives, and their like, an acquaintance with this emerging problematic is worthwhile. That is the case because European intellectuals like Ernest Renan, and before him De Sacy, Schlegel, and many other scholars of Arabic and Oriental languages, found themselves in charge of a partial body of knowledge, a constellation, that warranted attention and assessment. They exerted efforts that a number of them, including William Jones (dubbed as Oriental Jones by Johnson), were later to regret. While many scholars in the East India Company, the Arabists and scientists in the Napoleonic conquest of Egypt, and societies and academies in France, Germany, and the Netherlands were drawn to "solid" scholarship, especially in the field of language, poetry, and religion, they felt some unease with respect to a raging style associated with the advent of *A Thousand and One Nights*. Although *fiqh al-lughah* ("philology") was already in use in Arabic some seven centuries earlier,[18] its use and practice as a profession in Europe was "born the day in 1777 when F. A. Wolf invented for himself the name stud.philol." Said qualifies this use by referencing Nietzsche, who castigated professionals in the classics as people who "never reach *the roots of*

[16] Cited and translated from Renan, *Histoire générale*, in Said, *Orientalism*, 143.
[17] Johnson, *The History of Rasselas*. More in al-Musawi, "Rasselas."
[18] See, for example, Aḥmad ibn Fāris al-Qazwīnī (d. 390/999), *al-Ṣāḥib fī fiqh al-lughah*; and Abū Manṣūr al-Thaʿālibī (961–1039), *Kitāb fiqh al-lughah wa-asrār al-ʿArabiyyah*.

the matter: they never adduce philology as a problem."[19] The exception was the new philologists, like Renan who conceives the job of the practitioner as being to "continue to see reality and nature clearly, thus driving out supernaturalism, and to continue to keep pace with discoveries in the physical sciences."[20] De Sacy prepared the field work for new philologists, and his work on the *Arabian Nights* continues to inform scholars. Said describes de Sacy's general contribution, minus the *Nights*, as follows: "Sacy's anthologies not only supplement the Orient; they supply it as Oriental presence to the West."[21] Moreover, "Sacy's work canonizes the Orient; it begets a canon of textual objects passed on from one generation of students to the next."[22] However, Said recognizes this achievement as one of restoration that runs counter to dismissals from others: "Sacy's genealogical originality was to have treated the Orient as something to be restored not only because of but also despite the modern Orient's disorderly and elusive presence."[23] Although he was the "father of Orientalism, he was the discipline's first sacrifice"[24] because his work was soon to be supplanted by others like Renan. This turn toward new philology was not unique to Renan, however. Ethnologists and Arabists like Lane had already embarked on a restoration project in line with the efforts of de Sacy and von Hammer.[25] At the time his restorative method meant disorienting or even effacing Galland's popular project, displacing it while aligning himself with more than one Arab philologist. If Galland failed insofar as Lane perceived his translation as defective, unaccountable, discordant, and not in keeping with its proposed claims of fidelity, then someone else, a hero, should take over and restore the original as a mission among larger ones to restore the Arab and the Orient. Unlike Jonathan Scott, the Rev. G. Lamb, John Richardson, or even Henry Torrens, and better equipped than the French endeavors of Galland and Trébutien, Lane saw the *Nights* as an inviting site to demonstrate, point by point, the knowledge that he acquired in Egypt, with its everyday life, religious and social practices, institutions, learned people, and booksellers. From now on, nobody, not even in the twenty-first century, could escape this institutionalization of knowledge that took the *Nights* as a repository. Said's concern with Lane's *Modern Egyptians*, and – almost at the same time – Leila Ahmed's *Edward W. Lane: A Study of His Life and Works and of British Ideas of the Middle East in the*

[19] Cited in Said, *Orientalism*, 131. [20] Ibid., 132. [21] Ibid., 129. [22] Ibid.
[23] Ibid., 129–30. [24] Ibid., 130.
[25] For more on the genealogy of the manuscript tradition and role of Henry Salt, as the British consul general in Egypt, in hiring Egyptian scribes to compile an edition of 1001 tales, see Horta, *Marvellous Thieves*, 110–11.

Nineteenth Century (1978),[26] along with reprints of Lane's works and especially his translation, testify to a lasting presence that prioritizes social science at the expense of the art of storytelling.[27] An explosive nexus, a crucial intersection, has been set that Burton and others would try hard to control by beating a recent antecedent. Armed with all the sympathy, knowledge, and experience of life in Cairo for almost five years, Lane could claim what other philologists could not. In the words of the *Foreign Quarterly Review*, Lane and the *Nights* were made for each other: "as if the work and the translator were made expressly for each other."[28] Here one can reference Walter Benjamin's endorsement of the call for translators to bring something of the original to their own language. Set against Galland's literary translation "through the haze of his own culture," Lane's style sounds uncouth, heavily burdened with stylistic "peculiarities" that have a semiscriptural and biblical ring even in passages that are meant to be humorous.[29] He certainly places himself in the genealogy of von Hammer and de Sacy as is demonstrated by his extensive notes in the appended review to the third volume of his translation,[30] but he was more empowered by two other factors: actual experience of life in Cairo and the support of Arab philologists. In his pleasant manner, the author of the *Lexicon* saw himself as "a hero rescuing the Orient from the obscurity, alienation, and strangeness"[31] that Galland's translation evoked. In other words, his effort was to remove the literariness of the text. To understand his method, we need to follow his argument. It focuses on the reasons behind his undertaking of this translation of *A Thousand and One Nights*.[32] He explains:

> My undertaking to translate anew the Tales of "The Thousand and One Nights" implies an unfavorable opinion of the version which has so long amused us; but I must express my objections with respect to the latter in plain terms, and this I shall do by means of a few words on the version of Galland, from which it is derived; for to him alone its chief faults are to be attributed.[33]

[26] Leila Ahmed, *Edward W. Lane: A Study of His Life and Works and of British Ideas of the Middle East in the Nineteenth Century* (London and New York: Longman, 1978).

[27] On a reading of the translation movement, see Haifa Kraid, "Translation and Empire," with a translated text by G. Bell (PhD diss., New York University, 1998).

[28] *Foreign Quarterly* 24 (October 1839), 157. See also Ahmed, *Edward W. Lane*, 156. This article was by B. E. Pote; see al-Musawi, *Scheherazade in England*, 169, 91–113.

[29] See Ahmed's review of articles, *Edward W. Lane*, 156–57; and al-Musawi, *Scheherazade in England*, 95–96.

[30] See Lane, "Review," 3:675, 680, 684.

[31] Said, *Orientalism*, 121.

[32] I am making use of https://gutenberg.org/files/34206/34206-h/34206-h.htm.

[33] Edward William Lane, trans., *The Thousand and One Nights; Commonly Called the Arabian Nights' Entertainment*, illus. William Harvey, 3 vols. (London: Chatto and Windus, 1912).

Highly appreciated by the *Eclectic Review* (n.s. VIII, 1840, 641–60) for preservation of *peculiarities*, Lane's translation, with its use of extant Arabic manuscripts along with its main Bulaq text, was to set rules for any forthcoming translation or adaptation.

Lane as Heir to De Sacy's Legacy

His justification for criticism of Galland's version was taken very seriously by his contemporaries, and his version was to be a serious contender against Galland's. The argument helped in the ongoing readjustment of the field of discussion: Instead of issues like Huet's treatise on the origin of fiction, or the placement of Arabic in medieval strictures of Christianity versus Islam, there emerged domains of philological inquiry whereby language was approached as human bound, and not God-given. Thus, Lane's reasoning situates it in secular terms as a field of restoration that complements the mission of the Orientalist as ethnologist. It speaks to a *new* philology and a secular discourse that was pivotal to colonialism and modernity. His critique of Galland's version was contextualized in a process of compromise with other colleagues in the field to whom he alludes as being enthusiasts for Galland's version. This recognition by his peers indicates the existence of a field wherein cordial discussions could take place. This is even more so if we read it in the context of Said's conclusion with respect to this field:

> As if carrying on such methods and such positions beyond the life-span of any individual Orientalist, there would be a secular tradition of continuity, a lay order of disciplined methodologists, whose brotherhood would be based, not on blood lineage, but upon a common discourse, a praxis, a library, a set of received ideas, in short, a doxology common to everyone who entered the ranks.[34]

This is why Lane feels obliged to explain himself to his fellow scholars:

> I am somewhat reluctant to make this remark, because several persons, and among them some of high and deserved reputation as Arabic scholars, have pronounced an opinion that his [Galland's] version is an improvement upon the original. That "The Thousand and One Nights" may be greatly improved, I most readily admit; but as confidently do I assert that Galland has excessively *perverted* the work.

This conversation speaks directly to the evolving constellation of *Arabian Nightism*, as a field of study whereby the Arabist/Orientalist, and, in Lane's case, ethnologist, was in charge, a master aiming to improve on

[34] Said, *Orientalism*, 121.

a work which was obviously available in the eleventh and twelfth centuries but continued to be reported by storytellers.[35] An undervalued narrative in comparison with a formidable classical Arabic tradition was thus being raised to another elevated status through the mediation of the translator and annotator. Lane was not opposed to Galland's decorum because he exercised a rather prudish politics to move a book – in his case, the Bulaq edition, which was relatively "sanitized" in vocabulary, syntax, and scenes, from the street to the salon and drawing room. Thus, he explains in his "Review" that

> learned sheykhs (as the editors of the Cairo edition and the Calcutta edition of the first two hundred Nights) have taken pains to *improve* the style. I therefor believe that all the copies of it are from manuscripts which, with respect to language, were unworthy of being faithfully transcribed.[36]

Throughout this endeavor, Lane felt that he was on solid ground in responding to critics, especially the writer for the *London and Westminster Review* (no. lxiv, 113).[37] The latter castigated him for his style and omissions:

> it is impossible that the impression made upon the audience of the native story-tellers can be of the same uncolloquial and semi-scriptural sort, apart from their every-day experience, as that which the English reader receives from the unfamiliar style of Mr. Lane. It must be far more easy, natural, impulsive, and unobstructed by a constant sense of strangeness.

This is the critic's stepping-stone by which to discredit Lane's claim to "peculiarity." He recapitulates: "In this respect, therefore, he has missed even the Arab peculiarity; at least, he has sacrificed Arab spirit to Arab letter, and consequently the greater peculiarity to the less, and so become the victim of his own 'excessive exactitude.'"[38]

While this criticism speaks even more to the turn toward the literary side of the tales, it also raises issues of relevance to the "task of the translator," and also to what Borges articulates about the art in view of the discussion that had been in progress ever since the debate between Matthew Arnold and Newman, which he references in his reading of "The Translators of the *Arabian Nights*." He explains: "The beautiful Newman-Arnold exchange (1861–62) – more memorable than its two interlocutors extensively argued the two general ways of translating."[39] It was beautiful because both had different approaches: "Newman

[35] Lane made references to de Sacy, von Hammer, the *Athenaeum* reviewer on available documentation of the mention of the *Nights*, and also its circulated editions. See nn2, 6, 18, 22, 38.

[36] Lane, "Review," 3:679. [37] Ibid., 686. [38] Ibid., 685.

[39] Borges, "The Translators," 95.

championed the literal mode, the retention of all verbal singularities: Arnold, the severe elimination of details that distract or detain."[40] Rather than a digression, the reference to these two approaches that he supplements with further qualifications leads to his view of Lane's version: "Lane's syntax is delightful, as befits the refined parlor table. His vocabulary is often excessively festooned with Latin words, unaided by any artifice of brevity."[41]

Nevertheless, Lane's very omissions or "improvements" were the source of his popularity with the Victorians, and almost everywhere. Lane was not enthusiastic about showing us the nature of Galland's perversion of the text; rather he criticized him for lack of familiarity with Arab life, manners, and language. Nevertheless, more than a century earlier Galland had a different say: He wrote of the *Nights* not only as a consummate art of storytelling, but also as an adequate representation of Eastern – meaning Arab – customs and manners. For one reason or another, almost every major translator claimed the *Nights* as documents. Although the least disposed to annotation and documentation, Galland set the tone for reading the tales as representations, probably to appease his upper-class readership whose sensibilities could have been compromised by a presumed vraisemblance. Although Horace Walpole and William Beckford, for example, were not given to this equation between the *Nights* and the Orient, one may agree with Muhsin Mahdi that for "the eighteenth-century, the *Nights* was the 'Orient' and the Orient was the world of Muslims and Ottomans." Galland writes in the preface:

> They [the tales] must also be pleasing, because of the account they give of the customs and manners of the eastern nations, and of the ceremonies of their religion, as well Pagan as Mahometan, which are better described here than in any author that has wrote of them, or in the relations of travelers. All the eastern nations, Persians, Tartars, and Indians, are here distinguished, and appear such as they are, from the foreign to the meanest subject; so that without the fatigue of going to see those people in their respective countries, the reader has here the pleasure to see them act, and hear from them speak. Care has been taken to preserve their characters, and to keep their sense; nor have we varied from the text, but when modesty obliged us to it.[42]

While such a promise was enough to appease early eighteenth-century British, French, Dutch, and German audiences, the last decades of the eighteenth century witnessed a closer scrutiny of such a claim. Powerful venues of public and learned circles, like the *Gentleman's Magazine*, published articles on the issue of fidelity to

[40] Ibid. [41] Ibid.
[42] Antoine Galland, "The Translator's Preface," *Novelist's Magazine* 18 (1785).

manuscripts.[43] The conversation then focused on the *Nights* as a text that was once a manuscript or a number of manuscripts, possessed by those who resided in Aleppo, Turkey, and Cairo, and were sold or given later to certain libraries. The ramifications of this conversation draw on issues of authenticity, translators' faithfulness, documentation, relation to other books or manuscripts, and the ultimate evolution of the *Nights* as a centerpiece in reading the East and its pseudo-Orient. This is why the *Nights* turned into a "node within a network."[44] In other words, and regardless of the rambling introductions prefacing partial translations or reeditions throughout the second half of the eighteenth century and even the first decades of the nineteenth century, European publics were prepared for a more tabulated field that could take the *Nights* as fulcrum, nexus, and pivot in a growing constellation under the heading of *A Thousand and One Nights*.

Since then and in tandem with the growth of social science (with Orientalism as a part of that), a discussion erupted that continued to branch off in a number of directions that often (and with the exception of pure literary criticism) divest the *Nights* in its multiple recensions of any folk or literary dimensions. In other words, since that time the *Nights* has had to suffer a colonization, an encroachment on its properties for the sake of reading it as document, "an inert material through which [history] tries to reconstitute what men have done or said, the events of which only the trace remains."[45] Lane was the pioneer in offering this document, not only because of his heavy annotation and use of Calcutta I and Breslau alongside Bulaq, but also because of the ongoing dialogue with reviewers, critics, philologists like de Sacy, and deceased ones like von Hammer. This was Lane's mission. True to the philologist's *new* undertaking, Lane overlooked the classical Arabic tradition's dismissal of writing down tales in their reported, recited, and narrated form in squares and assemblies. The canon of refined writing prompted Ibn ʿAbdūs to rewrite storytellers' versions to offer urban classes a text that had been sanitized in both matter and manner. But the *Nights* made its way to Europe and acquired its mixed language of classical and colloquial mediated through translation. It therefore lost its twists and turns of phrase, its paradoxical doxology that collapses grammatical forms, and plays havoc with rules of composition. Moreover, Lane's edition initiated a criticism that takes the *Nights* as representative of manners and customs, a faithful picture of life in Egypt.[46] Thus, his rejection of Galland runs as follows:

43 al-Musawi, *Scheherazade in England*, 170–71.
44 Foucault, *Archaeology of Knowledge*, 23. 45 Ibid., 7.
46 See al-Musawi, *Scheherazade in England*, 91–145.

His acquaintance with Arab manners and customs was insufficient to preserve him always from errors of the grossest description, and by the style of his version he has given to the whole a false character, thus sacrificing, in a great measure, what is most valuable in the original work, – I mean its minute accuracy with respect to those peculiarities which distinguish the Arabs from every other nation, not only of the West, but also of the East.[47]

The Philologist's Skills at Work

Galland was not only a stepping-stone, a justification for the new translation, but also a model for an outdated breed that had to give way to the new philologist, armored with "scientific statement and the ambience of corrective study."[48] In his capacity as Arabist, and very much in line with de Sacy, Lane differs from Renan and company on a number of issues. His emphasis on "those peculiarities which distinguish the Arabs from every other nation, not only of the West, but also of the East" disposes of the Aryan/Semite polarity proclaimed by Gobineau and Renan and company. His "Arab" defies the stratification that Renan applies to his reading of "the Semitic race [that] appears to us to be an incomplete race, by virtue of its simplicity. This race – if I dare use the analogy – is to the Indo-European family what a pencil sketch is to painting; it lacks that variety, that amplitude, that abundance of life which is the condition of perfectibility."[49] After almost seventeen years as student of Arabic and five years of residence in Egypt, Lane was well positioned to deesssentialize such a sweeping premise. His method was one of particularization that focuses on "the peculiarities" of Arabs as is demonstrated by his extensive notes and also his concluding review. Every detail has to find a place and meaning in a vast canvas of manners and customs. Does this "peculiarization" essentialize the Arab as a different species? Lane, as author of both *Manners and Customs of the Modern Egyptians* and the *Arabic-English Lexicon*, was not given to an essentialization as a derogatory application, but he was the product of current methods of reading the Orient in terms of the needs of the growing empire. His pro-Arab or pro-Egyptian disposition was also the outcome of his extensive reading, something that saved him from being in agreement with the three dominating lines of inquiry – the reductionist atomization of Sir Alfred Lyall, the brother of the celebrated translator of the pre-Islamic odes Sir Charles James Lyall (1845–1920), the romanticization of Schlegel that

[47] Lane, trans., *The Thousand and One Nights*, 1:ix. See also Bruce Fudge's summary, "More Translators of The Thousand and One Nights," *The Journal of the American Oriental Society* (2016), https://bit.ly/2Pi8Pcg.
[48] Said, *Orientalism*, 149. [49] Ibid.

perceives an "'orient' as "salutary derangement of their European habits of mind and spirit,"[50] or of Schelling's traces in that Orient of pantheistic, spiritual, and ultimately primitive originary, and Renan's debasing stratification. Lane's *Modern Egyptians*, *Lexicon*, and the profusely annotated translation of *A Thousand and One Nights* present him as a dispassionate observer, a raconteur, and a diligent archivist who is often engaged in one-way traffic so as to provide information as befitting a scholar. In Said's neat reading of *Modern Egyptians*, Lane appears "only in the official persona of annotator and retranslator,"[51] who "wrote his work, and sacrificed his ego."[52] Lane's prose, even in the translation and even more so in the annotations, is robust but uninspiring. It lacks Galland's finesse, his touch that won him a reading public and a large number of Romantic writers. But that same prose style presents Lane as a supplier of knowledge useful to empires that need more than Galland's endearing narrative. His vast body of annotations – that his nephew Stanley-Lane Poole published later as a separate book entitled *The Arabian Society in the Middle Ages* – presents him as a detached observer who "literally abolishes himself as a human subject by refusing to marry into human society."[53] In this sense, he is even more influential than de Sacy in developing a field of knowledge, scholarly Orientalism, simply because his life experience in Egypt, informants, readings, and acquaintance with many Egyptians consolidate his image as a credible and legitimate authority as befitting scholars in the Royal Asiatic Society. Thus, while appreciated but shunned in preference for Galland, his *Nights* for the Romantics is more of a treatise than a narrative of enchantment. Nevertheless, his project aborted that of Torrens, who felt superseded and surpassed by the learned Arabist. However, Lane felt that it was time to outdo every other competitive project by claiming the Egyptian Bulaq edition as the more legitimate for being complete and compiled in Egypt. His use of this edition enabled him to dispute von Hammer's. "The work from which my translation is made I conceived to be extremely different from that which Von Hammer regarded as its basis."[54] The Bulaq edition corroborates the role of the ethnologist whose residence in Cairo gives him more credibility than others. Thus, he fits well and very strongly with the recension of the Orientalist and Arabist Hermann Zotenberg (1836–94), that is, Egyptian manuscripts since the last decades of the eighteenth century, and the rise of a European mania in this direction. To oust Galland's version, there is a recension prompted by an increasing search for a competing text to undo Galland and the sweeping popularity of his

[50] Ibid., 150. [51] Ibid., 164. [52] Ibid., 165. [53] Ibid., 163.
[54] Lane, "Review," 3:675.

translation. Lane justifies the Bulaq (Cairo) Arabic edition as the most suitable, especially in relation to that of von Hammer:

I have taken as my general standard of the original text the Cairo edition lately printed; it being greatly superior to the other printed editions, and probably to every manuscript copy. It appears to agree almost exactly with the celebrated MS. of Von Hammer, than which no copy more copious, I believe, exists; and contains all the tales in the old version except those which, as Von Hammer says, Galland appears to have taken from other works, Arabic, Persian, and Turkish, in the Royal Library of Paris.[55]

As his annotations show, he made use of Calcutta I with 200 tales, Breslau and Galland's. He collates and changes when necessary, explaining to the reader the nature of complementation, abridgment, or collation. This guided amalgamation and patching was already followed by Scott, and more so in Breslau.

This Egyptian recension was important not only to the Royal Asiatic Society and similar academies but also to the Society for the Diffusion of Useful Knowledge, or SDUK (1826), an imperial museum with a keen interest in inculcating specific "useful" knowledge in the minds of the reading public. This Egyptian recension was a recent outgrowth of a number of eighteenth-century manuscripts that, along other things, could compete with and probably dislodge Galland's Syrian recension.[56] Its reliance on living human informants, sheikhs, and other learned people brought it closer to a striding utilitarian drive that was thriving in England. Insofar as *A Thousand and One Nights* is concerned, the recensions represent the battle over a body of tales between French mobilization of storytellers and bibliophiles, and British monopoly over India before invading Egypt. As reviews make clear, the urge to support this Egyptian recension led some Arab philologists to give it a warm welcome, and it was duly celebrated by societies of useful knowledge. These philologists were perceived as the national elite with whom Napoleon's experts had previously coordinated and who were to be supplementary to colonial administration. It was, then as always, a sign of experience, skill, and mastery to maintain the collaboration of native scholars, an attitude that was the mainstay of colonialism. This is why Lane felt compelled to recognize the support he got from Egyptian scholars:

The manuscript from which it was printed was carefully collated and corrected by a very learned man, the sheykh 'Abd-Er-Raḥmán Eṣ-Ṣaftee Esh-Sharḳáwee, who

[55] Ibid., cited in Lane's preface to his translation (1838–41), in his nephew's reedition, 1:xii.

[56] For further discussions of this recension, and the justifications for a complete version of the *Nights* by British officials in Egypt and Bengal, see Horta, *Marvellous Thieves*, 110–11.

also superintended the progress of the work through the press. But in addition to the value conferred upon it by the corrections of this sheykh, the copy from which the whole of my translation is made, except in a few instances, possesses an advantage which, I believe, renders it incomparably superior to any other now existing.[57]

After establishing this authentication process that adds more value to the text and presents it as an improvement on every other text, Lane, as the future author of a *Lexicon* (1863), had to assure the learned among his fellow Orientalists and Arabists that he even checked everything in consultation with the best Egyptian philologists. Established as such, the translation is more of a restoration of a tradition than a Grub Street *Arabian Nights' Entertainments*. Although the publisher kept as subtitle "commonly called in England *The Arabian Nights' Entertainments*," Lane retained the title mentioned by Arab authorities of the tenth century, the *Thousand and One Nights*, "subjoining" a translation of al-Nadīm's passage in his *Fihrist*,[58] and made it clear that he secured the support of the best Arab minds in the field. With this in mind, he acquainted his readers in the review essay with an institutionalization of knowledge that had in the process the collaboration of a national elite:

it has been again revised and corrected, and illustrated with numerous manuscript notes, by a person whom I think I may safely pronounce the first philologist of the first Arab college of the present day, the sheykh Moḥammad 'Eiyád Eṭ-Ṭanṭáwee, or, more properly, Eṭ-Ṭanditáee.[59]

Lane's wording is carefully crafted. While very generous in admitting the help obtained from Egyptian scholars, a recognition that also consolidates his image as a well-established scholar in conversation with local authorities in culture and language, Lane divides philology into two fields, one is in the line of de Sacy, and also an Egyptian scholar who "collated" material and supervised print; and the other as applied to "the first philologist of the first Arab college." Across both divides, he remains intact as the master of the effort to bring the Bulaq edition to the attention of his society and its learned coterie who mattered more. This is why Said's reading of *Modern Egyptians* seems as equally pertinent to Lane's translation and annotation. "The subordination of genetic ego to scholarly authority in Lane corresponds exactly to the increased specialization and institutionalization of knowledge about the Orient represented by the various Oriental societies."[60]

[57] Cited in Lane's preface, 1:xii.
[58] Lane, "Review," 3:675.
[59] Cited in Lane's preface, 1:xii.
[60] Said, *Orientalism*, 164.

Having mastered the field, Lane can tell us the scope and also limits of interventions received from local Egyptian scholars. Thus, he qualifies his appreciation by reminding us of the following:

His [sheykh Moḥammad 'Eiyád Eṭ-Ṭanṭáwee's] notes are chiefly philological, and explanatory of words which do not belong to the classical language; and many of them are of very great assistance to me; though most of them I find unnecessary, from the knowledge of the modern Arabic which I have acquired during my intercourse with the people who speak it. His corrections of the text are numerous; and as they would interest very few persons, I have mentioned but few of them in the notes to my translation, notwithstanding a strong temptation that I felt to do otherwise that Arabic scholars might be assisted to judge of the fidelity of my version by comparing it with the text of the Cairo edition. To the pieces of poetry which are interspersed throughout the work he has paid especial attention; not only correcting the errors which he found in them, but also always adding the vowel-points, and generally, commentaries or explanations. Thus I have shewn that I am very greatly indebted to him for his learned labours.[61]

There is, however, something in the annotations that militates against a reliance on *Modern Egyptians* in approaching the *Nights*. There is a personal touch that shows Lane as a jovial fellow on good terms with people around him. While his prose is opaque and less poetic than Galland's, his massive annotations display a number of things: experience of everyday life in Cairo, readings in annals and histories written by Egyptian scholars over time, interaction with his contemporaries among the learned, and passion for tricks to be played on bean-sellers around his residence.[62] This last point presents him as a human being who is given to mirth alongside his other serious undertakings. Had we had a record left by his Egyptian contemporaries, we could have even substantiated his already recognized place as an Arabist, an ethnologist, and less as a stratified Orientalist.

When perceived in view of reprints, retranslations, and reeditions, Lane's translation was no less epoch making than Galland's. The latter was the least given to annotation to supply a smooth, delightful narrative. His effort was no less in keeping with the cultural needs of the new reading publics, the demand for entertaining and somehow slightly instructive narrative. Galland's admirers wrote at length about the drastic transformation that his tales brought into the literary scene. Lane's edition was no less so for the Victorian family, learned societies, and the empire. He brought along a heavy arsenal, one that would be a source for efforts to

[61] Lane, "Preface," xii. [62] See, for example, his notes on chapter 9, n25.

control and master Egypt and the region. In the end we have two different translations that set the stage for further engagements.

With this heavy apparel, was it possible for the *Nights* to retain a protean self? This heavy textual arsenal of annotations (and regardless of how useful it was to its immediate and even later readers) incited further efforts either to retain a storytelling mediated anew,[63] or to reclaim Arabic and Anglicize it for the English-speaking world as if anticipating Benjamin's thesis. He argues, "[I]nstead of resembling the meaning of the original, [a translation] must lovingly and in detail incorporate the original's mode of signification."[64] After Lane, the textual *Nights* was to pass through processes of literary retention, massive annotation, and/or retelling. The first process is exemplified by John Payne, the second by Richard F. Burton, and the third by Housman's popular 1907 version. As argued earlier, but more in line of a "decolonizing" politics, it is reasonable to suggest that Payne's edition substantially released itself from the heavy paraphernalia of "useful knowledge"; its translator could not totally free himself from an aesthete's disposition to finesse. In a remarkable turn of fortunes, this translation, with its thirteen volumes, lent itself to Burton to serve his own enterprise and allow him to claim to be the most knowledgeable and widely traveled all over Europe, and Britain in particular. Giving Payne's style twists and turns that he thought would bring it closer to Arabic storytelling, Burton was free to present extensive but not necessarily relevant notes to his version that superseded Lane's and aborted further documentation. In other words, Burton's *Nights* has the advantage of a repository, a container, that made use of every inviting and available tale, dressing it with annotations and presenting it as a treasury of knowledge not within the reach of others, even Arabs. Burton's legacy has many anthropological advantages, and his inclusion of unrelated tales helped in establishing another canon that competes very strongly with Galland's. Defective in other issues, this translation/edition would give birth to many reprints and translations that are "merely a confirmation of Sir Richard's primacy over the Arabs."[65] Said's pertinent remarks with respect to Burton's *Pilgrimage* may apply to his heavy annotation of the *Nights*. His "knowledgeable (and often prurient) interventions" often "remind us . . . how he had taken management of Oriental life for his purposes."[66] With a mastery of this knowledge and a strong

[63] See, for example, *The Arabian Nights' Entertainments – or The Thousand and One Nights*, the complete, original translation of Edward William Lane, with the translator's complete, original notes and commentaries on the text (New York: Tudor Publishing Company, 1927).

[64] Benjamin, "The Task of the Translator," 78.

[65] Borges, "The Translators," 107.

[66] Said, *Orientalism*, 196.

individualistic and rebellious spirit, Burton's "individuality perforce encounters and indeed merges with the voice of Empire."[67]

Commoditization and Revolt

Insofar as the *Arabian Nights* is concerned, the print industry enables readerships to interact through the mediation of authors, translators, editors, and publishers with a vast compelling audiovisual industry. Its illustrators as well as film industry and theater entrepreneurs situate the *Nights* at the center of culture industry. Audiovisual culture and its other varieties live on print industry, but in time there is a gradual disconnect, a departure from one text or another. This shows more in the history of specific tales adapted for cinematic production, like Aladdin and Ali Baba, and also in new or reproduced illustrations of nineteenth-century publications. Although these sites present the complexity of production, they often show how the *Arabian Nights*, and its orphan or popular tales, are gradually acted on as commodities to be prepared and supplied upon demand. Exceptions, like Chagall's paintings, for example, are so because they attempt to connect to the source only as an impression mediated through the illustrator's or producer's redirection of art away from the overwhelming attraction of a consumer economy. In this context, decolonizing the *Nights* means rereading it as a literary production inviting the engagement of a visual culture that is free from stereotyping, profiling, and politically and economically driven motivations. But it also involves the laying bare of tactics and strategies used to derail and halt the act of questioning texts, screen, labels, and other visual manifestations of manipulation and appropriation. This is one way of combating commodity as "crucial for the subjugation of men's consciousness to the form in which this reification [produced by commodity relations] finds expression."[68]

If book illustration, which was a thriving business in nineteenth-century Europe, often complements words, the artist as individual, like Arthur Boyd Houghton, Albert Letchford, or Edmund Dulac, allowed their own aesthetics to depart from what Harvey tried hard to particularize in view of Lane's meticulous supervision. This turn toward less particularized art must not be confused with the increasing attention to demons and jinn, a demonizing alterity that puts so much emphasis on the strange and menacing that it leaves the reader with an impression of an

[67] Ibid.
[68] Georg Lukacs (György Lukács), *History and Class Consciousness: Studies in Marxist Dialectics* (Cambridge, MA: MIT Press, 1971), 86.

alien Other. A different lexicon appears that speaks of a problematic "East," later the Middle East, in haughty imperial rhetoric with respect to Arab sites and cultures. The departure from the pictorial representations of Harvey and Houghton shows forth in paintings that deliberately exoticize a menacing or voluptuous East as in Wilhelm Vita's (1891) "Sheherazade" that Codrescu and publisher take as jacket art, a point that I have already mentioned. Representations of a perilous "East" show in films of thieves, sorcery, and in an abundant production of jinn. The turn derives some momentum from an epistemic stance whereby there is, as Jacques Rancière argues, a "revocation of the subordination of pictorial forms to poetic hierarchies."[69] Although Rancière does not specify a historicity, this understanding remains central to revolutionary or independent art. He explains, "The power of words is no longer the model that pictorial representation must take as its norm."[70]

This articulation is ahistorical, however. There is always a tension that keeps art and literary products suspended between Dulac's aesthetics of the sublime and the grotesque, as in Scheherazade and other women, on the one hand, and the genie, on the other, and Houghton's recognition of the beauty of the commonplace: "the ordinary becomes beautiful as a trace of the true."[71] Houghton could not go as far as to have the ordinary "torn from its obviousness to become a hieroglyph, a mythological or phantasmagoric figure."[72] Since the second half of the nineteenth century, there has been a conspicuous rise of the visual at the expense of the poetic or the written. But even later illustrators of the *Nights* cannot dissociate their experimentation from the solid base set by Harvey, Houghton, Letchford, and Dulac. In other words, the relation between the pictorial and the poetic remains tenuous even when an epistemic independence of the pictorial seems paramount. A better way to theorize this relationship is to contextualize it in terms of imperial exhibitions. The phenomenal rise of imperial exhibitions – such as the Great Exhibition of May 1, 1851 (The Crystal Palace), opened by Queen Victoria; the New York Great Exhibition 1853; and followed by French exhibitions in 1878, 1900, 1906, and 1922, which put samples of its colonial Others on display – ushered the spectacle in a new stage of imperial supremacy over its Other. Even if we assume that a brilliant poster designer, illustrator, and draughtsman, a leader in the aesthetic movement like Aubrey Vincent Beardsley (1872–98), was not sympathetic to that

[69] Jacques Rancière, *The Future of the Image* (London and New York: Verso, 2007), 76.
[70] Ibid.
[71] Jacques Rancière, *The Politics of Aesthetics* (New York: Continuum, 2004), 34.
[72] Ibid.

Figure 18 Aubrey Vincent Beardsley: Ali Baba.

overbearing imperial manner, his drawings convey the "pampered Oriental as Europe saw him, plump, sensual, cynical, heavy of thigh and jowl, with narrow eye and spirited moustache and be gemmed turban."[73] His cover illustration for Ali Baba shows as much (see Figure 18). However, and as shown in recent scholarship on visual culture,[74] new print technologies, like chromolithography, and the advent of kinetograph and kinetoscope happened to accelerate the book industry and motion pictures.

In both spheres the *Arabian Nights* proved the most accessible and saleable. Albert Ludwig Grimm made use of chromolithography in 1889 in the production of "eight original water colors" for an adaptation of the *Nights* for children. Earlier in 1880, Theodor von Pichler had boasted of six *Transparent-Verwandlungs-Bilder*, for his adaptation of six stories from the same collection. Pictorial independence becomes, in some cases, a sharp critique of the postcapitalist culture as in the paintings of Paul Klee. Art critics give credit to the Swiss-born and German artist, poet, and writer, Klee, claimed as a natural draftsman, whose *Notebooks* on form and design theory are of special importance to art theory. The

[73] Kiernan, *The Lords of Human Mind*, 139. [74] Haase, "The Arabian Nights."

known qualities of his paintings of Sindbad are usually described as musicality, dry humor, childlike perspective, and careful color design. His bright colors of the sailor, sea monsters, and sea are set against a dark color of geometrical patterns, irregular "magic squares," that impose a certain unified impression. His travels to Tunisia, and Qairawan in particular,[75] endow his sharp awareness of the *turkuaz* (turquoise) color with a deep magical meaning. Amulets and talismans appear in the faint scribbles across his paintings. In a painting of 1923,[76] Klee hints at the disparity between vision and achievement, the limits of the human in the face of existential challenge, a point that Ferial Ghazoul addresses in her reading of the modern Sindbad.[77] In *Pedagogical Sketchbook*, he explains: "The contrast between man's ideological capacity to move at random through material and metaphysical spaces and his physical limitations is the origin of all human tragedy. . . . Half winged – half imprisoned, this is man."[78]

Visual Narrative

In the first three decades of the twentieth century, there were more achievements in the film industry, and the *Nights* proved again to be a resourceful investment. After enumerating a number of examples in the print and film industries, Haase argues, "the pioneers of visual culture seem to adapt the *Arabian Nights* to work through the transition from print to film."[79] There is, however, an inherent pictorial quality in the *Nights* that *invites* further illustration or performance. It comes as no surprise to have Hermann Hesse depict the *Nights* in 1929 as "the richest picture book in the world."[80] This may sound contrary to the wide acceptance of the *Nights* as rather a narrative of events, encounters, and "narrative men." The power to evoke scenes and sites could reside in the sequence of events, but this evocation can stimulate further discourse (narrative) or illustration, and painting. The shift in recognition is important in a number of ways. Although the scene was still relatively bound to claims regarding the *Nights*' depiction of "manners and customs" as stressed by Lane and Burton, the accessibility of colonies and the amount

[75] Paul Klee, *The Diaries of Klee, 1898–1918*, ed. Felix Klee (Berkeley, CA: University of California Press, 1964), 297. Nacer Khemir and Bruno Moll prepared and directed a film covering his travels (1914) in Tunisia, *Le voyage à Tunis* (Ennetbaden: Trigon-Film/Fama Film, 2007), in which the itinerary of Paul Klee in Tunisia on April 1914 is redrawn. See also Jean Duvignaud, *Klee en Tunisie* (Tunis: Ceres, 1980).

[76] For Paul Klee's paintings of Sindbad the Sailor, see www.icanvas.com/canvas-print/sinbad-the-sailor-1359#1PC6-40x26.

[77] Ghazoul, "Sindbad the Sailor." [78] Cited in ibid., 251.

[79] Haase, "The Arabian Nights," 2. [80] Cited in ibid., 4.

of writing on the region devalued this documentary proposition. Moreover, new print technologies and the growth of a visual culture shifted attention to the visual properties that had already been drawing the attention of artists and craftsmen or film directors. Along with these, there were new historical dynamics: national uprisings (e.g., Egypt 1919, Iraq 1920) and the October Revolution in Russia in 1917, events that forced a new understanding of the "politics of aesthetics." It is only logical for a storytelling monument addressing common audiences to appeal even more to artists and entrepreneurs of visual culture. Like many other twentieth-century writers who find no contradiction in verbal and pictorial properties, and probably in conversation with what was already in circulation with respect to richness of detail, Hugo von Hofmannsthal introduced Felix Paul Greve's German illustrated edition of 1907 with an emphasis on these combined properties: "The boldest intellectuality [*Geistigkeit*] and the most complete sensuousness are woven here in one."[81] As noted in writings on the *Nights*, Enno Littmann argues a similar point in his lecture of 1923:

> One is often astonished at how many different colors are united there in a single image, which nonetheless remains unified precisely because, like the meadow, it has grown that way naturally, or, like the rug and the artful title page, is modeled on nature.[82]

Do these properties veer away from storytelling toward other means of appropriation that accelerate the decline of the art? Before trying to account for the switch toward visual culture, we need to focus on the ideological turn toward profiling the Other. While illustration was part of a print industry and its effort to draw on pictorial resemblance as a prop to a written text, the literary quality of Galland's translation and appropriation offered little that alienates its subject matter. On the contrary, style and content underwent some trimming and amelioration to meet the audience's needs and expectations. While harping on the fantastic to evoke unease, there was little to disturb the endearing quality of the *Nights*. Although the East/West dichotomy exists in the title and advertisement of Galland's version, a counter endearment prevails that enumerates the beauties of the *Nights*. If there is a supernatural presence like the genie, its menace applies to the society of the *Nights*, but not to the receiving milieu. Anne Duggan is right when she argues that Galland's version and its genealogy of Oriental tales "have presented the text as a work of fiction as well as an ethnographic document, as a representation of an imaginary space as

[81] Haase's translation and citation, ibid. [82] Ibid., 5.

well as a real, geographical one."[83] Moreover, the supernatural is naturalized in Lane's version by his heavy annotation that relies on his experience as resident of Egypt where the natural and supernatural presumably coexist. This naturalization of the genie also intensifies the polarity between the Egyptian society and the one he is addressing as his own.

> I have resided in a land where genii are still firmly believed to obey the summons of the magician or the owner of a talisman . . . and I have listened to stories of their deeds related as facts by persons of the highest respectability, and by some who would not condescend to read the Tales of the "Thousand and One Nights," merely because they are fictions, and not written in the usual polished style of literary compositions.[84]

While supernatural beings and local inhabitants of islands and offshore locations are often profiled as different, representation until the mid-nineteenth century is often contained in terms of alterity but not rejection. Efreets might be described as monstrous and hideous, but not the two kings and their women. Hierarchy holds there, and in one way or another corresponds to human hierarchies in mercantile and capitalist societies. As noticed by Henscher and also endorsed by Duggan, there is "a degree of hierarchization" in human relations and also between human and the world of demons and jinn that shows in illustrations by Pierre-Clémenet Marillier.[85] Lane's profuse description of genies and efreets[86] allows for significant differentiation between good and bad supernatural beings. Hence, Harvey in his illustrations sticks to profiling the monstrosity of bad genies in racial terms that are part of an ongoing racial discourse. But, alongside imperial exhibitions, illustrations and also textual meanderings like Mardrus's *Nights*, a totally racist stereotyping takes over, as in René Bull's illustrations for an edition of the *Nights* that has gone through many reprints. The illustrator, who was born to a French mother and English father, was in tune with an imperial haughtiness and debasement of others. The trend is already noticeable in Mardrus's own inventions and fraudulent insertions,[87] which strangely won him the acclaim of

[83] Anne E. Duggan, "From Genie to Efreet: Fantastic Apparitions in the Tales of the 'Arabian Nights,'" *Journal of the Fantastic in the Arts* 26, no. 1 (2015), 116.

[84] Lane, trans., *The Thousand and One Nights; Commonly Called, in England, the Arabian Nights*, 1:xviii–xix. Also cited in Duggan, "From Genie to Efreet," 117.

[85] Jonathan Hensher, "Engraving Difference: The Representation of the Oriental Other in Marillier's Illustrations to the Mille et Une Nuits and Other Contes orientaux in Le Cabinet des fees (1785–1789)," *Journal for Eighteenth-Century Studies* 31, no. 3 (2008), 381; Duggan, "From Genie to Efreet," 119.

[86] See Edward William Lane, *The Arabian Nights* (New York: Tudor Publishing Company, 1927), 979.

[87] See Duggan, "From Genie to Efreet," 122.

prominent writers who probably read his *Nights* as a worthy supplement to an art already started by Galland.[88]

In sum, there is a line of demarcation between early pictorial depiction of supernatural beings as if from "an Other ontological – and not geographical – world"[89] and a late nineteenth-century shift in perception that was conversant with an imperial imagination.[90] Dana S. Hale points out another side of the large tendency to racialize colonies and their beliefs, the trademark,[91] that, though seemingly unconnected to the vogue of illustrated editions of the *Nights* and the rise of motion pictures, infiltrates into the spectacle as an imperial manifesto of stereotypes that will continue to feed culture industry. It takes gestures and codes from the *Nights*, like "open sesame," to make the product saleable worldwide. However, the pictorial depiction of the genie should not be taken as the most demarcating point of this differentiation. The fear of the supernatural is more of a European phenomenon whenever perceived in light of the Age of Reason and its impact on culture. To have Dulac and his imitators like the American art editor of childcraft books Milo Winter (1888–1956)[92] retain differential images of the genie and the human is part of this fear that demonizes the unseen.

More significant for decolonizing the *Nights* is the wording and imaging of the tales as they reach readers and audiences. Winter racializes physique, attire, and color to convey difference, whereas Dulac tames scenes and humans other than the supernatural. Processes of taming, domestication, or alienation take place along this trajectory of textual faring. Peterson suggests that global folklore takes over from the *Nights* its "free-willed" and "dangerous jinn" who become in this contextualizing process "the enslaved gift-giving genies."[93] As noticed by Nance, however, a postcapitalist culture industry is rather concerned with confiscating and appropriating Scheherazade's rich referential treasury. Confiscation takes place in a cultural terrain as it does in invasions, or other forms of occupation.

[88] On this reception, see Lynne Thornton, *Women as Portrayed in Orientalist Painting* (Paris: ACR Edition, 1994), 16; also cited in Duggan, "From Genie to Efreet," 123.

[89] Duggan, "From Genie to Efreet," 124.

[90] See also in this relation, Mark Allen Peterson, "From Jinn to Genies: Intertextuality, Media, and the Making of Global Folklore," in *Folklore/Cinema: Popular Film as Vernacular Culture*, ed. Sharon R. Sherman and Mikel J. Koven (Logan, UT: Utah State University Press, 2007), 93–112.

[91] Dan S. Hale, *Races on Display: French Representation of Colonized Peoples, 1886–1940* (Bloomington, IN: Indiana University Press, 2008), 21.

[92] For Milo Winter, see *The Arabian Night Entertainments* (Chicago, IL: Rand McNally & Co., 1914), cited in Duggan, "From Genie to Efreet," 131, figure 11.

[93] Peterson, "From Jinn to Genies," 93–94.

The colossal postindustrial globalization manipulates every image, especially made known through popular works like the *Nights*, to commodify cultural products.

Imperial Representations: Compliance and Resistance

Book illustration, and that of the *Nights* in particular, was only part of this universalization of the spectacle as the glaring manifestation of imperial representation of its Others. Artists, printers, readers, and editors and translators are all part of the scene, and no matter how significant their acts of resistance to the imperial onslaught is, these acts are too marginal to halt the sweeping capitalist mastery that makes the "spectacle . . . the moment when the commodity has attained the total occupation of social life."[94] The Dutch artist Anton Franciscus Pieck (1895–1987) offers us examples of the struggle to work in and out of an overpowering system. Although derided for his kitsch and highly nostalgic tone, his stand as an independent craftsman, free from trendy art movements, enabled him at times to ridicule the practice of demonizing the aliens of the *Arabian Nights*, like the genie of the lamp in Aladdin.[95] His paintings for the *Arabian Nights*, 1943–56, demonstrate a hybrid tableau of rich color where grotesquery and refinement coexist as if simultaneously to embrace and repel what Debord calls "society of the spectacle."[96] Particular tales like Aladdin, Ali Baba, and Sindbad receive more attention for a number of reasons. Apart from their adaptability to cultural transaction and their malleability, they converse easily with a consumer culture. Dreams of wealth and supremacy find their venues in Aladdin's magic lamp, in outwitting others as in Ali Baba, and in adventures of material achievement in Sindbad. As shown by Jack Shaheen, and in detail by Ulrich Marzolph and Christopher Wise,[97] the era of multinational capitalism finds in these tales sources for a self-generative culture industry as befitting a consumer economy. Shaheen (d. 2017) set the path toward decolonizing Aladdin in particular, but his contributions continued to criticize and correct Disney's recent musical of Aladdin (2011, 2013, etc.) and force the company to relent and change a few things that carry the stamp of racialization.[98] The film and print industries have been feeding culture in

[94] Guy Debord, *Society of the Spectacle* (Detroit, IL: Black and Red, 1983), 42.
[95] www.lambiek.net/artists/p/pieck_anton.htm.
[96] For more on this, see Duggan, "From Genie to Efreet," 116.
[97] Ulrich Marzolph, "Aladdin Almighty: Middle Eastern Magic in the Service of Western Consumer Culture," *The Journal of American Folklore* 132, no. 525 (Summer 2019), 275–90. Shaheen, *Reel Bad Arabs*. See also Wise, "Notes from the Aladdin Industry"; Macleod, "The Politics of Vision"; and White and Winn, "Islam, Animation and Money."
[98] www.latimes.com/local/obituaries/la-me-jack-shaheen-20170713-story.html.

multiple ways, to such an extent that names, labels, images, and motifs slip into media, stock markets, enterprises, and news, to denote or connote one thing or another. In an extensive survey of the uses of Aladdin in contemporary culture, Marzolph also cites the following in which "Aladdin" is no longer a noun, but also an active verb intended to effect transformation, interaction, and creativity: "[P]rincipal Bernie McVeigh from the Scoil Mhuire C.B.S. (Christian Brothers School), Mullingar, is even quoted as enthusiastically saying 'Aladdin is now a verb in our school . . . Just as other people google, we aladdin.'"[99] While that sounds like a positive response to Aladdin as a tale of magic and achievement, the film of 1992 was different. Shaheen lays bare its underlying racism, starting with the opening song that describes "home" as a cruel desert where wrongdoings are punished severely. Shaheen's masterly synthesis shows how screening, narration, and demonization work together to intensify Hollywood images of terrorism and/or fanaticism. "Aladdin, a $35 million film aimed at children, crosses the racist line in no uncertain terms. Consider the film's opening song, 'Arabian Nights.' It is belted out by a shady-looking *al-rawi* (storyteller) sitting atop a camel crossing the desert. The ditty goes like this: Oh I come from a land / From a faraway place / Where the caravan camels roam. / Where they cut off your ear / If they don't like your face. / It's barbaric, but hey, it's home." Shaheen adds, "The viewer can't say, 'Hey, that's just Hollywood,' for this song effectively slanders the heritage of 300,000,000 Arabs."[100]

Although Aladdin was the most popular with the cinema, other general productions all over the globe made use of the *Nights* for one case and event or another. A countermovement to this massive use in visual culture has begun to gather momentum since the first decades of the twentieth century. Benjamin was not alone in critiquing the "Age of Mechanical Production," or lamenting the waning of storytelling.[101] Hesse was another, and yet approaches differ. While Hesse was more concerned with the art in general and the *Arabian Nights* in particular, Benjamin speaks of the "art of storytelling" as "reaching its end because the epic side of truth, wisdom, is dying out."[102] Rather than looking at it in terms of narrative in its multiple forms, he draws a comparison with the novel: "The earliest symptom of a process whose end is the decline of storytelling is the rise of the novel at the beginning of modern

[99] Marzolph, "Aladdin Almighty," 281. Cited from www.aladdin.ie/testimonials.html.
[100] Jack Shaheen, "Aladdin Animated Racism," *Cinéaste* 20, no. 1 (1993), 49.
[101] Walter Benjamin, "The Work of Art in the Age of Mechanical Production," in *Illuminations: Essays and Reflections*, trans. Harry Zohn (New York: Schocken Books, 1968), 217–51; and "The Storyteller" in ibid., 83–110.
[102] Benjamin, "The Storyteller," 87.

times."[103] If the storyteller draws on experience, the novelist is a solitary individual, someone who is "uncounseled, and cannot counsel others."[104] The disparity between a flowing storytelling that aspires to enthrall an assembly, and a novelistic tradition whose authors are forlorn and worried, is even greater when estrangement is perceived in terms of the age of mechanical reproduction. Relying on Pirandello's words in describing the strangeness overcoming the "the actor before the camera," Benjamin further explains, "While facing the camera, he knows that ultimately he will face the public, the consumers who constitute the market," which is "beyond his reach."[105] Certainly there was a history for this anxiety. If Edgar Allan Poe raises the issue of incompatibility between storytelling and a new industrial and highly positivist age in "The Thousand-and-Second Tale of Scheherazade" (1845), Isabelle de Montolieu in her *Histoire de la princesse Una* (1803) presents a faltering narrator whose conclusion to *A Thousand and One Nights* is saved only by an agreement to raise children.[106] But, like Shahrayar, the reading publics and publishers had Lane's edition in thirty-two parts holding the public in suspense while waiting anxiously for the next part. Other versions and imitations were serialized in a phenomenon that the French dubbed *querelle du roman feuilleton.*[107] Although the theater was up to speed with the exhilarating production of the *Night*s and its imitations, a more developed art of illustration became an asset to this serialized production, inviting others to participate in a gradual shift to visual culture.

Realized as such, this experience brings us to the production of the *Nights* in the film industry. How far was that industry successful in reproducing the *Nights*? Could a sense of alienation overcoming actors generate incommensurability, if not indifference? The German-born Swiss poet, novelist, and painter Hesse (d. 1962) argues a case for storytelling in the age of mechanical reproduction in light of Littmann's translation of Arabic tales (*Arabische Märchen*) in 1935. Hesse characterizes the *Nights* as different from these tales because in the *Nights* there is "the naïve passion for narration in tandem with an extremely sophisticated literary and religious-intellectual background."[108] But the "genuine tradition of Oriental storytelling" suffers decline because the "Orient of the fairy tale, of the pleasure taken in images, of contemplation has been destroyed more thoroughly by the books, newspapers, business practices, and work ethic of the West than by its armies and machine guns."[109] This rings true, especially if read to mean the forced imposition of an imperial

[103] Ibid. [104] Ibid. [105] Benjamin, "The Work of Art," 230–31.
[106] See more in Gipson, "Writing the Storyteller," 7, 27. [107] Ibid., 7–8.
[108] Cited in Haase, "The Arabian Nights," 3. [109] Ibid.

image on other societies and cultures. It also invites us to retain the comparison between storytelling and the rise of the novel. Which one needs the other? As shown in novelists' metafictional digressions, the *Nights* remains a source, albeit the focus is on its frame tale. This dependency on or accountability to a source should redirect narratologists' attention to the *Nights* as an exemplary mine for the art of narrative. Decolonizing lenses have to set theory free from boundaries of a Eurocentric understanding of fiction. An imaginary that was born out of the *Nights* as an Orient of poets, which Leigh Hunt saw challenged by the prosaic and heavily annotated Lane's translation, 1838–41, appears in twentieth-century German literature as an interstice of confrontation and challenge in an age of mechanical reproduction.

Rich with properties, but now in print and not narrated by storytellers, is the *Nights* bound to suffer in book form? Many electronic versions have already made use of virtual space to show readers illustrations of renowned painters; while some publishers have struck deals with other investors to have musicals and films available online. Can a work with a mixed history of oral and written traditions survive in these multiple milieus without some inherent propensity to theater, cinema, and musicals? Moreover, how is it possible to disengage a "genuine" *Thousand and One* from its metamorphoses in these different domains of production? French, German, and English adaptors, translators, and editors argue widely in favor of an undying *Arabian Nights*. The Leipzig Arabist Max Henning, whom Borges castigates for his "dogged and flat" style,[110] suggests in an afterword to his Philipp Reclam *Universalbibliothek* (1897) that the *Nights* is a panorama "of countless images that were magnificently colored, sometimes fantastic and grotesque, sometimes true-to-life, gentle and charming or crudely humorous."[111] One can argue the case for illustrations as a middle ground between plain storytelling and cinematography. Like the theater director, the filmmaker puts on the garb of the storyteller to grapple with an audience that he knows is disconnected from his team of actors and actresses. While print industry stands as an obstacle between the storyteller and reader, the same applies to the actor, as argued by Benjamin. The *Nights*' appeal to cinematic reproduction is enormous, however, because of the successions of events, the colorful life, and the vicissitudes of fortune that usually concede to the benefit of good and needy human beings. The "magic of this magical world" offers a "psychological moment" of a retention of a dream world,

[110] Borges, "The Translators," 107.

[111] Translated and cited by Haase, "The Arabian Nights," 6. See also Hackford, "Fantastic Visions."

as explained by Carl Theodor Ritter von Riba in his German edition of *Oriental Love Stories* from *A Thousand and One Nights* (1913).[112] Not all the tales are love stories, nor is the cinematic reproduction often faithful to one version of the *Nights* or another. As it is impossible to uncover the problems involved in this massive investment,[113] its true moments, and stereotypical others, a sustained critical reading can help in decolonizing the *Nights*, freeing it from bondage, and setting it back in conversation with its perennial moments of storytelling. While decolonizing the *Nights* often takes us from its immediate orientations, its re-orientation in Europe deserves a further note. After all, Galland was not the originator or the sole proprietor of tales like Aladdin. As noticed earlier (Chapter. 4, p. 133, fn.2), the upsurge of scholarly interest in Ḥānnā Diyāb's Vatican manuscript shows another direction in decolonizing the *Nights*: The Aleppo storyteller acted as the inheritor of an Arab tradition that connects written and oral practices in the land of the *Arabian Nights*. Even when seen as a textual-oral meeting ground, an amalgam of narration, translation, and appropriation, Aladdin is reclaimed, albeit as an exemplary case in cultural negotiation between Paris and Aleppo. However, working alongside Scheherazade to critique a case, a situation, in parodic stylization or covert political and social criticism is another decolonizing strategy, in that it challenges and destabilizes common platitudes through Scheherazade's lenses, an effort that scholarship in the field has been doing recently to liberate the tales not only from a heavy paraphernalia of stock images and stereotypes, but also from their use as documents.[114]

[112] Haase, "The Arabian Nights," 6.

[113] For more on the cinema, see Karl Sabbagh, "The *Arabian Nights* in British Pantomime," in *Scheherazade's Children*, ed. Philip Kennedy and Marina Warner (New York: New York University Press, 2013), 265–73; see also in ibid. Yuriko Yamanaka, "The *Arabian Nights* in Traditional Japanese Performing Arts," 274–81; Berta Joncus, "'Nectar if You Taste and Go, Poison if You Stay': Struggling with the Orient in Eighteenth-Century British Musical Theater," 282–321; Elizabeth Kuti, "Scheherazade, Bluebeard, and Theatrical Curiosity," 322–46; Tetsuo Nishio, "The Takarazuka Revue and the Fantasy of 'Arabi' in Japan," 347–61; and Rosie Thomas, "Thieves of the Orient: The *Arabian Nights* in Early Indian Cinema," 362–94. On the return journey from the West to Egypt in cinematic production, see Peterson, "From Jinn to Genies." For a general survey of Anglo-American films, see Marina Warner, *Stranger Magic* (London: Vintage Books, 2012). A general survey of the *Nights* in Japan is by Sugita Hideaki, *Arabian-Naito to Nihon-Jin* (Tokyo: Iwanami Shoten, 2012).

[114] See, for example, Ana Vera, "Miguel Gomes's Arabian Nights Trilogy: Representing the Portuguese Crisis through the Imaginary World of the Thousand and One Nights," in *Endless Inspiration: One Thousand and One Nights in Comparative Perspective*, ed. Orhan Elmaz (Piscataway, NJ: Gorgias Press, 2020), 309–21.

8 Invitation to Discourse

> The idea of infinity is consubstantial with The Thousand and One Nights.
>
> Borges, "The Thousand and One Nights"

> [T]he orient is not something to be imitated: it only exists in the construction of a smooth space.
>
> Gilles Deleuze and Félix Guattari, *Nomadology*

The late tenth-century title of *A Thousand Nights and One*, ostensibly used to differentiate it from the Persian *Hezār afsāneh* (*Hazār afsān*), becomes a trope for infinitude, not only in storytelling, but also in criticism as an incitement to write. This invitation to discourse has created a rich field, to the extent that there are independent bibliographies of the *Nights*, *Arabian Nights Encyclopedia*,[1] alongside companions, selections, new editions, conference proceedings, and compilations. Scholarship and criticism are enormously invested in this rewarding field. In an early reading of the state of the art (1980),[2] I mentioned some conspicuous trends and attitudes in twentieth-century scholarly interest in the *Arabian Nights*. Since then, other trends and readings are mounting up, creating a field of multiple interests whereby fiction and nonfiction, philological and literary criticism abound. Not abating in its incitement to discourse, the *Nights* is drawing even further attention in the third millennium. Explorations vary, and some draw attention for being different. As mentioned earlier, Codrescu's margins and annotations vie, for example, with Burton's "Terminal Essay" and Lane's "Review." He tries to be translator, editor, and fiction writer, all in one. His effort to present to the reader a book that is self-sufficient but different from the original and other pseudo-Oriental

[1] Ulrich Marzolph and Richard van Leeuwen, eds., with the collaboration of Hassan Wassouf, *The Arabian Nights Encyclopedia* (Santa Barbara, CA: ABC-CLIO, 2004).

[2] See al-Musawi, "Growth of Scholarly Interest."

tales, a book that covers the history of the *Nights* in Europe but remains fictional, is worth considering in terms of the state of the field. No matter how much this attempt conveys an anxiety of both influence and authorship, it is different from other rewritings of the frame tale. Can the frame tale undergo growth while retaining its major properties? Can the reader enjoy reading it against annotations that attempt to engage, albeit briefly and not always successfully, with dynastic translations and translators' annotations? Codrescu's rewriting is both a replica and genuine attempt to depart from his immediate ghosts like John Barth, Najīb Maḥfūẓ (whom he does not mention), and Galland, Lane, and Burton. In this anxiety of authorship, we are offered a work that invites its placement in the growing corpus of scholarship. Had it been without annotations and margins, Codrescu's work would have passed on as a sensational fictive endeavor like many others.

Worldwide scholarship in the field has been growing stupendously to account for the history of the *Nights*; its origins, translations, receptions, and appropriations; and its permeation into consciousness that manifests itself in poetry, narrative, theater, cinema, and almost every other field. My early classification was followed by others. Peter Heath suggests such headings as the historical that deals with textual and literary developments of the collection; panoramic with a "holistic perspective, combining historical, philological, folkloristic, literary, and, occasionally, sociological concerns"; and a third path that cares for individual stories.[3] While the first heading can be classified with ease, the matter is not so smooth with the panoramic. Heath places Burton's "Terminal Essay," Gerhardt's *The Art of Storytelling*, and Elisseef's reading of themes and motifs under this heading.

John Payne Matters

We know that John Payne – and his contemporary dependents like Burton and Kirby – had already offered a classification of the genres that make up the colorful and highly entertaining body of the collection. As recognized and reproduced by Burton in his "Terminal Essay," Payne applies his literary scholarship to set first a basal structure or nucleus for the collection before searching for origins. Burton explains:

> as "justly observed by Mr. Payne, the first step when enquiring into the original date of *The Nights* is to determine the nucleus of the Repertory by a comparison of the four printed texts and the dozen MSS. which have been collated by scholars.

[3] See Peter Heath, "Romance as Genre in 'The Thousand and One Nights,'" Part I, *Journal of Arabic Literature*, no. 18 (1987), 1–21; Part II, no. 19 (1988), 1–26.

This process makes it evident that the tales common to all are the following thirteen: 1. The Introduction (with a single incidental story 'The Bull and the Ass'). 2. The Trader and the Jinni (with three incidentals). 3. The Fisherman and the Jinni (with four). 4. The Porter and the Three Ladies of Baghdad (with six). 5. The Tale of the Three Apples. 6. The Tale of Núr-al-Dín Ali and his son Badr al-Dín Hasan. 7. The Hunchback's Tale (with eleven incidentals). 8. Nur al-Dín and Anís al-Jalís. 9. Tale of Ghánim bin 'Ayyúb (with two incidentals). 10. Alí bin Bakkár and Shams al-Nahár (with two). 11. Tale of Kamar al-Zamán. 12. The Ebony Horse; and 13. Julnár the Seaborn."

Burton goes on to note:

These forty-two tales, occupying one hundred and twenty Nights, form less than a fifth part of the whole collection which in the Mac. Edit. contains a total of two hundred and sixty-four.

He corroborates this count by Dr. Patrick Russell, the author of the *Natural History of Aleppo* who "believed that the original Nights did not outnumber two hundred, to which subsequent writers added till the total of a thousand and one was made up." Furthermore, Dr. Jonathan Scott confirms that Russell "held it highly probable that the tales of the original *Arabian Nights* did not run through more than two hundred and eighty Nights, if so many."

In his study of the history and character of the work, Payne divides the tales into four main categories:
(1) Histories and romances partly founded on historical data;
(2) Anecdotes and short accounts concerned with historical figures and daily adventures;
(3) Romances and romantic fictions of different proportions; and
(4) Didactic stories.

In the section dealing with romantic fiction, Payne distinguishes between three cycles. Apart from the romantic stories that make free use of the supernatural agency, there are narratives in which the fictional blends with the realistic. More entertaining, however, are the "novellas" and tales of roguery, to which Payne traced back many medieval European romances.[4] In these classifications, Payne has worked out a basic pattern, which later scholars, including Heath, have continued to appropriate in their descriptive appraisals of the generic richness of the *Nights*.[5]

However, the third heading in Heath's classification that deals with specific tales also poses no problem, as these make up the titles and headings of articles and monographs. The effort to classify the different aspects and elements in this corpus indicates its multifarious nature. The

[4] John Payne, "The Thousand and One Nights," Part II, *New Quarterly Magazine*, n.s. 2 (April 1879), 378–80.
[5] See, for instance, Littmann, "Alf layla wa-layla," 1:363.

"growth" of scholarly interest is enormous. Heath also suggests a generic subdivision, to justify his reading of romance in the collection.[6] As already argued, at a later stage Payne, Burton, and Gerhardt all realized the need to break the collection into divisions, subdivisions, and cycles. As is obvious in Heath's contribution, the need for further research and criticism of subgenesis is as urgent as ever. The effort to specify rather than to generalize has the advantage of drawing attention to the literary nature of the collection, but it may downplay the composite evolution of the whole. The case invites meticulous analysis, and Heath later relies on Tzvetan Todorov to classify "internal literary analysis" according to Todorov's levels: the semantic, the syntactic, and the verbal, covering thereby themes, narrative units and structures, and rhetorical devices. Nevertheless, Heath supplements them by voicing the need for cultural substantiation.[7] The note is worthwhile, as the history and nature of the collection defies mere textual or structural analysis. In line with Todorov's insights on the literariness of the text and generic motivations of narrative, Jonathan Culler's reading of signs can be useful, especially in matters that relate to openings. Culler divides presuppositions that introduce storytelling into logical and literary or pragmatic. Such openings, like *Once upon a time*, he suggests, relate the story to a series of other stories, identify it with generic conventions, and impel the reader to respond accordingly. It is, for that matter, "a powerful intertextual operator."[8] While unconcerned with the *Nights*, Culler's insights are useful for the study of the art in its oral significations. At a later stage, and applying literary analysis to motivations, stylistic features, and techniques, David Pinault wrote his doctoral dissertation on some of them, specifying first "repetitive designation" of gardens and windows, for instance, where the emphasis is laid on a scene, a place that will prove quite functional in initiating narrative disequilibrium. Second is the "*leitwortstil*" or the "leading-word style," whereby words assume substantial significance, as they are loaded with religious and cultural connotations, encapsulating themes, and techniques. The third is "thematic techniques and formal patterning," with emphasis on an idea or an argument, or the very organization of events, leading to the pleasure of recognition. Part of the patterning relies on ransom motivations, but the emphasis on this is not new in literary scholarship, especially in Gerhardt's reading. The fourth is dramatic visualization, with the emphasis on both the mimetic and the descriptive.[9] These are useful suggestions, especially in Pinault's detailed and meticulous analysis. It is good that he entitled his work in such a general

[6] Heath, "Romance as Genre," Part I, 3. [7] Ibid., 7.
[8] See Jonathan Culler, *The Pursuit of Signs: Semiotics, Literature, Deconstruction* (London: Routledge, 1981), 115.
[9] See Pinault, *Story-Telling Techniques*, 16–30.

way, as techniques in this collection are far more numerous than what are discussed in his study. As I have argued in *Mujtama' alf laylah wa-laylah*,[10] there are verbal and nonverbal narratives and genres, and we need to make use of Roland Barthes's suggestion in his readings of narrative, to account for the multifarious technical nature of this collection. He argues, "[N]arrative is first and foremost a prodigious variety of genres, themselves distributed amongst different substances – as though any material were fit to receive man's stories."

He continues:

> Able to be carried by articulated language, spoken or written, fixed or moving images, gestures, and the ordered mixture of all these substances; narrative is presenting myth, legend, fable, tale, novella, epic, history, tragedy, drama, comedy, mime, painting ... stained glass windows, cinema, comics, news item, conversation.[11]

When making use of the enormous archival work and painstaking study of manuscripts by MacDonald's descendants like Chraïbi and Marzolph, Barthes's articulation not only broadens the field of excavation, but also consolidates our reading of the *Nights* as narrative. With this understanding of narrative, corroborated in the case of the *Nights* by the enormous production in textual, genealogical, historical, and comparative studies, the following summarization also attempts to define this corpus under a number of headings.

Critical Typologies: The New *Philological Inquiry*

As much as this inquiry has its solid grounds in historical documentation, its directions vary according to predispositions and the dominating cultural script. As mentioned earlier, basic to this *new* philological inquiry is "the discovery of language ... [as] a secular event that displaced a religious conception of how God delivered language to man in Eden."[12] By the last decades of the eighteenth century, a dissociation with religion took place, giving rise to other classifications of language on the basis of race. Has this classification in families touched research on the *Nights*? Not for von Hammer, despite Burton's biting remark ("Terminal Essay," n142) on his "customary inexactitude," but it can be traced in Sir William Jones's end of career reflections,[13] Friedrich Schlegel, and many

[10] al-Mūsawī, *Mujtama'*. [11] Barthes, "Introduction," 79.

[12] Said's reflection on Foucault's thesis, *Orientalism*, 135.

[13] Satya S. Pachori, *Sir William Jones: A Reader* (Delhi: Oxford University Press, 1993). As argued in al-Musawi, *Anglo-Orient*, 16–17, disappointments in his career led Oriental Jones back to the classical tradition where he finds "the superiority of European talents," for "the Athenian poet seems perfectly in the right, when he represents 'Europe' as

others. The *Nights* was either to be relocated in an urban space, with specific reference to Indo-Persian origins of the frame tale or placed in a societal Orient. MacDonald concludes this search for origins by pointing out the existence at a certain time since the Fatimid dynasty in Egypt of a number of manuscripts. But "there is evidence that our present Nights, from Galland MS. to ZER, is of specifically Arabic and not Persian origin."[14] To prove this, he directs attention to the first cycle of stories,

> where the merchant's life is saved by the stories told by three chance met travelers, is already to be found narrated by al-Mufaḍḍal b. Salam (fl.250 = 865) in his *Fākhir*, a book of proverbs (ed. Storey, pp. 137–140). It is all of pronounced desert and Arabic type and contrasts strongly with the immediately preceding and plainly Persian Frame-work Story.[15]

Since the mid-nineteenth century, efforts have been made to dislodge the discussion of the *Nights* and its composite nature from the ongoing supremacist and racist stipulations of language families, and to address it as either Arabic, Eastern, or almost a thing of "our own." Instead of a holistic reading, the search for origins conceded to a partial tracing of Sanskrit, Greek, and other elements. Even Burton's enormous anthropological erudition, noted but rarely read, could not disengage the *Nights* from its diffusion into the European unconscious. The history of the *Nights* in Europe provides an index of how far a fictional book like the *Nights* can penetrate structures of feeling. This explains in part how and why philological inquiry took a sharp turn toward other practices. Alongside the increasing interest in the *Nights* as a story book, this inquiry turns toward authentication of source material, manuscripts, resurrection of notebooks, echoes, and traveling narratives. Does this mean the end of a certain streak in Orientalist scholarship that tends to essentialize an Arab mind, society, or mentality? Edward Said argues against this presumption.

> At the same time that Friedrich Schlegel, Wilhelm von Humboldt, and Ernest Renan were making their distinction between organic, lively, wonderful Indo-European and inorganic, agglutinative, uninteresting Semitic, they were also constructing the doxology of twentieth-century anti-Arab and anti-Jewish Orientalist scholarship ... because of a desire to possess and control.[16]

a 'Sovereign princess' and 'Asia' as her Handmaid." Jones was privy to a racist debate regarding reason and imagination. Jones argues, "[R]eason and taste are grand prerogatives of European minds, while the Asiatics have soared to loftier heights in the sphere of imagination." William Jones, *Works, with the Life of the Author by Lord Teignmouth*, 13 vols. (London: John Stockdale and John Walker, 1807), 3:12.

14 MacDonald, "Alf laila wa-laila," 15. 15 Ibid.

16 Said, *The World, the Text and the Critic*, 264.

The search for roots and language families plagued the history of the tales for some time. Burton sums up the discussion in his "Terminal Essay" as follows: "[T]he chief authorities at once branched off into two directions. One held the work to be practically Persian: the other as persistently declared it to be purely Arab." August von Schlegel, Friedrich's brother, was the butt of sarcasm in Ameen al-Rihani's articles and book on *The Lore of the Arabian Nights*. His argument for a Sanskrit-Indian origin is ridiculed: "Even though the Book of the Nights were held in esteem by the eminent grammarian, to discover its origin were as futile as discovering the origin of the rose or of weighing a drop of dew."[17] Al-Rihani relates the problem to each Orientalist's specialization, the knowledge of a specific area of study. "August von Schlegel, whose hobby in his latter days was Sanskrit literature, discovered in India the source of all the mythology and folk-lore of the world!"[18]

Textual and Genealogical Criticism

Even a cursory survey of late nineteenth and early twentieth-century criticism of Scheherazade's tales will indicate a heavy bias in favor of textual and literary-historical research. Numerous essays have appeared dealing with the literary genesis of the tales and their place in fictional literature. At the close of the nineteenth century, the investigations of August Müller and others into the typological, generic, and genetic characteristics of the various layers of the work were widely known.[19] The immediate impact of this research is manifested not so much in the subsequent critical concern with specific tales and motifs as in the relative disappearance of sweeping generalizations about the composition of the *Nights*, a point that will become obvious in due course. No less influential, but more comprehensive and thorough, is Victor Chauvin's *Bibliographie des ouvrages arabes*, especially volumes IV–VII.[20] Besides the excellent listing of numerous European editions and imitations, Chauvin supplies exhaustive bibliographic references to Western criticism of the major translations. Unlike early nineteenth-century philologists, late

[17] Ameen F. Rihani, *The Lore of the Arabian Nights* (Washington, DC: Platform International, 2002), 54. Some of the articles appeared in 1912; and the manuscript "can be dated to between 1928 and 1930." See Geoffrey Nash's "Introduction," in ibid., 12.

[18] Ibid., 52.

[19] For a brief bibliographic survey of these, see Littmann, "Alf layla wa-layla," 1:361; C. Brockelmann, *Geschichte der Arabischen Litteratur*, 2nd ed. (Leiden: E. J. Brill, 1938), 2:72–74; Suppl. II (Leiden: E. J. Brill, 1938), 59–63; and Gerhardt, *The Art of Story-Telling*, 475–87.

[20] Chauvin, *Bibliographie des ouvrages arabes*.

nineteenth-century European scholars first embarked on examining and classifying individual stories before attempting to tackle the genealogical implications of the whole work. Their achievement in this respect is significant, for rather than adducing sporadic evidence from one exclusive portion; they wisely began establishing the different layers that form the collection, classifying each according to its prevailing topographical detail and generic characteristics. This endeavor quite legitimately entailed extensive search not only for internal circumstantial or stylistic peculiarities, but also for external evidence. Besides Arabic literary histories, Indo-Persian, Babylonian, and Greek documents were investigated to determine the milieu, origin, and possible transmission or migration of specific motifs and story elements. Again, this effort does not entail the end of sweeping generalizations. Even an eminent scholar like Enno Littmann (d. 1958) would go as far as introducing his entry to the *Encyclopedia of Islam* as follows:

> Like all Orientals the Arabs from the earliest times enjoyed imaginative stories; but since the intellectual horizon of the true Arabs in ancient times before the rise of Islam was rather narrow, the material for these entertainments was borrowed mainly from elsewhere, from Persia and India, as we gather from the accounts of the Prophet's competitor, the merchant al-Naḍr.[21]

He has also to draw on late eighteenth-century apologetic admirers of the tales who argued for "cultivating the garden," as noted by Robert Mack. The multifarious production is excused in terms of analogy: "[T]hey resemble in a way an Oriental meadow with many different beautiful flowers intermingled with a few weeds."[22] But before the bearings of these efforts on subsequent undertakings are sketched, it is worth stressing that late nineteenth-century and modern Oriental scholarship, especially in textual, philological, and historical matters and reception, owes more to early and mid-nineteenth-century scholarship than is readily acknowledged in current bibliographic surveys.[23] Moreover, late

[21] Littmann, "Alf layla wa-layla," 1:358–64, 358. [22] Ibid.

[23] Here are examples, listed by date, from this multifarious effort to account for the presence of the collection in European cultures, covering the whole twentieth century: Victor Charles Chauvin, *La recension égyptienne des Mille et une nuits* (Brussels: Société belge de librairie, 1899); MacDonald, "The Earlier History"; see also Richard Nykl, *Hispano-Arabic Poets in The 1001 Nights* (Wellesley, MA: Wellesley College, 1952); Sheila G. Shaw, "Early English Editions of the Arabian Nights: Their Value to Eighteenth Century Literary Scholarship," *Muslim World* 49 (1959), 232–38; Georges May, *Les mille et une nuit d'Antoine Galland, ou, Le chef-d'oeuvre invisible*, 1st ed. (Paris: PUF, 1986); Georges May, "Scheherazade et la paralitterature: Melanges de litt. gen. & de crit. romanesque offerts au Professeur Henri Coulet par ses amis," *In Letters et realites* (Aiz en Provence: PU de Provence, 1988), 227–45; Rene R. Khawam, "Les Mille et Une Nuit et l'aspect creative du langage," *Le Langage et l'Homme: Recheches Pluridisciplinaries sur le*

twentieth and early twenty-first-century philological inquiry has not given up on some issues of relevance to milieu and origin. Codrescu for one, and as late as 2011, has to engage with Muhsin Mahdi and Husain Haddawy, and somehow with Said, on certain points. On the issue of giving an imaginary a national identity, he argues: "The vehement introduction to his [Haddawy's] translation reveals a deep fissure among academic Arabists, some of whom, like Mahdi and Haddawy, attempted to claim the *Nights* for some kind of exclusive Arabic imaginary" (75n41).

Codrescu could have argued differently in relation to the revival of the discussion of origins and manuscripts upon the publication of Galland's manuscript, and Mahdi's contributions to the history of the book, but, as befitting an anxiety of authorship, Codrescu has to clear some space for his marginal notes. In her critique of the blame leveled at Galland by Mahdi, Mohamed Abdel-Halim, and Sylvette Larzul, Madeleine Dobie refers readers to the following statement of Galland: "In this genre up to now we have not seen anything so beautiful in any language."[24] Another direction is taken by Robert Irwin that associates translation with specific temporalities. Irwin considers Mahdi's critique of Galland "unkind." He explains:

> Mahdi could afford to write for a broad, well-funded academic readership, whereas Galland had no choice but to address his book to the favour and patronage of ladies at court. Translators translate not just into a language, but also into a time, and it is for this reason that Homer, Dostoevsky and Proust have had to be regularly retranslated.[25]

There is something more. Mahdi was concerned with a "scholarly" edition of a popular narrative. Haddawy had to cope with translating a text into a new medium – English – with different requisites from the ones

Langage, Louvain la Neuve, Belgium (Lang&H), 23, no. 1 (1988), 66–70; Edgard Weber, *Paroles d'Arabie et d'Afrique: violences dans le secret du dire* (Paris: Publisud, 1990); *Les Mille et Une Nuit: contes sans frontière*, papers presented at a conference held November 1993, Toulouse (Toulouse: AMAM, 1994); Sylvette Larzul, "L'Exotisme fantasmatique dans Les Mille et Une Nuit de Mardrus." *Revue de Litterature Comparee*, Paris, France (RLC), 68, no. 1 (269) (January–March 1994), 39–46; Sylvette Larzul, *Les traductions françaises des Mille et une nuits: etudes des versions Galland, Trébutien et Mardrus*. Précédée de Traditions, traductions, trahisons par Claude Bremond (Paris: Harmattan, 1996); Susan Van Deventer, "Re Orientations: 'The Thousand and One Nights' in France," in *Dissertation Abstracts International*, Section A: The Humanities, Ann Arbor, MI (DATA), 57:12 (PhD diss., Cornell University, 1997); Lethuy Hoang, *Les Mille et une nuits: à travers l'infini des espaces et des temps: le conteur Galland, le conte et son public* (New York: P. Lang, 2001).

24 Dobie, "Translation in the Contact Zone," 33.

25 Robert Irwin, "Night Classes," *The Times Literary Supplement*, April 17, 2015, www.the-tls.co.uk/articles/night-classes-robert-irwin/. Irwin has other reservations that relate to the date of the manuscript, its thematic layers, and the assumption that there is an UrText.

applied by the Grub Street translator in relation to Galland's version. Translations or their outgrowths, as is the case in the genesis of Galland's, work within certain prerogatives. Said has a point when he argues, "genesis is not a simple empirical idea like birthdate . . . but a conceptual test of critical interpretation."[26] In the genesis of the *Nights*, a modern edition has to justify its presence against a predecessor in a "hostile dynasty" syndrome.

The Comparatists' Pursuits

More than any ethnographic, anthropological, and pure philological inquiry, the literary comparative pursuit takes the *Nights* as a proper field for exploration, not only in terms of "translation in the contact zone," adroitly pursued by Dobie,[27] but also in terms of Said's "travelling theory" as studied by many, especially Srinivas Aravamudan. While taking into account Galland's departure from his original, Dobie argues that "as a project it is nonetheless fundamentally guided by an underlying perception of translation as a privileged site of intercultural contact,"[28] a point that also leads her to negotiate Georges May's *Les Mille et Une Nuit d'Antoine Galland, ou, Le chef-d'œuvre invisible* (1986) as "the most developed of a handful of attempts to evaluate Galland's translation as a work of literature in its own right."[29] Read as a literary text, the *Nights* departs from two points of origin: Galland's reproduction for a French milieu that, through delicate appropriation, changes the identity of the text to a French commodity with no drastic change to narrative events or the art of storytelling. The second relates to the probable oral dissemination and genesis of manuscripts over time. Said reiterates what others, like Macherey,[30] argue: "In one sense no text is finished, since its potential range is always being extended by every additional reader."[31] Although derived from multiple manuscripts, with nothing extant older than Galland's, the *Nights* sustains a core that MacDonald – and before him Payne and Burton – has already classified.[32] In its multiple versions and forgeries, the *Nights* has proved a power of its own, which may relate to what Aravamudan sums up a "as an internal dialectic between tropes of travel and stasis, as well as strangeness and familiarity."[33] These are broad

[26] Said, *The World, the Text, and the Critic*, 156.
[27] Dobie, "Translation in the Contact Zone"; and Aravamudan, "The Adventure Chronotope."
[28] Dobie, "Translation in the Contact Zone," 34. [29] Ibid., 41.
[30] Pierre Macherey, *A Theory of Literary Production* (London and New York: Routledge, 2006), 113.
[31] Said, *The World, the Text, and the Critic*, 157. [32] MacDonald, "The Earlier History."
[33] Aravamudan, "Adventure Chronotope," 237.

paradigms, to be sure, and we have a mass of comparative studies that require further classification. An overview of the field in a number of languages has already been done, preparing the groundwork for further research. *Scheherazade in England: Nineteenth-Century English Criticism of the Arabian Nights* appeared in 1981, to be followed in 1988 by Peter L. Caracciolo's edition of *The Arabian Nights in English Literature: Studies in the Reception of The Thousand and One Nights into British Culture*,[34] and Irwin's critical survey of the "Children of the Nights." Along with these studies, an increasing number of dissertations have begun to appear, studying one or another aspect in this comparative pursuit. To reflect on visible patterns in this pursuit, a retrospective look at early efforts in this direction is worthwhile.

Soon after the publication of Lane's, Payne's, and Burton's *Nights*, interested scholars embarked on studying the early history of the *Nights* and assessing its impact on world fictional and legendary lore.[35] William E. A. Axon admits, in a review of Lane's version,[36] that

> Prof. Victor Chauvin's "Bibliographie Arabe" is a perfect storehouse of information about the literary history of the "Thousand and One Nights," and of the analogues of the tales of which it is composed. It is in this direction we must look for the *scientific* value of the "Arabian Nights." (emphasis added)

No less indicative of Chauvin's influence was MacDonald's address of September 23, 1904, to the International Congress of Arts and Sciences at St. Louis. Obviously drawn by Chauvin's meticulous listing of analogous tales and conventions, MacDonald encouraged researchers to inquire more thoroughly into the impact of Arabic fiction on such romances as "Aucassin et Nicolette."[37] This rather specialized pursuit is a marked change in the criticism of the *Nights*. Whether seen as part of the rise of academic scholarship or as a manifestation of the evolving taste for the freshness and vitality of folklore and romance in tandem with a whole

[34] Caracciolo, ed., *The Arabian Nights in English Literature*.

[35] As far as Anglo-American studies are concerned, Duncan B. MacDonald's writings stand among the best scholarly researches in the history of the collection, while the literary accounts of Martha Pike Conant, R. C. Whitford, and William Axon represent early twentieth-century interest in the impact of the *Nights* on English (mainly eighteenth-century) literature. A comparison between MacDonald's output with the latter's brief and hardly exhaustive surveys will tell much about the bias in favor of philological, editorial, and ethnographic research early in the twentieth century. For MacDonald's writings, see *The MacDonald Presentation Volume, Essay Index Reprint Ser.* (1933; repr. New York: Books for Libraries Press, 1968), 473–86; and John Jermain Bodine, "The Romanticism of Duncan Black MacDonald" (PhD diss., Hartford Seminary Foundation, 1973), 232–44.

[36] *Bookman* 31 (March 1907), 258.

[37] Duncan B. MacDonald, "The Problems of Muhammadanism," *Hartford Seminary Record* 15 (November 1904–August 1905), 82.

comparatist drive, there was a growing Western interest, excluding France, in nationalism against such a broad cultural identity as Islam. The amount of work in this comparative domain is quite noticeable.

Due mention must be made of a number of nineteenth-century attempts to assess not only the impact of the *Nights* on medieval romance, but also its probable, although meager, indebtedness to Greek, ancient Egyptian, and Babylonian sources. A few late eighteenth- and early nineteenth-century writers proposed some ideas regarding possible Greek elements in the *Nights*. A century and a half later, the late Gustave von Grunebaum attempted to track down classical conventions in Scheherazade's intricate web.[38] Well acquainted with Arabic and Greek literatures, von Grunebaum came to some interesting conclusions concerning the process of borrowing and adapting literary patterns.[39] Nevertheless, his findings are worth attention only in the sense of his own deep classical grounding, which makes him read echoes in everything of value. Similarly, biblical and Sanskrit scholars have continued to search for relevant echoes in the *Nights* to substantiate their respective views of the transmission and diffusion of folk literature.[40] However, whether engendered by late eighteenth-century apologetic admirers of the *Nights* or by biblical and Oriental scholars, this search for foreign elements represents a mere eddy when set against the more solid tendency to

[38] G. E. von Grunebaum, "*The Arabian Nights*," *Midway: A Magazine of Discovery in the Arts and Sciences* 14 (1963), 40–63.

[39] See, for example, G. E. von Grunebaum, "Greek Elements in the Arabian Nights," *Journal of the American Oriental Society* 62 (1942), 277–92; and G. E. von Grunebaum, "Creative Borrowing: Greece in the 'Arabian Nights,'" in *Medieval Islam*, 2nd ed. (Chicago, IL: Chicago University Press, 1953), 294–319.

[40] Biblical scholars were rapturous to discover that the biblical story of Ahikar crept into the body of the *Nights*. See, for instance, George A. Barton, "The Story of Ahikar and the Book of Daniel," *American Journal of Semitic Languages and Literatures* 16 (July 1900), 242–47; and Eb. Nestle, "The Story of Ahikar," *Expository Times* 10 (1898), 276–77. The latter concluded as follows: "startling as it seemed at first, that a story from the *Thousand and One Nights* should have connexions with our Bible, not as the offspring of a Biblical book, but as an ancestor of it, it is no longer incredible, and this reason is enough for anyone who has his eyes wide open to join in Hutten's sentiment: 'Century, what a joy to live!'" Schlegel's controversial discourse on the Sanskrit origin of the *Nights* was partially echoed by Louis H. Gray in "The Sanskrit Novel and the Arabian Nights," *Wiener Zeitschrift für die Kunde des Morgenlandes* 18 (1904), 39–48. In "History as Told in the Arabian Nights," *Westminster Review* 143 (March 1895), 276, J. F. Hewitt argued: "*Arabian Nights* is not only a living picture of Eastern Mahommedan life, but a storehouse of the unwritten archives of primeval history derived from the tribal traditions and customs of northern and southern nations." A writer with grounding in Hindu mythology who contributed to the *British and Foreign Review* 11, no. 21 (1840), 224–74, studied the impact of Eastern fiction on European literature, concluding that most medieval writings "were indebted to the East for many of their 'findings,' and that the Hindus occupy an early and a prominent place in the History of Fiction" (274).

trace Arabian motifs and details in European literature.[41] It testifies, nevertheless, to the *Nights* as a desirable commodity.

Although mainly provoked by Huet's and, later, Warton's speculations on the origin of romance, late eighteenth- and early nineteenth-century attempts to tackle the involved genesis and growth of popular fiction evolved into two different schools. The first school accepted the theory of Benfey, Gödeke, Köhler, Nöldeke, and Liebrecht respecting the Oriental origin of a great body of European legendary and fictional lore, whereas the second followed Cox, Dasent, and Max Müller in stressing a direct Aryan descent.[42] As far as the present topic is concerned, it is worth mentioning that the most obvious medieval borrowings from Arabic romantic fiction were noticed by such scholars as Henry Weber, Dunlop, Charles Swan, Francis Douce, Thomas Keightley, B. E. Pote, and, later, Payne.[43] However, no matter how valuable these writings might be, they were done at a time when comprehensive surveys of the Arab presence in Sicilian and Spanish popular literatures were inaccessible and when the study of folklore was yet undeveloped. In fact, as late as

41 Eighteenth-century concern with influences was scanty. Alongside Beattie's remark on Swift's indebtedness to the *Nights* and Goldsmith's remark on the Arabian origin of Thomas Parnell's "Hermit," there appeared no other significant suggestions. The case is different with the nineteenth century. References to obvious dramatic adaptations abound. In 1875, George Brandes devoted a chapter to "The Lake School's Oriental Romanticism," whereas W. A. Clouston and James Mew wrote on Parnell's probable indebtedness to the *Nights* and the Qur'ān. See George Brandes's *Main Currents in Nineteenth Century Literature*, vol. 4 (1875; repr. London: Heinemann, 1905), 90–101; William A. Clouston's *Popular Tales and Fictions* (Edinburgh: Blackwood, 1887), 1:27–28; and Mew's "Some Unedited Tales from the 'Arabian Nights,'" *Tinsley's Magazine* (March 1882), 235–36. But there is an enormous body of allusions and manipulations in novels, articles, and adaptations for the theater. Earlier examples like Eliza Haywood's "Fruitless Enquiry "(1727) are less until later in the century. See Suzanne Byrl Gibson, "The Eighteenth-Century Oriental Tales of Eliza Haywood, Frances Sheridan and Ellis Cornelia Knight" (PhD diss., McMaster University, 1996). See also Christopher F. Loar, "The Exceptional Eliza Haywood: Women and Extralegality in 'Eovaai,'" *Eighteenth-Century Studies* 45, no. 4 (Summer 2012), 565–84.

42 On Warton and his indebtedness to Huet and Warburton, see Manzalaoui, "Pseudo Orientalism," in *William Beckford of Fonthill, 1760–1844, Bicentenary Essays*, ed. Fatma Moussa Mahmoud (1960; 2nd ed. Port Washington, NY: Kennikat Press, 1972), 135–38. Clouston supplies an excellent survey of these two schools in the "Introduction" to his *Popular Tales*. See also T. F. Crane, "Italian Popular Tales," *North American Review* 123, no. 252 (July 1876), esp. 26.

43 For an apt summary of Swan's and Douce's views, see Manzalaoui, "Pseudo-Orientalism," 138–39. For other explications, see Henry Weber's "Introduction" to *Tales of the East* (Edinburgh: Ballantyne, 1812); John C. Dunlop, *The History of Fiction* (1814; revised by Henry Wilson, London: G. Bell and Sons, 1888), 2:29–30, 39–42, 132, 211, 476–77; Thomas Keightley, *Tales and Popular Fictions* (London: Whittaker, 1834) (esp. on the Perso-Arabian origin of "Cleomades and Claremond," "Peter of Provence and the Fair Maguelone," in *Le Notti Piacevoli*, better known as the Pleasant Nights of Straparola), 40–127; Pote, "Arabian Nights"; and Payne, "The Thousand and One Nights," Part II.

July 1876, T. F. Crane complained that it was too soon to decide upon matters of transmission and diffusion of popular tales, for the science of folklore had not yet advanced beyond the primary stage of collecting and arranging materials.[44]

In the closing decades of the nineteenth century, and with the publication of sound surveys of South European and Asian popular fictions and the appearance of some detailed researches into the typology and semantics of the *Nights*, a solid foundation was established for the thorough analysis of single themes and motifs. Clouston's investigations into the Arabian origin of several European folktales must be cited among the prominent developments in the study of the *Nights*.[45] No less rewarding are the writings of Edward Yardley, E. Rehatsek, Henry Charles Coote, W. F. Kirby, Sidney Hartland, and, later, John W. Mackail.[46] Whether tracing the Arabian origin of some motifs, modes, and thematic conventions or examining the process of their migration and diffusion into European literatures, these and other writers have demonstrated a keen awareness of the debate on narrative migrations to European literature. Insofar as comparative studies are concerned, many penetrating remarks and sharp insights into the nature of this influx could be gathered from the foregoing surveys, to be synthesized and developed into a brilliant chapter in comparative literature. Regrettably, modern scholarship has left this field virtually untouched, despite the fact that, as a field, comparative literature was drawn to transmissions and intermediaries by the end of the nineteenth century. With this sad situation in mind, Joseph Campbell criticized those Occidental literary historians who, while collaborating in "a curious fiction of the virtual nonexistence of our debt beyond the boundaries of Europe," have continued to "rehearse the outdated schoolbook story about the Greeks and the Renaissance."[47]

[44] Crane, "Italian Popular Tales."

[45] In *Popular Tales and Fictions*, Clouston has quite intelligently discussed the nature of this diffusion in European literature. While taking into account the theories advanced by other mythologists, he handled the question of influx with great tact. He began establishing the origin of some tales and examining probable ways of transmission. Throughout, he has made good use of preceding investigations into the subject.

[46] See Edward Yardley, *The Supernatural in Romantic Fiction* (London: Longman & Green, 1880); E. Rehatsek, "A Few Analogies in 'The Thousand and One Nights' and in Latin Authors," *Journal of the Bombay Branch of the Royal Asiatic Society* 14 (1880), 74–85; Henry Charles Coote, "Folk-lore the Source of Some of M. Galland's Tales," *The Folk-lore Record* 3, no. 2 (1881), 178–91; W. F. Kirby, "The Forbidden Doors of the Thousand and One Nights," *Folk-lore Journal* 5, no. 2 (1887), 112–24; E. Sidney Hartland, "The Forbidden Chamber," *Folk-lore Journal* 3, no. 3 (1885), 193–242; and John W. Mackail, *Lectures on Poetry* (London: Longman & Green, 1911).

[47] Joseph Campbell, ed., *The Portable Arabian Nights* (New York: Viking Press, 1967), 35, 33, respectively.

This tendency persisted even among a number of well-known scholars throughout the first decades of the twentieth century, influencing through academic exchange many Arab minds.[48] Nevertheless, Müller's studies of old Middle Eastern civilizations led to different formulations. In Gladstone's speeches, with echoes from Müller, there developed a recognition of these civilizations in opposition to insularity and imperial rhetoric of disparagement. Nevertheless, such a shift in British imperial rhetoric should be understood as part of that growing interest in Arabism, sectarianism, ancient ethnicities and identities as part of a shift toward divide and rule in colonies and lands under mandatory rule. Rather than an outsider, the *Nights* happened to be referenced by politicians, ethnologists, eminent prose writers, and religious authorities as a source of knowledge. It is soon to become a recognized field in English, French, Italian, and Iberian studies. The comparative side, with a shift to political thought, is impacted by Said, whose detractors are also many, alongside less definite voices like Codrescu. Presumably addressing the claim to an Arab "imaginary," the latter says: "[I]t has even less reality than Edward Said's nearly successful attempt at lumping all oriental studies together with imperialism in the notion of 'orientalism'" (75).

To a certain extent, I agree with the editors of the *Arabian Nights in Historical Context* that Said's *Orientalism* "has shaped much of the recent and contemporary scholarship on the *Nights*."[49] It acquires validity when read in terms of the post-May 1968 cultural penchant in European and American campuses to deconstruct the dominating conservative discursive structures of knowledge. To recapitulate, *Orientalism* is not concerned with the *Arabian Nights* as text; its concern is with its translators: Galland, "who was the first European translator of *The Thousand and One Nights* and an Arabist of note";[50] Lane and " his uninspired translation of the *Arabian Nights*";[51] and Burton, with his "combativeness" toward "the uninformed teachers who ran Europe and European knowledge with such precise anonymity and scientific firmness," a combativeness "rarely with more candid contempt for his opponents than in the preface to his translation of the *Arabian Nights*."[52] Along with his *Pilgrimage*, Burton's notes to the *Arabian Nights* and his "Terminal Essay" are meant "to be testimony to his victory over the sometimes scandalous system of Oriental knowledge, a system he had mastered by himself."[53] While Galland's

[48] See Muḥsin Jāsim al-Mūsawī, *al-Istishrāq fī al-fikr al-'Arabī* (Beirut: al-Mu'assasah al-'Arabiyyah li-l-Dirāsāt, 1993).

[49] Saree Makdisi and Felicity Nussbaum, "Introduction," in *The Arabian Nights in Historical Context: Between East and West*, ed. Saree Makdisi and Felicity Nussbaum (Oxford: Oxford University Press, 2008), 9.

[50] Said, *Orientalism*, 64. [51] Ibid., 164. [52] Ibid., 194. [53] Ibid., 196.

translation falls outside the purview of *Orientalism*, Said distinguishes Galland as an "Arabist of note," not Orientalist.

Can translations be separated from their translators? Can we speak only of translators as arbiters and architects of taste without their "*Arabian Nights*"? It seems to me that Said sides with Arab classicists and Nahḍah intellectuals who dismiss the *Nights* as street storytelling. Nevertheless, as a dynamic force in cultural criticism, Said's works, *Orientalism* and *Culture and Imperialism*, and along with them *The World, the Text, and the Critic*, help to generate new methods and concerns in the field of comparative studies.

No matter what tracks comparative readings pursue, the increasing volume of relevant publications marks a development in the field. Writings in this comparative vein vary, and the following selected articles and books indicate such diversity. There is first conspicuous emphasis on migration, influx, and influence.[54] Roger Allen even suggests a burgeoning Arabic novel in relation to the voyages of Sindbad.[55]In other cases, the focus is on echoes and traces that new methodologies situate in nuanced readings of the art of fiction.[56] With the late twentieth-century shift to high modernists and nuanced understanding of the comparative pursuit as an intertextual enterprise, texts are read as mosaics, a body of quotes, where readings permeate consciousness in an endless dialogue. Evelyn Fishburn's reading of Borges may fit here, albeit within the context of a need for rigorous theorization in the matter of "acculturation and transculturation."[57] In that direction, and as engagement with Fishburn's significant analysis, is Philip Kennedy's study.[58] Traces are no longer what matter most because inventions and/or actual reference to the *Nights* are perceived as leading motifs in an intricate textual space. Writers

[54] Stephen Belcher, "Parallel Tracks? The Seven Sages, the Arabian Nights, and Their Arrival in Europe," *South Asian Review* 19, no. 16 (December 1995), 11–23; and Antoinette Saly, "Les Mille et Une Nuit au Xllle siècle: Conte oriental et matiere de Bretagne," *Travau de Litterature* 3 (1990), 15–24.

[55] Roger Allen, "Sindbad the Sailor and the Early Arabic Novel," in *Tradition, Modernity, and Postmodernity in Arabic Literature: Essays in Honor of Issa J. Boullata*, ed. Kamal Abdel-Malek and Wael Hallaq (Leiden: Brill, 2000), 78–85.

[56] Antonio L. Furtado, "The Arabian Nights: Yet Another Source of the Grail Stories?" *Quondam et Futurus: A Journal of Arthurian Interpretations* 1, no. 3 (1991), 25–40; Frederick Garber, "Assisting at the Light," *Prisms: Essays in Romanticism* 1 (1993), 1–30; and Sharon S. Geddes, "The Middle English Poem of Floriz and Blauncheflur and the Arabian Nights Tale of 'Ni'amah and Naomi': A Study in Parallels," *Emporia* 19, no. 1 (1970), 14–21, 23–24.

[57] Evelyn Fishburn, "Traces of the Thousand and One Nights in Borges," in *New Perspectives on Arabian Nights: Ideological Variations and Narrative Horizons*, ed. Wen-Chin Ouyang and Geert Jan van Gelder (London and New York: Routledge, 2005), 81–90.

[58] Kennedy, "Borges and the Missing Pages of the Nights."

like Barth draw attention by their use of parody, a self-reflexivity that claims lineage to Scheherazade and her sister. The archetypal storyteller provokes an anxiety for replenishment to escape from a literary canon that is exhausted and dead. As an allegory for replenishment and hence life, Scheherazade turns into a trope. Wen-Chin Ouyang's reading of "An American Tycoon in John Barth," as part of her article on Sindbad, is a postmodernist reading of parody as exemplified in Barth's *Last Voyage*, which "has not the success of Dunyazadiad."[59] While reading Barth is understandable, the return to Borges is like the discovery of Walter Benjamin. Under the impact of academic training, writers look at Borges afresh from a postmodernist perspective, finding in him an exemplary nuanced postmodernist poetics. Alongside this mounting interest, the issue of trace in an intertextual space remains the most popular among a large number of scholars.[60]

Since the last decades of the twentieth century, and in conversation with René Wellek's (d. 1995) landmarks in comparative literary criticism, like *Theory of Literature* (1942), *History of Modern Criticism* (1955), and especially *Concepts of Criticism* (1963), a noticeable interest in reflections, motifs, tropes, and story migration takes over. Other studies deal with authors and genres in the context of creative *Arabian Nightism*.[61] The

[59] Wen-Chin Ouyang, "Whose Story Is It? Sindbad the Sailor in Literature and Film," in *New Perspectives on Arabian Nights*, 1–16.

[60] Faris, "1001 Words" (discusses briefly the place of the *Arabian Nights* in the works of Barth, Borges, Nabokov, and Proust); Ferial Jabouri Ghazoul, "The Arabian Nights in Shakespearean Comedy: 'The Sleeper Awakened' and 'The Taming of the Shrew,'" in *1001 Nights: Critical Essays and Annotated Bibliography*, *Mundus Arabicus*, vol. 3 (Cambridge, MA: Dar Mahjar, 1985), 58–70; also Ferial Jabouri Ghazoul, "Poetic Logic in the Panchatantra and The Arabian Nights," *Arab Studies Quarterly* 5, no. 1 (1983), 13–21; Bonnie D. Irwin, "Narrative in the Decameron and the Thousand and One Nights," in *Approaches to Teaching Boccaccio's Decameron*, ed. and trans. James H. McGregor (New York: Modern Language Association of America, 2000), 21–30; Cynthia Ho, "Framed Progeny: The Medieval Descendants of Shaharzad," *Medieval Perspectives* 7 (1992), 91–107; Grace Eckley, "The Entertaining Nights of Burton, Stead, and Joyce's Earwicker," *Journal of Modern Literature* 13 (1986), 339–44.

[61] See, as examples, Eckley, "The Entertaining Nights"; Muhsin al-Musawi, "Writing Scheherazade Now: The Growth of Arabic Fiction," in *The Postcolonial Arabic Novel: Debating Ambivalence* (Leiden: Brill, 2003), 71–115; Jennifer R. Walters, "Michel Butor and 'The Thousand and One Nights,'" *Neophilologus* 59 (1975), 213–22; Nicasio Urbina, "Las mil y una noches y Cien anos de soledad: Falsas presencias influencias definitivas," *MLN* 107, no. 2 (March 1992), 321–41; Jonathan Glance, "Irving's Tales of a Traveler," *Harvard Library Bulletin* 14 (1960), 461–86; W. Grossman, "Rilke and the Arabian Nights with Two Unpublished Translations," *Harvard Library Bulletin* 14 (1960), 461–869; Robert G. Hampson, "Conrad, Guthrie, and 'The Arabian Nights,'" *Conradiana: A Journal of Joseph Conrad Studies* 18 (1986), 141–43; Katharina Mommsen, *Goethe und 1001 Nacht* (Berlin: Akademie-Verlag, 1960); John Brian, "Tennyson's 'Recollections of the Arabian Nights' and the Individuation Process," *Victorian Poetry* 4 (1966), 275–79; Aida Yared, "Joyce's Sources: Sir Richard F. Burton's Terminal Essay in Finnegans Wake," *Joyce Studies Annual* 11 (Summer 2000), 124–66.

actual impact of postmodernist poetics and postcolonial theories comes later, and mostly in the late 1980s and 1990s.

Nevertheless, the interest is unlimited, and scholars search for echoes and manipulations in other writings. They bring into the art deconstructionist methodologies to track down motifs and images.[62] But, as argued in the preceding text, the hold of a comparative literary method remains the most visible, hence showing the *Nights* as a worldwide text in different versions or claimed translations.

Littmann, among others, has already set the scene for further criticism involving themes or cultures, as in his two books: *Geschichten der Liebe aus den Tausendundein Nächten* and *Tausendundeine nacht in der arabischen literature.*[63] In this direction of cultural exchange, there are many contributions, including Jiri Becka, "Arabian Nights in Czech and Slovak Literature and Research";[64] Kevin Windle, "The Slavonic Nights: Observations on Some Versions of *The Book of a Thousand and One Nights* in Slavonic Languages";[65] Jan Pauliny, "Adaptation oder Übersetzung? Tausend und eine Nacht im europäischen Literaturkontext";[66] Veronika Bernard, "Stadt als Schein: Die Rezeption der Geschichte von der Messingstadt";[67] Ulrich Marzolph, "The *Arabian Nights* in Comparative Folk Narrative Research";[68] and Peter L. Caracciolo, "The House of Fiction and *le jardin anglo-chinois.*"[69] There are many more such studies that give us an impression of directions in comparative readings of the *Nights*. The mounting production in this domain is partly motivated by authors' affiliations with certain academic institutions and departments, and the publishers' interest

[62] Nancy Batty, "The Art of Suspense: Rushdie's 1001 Mid-Nights," *ARIEL: A Review of International English Literature* 18, no. 3 (July 1987), 49–65; David C. Cody, "Henry Adams and the City of Brass: A Historical Review of New England Life and Letters," *The New England Quarterly* 60, no. 1 (March 1987), 89–91; Yusur al-Madani, "Deconstructing and Reconstructing a Narrative of the Self: John Barth's The Last Voyage of Somebody the Sailor," *International Fiction Review* 26, no. 1–2 (1999), 8–18; Ulla Albreck, "Isak Dinesen and The Thousand and One Nights: Albondocani, an Analysis," in *Isak Dinesen: Critical Views*, ed. Olga Anastasia Pelensky, trans. William Mishler (Athens, OH: Ohio University Press, 1993), 304–13.

[63] Enno Littmann, *Geschichten der Liebe aus den Tausendundein Nächten* (Wiesbaden: Insel-Verlag, 1953); and Littmann, *Tausendundeine Nacht in der arabischen Literatur.*

[64] Jiri Becka, "Arabian Nights in Czech and Slovak Literature and Research," *Archiv Orientalni: Quarterly Journal of African, Asian, and Latin American Studies* 62, no. 1 (1994), 32–42.

[65] Windle, "The Slavonic Nights." [66] Pauliny, "Adaptation oder Übersetzung?"

[67] Veronika Bernard, "Stadt als Schein. Die Rezeption der Geschichte von der Messingstadt," *Wirkendes Wort* 47, no. 2 (August 1996), 189–93.

[68] Ulrich Marzolph, "The *Arabian Nights* in Comparative Folk Narrative Research," in *The Arabian Nights and Orientalism: Perspectives from East and West*, ed. Yuriko Yamanaka and Tetsuo Nishio (London: I.B. Tauris, 2006), 3–24.

[69] Peter L. Caracciolo, "The House of Fiction and *le jardin anglo-chinois*," in *New Perspectives on Arabian Nights*, 67–79.

in saleable commodities; but it also shows how the *Nights* invigorates the comparative enterprise. In conclusion to this section, one can argue that, with few exceptions, the presence of the *Nights* in comparative studies is often textual, with less probing into the politics of appropriation or migration. While significantly enriching the field, intertextuality as a mere pursuit of quotes and echoes can become, as Said argues in opposition to its Euro-American use, "the exact antithesis and displacement of what might be called history," tracing in this "the triumph of the ethic of professionalism."[70]

Literary Criticism: Genres and Translational Mediums

Although a large number of studies fit under this rubric, the matter is not as easy as it sounds, simply because the composite nature of the *Nights* often baffles researchers and critics and redirects their attention from specific genres and transgenres that hold narrative cycles together. The same composite nature also baffles the film industry and directors, and, as it is impossible to produce the whole in a sequential pattern, free from the formulas of storytelling that may appear as beginnings or conclusions, they are compelled to select and collapse tales. The matter is easier with illustrators who can select particular scenes and characters. Texts pose a problem, especially as the phenomenal intertextualization of the *Nights*, from Balzac, Thackeray, Dickens, and almost every writer of note down to Joyce, Borges, and Calvino, implies that their consciousness and memory find, reinvent, and exploit multiple ways and directions in their writing. Cross-textual spaces emerge that not only downplay Manichean polarities, but also negate space and time as boundaries.

At this juncture, other issues arise that relate to the meaning of literature. Is literature still conversant with its "modern" retention of the "living being of language"?[71] Is literature exercising a "counter-discourse," "finding its way back from the representative or signifying function of language to this raw being that had been forgotten since the sixteenth century"?[72] Foucault suggests freedom from discursive representation as the sign of "literature" in the modern period: "In the modern age, literature is that which compensates for (and not that which confirms) the signifying function of language."[73] He adds:

> Through literature, the being of language shines once more on the frontiers of Western culture – and at its center – for it is what has been most foreign to that culture since the sixteenth century; but it has also, since this same century, been at the very center of what Western culture has overlain.[74]

[70] Said, *The World, the Text, and the Critic*, 4. [71] Foucault, *The Order of Things*, 43.
[72] Ibid., 44. [73] Ibid. [74] Ibid.

This brings us to the crux of the matter: How can literary critics claim a status within this understanding of literature? When we look back at writings on the *Nights*, such as Leigh Hunt's, and, in the modern period, those of Borges, their literary criticism glitters with the smoothness and poetic flow of language. It still functions outside the realms of most academic discourse, where analysis takes over so as to produce an argument. This poses a problem because literary criticism can no longer fuse into the text, or, as Foucault argues, the "primary Text is effaced": as a separate consciousness takes over that works with signs, and hence representation becomes "discourse,"[75] for "[*C*]*ommentary* has yielded to *criticism*."[76] But the case is not resolved in this Foucauldian reading. Said thinks that, apart from Foucault's reading of discourse that he sides with, the focus on textuality to the exclusion of author and circumstance can be damaging to a "theory" that "proposed itself as synthesis overriding the petty fiefdoms within the world of intellectual production," covering "all the domains of human activity."[77] How does the *Nights* fare in this discussion of text, commentary, and criticism?

One can argue that both Galland and Payne offer a text, relatively free from the heavy apparel of annotations. Mardrus's text is different. Borges speaks of him as "the only Arabist whose glory was promoted by men of letters," for his "infidelity, his happy and creative infidelity, that must matter to us."[78] In other words, Mardrus offers a text. Between narrative and discourse, and outside the Russian formalists' patterning of *story* and *discourse*,[79] we have a text as offered by Galland, Payne, Mardrus, and Haddawy's translation of Mahdi's edition of Galland's manuscript. The evolving discursive space of literary criticism and academic scholarship is a metadiscoursal field. It feeds its components in an endless chain that is often citational. The question remains as to whether we can assort studies by their amount of literariness, and not only by the amount of research.

Since the publication of late nineteenth-century academic studies of the *Nights*, several literary critics have embarked on the effective use of these achievements to develop psychoanalytic, sociological, or general literary critiques. Numerous articles and book-length essays have appeared dealing with individual themes in the *Nights* and pursuing a variety of topics, ranging from its "teachings" and pictures of social conditions to its subtle Freudian implications.[80] The multifarious nature

[75] Ibid., 79. [76] Ibid., 80. [77] Said, *The World, the Text, and the Critic*, 3.
[78] Borges, "The Translators," 106.
[79] See Barthes, "Introduction," in *Image, Music, Text*, 87.
[80] For a good listing of these, see the bibliography in Gerhardt, *Art of Story-Telling*; and *Index Islamicus and Supplements*, Section XXXVII, "Arabic Literature," subsection "i. Legends and Stories."

of genres has drawn more attention, but there is always a historical context for literary criticism: The rise of structuralism and its application to narrative touched the academy and led to an upsurge in the application of structuralist poetics to the *Nights* as a visible domain of inquiry, as in the following subsection. On another front, there is more interest in structural/thematic constructions, like the fantastic, the therapeutic, and the mythical.[81] There are studies that find specific motifs and figures in tales that give an extra meaning to the narrative or convey a deeper layer. Others look upon space and outcome as elemental thematic lines of rupture.[82] Some basic structural patterns that, though applied specifically to one cycle or another, can also apply to others. Their concern is more generic and translational in the sense that the tale works within visual patterns of repetition, resumption, interruption, and thematic ruptures, like the wound that Ferial Ghazoul studies in her doctoral dissertation on structural analysis of the *Arabian Nights*.[83] A kind of undying and unhealable wound that meets the reader's or listener's eye evolves as a situational archetype that permeates and problematizes narrative. The wound plays out as thematic and structural poetics in wider patterns that study cycles, as in Gerhardt's pioneering work on storytelling techniques (1962), and, some thirty years later, in Sandra Naddaff's reading of Arabesque as a structural device of aesthetic repetition, a point that Marzolph applies in turn to understudied tales.[84] As customary in literary fields and narratives, no text stands alone, or, as Macherey argues, each a text rarely

[81] Roy D. Mottahedeh, "Aja'ib in the Thousand and One Nights," in *The Thousand and One Nights in Arabic Literature and Society*, ed. Richard G. Hovannisian and Georges Sabagh (Cambridge: Cambridge University Press, 1997), 29–39; Bruno Bettelheim, "The Frame Story of Thousand and One Nights," in *The Uses of Enchantment: The Meaning and Importance of Fairy Tales* (New York: Knopf, 1976), 86–90; Jerome W. Clinton, "Madness and Cure in The Thousand and One Nights," in *Fairy Tales and Society: Illusion, Allusion, and Paradigm*, ed. Ruth B. Bottigheimer (Philadelphia, PA: University of Pennsylvania Press, 1986), 35–51; Peter Molan, "Ma'ruf the Cobbler: The Mythic Structure of an Arabian Nights Tale," *Edebiyat* 3, no. 2 (1978), 121–36; Stanislav Segert, "Ancient Near Eastern Traditions in the Thousand and One Nights," in *The Thousand and One Nights in Arabic Literature and Society*, 106–13.

[82] See, for instance, Elliott Colla, "The Porter and Portability: Figure and Narrative in the Nights," in *Scheherazade's Children: Global Encounters with the Arabian Nights*, ed. Philip F. Kennedy and Marina Warner (New York: New York University Press, 2013), 89–108; Wendy Doniger, "The Rings of Budur and Qamar al-Zaman," in ibid., 108–26; al-Musawi, "The 'Mansion' and the 'Rubbish Mounds'"; and Roger Allen, "An Analysis of the 'Tale of the Three Apples' from The Thousand and One Nights," in *Logos Islamikos: Studia Islamica in Honorem Georgii Michaelis Wickens*, ed. Roger M. Savory and Dionisius A. Agius (Toronto: Pontifical Institute of Mediaeval Studies, 1984), 51–60.

[83] Ghazoul, *The Arabian Nights*.

[84] Moffitt Cecil's estimate forms part of his study of "Poe's 'Arabesque,'" *Comparative Literature* 18 (1966), esp. 63–65; see also Jacob Rama Berman, "Poe's Taste for the Arabesque," in *American Arabesque: Arabs and Islam in the Nineteenth-Century Imaginary*

appears unaccompanied. Thus, we need to look back retrospectively to trace a genealogy of writing on the *Nights*.

In a brief but very penetrating survey of the generic characteristics that distinguish the *Nights* as a work of fiction, Moffitt Cecil, for example, draws attention to the elemental aspects that incite Western narratives. Taking Edgar Allan Poe as a case in point, he shows how certain patterns strike different chords in each writer. As if anticipating structuralists, he highlights the narrated event as the center of attraction, which is also touched on by his contemporaries and early twentieth-century writers.[85] Whether causing wonder and terror or titillating one's desire for wealth and adulation, the story needs to be appealing enough to arouse the listener's curiosity and sustain her/his interest. The second narrative component is the casually identified narrator. A fisherman, a trader, or a barber may step in unexpectedly to narrate her/his own life story, which must always prove more fascinating than the preceding. A third point that may not show up in structuralist analysis is the absolute faith in God. Recapitulating Lane, Cecil also refers to the medieval Arab storyteller who draws no lines between the natural and supernatural in a universe that is one manifestation of God's sovereignty. Hence in Scheherazade's world, the "supernatural, ordinarily hidden from us, might at any moment crowd miraculously over into the sphere of the senses."[86] Not to have this mistaken for fatalism in the *Nights*, this dominating understanding of Providence and a world of multiple beings has to be compatible with human ingenuity, cunning, and perseverance. This is what the fisherman shows in dealing with the genie, and the same applies to Sindbad and Morgiana (Ali Baba's female slave), who also demonstrate effective ingenuity in averting impending disasters and turning events to their own benefit.

Cecil draws the reader's attention to Poe's acquaintance with medieval Arabic fiction and Islamic theology in general, as well as to his familiarity with the graphic implications of the term. Nevertheless, like all other critics of the *Nights*, Victorian or modern, Cecil fails to stress the applicability of the term "Arabesque" to medieval Arabic fiction. The Abbasid or medieval storyteller was no less susceptible to the prevailing religious

(New York: New York University Press, 2012), 109–37; Sandra Naddaff, *Arabesque: Narrative Structure and the Aesthetics of Repetition in 1001 Nights* (Evanston, IL: Northwestern University Press, 1991); and Ulrich Marzolph, "Making Sense of the Nights: Intertextual Connections and Narrative Techniques in the Thousand and One Nights," *Narrative Culture* 1, no. 2 (Fall 2014), 239–58.

85 See Hunt, "New Translations"; and for de la Mare, see "The Thousand and One," in his *Pleasures and Speculations* (1940; repr. New York: Books for Libraries Press, 1960), 71–76.

86 Cecil, "Poe's 'Arabesque,'" 65.

teachings and traditions than his contemporary, the graphic designer. Although the term is still exclusively applied to Islamic geometric, vegetal, calligraphic, and (only occasionally) figural ornaments and designs, its early genesis coincided with the origin and growth of the *Nights*. Its very form (a denaturalized vegetal ornament with leaves spreading from a spiral, interlaced, or undulating main stalk) is also similar to the involutedly presented structure of the *Nights*, a point that Naddaff associates with repetitious narrative motifs, images, events, and formulas.[87] In the end, the principles of "Arabesque," such as reciprocal repetition and density, are identical not only with the stereotyped formulas that begin and end each tale, but also with the abundant detail with which each story abounds.

A more impressive testimony to the value of academic research for the literary critic is Gerhardt's *Art of Storytelling*, mentioned previously. Using Littmann's sound edition of the *Nights* and drawing profitably on the outstanding scholarship of Chauvin, Elisseeff, Horovitz, MacDonald, and Oestrup, she produced the first thorough literary appraisal of the work. Aside from her fair evaluation of the major translations, she demonstrated a sharp insight and a great deal of meticulousness when analyzing the form and content of the work. While building on Payne's significant contribution, she divides the thematic contents into stories of love, crime, and travel; fairy tales; and tales of piety and learning. In so doing, Gerhardt supplies a comprehensive survey of the thematic diversity of the *Nights*. Because the Hārūn's cycle forms a major portion in the collection, she treated it in a separate section, where she dwells with particular care on the caliph's character as well as on the "bourgeois" substance and the narrative skill displayed in the whole cycle. No less rewarding is her description of the structure of the *Nights*. By pointing to the oblique and witnessing narrative systems employed in the work and classifying the thematic nature of the framing tales, she brought to the reader's mind the artistic richness and literary wealth of Scheherazade's peerless *Nights*. These multiple directions in literary analysis exist alongside new readings, especially of marginalized narrators like Dunayzad

[87] On "Arabesque," see E. Kühnel in *EI*, new ed. 1:559–61. In *Two Essays on Robert Browning* (Philadelphia: 1890), Felix E. Schelling devotes one essay to study the Arabesque in Browning's poetry. In this he explains that "Arabesque . . . was an elaborate style of ornamentation used among the earlier saracens or Arabs, in which the most indulgent play of the fancy was permitted, except that a literal interpretation of the second commandment forbade the representation of a living creature therein" (1). Richard A. Moulton beautifully describes this involution in the *Nights* where it "is perfectly carried through; all the dropped threads are regularly recovered and the whole brought into symmetry," *World Literature* (New York: Macmillan, 1927), 307.

who has been receiving attention as being no less dynamic for the motivation of the frame story.[88]

Literary Criticism: Poetics of Narrative

> Great novelist though she was – exquisite in her descriptions, tolerant in her judgements, ingenious in her morality, vivid in her delineations of character, expert in her knowledge of three oriental capitals – it was on none of these gifts that she relied when trying to save her life from her intolerable husband. They were but incidental. She only survived because she managed to keep the king wondering what would happen next.
>
> E. M. Forster, *Aspects of the Novel*

There is more than one reason to start with E. M. Forster's quote, as he directs attention to suspense as an inclusive dynamic that mutates and accelerates narrative action, generating the disorder (disequilibrium) that fascinates Todorov and other narratologists. As late as 2015, this dynamic still holds and invites Barth's high postmodernist interventions. His "Missy: A Postscript to 1001 Nights,"[89] as already discussed, is a pastiche, but also a literal ironic application of Scheherazade's children. Scheherazade's daughter, now the narrator Missy, rehearses, in an invited talk to an academy, how on a "dark stormy night" her mother's narrative ordeal began to continue for 1,001 nights. She gives credit to her aunt "Doony" who was not as busy as her mother with storytelling. The postscript grants Missy's aunt another role alongside her previous presence as an interlocutor/listener. This postscript complements Barth's "Dunyazadiad" in *Chimera,* but also reflects a tradition initiated by Anthony Hamilton (d. 1720) that presents Dinarzade not only as a sharp literary critic who cannot be amused easily, but also as a better narrator who can tell the sultan on the last night a story "more extraordinary than all you have related."[90] Forster's suspense emanates from situations that should witness a better narrative, either to appease somebody or to forestall death. What holds the *Nights* together is this string that has its outward manifestation in formulas. In terms of poetics, suspense operates in a liminal space between equilibrium and disequilibrium.

88 See, for example, Ros Ballaster, "Playing the Second String: Dinazade in Eighteenth-Century English Fiction," in *The Arabian Nights in Historical Context,* 83–102.

89 Barth, "Missy."

90 Cited in Anthony Hamilton, *Fairy Tales and Romances,* trans. M. Lewis, H. T. Ryde, and C. Kenney (London: Henry G. Bohn, 1849); and discussed by Ballaster, "Playing the Second String," 87. See also Ruth Clark, *Anthony Hamilton: His Life, Works, and His Family* (London: John Lane, 1921).

While Gerhardt is primarily interested in describing the thematic and technical generic richness of the tales, more theoretic critics have probed into the aesthetics of storytelling. Foremost among these is Todorov. Whether seen as a pure expression of the modernist concern with the intrinsic and total value of the work or assessed as an indirect flowering of late nineteenth-century researches into the generic and typological features of the tales, Todorov's formalist approach to the marvelous component in the tales represents a prominent current in modern literary criticism of the *Nights*.[91] His analysis is worth considering at some length because it deals with the aesthetic totality of the *Nights*, its musical blend of form and content.[92]

According to Todorov, the supernatural in the *Nights* is of the "marvelous" rather than the "uncanny" type, for it transcends the laws of reality and plunges into a world of very different obligations. Todorov classifies the marvelous into three categories: the hyperbolic, the exotic, and the instrumental. Under the first heading, the hyperbolic, he places Sindbad's descriptions of enormous fish, huge birds, and serpents. In such accounts the sailor reports about beings that are "supernatural" only by virtue of their superiority to the commonplace and familiar. Whether occurring as mere rhetoric or as an observation of strange lands, this element does no excessive violence to reason. From Sindbad's voyages, too, are cited examples to describe the "exotic marvelous." In this case, the listener is supposed to be ignorant of the remote regions that the sailor describes. He has no reason to doubt things with which he is unfamiliar. The "instrumental marvelous," however, denotes a different genre. As a term, it is applicable to such devices of magical nature, as the enchanted carpet and the healing apple in Prince Ahmed's story or the evolving stone in "Ali Baba" (*The Fantastic*, 54).

In analyzing the literary function of the "supernatural," Todorov explains that this element involves the collapse of limits between matter and mind and between the physical and spiritual. It claims its own conditioning laws that transcend our commonplace explanations of coincidence and chance. He cites the story of the second calender, the smitten son of a king into a monkey, to elaborate on the semantic function of the supernatural (*The Fantastic*, 107–10). In this tale, the realistic theme is sustained as long as the protagonist complies with certain taboos. Soon

[91] See Todorov, *The Fantastic*. Further citations are given in the text. See also Todorov, *The Poetics of Prose*, 66–79, for an analysis of actors as narrators. I make use here of an earlier article on "The Growth of Scholarly Interest."

[92] Although not a formalist, Andras Hamori deals with the story of "The Porter and the Three Ladies of Baghdad" from a similar perspective; see *On the Art of Medieval Arabic Literature* (Princeton, NJ: Princeton University Press, 1974), 164–80.

after violating them and transgressing the taboo of not messing with the supernatural, the latter intervenes in the shape of a wicked genie that is bent on punishing the princess hidden in the subterranean haven and her amorous companion. According to Todorov, the intrusion of the supernatural is a salient constant in the literature of the fantastic. Rather than merely symbolizing dreams of power, the existence of beings superior to us compensates for "a deficient causality." While most events in our daily life are explained by logical reasoning, many are inexplicable and, as such, are usually passed off as mere coincidence. Instances of coincidence or chance, however, have no place in the realm of the fantastic, for, although we tend to consider the intrusion of the genie upon the amorous frolic a sign of the calendar's bad luck, we have to realize that the protagonist herself/himself as well as her/his listeners consider this intrusion inevitable. To them, a conditioning and determining cause is no less so for being of a supernatural order (*The Fantastic*, 107–10).

Todorov assigns another function to the supernatural in imaginative writings. Apart from its literary significance, the supernatural is introduced as a cover to transgress institutionalized censorship or to escape self-imposed taboos. Nevertheless, as the nature of taboos varies from one society to another, the "social" function of the supernatural must be viewed in relation to the moral and religious standards of a given milieu. Thus, when considering the function of the supernatural in the Gothic romance or the *Nights*, we need to understand that the former was the product of a milieu that was puritan in its attitude toward sexual love. It should not be surprising, therefore, that, in the Gothic romance, the supernatural is usually used to elude such inhibitions and taboos. However, medieval Arabic fiction depicts a society that cherishes rather than condemns sexual love. Hence, the supernatural assumes another function. It is mainly introduced to transgress class distinctions and, thereby, to fulfill the protagonist's wish to marry the princess. In "Aladdin and the Wonderful Lamp," for example, Aladdin's love for the sultan's daughter "would have remained a dream forever without the intervention of the supernatural forces" (*The Fantastic*, 138; also 158–59, 166).

No less engaging is Todorov's discussion of the syntactical function of the supernatural, in which he cites a number of stories in which the supernatural intrudes to mobilize action and accelerate the narrative. In the story of Kamar al-Zaman (Figure 19), for instance, the imprisonment of the protagonist in the tower represents a static situation. However, as soon as the "jinniya" Maymūna intervenes, "the median disequilibrium" gives way to rapid action (*The Fantastic*, 164–65). The same explanation applies to the second calender's tale.

Figure 19 Arthur Boyd Houghton: The old gardener and Camaralzaman.

As long as the prince retains his sobriety and refrains from touching the talisman, he can live happily with the imprisoned princess. Such immobility means, however, the termination of the story, a thing that runs counter to the storyteller's design. To work out a good story, the narrator explains how a glass of wine provokes the prince into violating the ban and touching the genie's talisman, a move that brings about the intrusion of the genie to break the established equilibrium. In this, as in many other tales, the supernatural agency becomes identical with the artist's knack for storytelling. With this fact in mind, Todorov concludes that "every text in which the supernatural occurs is a narrative, for the supernatural event first of all modifies a previous equilibrium" (*The Fantastic*, 166).

It may be pertinent, and much in order, to reflect on the supernatural in the *Nights* in terms of its textual/contextual milieu. Abū Yaḥyā Zakariyā ibn Muḥammad ibn Maḥmūd al-Qazwīnī (ca. 1203–83 CE) composed his book *Kitāb ʿajāʾib al-makhlūqāt wa-gharāʾib al-mawjūdāt* (*Marvels of Creatures and Miracles of Things Existing*; a common short title is *The Wonders of Creation*), in Wasit, Iraq, in the mid-thirteenth century.[93] Homira Pashai sums up the significance of the work as follows:

> Qazwini's ʿAja'ib is a constant dialogue between contemplation and exploration; as Qazwini noted by contemplating the creation through the instrument of ʿulum (science) and purification of soul one can see the reality of the universe. Therefore, Qazwini's encyclopedia of natural history was a mirror to represent the divine unity through the multiplicity of the creation.

She continues, "Qazwini's boundless curiosity about science, history, geography, fantastic lands and creatures shaped the collective memory and imagination of generations of children and adults around the world." He describes the marvelous as "whatever is of less occurrence, strange to customary happenings and familiar scenes."[94] Among the unfamiliar or strange, al-Qazwīnī quotes from Yaʿqūb ibn Isḥāq al-Sarrāj a story reported by a merchant. He falls among strangers who crawl rather than walk. One of them almost strangles him with his legs when he asks the merchant to walk him around. The merchant cannot get rid of him until he distills for him grape juice that intoxicates the old man of the sea and causes him to relax his grip on the merchant's neck. Almost the same story occurs in the Sindbad tales (Būlāq, 2:26). Many reports and anecdotes in al-Qazwīnī's book of wonders resonate with tales in the *Nights*.[95]

Different from Todorov's structural approach, but indicative nonetheless of the increasing interest in the elemental charm of Scheherazade's art, are the early writings of such critics as Laura Spencer Portor, Forster, G. K. Chesterton, and P. H. Newby.[96] In his estimate of the irresistible

[93] al-Qazwīnī, *Kitāb ʿajāʾib*, 10–15. On original Arabic manuscripts, and the gorgeous illustrated ones, translated into Persian and Turkish, see Homira Pashai, "The Wonders of Creation," https://circulatingnow.nlm.nih.gov/2016/01/21/the-wonders-of-creation/. Manuscripts are at U.S. National Library of Medicine.

[94] al-Qazwīnī, *Kitāb ʿajāʾib*, 118; see also 150, 114–15, 108–9, respectively. For a discussion of the supernatural, and the marvelous, see Muḥsin Jāsim al-Mūsawī, "Makhābiʾ al-khayāl al-munthahil," in *Fī al-mutakhayyal al-ʿArabī* (Sousse, Tunis: 1995), 7–29.

[95] See al-Mūsawī, "Makhābiʾ al-khayāl," 7–29.

[96] See Laura Spencer Portor, "The Greatest Books of the World: The Arabian Nights," *Women's Home Companion* 40 (February 1913), 16; Chesterton, "The Everlasting Nights"; and P. H. Newby, "The 'Thousand and One Nights,'" *The Listener* 39 (January 29, 1948), 178–79.

appeal of this art, Newby elaborates on the most obvious thematic dimensions of the tales, stressing the obsession with luck, the belief in the supernatural, and the seeming indulgence in love and money fantasies. In these explications, as in his preference for the more realistic tales, Newby repeats what nineteenth-century critics have already said. What is new in his appraisal, however, is the awareness of the storyteller's extreme cynicism and raillery. Rather than mere willful fantasies, Newby traces in the *Nights* thematic patterns that are heavily charged with irony. According to the writer, the storyteller figures throughout as the "keenest mocker" of self-deceptions despite his seeming indulgence in agreeable illusions.

Both Portor and Chesterton were more attracted to the meaning of Scheherazade's experience as a storyteller. Early in the twentieth century, Portor regarded Scheherazade's involuted storytelling as no mere narrative thread. It is synonymous with the magic that permeates the whole work. As magic transforms the commonplace into lovely and majestic forms, so does Scheherazade's imagination recreate enchanting narratives from familiar themes, thereby engaging the sultan's attention and simultaneously transforming him into a perceptive admirer of literature. Portor's conclusion is not very different from Chesterton's estimate of Scheherazade's aesthetics. In "The Everlasting Nights," Chesterton looks upon the scenes of splendor in the *Nights* as symbols of the richness of life: "The richness of gold, silver, and jewels is a mere figure and representation of that which is the essential idea, the deep and enduring richness of life." Expounding on this point, he further explains that the "preciousness of emerald and amethyst and sandal-wood is only the parable and expression of the preciousness of stones, dust, and dogs running in the streets." The length of the tales is, therefore, essential to the meaning of the collection, for it signifies the devouring desire for life. As long as Scheherazade can engage the tyrant's attention and arouse his curiosity, she will continue to live:

> the tyrant can sway kingdoms and command multitudes, but he cannot discover exactly what happened to a fabulous prince or princess unless he asks for it. He has to wait, almost to fawn upon a wretched slave for the fag-end of an old-tale. Never in any other book, perhaps, has such a splendid tribute been offered to the pride and omnipotence of art.[97]

Chesterton was not the only one who dwelt on the aesthetic dimension of Scheherazade's experience. In his *Aspects of the Novel*, Forster had already elaborated on Scheherazade's capacity "to wield the weapon of suspense"

[97] Chesterton, *Spice of Life*, 58–60.

to escape her fate.[98] Although recognizing her other qualifications as an accomplished novelist (exquisite descriptions, tolerant judgments, ingenious incidents, advanced morality, vivid delineations of character, and expert knowledge of three Oriental capitals), Forster argues that Scheherazade "only survived because she managed to keep the king wondering what would happen next." Thus, in line with the general drift of his thesis, Forster cites her experience as conclusive testimony to the importance of a well-sustained narrative in novel writing.

Articles abound also on the subject of media and cinematic appropriation. No less visible is the belated awareness of Todorov's poetics, as carefully applied in Ghazoul's 1978 structural analysis; followed by Andras Hamori's analysis of some tales with a focus on repetition and interruption in the structure of the *Nights*; and David Pinault's study of techniques. Along with his book on the *Arabian Nights* in twentieth-century fiction, Richard van Leeuwen studies interruption, for example, "as a structuring principle, but also as a way to create a multi-layered perspective of reality and the suggestion of a rite of initiation."[99]

It is possible to place these analyses of narrative structuration under a number of headings: (1) narrative as loquacity and life, like Jean Pierre Picot's contribution;[100] (2) repetition as technique, as in Naddaff's *Arabesque*[101] and her article on magic;[102] Bonnie D. Irwin's reading of the hunchback cycle;[103] (3) narrative structural patterns, as in Pinault's book on techniques, and Eva Sallis's contribution on descriptive narrative, and a few other articles;[104] and (4) the fantastic as narrative, as in

[98] E. M. Forster, *Aspects of the Novel* (London: Penguin, 1927), 34. Further references are to this and the following page.

[99] Richard van Leeuwen, "The Art of Interruption: The Thousand and One Nights and Jan Potócki," *Journal Middle Eastern Literatures* 7, no. 2 (2004), 183–98.

[100] Jean Pierre Picot, "Silence de mort, parole de vie: Du recit cadre des Mille et Une Nuits," *Litteratures* 24 (Spring 1991), 13–27.

[101] Naddaff, *Arabesque*.

[102] Sandra Naddaff, "Magic Time: Narrative Repetition in the Thousand and One Nights," in *The 1001 Nights: Critical Essays and Annotated Bibliography*, ed. Kay Hardy Campbell, Ferial J. Ghazoul, Andras Hamori, Muhsin Mahdi, Christopher M. Murphy, and Sandra Naddaff (Cambridge, MA: Dar Mahjar, 1984), 41–57.

[103] Bonnie D. Irwin, "Framed (for) Murder: The Corpse Killed Five Times in the Thousand Nights and a Night," in *Telling Tales: Medieval Narratives and the Folk Tradition*, ed. Francesca Canadé Sautman, Diana Conchado, and Giuseppe Di Scipio (New York: St. Martin's Press, 1998), 155–70.

[104] Eva Sallis, "Playing on the Senses: Descriptive Narration in the Thousand and One Nights," *Journal of Semitic Studies* 45, no. 2 (Autumn 2000), 347–60. W. H. Trapnell, "Inexplicable Decisions in The Arabian Nights," *International Journal of Islamic and Arabic Studies* 10, no. 1 (1993), 1–12; Bonnie D. Irwin, "What's in a Frame? The Medieval Textualization of Traditional Storytelling," *Oral Tradition* 10, no. 1 (1995), 27–53; and Silvia Pavel, "La Proliferation narrative dans les 'Mile et une nuits,'" *Canadian Journal of Research in Semiotics* 2, no. 4 (Winter 1974), 21–40.

Todorov's indispensable reading. Under the same heading, we may cite Mikko Hakalin, "Flying Carpets and Talking Heads: The Elements of Fantasy and 'Science Fiction' in 1001 Night Stories."[105]

In addition, I should also draw attention to my own series of articles in the Egyptian quarterly *Fuṣūl*, also included in my book *Mujtamaʿ alf laylah wa-laylah*.[106] There I developed the argument that tokens, magical devices, food (especially defined dishes), painting, masks, and their like function with no less power than speech acts while sustaining verbal properties of narrative.[107] Although still undeveloped, some articles attempt to locate the *Nights* in a novelistic tradition. The attempt is worthwhile to pursue what Payne, Conant, Borges, and Byatt argue as a staple of a novelistic tradition.[108] The recurrence of novelistic elements in many tales should redirect our discussion of the art and develop broad cultural readings that can make use of anthropology to devise a poetics of great potentiality.

Cultural Criticism

The enormous focus on the visual arts in relation to the *Nights*, inclusive of print in Marshall McLuhan's groundbreaking *Gutenberg Galaxy*,[109] and the discursive analysis of issues of gender and race, and the politics of translation, all signify a noteworthy engagement with the *Nights*. This trend cannot be seen outside the rise of cultural studies, third-world feminisms, postcolonial theories, and the contributions of French, Italian, and German theorists. While French-oriented theory and, in particular, Foucault's reading of genealogy and discourse have left a visible mark on writings, the case is less so with the Frankfurt school of critical theory in Western academies, despite the fact that it had a better reception among the intelligentsia in the Arab world. A belated degree of attention probably began toward the end of the 1980s. Herbert Marcuse's early reading of the radical transformation in media and "technicity" and his singling out "women's liberation" movement, as being dynamic forces

105 Mikko Hakalin, "Flying Carpets and Talking Heads: The Elements of Fantasy and 'Science Fiction' in 1001 Night Stories," in *Studies in Folklore and Popular Religion*, ed. Ulo Valk (Tartu, Estonia: Department of Estonian and Comparative Folklore, University of Tartu, 1996), 81–85.

106 al-Mūsawī, *Mujtamaʿ*.

107 See also Muhsin Jassim al-Musawi, "Scheherazade's Nonverbal Narrative," *Journal of Arabic Literature* 36, no. 3 (2005), 338–62.

108 Valerie Porcello, "Slander and Continuity in the New Novel and the Old," *South Asian Review* 19, no. 16 (December 1995), 41–48; Walters, "Michel Butor."

109 Marshall McLuhan, *The Gutenberg Galaxy* (Toronto: University of Toronto Press, 1962).

in sociopolitical and economic transformation,[110] can also be traced in other domains of production, especially plastic arts, film industry, theater, and in some ways music. In other words, a cultural critique began to gather force in a post-May 1968 age. Under the rubric of cultural criticism, one may include feminist, psychological, sociological, linguistic, and social history writing and enunciation, and various visual arts. Examples in Arabic criticism abound, as some bibliographic entries at the end of this section indicate.[111] Raymond Williams tends to democratize culture, to move its discussion away from the penchant of high modernists like T. S. Eliot and F. R. Leavis.[112] Both Richard Hoggart and Williams look at cultural studies as a wide field because, for Hoggart, "culture" is "a whole way of life of a society, its beliefs, attitudes and temper as expressed in all kinds of structures, rituals and gestures, as well as in the traditionally defined forms of art."[113] In these, there is what Foucault calls "discursive formation," whenever "one can define a regularity (and order, correlations, positions and functionings, transformations)."[114] In every cultural manifestation, there is a narrative. Included under this rubric and also as a reflection on social science, we can draw attention to the recent exploration of Leo Strauss's papers that include a typescript of eighteen pages on the *Thousand and One Nights*, probably written in 1962.[115] The significance of the notes as preliminary material for a study of the *Nights* lies not only on how much light they shed on a scholar's mind that influenced generations of his students (including Mahdi, who lent his teacher Littmann's German translation of Calcutta II of the *Nights*), but also in their conversation with an increasing interest of American policymakers in the Middle East. As rightly argued by Namazi, the basic pattern that runs throughout the notes is Strauss's view of the *Nights* as a religio-political document that resorts to storytelling to protect its author from any repercussions. Strauss, who wrote and lectured on the renowned philosopher al-Fārābī (d. AD 950, Damascus), thinks that there is an underlying esotericism,

[110] https://plato.stanford.edu/entries/marcuse/.
[111] See also Akel, "Arabic Editions and Bibliography."
[112] Raymond Williams, *Culture and Society, 1780–1950* (London: Chatto and Windus, 1958); Raymond Williams, *Communications: Britain in the Sixties* (Harmondsworth, UK: Pelican-Penguin, 1968); and Raymond Williams, *Culture* (London: Fontana, 1981).
[113] Richard Hoggart, "Contemporary Cultural Studies: An Approach to the Study of Literature and Society," in *Contemporary Criticism*, ed. Malcolm Bradbury and David Palmer (London: Arnold, 1970), 156.
[114] Foucault, *Archaeology of Knowledge*, 38.
[115] Namazi, "Politics, Religion, and Love." For Leo Strauss's notes, see Leo Strauss Papers, box 20, folder 2, Special Collections Research Center, University of Chicago Library. Reproduced in full by Namazi.

a heterodox view in the tales, that speaks to the elect, not the common reader who takes them at their surface meaning. As argued by Ali A. Allawi in *The Occupation of Iraq*,[116] Strauss's unwavering faith in a leading conservative elite shows forth even in his reading of the *Arabian Nights*, which he reads as a sociopolitical document. Straussian thought is not an ordinary matter, not when perceived in relation to his disciples like Abram Shulsky in the Pentagon who was among the contributors to the project for the New American Century (PNAC). The road from *new* philology to a neoconservative discourse does not spare the *Nights*, as shown in Strauss's extensive notes. Strauss's notes lay emphasis on a number of thematic issues and leitmotifs, including patriarchy, authoritarianism, human intelligence, deception, jealousy, anger, demons and humans, slaves and masters, love, and everyday life practices as guiding thematic and structural patterns that run throughout the *Nights* in this late compilation. He also relates all these themes to the number of beggars, fools, barbers, jesters, and others whom he thinks the author of the *Nights* introduces as mouthpieces to distance his own position while enabling them to say what he cannot do in his own voice, thus escaping persecution while impacting the readership with his views. This line of thought coincides with Strauss's own ideas as expressed in *Persecution and the Art of Writing* (1952). He writes, "There would then be good reason for our finding in the greatest literature of the past so many interesting devils, madmen, beggars, sophists, drunkards, epicureans and buffoons."[117] Strauss's views and readings are more in tune with his own mind, not with current readings of the tales. They may prove of little use to scholarship on the *Nights*, but they surely convey a cultural turn in thought that reflects its own politico-religious interest in certain literatures and cultures. In Strauss's notes, the *Nights* loses innocence and storytelling forsakes its entertaining function to become a documentary record. Luckily, the cultural scene is wide enough to accommodate innovative explorations that try to regain for the *Nights* its earliest burgeoning.

As long as there is a counterview in the field, an argument against authoritative discourse, there is a possibility of further explorations in the *Nights*, as Tim Supple's production for the theater (Toronto, 2011) shows; or as Pasolini does in his swerve toward the marginalized groups that that have escaped the attention of cinematic production and also literary critics. Supple explains his purpose in producing the *Nights* for the

[116] Ali A. Allawi, *The Occupation of Iraq: Winning the War, Losing the Peace* (New Haven, CT, and London: Yale University Press, 2007), 81.

[117] Leo Strauss, *Persecution and the Art of Writing* (Chicago, IL: University of Chicago Press, 1952), 36.

theater as follows: "We are trying to create a theatrical version of *The Arabian Nights* which will do justice to the scale, depth, and richness of the stories."[118] Apart from his visits to the Middle East and North Africa to enroll actors, acrobats, and singers, he also worked with the Lebanese novelist Hanan al-Shaykh, "who spent last summer [2010] reading all 1,001 stories in their original Arabic."[119] Mark Brown adds: "Supple wants to try to discover the lost truths of the stories." Indeed, the version was a departure from other Western productions. The director tried to illustrate the hidden power of the *Nights* by minimizing the erotic, exhilarating action, using dance, collapsing stories, and creating an impression whereby an archetypal narrator, Scheherazade, presides with a mixture of certainty and apprehension. As I mentioned to Supple in a panel that was held after the first part show in Toronto, his Scheherazade shares the characteristics of some of al-Shaykh's women, usually held in suspense between desire and fear of male encroachment.[120] By sticking to the earliest Arabic version, without relying on the sensational orphan tales that have preoccupied cinema and theater production, Supple offers an alternative theater in line with alternative cinema. In *Visual Pleasure and Narrative Cinema* (1975), Laura Mulvey argues that "[t]he alternative cinema provides a space for the birth of a cinema which is radical in both a political and an aesthetic sense and challenges the basic assumptions of the mainstream film."[121] While the focus on Hollywood as a starting point for discussion allows space for alternatives in the same domain and outside it, Ella Shohat connects the issue to a broad cultural dynamic whereby a dominating and authoritative discourse allows less space for alternatives. Hence, she sees popular culture in the West as being imbued with "Eurocentric discursive continuum" in every field of knowledge.[122] This critical drive in visual culture is also in line with the feminist radicalization of the hermeneutics of the *Nights* as no less deserving of explicatory investigation than any other epochal production. In this sense,

[118] Mark Brown, "Tim Supple's Epic Odyssey to Create a New Arabian Nights," *The Guardian*, March 29, 2009, www.theguardian.com/stage/2009/mar/30/arabian-nights-theatre-midsummer-dream. The London-based Dash Arts project was funded by the Luminato festival in Toronto. The production premiered in June 2011.

[119] Hanan al-Shaykh has her version of the *Nights*, *One Thousand and One Nights* (London: Bloomsbury, 2011), upon which the adaptation for the stage was done with Tim Supple, *One Thousand and One Nights* (London: Methuen Drama, 2011).

[120] al-Shaykh and Supple, *One Thousand and One Nights*.

[121] Laura Mulvey, *Visual and Other Pleasures* (London: Macmillan, 1989), cited in *A Critical and Cultural Theory Reader*, ed. Anthony Easthope and Kate McGowan (Toronto: Toronto University Press, 2002), 159.

[122] See Ella Shohat, "Gender and Culture of Empire: Towards a Feminist Ethnography of the Cinema," in *Visions of the East: Orientalism in Film*, ed. Matthew Bernstein and Gaylyn Studlar (London: I.B. Tauris, 1997), 19–66.

cultural criticism opens up further venues to examine the *Nights* as a complex creation. The variety in approaches draws attention to the text as a rich field that provokes and invites engagement. As early as 1991, Fedwa Malti-Douglas devotes a chapter, "Narration and Desire: Shahrazād," to the frame story. She argues her case against a number of writers and approaches, for Scheherazade is not only a narrator, but "also a sexual being, who manipulates discourse (and men) through her body. It is the latter that permits her to speak, as male violence is met with her sexuality, articulated through her body and her words."[123] This is Malti-Douglas's stepping-stone, used to critique a large body of criticism by André Miquel, Jamel Eddine Benccheikh, Edgar Weber, Gerhardt, Bruno Bettelheim, and Jerome W. Clinton for being "prefeminist and pre-gender conscious, in the intellectual, not the chronological sense."[124] They either present Scheherazade as a "being of desire (or equating her with speech)," or "confining her to the role of healer." In both cases, this reading "draws attention away from both the strength of her personality and her mastery of the situation, while occulting male-female dynamics."[125] Malti-Douglas does not spare "the noted Moroccan feminist, Fatima Mernissi," who comes up with the idea that Scheherazade is "an innocent young girl whom a fatal destiny led to Chahrayar's bed," and whose "achievement" is "the miraculous triumph of the innocent."[126] This is a significant critique, in that it shifts the argument with respect to the frame tale to the issue of roles: Scheherazade has to undo "the lessons that have been instilled by another woman, the ʿifrīt companion." She and her sister "act as pair in the transition from sex to text,"[127] in a way that balances and also dislodges the homosocial desire connecting the two brothers. In this intervention and also in her "Shahrazad Feminist,"[128] Malti-Douglas develops a reading that other scholars have to reckon with when writing the dynamics of the frame tale. Having said that, there are some limitations that question such a reading: It focuses on a frame tale, the assumption being that it was in whole or in part of an Arabo-Islamic orientation. Malti-Douglas asserts that "the frame of the *Nights* is certainly in the Islamic mainstream."[129] There is also the underlying understanding that the frame tale converses with every other tale in the collection. While the frame encapsulates and informs an accretive process, the role of storytellers before the circulation of a creditable version cannot be underestimated. Malti-Douglas draws attention, however, to the presence of Scheherazade in her multiple roles,

[123] Malti-Douglas, *Woman's Body, Woman's Word*, 11. [124] Ibid., 13.
[125] Ibid., 12–13. [126] Ibid., 13. [127] Ibid., 23.
[128] Malti-Douglas, "Shahrazad Feminist."
[129] Malti-Douglas, *Woman's Body, Woman's Word*, 24.

a point that can be corroborated by the large number of articles that have Scheherazade as narrator, artist, and woman in their titles.[130] On the positive side, there is a movement toward exploring issues of gender, race, color, class, and other social and political issues that place the *Nights* at the center of humanities and social science.[131] Although marginalizing

[130] Gordon Poole, "The Drunken Scheherazade: Self Reflection in Jack London's The Road, Martin Eden and John Barleycorn," *RSA Journal: Rivista di Studi Nord Americani* 1 (1990), 69–80; David Gurewich, "Piccadilly's Scheherazade," *The New Criterion* 7, no. 7 (March 1989), 68–72; Gabriella Bedetti, "Women's Sense of the Ludicrous in John Barth's 'Dunyazadiad,'" *Studies in American Humor* 4, no. 1–2 (Spring–Summer 1985), 74–81; Patrick O'Neill, "The Scheherazade Syndrome: Gunter Grass' Mega Novel Der Butt," in *Adventures of a Flounder: Critical Essays on Gunter Grass' Der Butt*, ed. Gertrud Bauer Pickar (Munich: Fink, 1982), 1–15; Silvian Iosifescu, "Scheherazade 1977," *La Revue d'Esthetique* 31, no. 3–4 (1978), 234–41; Philip Stevick, "Scheherazade Runs Out of Plots, Goes on Talking; the King, Puzzled, Listens: An Essay on New Fiction," *TriQuarterly* 26 (1973), 332–62; Borisalva Sasic, "Nuruddin Farah's Sardines: The Construction of a Somali Novel on the Intersection of Transcultural Intertextuality," in *Across the Lines: Intertextuality and Transcultural Communication in the New Literatures in English*, ed. Wolfgang Kloss (Amsterdam: Rodopi, 1998), 167–74; and in relation to modes of writing and serialized models, Georges May, "Scheherazade et la paralitterature: Melanges de litt. gen. & de crit. romanesque offerts au Professeur Henri Coulet par ses amis," in *Lettres et réalités* (Aix-en-Provence: PU de Provence, 1988), 227–45.

[131] See, for example, Eliana S. Rivero, "Scheherazade Liberated: Eva Luna and Women Storytellers," in *Splintering Darkness: Latin American Women Writers in Search of Themselves*, ed. Cunningham Lucia Guerra (Pittsburgh, PA: Latin American Literary. Review, 1990), 143–56; Samar Attar and Gerhard Fischer, "Promiscuity, Emancipation, Submission: The Civilizing Process and the Establishment of a Female Role Model in the Frame-Story of *1001 Nights*," *Arab Studies Quarterly* 13, no. 3–4 (1991), 1–17; Judith Grossman, "Infidelity and Fiction: The Discovery of Women's Subjectivity in Arabian Nights," *The Georgia Review* 34 (1980), 113–36; Afsaneh Najmabadi, "Reading and Enjoying 'Wiles of Women' Stories as a Feminist," *Iranian Studies: Journal of the Society for Iranian Studies* 32, no. 2 (Spring 1999), 203–22; Lisa R. Perfetti, "Men's Theories, Women's Laughter: The Thousand and One Nights and Women's Comic Pleasures in Medieval Literature," *Exemplaria: A Journal of Theory in Medieval and Renaissance Studies* 10, no. 2 (Fall 1998), 207–41; Arthur J. Weitzman, "Scheherazade's Risk: Male Voyeurism and the Female Narrative Gambit," in *1650–1850: Ideas, Aesthetics, and Inquiries in the Early Modern Era*, ed. Kevin J. Cope et al. (New York: AMS, 2000), 151–61; Michel Matarasso, "In Praise of Double Sexuality in The Thousand and One Nights: The Geste of Boudour," *Diogenes* 118 (Summer 1982), 2–48; Kathrin Müller und Anton Spitaler, "Da war ihm, als müsse er fliegen vor Freuden: 'Tausendundeine Nacht'," *Fundus für arabische Phraseologie* (Munich: Verlag der Bayerischen Akademie der Wissenschaften, 2001); and Daniel Beaumont, "King, Queen, Master, and Slave: The Master/Slave Dialectic and The Thousand and One Nights," *Neophilologus* 82, no. 3 (July 1998), 335–56. Earlier, we have two important works by Andras Hamori: "The Magian and the Whore: Readings of Qamar al-Zaman," in *The 1001 Nights*, 25–40, and *On the Art of Medieval Arabic Literature*.

the literariness of the tales, these engagements highlight the place of the *Nights* in interdisciplinary studies.[132]

History as Narrative and Narrative as History

This is a problematic aspect of the *Nights*, simply because it relates to the history of the composition, its accretion over time but especially in the ninth to tenth centuries, and also because little analysis has been done to situate the collection properly in the history domain. There is an overlap between history and some tales in the collection. Amedroz's article "A Tale of the Arabian Nights Told as History"[133] represents a pioneering effort. Special mention should be made here of Mahdi's article "From History to Fiction: The Tale Told by the King's Steward in the *Thousand and One Nights*," which builds on Amedroz's previous study.[134] In *Mujtamaʿ alf laylah wa-laylah* (*The Society of the Thousand and One Nights*), I have cited a number of overlapping tales, and the surprising documentary and descriptive material involved in narrative, albeit with anachronisms that speak of storytellers' intrusions. Jamel Eddine Bencheikh and A. Gerard Gauntlett offer gleanings of some value on the disparity between the realistic and fictional in "Historical and Mythical Baghdad in the Tale of Ali b. Bakkar and Shams al-Nahar: Or, the Resurgence of the Imaginary."[135] The overlapping of history and fiction in a large number of tales takes a number of directions: There are historical narratives taken by storytellers from historical accounts related to prominent individuals like ʿUmar ibn al-Nuʿmān that combine anecdotal quality and powerful dramatic events. There are also historical anecdotes based in an affluent society such as Baghdad and Basrah, like the story of Ḍamrah, narrated by the poet al-Ḥusayn ibn al-Ḍaḥḥāk.

132 Mīkhāʾīl ʿAwwād, *Alf laylah wa-laylah, mirʾāt al-haḍārah* (Baghdad: Wizārat al-Thaqāfah, 1962); al-Qalamāwī, *Alf laylah wa-laylah*; Bin Ḥasan al-Munsif, *al-ʿAbīd wa-al-jawārī fī ḥikāyāt alf laylah wa-laylah* (Tunis: Sirās li-l-Nashr, 1994); Fāṭimah Hājī, *al-Qaṣaṣ al-shaʿbī fī alf laylah wa-laylah fī masrah al-ṭifl bi-l-Kuwayt: Namūdhaj masrahīyat al-Shātir Ḥasan taʾlīf al-Sayyid Ḥāfiẓ* (Alexandria: Markaz al-Diltā li-l-Ṭibāʿah, 1991); ʿAbd al-Ghanī Mallāh, *Riḥlah hadāriyyah wa-lamahāt turāthiyyah ʿabra alf laylah wa-laylah* (Baghdad: Dār al-Kitāb al-Jadīd, 1977); al-Mūsawī, *Mujtamaʿ*; Aḥmad Muḥammad Shaḥḥādh, *al-Malāmiḥ al-siyāsiyyah fī ḥikāyāt alf laylah wa-laylah* (Baghdad: Wizārat al-Thaqāfah wa-l-Iʿlām, Dār al-Shuʾūn al-Thaqāfiyyah al-ʿĀmmah, 1986); Muḥammad ʿAbd al-Raḥmān Yūnus, *al-Jins wa-al-sulṭah fī alf laylah wa-laylah* (Beirut: Muʾassasat al-Intishār al-ʿArabī, 1998); and Iḥsān Sarkīs, *Al-Thunāʾiyyah fī alf laylah wa-laylah* (Beirut: 1979).

133 Amedroz, "A Tale of the Arabian Nights."

134 Mahdi, "From History to Fiction." Also, in his *The Thousand and One Nights*, 165–80.

135 Jamel Eddine Bencheikh and A. Gerard Gauntlett, "Historical and Mythical Baghdad in the Tale of Ali b. Bakkar and Shams al-Nahar: Or, the Resurgence of the Imaginary," in *The Thousand and One Nights in Arabic Literature and Society*, 14–28.

Other tales that have an urban quality and take place in Cairo, Damascus, Baghdad, and Basra, including tales of love, adventure, or tricksters, jesters, barbers, merchants, *qāḍīs*, and craftsmen and professionals, are also historical and become part of the storytellers' material as dramatic tales dealing with vicissitudes of fortune and surprising events. Even tales that are corroborated by *ḥadīth*, like those of Khurāfah, assume the power of history for being authenticated by a prophetic tradition, authentic or fabricated. No wonder, then, that a number of books in Arabic address the "realistic" side of *A Thousand and One Nights* as being no less relevant than history proper.

However, Payne, Borges, Byatt, and many others have thought of the *Nights* as central to a novelistic tradition. In terms of cycles, involuted or embedded narrative and long stories like "Abū Khayr and Abū Ṣayr" (Būlāq, no. 928) have the properties of a short novel.[136] But the issue of narrative, historical and novelistic, is even more complicated in the case of the *Nights* than what Hayden White suggests in his Northrop Frye application of modes of emplotment in *Metahistory* (1973) (romance, tragedy, comedy, and satire), tropes (metaphor, metonymy, synecdoche, and irony), and modes of explanation by emplotment that imposes a form on "unprocessed" material, or by "formal argument" and ideological implication. White's argument tends toward better recognition of the creative factor in historical accounts.[137] Many tales of historical substance can conform easily to this accommodation.

The multivalent and multifarious composition defies categories and motif indices unless these are applied to specific tales.[138] Todorov is aware of that as his selective use of specific cases of the fantastic or narrative men makes clear. When we think of the composite nature of the *Nights* in relation to a worldwide novelistic referentiality, and its massive use by novelists and other writers and poets, we confront an issue that requires a different understanding of the novel as no longer a bourgeois epic, but rather a mosaic of texts and quotations that leave the well-wrought tale to the film industry.

[136] See al-Mūsawī, *al-Riwāyah al-'Arabiyyah*, 18–22. On the application of the term "short novel" to long tales, see Roger Allen, "The Novella in Arabic: A Study in Fictional Genres," *International Journal of Middle Eastern Studies* 18, no. 4 (November 1986), 473–84.

[137] Hayden White, *Metahistory: The Historical Imagination in 19th-Century Europe* (Baltimore, MD: Johns Hopkins University Press, 1973); see also Hayden White, *Tropics of Discourse: Essays in Cultural Criticism* (Baltimore, MD: Johns Hopkins University Press, 1978).

[138] Hasan al-Shamy, *A Motif Index of The Thousand and One Nights* (Bloomington, IN: Indiana University Press, 2006); and before him, Nikita Elisséeff, *Thèmes et motifs des Mille et une Nuits: Essai de Classification* (Beirut: Institut français de Damas, 1949).

Edited compilations and translations, corroborated by essays or footnotes, played a major role in impacting literary/historical recapitulations of the *Nights*. Patterns of relation and reaction to academic and critical investigations involved in historicizations mark a large portion of literary production in the early decades of the twentieth century. In such a consummate exercise in Oriental exoticism as Flecker's *Hassan*, for instance, the reader will notice that the author's picture of the caliph is inspired by a late nineteenth-century view of Hārūn al-Rashīd as less just and wise than Alfred Lord Tennyson's idealized hero.[139] Impressed perhaps by Payne's analysis of Hārūn's character, Flecker has willfully manipulated his source (the tale of Aladdin Abū al-Shamat) to present the caliph in a very unfavorable light.[140] An entirely different literary recreation of the Orient is Chesterton's deliberate use in "Lepanto" of a medieval image of the Muslim faith. Reacting to the accumulation of factual and historical information about Islam and the Arabs, Chesterton in that poem seizes upon an obsolete convention to retain a clerical picture of the Muslim East.[141]

In line with these early literary recreations, but more closely related to their authors' everyday experiences, are the attempts on the part of some modern storytellers to emulate Scheherazade's hypnotic art. Although no less dissatisfied with his reading public than was Poe,[142] William Sidney Porter (O. Henry) continued to derive inspiration from the *Nights*. Mainly

[139] On Flecker's grounding in Oriental studies, see Geraldine Hodgson, *The Life of James Elroy Flecker* (Oxford: Basil Blackwell, 1925).

[140] It is worth mentioning that Yeats strongly disapproved of Flecker's misrepresentation of the caliph's character, condemning *Hassan* as "nothing but the perversity and petulance of the disease from which its author was already fading." In Yeats's opinion, the *Nights* provides sufficient testimony to the amiability and justice of the caliph: "we know Harun al-Rashid through the *Arabian Nights* alone, and there he is the greatest of all traditional images of generosity and magnanimity"; "On the Boiler," in William Butler Yeats, *Explorations* (London: Macmillan, 1962), 447–48. For more on Yeats's poetry and the caliph's gift, see William Butler Yeats, "The Gift of Harun al-Rashid," first published in 1924 in *The Dial, Corps écrits* 31 (1989), 63–75.

[141] See *Collected Poems* (London: Cecil Palmer, 1927), 100–103. Chesterton's image of the East is worth contrasting with that of Kipling. Especially in *Kim*, Kipling manifests some intimacy with the Orient that also contrasts quite sharply with the apathetic attitudes of Southey and Moore. In this story, the exotic is absorbed into the homely and the whole picture overflows with liveliness and breathes robust understanding of other manners. After reading the story, the reader may feel, however, that Kipling's view is fixed within the larger imperialist contention that the East is a component part of the British Empire, known and cherished as such. See *Kim* (1908; repr. London: Macmillan, 1930).

[142] Although Poe's "Thousand-and-Second Tale of Scheherazade" is often cited as a parody of Scheherazade's framing tale in the *Nights*, it was meant as "a parable which deplores the plight of the story-teller, Poe himself, in the modern world." After listening with due admiration to her early stories, the king was outraged when she reported modern discoveries and inventions. Consequently, Poe's storyteller was bowstrung. According to Cecil, "the bowstringing of the modernized Scheherazade

fascinated by the caliph's role in this collection, Porter reads in the former's nocturnal adventures an expression of the Arabian storyteller's search for subject matter on the streets of Baghdad. These same adventures have suggested to Porter the idea of roaming his own "Baghdad-on-the-Subway" (as he used to call New York), looking for incidents and detail:

> You may be familiar with the history of that glorious and immortal ruler, the Caliph Harun Al Rashid, whose wise and beneficent excursions among his people in the city of Baghdad secured him the privilege of relieving so much of their distress. In my humble way, I walk in his footsteps. I seek for romance and adventure in city streets – not in ruined castles or in crumbling palaces.[143]

With Marcel Proust, Butor, and many others, authors or narrators exchange roles with Scheherazade. But instead of Poe's situational ironies and the feigned shock at the achievements of science, or Théophile Gautier's equation of a ruthless and demanding sultan and the penchant of a reading public for *feuilletoniste*,[144] the twentieth-century writer struggles with a fear of loss of the creative impulse, a point that this book has already considered. Postmodernists find an escape in parody, as Barth does.[145] Without saying as much, Barth only retraces Richard Moulton, who advised students of literature to return to the *Nights*, for "it alone brings us in touch ... with the processes of evolution which built up romance ... [and as such] has ... great interest for the student of literary form."[146] Comparing Barth to writers like Walter de la Mare is valuable as a way of understanding parody in relation to the art of storytelling as perceived and admired by a generation of writers who regard narrative as an art that needs no contextualization. Using "The Porter and the Three Ladies of Baghdad" to explain his point, de la Mare argues that

suggests ... Poe's own failure to gain admiration and support as an author in his day." Cecil, "Poe's 'Arabesque,'" 62–63.

In "A Madison Square Arabian Night," Porter is disillusioned with the public demand for mere amusement. Plumer the painter, who undertakes Scheherazade's role in the same story, explained how, after being a fashionable painter, he suddenly found himself out of business because he "had a knack of bringing out in the face of a portrait the hidden character of the original." People, he concluded, "don't want their secret meanness shown up in a picture." *The Trimmed Lamp* (New York: Doubleday, 1919), 28–29.

143 William Sidney Porter (O. Henry), "A Bird of Baghdad," in *Strictly Business* (New York: Doubleday, 1919), 188.

144 Évanghélia Stead, "On Inefficient Arabian Nights Tales: Théophile Gautier's 'The Thousand and Second Nights,'" *Middle Eastern Literatures* 19, no. 1 (2016), 99–110.

145 See Barth, *Chimera*, 20.

146 Richard Moulton, *World Literature* (New York: Macmillan, 1927), 306.

two black dogs are barbarously beaten with rods, their tears and lamentations are kissed away, the porter egged on by his betters, addressed but one intrusive little question to the fair ladies, and presto, all but a round dozen of narratives, opening out like incense – breathing water-lilies on some moon-haunted swamp, break one after another into full bloom under our noses.[147]

Barth is different. He is more concerned with a "parodic stylization," the double-voicing discussed by Bakhtin that distances the author, but clashes nevertheless with its original.[148] Finally, Barth's attempt to refract a historical context in the *Last Voyage*, to predicate it on another text that has the crucial years of the 1980s as a point of collision, downplays Scheherazade's original. In Bakhtin's analysis of parodic stylization, "The novelistic discourse dominating a given epoch is itself turned into an object and itself becomes a means of refracting new authorial intentions."[149] Experimentations with the *Nights*, starting with the New Novel (*nouveau roman*) and Butor (d. 2016) in particular,[150] are bound to conclude with Barth's parodic stylization, giving way to other forms of linkage with the *Arabian Nights* and its differential cycles.

147 de la Mare, "The Thousand and One," 70.
148 Mikhail Bakhtin, "Discourse in the Novel," in *The Dialogic Imagination: Four Essays*, ed. Michael Holquist, trans. Carl Emerson and Mikhail Holquist (Austin, TX: University of Texas Press, 1981), 306.
149 Ibid., 309.
150 Walters, "Michel Butor"; Pauliny, "Adaptation oder Übersetzung?"; see also Porcello, "Slander and Continuity."

A Way to Conclude?

If we agree with the readings of the additional One Night, its suggestions of ad infinitum, we may, then, conclude that Scheherazade's art resists closure. Its power derives from an accrual that implies a contrapuntal displacement and replacement invited by readership over time. Jorge Luis Borges's insertion of his tale in a collection in Spanish is not different from Barth's claims to have Dunyazade as storyteller rather than interlocutor or listener.[151] Nor is it different from Burton's insertion of many tales in his "unexpurgated" version. An incitement to participate in Scheherazade's anecdotal "feast" took place in Arabic throughout the ninth to fourteenth centuries. The *Nights* had to undergo another process of mediation, appropriation, imitation, and accretion when transferred to other languages. Because there is no definitive text, the *Nights* turned into a textual banquet. Although the analogy was used by Abū Muḥammad ibn Qutaybah (d. 889) for his *ʿUyūn al-akhbār* (*Springs of Information*; i.e., the best anecdotes), it might well apply to the *Nights*. He says, "This book is like a feast with different dishes as befitting the tastes and likings of guests." As such, "it is not meant to be solely for the seeker of this world, nor the seeker of the next. It is not solely for a privileged group at the expense of common people, nor for royalty to the exclusion of the rabble."[152] However, diverging from Ibn Qutaybah's collection of anecdotes is Scheherazade's treasury of other tropes like the Barmicide's (Barmakī's) imaginary feast to his guest, the barber's sixth brother (Figure 20). The Barmicide entertains guests with his imaginary banquet, an ironic playing out of the disaster that befell the family in 803, and left the remaining ones destitute.[153] As the tale has it, the barber's sixth brother has his counterresponse that ends up with an imaginary drunkenness that lets him raise his arm and "suddenly hit the host on the back of the neck," telling the Barmakī: "My lord, you have admitted your slave into your house, fed him, and given him wine to drink until he became drunk and unmannerly. You should be the first to tolerate his foolishness and pardon his offense."[154] Like the sumptuous feast, the *Nights*, in its Arabic growth or migration to other lands and languages, and subsequent

[151] Richard Burton and Jorge Luis Borges, *Las mil y una noches según Burton* (Madrid: Ediciones Siruela, 1985).

[152] Cited in al-Musawi, *The Islamic Context of the Thousand and One Nights*, 229.

[153] Julie Scott Meisami, "Masʿūdī on Love and the Fall of the Barmakids," *Journal of the Royal Asiatic Society* 2 (1989), 252–77; and Philip Kennedy, "The Fall of the Barmakids in Historiography and Fiction: Recognition and Disclosure," *Journal of Abbasid Studies* 3, no. 2 (2016), 167–238.

[154] For a discussion, and quotes, see al-Musawi, *The Islamic Context of the Thousand and One Nights*, 192.

Figure 20 Arthur Boyd Houghton: The barber's sixth brother, Shacbac, knocks down the Barmicide.

afterlife, invites translators, editors, redactors, film producers, illustrators, and media experts as guests and hosts to excercise an accrual of one sort or another. Fiction writers as well as poets, film producers, and painters have developed a composed attitude toward the *Nights*, simply because the extra One Night is an invitation to infinite appropriation and joy.

The implications of these stylistic and thematic engagements are many, and they suggest in turn the richness of a book that is much larger than its material and physical size. To sum up the elemental aesthetic fecundity of the *Arabian Nights* is almost beyond reach, not only because a constellation of knowledge has been growing around it, but also because its advent in Europe, and in France, England, and Germany in particular, touched sensitive chords and set up lines of discussion or narrative that were conversant with cultural transformations. Let's take the issue of licentiousness or coarse language that was raised against it in early Victorian England as an example: We know that Galland sanitized many passages, but the mid-nineteenth-century paterfamilias and the bourgeois sense of decorum required somebody like Lane to do further trimming and sanitization, "intensifying people's sense of it [sex] as a constant danger, and this in turn created a further incentive to talk about it."[155] Payne, Mardrus, Burton, and Littmann made use of that incentive to meet a demand to talk and discuss sex. Burton's "Biography of the Book and Its Reviewers Reviewed" sums up the raging controversy that takes the body of the *Nights* as battleground. As a site of displacement whereby British issues with prudery can be predicated on another culture, the *Nights* in its late nineteenth- and early twentieth-century versions allows sex to be "driven out of hiding and constrained to lead a discursive existence."[156]

This is only one index in the history of the *Night*s in Europe. Galland was not desperate to justify his new venture after the success of his translation of "The Seven Voyages of Sindbad the Sailor" (1701). He had to explain in the preface, however, that *Contes Arabes* is unsurpassed narrative, and that it also reflects manners and customs. His early or late contemporaries like Voltaire, Montesquieu, Addison, and Steele were given to discursive satire, moralism, and instruction. They used the mediated text of the *Thousand and One Nights* (*Arabian Nights*) as a forum for reaching their reading public. In other words, their works are discursive, that is, not poetic or literary, practices, unlike William Beckford's *Vathek*. The latter, along with a pre-Romantic movement, signals an inauguration of language as literature. Hence, the centrality of "the book" in a growing literary tradition; and hence its enormous appeal to such literary icons like Samuel Taylor Coleridge, John Keats, Hunt, Goethe, Tennyson, George Meredith, William Henley, James Joyce, Proust, and almost every prominent writer in Europe before the book could make its way to other continents and cultures. Foucault's conclusion with respect to issues of language, discourse, and literature may well apply to that enchantment of the *Nights* at the turn of the eighteenth century and after, its formative and also popular appeal: "It may be said in a sense that 'literature,' as it was constituted and so designated on the threshold of the modern age, manifests, at a time

[155] Foucault, *The History of Sexuality*, 1:31. [156] Ibid., 35.

when it was least expected, the reappearance, of the living being of language." Arguing against the separation of words from signified in discourse throughout the sixteenth century, he explains the poetic retention of language since the late eighteenth century as follows: "[H]enceforth, language was to grow with no point of departure, no end, and no promise. It is the traversal of this futile yet fundamental space that the text of literature traces from day to day."[157] Every engagement with the *Nights* becomes basically poetic. Even neoclassicists like Walter Bagehot had to recall that early aesthetic experience of reading the tales before the takeover of a rationality that prompts a discursive analysis. The same applies to Lane. His omissions notwithstanding, he offers a literary text while relegating the explanatory surplus to the margins.

Does the *Nights* in its multiple translations or appropriations, then, signal a literary phenomenon? If so, as shown in the enormous body of literature around it and the massive use of its properties in audiovisual and also virtual space, does the same apply to its genealogy in Arabic, ancient and modern? Although partly raised by Bonebakker,[158] the question is irrelevant, not only because it was not thought of in its storytelling concoction as belles lettres, or refined literary or prose writing, but also because we have no extant manuscripts other than Nabia Abbott's early ninth-century fragment, and Galland's fourteenth-century one. Hence, we are left with a few substantial and robust pieces of evidence, but a large body of conjectures. In conclusion, the One in the title turns into a talisman that resists containment.

[157] Foucault, *The Order of Things*, 300.

[158] Seeger Adrianus Bonebakker, "Nihil obstat in Storytelling?" in *The Thousand and One Nights in Arabic Literature and Society*, 56–77. He argues, "If one defines adab literature as collections of prose and poetry of artistic merit and, at the same time, embodying the old Arab traditions in the widest sense – moral, social, ethical, stylistic, and educational – The Thousand and One Nights clearly falls short of meriting the title adab" (70).

Appendix A: Editions Worldwide

Major Editions, Popular Abridgments, and Famous Illustrated Copies

This appendix dealing with editions consists of eighteenth-, nineteenth-, and twentieth-century Arabic, European, and Asian translations of the tales and their significant abridgments, excluding reprints, reissues, adaptations, and passing imitations which the interested can easily find in the British Museum and the Library of Congress catalogs of printed books as well as in the bibliographic aids and the Internet. Significant imitations and appropriations are included. Lists are under title, and names of translators and editors are arranged under authors for convenient cataloging. Whenever a second name comes before or after primary translators (Galland, Lane, Payne, Burton, etc.), he/she is an editor, secondary translator, or illustrator. On the other hand, some reprints recur as indices of literary taste. The listing minimizes transliteration to enable accessibility. It stops at 2008.

Arabic

Alf layla wa-laylah. Calcutta: The Asiatic Lithographic Company, 1829.
Bulaq: 1836.
Mumbai: Maṭbaʿat al-Ḥaydrī, 1879.
Miṣr: Maṭbaʿat al-Hilāl, 1922.
Cairo: Dār al-Hilāl, 1956.
Cairo: Dār al-Hilāl, 1958.
Miṣr: Maṭbaʿat al-Ḥalabī, 1960.
Cairo: Dār al-Hilāl, 1966.
Beirut: Sharikat al-Maṭbūʿat, 1995.
Beirut: Dār Ṣādir, 1999.
Miṣr: Dār al-Maʿārif, 1952.
Cairo: Muʾassasat Rūz al-Yūsuf, 1960–69?
Beirut: al-Maṭbaʿah al-Kathūlikiyyah li-l-Ābāʾ al-Yasūʿiyyīn, 1888–90.

Alf laylah wa-laylah: Min al-mubtadaʾ ilā al-muntahā: ṭabʿah muṣawwarah ʿan ṭabʿat Brislaw, ed. Christian Maximilian Habicht and Fleischer Heinrich Leberech. Cairo: Dār al-Kutub wa-l-Wathāʾiq al-Qawmiyyah, 1998.

Alf laylah wa-laylah, aʿnī, kitāb alf laylah wa-laylah yudʿā ʿumuman Asmar al-layali li-l-ʿArab mimma yataḍammanu al-fukahah wa-yurathu al-tarab, ed. W. H. Macnaghten. Calcutta: Thacker, 1839–42.

Alf laylah wa-layla or, The Arabian Nights Entertainments in the Original Arabic, ed. Ahmad ibn Mohammed Shirwanī. Calcutta: Hindoostanee Press, 1818.

Alf laylah wa-laylah: Wa-at al-ḥāwadith al-ʿajībah wa-l-qiṣaṣ al-muṭribah al-gharībah. Miṣr: Maktabat wa-Maṭbaʿat Muḥammad ʿAlī Subayḥ wa-Awlāduh, 1800–1899.

Alf laylah wa-laylah. al-Ṭabʿah al-ūlā, ṭubiʿa bi-maṭbaʿat Būlāq sanat 1252 Hijriyyah: Muqābalah wa-taṣḥīḥ Muḥammad Qitah ʿAdwī. Baghdad: Maktabat al-Muthannā, 1964.

Alf laylah wa-laylah: Dhāt al-nawādith al-ʿajībah, wa-qiṣaṣ al-maṭrabah al-gharībah, lialiha gharām fī gharām, ḥasab wa-ʿishq, wa-hiyām, ḥikāyat wa-nawādir fukahiyyah wa-laṭāʾif wa-ṭarāʾif adabiyyah, min ʿabdʾa mā kān min ʿajāʾib al-zamān. Beirut: Dār al-Hudā al-Waṭniyyah, 1981.

Alf laylah wa laylah: Ḥikāyat ʿajībah, qiṣaṣ gharībah, ḥubb wa-ʿishq, ḥikāyat wa-nawādir fukahiyyah, laṭāʾif wa-ṭarāʾif adabiyyah, uʿjubah min ʿajāʾib al-zamān. Beirut. Dār al-Tawfīq li-l-Ṭibāʿah wa-l-Nashr wa-l-Tawzīʿ, 1979.

Alf laylah wa-laylah: Ḥawādith ʿajībah, qiṣaṣ gharībah, ḥubb wa-ʿishq, ḥikāyat wa-nawādir fukahiyyah, laṭāʾif wa-ṭarāʾif adabiyyah, uʿjubah min ʿajāʾib al-zamān. Beirut: al-Sharikat al-ʿAlamiyyah li-l-Kitāb, 1990.

Alf laylah wa-laylah. al-Ṭabʿah al-ūlā, ṭubiʿa bi-maṭbaʿat Būlāq sanat 1252 Hijriyah: Muqābalah wa-taṣḥīḥ Muḥammad Qitah ʿAdwī. Baghdad: Maktabat al-Muthannā, 1946.

Alf laylah wa-laylah: Hiya al-riwāyah al-Sharqiyyah al-shahīrah tashraḥu aḥwāl al-ʿuṣūr al-Islāmiyyah al-wusṭā. Cairo: Maṭbaʿat al-Hilāl bi-al-Fajjalah bi-Miṣr, 1904.

Alif laila; or, Book of the Thousand Nights and One Night, Commonly Known as "The Arabian Nights' Entertainments" Now, for the First Time, Published Complete in the Original Arabic, from an Egyptian Manuscript Brought to India by the Late Major Turner Macan, ed. Willian Hay Macnaghten. London: W. Thacker and Co., 1983.

Arabian Nights Entertainments. In the Original Arabic. Reprinted from the Edition Published by Shuek Uhmud Son of Moohumud of Shirwan in Yumun the Two Vols. In One, Containing Two Hundred Nights, ed. Ahmad ibn Muhammad ibn 'Ali. Calcutta: Asiatic Lithographic Company's Press, 1829.

Asāṭīr al-ʿArab fī qiṣṣat alf laylah wa-laylah. Dakka: Maktabat al-Jīl, 1900.

ʿAṭārī, Ḥāmid ʿAlī, and Ḥasan ʿAbd al-Satār. *Ḥikāyāt min alf laylah wa-laylah*. Beirut: Maktabat Lubnān, 1988.

al-Juzʾ al-awwal [-al-juzʾ al-rābiʿ] min kitāb alf laylah wa-laylah. Cairo: al-Maṭbaʿah al-ʿĀmirah al-ʿUthmāniyyah, 1991.

Kitāb alf laylah wa-laylah. Beirut: al-Maṭbaʿah al-Adabiyyah, 1880–82.
  Cairo: al-Maṭbaʿah al-ʿĀmirah al-ʿUthmāniyya, 1885.
  Beirut: Maktabat Ṣādir, 1926.
  Beirut: Dār Maktabat al-Ḥayāh, 1980–85.

Kitāb alf laylah wa-laylah: Min uṣūlihi al-ʿArabiyyah al-ūlā, ed. Mushin Mahdi. Leiden: Brill, 1984. [a revised edition with a preface by Aboubakr Chraïbi and corrections by Ibrahim Akel].

Kitāb alf laylah walaylah. Ṭabʿat ūlā bi-maṭbaʿat Dār al-Kutub al-ʿArabiyyah al-Kubrā, muqābalah wa-muṣaḥḥah ʿalā al-nuskhah al-maṭbūʿah bi-maṭbaʿat Būlāq al-Amīriyyah sanat 1279, taṣḥīḥ al-shaykh Muḥammad Qitah al-ʿAdawī. Miṣr: Muṣṭafā al-Bābī al-Ḥalabī wa-Skhawayhi Bakrī wa-ʿĪsā, 1910.

Pérès, Henri, and Paul Mangion, eds. *al-Muntakhab min kitāb alf laylah wa-laylah.* al-Jazāʾir: Dār al-Maʿārif, 1954.

ʿUqābī, ʿAbd al-Ṣāhib. *Diwan alf laylah wa-laylah.* Baghdad: Dar al-Jāḥiẓ, Wizārat al-Thaqāfah wa-l-Iʿlām, al-Jumhūriyyah al-ʿIrāqiyyah: Tawzīʿ al-Dār al-Waṭaniyyah, 1980.

Chinese

See Wen-chin Ouyang, "The Arabian Nights in Chinese and English Translations: Differing Patterns of Cultural Encounter and World Literature," in *World Literature in Motion: Institution, Recognition, Location*, ed. Flair Donglai Shi and Gareth Guangmin Tan (Stuttgart: ibidem-Verlag, 2020), 435–474.

Alading shen deng. Taibei Xian San xia zhen: San feng chu ban she, 1996.

Lane, Edward William. *Dian fang ye dan*, trans. Lin Zunqian: Hong Kong: Hui tong shu dian, 1974.

Li Bingxuan. *Tian fang ye tan jing cui.* Beijing: Zhongguo shu ji chu ban she, 2005.

Li, Weizhong. *Jing xuan Yi qian ling yi ye.* Xianggang: Shang wu yin shu guan you xian gong si, 2006.

Qikang, Su. "Gushi zhong de gushi – Tian Fang Ye Tan," in *Tian Fang Ye Tan.* Taipei: Gueiguan, 1999 [1981, 1984, 1985, 1994, 1997].

Tian fang ye tan, trans. Xi Ruo. Taipei: Taiwan shang wu yin shu guan, 1966.

Beijing: Ren min wen xue chu ban she: Xin hua shu dian Beijing fa xing suo fa xing, 1988.

Trans. Ssu Chung. Taipei: Yuan jing chu ban shi ye gong si, 1981.

Tian fang ye tan 1: Alabo min jian gu shi. Gaoxiong Shi: Da zhong shu ju, 1983.

Tian fang ye tan: Stories from the Arabian Nights, trans. Li Shuzhen. Taibei Shi: Jiu yi chu ban she, 1999.

Tian fang ye tan, ed. and trans. Shuling Lin, Donghe Chen, and Tianci Zhang. Tainan Shi: Jin qiao chu ban she, 1983.

Xinbada li xian ji. Taibei Xian San xia zhen: San feng chu ban she, 1996.

Xinbada li xian ji, trans. Deng Miaoxiang. Tainan Shi: Shi yi shu ju, 1985.

Ming hua chu ban gong si: Fa xing zhe Wan li shu dian, 1983.

Yan, Chunyu, and Huang Yan. *Bao en he.* Gaoxiong Shi: Da zhong shu ju, 1986.

Yi qian ling yi ye. Beijing: Ren min wen xue chu ban she: Xin hua shu dian Beijing fa xing suo fa xing, 1900.

Trans. Li Weichong. Taibei shi: Yuan liu chu ban shi ye gu feng you xian gong si, 2000.

Wuhan Shi: Hubei mei shu chu ban she, 2004

Xianggang: Xin ya wen hua shi ye you xian gong si, 2007

Yi qian ling yi ye: The Arabian Nights, ed. and trans. Huiling Zhang. Taibei Shi: Chen xing chu ban you xian gong si, 2005.

Yi qian ling yi ye. One Thousand and One Nights, ed. and trans. Liu Jian'gang. Beijing: Zong jiao wen hua chu ban she, 1998.

Yi qian ling yi ye de gu shi. Na Xun yi. Xianggang: Zhongliu chu ban she, 1975.

"Yi qian ling yi ye" gu shi xuan. Chengdu: Sichuan shao nian er tong chu ban she: Sichuan sheng xin hua shu dian fa xing, 1983.

Croatian

Grebo, Dravko, and Semezdin Mehmedinovic. *Tausend und eine Nacht: Sarajevske price: sa dvadeset slika Fernand Schultz Wettel-a priredio Zdravko Grebo sa Semezdinom Mehmedinovicem.* Sarajevo: Izdavac Zid, 1993.

Hiljadu i jedna noc, trans. Stanislav Vinaver and Vojislav Vasiljevic. Wuppertal: Bosanska Rijec, 1998.

Czech

Hrubín, František, and Jirí Trnka. *Pohádky z Tisíce a jedné noci.* Prague: Státní nakl. detské knihy, 1956.

Petiška, Eduard, and Karel Teissig. *Príbehy tisice a jedné noci.* Prague: Melantrich, 1986.

Tauer, Felix. *Kniha tisíce a jedné noci.* Prague: Aventinum, 1928–34.

Zemla, J. *Milostné povídky z Tisice a jedné noci.* Prague: Nakladatel J. Svatek knihkupec, 1930.

Danish

Irwin, Robert. *1001 nat: en indføring*, trans. Ole Lindegård Henriksen. Copenhagen: Vandkunsten, 2005 Introduction.

Løkkegaard, Frede. *1001 [i.e. Tusind og en] nat.* Copenhagen: Rhodos, 1961.

Østrup, J. E., ed. *1001 nat*, trans. V. A. Thisted. Copenhagen: Det Schubotheske forlag, 1895–1896.

Rasmussen, J. L. *Tusende og een nat.* Copenhagen: J. H. Schultz, 1824.

Thisted, Valdemar. *Eventyr og fortællinger af Tusind og een nat.* Copenhagen: Schubothe, 1852–54.

Tusinde og een arabiske fortællinger. Copenhagen: I kommission hos Reitzel, 1832–33.

Winther, Christian. *1001 nats: smukkeste eventyr.* Copenhagen: Det Nordiske Forlag, 1900.

Dutch (Earlier Editions Mentioned in the Text)

Galland, Antoine. *Duizend en één nacht; arabische vertellingen*, trans. Henri van Booven. Amsterdam: J. M. Meulenhoff, 1829–31. [Available in many reprints.]

Keller, Gerard. *Duizend en een nacht.* Nijmegen, Arnhem, Gebr. E. & M. Cohen, 1889.

English

Here is not the place to dwell on the first appearance in English of Galland's *Nights* (see W. H. Mcburney, *Check List*, 10–11). One may notice in passing, however, that Bell's 1708 twelve-volume edition (*Term Catalogues*, III, 592) is probably a reissue of the 1704 copy. An advertisement for a newly published three-volume copy appeared in the *Diverting Works of the Countess D'Anois* (1707). A third edition in seven volumes was on sale in 1711 (*Term Catalogues*, III, 677–78). The following editions, mentioned in the British Museum and the Bodleian Library catalogs, will give a bibliographic indication of the vogue of the *Nights* in the eighteenth century: the fourth edition (in 12 vols., Andrew Bell, 1713–15); the fifth (bound in 4 vols., Andrew Bell, 1717–22); the sixth (12 vols., Osborne & Longman, 1725); the seventh (6 vols., bound in 4, Dublin: Powell & Risk, 1728); the eighth (8 vols., Longman, 1736); the tenth (4 vols., Dublin: Whitestone, 1776); the fourteenth (4 vols., London: Longman, 1778); the eighteenth (4 vols., Montrose: Buchanan, 1798); Harrison's (*The Novelist's Magazine*) with plates by E. F. Burney in 1785. For serialized issues, see Robert D. Mayo; and for cheap prints, see Chauvin, IV, and MLA bibliographic listings. Excepting some editions of individual tales, most of the items below are based on the major English translations that are marked with asterisks. Arrangement is mainly by author (redactor, translator, or editor) or by title in cases of anonymous editions and translations. Chronology is preserved whenever anonymous works bearing the same title are cited.

Adventure of the Hunch-back, and the Stories Connected with It. From the Arabian Nights Entertainments. With engravings by William Daniell from pictures by Robert Smirke. London: Daniell, 1814.

Aladdin; or, the Wonderful Lamp. A Delightful Story, Selected from the Arabian Nights' Entertainments, and on Which the Pantomime of That Name Is Founded; Which Is Now Performing, with Universal Applause, at the Theatre Royal. London: Hardy & Co., 1789.

London: Tabart, 1805.

A new and corrected edition. London: New Juvenile Library, 1816.

Corrected and adapted for juvenile readers by a lady. London: Dean, 1840.

With an introductory sketch. New York: Maynard, Merrill, 1894.

Retold in rhyme by Arthur Ransome. London: n.d.

Arabian Nights Entertainments: Consisting of One Thousand and One Stories: Translated into French from the Arabian MSS. by M. Galland of the Royal Academy; and Now Done into English from the Last Paris Edition. 4 vols. London: Longman, 1783.

3 vols. London: Suttaby, 1807.

To which Is Added a Continuation of the Arabian Nights' Entertainments. 2 vols. Liverpool: Nuttall & Fisher, 1814.

4 vols. London: Brockers & Baldwin, 1819.

Selected and Revised for General Use, to Which Are Added Other Specimens of Eastern Romance. 2 vols. London: James Burns, 1847.

London: Lloyd, 1847.

A New and Complete Edition with Illustrations by S. J. Groves. 2 vols. Edinburgh: Nimmo, 1865.
In Which Vathek Is Included. London: Griffin, 1866.
London: Dicks, 1868.
London: Routledge, 1877.
Sixpenny Series. London: Routledge, 1882.
Aldine edition. London: Pickering & Chatto, 1890.
Lubbock's Hundred Books, no. 57. Routledge, 1893.
London: Service & Paton, 1898.
London: Newnes, 1899.
6 vols. London: Dent, 1901.
Gardners Books, 2007.
W. W. Norton & Co. Inc., 2007.
"Arabian Story," *Classical Journal* 21 (1820), 33–35.
* *Arabian Tales; or, A Continuation of the Arabian Nights Entertainments*, trans. William Beloe. 3 vols. London: Faulder, Hookham and Carpenter, 1794.
Arberry, A. J. *Tales from the Thousand and One Nights*. London: Allen & Unwin, 1953.
Atwater, Richard-Merlin. *Selections from the 1,001 Nights: Stories Told by Sheherazade*. Palm Harbor, FL: Three Swans, 2005
Baskett, George C., ed. *Selections from the "Arabian Nights." Rewritten from the Original English Version of Dr. Scott, for Use in Schools*. London: Bell's Reading Books, 1885.
Beaumont, G. S. *Arabian Nights' Entertainments: or, the Thousand and one Nights, Accurately Describing the Manners, Customs, Laws, and Religion of the Eastern Nations*. 4 vols. London: Mathews & Leigh, 1811
Beauties of the Arabian Nights Entertainments, Consisting of the Most Entertaining Stories. London: 1792.
*Beloe, William. *Miscellanies, Consisting of Poems, Classical Extracts, and Oriental Apologues*. 3 vols. London: 1795.
Bleeck, A. H. "Story of the Cadi and the Robber," *New Monthly Magazine* 99 (1853), 85–91.
Braddon, M. E. ed. *Aladdin; or, the Wonderful Lamp, Sindbad the Sailor; or, the Old Man of the Sea, Ali Baba; or, the Forty Thieves*. London: Maxwell, 1880.
Burnside, Helen M., ed. *Arabian Nights*. London: Tuck, 1893.
*Burton, Sir Richard F. *The Book of the Thousand Nights and a Night: A Plain and Literal Translation of the Arabian Nights Entertainments*. 10 vols. Kamashastra Society for private subscribers only, 1885–86.
Supplemental Nights to the Book of the Thousand Nights and a Night, with Notes Anthropological and Explanatory. 6 vols. 1886.
Lady Burton's Edition of Her Husband's Arabian Nights Entertainments Translated Literally from the Arabic. 6 vols. London: Waterlaw, 1887.
The Library Edition of the Arabian Nights' Entertainments. 12 vols. London: Nichols, 1894.
Tales from the 1001 Nights. Ann Arbor, MI: Borders Classics, 2004
The Arabian Nights Entertainments. Whitefish, MO: Kessinger Pub., 2004, 2005.

Bussey, G. Moir, ed. *Arabian Nights' Entertainments*, trans. the Reverend Edward Forster: London: J. Thomas, 1839.

Cardonne, Denis Dominique. *A Miscellany of Eastern Learning: Translated from Turkish, Arabian, and Persian Manuscripts, in the Library of the King of France*. London: Printed for J. Wilkie ... and B. Law, 1771. [Containing some tales, and a useful preface.]

Clarke, Michael, ed. *Stories from the Arabian Nights*. Eclectic School Readings. New York: American Book Co., 1897.

Collection of Tales, Extracted from the Arabian Nights' Entertainments. Karlsruhe: Brawn, 1828.

Cooper, J. *The Oriental Moralist; or the Beauties of the Arabian Nights Entertainments*. London: Newbery, 1790.

Dalziels' Illustrated Arabian Nights' Entertainments. London: Ward & Lock, 1864.

Daniel, G., ed. *Aladdin; or the Wonderful Lamp: A Grand Romantic Spectacle in Two Acts*. London: n.d.

Davidson, Gladys, ed. *Arabian Nights' Entertainments*. London: Blackie, 1906.

Dawood, N. J., and William Harvey, ed. and trans. *Tales from the Thousand and One Nights*. London: Penguin, 2003.

Dixson, C., ed. *Fairy Tales from the Arabian Nights*. London: Dent, 1893.

Dulcken, H. W., ed. *Dalziel's Illustrated Arabian Nights' Entertainments*. 1878.

Eliot, Samuel, ed. *Arabian Nights' Entertainments*. Boston: Lee & Shepard, 1880.

Enchanted Horse and Other Tales from the Arabian Nights' Entertainment. London: Blackwood, 1877.

Fairy Tales from the Arabian Nights. London: Dent, 1899.

Far-Famed Tales from the Arabian Nights' Entertainments. London: Addey, 1852.

Finter, Edward. *Arabian Nights Entertainments*. 5 vols. 1810. [Scarce, see Macdonald's marginal notes and clippings in his own copy of Chauvin, Case Memorial Library, Hartford Seminary.]

*Forster, Edward. *The Arabian Nights*. 5 vols. London: Miller, 1802. [With a preface.]

Forty Thieves; or, the Banditti of the Forest. New York: Turner & Fisher, 1841. [With moral reflections interspersed.]

*Gough, Richard, ed. and trans. *Arabian Nights Entertainments*. 4 vols. London: Longman, 1798. [With a preface.]

Green, Mrs. F. G., ed. *Arabian Nights*. London: Dean, 1904.

Griffis, W. E., ed. *Alif Laila wa Leila: The Arabian Nights Entertainments; Adapted for American Readers from the Text of Jonathan Scott, with an Introduction*. 4 vols. Boston: Lothrop, 1891.

Haddawy, Husain. *The Arabian Nights*. London: Norton, 1990.

Hale, Edward E., ed. *A Selection of Stories from Alif Laila wa Laila, the Arabian Nights Entertainments*. Boston: Ginn & Co., 1888.

*Hanley, Sylvanus, ed. and trans. *Caliphs and Sultans: Being Tales Omitted in the Usual Editions of the Arabian Nights Entertainments*. London: Reeve, 1868.

*Heron, Robert. *Arabian Tales; or the Continuation of the Arabian Nights Entertainments*. Edinburgh: Bell & Bradfute, 1792. [With a preface.]

History of Ali Baba or the Forty Thieves Destroyed by a Slave. Newcastle: W. & E. Fordyce, 1890.

"History of Djouder," *Lady's Magazine* (1830), 11–15. [Hurried in style, annotated with remarks on Eastern manners and customs.]

Holden, Edward Singelton, ed. *Stories from the Arabian Nights*. Appleton's Home Reading Books. New York: Appleton & Co., 1900.

Horch, Daniel. *The Angel with one Hundred Wings: A Tale from the Arabian Nights*. New York: St. Martin's Griffin, 2004, 2002.

Housman, L., ed. *Stories from the Arabian Nights*. New York: Scribner's, 1907.

Jacobs, J., ed. *The Thousand and One Nights; or the Arabian Nights Entertainments*, trans. Edward W. Lane. 6 vols. London: Gibbings, 1896. [With an introduction and appendices.]

Johnson, Clifton, ed. *Arabian Nights' Entertainments*. London: Macmillan, 1904.

Kim Yoon-soo, Kim Jisu, and Kim Jong-min. *The Arabian Nights*. Taipei: Caves Books, 2006.

*Kirby, W. F., trans. *New Arabian Nights: Select Tales Not Included in Galland or Lane*. London: Sonenschein, 1882.

*Lamb, George. *New Arabian Nights' Entertainments, Selected from the Original MS. by Jos. von. Hammer; Now First Translated into English*. 3 vols. London: Henry Colburn, 1826. [With a preface.]

*Lane, Edward William, ed. and trans. *A New Translation of the Tales of a Thousand and One Nights; Known in England as the Arabian Nights' Entertainments*. London: Charles Knight & Co., 1838–40. [In 32 parts.]

The Thousand and One Nights, Commonly Called, in England, the Arabian Nights' Entertainments. 3 vols. London: Charles Knight, 1839–41. [With a foreword and substantial review.]

Arabian Tales and Anecdotes: Being a Selection from the Notes to the New Translation of "The Thousand and One Nights." London: Charles Knight, 1845. [Part of Knight's weekly vols.]

Lane-Poole, Stanley, ed. and trans. *Stories from the Arabian Nights*.3 vols. New York: Putnam, 1890. [With a preface and notes.]

Lane-Poole, Stanley, ed. *The Thousand and One Nights: The Arabian Nights' Entertainments*, trans. Edward William Lane. 4 vols. London: George Bell, 1906.

Sindbad the Sailor. London: Blackie, 1908.

Stories from the Thousand and One Nights. New York: Harvard Classics, 1909.

Lang, Andrew. *The Arabian Nights Entertainments*. New York: Cosimo Classics, 2005.

Little Hunchback, from the Arabian Nights Entertainments. London: Harris, 1817.

Little Hunchback, the Barber, the Sleeper Awakened, and the Forty Thieves: From the Arabian Nights' Entertainments. London: Ward & Lock, 1886.

Macnaghten, William Hay. *The Alif laila; or, Book of the Thousand Nights and One Night, Commonly Known as 'The Arabian Nights Entertainments."* Calcutta and London: W. Thacker and Co., W. H. Allen and Co., 1839.

Mahfuz, Najib, Denys Johnson-Davies, Nazli Madkur, et al. *Arabian Nights and Days: Layali alf laylah*. New York: Ltd. Editions Club, 2005.

Mardrus, J. C., and E. Powys Mathers. *The Arabian Nights: The Book of the Thousand Nights and One Night*. London: Folio Society, 2003; New York: Assouline Pub., 2005.

The Arabian Nights: The Book of the Thousand Nights and One night. Vol. 4. Vol. 5. Vol. 6. London: Folio, 2003.

Martin, A. T., ed. *Stories from the Arabian Nights*. London: Macmillan, 1908.

Martin, Theodore. *Aladdin, or the Wonderful Lamp*.

Mason, J., ed. *Arabian Nights' Entertainments*. Revised and annotated. London: Cassell, 1875.

McCaughrean, Geraldine, and Rosamund Fowler. *One Thousand and One Arabian Nights*. Oxford: Oxford University Press, 2003.

Mew, James. "Some Unedited Tales from the 'Arabian Nights.'" *Tinsley's Magazine* (1887). [Later incorporated in Kirby's.]

Mord, W. *Tales from the East: A Picture-Book for Children by Harlequin. Containing Sixteen Coloured Plates and about Fifty Line Illustrations, with Tales Adapted from the Arabian Nights' Entertainments*. London: Fisher & Unwin, 1908.

Thousand and One Nights, or the Arabian Nights' Entertainments: A New Edition Adapted to Family Readings. Boston, MA, 1869.

Trans. Jonathan Scott, with etchings by A. Lalauze. 4 vols. London: Nimmo, 1883.

With the Addition of Aladdin and Ali Baba, trans. Stanley Lane-Poole. London: Bliss, 1895.

Oliver, Edwin, ed. *Arabian Nights*. London: Treherne, 1909.

Ouyang, Wen-Chin. *The Arabian Nights*. London and New York: Everyman, 2014.

Oriental Anecdotes: or, the History of Haroun Al Raschid. 2 vols. in 1. Dublin: 1764.

Oriental Tales: Being Moral Reflections from the Arabian Nights' Entertainments: Calculated Both to Amuse and Improve the Minds of Youth. 2 vols. London: Tegg, 1829.

*Payne, John, trans. *The Book of the Thousand Nights and One Night: Now First Completely Done into English Prose and Verse, from the Original Arabic*. 9 vols. London: Printed by Villon Society for private subscription and private circulation, 1882–84. [With well-informed book-length essay appended to vol. 9.]

* *Tales from the Arabic of the Breslau and Calcutta (1814–1818) Editions of the Book of the Thousand Nights and One Night, Not Occurring in the Other Printed Texts of the Work, Now First Done into English*. 3 vols. London: Villon Society, private subscription and circulation, 1884.

* *Alaeddin and the Enchanted Lamp; Zein ul Asnam and the King of the Jinn: Two Stories Done into English from the Recently Discovered Arabic Text*. London: private subscription, 1889.

* *Abou Mohommed the Lazy, and Other Tales from the Arabian Nights*. Publications of John Payne Society. Olney: Thomas Wright, 1906.

People's Edition of the Arabian Nights' Entertainments. London: Ward & Lock, 1882.

Pictorial Penny Arabian Nights' Entertainments. Part 1. London: Moore, 1845.

Piguenit, C. P., ed. *Arabian Nights Entertainments: Consisting of One Thousand and One Stories Freely Transcribed from the Original Translation*. 4 vols. London: C. D. Piguenit, 1792.

Poole, Edward Stanley, ed. *The Thousand and One Nights, Commonly Called in England the Arabian Nights' Entertainments.* 3 vols. London: Murray, 1859. [Reprinted many times; Bickers' 1977 three-volume copy used; Lane's foreword incorporated in Poole's.]

3 vols. London: Chatto & Windus, 1883. [Same edition with a preface by Stanley Lane-Poole.]

Readings from the Arabian Nights' Entertainments. Murray's Railway Readings. Glasgow: 1867.

Robinson, W. Heath, ed. *Child's Arabian Nights.* London: Grant Richards, 1903.

Rouse, W. H. D., ed. *Arabian Nights.* London: Nister, 1907.

Savile, the Hon. C. Stuart, ed. and trans. "The Adventures of Khodadad," *Colburn's New Monthly Magazine* 58 (1840), 180–93, 373–84.

*Scott, Jonathan, ed. and trans. *Tales, Anecdotes, and Letters, Translated from the Arabic and the Persian.* Shrewsbury: J. & W. Eddowes, 1800.

* *The Arabian Nights Entertainments: Carefully Revised and Occasionally Corrected from the Arabic. To Which Is Added, a Selection of New Tales, Now First Translated from the Arabic Originals.* 6 vols. London: Longman & Hurst, 1811.

Sindbad the Sailor, Aladdin, and Other Stories from the Arabian Nights' Entertainments. London: Ward & Lock, 1886.

Sindbad the Sailor and Ali Baba and the Forty Thieves. London: Lawrence & Bullen, 1896.

Stead, W. T., ed. *The Story of Aladdin and the Wonderful Lamp.* Philadelphia, PA: 1908.

Steedman, Amy, ed. *Stories from the Arabian Nights.* London and New York: Jack, Dutton, 1907.

Stories from the Arabian Nights, with an Introductory Note. Boston: Houghton & Mifflin, 1897.

Story of Ali Baba and the Forty Thieves, an Extract from Dr. Weil's German Translation of the Arabian Nights. Boston: L. H. Kilborn, 1888.

Sugden, the Hon. Mrs., ed. *Arabian Nights' Entertainments; Arranged for the Perusal of Youthful Readers.* London: Whittaker, 1863; New York: Routledge, 1863.

Tales from the Arabian Nights' Entertainments, as Related by a Mother for the Amusement of Her Children with Engravings by Butler, from Designs by J. Gilbert. New edition. New York: Walker, 1848.

Tales from the Arabian Nights' Entertainments. Included in H. B. Stowe's *Library of Famous Fiction.* New York: Ford, 1873.

English School Texts. London: Blackie, 1905.

Aladdin and the Wonderful Lamp, Ali Baba and the Forty Thieves, Sindbad the Sailor. Chamber's Supplementary Readers. London: Edinburgh, 1908.

*Torrens, Henry. *Book of the Thousand Nights and One Night: From the Arabic of Aegyptian MS. as Edited by Wm. Hay Mcnaghten.* London: Allen, 1838.

Townsend, the Rev. George Fyler, ed. *The Arabian Nights' Entertainments: A New Edition, Revised, with Notes.* London: F. Warne & Co., 1866. [With a preface.]

Tweed, Anna, ed. *Arabian Nights.* New York: Baker & Taylor, 1910.

Valentine, Mrs., ed. *Eastern Tales by Many Story-Tellers*. London: Warne, n.d.
Warner, A. & A., ed. *Five Favourite Tales from the Arabian Nights in Words of One Syllable*. London: Lewis, 1871.
Weber, Henry, ed. *Tales of the East: Comprising the Most Popular Romances of Oriental Origin; and the Best Imitations by European Authors. To Which Is Prefixed an Introductory Dissertation*. 3 vols. Edinburgh: James Ballantyne, 1812.
Wiggin, Kate Douglas, and Nora Smith, eds. *The Arabian Nights: Their Best-Known Tales Retold. With Illustrations by Maxfield Parrish*. New York: Scribner's, 1909.
Willingham, Bill, Mark Buckingham, and Steve Leialoha. *Arabian Nights (and Days)*. London: Titan, 2006.
Wilson, Epiphanius, ed. *Arabic Literature ... with Critical and Biographical Sketches*. London and New York: Colonial Press, 1902. [Containing selections from the *Nights*.]
Zipes, Jack David. *Arabian Nights: The Marvels and Wonders of the Thousand and One Nights*. New York: Penguin Group, 1991.
Zipes, Jack David, and Richard Francis Burton. *Arabian Nights: The Marvels and Wonders of the Thousand and One Nights*. New York: Signet Classic, 1991.
Arabian Nights: More Marvels and Wonders of the Thousand and One Nights Volume II. New York: Signet Classic, 1999.
The Arabian Nights. Vol. 1, The Marvels and Wonders of the Thousand and One Nights. New York: Signet Classics, 2007.

French

Reprints of Galland's translation are mentioned below to show the popularity of this translation.

Alger, J. Carbonel, ed. *Histoire de Djoûdhar le pêcheur et du sac enchanté; conte extrait des Mille et une nuits. Texte établi d'après quatre éditions accompagné de variantes et suivi d'un glossaire*. 1944.
Bauer, Marius Alexander Jacques, and Antoine Galland, eds. *Histoire d'Aboulhassan Ali Ebn Becar, et de Schemselnihar, favorite du Calif Haroun Al-Raschid*. Harlem: F. Bohn, 1929.
Bencheickh, Jamel Eddine. *Les Mille et Une Nuit ou la parole prisonnière*. Paris: Gallimard, 1988.
Bencheikh, Jamel Eddin, and André Miquel. *Les Mille et Une Nuit*. Paris: Gallimard, 2007.
Cazotte, Jacques, ed. *Suite des Milles et une nuits: le diable en Arabie*. Monaco: Editions du Rocher, 1996.
Cinquante contes de l'Orient; choix des Mille et un contes de l'arabe. Brussels: Libraire belge-française, 1847.
Deslongchamps, Auguste-Louis-Armand-Loiseleur, and Louis-Aimé Martin, eds. *Les Mille et Une Nuit contes arabes*. Paris: A. Desrez, 1838.
Dulac, Edmund, ed. *Sindbad le marin et d'autres contes des Mille et une nuits*. Paris: H. Piazza, 1919.

Galland, Antoine, ed. *Les Mille et Une Nuit: contes arabes.*
Lyon: Chez les frères Bruyset, 1706–20.
La Haye: Chez Pierre Husson, Marchand Libraire, sur le capel-brug, 1728.
La Haye: Chez Jean Mart. Husson, 1743.
Paris: Compagnie des libraires, 1745.
Leide: Chez J. de Wetstein & fils, 1768.
Paris: Par la Compagnie des Libraires, 1773.
Lille: C. F. J. Lehoucq, 1781.
Paris: Laplace, Sanchez & Cie, 1800s.
Paris: Ledentu, 1818.
Paris: Felix Locquin, 1843.
Paris: Gustave Havard, 1849.
Paris: F. Béchet, 1851.
Paris: Librairie de L. Hachette. Publication de C. H. Lahure, 1865.
Tours: Alfred, Mame et Fils, 1873.
Paris: Garnier Frères, 1921.
Paris: Garnier, 1900–1909?
Paris: Flammarion, 1965.
Paris: Jean de Bonnot, 1972.
Paris: Flammarion, 2004.
Montréal: Librairie Beauchemin, n.d.
Les Mille et Une Nuit: récits d'Orient. Paris: Hachette, 1978.

Galland, Antoine, and François Pétis de la Croix, eds. *Les mille & une nuit: contes arabes.* Paris: Chez la veuve de Claude Barbin, 1704–17.

Galland, Antoine, and A. Caussin de Perceval, eds. *Les mille et une nuit; contes arabes.* Paris: Chez Le Normant, 1806.

Galland, Antoine, and Denis Chavis, eds. *Continuation des Mille et une nuit, contes arabes.* Genève, Paris: Barde, Manget & compagnie; Cuchet, 1788–89.

Galland, Antoine, and L. E. Gauttier du Lys d'Arc, eds. *Les mille et une nuit, contes arabes.* Paris: J. A. S. Collin de Plancy, 1822–23.

Galland, Antoine, and Eugène Destains, eds. *Les mille et une nuit, contes arabes.* Paris: A. Dupont et cie., 1827.

Galland, Antoine, and Jules Gabriel Janin, eds. *Les mille & une nuit: contes arabes.* Pourrat Frères: éditeurs, rue des Petits-Augustins, 1838.
Paris: Librairie de Bibliophiles, 1880–89?
Paris: Librairie des bibliophiles, E. Flammarion, successeur, 1920–29.

Galland, Antoine, and A. I. Silvestre de Sacy, eds. *Les mille et une nuit: contes arabes.* Paris: E. Bourdin, 1839–40, 1860.

Galland, Antoine, and Andrè Lejeune, eds. *Les mille et une nuit, contes arabes.* Paris: Ducrocq, Libraire Éditeur, 1872.

Galland, Antoine, and Adolphe Lalauze, eds. *Les mille et une nuit, contes arabes; réimprimés sur l'édition originale.* Paris: Librairie des bibliophiles, 1881.

Galland, Antoine, and Paul De Maurelly, eds. *Les mille et une nuit: contes arabes choisis pour la jeunesse, adaptation nouvelle d'après la traduction de Galland.* Paris: Émile Guérin, Librairie de Théodore Lefèvre et Cie, 1905.

Gaudefroy-Demombynes, Maurice, ed. *Les cent et une nuit.* Paris: E. Guilmoto, 1911.

Paris: Sindbad, 1982.
Guillon, M. N. S. Nouveaux, ed. *Contes arabes; ou, Supplément aux Mille et une nuits, suivis de Mélanges de littérature orientale et de letters*. Paris, Prault, 1788.
Histoire de Chems-Eddine et de Noureddine; extraite des Mille et une nuits expliqués d'apres une nouvelle méthode par deux traductions francaises, l'une, littérale et juxtalinéaire, présentant le mot a mot francais en regard de mots arabes correspondants, l'autre, correcté et precédée du texte arabe. Paris, Hacette, 1853.
Henri, Auguste, ed. *Choix des plus jolis contes arabes tirés des Mille et une nuits*. Leipzig: C. Cnobloch, 1810.
Khawam, René R., ed. *Les Mille et une nuit: dames insignes et serviteurs gallants. tome 1*. Paris: Phébus, 1986.
Laboulaye, Edouard, ed. Abdall*ah: ou, Le trèfle a quatre feuilles, conte arabe suivi de Aziz et Aziza, conte des Mille et une nuits*. Paris: G. Charpentier, 1882.
Laforge, Lucien. *Les 1001 [i.e. mille et une] nuits*. Paris: J. Tallandier, 1912.
La Haye, J. M. Husson. *Les mille et une nuit, contes arabes.*
Le Gal, Lydie, and Abdelghani Boudaakkar. *Les Mille et Une Nuit: les Amphores de Salomon*. Beirut: Albouraq, 2004.
Les mille et une nuit: contes arabes. Paris: chez Salmon, 1825.
Paris: J. Lecoffre, 1844–46.
Paris: Gustave Havard, 1850.
Les mille et une nuit: contes choisis: Aladdin, Ali Baba, Ali Cogia. Paris: A. Bédelet, 1840–65.
Les milles et une nuit: choix de contes Arabes. Paris: Chez Tirpenne, 1850.
Mardrus, J. C., ed. *Le livre des mille nuits et une nuit*. Paris: Éditions de la Revue blanche, 1899–1929, 1900–1904.
Paris: Charpentier et Fasquelle, 1903–14.
Paris: Charpentier et Fasquelle, 1924–27.
Paris: L'Édition d'art H. Piazza, 1926.
Brussels: Éditions La Boétie, 1947.
Mardrus, J. C., and Léon Carré. *Le livre des Mille Nuits et Une Nuit: Extraits Choisis*. Paris: Assouline, 2005.
Mille et une Nuits, Les. Alf Layla wa-layla Dossier documentaire, éléments bibliographiques. Paris: Institut du Monde arabe, 1995.
Pixérécourt, R.-C. Guilbert, ed. *Ali-Baba; ou, Les quarante voleurs. Mélodrame en trois actes à spectacle, tiré des Milles et une nuits*. Paris: Pollet, 1822.
Savary, Claude-Etienne. ed. *Les amours D'Anas-Eloujoud et de Ouardi*. Baghdad and Paris: Onfroy, 1789.
Schoummel, Jean Théophile, ed. *Recueil des plus jolis contes tirés des Mille et une nuit: à l'usage des écoles*. Leipzig: S. L. Crusius, 1780.
Silvestre de Sacy, Antoine Isaac (1758–1838), and Antoine Galland, eds. *Les mille et une nuit*. Paris: Bourdin, 1860. Les Mille et Une Nuit, contes arabes, traduits par Galland. Illustrés par MM. Francais, H. Baron, Ed. Wattier, Laville, etc. Revus et corrigés sur l'édition princeps de 1704, augmentés d'une dissertation sur les Mille et une nuit, par Sylvestre de Sacy [The thousand and One Nights, Arabian tales, translated by Galland. Illustrated by MM. Francais, H. Baron, Ed. Wattier, Laville, etc. Revised and corrected

on the original 1704 edition, supplemented by a dissertation on the Thousand and One Nights, by Sylvestre de Sacy], https://bit.ly/32QtCXo.
Sironval, Margaret. *Album Mille et Une Nuits*. Paris: Gallimard, 2005.

German (Earlier Editions Mentioned in the Text)

Dalziel's illustrirte Tausend und eine Nacht. Sammlung persischer, indischer und arabischer Märchen. Leipzig: A. Schumann, 1899?

Die Tausend und eine Nacht worinnen seltzame arabische Historien und wunderbare Begebenheiten, benebst artigen Liebes-Intriguen, auch Sitten und Gewohnheiten der Morgenländer. Leipzig: Moritz Georg Weidmann, 1719.

Dulac, Edmund, illus. *Arabische Nächte: Erzählungen aus Tausend und eine Nacht*. Bergen: Müller & Kiepenheuer, 1953.

Ernst, Paul, ed. *Tausend und ein Tag: Orientalische Erzählungen*. Leipzig: Insel, 1909.

Greve, Felix Paul, ed. *Die schönsten Geschichten aus tausendundeiner Nacht*. Leipzig, Weimar: G. Kiepenheuer, 1964.

Habicht, Maximilian, ed. *Arabische Miniaturen: Die schönsten Nächte*. Paris: Éditions du Sud, 1968.

Habicht, Maximilian, and Friedrich Heinrich von der Hagen, eds. *Tausend und eine Nacht: arabische Erzählungen*. Breslau: Josef Max und Komp, 1825.

Hammer-Purgstall, Joseph, and A. E. Zinserling. *Märchen aus Hundert und einer Nacht*. Nördlingen [West Germany]: Franz Greno, 1986.

Henning, Max, ed. *Tausend und eine Nacht*. Leipzig: P. Reclam, 1896–1901, 1924.

Hepner, Clara, ed. *Frauen des Morgenlandes: Die schönsten Liebesgeschichten aus 1001 Nacht*. Stuttgart: Heimat und Welt, 1924.

Hermann, Schrader, and Hilde Schlotterbeck, eds. *Liebesabenteuer aus 1001 Nacht*. Olten: Fackelverlag, 1962.

Janschka, Fritz, ed. *Die schönsten Geschichten aus Tausendundeiner Nacht*. Dortmund: Harenberg, 1986.

Littmann, Enno, ed. *Die Erzählungen aus den Tausend und ein Nächten*.Leipzig: Insel, 1924; Wiesbaden: Insel, 1953.

Geschichten der Liebe aus den 1001 Nächten: Aus dem arabischen Urtext übertragen. Frankfurt am Main: Insel, 1953.

Märchen aus Tausend und einer Nacht: Eine Auswahl für die Jugend. Leipzig; F. Loewe, 1962.

Ott, Claudia, trans. *Tausendundeine Nacht*. Munich: Beck, 2004.

Riba, Karl Theodor. *Die Erzählungen aus den tausend Nächten und der einen Nacht*. Berlin: W. Borngräber, 1913.

Riba, Karl Theodor, and Wilhelm Franz Bayros, eds. *Die Liebesgeschichten des Orients: Tausend und eine Nacht*. Berlin: W. Borngräber, 1916.

Sachse, Günter, ed. *Sindbad der Seefahrer*. Gottingen: W. Fischer-Verlag, 1974.

Tauer, Felix, ed. *Die Erzählungen aus den Tausendundein Nächten: Die in anderen Versionen von 1001 Nacht nicht enthaltenen Geschichten der Wortley-Montague-Handschrift der Oxforder Bodleian Library*. Frankfurt am Main: Insel, 1966.

Erotische Geschichten aus den Tausendundein Nächten. Frankfurt am Main: Insel, 1983.

Tausend und eine Nacht; arabische Erzählungen. Leipzig: G. Wigand, 1841.
Thanner, Josef, ed. *Von Torheit, List und Schelmen: Drei Erzählungen aus Tausendundeiner Nacht*. Basel: Birkhäuser, 1959.
Wehr, Hans, ed. *Arabische Märchen aus der Welt von Tausendundeine Nacht*. Munich: Wilhelm Goldmann, 1900 [this date is not correct; should be around 1960].
Weil, Gustav, ed. *Tausend und eine Nacht: Arabische Erzählungen*. Stuttgart: Rieger, 1871.
Bonn: E. Strauss, 1897.
Munich: Keysersche Verlagsbuchhandlung, 1961.
Weil, Gustav, and Arwed D.Gorella, eds. *Tausendundeine Nacht: die schönsten Geschichten*. Im Bertelsmann Lesering, 1900.
Weil, Gustav, and Karl Heinz Berger, eds. *Die schönsten Geschichten aus 1001 Nacht*. Berlin: Kinderbuchverlag, 1970.
Zinserling, A., ed. *Der tausend und einen Nacht noch nicht übersetzte Mährchen, Erzählungen und Anekdoten zum erstenmale aus dem Arabischen in's Französische übersezt*. Stuttgart: J.G. Cotta, 1823–1924.

Greek

For a survey, see Papachristophorou, Marilena. "The Arabian Nights in Greece: A Comparative Survey of Greek Oral Tradition." *Fabula* 45, 3–4, 2004. 311–329; revised version in *The Arabian Nights in Transnational Perspective*. ed. by Ulrich Marzolph. Detroit: Wayne State Univ. Press 2007, pp. 291–311.

Hebrew

Almagor, Dan. *Lailah ha-69: mi-tokh Elef lailah ve-lailah*. Tel Aviv: Modan, 1984.
Rivlin, Joseph Joel. *Elef lailah ve-lailah*. Jerusalem: Kiryat sefer; Israel, 1947–71.
Williams-Ellis, Amabel, and Zvi Arad. *ʿAli Baba ve-arbaʿim ha-shodedim: ve-ʿod tishʿah ʿasar sipurim*. Tel Aviv: Mahberot le-sifrut, 1988.
Yellin, David, ed. *Sipure Elef oteh ve-lailah*. Yerushalayim: Turgeman, 1912.

Italian

Dominicis, Armando, ed. *Le mille e una ote; novelle arabe*.
Florence: Salani, 1915.
Rome: Grandi Tascabili Economici Newton, 1991.
Franchi, Anna. *Le mille e una notte*. Milan: V. Nugoli & Co., 1921–29.
Jevolella, Massimo, and Armando Dominicis. *Le mille e una notte*. Milan: Mondadori, 1984.
Oddone, Teresita, and Flora Oddone, eds. *Le migliori novelle delle mille e una ote; narrate alla gioventù italiana de Teresita e Flora Oddone*. Milan: Hoepli 1922.
Spina, Alessandro, ed. *Storia della Città di Rame*. Brescia: L'obliquo, 2007.
Tibaldi Chiesa, Mary, and Vsevolode Nicouline, eds. *Le mille e una notte*. Milan: Hoepli, 1952.

Japanese

Borges, Jorge Luis, ed. *Sen'ya ichiya monogatari: Galland Edition*, trans. Teruo Inoue. Babel Toshokan: Tosho Kankokai, 1990. A new translation of Galland by Tetsuo Nishio (2019/20)

Burton, Sir Richard Francis, ed. *Sen'ya ichiya mongatari: Baton-ban*, trans. Masafumi Oba. Tokyo: Kawade Shobo, 1966–67.

Burton, Sir Richard Francis, ed. *Baton-ban Sen'ya ichiya monogatari*, trans. Masafumi Oba. Tokyo: Chikuma Shobo, 2003–4.

Dixon, E., and Yoshio Nakano, eds. *Arabian, naito*. Tokyo: Iwanami Shoten, 1959.

Maejima, Shinji, ed. *Arabian naito*. Tokyo: Heibonsha, 1966.

Maejima, Shinji, and Osamu Ikeda. *Arabian naito*. Tokyo: Heibonsha, 1966.

Mardrus, J. C., and Yaso Saijo. *Gafu Issen ichiya monogatari*. Tokyo: Kokusai Bunken Kankokai, 1929.

Morita, Sohei, ed. *Arabiya yawa*. Tokyo: Meicho Fukyukai, 1927.

Oya, Soichi., ed. *Sen'ya ichiya: kan'yaku arabian naito*. Tokyo: Chuo Koronsha, 1930.

Sohei, Morita, ed. *Arabiya yawa*. Tokyo: Meicho Fukyukai, 1927.

Tatsuro, ed. *Arabian naito sutori*. Tokyo: Shinkigensha, 2006.

Toyoshima, Yoshio. *Sen'ichiya monogatari: Marudoryusu-ban*. Tokyo: Iwanami Shoten, 1982–83.

Toyoshima, Yoshio, ed. *Arabian naito bekkan*. Tokyo: Iwanami Shoten, 1988.

Toyoshima, Yoshio, et al. *Kanyaku Sen'ichiya monogatari*. Tokyo: Iwanami Shoten, 1988 [Mardrus edition].

Korean

Burton, Richard Francis, ed. *Ch'onya irya: The Book of the Thousand Nights and a Night*, trans. O Chong-hwan. Seoul T'ukpyolsi: Tongso Munhwasa, 1975.

Gebert, Helga, ed. *Helga Gebot'u ui 1001-pam tonghwa*, trans. Kim Kyong-yon. Seoul: Saemt'o, 1998.

Ha, Il-chi, ed. *Arabian nait'u*. Soul-si: Minumsa, 1997.

Yi, Chong-hui, ed. *Arabian nait'u*. Seoul: Han'guk Chayu Kyoyuk Hyophoe, 1972.

Persian

Afrasiyabi, Bahram. *Hizar va yik shab*. Tehran: Intisharat-i Sukhan, 1999.

Dastanha-yi hazar va yak shab. [Tehran?]: Iqbal, 1998.

Farhang, Musá. *Hizar va yik shab*. [Tehran]: Bungah-i Matbuʻati-i Gutinbirg, 1990.

Hazar va yak shab: tarjumah-ʼi Abd al-Latif Tasuji. Sweden: Arash Tryck & Förlag, 1990.

Hizar va yik shab. [France?]: Sazman-i Intisharat-i Ruzgar-i Naw, 1984.

Mazdapur, Katayun. *Rivayati-i digar az dastan-i Dalilah-i muhtalah va makr-i zanan*. Tehran: Rawshangaran, 1995.

Samini, Naghmah. *Kitab-i ʻishq va shaʻbadah: pazhuhishi dar Hazar va yak shab*. Tehran: Nashr-i Markaz, 2001.

Tasuji, ʿAbd al-Latif. *Hizar va yik shab*. Istuk'hulm: Muʾassasah-i Chap va Intisharat-i Arash, 1991.
Tehran: Dunya-i Kitab, 1998.

Romanian

Gramescu, Haralambie, ed. and trans. *O mie si una de nopti*. Confrontation of three editions: French (J. C. Mardrus), Russian (M. A. Salie), and German (Max Henning). Editura Erc Press, 2010.
Mardrus, J. C. *O mie si una de nopti*. Editura Saeculum I.O. Editura Vestala, 1996.
Povestiri din halimà. Bucharest: Romania noua, 1924.

Russian

Novyia arabskiia skazki sostoiashchiia v os'mi tomakh. Smolensk: V tip. Prikaza obshchestvennago prizrieniia, 1796.
Ridley, James. *Skazki dukhov: ili zabavnyia nastavleniia Gorama, syna Asmarova*. Moscow: 1785.
Sal'e, M. A. *Khalif na chas; novye skazky iz knigi "Tysiacha i odnoi nochi."* Moscow: Izd-vo vostochnoi lit-ry, 1961.
Sindbad-morekhod: izbrannye skazki i rasskazy iz "Tysiachi i odnoi nochi." Moscow: Ermak, 2003.
Sal'e, M. A., and I. Fil'shtinskii. *Maruf-bashmachnik: izbrannye skazki, rasskazy i povesti iz "Tysiachi i odnoi nochi."* Moscow: Pravda, 1986.
Sal'e, M. A., and I. Krachkovskii. *Kniga tysiachi i odnoi nochi: Alf laylah wa-laylah*. Moscow: Novosti, 1992.
Sal'e, M. A., and Betsi Iakovlevna Shidfar. *Tysiacha i odna noch': i zbrannye skazki*. Moscow: EKSMO, 2004.
Shidfar, Betsi Iakovlevna, and Rustam M. Aliev. *Srednevekovye arabskie povesti i novelly*. Moscow: Izd-vo "Nauka," Glav. red. vostochnoi lit-ry, 1982.
Smirnova, T. G. *Tysiacha i odna noch*. Leningrad: EGO, 1991.

Spanish

Aguado de Lozar, Gaspar A. *Las mil y una noches, cuentos árabes*. Paris: Garnier Hermanos, 1880.
Burton, Richard, and Jorge Luis Borges. *Las mil y una noches según Burton*. Madrid: Ediciones Siruela, 1985.
Cansinos Assens, Rafael. *Libro de las mil y una noches: el de los conocimientos maravillosos*. Mexico: D. F. Aguilar, 1963.
Cuentos de las Mil y Una Noches/Tales from a Thousand and One Nights. Diana, Mexico: 2007.
Galland, Antoine. *Las mil y una noches, cuentos árabes*. Barcelona: Editorial Ramon Sopena, 1974.
Las Mil y una noches. Barcelona: Editorial Optima, 2003.

Galland, Antoine, and Pedro José Pedraza y Páez. *Las mil y una noches, cuentos árabes*. Barcelona: Casa Editorial Maucci, 1902.

Jimenez, Juan F., and Dimitri Makhashvili. *Las Mil y una noches*. Barcelona: Plaza Joven, 1990.

Larraya, Juan A. G., Leonor Martínez Martín, and Juan Vernet Ginés. *Las Mil y una noches*. Barcelona: Editorial Vergara, 1965.

Las Mil y una noches. Barcelona: Editorial Mateu, 1967.

Barcelona: Ediciones 29, 1981.

Madrid: Pérez del Hoyo, 1975.

Nezahualcóyotl: Ediciones Leyenda, 2003.

Madrid: Edimat Libros, 2004.

Trans. Luis Rutiaga. Mexico, D.F.: Grupo Editorial Tomo, 2004.

Ed. and trans. José María Sicilia, Enrique Morente, Juan Goytisolo, et al. Gran Canaria, Canary Islands: Centro Atlántico de Arte Moderno, 2005.

Mexico: Editores Mexicanos Unidos, 2006.

Las mil y una noches, cuentos árabes. Barcelona: Imprenta de D. Antonio Bergnes y compañia, 1841.

Bogotá, Colombia: Ediciones Universales, 1984.

Las Mil y Una Noches: Esmerada Selección de Cuentos Arabes. Barcelona: Ediciones Obelisco, 2006.

Las mil y una noches: selección cuidadosa y expurgada de la famosa colección de cuentos arábes que tradujo al frances Galland en el siglo xvii. Madrid: Editorial Saturnino Calleja, 19–?

Las mil y una noches: Thousand and one nights. Buenos Aires: NEED, 1999.

Las mil y una noches: traducción espaõla según la versión francesa de A. Galland. Barcelona: Ramon Sopena, 1981, 1962.

Mahfuz, Najib. *Las noches de las mil y una noches*. Barcelona: Plaza & Janés, 1996.

Mardrus, J. C., and Vicente Blasco Ibáñez, *Las Mil y una noches*. Bogotá, Colombia: Editorial La oveja negra, 2003.

Rodrigo, Argüello G. *Sherezada cuenta de Nuevo*. Santa Fe, Bogotá: Editorial Letra Escarlata, 1998.

Rodríguez, Acero, and Huadi Margarita. *Las Mil y Una Noches: Versión Completa*. Buenos Aires: Longseller, 2005.

Rohde, Teresa E. *Las Mil y una noches*. México: Editorial Porrúa, 1972.

Samsó, Julio, ed. *Antología de Las mil y una noches*. Madrid: Alianza Editorial, 1975.

Selección de Las mil y una noches, ed. Kenneth Dillard Dills. Barcelona: Círculo de lectores, 1969.

Vernet Ginés, Juan. *Las Mil y una noches*. Barcelona: Editorial Planeta, 1970–75, 2003.

Las mil y una noches: antología. Barcelona: Salvat Alianza, 1970.

Las mil y una noches: Aladino y la Lámpara Maravillosa; Sindbad, el marino; Alí Babá y los Cuarenta Ladrones. Barcelona: Planeta DeAgostini, 2003.

Weil, Gustav, and Antoine Isaac Silvestre de Sacy. *Las Mil y una noches*. Paris: 1855.

Swedish

Bergman, H. F. E. *Tusen och en natt; en sagokrans från Österlandet*, ed. Sir Richard Francis Burton, trans. Ernst Gustaf Lundquist and R. Heijll. Stockholm: A. Bonnier, 1921–27.

Holmberg, Nils. *Tusen och en natt; en sagokrans från Österlandet*. Stockholm: Tidens Bokklubb, 1958.

Moberg, Axel. *Tusen och en natt; en sagokrans från Österlandet*. Stockholm: Bonnier, 1928.

Tengström, Edvin. *Tusen och en natt; en sagokrans från Österlandet*. Gotheburg: Mellgrens förlag, 1926.

Wahlenberg, Anna, and Louis Maria Moe. *Tusen och en natt; en sagokrans från Österlandet*. Stockholm: Svensk Läraretidnings, 1899.

Weil, Gustav. *Tusen och en natt; en sagokrans från Österlandet*. Stockholm: P.A. Huldberg, 1875.

Turkish

See Birkalan(-Gedik), Hande E. "The Thousand and One Nights in Turkish: Translations, Adaptations, and Related Issues." *Fabula* 45, 3–4: 2004. 189–206; revised version in *The Arabian Nights in Transnational Perspective*. ed. by Ulrich Marzolph. Detroit: Wayne State Univ. Press 2007, pp. 201–220.

Appendix B: Selections from a Comparative Study between the Grub Street Translation of Galland (Reprinted in *The Novelist's Magazine*), and Haddawy's Translation of Muhsin Mahdi's Edition of Galland's Original Arabic Manuscript

This is a selection of samples from the Grub Street translation of Galland's French version (left column), reproduced in Harrison's *Novelist's Magazine*, 1785. It is compared to Husain Haddawy's translation from the manuscript which Galland used, edited by Muhsin Mahdi (right column). The translator often ascribes different emotions to a scene. Apart from known deviations from the manuscript, already noticed by Mahdi and others, there are other departures and omissions and additions that were much in keeping with what Galland justified as decorum, or accommodation. Other departures are in keeping with his knack for storytelling. Sometimes the additions serve the purpose of distancing or exoticizing the scene by saying something to the effect of "In the ways of the Arabians," or "In the custom of Eastern princes," and so on.

Abbreviations

AD	additional description
CAE	the story has been altered in order to fit a different cultural context – emotional
CAP	the story has been altered in order to fit a different cultural context – political
CAS	the story has been altered in order to fit a different cultural context – social/moral
CR	a specific cultural reference has been omitted
EC	edited due to claims of modesty and decorum
OM	omission that alters the story significantly
RG	a reference to God has been omitted
VO	verse omitted

Volume the First	**Prologue**
(Page 7: Paragraph 1) *No reference to God.*	(Page 3: Paragraph 1) . . . but God knows and sees best what lies hidden in the old accounts of bygone peoples and times.
The chronicles of the Sussians . . . acquaint us that there was formerly a king of that potent family . . .	It is related . . . during the time of the Sasanid dynasty, there lived two kings who were brothers.
All subsequent qualities are ascribed to the King.	*All subsequent qualities are ascribed to Shahrayar.*
(7:2) *Most of this paragraph conforms with (3:1) in HH. Here we find references to Shahzaman's status within the empire and an account of his feelings for his brother that we don't see in HH.*	
(7:3) . . . and went out to meet him with the principle lords of his court, who, to put the more honor on the Sultan's minister, appeared in magnificent apparel.	(3:2) He went out with his retainers . . . to meet him . . .
A long dialogue occurs at this point.	*No dialogue appears here.*
	(3:3) At midnight he returned to his palace in the city, to bid his wife goodbye.
(7:4) But willing once more to embrace the queen, whom he loved entirely, he returned alone to his palace . . . [He] went straight to her majesty's apartment; who, not expecting his return, had taken *one of the meanest officers of the household* to her bed . . .	But when he returned to his palace, he found his wife lying in the arms of *one of the kitchen boys*.
(8:1) . . . by the light of the flambeaux which burn all night in the apartments of those eastern princes . . .	"No. Women are not to be trusted."
No reference to the character of women. *Uses the term "scimitar."*	*Uses the term "sword."*
(8:2) . . . with kettle drums and other instruments of music, that filled everyone with joy, except the King; who was so much troubled at the disloyalty of his wife that *he was filled with extreme melancholy* . . .	The drum was struck, and they set out on their journey, while Shahzaman's *heart was on fire* because of what his wife had done to him.
(8:3) The Sultan conducted his brother to the palace he had provided for him, which had communication with his own by means of a garden; and was so much more the magnificent because it was set apart as a	(4:1) He offered him quarters in a palace adjoining his own, for King Shahrayar had built two beautiful towering palaces in his garden, one for guests, the other for women and members of his household. *HH has not yet used the word "Sultan," only "King."*

banqueting house for public entertainment and other diversions of the court . . .

(8:5) . . . though the conversation of his brother had suspended hi grief for some time, it returned on him with more violence; so that instead of taking his necessary rest, he tormented himself with cruel reflections. All the circumstances of his wife's disloyalty represented themselves afresh to his imagination in so lively a manner that he was like one beside himself. In a word, not being able to sleep, he got up and, giving himself over to afflicting thoughts, they made such an impression upon his countenance that the Sultan could not help but take notice of it. *The Sultan reflects*: "What can be the matter with the King of Tartary, that he is so melancholy? Has he any cause to complain about his reception? No, surely I have received him as a brother whom I love, so that I can charge myself with no omission in that respect. Perhaps it grieves him to be at such a distance from his dominions and from the Queen, his wife . . ."

(9:2) He observed that the persons who accompanied the Sultaness threw off their veils and long robes, that they might be at more freedom; but was wonderfully surprised when he saw that ten of them were blacks, and that each of them took a mistress. The Sultaness, on her part, was not long without her gallant; she clapped her hands and called "Masoud! Masoud!" and immediately a black came down form a tree, and ran to her in all haste."

(9:3) Modesty will not allow, nor is it necessary to relate, what passed between the blacks and the ladies . . .
They carried on until midnight . . .

(9:4) "How little reason had I," he said, "to think that no one was so unfortunate as myself? It is certainly the unavoidable fate of all husbands, since the Sultan, my brother, who is sovereign of so many dominions, and the greatest prince on earth, could not escape it . . . "

But whenever he found himself alone and thought of the ordeal with his wife, he would sigh deeply, then stifle his grief, and say, "Alas, that this great misfortune should have happened to one in my position!" Then he would fret with anxiety, his spirit would sag and he would say, "None has seen what I have seen." In his depression, he ate less and less, grew pale, and his health deteriorated. He neglected everything, wasted away, and looked ill.

(4:2) When King Shahrayar looked as this brother and saw how day after day he lost weight and grew thin, pale, ashen and sickly, he thought that this was because of his expatriation and homesickness for his country and family . . .

(5:1) Then they sat down, took off their clothes, and suddenly there were ten slave-girls and ten black slaves dressed in the same clothes as the girls. Then the ten black slaves mounted the ten girls, while the lady called "Mas'ud, Mas'ud!" and a black slave jumped from a tree to the ground, rushed to her, and, raising her legs, went between her thighs and made love to her. Mas'ud topped the lady, while the ten slaves topped the ten girls, and they carried on till noon.

(5:2) "This is our common lot. Even though my brother is king and master of the whole world, he cannot protect what is his, his wife and concubines, and suffers misfortune in his very home. What happened to me is little by comparison. I used to think that I was the only one who suffers, but from what I have seen, everyone suffers. By God, my misfortune is lighter than that of my brother."

(10:1) "I imagined it might be occasioned by the reason of your distance from your dominions; or that love might have a great share in it, and that the Queen of Samarcande, who no doubt is an accomplished beauty, might be the cause."
(10:2) "Oh my brother!" said the Sultan, in a tone that shewed that he had the same sentiments in the matter as the King of Tartary . . ."

(6:1) "As you continued like this, I thought what ailed you was your homesickness for your family and your country . . .

(6:2) When King Shahrayar heard his brother's explanation, he shook his head, greatly amazed at the deceit of women, and prayed to God to protect him from their wickedness, saying, "Brother, you were fortunate in killing your wife and her lover . . ."

(10:3) " . . . yet I am afraid that my obedience will occasion your trouble to be greater than mine ever was; but you must blame yourself for it, since you force me to reveal a thing which I should otherwise have buried in eternal oblivion . . . "

Shahzaman: "King, I wish for God's sake you would excuse me from telling you . . . I fear that you will feel even more troubled and careworn than I."

The King of Tartary being no longer able to refuse gave him all the particulars . . . "After being witness to these infamous actions," said he, "I believed all women to be naturally that way inclined, and that they could not resist those violent desires. Being of this opinion, it seemed to me to be an unaccountable weakness of men to make themselves uneasy at their infidelity . . . I thought the best thing I could do was make myself easy . . . if you will take my advice, you shall follow my example."

(7:1) Shazaman then told him about what he had seen from the palace window and the calamity in his very home . . . He told him everything from beginning to end (but there is no point in repeating that) . . .

(11:1) "What!" says he, "is the Sultaness of the Indies capable of prostituting herself in so base a manner? No Brother, I cannot believe what you say, except I saw it with my own eyes."
(11:2) Next day the two princes set out . . . They had scarce placed themselves in the frame window . . . but the secret gate opened, and the Sultaness and her ladies entered the garden with the blacks; and having called upon Masoud, the Sultan saw more than enough to convince him plainly of his dishonour and misfortune."

(7:2) When the King Shahrayar heard what his brother said and found out what happened to him, he was furious and his blood boiled. He said, "Brother, I can't believe what you say unless I see it with my own eyes."
(7:3) . . . when God's morning broke, the two rode out of the city . . .
When they awoke, they sat at the palace window, watching the garden and chatting until the light broke, the day dawned, and the sun rose. As they watched, the private gate opened . . . They then took off their women's clothes, and suddenly there were ten slaves, who mounted the girls and made love to them. As for the lady, she called, "Mas'ud, Mas'ud" and a black slave jumped from the

	tree to the ground, came to her and said, "What do you want, you slut? Here is Sa'ad al Din Mas'ud." She laughed and fell on her back, while the slave mounted her and like the others did his business with her.
(11:3) Shahzaman did not at all approve of this resolution; but did not think fit to contradict Shahrayar in the heat of his passion.	(8:1) Then he turned to his brother and asked, "Would you like to follow me in what I shall do?" Shahzaman answered, "Yes. I will . . . This is an excellent idea. I shall follow you."
They sat down under those trees to rest a refresh themselves; and the chief subject of their conversation was the lewdness of their wives.	(8:2) While they sat in a meadow amid thick plants and trees, discussing their misfortunes and recent events . . .
(11:4) . . . but in a little time they found it was one of those malignant Genii who are mortal enemies to mankind, and always doing them mischief.	When they looked again they saw it was a black demon . . .
(12:2) When they came down, the lady took them by the hand, and, going a little farther with them under the trees, made a very urgent proposal to them. At first they rejected it; but she obliged them to accept it by her threats. Having obtained what she desired . . .	(9:1) She kept gesturing and pressing until they came down very slowly and stood before her. Then she lay on her back, raised her legs, and said, "Make love to me and satisfy my need, or else I shall wake the demon, and he will kill you." They replied, "For God's sake, don't do this to us . . ." As she persisted, they could no longer resist and they made love to her, first the older brother, then the younger.
(12:3) "And do you not agree that there is no wickedness equal to that of a woman's?"	*No such quote.*
No such quote.	(10:2) "There is not a single chaste woman anywhere on the entire face of the earth."
[When a method of execution mentioned in reference to the murder of the Sultaness and other women, it is death by strangulation.]	*[When a method of execution mentioned in reference to the murder of the Sultaness and other women, it is death by sword.]*
(13:4) The rumor of this unparalleled barbarity . . .	*No such judgment of Shahrayar's actions given.*
So that, instead of the commendations and blessings which the Sultan had hitherto received from his subjects, their mouths were now filled with imprecations against him.	(10:3) . . . and there arose a clamor among the fathers and mothers, who called the plague upon his head, complained to the Creator of the heavens, and called for help on Him who hears and answers prayers.
(13:5) . . . but the elder had courage, wit, and penetration, infinitely above her sex . . .	(11:1) She was intelligent, knowledgeable, wise and refined. She had read and learned.
No mention of a popular saying.	As the popular saying goes, "I would be sitting pretty, but for my curiosity."

THE TALE OF THE OX AND THE DONKEY

[Again, the translator confuses night and day. What, in HH is said to be nighttime, is called day here.]

No such saying.

(14:5) The ox took the ass's advice in very good part, and he owned he was very much obliged to him for it: "Dear Sprightly," added he, "I will not fail to do all that you have said, and you shall see how I acquit myself."

(15:2) He was glad at the heart that he had followed the ass's advice, blessed him a thousand times for it, and did not fail to compliment him upon it when he saw him come back.

(15:3) "Alas! What did you hear?" said the ox. "As you love me, hide nothing from me, my dear Sprightly!"

(16:1) This discourse had the effect which the ass designed; the ox was strangely troubled at it; and bellowed out for fear.

"If you do not satisfy me presently, what you laugh at, and tell me the ox and the ass said to one another, I swear by heaven that you and I shall never bed together again."

... finding that the next morning, she continued in the same humor, told her she was a very foolish woman to afflict herself in that manner ...

[This scene is framed differently in the two translations. Here, it is the wife who is willing to die in order to discover what her husband heard; her family is called in to see her before her death. The paragraph closes with:] ... the merchant himself was like a man out if his senses, and was almost ready to risk his own life to save that of his wife, whom he loved dearly.

THE TALE OF THE OX AND THE DONKEY

(12:1) "Have you not heard the saying, 'Out of bad luck, they hastened on the road.'"

(12:2) He thanked him, commended him to God, and invoked his blessings upon him, and said, "May you stay safe from harm, watchful one."

(13:1) All day long he kept praising the donkey's advice and invoking God's blessing upon him ... "Good evening, watchful one! You have done me a favor beyond description, for I have been sitting in comfort. God bless you for it."

HH inserts a title here while NM does not:

THE TALE OF THE MERCHANT AND HIS WIFE

(14:1) The ox asked, "What?"

The ox farted and bellowed.

-(14:2) His wife said, "By God, you are lying. This is nothing but an excuse. I swear by God, the Lord of Heaven, that if you don't tell me and explain the cause of your laughter, I will leave you."

The merchant said, "Damn it! Tell me why you are crying. Ask for God's forgiveness, and stop questioning and leave me in peace."

[Here, it is the husband who will die if he imparts what he has heard. He calls in the family to see him before he dies and makes out his will. The paragraph ends:] "Desist, for if your husband had not known for certain that he would die if he revealed his secret, he wouldn't have gone through all this." She replied, "I will not change my mind," and everybody cried and prepared to mourn his death.

(15:1) ... he overheard a dog of his say something in dog language to the rooster,

(16:2) . . . and considering what he had left to do, saw his dog run towards the cock as he was treading a hen . . .
(17:2) . . . he went that minute to acquaint the Sultan that next night he would bring him Shahrazad.
(17:3) *[A long dialogue unfolds between the King and his vizier that is not present in HH. In it, the vizier proclaims that his daughter prefers the honor of being the Sultan's bride over the value of her own life.]*
(18:1) The Sultan went to bed with Shahrazad upon an alcove raised very high, according to the custom of monarchs of the East . . .

who, beating and clapping his wings, had jumped on a hen, and finishing with her, jumped down and jumped on another . . .
(16:1) Tired and exhausted the vizier went to King Shahrayar and, kissing the ground before him, told him about his daughter . . .
(16:2) *Again, a reference to God not found in Galland:* "Vizier, how is it that you have found it possible to give me your daughter, knowing that I will, by God, the Creator of heaven, ask you to put her to death . . ."

NIGHT 1: THE MERCHANT AND THE GENIUS

(18:5) He had abundance of deputies, factors and slaves.
. . . he took horse, and put a portmanteau behind him, with some biscuits and dates because he had a great desert to pass over . . .
He arrived without any incident at the end of his journey . . .
(18:6) When he had done eating, being a good Mussulman, he washed his hands, his face, and his feet, and said his prayers.
Throughout the scene, the translator uses the word "scimitar."
"Ah my lord, pardon me!" cried the merchant. "No pardon" answered the Genius, "No mercy. Is it not unjust to kill him who has killed another?" "I agree to it" said the merchant, "but certainly I never killed your son; and if I have, it was unknown to me, and I did it innocently, therefore I beg you to pardon me, and to suffer me to live."
(19:1) The merchant . . . spoke to the Genius in the most moving expressions that could be uttered.

No verse.

NIGHT 1: THE STORY OF THE MERCHANT AND THE DEMON

(17:1) He had many women and children and kept many servants and slaves.
No mention of a desert.

. . . he journeyed under God's care until he reached his destination.
Then he got up, performed his ablutions, and performed his prayers.

Throughout the scene, the translator uses the word "sword."
(17:2) The merchant said, "O my lord, please don't kill me." The demon replied, "I must kill you as you killed him – blood for blood." The merchant said, "To God we belong and to God we return. There is no power or strength, save God the Almighty, the Magnificent. If I killed him, I did it by mistake. Please forgive me." Again the demon raised his sword to strike, while the merchant cried until he was drenched with tears, saying, "There is no power or strength, save in God the Almighty, the Magnificent."
There is a long verse given here.

NIGHT 2	**NIGHT 2**
(19:9) I swear by all that is sacred that I will come here and meet you without fail."	(19:1) "I swear to keep my pledge to come back, as the God of Heaven and Earth as my witness."
(20:1) *[A good example of the different translation styles of the two versions:]* When he came home his wife and children received him with all the demonstrations of perfect joy; but he, instead of making them suitable returns, began to weep bitterly; from whence they readily conjectured that something extraordinary had befallen him.	(19:2) *[A good example of the different translation styles of the two versions:]* He journeyed until he reached his home and came to his wife and children. When he saw them he wept bitterly, and when his family saw his sorrow and grief, they began to reproach him for his behavior . . .
(20: 4) "I obey the order of Heaven in quitting you; follow my example, submit courageously to this necessity, and consider that this is the destiny of man, to die."	"He said to them, "Children, this is God's will and decree, for man was created to die."
NIGHT 3	**NIGHT 3**
[Shahrazad's stories all begin with "Sir."]	*[Shahrazad's stories all begin with "O happy King."]*
NIGHT 4	**NIGHT 4**
(21:8) "I will tell you the history of my life, and of the bitch you see; and, if you think it more wonderful and surprising than the adventure of the merchant you are going to kill, I hope you will pardon the poor, unfortunate man the third of his crime."	(22:1) " . . . if I tell you what happened to me and that deer, and you find it strange and amazing, indeed stranger and more amazing than what happened to you and the merchant, will you grant me a third of your claim on him for his crime and guilt?"
The History of the First Old Man and the Bitch	**The First Old Man's Tale**
(21:10) The desire of having children only made me buy a slave, by whom I had a son, who was extremely promising. She made use of that time to satisfy her hatred; she applied herself to magic; and when she knew enough of that diabolical art to execute her horrible contrivance, the wretch took my son to a desolate place, where by her enchantment she turned him into a calf . . .	(22:2) Then I took a mistress, and she bore me a son, who grew up to look like a slice of the moon. In my absence my wife, this cousin of mine, learned soothsaying and magic and cast a spell on him and turned him into a young bull.
(22:3) The farmer, being less compassionate than I, sacrificed her . . .	(22:3) The shepherd butchered her . . .
(22:4) I was more surprised and affected with this action than with the tears of the cow; I felt a tender pity, which made me concern myself with him, or, rather, nature did its duty.	(23:1) I was astonished and touched with sympathy, pity, and mercy, for blood hearkened to blood and the divine bond, and my heart throbbed within me when I saw the tears coursing over the cheeks of my son the young bull, as he dug into the earth with his hoofs.

NIGHT 5

(23:4) At these words, added the old man, I leave you to think, my Lord Genius, how much I was surprised . . .

"As to what related to my wife, I also agree to it . . . I leave her to you; only I must pray that you not take her life . . . "

. . . said she, "if thou wast created by the Almighty and Sovereign Master of the world such as you appear at this time . . ." *[This translation agrees with that of HH, even in the evocations of God.]*

NIGHT 5

(24:1) Demon, when I heard that, I uttered a cry and fainted, and when I came to myself . . .

As for my wife . . . her life is forfeit to you."

She said, "No, but I will let her taste what she has inflicted on others."

NIGHT 6

(24) **The Story of the Second Old Man, and the Two Black Dogs**

(25:2) But when we were to make out preparations for our voyage, and to buy the goods necessary for our undertaking, I found they had spent all . . .

NIGHT 6

(26) **The Second Old Man's Tale**

(26:3) I found that they had eaten and drunk and squandered everything that they had . . .

NIGHT 7

(25:9) I made some difficulty to agree to it; but she said so many things to persuade me that I ought to make no objection to her poverty, and that I should have all the reason to be satisfied with her conduct, that I yielded.

. . . having married her according to form, I took her onboard and we set sail.

(26:1) My wife was a fairy . . .

"You must know that I am a fairy . . . "

(26:2) "No, my good lady," replied I, "For Heaven's sake, do not do so! Moderate your anger; consider that they are my brothers, and that we must do good for evil."

NIGHT 7

(27:4) . . . as your wife, I wish to give myself to you. I, in turn, will reward you for your kindness and charity, the Almighty God willing. . . . When I heard her words, I felt pity for her, and guided by what God the Most High had intended for me, I consented. Then I took her to the boat, spread the bed and we consummated our marriage.

(28:1) When we awoke, my wife turned into a she demon . . .

"Husband . . . I am one of those demons who believe in God."

I entreated her, saying "For God's sake don't. The proverb advises, 'Be kind to those that hurt you.'"

NIGHT 8

(27) **The Story of the Fisherman**

(27:10) He went one morning by moonlight; and coming to the sea bank . . .

. . . he was mightily vexed.

NIGHT 8

(30) **The Story of the Fisherman and the Demon**

(30:1) One day, while the mon was still up, he went out with his net at the call for the early morning prayer.

The fisherman felt sad and depressed and said to himself, "There is no power and so

	strength save in God the Almighty, the Magnificent . . . *There follows a verse that is omitted in Galland's.*
NIGHT 9	**NIGHT 9**
(28:1) *No exclamation to God.* *Verse:* But I am in the wrong to complain to thee; Thou take pleasure to persecute honest people, and to leave great men in obscurity.	(31:1) "God's we are and to God we return" (31-verse)*[Interestingly, both translations have this verse, with the following notable difference:]* The Pleides many fools attain While sages sit in dark disdain
Verse omitted. (28:2) However, when day began to appear, he did not forget to say his prayers, like a good Mussalman . . .	*Verse present.* (32:1) The fisherman raised his eyes to heaven . . . and said . . .
(28:4) . . . of which formed a Genius twice as high as the greatest of Giants.	(32:2) He had a head like a tomb, fangs like pincers, a mouth like a cave, teeth like stones, nostrils like trumpets, ears like shields, a throat like an alley, and eyes like lanterns.
NIGHT 10	**NIGHT 10**
(29:1) "It is above eighteen hundred years since the prophet Solomon died, and we are now at the end of time."	(33:3) ". . . It has been more than one thousand eight hundred years since the prophet Solomon died, and we are now ages later."
"You must speak to me with more civility; thou are very bold to call me a proud spirit." "Very well," replied the fisherman, "shall I speak to you with more civility and call you the owl of good luck?"	When the demon heard the fisherman, he said, "Be glad!" The fisherman cried, "O happy day!" The demon added, "Be glad that you will soon be put to death."
(29:4) Solomon, the son of David, commanded me to quit my way of living, to acknowledge his power, and to submit myself to his commands: I bravely refused to obey . . .	When the prophet saw me, he invoked God to protect him from me and my looks and asked me to submit to him, but I refused.
(29:6) This discourse afflicted the poor fisherman extremely. "I am very unfortunate," cried he, "to come hither and do such a piece of good service to one that is so ungrateful. I beg you to consider your injustice, and revoke such an unreasonable oath: pardon me and Heaven will pardon you; if you grant me my life, Heaven will protect you from all attempts against yours."	(34:1) When the fisherman heard what the demon had said, he replied, "To God we belong and to Him we return . . .. Forgive me and God will grant you forgiveness. Destroy me, and God will inflict on you one who will destroy you."
"The proverb says, 'That he who does good to one who deserves it not, is always ill rewarded."	"How true is the sentiment of the following lines: Our kindness they repaid with ugly deeds Upon my life, the deeds of men depraved He who the undeserving aids will meet

The fate of him who the hyena saved"

(30:1) Necessity is the mother of invention: the fisherman bethought himself a stratagem . . .

(34:2) The fisherman thought to himself, "He is only a demon, while I am a human being, whom god has endowed with reason and thereby made superior to him. He may use his demonic wiles on me, but I will use my reason to deal with him."

NIGHT 11

(30:6) . . . thou mayest very well stay till the day of judgment.

The Tale of the Grecian King and the Physician Douban

(31:2) There was in the country of Zouman, in Persia, a king whose subjects were originally Greeks.

[The Grub Street translator uses physician, not sage. Douban is always called "physician."]

(31:3) As soon as he was informed of the king's distemper, and understood that his physicians had given him over, he clad himself as best he could, and found a way to present himself to the king.

(31:4) "I promise myself success, through God's assistance . . . "

NIGHT 11

(35:4) This time I will let you stay there until Doomsday.

The Tale of King Yunan and the Sage Duban

(36:2) Demon, there was a king called Yunan, who reigned in one of the cities in Persia, in the Province of Zuman. *The translator identifies, in a footnote, this province as modern Armenia.*

On the following day, when God's morning dawned and His sun rose, the sage Duban put on his best clothes and went to King Yunan . . .

The sage replied, "I hear and obey. I'll do it tomorrow morning, the Almighty God willing."

NIGHT 12

Omitted

(32:3) As soon as he was dressed, he came to the hall of public audience, where he mounted his throne and showed himself to his courtiers . . .

. . . and gave him all the commendation he deserved.

NIGHT 12

(38:1–38:2) "As for the sage Duban" to "as clear and pure as silver."

(38:2) Thus when he went in the morning to the reception hall and sat on his throne, attended by Mamluks . . .

Then the King bestowed on him robes of honor, gave him gifts and endowments, and granted his wishes.

NIGHT 13

(32:5) Dinarazade, willing to keep the Sultan in ignorance of her design, cried out, as if starting suddenly from her sleep, "O dear sister! I have had a troubling dream; and

NIGHT 13

(39:2) The following night, Dinarzad said to her sister, "Sister, if you are not sleepy, tell us one of your lovely tales to while away the night."

nothing will sooner make me forget it than the remainder of your story . . . "	
(32:7) "The Grecian King . . . was not satisfied with having admitted the physician Douban to his table; but towards night when he was about to dismiss the company, he caused him to be clad in a long, rich robe, like those which his favorites usually wore in his presence . . .	(39:3) I heard, O happy King who is praiseworthy by the Grace of God, that King Yunan bestowed favors on the sage, gave him robes of honor . . .
No comparable sentence.	The Sage went home and spent the night with his wife, feeling happy and thankful to God the Arbiter.
To effect this, he went to the king, and told him in private that he had some advice to give him which was of the greatest concernment.	(39:4) The envious vizier approached the king . . . and said, "O excellent King and glorious Lord, it was by your kindness that I rose to prominence; therefore, if I fail to advise you on a grave matter, I am not my father's son."
(33:4) "I am very well pleased that Grecian King, said Dinarzade, had so much firmness of spirit to reject the false accusation of the vizier." If you commend that firmness today" said Scheherazade, "you will as much condemn his weakness, if the Sultan will be pleased to allow me to finish this story."	(40:2) Then her sister, Dinarzad, said, "Sister, what a lovely story!" Shahrazad relied, "What is this compared with what I shall tell you tomorrow night . . ."
NIGHT 14 **The Story of the Husband and the Parrot**	**NIGHT 14** **The Tale of the Husband and the Parrot**
(34:1) A certain man had a fair wife whom he loved so dearly that he could scarce allow her to be out of his sight.	(41:2) I have heard it told that there was once a very jealous man who had a wife so splendidly beautiful that she was perfection itself. The wife always refused to let her husband travel and leave her behind . . .
At his return, he took care to ask the parrot concerning what had passed in his absence, and the bird told him things that gave him the occasion to upbraid his wife.	The parrot gave him a day-by-day account of what his wife had done with her lover and how the two carried on in his absence.
NIGHT 15 **The Story of the Vizier Who Was Punished**	**NIGHT 15** **The Tale of the King's Son and the She-Ghoul**
(35:1) As they passed by the ruins of a house, they lady signified a desire to alight on some occasion.	(42:5) As they passed some ruins, she said, "O my lord, I wish to relieve myself here."
. . . and other voices, which answered immediately, "Mamma, where is he, that we may eat him presently, for we are very hungry."	They replied, "Mother, bring us to him so we may feed on his innards."
(35:2) . . . and then he perceived that the lady who called herself daughter to an Indian	

King was a Hogress, wife to one of those savage demons, called Hogres, who stay in remote places and make use of a thousand wiles to surprise and devour passengers.

When the young prince heard what they had said, he shook with terror, and, fearing for his life, ran outside.

NIGHT 16

(36:4) The Grecian King, who naturally had very little sense, was not able to discover the wicked design of his vizier; nor had he the firmness enough to persist in his first opinion. This discourse staggered him . . .
Verse omitted.

(36:7) *Two verses omitted.*
No similar passage.

(37:3) . . . and to bequeath my books to those who are capable of making good use of them. I have one, particularly, I would present it to your majesty; it is a very precious book, and worthy to be laid up very carefully in your treasury. "Well," replied the king, "Why is that book so precious as you talk of?" "Sir," said the physician, "It is because it contains an infinite number of curious things . . . "

(37:5) The physician Douban was soon brought in . . . with a great book in his hand; there he called for a basin, upon which he laid the cover that the book was wrapped in.
The translator is taking more and more liberties with the frame tale, adding whole sections of dialogue between Dinarzad, Shahrazad, and the King.

NIGHT 16

(44:1) King Yunan, who was beginning to feel angry, replied . . .

(45:2) Then the sage added, "Is this my reward from your Majesty? It is like the reward of the crocodile." The king asked, "What is the story of the crocodile?" The sage replied, I am in no condition to tell you a story. For God's sake spare me, and God will spare you . . .

(46:1) I have a particular book entitled the *Secret of Secrets*, which I should like to give you for safekeeping in your library." The king asked, "What is the secret of this book?" The sage replied, "It contains countless secrets . . ."

(46:2) The sage Duban entered, carrying an old book and a khol jar containing powder. He sat down, ordered a platter, and poured out the powder and smoothed it on the platter.

NIGHT 17

(38:5) "Tyrant," it cried, "now you see how princes are treated, who, abusing their authority, cut off innocent men: God punishes soon or late, their injustice and cruelty."

NIGHT 17

(47:3) For long they ruled us arbitrarily
But suddenly vanished their powerful rule
Had they been just, they would have happily
Lived, but they oppressed, and punishing fate
Afflicted them with ruin deservedly,
And on the morrow the world taunted them
"Tis tit for tat; blame not just destiny."

NIGHT 18

(38:9) "No," said the fisherman, "I will not let thee out; it is in vain to talk of it . . . "

NIGHT 18

(48:1) The fisherman said, "I must throw you into the sea . . . when you treated me this way I realized that you were unclean from birth . . ."

"Hear me one more word," cried the Genius, "I promise to do thee no hurt, nay, far from that, I will shew thee a way how thou may become exceedingly rich."
(39:1) The hope of delivering himself from poverty prevailed with the fisherman . . .

(39:3) The Genius laughed at the fisherman's fear and answered, "No, fisherman, be not afraid, I only did it to divert myself, and to see if thou would be alarmed at it, but to persuade thee that I am in earnest, take thy nets and follow me."

The demon replied, "Set me free this time, and I pledge never to bother you or harm you, but to make you rich." When he heard this, the fisherman made the demon pledge covenant that if the fisherman released him and let him out, he would not harm him but would serve him and be good to him.
(48:2) When the demon heard what the fisherman said, he laughed, and the fisherman cried out again, "Demon, spare me," he replied, "Fisherman, follow me," and he followed him . . .

NIGHT 19

(39:9) "Take those fishes," said he to his prime vizier, "and carry them to the fine cook maid that the emperor of the Greeks has sent me."
(40:1) "Look ye," he said, "here are four fishes newly brought to the sultan; he orders you to dress them."

(40:2) The fisherman, who had never seen so much cash in his lifetime, could scarce believe his own good fortune, but thought it must be a dream, till he found it to be real, when he provided necessaries for his family with it.

(40:6) . . . but without speaking a word of it to the sultan, he invented an excuse that would satisfy him; and sending immediately for the fisherman, bid him bring four more such fish . . . The fisherman, without saying anything the Genius had told him, in order to excuse himself from bringing them that very day, told the vizier that he had a great way to go for them, but would certainly bring them tomorrow.

NIGHT 19

(49:3) Then he said to his vizier, "Take them to the cook whom the emperor of Byzantium has given us as a present."

"Girl, as the saying goes, 'I save my tears for the time of trial.' The king has been presented these four fish, and he bids you fry them well."
The vizier gave the money to the fisherman, who, receiving it, gathered it in the folds of his robe and went away, running, and as he ran, stumbled and kept falling and getting up, thinking that he was in a dream. Then he stopped and bought some provisions for his family.
(50:2) The vizier was astonished and said, "This is very strange." Then he sent an officer after the fisherman, and he returned a while later with the fisherman. The vizier shouted at him, saying, "Bring us at once four more fish like the ones you brought us before, for we had an accident with them." When he followed with threats, the fisherman went home and, taking his fishing gear, went outside the city . . .

NIGHT 20

(41:3) . . . then the wall of the closet opened, but instead of the young lady, there came out a black, in the habit of a slave, and of gigantic

NIGHT 20

(52:1) When they were almost done, the palace wall split open . . . and when they looked up, they saw a black slave who stood towering like a mountain, or a giant stature, with a great green battoon in his hand.

(42:2) . . . and then he saw before him, at a considerable distance, a great building . . . When he came near. he found it was magnificent palace, or rather a very strong castle . . .

descendant of the tribe of 'Ad. He was as tall as a reed, as wide as a stone bench, and held a green palm leaf in his hand.

(53:2) . . . and when he arrived, he found a palace, built under a lucky star . . .

NIGHT 21

(42:8) The sultan, perceiving nobody in the court, entered the great halls which were hung with silk tapestry, the alcoves and sofas were covered with stuffs from Mecca; and the poches with the richest stuffs of the Indies, mixed with gold and silver.

. . . water issued from the mouths of the four lions . . . which, springing from the middle of the fountain, rose as high almost as the bottom of a cupola, painted in the Arabian manner. *[more details that are Galland's invention]*

NIGHT 21

(54:3) The palace was furnished with silk carpets and leather mats and hung with drapes. There were also settees, benches, seats with cushions, as well as cupboards.

(43:1) He listened with attention, and heard distinctly these sad words: "O Fortune! thou who wouldst not suffer me longer to enjoy a happy lot; and hast made me the most unfortunate man in the world, forbear to persecute me, and by a speedy death put an end to my sorrows. Alas! Is it possible that I am still alive, after the many torments I have suffered?"

(54:3) . . . when he heard sad moans and lamentations and the following plaintive verses:

My soul is torn between peril and toil / O life dispatch me with one mighty blow / Lover, neither bankrupt nor a noble man / Humbled by love's law do you pity show / Ev'n from the breeze I jealously used to guard you / But at the blow of fate the eyes blind go / When, as he pulls to shoot, the bowstring breaks / What can the bowman facing foes do? / And when the foes begin to congregate / How can he escape his cruel fate?

(43:2) . . . and saw a handsome young man, richly habited, set upon a throne raised a little above the ground. Melancholy was painted on his looks.

(54:4) He was a handsome young man, with a full figure, clear voice, radiant brow, bright face, downy beard and ruddy cheeks, graced with a mole like a speck of amber, just as the poet describes it: Here is a slender youth whose hair and face / All mortals envelope with light or gloom. / Mark on his cheek the mark of charm and grace / A dark spot on red anemone. *More physical descriptions, absent in Galland's.*

"Being drawn hither by your complaints, and afflicted by your grief, I come to offer you my help, would to God it lay in my power to ease your troubles . . . I flatter myself that you will willingly tell me the history of your

(55:1) The king replied, "Young man, you are pardoned. I myself have come on a serious mission. Pray tell me the story behind the lake . . ."

misfortunes; but pray tell me first the meaning of the pond near the palace …	
(43:3) Instead of answering those questions, the young man began to weep bitterly, "O how inconstant is fortune!" cried he, "she takes pleasure to pull down those men she has raised up. Where are they who enjoy quietly the happiness which they hold of her, and whose day is always clear and serene?"	When the young man heard this, his tears began to flow over his cheeks until they drenched his breast. Then he sang the following *Mawwaliya* verses: Say to the man whom life with arrows shot / "How many men have felt the blows of fate!" / If you did sleep, the eyes of God had not / Who can say time is fair and life in constant state?
NIGHT 22	**NIGHT 22**
(43:7) "That which you shew me," said he, "as it fills me with horror, whets my curiosity, so that I am impatient to hear your history, which, no doubt, is very strange, and I am persuaded that the pond and the fishes make some part of it, therefore I conjure you to tell it to me. You will find comfort in it, since it is certain, that unfortunate people find some sort of ease in telling their misfortune."	(56:1) "Young man, you have added one more worry to my worries. I came here to look for an answer to the mystery of the fish, in order to save them, but ended up looking for an answer to your case as well as the fish. There is no power and no strength save in God, the Almighty, the Magnificent. Hurry up young man, and tell me your story."
The History of the Young King of the Black Isles	**The Tale of the Enchanted King**
(44:1) "You must know, my lord," continued he, "that my father, who was called Mahmoud …	(56:2) My story, and the story of the fish, is a strange and amazing one, which, if it could be engraved with needles at the corner of the eye, would be lesson to those who would consider. My father was the king of this city, and his name was King Mahmud.
(44:2) I had all the reason imaginable to be satisfied in her love for me; and for my part, had so much tenderness for her that nothing was comparable to the good understanding betwixt us, which lasted for five years, at the end of which time, I perceived the queen, my cousin, had no more delight in me.	She loved me very much, so much so that if I was away from her for even a single day, she would refuse to eat and drink until I returned to her. In this way we lived together for five years until one day she went to the bath and I ordered the cook to grill meat and prepare a sumptuous supper for her.
(44:3) Two of her ladies, who were in my chamber, came and sat down, one at my head, the other at my feet, with fans in their hands, to moderate the heat, and hinder the flies from troubling my sleep.	Then I entered this palace, lay down in this very spot where you are sitting now, and ordered two maids to sit down, one at my head and one at my feet, to fan me.
(44:4) One of them said to the other, "Is not the queen much in the wrong not to love such an amiable prince as this?" "Aye, certainly!" replied the other, "for my part I do not understand it; and I know not why she goes out every night and leaves him alone …"	The other one replied, "what can one say? May God damn all treacherous, adulterous women. Alas, it is not right that such a young man like our master lives with this bitch who spends every night out." … The other replied, "Alas, may God trip the bitch, our mistress."

(44:7) We went to bed together; and soon after, believing I was asleep, though I was not, she got up with so little precaution, that she said, so loud that I could hear it distinctly, "Sleep, and may you never wake again." She dressed herself speedily, and went out of the chamber.

(57:1) No sooner had I fallen on my side than my wife said, "Go to sleep, and may you never rise again. By God, your sight disgusts me and your company bores me." The she put on her clothes, perfumed herself with burning incense and, taking my sword, girded herself with it. Then she opened the door and walked out.

NIGHT 23

(45:2) I went thither by another way; and slipping behind the pallisadoes of a long walk, I saw her walking there with a man. I gave very good heed to their discourse, and heard the queen say thus to her gallant, "I do not deserve to be upbraided by you for want of diligence; you know very well what hinders me; but if all the marks of love that I have already given you be not enough, I am ready to give you greater marks of it; you need but command me; you know my power. I will, if you desire it, before sun-rising, change this great city, and this fine palace, into frightful ruins, which shall be inhabited by nothing but wolves, owls and ravens. Would you have me transport all the stones of these walls, so solidly built, beyond Mount Caucasus and out of the bounds of the habitable world . . ."

The following does not appear in the HH edition:
(45:5) In the meantime, the blow I had given to her gallant was mortal; but she preserved his life by the force of her enchantments; in such a manner however, that he could not be said to be either alive or dead. As I crossed the garden to return to the palace I heard the queen cry out lamentably; and judging by how much she was grieved, I was pleased that I had spared her life.

NIGHT 23

(57:4) . . . I saw my wife standing before a decrepit black man sitting on reed shavings and dressed in tatters. She kissed the ground before him and, her raised his head and said, "Damn you, why are you so late? My black cousins were here. They played with the bat and the ball, sang and drank brewed liquor. They had a good time, each with his own girlfriend, except for myself, for I refused to even drink with them because you were absent."

(58:1) My wife replied, "O my lord and lover, don't you know that I am married to my cousin, who finds me most loathsome and detests me more than anyone else? Were it not for your sake, I would not have let the sun rise before reducing this city to rubble, a dwelling place for bears and foxes, where the owl hoots and the crow crows, and would have hurled the stones beyond Mount Qaf."

From, He replied, "Damn you, you are lying . . ." *to*, "Then she undressed and slipped under his tatters . . ." *is omitted in Galland's. The HH edition ends the twenty-third night here, whereas Galland's continues.*

NIGHT 24

(46:2) "Madam," said I, "I am so far from blaming for your grief, that I assure you, I am willing to bear whatever share of it is proper

NIGHT 24

(59:1) When I heard what she said, I did not reply, except to say, "I do not reproach you. Do as you wish."

for me. I should wonder if you were insensible of so great a loss! Mourn on; your tears are so many proof of your good nature; but I hope, however, that time and reason will moderate your grief."

(46:5) *In this edition, the lament of the queen to her lover is given in prose.*

(59:2) *In this edition, the lament of the queen to her lover is given in verse and song.*

(46:6) "Madam, you have mourned enough; it is time to give over this sorrow which dishonors us both: you have too much forgot what you owe to me and to yourself." "Sir," said she, "if you have any kindness of compliance left for me, I beseech you to put no force upon me; allow me to give myself up to mortal grief; it is impossible for time to lessen it."

(60:3) When she stopped crying, I said to her, "Wife, you have mourned and wept enough and further tears are useless." She replied, "Husband, do not interfere with my mourning. If you interfere again I will kill myself."

(46:8) . . . and heard her speak thus to her gallant: It is now three years since you last spoke one word to me; you return no answer to the marks of love I give you by my discourse and groans. Is it from want of sense, or out of contempt? O tomb, have you abated that excessive love he had for me? Have you shut those eyes that shewed me so much love, and were all my joy? No, no! I believe nothing of it! Tell me rather by what miracle you became entrusted with the rarest treasure that ever was in the world?"

"My lord, I have not had any word from you. For three years I have had no reply." Then she recited the following verses: O tomb, O tomb, has his beauties lost / Or have you lost yourself that radiant look? / O tomb, neither a garden or a star, / The sun and moon at once how can you host?

(47:1) I must confess my lord, I was enraged at these words; for in short, this gallant, so much doated upon, this adored mortal, was not such a one as you would have imagined him to have been. He was a black Indian, a native of that country . . . "O tomb," cried I, "why do you not swallow up that monster in nature, or, rather, why do you not swallow up the gallant and his mistress?"

(60:4) These verses added anger to my anger, and I said to myself, "Oh, how much longer shall I endure." Then I burst out with the following verses: O tomb, O tomb has he blackness lost, / Or have you lost that filthy look? / O tomb, neither a toilet nor a heap of dirt / Charcoal and mud at once how can you host?

(47:2) I had scare finished these words, when the queen, who fat by the black, rose up like a fury, "Ah, cruel man . . . "

(60:5) When my wife heard me she sprang up and said, "Damn you dirty dog . . ."

"Yes!" I said in a rage, "it was I who chastised this monster according to his desert! I ought to have treated thee in the same manner: I repent now that I did not do it; thou has abused my goodness too long."

I said to her, "You, dirtiest of whores and filthiest of all venal women who desired and copulated with black slaves, yes it was I who did it to him."

NIGHT 25

(48:2) "Oh unfortunate prince!" said the sultan, "you can never enough be bewailed!

NIGHT 25

(62:1) The king replied, "By God young man, I shall do something for you that will go

Nobody can be more sensibly touched with your condition than I am; never did such an extraordinary misfortune befall any man; and who write *your* history will have the advantage to relate a passage that surpasses that has ever yet been written. The only thing wanting; the revenge which is due to you; and I will omit nothing that can be done to procure it."

down in history and commemorate *my* name."

NIGHT 27

NIGHT 27

(65:3) *From,* "Do you have any children?" *until* "*with* daughters married to kings" *does not correspond with Galland's version.*

NIGHT 28

The Story of the Three Calenders, Sons of Kings; and of the Five Ladies of Baghdad

(51:8) In the reign of Caliph Haroun al-Raschid, there was at Baghdad, the place of his residence, a porter who, notwithstanding his mean and laborious business, was a fellow of wit and good humor.

. . . a young handsome lady, covered with a great muslin veil, came to him and said . . .

NIGHT 28

The Tale of the Porter and the Three Ladies

(66:2) I heard, O happy king, that once there lived in the city of Baghdad a bachelor who worked as a porter.

. . . when a woman approached him. She wore a Mosul cloak, a silk veil, a fine kerchief embroidered with gold, and a pair of leggings ties with fluttering laces. When she lifted her veil, she revealed a pair of beautiful dark eyes graced with long lashes and a tender expression, like those celebrated by the poets. Then with a soft voice and a sweet tone, she said to him . . .

(66:2 – 67:2) *[This version is far more specific regarding the items purchased than the English translation from the French of Galland.]*

NIGHT 29

(52:7) . . . another lady came to open the gate, and appeared so beautiful to him, that he was perfectly surprised, or rather so much struck by her charms that he was like to have let his basket fall, for he had never seen any beauty that came near her.

NIGHT 29

(68:2) The porter, looking to see who opened the door, saw a full-bosomed girl, about five feet tall. She all charm, beauty, and perfect grace, with a forehead like a new moon, eyes like those of a deer or wild heifer, eyebrows like the crescent in the month of Sha'ban, cheeks like red anemones, mouth like the seal of Solomon, lips like red carnelian, teeth like a row of pearls set in coral, neck like a cake for a king, bosom like a fountain, breasts like a pair of big pomegranates resembling a rabbit with uplifted ears, and a belly with a navel like a cup that holds a pound of benzoin ointment.

No verse here.

(53:1) In the middle of the court there was a great fountain, faced with white marble, and full of clear water, which fell into it abundantly out of the mouth of lion made of brass.

(69:1) In the middle stood a large pool of water, with a fountain in the center . . .

(53:2) . . . but that which particularly captivated his attention was a third lady, who seemed to be of greater beauty than the second, and was set upon the throne just mentioned.

The curtain was unfastened, and a dazzling girl emerged, with genial charm, wise mien, and features as radiant as the moon. She had an elegant figure, the scent of ambergris, sugared lips, Babylonian eyes, with eyebrows as arched as a pair of bent bows, and a face whose radiance put the shining sun to shame, for she was like a great star soaring in the heavens, or a dome of gold, an unveiled bride, or a splendid fish swimming in a fountain, or a morsel of luscious fat in a bowl of milk soup. She was like her to whom the poet said . . . *[verse follows]*.

Verse omitted.

Galland gives names: This lady was called Zobeide, she who opened the gate was called Sasie, and Amine was the name of the one who went out to buy provisions.

No names are given here.

NIGHT 30

(53:7) "Madam," replied the porter, "it is not that which stops me; I am over and above paid. I am sensible that I am unmannerly to stay longer than I ought, but hope that you will be so good as to pardon me, if I tell you, that I am astonished to see that there is no man with three ladies of such extraordinary beauty; and you know that a company of women without men is as melancholy a thing as a company of men without women." To which he added several other pleasant things to prove what he said, and did not forget the Baghdad proverb, that one is never well at a table, except there be four in company, and so concluded that since there were but three, they were in need of a fourth.

(53:8) The girls laughed heartily at the porter's discourse, after which Zobeide said to him very gravely – "Friend, you are a little

NIGHT 30

(70:2) "By God ladies, my pay is not little, for I deserve not even two dirhams, but I have been wondering about your situation and the absence of anyone to entertain you. For as a table needs four legs to stand on, you being three, likewise need a fourth, for the pleasure of men is not complete without women, and the pleasure of women in not complete without men. The poet says: For our delight four things we need, the lute / The harp, the zither and the double flute, / Blending with the scent of four lovely flowers, / Roses, myrtles, anemones, and gillyflowers. / Only in four such things join together, / Money, and wine, and youth, and a lover. You are three, and you need a fourth, a man."

His words pleased the girls, who laughed and said, "How can we mange that, being girls who keep our business to ourselves, for we

too bold, and though you do not deserve that I should enter into particulars with you, yet I am willing to tell you, that we are three sisters, who do our business so secretly that no one knows anything of it. We have too great reason to be cautious of acquainting indiscreet persons of it, and a good author that we have read says . . ."

fear to entrust out secrets where they may not be kept. We have read in some book what Abu Tammam has said . . ."

(54:1) "My ladies," replied the porter, "by your very air, I judged at first that you were persons of extraordinary merit, and I conceive that I am not mistaken; though fortune has not given me wealth enough to raise me above my mean profession, yet I have not failed to cultivate my mind as much as I could, by reading books of science and history; and allow me, if you please, that I have also read, in another author, a maxim which I have always happily practiced: 'We do not our secrets' says he 'but from such persons as are known to all the world to want discretion, and would abuse the confidence we put in them; but we make no scruple to discover them to prudent persons, because we know they can keep them.' A secret with me is as sure as if it were in a closet whose key is lost and the door sealed up."

(71:1) When the porter heard these words he replied, "Trust me: I am a sensible and wise man. I have studied the sciences and attained knowledge; I have read and learned, and presented my knowledge and cited my authorities. I reveal the good and conceal the bad, and I am well behaved. I am like the man of whom the poet said: Only the faithful does a secret keep; / None but the best can hold it unrevealed. / I keep it secret in a well shut house / Of which the key is lost and the lock is sealed.

(54:2) "Friend, have you never heard that which is commonly said, 'If you bring anything with you, you shall be welcome; but if you bring nothing, you must get you gone with nothing."

The thirtieth night ends here in this edition.

(71:2) The mistress of the house said, "Without gain, love is not worth a grain." The doorkeeper added, "have you got anything, my dear? If you are empty handed, go empty handed."

NIGHT 31

(55:1) Zobeide would not take back the money from the porter, but said – "My friend, in consenting that you stay with us, I must forewarn you, that it is not only on the condition that you keep secret what we have required of you, but also that you observe exactly the rules of good manners and civility."

NIGHT 31

No similar passage.

Amine, who sat next to the sideboard, took up a bottle and a cup, filled out wine, and drank first herself, according to the custom of the Arabians . . .

(71:3) She filled the first cup and drank it . . .

. . . and at last filled it a fourth time, to the porter, who, as he received it, kissed Amine's hand; and before he drank, sung a song to this purpose – That as the wind brings along with it the sweet scents of the perfumed palaces through which it passes, so the wine he was going to drink, coming from her fair hands, received a more exquisite taste than what it had of its own nature.

A large section of text has been edited out from this point onward, corresponding to four pages of the HH edition. It likewise skips what in HH is all of night 31, and half of 32. The missing portion of the original is glossed over with the words: In short, they were extraordinarily merry all the time of dinner, which lasted a long time, for nothing was wanting that could make it agreeable.

The scene reconnects with that of the HH edition with the lines: The day being almost spent, Sasie, speaking the names of the three ladies, said to the porter – "Arise and be gone, it is time for you to depart."

But the porter, not willing to leave such good company, cried, "Alas, ladies! Whither do you command me to go in the condition I am in? I am quite beside myself, by what I have seen since I came hither; and having drunk above my ordinary quantity, I shall never find my way home . . ."

. . . and filled a fourth and gave it to the porter, who held it in his hand and, saluting with a bow, thanked her and recited the following verses: Drink not the cup, save with a friend you trust / One whose blood to noble forefathers owes. / Wine, like the wind, is sweet if o'er the sweet, / And foul if o'er the foul it haply blows.

NIGHT 32

(56:7) . . . having by chance cast their eyes upon the porter, whom they saw clad almost like one of those other calenders with whom they are in controversy about several points of discipline because they neither shave their beards or eye-brows, one of them said, "Look here, I believe we have got one of our revolted Arab bretheren."

NIGHT 32

(75:3) *The two texts reconnect:* When it was dark, they said to the porter, "Sir, it is time that you get up, put on your slippers, and show us your back."

The porter replied, "Where do I go from here? The departure of my soul from my body is easier for me than my departure from your company . . ."

(78:2) When they turned and looked at the porter, who, sore from the beating and the slapping and intoxicated with wine, lay almost unconscious, they said, "Whether an Arab or a foreigner, he is a brother dervish."

NIGHT 33

(57:4) The Caliph, Haroun al-Rashid, was accustomed to walk abroad in disguise often

NIGHT 33

(77:4) . . . it happened that on that very night that the Caliph Harun al-Rashid and Ja'far

by night, that he might see with his own eyes if everything was quiet in the city, and that no disorders were committed in it . . . and passing through the street where these ladies dwelt, he heard the sound of music and the great fits of laughter upon which he commanded the vizier to knock, because he would go in and know the reason of the jollity.

came into the city, as they used to do every now and then, and as they walked, they passed the door and heard the music of the flute, the harp and the tambourine, the singing of the girls and the sounds of people partying and laughing. The caliph said, "Ja'far, I would like to enter this house and visit the people inside."

NIGHT 34

(59:3) The three calenders and the caliph, with his companions, were extremely surprised at this execution, and could not comprehend why Zobeide, after having so furiously whipped those two bitches, that by the Mussalman religion are reckoned unclean animals, should cry with them, wipe off their tears, and kiss them . . .

NIGHT 34

No such detail.

NIGHT 35

No poetry.

(60:5) "Sister, you have done wonders, and we may easily see that you have a feeling of the grief you have expressed so much of your life." Amine was prevented from answering this civility, her heart being so sensibly touched at the same moment, that she was obliged, for air, to uncover her neck and breast . . . "

NIGHT 35

(81:2) *Poetry and song.*

(82:1) When the girl finished the poem, her sister let out a loud cry and moaned, "Oh, oh, oh!" Then she grabbed her dress by the collar and tore it down to the hem, baring her entire body, and fell down in swoon.

The remainder of the description of this night events are absent in Galland's.

NIGHT 36

(62:4) *This edition simply reads:* ". . . do them no hurt, let them go where they please."

NIGHT 36

(85:1) *This edition uses a saying that seems to be common:* ". . . let him stroke his head and go."

NIGHT 37

The History of the First Calender, A King's Son

There are several slight differences in the two accounts:

(63:4) "Cousin, you will hardly be able to guess how I have been employed since your last departure from hence, which is now a year past. I have had a great many men at work to perfect a design I had in my mind; I have caused an edifice to be built."

And accordingly he came in with a lady in his hand, of singular beauty, and magnificently

NIGHT 37

The First Dervish's Tale

(86:4) "Cousin, I would like to acquaint you with something that I have been preparing for a whole year, provided you do not try to hinder me."

. . . but a while later he came back with a woman wearing a cloak, a kerchief, a

apparelled; he did not discover who she was; neither did I think it any wise prudent to ask.	headdress, and smelling of a perfume so sweet as to make us even more intoxicated.
(64:1) Then my cousin, speaking to the lady, said, "It is by this way that we are to go to the place I told you of."	Then, turning to the lady, he said with a sign, "Make your choice."
"Be content," replied he, "you may return back the same way you came."	"After I descend into this place, place the iron plate and earth back over us."
NIGHT 38	**NIGHT 38**
(65:1) Two verses are missing, one sung by the dervish to his executioner begging for his life, and one, quoting a poet, sung after the executioner releases him.	(88:1–89:1) *The two verses are present in this edition.*
(65:3) "Alas," he cried, "was it not enough for me to have lost my son, but must I have also news of the death of my brother whom I loved so dearly, and see you reduced to this deplorable condition?"	(89:2) When I went to him and told him about my father's death and the loss of my eye, he said to me, "I too have enough woes, for my son is missing, and I do not know what has happened to him, nor do I have any news about him."
(65:4–5) But he had another reason for keeping the matter secret, which he did not tell me; and an important reason it was, as you will perceive by the sequel of my discourse.	*This passage does not appear in this edition.*
No exclamation to God.	My uncle cried, "There is no power and no strength, save in God, the Almighty, the Magnificent."
NIGHT 39	**NIGHT 39**
(66:5) I did not hinder their growing love, because I did not foresee the pernicious consequences of it. This tenderness increased as they grew in years and came to such a head that I dreaded the end of it.	(90:3) But when they grew up, they did the ugly deed and I heard about it, hardly believing my ears.
But that unfortunate creature had swallowed so much of the poison, that all obstacles which, by my prudence, I could lay in the way, served only the more to enflame her love.	. . . but the cursed girl was in love with him, for the devil possessed her and made the affair attractive in her eyes.
(67:4) I avoided passing through towns, till I was got into the empire of the mighty governor of the Mussulmen, the glorious and renowned Caliph Haroun Alrashid, when I thought myself out of danger; and considering what to do, I resolved to come to Baghdad, intending to throw myself at that monarch's feet. whose generosity is everywhere applauded.	(91:1) Then I left the city, undetected by anyone, and journeyed to this country, with the intention of reaching Baghdad, hoping that I might be fortunate to find someone who would assist me to the presence of the Commander of the Faithful, the Vice Regent of the Supreme Lord, so that I might tell him my tale and lay my case before him.
(67:6) But good fortune, having brought us before your gate . . .	But God drove us to your house . . .

NIGHT 40
The Story of the Second Calender, A King's Son

(68:5) *A list of subjects studied by the Dervish in this edition:*

The Quran
The Hadith
History
Poetry/Prosody
Geography
Genealogy
Arabic Grammar

(68:6) [The king, his father] was very glad of this embassy for several reasons; he was persuaded that nothing could be more commendable in a prince of my age than to travel to see foreign courts; and besides, he was glad to gain the friendship of the Indian Sultan.

(68:7) . . . we saw very soon fifty horsemen, well-armed, who were robbers, coming towards us at a full gallop.

NIGHT 40
The Second Dervish's Tale

(92:5) *A list of subjects studied by the Dervish in this edition:*

The Qurʾān, in seven different editions
Jurisprudence through the works of al-Shāṭibī
Classical Arabic Grammar
Calligraphy

(92:6) One day the king of India sent my father gifts and rarities worthy of a king and asked him to send me to him. My father fitted me with six riding horses and sent me along with posted couriers.

. . . when a little later the wind blew the dust away and cleared the air, we saw fifty horsemen who, looking like glowering lions in steel armor . . .

NIGHT 41

No mention of this.

NIGHT 41

(93:4) I was mighty and became lowly; I was rich and became poor.

NIGHT 42

(69:5–6) I came to a large town well inhabited, and situated so much the more advantageously, that it was surrounded by several rivers, so that it enjoyed a perpetual spring. The pleasant objects which then presented themselves to my view, afforded me some joy, and suspended for some time the mortal sorrow with which I was overwhelmed to find myself in such a condition.

(70:5) . . . but seeing a lady of a noble and free air, and extraordinarily beautiful, coming towards me, I turned my eyes from beholding any other object but her alone.

NIGHT 42

(94:2–3) . . . until I came to a fair, peaceful and prosperous city, teeming with people and full of life. It was the time when winter had departed with its frost and spring had arrived with its roses. The streams were flowing, the flowers blooming, and the birds singing. It was like the city of which the poet said: Behold a peaceful city, free from fear / Whose wonders make it a gorgeous heaven appear. I felt both glad and sad at the same time, glad to reach the city, sad to arrive in such a wretched condition.

(95:1) I walked inside and saw a beautiful girl who looked as radiant as a brilliant pearl or the shining sun and whose speech banished all sorrow and captivated even the sensible and the wise. She was about five feet tall, with a beautiful figure, firm breasts, soft cheeks and a fair complexion. Through her tresses, her face beamed, and above her smooth bosom, her mouth gleamed, as the poet said for one like her: Four things that never meet do here unite / To shed my blood and ravage my heart / A radiant brow and tresses beguile / And rosy cheeks and a glittering smile

NIGHT 43

(71:2) Her great beauty, which had already smitten me, and the sweetness and civility wherewith she received me, emboldened me to say to her, "Madam, before I have the honor to satisfy your curiosity, give me leave to tell you, that I am infinitely satisfied with this unexpected rencounter, which offers me the occasion of consolation in the midst of my affliction; and perhaps it may give me the opportunity to make you also happier than you were."

(71:5) The princess made me go into a bagnio, the most handsome, the most commodious, and the most sumptuous that could be imagined; and when I came forth, instead of my own clothes, I found a very costly suit . . .

No verses.

NIGHT 43

(95:5) I said – for I found her words sweet and touching and she captivated my heart – "My good fortune brought me here to dispel my care, or perhaps your good fortune, to banish your sorrow."

(96:1) She was pleased, and she rose and took me by the hand through an arched doorway that led to a bath. She took off my clothes and took off hers and, entering the bath, she bathed and washed me. When we came out, she dressed me in a new gown . . . (96:1 and 97)

Two verses follow.

NIGHT 44

(72:6–7) At this answer, the furious Genius told her, "You are a false woman and a liar!" . . . The Genius made no other answer but what was accompanied with reproaches and blows, of which I heard the noise.

I let down the trapdoor, covered it again with earth, and returned to the city with a burden of wood, which I bound up without knowing what I did, so great was my trouble and sorrow.

(73:4) At this discourse I changed color and fell a trembling. While the tailor was asking me the reason, my chamber door opened at once, and the old man, having no patience to

NIGHT 44

(97:4) The demon cried, "You are lying, you whore," . . . "I will not be deceived by this ruse, you slut." The he seized her, stripped her naked and, binding her hands and feet to four stakes, proceeded to torture her and make her confess.

(98:1) I placed the trapdoor as it was before . . . And when I remembered my father and my country, how life turned against me and I became a wood cutter, and how for a brief moment it befriended me and punished me again, I wept bitterly, blamed myself, and repeated the following verse: My fate does fight me like an enemy / And pursues helpless me relentlessly / If once it chooses to treat me kindly / At once it turns, eager to punish me.

(98:2) When I heard what he said, I felt faint and turned pale and, while we stood there talking, the floor of my recess was torn asunder and there emerged the old Persian

stay, appeared to us with my hatchet and chords. This was the Genius, the ravisher of the fair princess of the Isle of Ebene, who had disguised himself after he treated her with such barbarity. "I am a Genius," said he, "son of the daughter of Ebis, Prince of Genii. Is this not your hatchet?

man, who was that demon. He tortured the girl almost to her death, but she did not confess. So he took the axe and the sandals, saying, "If I am truly the son of Satan's daughter, I shall bring you back the owner of the axe."

NIGHT 45

(73:8) "Oh, then," said the Genius, pulling out a scimitar and presenting it to the princess, "If you never saw him before, take the scimitar and cut off his head." – "Alas!" replied the princess, "how is it possible that should I execute what you would force me to do?"

NIGHT 45

(99:4) He replied, "If you do not know this man, take this sword then and strike him in the head." She took the sword and, coming up to me, stood facing me. I signaled to her with my eyes, and she understood and winked back, meaning, "Aren't you the one who has brought all this upon us?" I signaled again, "This is the time for forgiveness," and she replied with words written in tears on her cheeks *[a verse follows]* Then the girl threw the sword away and stepped back saying, "How can I strike the neck of one I do not know . . ."

NIGHT 46

A verse is missing.

(74:5) Upon this I stepped back, and threw the scymetar to the ground, "I shall for ever," said I to the Genius, "be hateful to all mankind, should I be so base as to murder, I do not only say a person I do not know, but a lady like this, who is ready to give up the ghost: do with me what you please, since I am in your power; I cannot obey your barbarous commands."

NIGHT 46

(100:4) *The verse is given here.*

(100:5) I threw the sword away, stepped back, and said, "Mighty demon, if a woman, who is befuddled, thoughtless, and inarticulate, refuses to strike off the head of a man she does not know, how can I, a man, strike off the head of a woman I do not know? I can never do such a deed, even if I have to die for it."

The Story of the Envious Man, and of Him Who He Envied
NIGHT 47

(76:2) "This old well," he said, "was inhabited by Fairies and Genii . . .
He clearly perceived that there was something extraordinary in his fall, which otherwise would have cost him his life; whereas he neither saw nor felt a thing.
"Then I will tell you. This man, out of charity, the greatest that ever was known, left the town he lived in, and has established himself in this place, in hopes to cure one of

The Tale of the Envious and the Envied
NIGHT 47

(102:4) That well happened to be haunted by a group of demons . . .
"This man is the envied who, flying from the envious, came to live in our city, built this hermitage, and has ever since delighted us with his litanies and his recitals of the Quran."

his neighbors of the envy he had conceived against him . . ."

(76:8) The prince, transported with joy, sent immediately to fetch his daughter, who very soon appeared, with a numerous train of ladies and Eunuchs, but masked so that her face was not seen.

(103:1) The king gladly sent for his daughter, and they brought her in, bound and fettered.

NIGHT 48

(77) *Verse omitted.*

(78:4) Our vessel was speedily surrounded with an infinite number of boats full of people, who either came to congratulate their friends upon their safe arrival, to enquire for those they had left behind them in the country from whence they came, or out of curiosity to see a ship which came from a difference country.

(78:6) I took the pen and wrote, before I had done, using six sorts of hands used among the Arabians; and each specimen contained an extemporary distich or quatrain in praise of the sultan.

NIGHT 48

(104:4) *Verse*

(105:2) No sooner had we entered port and cast anchor than we were visited by messengers from the king of that city.

(106:all) *The end of this night contains the verses that the dervish/ape wrote in the following scripts: Ruqʿa, Muḥaqqiq, Rayḥānī, Naskhī, Thuluth, and Tumar.*

NIGHT 49

Three verses, present in the HH edition, are omitted from this night. In this edition, the translator makes some attempt to describe the intent of the verse, though he is not always right. In place of the first verse he writes: (80:2) "I wrote upon a large peach, some verses after my way . . ." *Instead of quoting the second verse, he gives an incorrect assessment of its intent:* "I drank, and wrote some new verses upon it. which explained the state I was in, after a great many suffering." *For the third verse he gives a prose rendering that does match the meaning of the verse, but this edition states that the verse was written to pacify the King, angered by losing at chess, whereas the HH edition makes no mention of the King's anger.*

NIGHT 49

NIGHT 50

(81:3) . . . and within it wrote several words in Arabian characters, some of them ancient, and others those which they call the character of Cleopatra.

NIGHT 50

(109:4) . . . drawing a perfect circle in the middle of the palace hall, inscribed on it names in Kufic letters, as well as other talismanic words.

(81:4) . . . where she began adjurations and repeated verses out of the Alcoran [Qur᾽ān].	Then she muttered charms and uttered spells . . .
NIGHT 51	**NIGHT 51**
(82:4) *No mention of God.*	(111:2) . . . we cried, "There is no power and no strength save in God the Almighty, the Magnificent."
. . . when we heard the cry, "Victory! Victory!"	. . . we heard a cry, "God is great, God is great! He has conquered and triumphed; he has defeated the infidel."
(82:5) "If thou become an ape by enchantment, change thy shape and take that of a man, which thou hadst before."	(111:3) "In the name of Almighty God and His covenant, be yourself again . . ."
NIGHT 52	**NIGHT 52**
(83:7) He had not fully recovered his strength when he sent for me . . . *Absence of a reference to the beard here.*	(112:5) . . . but when God granted him recovery and he regained his health and his beard grew again, he summoned me before him.
No verse.	(113:1) *Verse*
NIGHT 53	**NIGHT 53**
The History of the Third Calender, A King's Son	**The Third Dervish's Tale**
(85:1) I afterwards caused my whole fleet to be fitted out and manned, and went twice to my islands with a view of gaining the hearts of my subjects by my presence, and to confirm them in their loyalty. *[An instance where Galland incorrectly interpreted the intent of the character or distorted the meaning to suit his own cultural circumstances.]*	(114:3) One day I decided to go on an excursion to the islands and I carried with me a month's supply and went there, enjoyed myself, and came back.
[Another culturally specific proverb going untranslated in this edition.]	We gave ourselves up for lost and said, "Even if he escapes, the foolhardy deserve no praise."
(85:3) The pilot changed color at this relation, and throwing his turban on the deck with one hand, and beating his breast with the other, cried, "Oh sir, we are all lost! Not one of us will escape. And with all my skill, it is not in my power to prevent it." . . . "and as the adamant has the virtue to draw all iron to it . . . " **[CA, RG]**	(114:4) When the captain heard what the lookout man said, he threw his turban on the deck, plucked out his beard, beat his face and said, "O King, I tell you we are about to perish. There is no power and no strength save in God, the Almighty, the Magnificent." . . . "As soon as we sail below the mountain, the ship's sides will come apart and every nail will fly out and stick to the mountain, for the Almighty God has endowed the magnetic stone with a mysterious virtue that makes the iron love it."

NIGHT 54

(86:8) The first thing I did was to strip and wring the water out of my clothes, and then laid them down on the dry land, which was still pretty warm by the heat of the day. **[AD]**

(87:2) I saw them once more go to the ship, and return soon after with an old man, who led a very handsome young lad in his hand . . . **[CR, VO]**

. . . who led a very handsome young lad in his hand, of about fourteen or fifteen years of age. **[CR,VO]** *I have rarely, if at all, seen passages in this edition describing male beauty, especially with any subtle eroticism.*

NIGHT 54

(116:4) I walked ashore, wring out my clothes, and spread them to dry.

(117:1) When they came out of the ship gain there was a very old man in their middle. Of this man nothing much was left, for time had ravaged him, reducing him to bone wrapped in a blue rag through which the winds whistled east and west. *A verse follows.*

(117:2) The old man held by the hand a young man so splendidly handsome that he seemed to be cast in beauty's mold. He was like the green bough or the tender young of the roe, ravishing every heart with his loveliness and captivating every mind with his perfection. Faultless in body and face, he surpassed everyone in looks and inner grace . . . *[a verse follows].*

NIGHT 56

(90:1) . . . after this misfortune I would have embraced death without any reluctance, had it presented itself to me, but what we wish, to ourselves, whether good or bad, will not always happen. **[CAE]**

[VO]

(90:8) The old man, overcome with sorrow, and not being able to stand, was laid upon a litter and carried to the ship. **[OM, VO]**

NIGHT 56

(121:4) My lady, when I was sure that I had killed him, as the God above had foreordained, I rose and, ascending the stairs, replaced the trapdoor and covered it with earth.

A long verse of lament by the boy's father appears here.

(122:1) Then the old man took a breath, and with a deep sigh his soul left his body. The black servants shrieked and, throwing dust on their heads and faces, wailed and cried bitterly. Then they carried the old man and his son to the ship . . . *[a short verse follows].*

NIGHT 57

(91:6) "This is the fruit of our idleness and debaucheries." **[CAS]**

(92:3) I earnestly prayed them to satisfy me, or show me how to return to my kingdom, for it was impossible for me to keep them company any longer. **[CR]**

NIGHT 57

(123:5) "We would be sitting pretty but for our curiosity."

(125:1) . . . for as the saying goes, "Better for me and meet to see you not, for if the eye sees nought, the heart grieves not."

NIGHT 58

(93:6) This roc is a white bird of monstrous size; his strength is such that he can lift up elephants from the plains and carry them to the tops of mountains where he feeds upon them. **[AD]**

NIGHT 58

No such description.

NIGHT 59	**NIGHT 59**
(94:4) The others began a sort of ball, and danced two one after another, with a wonderful good grace. **[CAS]**	*No mention of a "ball" or dancing of any kind.*
(94:5) I answered that I knew better things than to offer to make my own choice, since they were all equally beautiful, witty and worthy of my respects and service, and that I would not be guilty of so much incivility as to prefer one over the other.	(127:3) I chose a girl who had a lovely face and dark eyes . . . *[then follows a poetic description of the girl, followed by a verse]* . . . That night I slept with her and spent the best of nights.
(94:6) The lady who spoke to me before, answered, "We are very well convinced of your civility, and find you are afraid to create jealousy between us . . . I was obliged to yield to their entreaties, and offered my hand to the lady that spoke . . . **[OM, AD, CAE, CAS, VO, EC]**	
NIGHT 60	**NIGHT 60**
(95:1) *This edition skips over the choice of the second girl.* **[EC, VO]**	(128:4) I chose a girl with a lovely face and a soft body, like her of whom the poet said: *verse follows*.
(95:2) "For God's sake, fair ladies, let me know if it be in my power to comfort you, or if my assistance can in any way be useful to you." **[CR, CAE]**	(128:5) I asked, "Why do you weep, for to me your tears are gall."

Select Bibliography

Abbott, Nabia. "A Ninth-Century Fragment of the 'Thousand and One Nights': New Light on the Early History of the Arabian Nights," *Journal of the Near Eastern Studies* 8, no. 3 (July 1949), 129–64.

Ahmed, Leila. *Edward W. Lane: A Study of His Life and Works and of British Ideas of the Middle East in the Nineteenth Century*. London and New York: Longman, 1978.

Ahmed, Zubair, and Krishnaswamy Nachimuthu. "Reception of The Arabian Nights in Tamil: The Story of Medinatun Nuhas in Tamil Adaptation," in *Essays on The Arabian Nights*, ed. Risvanur Rahman and Syed Akhtar Husain (New Delhi: India International Centre, 2015), 25–39.

Alahmedi, Sami. "Wieland und 1001 Nacht," PhD diss., Leipzig University, 1969.

Akel, Ibrahim. "Arabic Editions and Bibliography," in *Arabic Manuscripts of the "Thousand and One Nights": Presentation and Critical Editions of Four Noteworthy Texts; Observations on Some Osmanli Traditions*, ed. Aboubakr Chraïbi (Paris: Espaces et signes, 2016), 431–91.

"Liste des Manuscrits Arabes des Nuits," in *Arabic Manuscripts of the "Thousand and One Nights": Presentation and Critical Editions of Four Noteworthy Texts; Observations on Some Osmanli Traditions*, ed. Aboubakr Chraïbi (Paris: Espaces et signes, 2016), 65–114.

"Quelques remarques sur la bibliothèque d'Antoine Galland et l'arrivé des Mille et une nuits en Occident." In *Antoine Galland et l'Orient des savants*. ed. by Pierre-Sylvain Filliozat and Michel Zink. Paris: Académie des Inscriptions et Belles-Lettres, 2017. 197–215.

Akel, Ibrahim, and William Granara, eds. *The Thousand and One Nights: Sources and Transformations in Literature, Art, and Science*. Leiden: Brill, 2020.

Akhtar, Syed Hasnain. "Reception of Alf Layla in India with Special Reference to Urdu," in *Essays on The Arabian Nights*, ed. Risvanur Rahman and Syed Akhtar Husain (New Delhi: India International Centre, 2015), 105–10.

Albreck, Ulla. "Isak Dinesen and The Thousand and One Nights: Albondocani, an Analysis," in *Isak Dinesen: Critical Views*, ed. Olga Anastasia Pelensky, trans. William Mishler (Athens, OH: Ohio University Press, 1993), 304–13.

Aliakbari, Rasoul. "American Nights: The Introduction and Usage of the Arabian Nights within the US's Print Modernity," in *The Thousand and One Nights: Sources and Transformations in Literature, Art, and Science*, ed. Ibrahim Akel and William Granara (Leiden: Brill, 2020), 255–69.

Allen, Roger. "An Analysis of the 'Tale of the Three Apples' from The Thousand and One Nights," in *Logos Islamikos: Studia Islamica in Honorem Georgii Michaelis Wickens*, ed. Roger M. Savory and Dionisius A. Agius (Toronto: Pontifical Institute of Mediaeval Studies, 1984), 51–60; also in *The Arabian Nights Reader*, ed. Ulrich Marzolph (Detroit, MI: Wayne State University Press, 2006), 239–48.

"Sindbad the Sailor and the Early Arabic Novel," in *Tradition, Modernity, and Postmodernity in Arabic Literature: Essays in Honor of Issa J. Boullata*, ed. Kamal Abdel-Malek and Wael Hallaq (Leiden: Brill, 2000), 78–85.

Almeida, Rochelle. "A Thousand and One Nights in the Pedagogic Global Village: Cross-cultural and Transnational Connections," in *La Réception mondiale et transdisciplinaire des Mille et une Nuits*, ed. Waël Rabadi and Isabelle Bernard (Amiens: Presses du Centre d'Études Médiévales, 2012), 17–30.

Amedroz, Henry F. "A Tale of the Arabian Nights Told as History in the 'Muntazam' of Ibn al-Jauzi," *Journal of the Royal Asiatic Society* (April 1904), 273–93.

Aoyagi, Etsuko. "Repetitiveness in the Arabian Nights: Openness as Self-Foundation," in *The Arabian Nights and Orientalism*, ed. Yuriko Yamanaka and Tetsuo Nishio (London: I.B. Tauris, 2006), 68–90.

Aravamudan, Srinivas. "The Adventure Chronotope and the Oriental Xenotrope: Galland, Sheridan, and Joyce Domesticate *The Arabian Nights*," in *The Arabian Nights in Historical Context: Between East and West*, ed. Saree Makdisi and Felicity Nussbaum (Oxford: Oxford University Press, 2008), 235–63.

ʿAwwād, Mīkhāʾīl. *Alf laylah wa-laylah, mirʾāt al-haḍārah*. Baghdad: Wizārat al-Thaqāfah, 1962.

al-Azdī, Abū al-Muṭahhar Muḥammad ibn Aḥmad. *Ḥikāyat Abī al-Qāsim al-Baghdādī*, ed. Adam Mitz. Baghdad: Maktabat al-Muthannā, 1902.

Azouqa, Aida. *Magical Realism between East and West: The Arabian Nights, Gabriel Garcia Márquez and Novelists of the Arab World*. Lewiston, NY, and Lampeter, UK: The Edwin Mellen Press, 2019.

Bagehot, Walter. "The People of the Arabian Nights," *National Review* 9 (July 1859), 44–71.

Bakhtin, Mikhail. "Discourse in the Novel," in *The Dialogic Imagination: Four Essays*, ed. Michael Holquist, trans. Carl Emerson and Mikhail Holquist (Austin, TX: University of Texas Press, 1981), 259–422.

Rabelais and His World, trans. Helene Iswolsky. Bloomington, IN: Indiana University Press, 1984.

Barth, John. "Muse, Spare Me," *Book Week* (September 26, 1965), 28.

"Literature of Exhaustion," *Atlantic Monthly* (August 1967), 29–35.

"Muse, Spare Me," in *The Sense of the Sixties*, ed. Edward Quinn and Paul J. Dolan (New York: Free Press, 1968), 440–44.

"Dunyazadiad," in *Chimera* (New York: Fawcett, 1973), 11–63.

"The Scheherazade Factor: Conversation with Alvin P. Sanoff," *U.S. News and World Report* (August 31, 1987), 55.

The Last Voyage of Somebody the Sailor. Boston, MA: Little, Brown and Company, 1991.

"Missy: A Postscript to *The 1001 Nights*," *The Iowa Review* 45, no. 3 (Winter 2015–16), 161–64.

Barthes, Roland. "An Introduction to the Structural Analysis of Narrative," *New Literary History* 6, no. 2 (Winter 1975), 237–72.

"Introduction to the Structural Analysis of Narratives," in *Image, Music, Text*, trans. Stephen Heath (New York: Hill and Wang, 1977), 79–124.

"Introduction to the Structural Analysis of Narratives," in *A Barthes Reader*, ed. Susan Sontag (New York: Barnes and Noble 2009), 212–49.

Bāshā, Aḥmad Zekī, ed. *Kitāb al-tāj*. Cairo: al-Amīriyyah, 1914.

Basset, René. "Notes sur les Mille et une Nuit," *Revue des Traditions Populaires* 9 (1894), 377–80; 11 (1896), 146–87; 12 (1897), 146–52; 13 (1898), 37–87, 303–8; 14 (1899), 20–37, 687–89; 16 (1901), 28–35, 74–88; 18 (1903), 311–14.

Batty, Nancy. "The Art of Suspense: Rushdie's 1001 Mid-Nights," *ARIEL: A Review of International English Literature* 18, no. 3 (July 1987), 49–65.

Beaumont, Daniel. "Literary Style and Narrative Techniques in the Arabian Nights," in *The Arabian Nights Encyclopedia*, ed. Ulrich Marzolph and Richard van Leeuwen (Santa Barbara, CA: ABC-CLIO, 2004), 1–5.

"Bedtime Story: The *1001 Nights* in Proust's À la recherche du temps perdu," in *Tradition and Reception in Arabic Literature: Essays Dedicated to Andras Hamori*, ed. Margaret Larkin and Jocelyn Sharlez (Wiesbaden: Harrassowitz, 2019), 221–32.

Becka, Jiri. "Arabian Nights in Czech and Slovak Literature and Research," *Archiv Orientalni: Quarterly Journal of African, Asian, and Latin American Studies* 62, no. 1 (1994), 32–42.

Beckford, William. *The History of the Caliph Vathek*. London: Cassell and Co., 1887.

Bedetti, Gabriella. "Women's Sense of the Ludicrous in John Barth's 'Dunyazadiad,'" *Studies in American Humor* 4, no. 1–2 (Spring–Summer 1985), 74–81.

Belcher, Stephen. "Parallel Tracks? The Seven Sages, the Arabian Nights, and Their Arrival in Europe," *South Asian Review* 19, no. 16 (December 1995), 11–23.

Benjamin, Walter. "The Task of the Translator," in *Illuminations: Essays and Reflections*, trans. Harry Zohn (New York: Schocken Books, 1968), 69–82.

"The Work of Art in the Age of Mechanical Production," in *Illuminations: Essays and Reflections*, trans. Harry Zohn (New York: Schocken Books, 1968), 217–51.

Bernard, Veronika. "Stadt als Schein. Die Rezeption der Geschichte von der Messingstadt," *Wirkendes Wort* 46, no. 2 (August 1996), 189–93.

Bernier, Georges. *La revue blanche; ses amis, ses artistes*. Paris: Hazan, 1991.

Bettelheim, Bruno. "The Frame Story of Thousand and One Nights," in *The Uses of Enchantment: The Meaning* and *Importance of Fairy Tales* (New York: Knopf, 1976), 86–90.

Bhabha, Homi. *The Location of Culture*. London and New York: Routledge, 1994.

Bonebakker, Seger Adrianus. "Nihil obstat in Storytelling?" in *The Thousand and One Nights in Arabic Literature and Society*, ed. Richard C. Hovannisian and Georges Sabagh (Cambridge: Cambridge University Press, 1997), 56–77.

Borges, Jorge Luis. "Borges and I," trans. James E. Irby in *Labyrinths: Selected Stories and Other Writings* (New York: New Directions, 1964), 246–47.

"The Garden of Forking Paths," trans. Donald A. Yates in *Labyrinths: Selected Stories and Other Writings* (New York: New Directions, 1964), 19–29.

"Metáforas de Las Mil y Una Noches," trans. Jack Ross, *Historia de la noche* (1977), 36–38.

"The Thousand and One Nights," trans. Eliot Weinberger, *The Georgia Review* 38, no. 3 (Fall 1984), 564–74.

Collected Fiction, trans. Andrew Hurley. New York: Penguin, 1998.

"Arthur Waley, *Monkey*," in *Selected Non-fictions*, ed. Eliot Weinberger, trans. Esther Allen, Suzanne Jill Levine, and Eliot Weinberger (New York and London: Penguin Books, 1999), 252–54.

"H. G. Wells' Latest Novel," in *Selected Non-fictions*, ed. Eliot Weinberger (New York: Penguin Books, 1999), 193.

"Literary Pleasure," trans. Suzanne Jill Levine in *Selected Non-fictions*, ed. Eliot Weinberger (New York: Penguin Books, 1999), 28–31.

"The Translators of the Thousand and One Nights," in *Selected Non-fictions*, ed. Eliot Weinberger (New York: Penguin, 1999), 92–109.

"When Fiction Lives in Fiction," trans. Esther Allen in *Selected Non-fictions*, ed. Eliot Weinberger (New York: Penguin, 1999), 160–62.

Bosworth, Clifford Edmund. *The Medieval Islamic Underworld: The Banu Sasan in Arabic Society and Literature*. Leiden: Brill, 1976.

Bottigheimer, Ruth B. "East Meets West: Hannā Diyāb and The Thousand and One Nights," *Marvels & Tales* 28, no. 2 (2014), 302–24.

Bray, Julia. "A Caliph and His Public Relations," in *New Perspectives on the Arabian Nights*, ed. Wen-Chin Ouyang and Geert Jan van Gelder (London and New York: Routledge, 2005), 27–38.

Brontë, Charlotte. *Jane Eyre*. Introduced by D. Leavis. London: Penguin, 1966.

Brontë, Emily. *Wuthering Heights*. Preface by Charlotte Brontë, ed. Frederick T. Flahiff. Toronto: MacMillan, 1968.

Brown, Mark. "Tim Supple's Epic Odyssey to Create a New Arabian Nights," *The Guardian*, March 29, 2009, www.theguardian.com/stage/2009/mar/30/arabian-nights-theatre-midsummer-dream.

Buckley, Jerome Hamilton. *Tennyson: The Growth of a Poet*. Cambridge, MA: Harvard University Press, 1960.

Burton, Richard F., trans. *A Plain and Literal Translation of The Arabian Nights' Entertainments, Now Entitled The Book of the Thousand Nights and a Night: With Introduction, Explanatory Notes on the Manners and Customs of Moslem Men and a Terminal Essay upon the History of the Nights*. 10 vols. Benares [= Stoke-Newington]: Kamashastra Society, 1885.

"Biography of the Book and Its Reviewers Reviewed," *Supplemental Nights* 6 (1886–88), 311–66.

Supplemental Nights to the Book of the Thousand Nights and a Night. 6 vols. London: Burton Club Edition, 1886–88.

"Terminal Essay," the Burton Club Edition (n.d., vol. 10).
Buschinger, Danielle. "*Les Mille et Une Nuit* et la littérature européenne: quelques rapprochements," in *La Réception mondiale et transdisciplinaire des* Mille et une Nuits, ed. Waël Rabadi and Isabelle Bernard (Amiens: Presses du Centre d'Études Médiévales, 2012), 117–39.
Byatt, A. S. "Narrate or Die: Why Scheherazade Keeps on Talking," *The New York Times Magazine* (1999), https://archive.nytimes.com/www.nytimes.com/library/magazine/millennium/m1/byatt.html.
"The Greatest Story Ever Told," in *On Histories and Stories: Selected Essays* (London: Chatto and Windus, 2000), 165–84.
Calvino, Italo. *If on a Winter's Night a Traveller*, trans. William Weaver. Orlando, FL: Harcourt, Inc./Helen and Kurt Wolff, 1981.
"Cybernetics and Ghosts," in *The Uses of Literature*, trans. Patrick Creagh (San Diego, CA: Harcourt Brace & Company, 1986), 3–27.
Campbell, Joseph, ed. *The Portable Arabian Nights*. New York: Viking Press, 1967.
Caracciolo, Peter L. "The House of Fiction and *le jardin anglo-chinois*," in *New Perspectives on the Arabian Nights: Ideological Variations and Narrative Horizons*, ed. Wen-Chin Ouyang and Geert Jan van Gelder (London and New York: Routledge, 2005), 67–79.
Caracciolo, Peter L., ed. *The Arabian Nights in English Literature: Studies in the Reception of the Thousand and One Nights into British Culture*. New York: St. Martin's Press, 1993.
Cecil, Moffitt. "Poe's 'Arabesque,'" *Comparative Literature* 18 (1966), 55–70.
Chagall, Marc. *Arabische Nächte; 26 Lithographien zu 1001 Nacht*. Zürich: R. Piper & Co Verlag, 1975.
Chauvin, Victor. *Bibliographie des ouvrages arabes ou relatifs aux arabes*. 12 vols. Liège: Vaillant-Carmanne, 1892–1922.
"Abou Nioute et Abou Nioutine," *Wallonia* 6 (1898), 188–91.
La récension égyptienne des Mille et une nuits. Brussels: Société belge de librairie, 1899.
"Homère et les 1001 Nuits," *Le Musée belge* 3 (1899), 6–9.
Bibliographies des ouvrages arabes, vols. 4–7. Liège: H. Vaillant-Carmanne; Leipzig: O. Harrassowitz, 1900–3.
"Les Mille et Une Nuit de M. Mardrus," *Revue des bibliothèques et archives de Belgique* (1905), 200–5.
Chavis, Dom, and M. Cazotte, trans. *La Suite des Mille et une Nuits, Contes Arabes*. Cabinet des Fées. 4 vols. Geneva: Barde & Manget, 1788–89.
Cheikho, Louis. *Majānī al-adab fī ḥadāʾiq al-ʿArab*. Beirut: Maṭbaʿat al-Ābāʾ al-Yasūʿiyyīn, 1882.
Chesterton, G. K. "The Everlasting Night," in *The Spice of Life and Other Essays*, ed. Dorothy Collins (Beaconsfield, UK: Darwin Finlayson), 58–60.
Chouliaraki, Lilie. *Spectatorship of Suffering*. London: Sage Publications, 2006.
Chraïbi, Aboubakr. "Un Thème de l'adab repris dans les Mille et une Nuit: L'homme qui demande au Calife sa favorite," *Studia Islamica* 76 (1992), 119–36.
Contes nouveaux des 1001 Nuits: Étude du manuscrit Reinhardt. Paris: J. Maisonneuve, 1996.

"Les à-côtés du Récit ou l'enchâssement à l'orientale," *Poétique* 30 (1999), 1–15.
"Les jinns penseurs de Naguib Mahfouz," in *L'Orient au cœur, en l'honneur d'André Miquel*, ed. F. Sanagustin (Paris: Maisonneuve et Larose, 2001), 171–83.
"Galland's 'Ali Baba' and Other Arabic Versions," *Marvels & Tales* 18, no. 2 (2004), 159–69.
"Idéologie et littérature: Représentativité des *Mille et une Nuits*," in *Les Mille et une Nuit en partage*, ed. Aboubakr Chraïbi (Paris: Sindbad, 2004), 95–104.
"Situation, Motivation, and Action in the *Arabian Nights*," in *The Arabian Nights Encyclopedia*, ed. Ulrich Marzolph and Richard van Leeuwen (Santa Barbara, CA: ABC-CLIO, 2004), 5–9.
"À Propos d'une version maghrébine manuscrite du conte de *Khalife le pêcheur*," in *Les Mille et Une Nuit. Du texte au mythe*. Actes du colloque international de littérature comparée. Rabat, les 30, 31 octobre et 1er novembre 2002, Série Colloques et séminaires 127, ed. Jean-Luc Joly and Abdelfattah Kilito (Rabat: Publications de la Faculté des Lettres et des Sciences Humaines, 2005), 43–56.
"Texts of the *Arabian Nights* and Ideological Variations," in *New Perspectives on [the] Arabian Nights: Ideological Variations and Narrative Horizons*, ed. Wen-Chin Ouyang and Geert Jan van Gelder (London and New York: Routledge, 2005), 17–25.
"Galland's 'Ali Baba' and Other Arabic Versions," in *The Arabian Nights in Transnational Perspective*, ed. Ulrich Marzolph (Detroit, MI: Wayne State University Press, 2007), 3–15.
"Des hommes dans le harem," in *Le répertoire narratif arabe médiéval: transmission et ouverture*, ed. Aboubakr Chraïbi, Frédéric Bauden, and Antonella Ghersetti (Geneva: Droz, 2008), 37–46.
"Île flottante et œuf de rukhkh," *Quaderni di Studi Arabi*, n.s. 3 (2008), 83–95.
Les Mille et une nuit. Histoire du texte et Classification des contes. Paris: L'Harmattan, 2008.
"Iram, Labta, les pyramides et l'oiseau rukh ou le paradis sur terre," in *Sulle orme di Shahrazàd: le "Mille e una note" fra Oriente e Occidente*. VI Colloquio Internazionale, Ragusa, 12–14 ottobre 2006, ed. Mirella Cassarino (Soveria Mannelli: Rubbettino, 2009), 43–59.
"La porte de l'Andalousie," in *Les Mille et une nuit et le récit oriental. En Espagne et en Occident*, ed. Aboubakr Chraïbi and Carmen Ramirez (Paris: L'Harmattan, 2009), 19–42.
"Quand les amoureux s'en vont," *Annali di Ca' Foscari* 48 (2009), 63–78.
"Pouvoir et religion dans les *Mille et Une Nuit*," in *Les mille et une nuit. Catalogue of an Exhibition at the Institut du Monde Arabe*, ed. Élodie Bouffard and Anne-Alexandra Joyard (Paris: Institut du monde arabe, 2012), 333–36.
"Qu'est-ce que les *Mille et Une Nuit* aujourd'hui? Le livre, l'anthologie et la culture oubliée," in *Les mille et une nuits. Catalogue of an Exhibition at the*

Institut du Monde Arabe, ed. Élodie Bouffard and Anne-Alexandra Joyard (Paris: Institut du monde arabe, 2012), 33–39.

"Le grand puzzle des Nuits," *al-Qantara* 86 (January 2013), 32–37.

"Une approche fantaisiste des Nuits: le Dictionnaire amoureux des Mille et une nuits de Malek Chebel," *Arabica* 60 (2013), 1–8.

"La Magie, les deux anges et la femme," in *Babylone, Grenade, villes mythiques: Récits, réalités, representations*, ed. Katia Zakharia (Lyon: Maison de l'Orient et de la Méditerranée – Jean Pouilloux, 2014), 113–25.

"Personnification, enchâssement, étonnement et littérature arabe médiane," *Cahiers de recherches médiévales et humanistes* 29 (2015), 23–42.

"Introduction," in *Arabic Manuscripts of the "Thousand and One Nights": Presentation and Critical Editions of Four Noteworthy Texts; Observations on Some Osmanli Traditions*, ed. Aboubakr Chraïbi (Paris: Espaces et signes, 2016), 15–64.

"L'étonnante générosité des *mille et une nuits*," in *Terra ridens – terra narrans: Festschrift zum 65. Geburtstag von Ulrich Marzolph*, vol. 1, ed. Regina Bendix and Dorothy Noyes (Dortmund: Verlag für Orientkunde, 2018), 11–27.

"Quatre personnages éduqués du début des *Mille et nue nuits*," in *Savants, amants, poètes et fous: Séances offertes à Katia Zakharia*, ed. Catherine Pinon (Beirut and Damascus: Presses de l'Institut francais du Proche-Orient, 2019), 85–112.

"Le leçon des *Mille et Une Nuits*," *Europe: revue littéraire mensuelle* 1–2 (2020), 9–23.

Chraïbi, Aboubakr, ed. *Les Mille et une Nuit en partage*. Paris: Sindba, 2004.

Arabic Manuscripts of the "Thousand and One Nights": Presentation and Critical Editions of Four Noteworthy Texts; Observations on Some Osmanli Traditions. Paris: Espaces et signes, 2016.

Chraïbi, Aboubakr, and Carmen Ramirez, eds. *Les Mille et une nuit et le récit oriental. En Espagne et en Occident*. Paris: L'Harmattan, 2009.

Chraïbi, Aboubakr, and Ilaria Vitali. "Les *Mille et Une Nuit*: Variations françaises," *Francofonia* 69 (Autumn 2015), 3–14.

Clair, Justin St. "Mahfouz and the Arabian Nights Tradition," in *Approaches to Teaching the Works of Naguib Mahfouz*, ed. Waïl S. Hassan and Susan Muaddi Darraj (New York: The Modern Language Association of America, 2012), 105–17.

Clinton, Jerome W. "Madness and Cure in The Thousand and One Nights," *Fairy Tales and Society: Illusion, Allusion, and Paradigm*, ed. Ruth B. Bottigheimer (Philadelphia, PA: University of Pennsylvania Press, 1986), 35–51.

Codrescu, Andrei. *Whatever Gets You through the Night*. Princeton, NJ: Princeton University Press, 2011.

Cody, David C. "Henry Adams and the City of Brass: A Historical Review of New England Life and Letters," *The New England Quarterly* 60, no. 1 (March 1987), 89–91.

Cohen, Matthew Isaac. "Thousand and One Nights at the Komedie Stamboel: Popular Theatre and Travelling Stories in Colonial Southeast Asia," in

New Perspectives on [the] Arabian Nights: Ideological Variations and Narrative Horizons, ed. Wen-Chin Ouyang and Geert Jan van Gelder (London and New York: Routledge, 2005), 103–14.

Conant, Martha Pike. The *Oriental Tale in England in the Eighteenth Century*. New York: Columbia University Press, 1908.

Cook, Thomas. *The Traveller's Handbook for Algeria and Tunisia*. London: Simpkin, Marshall, Hamilton, Kent and Co., 1913.

Coote, Henry Charles. "Folk-lore the Source of Some of M. Galland's Tales," *The Folk-lore Record* 3, no. 2 (1881), 178–91.

Corrao, Francesca Maria. "The Arabian Nights in Sicily," *Fabula* 45, no. 3–4 (2004), 237–45; also in *The Arabian Nights in Transnational Perspective*, ed. Ulrich Marzolph (Detroit, MI: Wayne State University Press, 2007), 279–89.

Cortés Garcia, Manuela. "Les Mille et une Nuit dans une zarzuela espagnole: El Asombro de Damasco," in *Les Mille et une Nuit dans les imaginaires croisés*, ed. Lucette Heller-Goldenberg (Cologne: Romanisches Seminar der Universität Köln, 1994), 204–10.

Crane, T. F. "Italian Popular Tales," *North American Review* 123, no. 252 (July 1876), 25–60.

Culler, Jonathan. *Structuralist Poetics: Structuralism, Linguistics and the Study of Literature*. London: Routledge and Kegan Paul, 1975.

The Pursuit of Signs: Semiotics, Literature, Deconstruction. London: Routledge, 1981.

Ḍayf, Aḥmad. "Baḥth tārīkhī naqdī fī alf laylah wa-laylah," *al-Muqtaṭaf* 86, no. 3 (1935), 265–70.

Dobie, Madeleine. "Translation in the Contact Zone: Antoine Galland's *Mille et une nuits: contes arabes*," in *The Arabian Nights in Historical Context: Between East and West*, ed. Saree Makdisi and Felicity Nussbaum (Oxford: Oxford University Press, 2008), 25–49.

Duggan, Anne E. "From Genie to Efreet: Fantastic Apparitions in the Tales of the 'Arabian Nights,'" *Journal of the Fantastic in the Arts* 26, no. 1 (2015), 113–35.

Easthope, Anthony, and Kate McGowan, eds. *A Critical and Cultural Theory Reader*. Toronto: Toronto University Press, 1992.

Eckley, Grace. "The Entertaining Nights of Burton, Stead, and Joyce's Earwicker," *Journal of Modern Literature* 13 (1986), 339–44.

Eco, Umberto. *The Name of the Rose*, trans. William Weaver. San Diego, CA: Harcourt, Inc., 1983.

Elisséeff, Nikita. *Thèmes et motifs des Mille et une Nuits: Essai de Classification*. Beirut: Institut français de Damas, 1949.

Elmaz, Orhan, ed. *Endless Inspiration: One Thousand and One Nights in Comparative Perspective*. Piscataway, NJ: Gorgias Press, 2020.

Estevez, Abilio. *Thine Is the Kingdom: A Novel*, trans. David Frye. New York: Arcade Publishing, 1999.

Fairclough, Norman. *Discourse and Social Change*. Cambridge: Polity Press, 1992.

Fanon, Frantz. *Black Skin, White Masks*, trans. Charles Lam Markmann. New York: Grove Press, 1968.

Faris, Wendy B. "1001 Words: Fiction against Death," *Georgia Review* 36, no. 4 (1982), 811–30.

"Scheherazade's Children: Magic Realism and Postmodern Fiction," in *Magic Realism: Theory, History, Community*, ed. Lois Parkinson Zamora and Wendy B. Faris (Durham, NC: Duke University Press, 1995), 163–90.

Fishburn, Evelyn. "Traces of the *Thousand and One Nights* in Borges," *Middle Eastern Literatures* 7, no. 2 (2004), 213–22.

"Traces of the Thousand and One Nights in Borges," in *New Perspectives on Arabian Nights: Ideological Variations and Narrative Horizons*, ed. Wen-Chin Ouyang and Geert Jan van Gelder (London and New York: Routledge, 2005), 81–90.

Forster, E. M. *Aspects of the Novel*. London: Penguin, 1927.

Foucault, Michel. *The Archaeology of Knowledge and the Discourse on Language*, trans. A. M. Sheridan Smith. New York: Pantheon Books, 1971.

Discipline and Punish: The Birth of the Prison, trans. Alan Sheridan. New York: Random House, 1977.

The History of Sexuality, vol. 1, trans. Robert Hurley. New York: Random House, 1990.

"The Repressive Hypothesis," in *The History of Sexuality*, vol. 1, trans. Robert Hurley (New York: Random House, 1990), 17–49.

The Order of Things: An Archaeology of the Human Sciences. New York: Random House, 1994.

Francis, Henry S. "Chagall's Illustrations for the One Thousand and One Nights," *The Bulletin of the Cleveland Museum of Art* 37, no. 3 (March 1950), 57–59.

Fuentes, Carlos. *Cervantes o la critica de la lectura*. Mexico: Joaquín Mortiz, 1976.

Furtado. Antonio L. "The Arabian Nights: Yet Another Source of the Grail Stories?" *Quondam et Futurus: A Journal of Arthurian Interpretations* 1, no. 3 (1991), 25–40.

Galland, Antoine, trans. *Arabian Nights' Entertainments: Consisting of One Thousand and One Stories. Told by the Sultaness of the Indies, to divert the Sultan from the Execution of a bloody Vow he had made to marry a Lady every day, and have her cut off next Morning, to avenge himself for the Disloyalty of his first Sultaness, &c. Containing a better Account of the Customs, Manners, and Religion of the Eastern Nations, viz. Tartars, Persians, and Indians, than is to be met with in any Author hitherto published. Translated into French from the Arabian Mss. by M. Galland of the Royal Academy, and now done into English from the last Paris Edition (London: Andrew Bell, 1706–17)*. 16th ed. 4 vols. London: Longman, 1783.

Garber, Frederick. "Assisting at the Light," *Prisms: Essays in Romanticism* 1 (1993), 1–30.

Gauttier, Edouard, trans. *Les Mille et une nuit, contes arabes, traduits en français par Galland. Nouvelle édition revue … avec les continuations et plusieurs contes, traduits pour la première fois du persan, du turc et de l'arabe*. 7 vols. Paris: Société de traduction, 1822–23.

Geddes, Sharon S. "The Middle English Poem of Floriz and Blauncheflur and the Arabian Nights Tale of 'Ni'amah and Naomi': A Study in Parallels," *Emporia* 19, no. 1 (1970), 14–21, 23–24.

Genette, Gérard. *Narrative Discourse: An Essay in Method*. Ithaca, NY: Cornell University Press, 1983.

Gerhardt, Mia I. *The Art of Story-Telling: A Literary Study of the Thousand and One Nights*. Leiden: Brill, 1963.

Ghazoul, Ferial Jabouri. *The Arabian Nights: A Structural Analysis*. Cairo: National Commission for UNESCO, 1980.

"Poetic Logic in the Panchatantra and The Arabian Nights," *Arab Studies Quarterly* 5, no. 1 (1983), 13–21.

"The Arabian Nights in Shakespearean Comedy: 'The Sleeper Awakened' and 'The Taming of the Shrew,'" in *In 1001 Nights: Critical Essays and Annotated Bibliography, Mundus Arabicus*, vol. 3 (Cambridge, MA: Dar Mahjar, 1985), 58–70.

Nocturnal Poetics: The Arabian Nights in Comparative Context. Cairo: American University in Cairo Press, 1996.

"Sindbad the Sailor: Textual, Visual, and Performative Interpretations," in *Scheherazade's Children: Global Encounters with the Arabian Nights*, ed. Philip F. Kennedy and Marina Warner (New York: New York University Press, 2013), 243–62.

Gilbert, Sandra M., and Susan Gubar. *The Madwoman in the Attic: The Woman Writer and the Nineteenth-Century Literary Imagination*. New Haven, CT: Yale University Press, 1979.

Gipson, Jennifer Lynn. "Writing the Storyteller: Folklore and Literature from Nineteenth-Century France to the Francophone World," PhD diss., University of California, Berkeley, 2011.

Godard, Barbara. "[F(r)ictions: Feminists Re/Writing Narrative," in *Gender and Narrativity*, ed. Barry Rutland (Ottawa, ON: Carleton University Press, 1997), 115–46.

Goitein, S. D. "The Oldest Documentary Evidence for the Title Alf Laila wa-Laila," *Journal of the American Oriental Society* 78 (1958), 301–2.

Gubar, Susan. "'The Blank Page' and the Female Creativity," in *The New Feminist Criticism*, ed. Elaine Showalter (London: Virago, 1989), 243–63.

Gurewich, David. "Piccadilly's Scheherazade," *The New Criterion* 7, no. 7 (March 1989), 68–72.

Haase, Donald. "The Arabian Nights, Visual Culture, and Early German Cinema," *Fabula* 45, no. 3–4 (2007), 237–45.

Hackford, Terry Reece. "Fantastic Visions: Illustration of the Arabian Nights," in *The Aesthetics of Fantasy Literature and Art*, ed. Roger C. Schlobin (Notre Dame, IN: University of Notre Dame, 1982), 143–75.

Haddawy, Husain Fareed Ali. "English Arabesque: The Oriental Mode in Eighteenth-Century English Literature," PhD diss., Cornell University Press, 1962.

Haddawy, Husain Fareed Ali, trans. *The Arabian Nights*. New York and London: W. W. Norton & Company, 1990.

Hājī, Fāṭimah. *al-Qaṣaṣ al-sha'bī fī alf laylah wa-laylah fī masraḥ al-ṭifl bi-l-Kuwayt: Namūdhaj masraḥīyat al-Shāṭir Ḥasan ta'līf al-Sayyid Ḥāfiẓ*. Alexandria: Markaz al-Diltā li-l-Ṭibā'ah, 1991.

Hakalin, Mikko. "Flying Carpets and Talking Heads: The Elements of Fantasy and 'Science Fiction' in 1001 Night Stories," in *Studies in Folklore and Popular Religion*, ed. Ulo Valk (Tartu, Estonia: Department of Estonian and Comparative Folklore, University of Tartu, 1996), 81–85.

Hale, Dan S. *Races on Display: French Representation of Colonized Peoples, 1886–1940*. Bloomington, IN: Indiana University Press, 2008.

Hartland, E. Sidney. "The Forbidden Chamber," *Folk-lore Journal* 3, no. 3 (1885), 193–242.

Havelock, Eric A. *The Muse Learns to Write: Reflections on Orality and Literacy from Antiquity to the Present*. New Haven, CT, and London: Yale University Press, 1986.

Heath, Peter. "Romance as Genre in 'The Thousand and One Nights,'" Part I, *Journal of Arabic Literature*, no. 18 (1987), 1–21.

"Romance as Genre in 'The Thousand and One Nights,'" Part II, *Journal of Arabic Literature*, no. 19 (1988), 1–26.

Henning, Max, trans. *Tausend und eine Nacht. Aus dem Arabischen übertragen*. 24 vols. Leipzig: Reclam, 1895–99.

Tausend und eine Nacht. 1895–99, ed. Hans W. Fischer. Berlin and Darmstadt: Deutsche Buch-Gemeinschaft, 1957.

Hensher, Jonathan. "Engraving Difference: The Representation of the Oriental Other in Marillier's Illustrations to the Mille et Une Nuits and Other Contes orientaux in Le Cabinet des fees (1785–1789)," *Journal for Eighteenth-Century Studies* 31, no. 3 (2008), 377–91.

Ḥikmat, 'Alī Aṣghar. "Min Hazār Afsan ilā Hazār distān: Dirāsah tarīkhiyyah li-kitāb alf laylah wa-laylah," *al-Dirāsāt al-Adabiyyah* 4 (1960), 5–35.

Ho, Cynthia. "Framed Progeny: The Medieval Descendants of Shaharzad," *Medieval Perspectives* 7 (1992), 91–107.

Holmberg, Arthur. "Carlos Fuentes Turns to Theater," *New York Times*, June 6, 1982.

Horta, Paulo Lemos. *Marvellous Thieves: Secret Authors of The Arabian Nights*. Cambridge: Harvard University Press, 2017.

Hunt, Leigh. "New Translations of the Arabian Nights," *Westminster Review* 33 (October 1839), 101–37.

Ḥusayn, Ṭāhā, and Tawfīq al-Ḥakīm. *al-Qaṣr al-masḥūr*. Cairo:Dār al-Nashr al-Ḥadīth, 1936.

Hutcheon, Linda. *Politics of Postmodernism*. London: Routledge, 1991.

Ibn 'Abd Rabbihi. *al-'Iqd al-farīd*, vol. 8. Beirut: Dār al-Kutub al-'Ilmiyyah, 1983.

Ibn Abī al-Ḥadīd. *Sharḥ Nahj al-balāghah*, 20 vols., ed. Muḥammad Abū al-Faḍl Ibrāhīm. Beirut: Dār al-Kutub al-'Ilmiyyah, n.d.

Ibn Qutaybah. *'Uyūn al-akhbār*, vol. 1. Beirut: Dār al-Kutub al-'Ilmiyyah, 1986.

Irwin, Bonnie D. "What's in a Frame? The Medieval Textualization of Traditional Storytelling," *Oral Tradition* 10, no. 1 (1995), 27–53.

"Framed (for) Murder: The Corpse Killed Five Times in the Thousand Nights and a Night," in *Telling Tales: Medieval Narratives and the Folk Tradition*, ed.

Francesca Canadé Sautman, Diana Conchado, and Giuseppe Di Scipio (New York: St. Martin's Press, 1998), 155–70.

"Narrative in the Decameron and the Thousand and One Nights," in *Approaches to Teaching Boccaccio's Decameron*, ed. and trans. James H. McGregor (New York: Modern Language Association of America, 2000), 21–30.

Irwin, Robert. *The Arabian Nights: A Companion*. London: The Penguin Press, 1994.

"A Thousand and One Nights at the Movies," in *New Perspectives on Arabian Nights: Ideological Variations and Narrative Horizons*, ed. Wen-Chin Ouyang and Geert Jan van Gelder (London and New York: Routledge, 2005), 91–102.

"Night Classes," *The Times Literary Supplement*, April 17, 2015, www.the-tls.co.uk/articles/night-classes-robert-irwin/.

Jabrā, Jabrā Ibrāhīm. "al-Dhirwah fī al-adab wa-al-fann," *al-Adīb* (February 1950), 3–7.

"al-Riwāyah wa-l-insāniyyah," *al-Adīb* (January 1954), 31–36.

al-Bi'r al-Ūlā: The First Well: A Bethlehem Boyhood, trans. Issa J. Boullata. Fayetteville, AR: University of Arkansas Press, 1995.

al-Jāḥiẓ, Abū ʿUthmān ʿAmr ibn Baḥr. *al-Bukhalāʾ*, ed. Ṭāhā al-Ḥājirī. Cairo: Dār al-Maʿārif, n.d.

al-Maḥāsin wa-l-aḍdād, ed. Fawzī ʿAṭwī. Beirut: al-Sharikah al-Lubnāniyyah, 1969.

Jakobson, Roman. "On Linguistic Aspects of Translation." 1959. https://complit.utoronto.ca/wp-content/uploads/COL1000H_Roman_Jakobson_LinguisticAspects.pdf.

James, Henry. *The Art of the Novel*. New York: Oxford, 1948.

Jameson, Fredric. *The Political Unconscious: Narrative as a Socially Symbolic Act*. Ithaca, NY: Cornell University Press, 1981.

Jeffares, A. Norman, and K. G. W. Cross, eds. *In Excited Reverie: Centenary Tribute to W. B. Yeats*. London: Macmillan, 1965.

Jianping, Wang. "Imagining Iraq and the Cultural Politics of Misreading: John Barth's *The Last Voyage of Somebody the Sailor*," *Journal of American Studies of Turkey* 21 (2005), 27–40.

Johnson, Samuel. *The History of Rasselas, Prince of Abissinia*. Harmondsworth, UK: Penguin Books, 1976.

Joubin, Rebecca. "Islam and Arabs through the Eyes of the Encyclopédie: The 'Other' as a Case of French Cultural Self-criticism," *International Journal of Middle East Studies* 32, no. 2 (May 2000), 197–217.

Jullien, Dominique. "Ailleurs ici: Les Mille et une Nuit dans À la Recherche du Temps Perdu," *Romantic Review* 79 (1988), 466–75.

"Biography of an Immortal," *Comparative Literature* 47, no. 2 (Spring 1995), 136–59.

"Hârûn al-Rashîd, du conte au feuilleton," in *Les mille et une nuit. Catalogue of an Exhibition at the Institut du Monde Arabe*, ed. Élodie Bouffard and Anne-Alexandra Joyard (Paris: Institut du monde arabe, 2012), 147–50.

Kabbani, Rana. "The Arabian Nights as an Orientalist Text," in *The Arabian Nights Encyclopedia*, ed. Ulrich Marzolph and Richard van Leeuwen (Santa Barbara, CA: ABC-CLIO, 2004), 25–29.

Kefala, Eleni. *Peripheral (Post)Modernity: The Syncretist Aesthetics of Borges, Piglia, Kalokyris and Kyriakidis*. New York: Peter Lang, 2007.

Kennedy, Philip. "Borges and the Missing Pages of the Nights," in *Scheherazade's Children: Global Encounters with the Arabian Nights*, ed. Philip Kennedy and Marina Warner (New York: New York University Press, 2013), 195–217.

Khoury, Elias. *Awlād al-ghītū: Ismī Ādam*. Beirut: Dār al-Ādāb, 2016.

The Children of the Ghetto, trans. Humphrey Davies. New York: Archipelago Books, 2019.

Kiernan, Victor. *The Lords of Human Mind*. London: Serif, 1969.

Kirby, W. F. "The Forbidden Doors of the Thousand and One Nights," *Folk-lore Journal* 5, 2 (1887), 112–24.

"Contributions to the Bibliography of the Thousand and One Nights," in *A Plain and Literal Translation of The Arabian Nights' Entertainments, Now Entitled The Book of the Thousand Nights and a Night: With Introduction, Explanatory Notes on the Manners and Customs of Moslem Men and a Terminal Essay upon the History of the Nights*, trans. Richard F. Burton (Benares [= Stoke-Newington]: Kamashastra Society, 1885), vol. 10, appendix II, 92–94 and 414–18.

Klee, Paul. *The Diaries of Klee, 1898–1918*, ed. Felix Klee. Berkeley, CA: University of California Press, 1964.

Knipp, Christopher. "The *Arabian Nights* in England: Galland's Translation and Its Successors," *Journal of Arabic Literature* 5, no. 1 (1974), 44–54.

Krachkovski, Ignati Iulianovich. *Istoria Arabskoi Geograficheskoi Literatury*. Beirut: Dār al-Gharb al-Islāmī, 1963–65.

Kristal, Efraín. *Invisible Work: Borges and Translation*. Nashville, TN: Vanderbilt University Press, 2002.

Kubarek, Magdalena. "The Reception of One Thousand and One Nights in Polish Contemporary Literature," in *The Thousand and One Nights: Sources and Transformations in Literature, Art, and Science*, ed. Ibrahim Akel and William Granara (Leiden: Brill, 2020), 216–26.

Lahusen, Thomas. "Thousand and One Nights in Stalinist Culture: Far from Moscow," *Discourse: Theoretical Studies in Media and Culture* 17, no. 3 (1995), 58–74.

Lane, Edward William, trans. *The Thousand and One Nights; Commonly Called, in England, The Arabian Nights' Entertainments. A New Translation from the Arabic, with Copious Notes*. 3 vols. London: Charles Knight, 1839–41.

The Thousand and One Nights; Commonly Called the Arabian Nights' Entertainments, illus. William Harvey. 3 vols. London: Chatto and Windus, 1912.

Larzul, Sylvette. "Les Mille et une Nuit d'Antoine Galland: Traduction, Adaption, Création," in *Les Mille et une Nuit en partage*, ed. Aboubakr Chraïbi (Paris: Sindbad, 2004), 251–66.

Levine, Neil. *The Architecture of Frank Lloyd Wright*. Princeton, NJ: Princeton University Press, 1996.

Lewis, Bernard. "The Question of Orientalism," *The New York Review of Books*, June 24, 1982, https://bit.ly/3cK4bvk.

Life, Allan. "Scheherazade's 'Special Artists': Illustrations by Arthur Boyd Houghton for The Thousand and One Nights," in *Haunted Texts: Studies in Pre-Raphaelitism*, ed. David Latham (Toronto: University of Toronto Press, 2003), 145–75.

Littmann, Enno. *Tausendundeine Nacht in der arabischen Literatur*. Tübingen: J. C. B. Mohr, 1923.

Geschichten der Liebe aus den Tausendundein Nächten. Wiesbaden: Insel-Verlag, 1953.

"Alf layla wa-layla," *Encyclopedia of Islam (EI)*. Leiden: Brill, 1960, 1:358–64.

Lonsdale, Roger. "Introduction," in *Vathek* (London: Oxford, 1970), 167–70.

Lowes, John Livingston. *The Road to Xanadu: A Study in the Ways of the Imagination*. Boston, MA: Riverside Press, 1927.

Lukacs, Georg. *History and Class Consciousness: Studies in Marxist Dialectics*. Cambridge, MA: MIT Press, 1971.

Lundell, Michael James. "Pasolini's Splendid Infidelities: Un/Faithful Film Versions of The Thousand and One Nights," *Adaptation: The Journal of Literature on Screen Studies* 6, no. 1 (2013), 120–27.

Lynn, Catherine. "Dream and Substance: Araby and the Planning of Opa-Locka," *The Journal of Decorative and Propaganda Arts* 23 (1998), 162–89.

Lyons, Malcolm C., and Ursula Lyons. *The Arabian Nights: Tales of 1001 Nights*. 3 vols. Harmondsworth, UK: Penguin, 2008.

Lyotard, Jean-Francois. *The Postmodern Condition: A Report on Knowledge*, trans. Geoff Bennington and Brian Massumi. Minneapolis, MN: University of Minnesota Press, 1984.

MacCabe, Colin. "*Arabian Nights*: Brave Old World," The Criterion Collection, November 13, 2012, www.criterion.com/current/posts/2552-arabian-nights-brave-old-world.

MacDonald, Duncan B. "On Translating the Arabian Nights," *The Nation* 71 (August 30, 1900), 167–68, 185–86.

"The Problems of Muhammadanism," *Hartford Seminary Record* 15 (November 1904–August 1905), 77–97.

"The Story of the Fisherman and the Jinnî: Transcribed from Galland's MS of 'The Thousand and One Nights,'" in *Orientalische Studien: Th. Nöldeke zum 70. Geburtstag gewidmet*, vol. 1, ed. Carl Bezold (Giessen: Toepelmann, 1906), 357–83.

"Lost Manuscripts of the 'Arabian Nights' and a Projected Edition of That of Galland," *Journal of the Royal Asiatic Society* (1911), 219–21.

"A Missing MS of the Arabian Nights," *Journal of the Royal Asiatic Society* (1913), 432.

"Alf laila wa-laila," *The Encyclopedia of Islam*. Supplement. Leiden: Brill, 1913–38, 17–21.

"From the Arabian Nights to Spirit," *Muslim World* 9 (1918), 336–48.

"A Preliminary Classification of Some Mss. of the Arabian Nights," in *A Volume of Oriental Studies: Presented to Edward G. Browne on His 60th Birthday*, ed. Thomas W. Arnold and Reynold A. Nicholson (Cambridge: Cambridge University Press, 1922), 304–21.

"The Earlier History of the Arabian Nights," *Journal of Royal Asiatic Society* 3 (July 1924), 353–97.

"A Bibliographical and Literary Study of the First Appearance of the Arabian Nights in Europe," *The Library Quarterly* 2, no. 4 (October 1932), 387–420.

Mack, Robert L., ed. *Arabian Nights' Entertainments*. Oxford: Oxford University Press, 1995.

"Cultivating the Garden: Antoine Galland's Arabian Nights in the Traditions of English Literature," in *The Arabian Nights in Historical Context: Between East and West*, ed. Saree Makdisi and Felicity Nussbaum (Oxford: Oxford University Press, 2008), 51–81.

Mackail, John W. *Lectures on Poetry*. London: Longman & Green, 1911.

Macleod, Dianne Sachko. "The Politics of Vision: Disney, Aladdin, and the Gulf War," in The *Emperor's Old Groove: Decolonizing Disney's Magic Kingdom*, ed. Brend Ayers (New York: Peter Lang, 2003), 179–92.

al-Madani, Yusur. "Deconstructing and Reconstructing a Narrative of the Self: John Barth's The Last Voyage of Somebody the Sailor," *International Fiction Review* 26, no. 1–2 (1999), 8–18.

Madelung, Wilfred. *The Succession to Muhammad*. Cambridge: Cambridge University Press, 1996.

Mahdi, Muhsin. "Remarks on the *1001 Nights*," *Interpretation* 3 (1973), 157–68.

"Mazâhir al-riwâya wa-'l-mushâfaha fî usûl 'Alf layla wa-layla,'" *Revue de l'Institut des manuscrits arabes* 20 (1974), 125–44.

The Thousand and One Nights (Alf Layla wa-Layla) from the Earliest Known Sources. Leiden: Brill, 1984–94. [Part I: "Arabic Text" (1984[a]); Part II: "Critical Apparatus. Description of Manuscripts" (1984[b]); Part III: "Introduction and Indexes" (1994). Contents of Part III: "Antoine Galland and the Nights," 11–49; "Galland's Successors," 51–86; "Four Editions: 1814–1843," 87–126; "Three Interpretations," 127–80.]

"From History to Fiction: The Tale Told by the King's Steward in the 1001 Nights," *Oral Tradition* 4, no. 1–2 (1989), 65–79.

"The Sources of Galland's Nuits," *International Journal of Islamic and Arabic Studies* 10, no. 1 (1993), 13–26.

Malek, Anwar Abdel. "Orientalism in Crisis," *Diogenes* 44 (Winter 1963), 104–12.

Mallāh, ʿAbd al-Ghanī. *Riḥlah haḍāriyyah wa-lamaḥāt turāthiyyah ʿabra alf laylah wa-laylah*. Baghdad: Dār al-Kitāb al-Jadīd, 1977.

Malti-Douglas, Fedwa. "Narration and Desire: Shahrazâd," in *Woman's Body, Woman's Word: Gender and Discourse in Arabo-Islamic Writing* (Princeton, NJ: Princeton University Press, 1991), 11–28.

Woman's Body, Woman's Word: Gender and Discourse in Arabo-Islamic Writing. Princeton, NJ: Princeton University Press, 1991.

"Shahrazad Feminist," in *The Thousand and One Nights in Arabic Literature and Society*, ed. Richard G. Hovannisian and Georges Sabagh (Cambridge: Cambridge University Press, 1997), 40–55.

al-Maqrīzī, *al-Khiṭaṭ*, vol. 1. Cairo: Būlāq, 1854.

Marzolph, Ulrich. "In the Studio of the Nights," *Middle Eastern Literatures* 17:1, 43–57, 2014.
"The Man Who Made the Nights Immortal: The Tales of the Syrian Maronite Storyteller Ḥannā Diyāb," *Marvels & Tales* 32, no. 1 (Spring 2018), 114–29.
"Aladdin Almighty: Middle Eastern Magic in the Service of Western Consumer Culture," *The Journal of American Folklore* 132, no. 525 (Summer 2019), 275–90.
Marzolph, Ulrich, ed. *The Arabian Nights Reader*. Detroit: Wayne State University Press, 2006.
"Arabian Nights". *Encyclopaedia of Islam* 1. Third Edition. Leiden: Brill, 2007. 137–145.
The Arabian Nights in Transnational Perspective. Detroit, MI: Wayne State University Press, 2007.
Matar, Hisham. *In the Country of Men*.New York: Dial Press, 2008.
Mathers, Edward Powys, trans. *The Book of the Thousand Nights and One Night: Rendered from the Literal and Complete Version of Dr. J. C. Mardrus; and Collated with Other Sources*. 8 vols. London: The Casanova Society, 1923.
Maynard, T. G. J. "The Literary Relevance of the Enclosed Garden as an Image in the Oriental Tale, 1704–1820," PhD diss., University of London, 1970.
McClintock, Anne. *Imperial Leather: Race, Gender, and Sexuality in the Colonial Conquest*. London: Routledge, 1995.
Melville, Lewis. *Life and Letters of William Beckford of Fonthill*. London: Heinemann, 1910.
Metlitzki, Dorothee. *The Matter of Araby in Medieval England*. New Haven, CT: Yale University Press, 1977.
Meyer, Susan L. "Colonialism and the Figurative Strategy of *Jane Eyre*," *Victorian Studies* 33, no. 2 (Winter 1990), 247–68.
Molan, Peter. "Maʿruf the Cobbler: The Mythic Structure of an Arabian Nights Tale," *Edebiyat* 3, no. 2 (1978), 121–35.
Morsy, Faten I. "Frame-Narrative and Short Fiction: A Continuum from 'One Thousand and One Nights' to Borges," PhD diss., University of Essex, 1989.
Mottahedeh, Roy D. "Aja'ib in the Thousand and One Nights," in *The Thousand and One Nights in Arabic Literature and Society*, ed. Richard G. Hovannisian and Georges Sabagh (Cambridge: Cambridge University Press, 1997), 29–39.
Muller, Bernhardt E. "Bernhardt Muller's Dream of Arabian City in Florida Is Reality," *Opa-locka Times*, February 23, 1927, 1–2.
"Arabian Nights in America: Fascinating Architectural Fantasy," *Country Life* 55 (November 1928), 67–69.
Mulvey, Laura. *Visual and Other Pleasures*. London: Macmillan, 1989.
al-Munṣif, Bin Ḥasan. *al-ʿAbīd wa-al-jawārī fī ḥikāyāt alf laylah wa-laylah*. Tunis: Sirās li-l-Nashr, 1994.
al-Mūsawī, Muḥsin Jāsim. *al-Istishrāq fī al-fikr al-ʿArabī*. Beirut: al-Muʾassasah al-ʿArabiyyah li-l-Dirāsāt, 1993.
"Makhābiʾ al-khayāl al-munthahil," in *Fī al-mutakhayyal al-ʿArabī* (Sousse, Tunis: 1995), 7–29.

Sardiyyāt al-ʿaṣr al-ʿArabī al-Islāmī al-wasīṭ. Beirut: al-Markaz al-Thaqāfī al-ʿArabī, 1997.

Mujtamaʿ alf laylah wa-laylah. Tunis: University Publication Center, 2000.

al-Dhākirah al-shaʿbiyyah li-mujtamaʿāt alf laylah wa-laylah. Beirut: al-Markaz al-Thaqāfī al-ʿArabī, 2016.

al-Musawi, Muhsin Jassim. "The Arabian Nights in Eighteenth-Century English Criticism," *Muslim World* 67 (1977), 12–32.

"The Growth of Scholarly Interest in the *Arabian Nights*," *Muslim World* 70 (1980), 196–212.

Scheherazade in England: A Study of Nineteenth-Century English Criticism of the Arabian Nights. Boulder, CO: Three Continents, 1981.

"Rasselas as a Colonial Discourse," *CIEFL Bulletin*, n.s. 8, no. 1 (June 1996), 47–60.

"Cultural Contestation and Self-definition," in *The Postcolonial Arabic Novel: Debating Ambivalence* (Leiden: Brill, 2003), 337–73.

"Scheherazade's Gifts: Maḥfūẓ's Narrative Strategies in *Layalī alf laylah*," in *The Postcolonial Arabic Novel: Debating Ambivalence* (Leiden: Brill, 2003), 375–88.

"The 'Mansion' and the 'Rubbish Mounds': The *Thousand and One Nights* in Popular Arabic Tradition," *Journal of Arabic Literature* 35, no. 3 (2004), 329–67.

"Scheherazade's Nonverbal Narrative," *Journal of Arabic Literature* 36, no. 3 (2005), 338–62.

"Abbasid Popular Narrative: The Formation of Readership and Cultural Production," *Journal of Arabic Literature* 38, no. 3 (2007), 261–92.

The Islamic Context of the Thousand and One Nights. New York: Columbia University Press, 2009.

The Medieval Islamic Republic of Letters: Arabic Knowledge Construction. Notre Dame, IN: University of Notre Dame Press, 2015.

"Postcolonial Theory in the Arab World: Belated Engagements and Limits," *Interventions* 20, no. 2 (February 2018), 174–91.

Naddaff, Sandra. "Magic Time: Narrative Repetition in the Thousand and One Nights," in *The 1001 Nights: Critical Essays and Annotated Bibliography*, ed. Kay Hardy Campbell, Ferial J. Ghazoul, Andras Hamori, Muhsin Mahdi, Christopher M. Murphy, and Sandra Naddaff (Cambridge, MA: Dar Mahjar, 1984), 41–57.

Arabesque: Narrative Structure and the Aesthetics of Repetition in the 1001 Nights. Evanston, IL: Northwestern University Press, 1991.

al-Nadīm, Abū al-Faraj Muḥammad ibn Isḥāq. *The Fihrist: A 10th Century AD Survey of Islamic Culture*, ed. and trans. Bayard Dodge. New York: Columbia University Press, 1998.

Namazi, Rasoul. "Politics, Religion, and Love: How Leo Strauss Read the Arabian Nights," *The Journal of Religion* 100, no. 2 (April 2020), 189–231.

Nance, Susan. *How the Arabian Nights Inspired the American Dream, 1790–1935*. Chapel Hill, NC: University of North Carolina Press, 2009.

O'Neill, Patrick. "The Scheherazade Syndrome: Gunter Grass' Mega Novel Der Butt," in *Adventures of a Flounder: Critical Essays on Gunter Grass' Der Butt* (Munich: Fink, 1982), 1–15.

Oliver, J. W. *Life of William Beckford.* London: Oxford, 1932.
Ostriker, Alicia. "The Thieves of Language: Women Poets and Revisionist Mythmaking," in *The New Feminist Criticism,* ed. Elaine Showalter (London: Virago Press, 1989), 314–38.
Ouyang, Wen-Chin. "Whose Story Is It? Sindbad the Sailor in Literature and Film," in *New Perspectives on Arabian Nights: Ideological Variations and Narrative Horizons,* ed. Wen-Chin Ouyang and Geert Jan van Gelder (London and New York: Routledge, 2005), 1–15.
Ouyang, Wen-Chin, and Geert Jan van Gelder, eds. *New Perspectives on Arabian Nights: Ideological Variations and Narrative Horizons.* London and New York: Routledge, 2005.
"From The Thousand and One Nights to Magical Realism: Postnational Predicament in The Journey of Little Ghandi by Elias Khoury," in *A Companion to Magical Realism,* eds. Stephen M. Hart and Wen-Chin Ouyang. Woodbridge: Tamesis, 2005, 367–380.
Poetics of Love in the Arabic Novel. Edinburgh: Edinburgh University Press, 2012.
Parreaux, Andre. *William Beckford, auteur de Vathek, 1760–1844.* Paris: A. G. Nizet, 1960.
Pauliny, Jan. "Adaptation oder Übersetzung? Tausend und eine Nacht im europäischen Literaturkontext," *Graecolatina et Orientalia* 15–16 (1983–84), 115–31.
Pavel, Silvia. "La Proliferation narrative dans les 'Mile et une nuits,'" *Canadian Journal of Research in Semiotics* 2, no. 4 (Winter 1974), 21–40.
Payne, John. "The Thousand and One Nights," Part I, *The New Quarterly Magazine,* n.s. 1 (January 1879), 154–61.
"The Thousand and One Nights," Part II, *The New Quarterly Magazine,* n.s. 2 (April 1879), 379–80.
Picot, Jean Pierre. "Silence de mort, parole de vie: Du recit cadre des Mille et Une Nuits," *Litteratures* 24 (Spring 1991), 13–27.
Pinault, David. *Story-Telling Techniques in the Arabian Nights.* Leiden: Brill, 1992.
Poe, Edgar Allan. "The Thousand-and-Second Tale of Scheherazade," *Godey's Lady's Book* (February 1845). [Reprinted in *The Works of the Late Edgar Allan Poe, Volume 1: Tales* (1850), 131–49.]
Poole, Gordon. "The Drunken Scheherazade: Self Reflection in Jack London's The Road, Martin Eden and John Barleycorn," *RSA Journal: Rivista di Studi Nord Americani* 1 (1990), 69–80.
Porcello, Valerie. "Slander and Continuity in the New Novel and the Old," *South Asian Review* 19, no. 16 (December 1995), 41–48.
Pote, B. E. "Arabian Nights," *Foreign Quarterly Review* 24 (October 1839), 144–46.
Prince, Gerald. "Narratology, Narrative, and Meaning," *Poetics Today* 12, no. 3 (Autumn 1991), 543–52.
"On a Postcolonial Narratology," in *A Companion to Narrative Theory,* ed. James Phelan and Peter J. Rabinowitz (Maiden, MA: Blackwell, 2005), 372–81.
Proust, Marcel. *On Remembrance of Things Past,* trans. C. K. Scott Moncrieff and Terence Kilmartin. New York: Random House, 1981.

Time Regained: In Search of Lost Time, vol. 6. New ed. edition. New York: Penguin Random House, Modern Library, 1999.

al-Qalamāwī, Suhayr. *Alf laylah wa-laylah*. Cairo: Dār al-Maʿārif, 1943.

al-Qayrawānī, al-Ḥuṣrī. *Zahr al-ādāb wa-thimār al-albāb*, ed. ʿA. M. al-Bajāwī. Cairo: al-Bābī al-Ḥalabī, 1970.

al-Qazwīnī, Abū Yaḥyā Zakariyyā ibn Muḥammad. *ʿAjāʾib al-makhlūqāt wa-gharāʾib al-mawjūdāt*. Beirut: Dār al-Sharq al-ʿArabī, n.d.

Rancière, Jacques. *The Politics of Aesthetics*. New York: Continuum, 2004.

The Future of the Image. London and New York: Verso, 2007.

The Emancipated Spectator, trans. Gregory Elliott. London and New York: Verso, 2011.

Rehatsek, E. "A Few Analogies in 'The Thousand and One Nights' and in Latin Authors," *Journal of the Bombay Branch of the Royal Asiatic Society* 14 (1880), 74–85.

Riffaterre, Michael. *Fictional Truth*. Baltimore, MD: Johns Hopkins University Press, 1990.

Rihani, Ameen F. *The Lore of the Arabian Nights*. Washington, DC: Platform International, 2002.

Ritter, H. *Kitāb al-ḥikāyāt al-ʿajībah waʾl-akhbār al-gharībah: Tales of the Marvelous and News of the Strange*, ed. Hans Wehr; trans. Malcolm C. Lyons. London: Penguin, 2014.

Rivkin, Julie, and Michael Ryan. "Introduction: 'The Class of 1968-Post-Structuralism par lui-meme,'" in *Literary Theory: An Anthology*, ed. Julie Rivkin and Michael Ryan (Malden, MA: Blackwell, 1998), 334–57.

Rodinson, Maxime. *Europe and the Mystique of Islam*, trans. Roger Veinus. Seattle, WA: University of Washington Press, 1991.

Rushdie, Salman. *Midnight's Children*. London: Jonathan Cape, 1981.

Haroun and the Sea of Stories. London: Granta, 1990.

Two Years Eight Months and Twenty-Eight Nights. London: Jonathan Cape, 2015.

Russell, Frances Theresa. *Satire in Victorian Fiction*. New York: Macmillan, 1920.

Said, Edward W. *Orientalism*. New York: Random House, 1979.

The World, the Text, and the Critic. London: Vintage, 1991.

Culture and Imperialism. New York: Random House, 1993.

Sallis, Eva. "Playing on the Senses: Descriptive Narration in the Thousand and One Nights," *Journal of Semitic Studies* 45, no. 2 (Autumn 2000), 347–60.

Saly, Antoinette. "Les Mille et Une Nuit au XIlle siècle: Conte oriental et matiere de Bretagne," *Travau de Litterature* 3 (1990), 15–24.

Sarkīs, Iḥsān. *Al-Thunāʾiyyah fī alf laylah wa-laylah*. Beirut: 1979.

Sasic, Borisalva. "Nuruddin Farah's Sardines: The Construction of a Somali Novel on the Intersection of Transcultural Intertextuality," in *Across the Lines: Intertextuality and Transcultural Communication in the New Literatures in English*, ed. Wolfgang Kloss (Amsterdam: Rodopi, 1998), 167–74.

Segert, Stanislav. "Ancient Near Eastern Traditions in the Thousand and One Nights," in *The Thousand and One Nights in Arabic Literature and Society*, ed. Richard G. Hovannisian and Georges Sabagh (Cambridge: Cambridge University Press, 1997), 106–13.

Severin, Tim. "In the Wake of Sindbad," *National Geographic* 162, no. 1 (July 1982), 2–41.

Shaheen, Jack. "Aladdin Animated Racism," *Cinéaste* 20, no. 1 (1993), 49.

Reel Bad Arabs: How Hollywood Vilifies a People. 3rd ed. Northampton, MA: Olive Branch Press, 2014.

Shaḥḥādh, Aḥmad Muḥammad. *al-Malāmiḥ al-siyāsiyyah fī ḥikāyāt alf laylah wa-laylah*. Baghdad: Wizārat al-Thaqāfah wa-l-I'lām, Dār al-Shu'ūn al-Thaqāfiyyah al-'Āmmah, 1986.

al-Shāljī (Also al-Shālchī), 'Abbūd. *al-Faraj ba'd al-shiddah*, 5 vols., ed. Muḥassin al-Tanūkhī. Beirut: Dār Ṣādir, 1978.

al-Shamy, Hasan. *A Motif Index of The Thousand and One Nights*. Bloomington, IN: Indiana University Press, 2006.

Shaw, Ronald E. *Erie Water West: A History of the Erie Canal, 1792–1854*. Lexington, KY: University Press of Kentucky, 2013.

al-Shaykh, Hanan, and Tim Supple. *One Thousand and One Nights: Media of One Thousand and One Nights*. London: Methuen Drama, 2011.

Shohat, Ella. "Gender and Culture of Empire: Towards a Feminist Ethnography of the Cinema," in *Visions of the East: Orientalism in Film*, ed. Matthew Bernstein and Gaylyn Studlar (London: I.B. Tauris, 1997), 19–66.

Sironval, Margaret. *Album Mille et Une Nuits: Iconographie Choisie et Commentée*. Paris: Gallimard, 2005.

Siry, Joseph M. "Wright's Baghdad Opera House and Gammage Auditorium: In Search of Regional Modernity," *The Art Bulletin* 87, no. 2 (June 2005), 265–311.

Stead, Évanghélia. "Joseph-Charles Mardrus: Les Riches Heures D'un Livre-Monument," *Francofonia* 69 (2015), 105–25.

"On Inefficient Arabian Nights Tales: Théophile Gautier's 'The Thousand and Second Nights,'" *Middle Eastern Literatures* 19, no. 1 (2016), 99–110.

Steele, David. "Galland and Mardrus: André Gide's Reading of The Arabian Nights," in *La Réception mondiale et transdisciplinaire des Mille et une Nuits*. Medievales 51, ed. Waël Rabadi and Isabelle Bernar (Amiens: Presses du Centre d'Études Médiévales, 2012), 336–56.

Stetkevych, Jaroslav. *The Hunt in Arabic Poetry: From Heroic to Lyric to Metapoetic*. Notre Dame, IN: University of Notre Dame Press, 2015.

Stevick, Philip. "Scheherazade Runs Out of Plots, Goes on Talking; the King, Puzzled, Listens: An Essay on New Fiction," *TriQuarterly* 26 (1973), 332–62.

Strauss, Leo. *Persecution and the Art of Writing*. Chicago, IL: University of Chicago Press, 1952.

al-Tanūkhī, Abū 'Alī Muḥassin. *The Table-Talk of a Mesopotamian Judge*, trans. D. S. Margoliouth. London: The Royal Asiatic Society, 1921–22.

Nishwār al-muhāḍarah wa-akhbār al-mudhākarah, ed. ʿAbbūd al-Shālchī. Beirut: Dār Ṣādir, 1971–73.

Tauer, Felix. "Einige Randglossen zu Tausendundeiner Nacht," *Acta Universitatis Carolinae, Philologica 1, Orientalia Pragensia* 1 (1960), 13–22.

"Tausendundeine Nacht im Weltschrifttum als Gegenstand der Lektüre un der Forschung," in *Irrgarten der Lust: 1001 Nacht, aufsätze, stimmen, illustrationen* (Frankfurt: Insel Verlag, 1968), 122–47.

al-Tawḥīdī, Abū Ḥayyān. *Kitāb al-imtāʿ wa-l-muʾānasah*, ed. Aḥmad Amīn and Aḥmad al-Zayn. Beirut: al-ʿAṣriyyah, n.d.

Todorov, Tzvetan. *The Fantastic: A Structural Approach to a Literary Genre*, trans. Richard Howard. Ithaca, NY: Cornell University Press, 1975.

"Narrative Men," in *The Poetics of Prose*, trans. Richard Howard (Oxford: Basil Blackwell, 1977), 226–38.

The Poetics of Prose, trans. Richard Howard. Oxford: Basil Blackwell, 1977.

Tonna, Jo. "The Thousand and One Nights and the Poetics of Arab-Islamic Architecture," in *Les Mille et une Nuit dans les imaginaires croisés*, ed. Lucette Heller-Goldenberg (Cologne: Romanisches Seminar dans Universität Köln, 1994), 171–76.

Trapnell, W. H. "Inexplicable Decisions in The Arabian Nights," *International Journal of Islamic and Arabic Studies* 10, no. 1 (1993), 1–12.

Uba Adamu, Abdalla. "'We Are Not in Baghdad Anymore': Textual Travels and Hausa Intertextual Adaptation of Selected Tales of One Thousand and One Nights in Northern Nigeria," in *Endless Inspiration: One Thousand and One Nights in Comparative Perspective*, ed. Orhan Elmaz (Piscataway, NJ: Gorgias Press, 2020), 35–59.

van den Boogert, Maurits H. "Patrick Russell and the Arabian Nights Manuscripts," in *Scholarship between Europe and the Levant: Essays in Honour of Alastair Hamilton*, ed. Jan Loop and Jill Kraye (Leiden: Brill, 2020), 276–98.

van Leeuwen, Richard. "Orientalisme, genre et réception des Mille et une Nuits en Europe." In *Les Mille et une Nuit en partage*. ed. by Aboubakr Chraïbi. Paris: Sindbad, 2004. 120–141.

"Translation and Referentiality: The European Translations of the Thousand and One Nights." In *Orientalismo, Exotismo y Traducción*. ed. by Gonzalo F. Parrilla and Manuel C. Feria García. Cuenca: Ediciones de la Universidad de Castilla, 2000. 191–207.

"The Art of Interruption: The Thousand and One Nights and Jan Potócki," *Journal Middle Eastern Literatures* 7, no. 2 (2004), 183–98.

"The Iconography of the Thousand and One Nights and Modernism: From Text to Image," *Relief* 4, no. 2 (2010), 213–36.

The Thousand and One Nights and Twentieth-Century Fiction: Intertextual Readings. Leiden: Brill, 2018.

Vargo, Lisa. "The Case of Anna Laetitia Barbauld's 'To Mr C[olerid]ge.'" www.usask.ca/english/barbauld/criticism/vargo98.html.

von Grunebaum, Gustave Edmund. "Greek Elements in the Arabian Nights," *Journal of the American Oriental Society* 62 (1942), 277–92.

"Creative Borrowing: Greece in the 'Arabian Nights,'" in *Medieval Islam*, 2nd ed. (Chicago, IL: Chicago University Press, 1953), 294–319.

"*The Arabian Nights*," *Midway: A Magazine of Discovery in the Arts and Sciences* 14 (1963), 40–63.

von Schlegel, Friedrich. *Philosophical Fragments*, trans. Peter Firchow. Minneapolis, MN: University of Minnesota Press, 1998.

Waelti-Walters, Jennifer. *Michel Butor*. Amsterdam and Atlanta, GA: Rodopi, 1992.

Wagner, Erica. "Two Years, Eight Months and Twenty-Eight Nights by Salman Rushdie Review – Stories Told against Disaster," *The Guardian*, September 13, 2015, www.theguardian.com/books/2015/sep/13/two-years-eight-months-twenty-eight-nights-review-salman-rushdie.

Waisman, Sergio Gabriel. "The Thousand and One Nights in Argentina: Translation, Narrative, and Politics in Borges, Puig, and Piglia," *Comparative Literature Studies* 40, no. 4 (2003), 351–71.

Walsh, Catherine E. "Decoloniality in/as Praxis," in *On Decoloniality: Concepts, Analytics, Praxis*, ed. Walter D. Mignolo and Catherine E. Walsh (Durham, NC, and London: Duke University Press, 2018), 15–32.

Walters, Jennifer R. "Michel Butor and 'The Thousand and One Nights,'" *Neophilologus* 59 (1975), 213–22.

Wehr, Hans (Hg.): *Das Buch der wunderbaren Erzählungen und seltsamen Geschichten*. Mit Benutzung der Vorarbeiten von A. von Bulmerincq. Wiesbaden: Steiner, 1956. [Ḥikāyāt 'aǧība wa-aḫbār ġarība.] Rez.: O. Spies: Der Islam 35 (1960), 155–159.

White, Hayden. *Metahistory: The Historical Imagination in 19th-Century Europe*. Baltimore, MD: Johns Hopkins University Press, 1973.

Tropics of Discourse: Essays in Cultural Criticism. Baltimore, MD: Johns Hopkins University Press, 1978.

White, Timothy R., and James Emmet Winn. "Islam, Animation and Money: The Reception of Disney's Aladdin in Southeast Asia," *Kinema* (1995), 58–59, https://doi.org/10.15353/kinema.vi.778.

Williams, Raymond. *Culture and Society, 1780–1950*. London: Chatto and Windus, 1958.

Communications: Britain in the Sixties. Harmondsworth, UK: Pelican-Penguin, 1968.

Windle, Kevin. "The Slavonic Nights: Observations on Some Versions of *The Book of a Thousand and One Nights* in Slavonic Languages," *The Modern Language Review* 88, no. 2 (April 1993), 389–405.

Winter, Milo. *The Arabian Night Entertainments*. Chicago, IL: Rand McNally & Co., 1914.

Wise, Christopher. "Notes from the Aladdin Industry: Or, Middle Eastern Folklore in the Era of Multinational Capitalism," in The *Emperor's Old Groove: Decolonizing Disney's Magic Kingdom*, ed. Brenda Ayers (New York: Peter Lang, 2003), 105–14.

Wood, Michael. "A Romance of the Reader," *New York Times*, June 21, 1981, www.nytimes.com/1981/06/21/books/a-romance-of-the-reader.html.

Woodbull, Winifred. *Transfigurations of the Maghreb*. Minneapolis, MN: University of Minnesota Press, 1993.

Yardley, Edward. *The Supernatural in Romantic Fiction*. London: Longman & Green, 1880.

Yūnus, Muḥammad ʿAbd al-Raḥmān. *al-Jins wa-l-sulṭah fī alf laylah wa-laylah.* Beirut: Muʾassasat al-Intishār al-ʿArabī, 1998.

Zadeh, Travis. "The Wiles of Creation: Philosophy, Fiction, and the 'Aja'ib Tradition," *Middle Eastern Literatures* 13, no. 1 (2010), 21–48.

Zakharia, Katia. 2016. "Jean-Georges Varsy et l'Histoire d'Ali Baba: révélations et silences de deux manuscrits récemment découverts." *Arabica* 62, 2016. 652–687.

"La version arabe la plus ancienne de l'Histoire d'Ali Baba: si Varsy n'avait pas traduit Galland? Réhabiliter le doute raisonnable." *Arabica* 64, 2017. 50–77.

Zonana, Joyce. "The Sultan and the Slave: Feminist Orientalism and the Structure of *Jane Eyre*," *Signs* (Spring 1993), 592–617.

Zotenberg, M. H. "Notice sur quelques manuscrits des Mille et une nuits," *Notices et extraits des manuscrits de la Bibliothèque nationale* 27 (1887), 167–235.

Index

Abbasid, 41, 204
  Baghdad, 48, 200
  caliph al-Muqtadar, 196
  caliph al-Rāḍī, 202
  caliph al-Rashid, 187
  cultural production and narrative, 78
  storyteller, 302
Abbott, Nabia, 12, 190, 209, 325
  complete translation location, 177
  debate on origins of the *Arabian Nights*, 208
  double argument, 178
  "fragment . . . ," 12
  fragment/importance, 176
  frame tale of Scheherazade/ Shahrayar, 176
  genealogy of tales, 50
  Hazār afsānah's translation, 177
  impact on study of origins, 212
  khurāfah as a proper name, 186
  Littmann's argument, 175
  Mahdi's mentor, 12
  manuscript, fragment of, 78
  on issue of *khurāfāt*, 186
  on popularity of storytelling, 30
  paleography expertise, 177
  Samarqand paper, 185
  significant finding, 172
  al-Ṣūlī's report, 178
  the Oriental Institute (Chicago), 185
'Abd al-Ṣabūr, Ṣalāḥ, 5
Abdel-Halim, Mohamed, 289
abductor
  Scheherazade and al-Ḥakīm's representation, 241
'Abdullāh, Yaḥyā al-Ṭāhir, 242
abridgments, 20
  Burton's version, 152
  collective unconscious, 45
absence
  in periodical criticism and Poe's counteruse, 42
  nonverbal narrative, 81
  of relative emphasis, 42
  of tales, 24
  on structural level, 88
  "one" in the title and Abbott, 172
  Pahlavi book, 179
  signifies death, 74
  Todorov on James's narrative, 85
al-Abshīhī, Shihāb al-Dīn ibn-Aḥmad, 199
Abū al-'Āliyah, 193
Abū al-'Aynā, Muḥammad ibn al-Qāsim, 193, 199, 206
Abū Dulāmah, 193
Abū al-'Ibar, 193
Abū al-Ṭayyib, 187
Abū 'Ubaydah, 193
Addison, 324
aesthetics, politics of, 273
Afghanistan, 211
Afsānah, Hazār (*Thousand Fanciful Tales*), 30, 101, 172, 174–75, 177, 179, 185–87, 189, 200–2, 204, 206
  al-Mas'ūdī, 31
  al-Nadīm's reference, 30
  and the Orientalist restorative effort, 215
  Ibn 'Abdūs al-Jahshiyārī, 31
  Islamized, 209
  similar collections, 31
age, industrial, 106
Akhbār, 179
Akkadian, 125
Aladdin, 6, 15, 25, 33, 102, 110, 135, 153, 166, 219, 226, 245, 249–51, 269, 277, 306, 319
  an active verb, 277
  and racism, 277
  Disney's, 6
  Jack Shaheen on, 7
  multinational capitalism, 276
  raids on, 7
  receive more attention, 276
  song slanders the heritage of Arabs, 277

Scheherazade (cont.)
Barth wrote heterosexual history of, 251
Barth's quintessential artist, 60
Barth's tales of, 120
Borges's comment, 43
Byatt on, 23
Charlotte Brontë's heroine emulate, 230
Codrescu's jacket art, 270
confabulator nocturne, 20
criticism of the tales of, 287
end to vengeance and terror, 64
engage the tyrant's attention, 309
fecund memory, 189
feminist discourse, 10
her images in Butor's, Barth's, and Maḥfūẓ's, 20
in danger of exhaustion, 118
in male writing, 10
in Sarajevo, 23
John Payne on, 43
like Prometheus, 251
Mahdi's point on the meaning of, 58
multidimensional universe and the tales of, 5
narrative globe trotter, 20
nocturnal narration, 68
on the role of the savior of women, 218
outsider to histories of literature, 43
poetics of storytelling and the tales of, 38
Portor and Chesterton attraction to a storyteller, 309
pose further challenge, 57
Proust, another remembrance of, 108
shifts the problem of desire, 109
storytelling against destruction, 23
supply of invention and the tales of, 28
surviving the process of replacemnt and deflection, 103
tales counteract relativism, 64
tales of, 95
the experience and capacity of, 309
the triumph of art, 250
use and distruction, 14
waiting for the imperial savior, 145
Scheherazade factor
and Arab writers, 58
and European writers, 58
and Jabra, 94
and Proust, 108
Barth's, 117
Barth's engagement with, 94
Barth's phrase, 19
Borges reinvents, 97
dynamic germinator for writing, 94
frame tale, 19
narrative dynamic, 110
narrative engagement, 95
not a container, 19
preludinal site, 19
resuscitation in Barth's, 111
signifies the power of storytelling, 53
spectacle, 19
staple of high modernist and postmodernist, 53
storyteller's vocation, 52
the function of, 93
the power of, 58
the properties of, 58
Scheherazadian, 98
Schlegel, 49, 207, 209–11, 213, 256, 287
scholarship
critics, literary historians, and folklorists, 46
Scott, Jonathan, 45, 136, 140–42, 148–49, 165, 257, 265, 283
Pickering and Chatto edition, 156
Scott, Walter, 140
script, cultural, 8–9, 11, 46, 116, 139, 154, 186, 285
demonized by Barth's rewritings, 117
Seduri, 126
self-reflexive
Barth more than many, 109
night 602, 110
self-reflexivity, 53, 297
Semites, 255, 256
Semitic, 20, 22, 155, 263, 286
Semitic/Aryan
in new philology, 46
Serendib (Siri Lanka), 121
serialization
and journalism, 132
tales, 58
Severin, Tim, 120, 121
al-Shāfiʿī, 187
Shaheen, Jack, 7, 276–77
Shahrayar, 33, 52, 58, 67–69, 72, 79, 84–86, 89, 98, 108–9, 116–18, 126–31, 132, 188, 201, 216, 229, 230, 242, 251, 278
appears passive, 87
changes in the character of, 65
curiosity as pronlematic, 84
death and, 118
excursion in manliness, 88
frailty and weakness, 62
haunting on the structural level, 88
lack of knowledge regarding, 85
mirthful psychologizing of, 251
Rochester as, 234

For EU product safety concerns, contact us at Calle de José Abascal, 56–1°,
28003 Madrid, Spain or eugpsr@cambridge.org.

www.ingramcontent.com/pod-product-compliance
Ingram Content Group UK Ltd.
Pitfield, Milton Keynes, MK11 3LW, UK
UKHW020403140625
459647UK00020B/2628